Experiential Legal Writing

Aspen Coursebook Series

Experiential Legal Writing

Analysis, Process, and Documents

Diana R. Donahoe

Professor of Legal Research and Writing
Georgetown Law Center

Wolters Kluwer
Law & Business

Published by Wolters Kluwer Law & Business in New York.

Wolters Kluwer Law & Business serves customers worldwide with CCH, Aspen Publishers, and Kluwer Law International products. (www.wolterskluwerlb.com)

To contact Customer Service, e-mail customer.service@wolterskluwer.com, call 1-800-234-1660, fax 1-800-901-9075, or mail correspondence to:

Wolters Kluwer Law & Business
Attn: Order Department
PO Box 990
Frederick, MD 21705

Printed in the United States of America.

1 2 3 4 5 6 7 8 9 0

ISBN 978-0-7355-0963-4

Library of Congress Cataloging-in-Publication Data

Donahoe, Diana R., 1964-
 Experiential legal writing : analysis, process, and documents / Diana R. Donahoe.
    p. cm. — (Aspen coursebook series)
 ISBN 978-0-7355-0963-4
 1. Legal composition. 2. Law—United States—Language. I. Title.
 KF250.D66 2011
 808'.06634—dc23

                                                             2011026042

About Wolters Kluwer Law & Business

Wolters Kluwer Law & Business is a leading global provider of intelligent information and digital solutions for legal and business professionals in key specialty areas, and respected educational resources for professors and law students. Wolters Kluwer Law & Business connects legal and business professionals as well as those in the education market with timely, specialized authoritative content and information-enabled solutions to support success through productivity, accuracy and mobility.

Serving customers worldwide, Wolters Kluwer Law & Business products include those under the Aspen Publishers, CCH, Kluwer Law International, Loislaw, Best Case, ftwilliam.com and MediRegs family of products.

CCH products have been a trusted resource since 1913, and are highly regarded resources for legal, securities, antitrust and trade regulation, government contracting, banking, pension, payroll, employment and labor, and healthcare reimbursement and compliance professionals.

Aspen Publishers products provide essential information to attorneys, business professionals and law students. Written by preeminent authorities, the product line offers analytical and practical information in a range of specialty practice areas from securities law and intellectual property to mergers and acquisitions and pension/benefits. Aspen's trusted legal education resources provide professors and students with high-quality, up-to-date and effective resources for successful instruction and study in all areas of the law.

Kluwer Law International products provide the global business community with reliable international legal information in English. Legal practitioners, corporate counsel and business executives around the world rely on Kluwer Law journals, looseleafs, books, and electronic products for comprehensive information in many areas of international legal practice.

Loislaw is a comprehensive online legal research product providing legal content to law firm practitioners of various specializations. Loislaw provides attorneys with the ability to quickly and efficiently find the necessary legal information they need, when and where they need it, by facilitating access to primary law as well as state-specific law, records, forms and treatises.

Best Case Solutions is the leading bankruptcy software product to the bankruptcy industry. It provides software and workflow tools to flawlessly streamline petition preparation and the electronic filing process, while timely incorporating ever-changing court requirements.

ftwilliam.com offers employee benefits professionals the highest quality plan documents (retirement, welfare and non-qualified) and government forms (5500/PBGC, 1099 and IRS) software at highly competitive prices.

MediRegs products provide integrated health care compliance content and software solutions for professionals in healthcare, higher education and life sciences, including professionals in accounting, law and consulting.

Wolters Kluwer Law & Business, a division of Wolters Kluwer, is headquartered in New York. Wolters Kluwer is a market-leading global information services company focused on professionals.

SUMMARY OF CONTENTS

CONTENTS

ACKNOWLEDGMENTS

Many people contributed to this book. Special thanks to: Noelle Adgerson for her continuous support in helping to produce the manuscript; my research assistants over the last few years for their many contributions, including: Daniel Solomon, Robyn English, Life Marshall, Stephen Winslow, Jackie Bean; Hanna Hickman; faculty and librarians for their input into the content and design, including Sara Sampson, Susan Sloane, Andrea Funk and the faculty at Whittier Law School, Dave Simon, Mitch Fleischmann, Michael Cedrone, Julie Ross, Michael Golden, David Wolitz, Sonya Bonneau, and Rima Sirota; the people at Aspen, including Barbara Roth, Emily Bender, Susan Boulanger, John Chatelaine, Carol McGeehan, and Richard Mixter. Thanks also to the support of Georgetown University Law Center.

A special thanks to: my family for their support, including my husband, Keith Donahoe, and my children Allie and Peter Donahoe, who have put up with my constant work during evenings and weekends; to my parents, Robert and Norma Roberto, for their support through the years; and to my family of Law Fellows, too numerous to name, who have been an integral part of my development of innovative material to engage students in the classroom.

I would also like to acknowledge the publishers and organizations that permitted me to reprint copyrighted material in this text:

ALWD Manual Front Cover
Reprinted from ALWD Citation Manual: A Professional System of Citation, 4th edition (ISBN 07355-8930-8) by the Association of Legal Writing Directors, with the permission of Wolters Kluwer Law and Business.

Bluebook Front Cover
Reprinted by permission of The Harvard Law Review Association. The Bluebook A Uniform System of Citation (19th Edition, The Harvard Law Review Association 2010)

PREFACE

"One can't become skilled simply by reading about skills."[1]

This book is designed to teach today's law students using experiential learning pedagogy. Instead of simply reading about writing techniques and documents, students using this book become actively engaged in their learning process through problem-based simulations, interactive exercises, immediate feedback, and thoughtful reflection. Through active engagement, students retain the material, understand the relevance and importance of what they are learning, and become effective and efficient with their new skills. This unique book is a powerful tool to help students form long-term professional habits, become efficient problem-solvers, and think and behave like lawyers.

The content of this book focuses on legal analysis, the writing process, a variety of legal documents, grammar, and citation, including the 4th Edition of ALWD and the 19th Edition of the Bluebook. Annotated samples, quizzes, and self-assessments provide the students with immediate feedback and help the learning process through engaging and enriching exercises. Some of the highlights of the book include the following:

- **Legal Analysis:** discusses legal rhetorical devices in an easy-to-understand fashion by focusing on statutory interpretation, common law analysis, policy arguments, and cohesive legal arguments.
- **Writing Process:** provides useful strategies for students to become efficient and effective writers by breaking down the process into multiple steps.
- **Legal Documents:** addresses a variety of legal documents including memos, briefs, client letters, pleadings and motions, scholarly writing and write-on competition papers. For each product, the book addresses audience, purpose, scope, and view; formal (as well as informal) requirements; and multiple annotated samples.
- **Grammar and Citation:** covers citation rules in the 19th Edition of the Bluebook and the 4th Edition of ALWD as well as grammar rules with quizzes and self-assessments for the students.
- **Annotated Samples:** provides a plethora of annotated samples, within each document (such as questions presented and issue statements) as well as full documents (such as memos, briefs, client letters, and motions).
- **Quick References and Checklists:** acts as study aid material for the students to reinforce and test their understanding of the material.
- **Quizzes and Self-Assessments:** provides interactive tools and immediate feedback for students and teachers to test the students' understanding of the materials.

---

1. Roy Stucky et al., Best Practices for Legal Education, p. 170-71 (Clinical Legal Education Association 2007).

This writing book can be used in conjunction with its research book counterpart, *Experiential Legal Research: Sources, Strategies, and Citation*. When used together, the two books provide all the required reading material in a typical modern legal research and writing course:

- Research (including Westlaw, WestlawNext, Lexis, Lexis Advance);
- Writing (memos, briefs, client letters, motions, pleadings, scholarly documents);
- Analysis (statutory interpretation, common law analysis, policy, etc.);
- Citation (ALWD 4th Edition and the Bluebook 19th Edition); and
- Grammar (included self-assessments and quizzes).

This book is designed as a standalone print book. However, it can also be used, if desired, in conjunction with its online version, *TeachingLaw.com*. The online version provides extra functionality such as (1) a courseware program that links directly with the content, (2) idea banks for professors to share information, assignments, and projects, (3) direct links to other useful web sites so students can research while they learn about sources, (4) self-assessments that report to the professors, and (5) more interactive features for students. Professors may choose to offer the print book, the online version, or both for their students. Appendix B at the end of this book provides a table of contents with both page numbers and screen numbers so that students can be "on the same page" regardless of which version they choose.

A Teacher's Manual accompanies this book. It provides both pedagogical theories and substantive techniques for teaching an experiential learning course:

- Experiential learning pedagogy techniques, including preparing research and writing assignments, designing simulations and class exercises, and crafting the syllabus for both objective and persuasive semesters.
- Specific assignments with accompanying research in multiple jurisdictions, similar to an idea bank or shared bank for professors;
- Ready-made research projects and accompanying answer keys;
- In-class exercises for experiential learning pedagogy and accompanying answer keys;
- Detailed lesson plans that highlight experiential learning pedagogy to actively engage students in and out of the classroom; and
- Techniques for providing effective and efficient professor feedback and student reflection on draft and final papers.

Reading about legal writing is not enough. Students need to be actively engaged in the process to understand the various strategies to succeed in today's legal world. By using experiential learning pedagogy, professors can help their students attain and retain the material and skills needed so that they can become professional, effective, and efficient legal writers. When these students become practicing lawyers, they will be able to learn to write any legal document in an efficient process because they have been actively engaged in the learning process throughout their academic lives.

Diana R. Donahoe

CHAPTER 1

Legal Analysis

Legal analysis is the use of law to create reasoned, logical arguments. In this chapter, you will learn how to gather and analyze the facts as well as how to interpret rules before you begin to analyze the law. In addition, you will learn basic jurisprudence and the classical rhetorical devices of deductive and inductive reasoning and then employ both types of reasoning to create logical legal analysis through statutory interpretation, case analysis, and policy arguments.

I.   INTRODUCTION

Legal analysis is the art of creating reasoned, logical, legal arguments and applying those arguments to a particular set of facts. To create sound legal analysis, you must find and analyze the facts as well as the law.

A.   *Collecting the Facts*

As a law student, you will probably be given a set of hypothetical facts to begin your analysis. However, as a lawyer, you will never receive such a "fact pattern." Instead, you will work for a client, and the facts will unfold in anything but a timely or thorough manner. Typical sources for collecting facts will be the client, other witnesses, documentation and tangible evidence, experts, and often a site visit (e.g., to a crime scene). Be sure to prepare questions before you investigate, interview, or depose. The questions you ask should not only center around understanding the background, history, or client's story, but they should also help you to find relevant law. Questions organized by editorial categories are often helpful:

Table 1.1. Examples of Editorial Categories Useful for Collecting Facts

Parties	Persons
Places, Objects, Things	Places
Basis or Issue	Acts
Defense	Things
Relief Sought	

Keep in mind that facts will often change as you collect more information. In addition, you will need to retrace many of your steps in the fact-finding process, so do not assume that you will need to visit a crime scene or interview a client only once.

B.   *Analyzing the Law*

Once you have a general sense of the facts of the case, you will need to begin to apply the law to those facts. Remember to be flexible; as the facts change, your analysis of the law might change as well. Applying the law to the facts requires a number of steps. You need to identify legal issues, find controlling law, understand the relationship among the various legal branches, and then apply a variety of legal reasoning techniques to create sound, logical, legal arguments.

1. Identifying Legal Issues

As a law student, you will often be told the exact legal issue for the hypothetical. However, as a lawyer, you will need to identify the legal issues by analyzing the client's facts. Keep in mind that there are usually many issues in every case. The plaintiff's lawyer or prosecutor often defines the issues. The defense lawyer can also help define issues by providing counterclaims and defenses.

2. Finding Controlling Law

Once you have identified the issues, you need to find the law that controls on each issue. Basically, you will be looking for a "rule of law" from statutes, cases, or regulations. You will need to determine whether this particular law controls the issue. For example, if you find a statute that applies to "only property owned" and your client leases the property, then that particular statute does not control. Often, the terms are ambiguous, and part of your legal argument will focus on what law controls. For example, if a statute applies to "all employees," you might need to argue that your client, who contracts with this employer, is actually an employee.

For information on finding law, see the corresponding research book, Donahoe, *Experiential Legal Research: Sources, Strategies, and Citation* (Wolters Kluwer Law & Business, 2011).

3. Understanding the Relationship Among the Legal Branches

Statutes are usually the starting point in the law. A statute binds the courts of that jurisdiction (a Maryland statute binds Maryland courts), but courts have two roles in interpreting a statute. First, a court may find a statute to be unconstitutional; such a finding makes the statute invalid unless the legislature amends the statute to cure the problem. Second, assuming the statute is constitutional, a court interprets the meaning of a statute. Once a court has written a decision interpreting the statute, other courts in that jurisdiction are bound by that interpretation under the doctrine of stare decisis. However, if the legislature disagrees with the courts' interpretation, the legislature can amend the statute to clarify its intent. For more on stare decisis, see page 28.

In addition, sometimes the law starts as common law or case law. A legislature might codify the common law. Thus, when finding law in the jurisdiction, you might find common law that predates the statute; these cases can still be applicable and binding as long as they are consistent with the way the law was codified.

Therefore, when finding controlling law, it is important to pay attention to any history of the law and look for dates of enforcement and amendments.

4. Applying a Variety of Techniques to Create Logical Legal Arguments

Lawyers use a variety of techniques to produce sound legal arguments. The most pervasive techniques are reasoning based on (a) rules, (b) analogies, and (c) policies.

a. **Rule-Based Reasoning:** The starting point for most legal analysis is rule-based reasoning. Here, a statute or case law dictates the rule to be applied. A lawyer's job is to break down the rule into its component elements. Oftentimes, a rule will clearly enumerate these elements; other times, a rule can be structured in many different ways. Once the elements of a rule are enumerated, the lawyer analyzes each element separately, applying the general rule to the particular client's facts to come to a conclusion. This type of analysis is similar to deductive reasoning (see pages 12-13) in that the lawyer starts with a premise and then applies his client's facts to that premise. Rule-based reasoning is addressed in statutory interpretation (see pages 14-23) and case synthesis (see pages 32-34).

b. **Analogies:** To analyze the elements of the law, lawyers use analogies. Here, the lawyer compares his client's case to cases that have already been decided. A lawyer will argue that his client's facts are similar to the facts of a prior case to show that the outcome should be the same. This technique is called an analogy. When a lawyer argues that his client's facts are different from the prior case, he is distinguishing that case. A good lawyer will use the facts and the reasoning of the prior case to show why the client's case should have a similar or different holding. Analogies use inductive reasoning (see pages 13-14) and are addressed in case analysis (see pages 31-40).

c. **Policies:** Lawyers make policy arguments when there is no applicable rule on the subject (this is called a case of first impression), when existing rules are ambiguous, and to bolster other legal arguments. A policy argument will show why an interpretation of the law is consistent or inconsistent with the goals of the rule (if there is one) or of society in general. Policy arguments use both deductive and inductive reasoning (see pages 12-14) and are addressed in policy arguments (see pages 39-40).

II.   UNDERSTANDING LEGAL RULES

The rule of law is the starting point for most legal analysis. Rules can come from statutes, regulations, or cases, and they come in a variety of forms. As a lawyer, you need to determine what type of rule you are applying, understand which terms of the rule are in contention, and break down the rule into its component parts and important terms so that you can apply your client's facts in a cohesive argument.

A. Types of Rules

The first step in rule application is determining the type of rule that applies. Rules come in many forms, including (but not limited to) an elements test, a balancing of factors test, a totality test, a test with exceptions, and a combination of these tests.

1. The Elements Test

An elements test may be very simple and have only one element that must be met or it may be more complicated. Some rules have two-part tests, three-part tests, or even more. Sometimes the elements are clearly enumerated (e.g., 1,2,3 or a,b,c). Oftentimes a rule will have only one sentence but will have multiple parts; you will need to break down that rule into subelements.

Elements Tests

One-Part Test

For the deed to be valid, it must be signed by a notary public. — The one element here is the notary's signature.

Multiple-Part Test

To maintain a cause of action under CEPA, the employee must establish the following:

Here, all five elements must be met.

1. The existence of a *clear mandate of public policy* that the employer's conduct has violated;
2. Employee's *reasonable belief* that employer's conduct was in violation;
3. Performance of a *whistle-blowing activity;*
4. That the employee has suffered an *adverse employment action;* and
5. A *causal connection* between the whistle-blowing activity and the adverse employment action.

One-Sentence Test That Breaks Down into Multiple Elements

The use of the name, portrait, or picture of any living person for advertising purposes without written consent constitutes a misdemeanor.

Here, the rule can be broken down into the following elements:
1. Use of name, portrait, or picture of any living person;
2. For advertising purposes; and
3. Without written consent.

---

2. The Balancing of Factors Test

A balancing of factors test sets out two or more considerations that must be weighed against each other. Here, factors may be used to add weight to each side of the argument. This test truly conjures up an image of the scales of justice.

Balancing of Factors Test

The evidence of prior bad acts will be admitted if the probative value outweighs the prejudice to the defendant.

---

3.   The Totality Test

A totality test sets out a number of factors but they need not all be met; instead, they are all considered and added up together into a totality. In this type of test, some of the factors may be more important than other factors, and not all factors need be met.

Totality Test

> Under the totality of circumstances test, a reasonable person would not have understood the meeting with the police to constitute custody. Factors that determine custody include the defendant's age and experience with the law, the length of the meeting, the number of police officers, and the time of day the meeting took place.

4.   The Exceptions Test

Here, a rule is set out with one or more exceptions. Therefore, to argue that the rule does not apply, you must argue that the exception applies. To argue that the rule applies, you will need to argue that one or more of the exceptions do not apply.

Exceptions Test

> In order to search a home, police need a warrant and probable cause except to perform a protective sweep or a search incident to an arrest.

At times, rules combine a number of these tests. So, in a factors test, one factor might include some sort of balancing or an exception. In a balancing test, many factors might apply to one (or both) sides. The trick is to understand what type of test (or tests) your rule uses to begin to decipher the rule itself.

B.   *Terms Within Rules*

Once you have an understanding of the type of rule you are applying, you must look closely at its terms and phrases. First, you should be familiar with terms that always carry a specific meaning.

1.   And vs. Or

The term *and* has a conjunctive meaning. For example, when *and* appears within a factors test, both or all parts of the factors must be met. *Or* has the opposite effect. When *or* appears in a factors test, only one of the factors need be proven.

And vs. Or

Or
To prove damages, the plaintiff must demonstrate either emotional harm or physical harm.
And
To prove damages, the plaintiff must demonstrate emotional and physical harm.

— Here, the plaintiff needs to prove only one type of harm to recover damages.

— Here, the plaintiff needs to prove both types of harm to recover damages.

2. Shall vs. May

Shall and *may* also have very different meanings. *Shall* is mandatory—it leaves no discretion to the judge or the subject of the rule. *May* is discretionary—a judge or the actor has some discretion to decide whether to take some action. (Often factors or some sort of balancing will help the judge decide.)

Shall vs. May

Shall
The court shall consider these factors when applying the balancing test.
May
The court may consider these factors when applying the balancing test.

Here, the court must consider all the enumerated factors.

Here, the court can consider some of the factors, but need not consider all of them.

Second, you need to determine the terms of the rule that are in dispute. While *and, or, shall,* and *may* will never be in dispute, many of the other terms will be. Therefore, you need to parse out the rule by looking at each word or term individually and asking yourself whether each side has an argument regarding that particular term. Terms may be a combination of words *(clear mandate of public policy)* or they can be a single word *(causation)*.

C. Organizing Around the Rule of Law

Once you have determined the type of rule you are analyzing and have made an initial determination of the terms in dispute, you will be better able to organize the rule into its elements or subcategories. This process is important because legal documents are organized around the legal rule. To organize the rule, you should first break it down into its component parts and then analyze the terms in dispute.

Breaking the rule down into its component parts should be easy if you have identified the rule's test. If it is an elements test, list the elements. If it is a balancing of factors test, write down the two conflicting considerations that must be balanced. Next, determine how those factors relate to each other. Is there an *or* or an *and* in the test? Is it a mandatory test or a discretionary test? Third, within each factor or consideration, highlight the terms of art that will come into play. One factor might have three terms in dispute; another factor may have no terms in dispute.

To analyze the terms of art, you will need to look at each term separately. Here, you will determine the meaning of each term. In persuasive writing, you will argue that it means one thing while your opponent will likely argue that it means another. In objective writing, you will predict what the term means. Here, you might use statutory interpretation (see pages 14-23), case analogy and distinction (see pages 34-35), and policy arguments (see pages 40-41) to interpret the meaning. Words and their meanings become especially important to lawyers because of this process. By analyzing each term within a rule, one word can change the outcome for your client. The best lawyers are able to spot ambiguities within terms and argue their meanings.

While this process of organizing a rule of law may seem simple, it can become quite complicated. For example, some statutes are relatively simple and confined to a few lines. However, others can be quite elaborate and cover pages and pages of the code. These complicated rules will require you to parse through all the different pieces of the rule, pull out the applicable sections, and piece them together in a coherent organizational scheme. In addition, even if concise, rules are not always enunciated clearly. For example, when a rule comes from common law, all the judges writing opinions on the same issue may not articulate the rule in exactly the same way. Some may add language to an already existing rule, and others might actually slightly change the interpretation of the rule. In this situation, you will need to either synthesize (see pages 32-34) the cases into one coherent rule or articulate a few possible readings of the rule and analyze them separately.

III.   JURISPRUDENCE

Before you begin making legal arguments, it is helpful to have a basic understanding of legal philosophy—or jurisprudence. If you understand where legal arguments come from, how they have been applied, and when they have changed, you will be able to craft more creative and reasoned arguments in your own writing. American jurisprudence has developed over time. Below you will read about some major legal trends in our history: natural law, formalism (or positivism), realism, and a variety of critical legal studies.

A.   *Historical Legal Trends*

1.   Natural Law

When the Declaration of Independence was signed, American jurisprudence centered around natural law, a philosophy inherited from English law. Natural law intertwines morality with the law. Naturalists argue that our beliefs in what is right are grounded in nature (and sometimes God), and the law should be built around these natural moralities. Our "inalienable rights," "due process," and "equal protection" come from natural law theory. When making a natural law argument, lawyers rely on arguments based on reasonableness, equity, and fairness.

2. Formalism or Positivism

During the nineteenth century, natural law was replaced by the theory of formalism (also known as positivism). Under this theory, law is created not by natural forces but by those rules formulated by the government. These rules can be categorized and then easily followed uniformly and objectively. The key number system and the Langdell method of teaching were developed during this time of jurisprudence and reflect the categorization of legal rules. When making a formalism argument, lawyers enumerate the applicable rules and then apply those rules with legal precedent.

3. Realism

Realism grew out of a reaction to formalism. Realists believe that law cannot be applied uniformly and objectively as in the formalist approach; instead, they believe that law is interpreted subjectively. Rules vary based on the judges making the decisions, not on the law itself. When making an argument based on realism, lawyers will make creative policy arguments (see pages 40-41) and try to play to the judge's emotions to influence the decision.

4. Critical Legal Studies (CLS)

Critical legal studies (CLS) comes directly from realism. The theory behind CLS is that law is not only subjective, it is political. CLS theorists believe that laws are not neutral; instead, they are created to perpetuate political agendas—specifically the agenda of the white, male majority. As a result, there are a number of CLS movements, including critical race theory and feminist legal theory. A lawyer making a CLS argument will rely less on existing law and more on policies based on helping the underprivileged or marginalized members of society.

5. Law and Economics Theory

Law and economics theory is based on the principles of economics and wealth. These theorists believe that law should be based less on government interference and more on market controls. Lawyers making law and economics arguments often rely on economic policy, pointing to economic growth and wealth maximization as reasons for the judge to rule in their favor.

B.　Classical Rhetoric: Deduction vs. Induction

The classical rhetorical devices of deduction and induction are both used in legal reasoning. Lawyers should have some basic understanding of these types of reasoning to create logical arguments and to find weaknesses in opponents' reasoning.

1.　Deduction and Syllogisms in the Law

Deduction is a type of logic that leads to conclusive results. The syllogism is the basic form of this reasoning. A syllogism is a statement that contains each of the following:

1.　A first premise: $A = B$
2.　A second premise: $B = C$
3.　A conclusion: $A = C$

If the first and second premises are true, then the conclusion is valid through deductive reasoning. For example:

First premise	All humans are mammals.	$A = B$
Second premise	Mammals breathe air.	$B = C$
Conclusion	All humans breathe air.	$A = C$

However, if one of the premises is invalid, then the conclusion is invalid. For example:

First premise	All fish are mammals.	$A \neq B$
Second premise	Mammals breathe air.	$B = C$
Conclusion	Fish breathe air.	$A = C$

Here, because the first premise is wrong, the conclusion is not valid.

Syllogisms can also be invalid if the premises are not logical. For example,

---

First premise	All mammals breathe air.	$A = B$
Second premise	Reptiles breathe air.	$C = B$
Conclusion	Reptiles are mammals.	$C = A$

Here, because there is nothing to indicate that breathing air makes mammals equivalent to reptiles, the logic is flawed.

Syllogisms are used frequently in legal arguments. For example, here is a valid syllogism:

First premise	A conviction for solicitation is a minor offense.	A = B
Second premise	If convicted of a minor offense, a defendant will receive no jail time.	B = C
Conclusion	If convicted of solicitation, a defendant will receive no jail time.	A = C

This syllogism correctly follows the formula and contains valid premises. Therefore, the conclusion shows valid deductive reasoning.

However, the syllogism is invalid if one of the premises is invalid. For example:

First premise	A conviction for murder is a minor offense.	A ≠ B
Second premise	If convicted of a minor offense, a defendant will receive no jail time.	B = C
Conclusion	If convicted of murder, a defendant will receive no jail time.	A = C

Because the first premise is invalid, the conclusion is invalid.

The syllogism is also invalid if the premises are not logically ordered. For example:

First premise	A conviction for solicitation is a minor offense.	A = B
Second premise	A conviction for shoplifting is a minor offense.	C = B
Conclusion	A conviction for shoplifting is a conviction for solicitation.	C = A

Because the second premise does not use the B = C formula, the conclusion is invalid.

A good lawyer will be able to create valid syllogisms and find the faults with invalid syllogisms. The simple A = B, B = C, A = C series of equations will help you to write and dissect syllogisms to create arguments and to poke holes in your oppositions' arguments. Oftentimes, rule-based reasoning such as **statutory interpretation** (see pages 14-23) and **case synthesis** (see pages 32-34) takes the form of deductive reasoning.

2. Induction and Inductive Reasoning in the Law

While deductive reasoning creates absolute conclusions, inductive reasoning creates probable conclusions. In induction, the writer shows why a conclusion is more likely than another conclusion. An analogy is a typical form of inductive reasoning. For example:

- A whale breathes air and births its young live.
- A human breathes air and births its young live.
- A snake breathes air and lays eggs.
- A human is more like a whale than a snake because while both breathe air, a human also births its young live and a snake lays eggs.

Here, through inductive reasoning, the writer shows why one conclusion is more likely than another. The trick with the analogy is deciding which characteristics are more important in the comparison.

In law, the analogy is often used to show why a case is more likely to be decided one way instead of another. Usually, prior cases are the basis for the comparison. For example, in a case involving the solicitation of a minor, note the different analogies:

A defense lawyer's argument

"My client should not go to jail for his first offense of solicitation because in most prior cases that involved first offenses, similar defendants received only fines."

Here, the lawyer is using an analogy, comparing a number of offenses to make a conclusion.

The prosecutor's argument

"The defendant should get jail time because in other cases in which the person solicited was a minor, jail time was the usual sentence."

Here, the lawyer bases his inductive reasoning on a different characteristic—age.

In both analogies, the lawyers use inductive reasoning to create sound logic. However, the different characteristic used in the comparisons makes a difference in the conclusions. In this example, the judge needs to decide which characteristic (or which prior case) is more compelling to decide the outcome. A lawyer's job in using inductive reasoning, then, is to provide enough reasoning of the prior case to show why one characteristic is more compelling than another. As you read through case analysis (see pages 31-40), you will see analogies in the law and learn techniques to show how a prior case can be effectively analogized.

IV.   STATUTORY INTERPRETATION

A.   Statutory Language

Statutory interpretation is rule-based reasoning. The lawyer starts with a rule, the statute, and then uses deductive reasoning (see pages 12-13) to apply the general rule to the particular facts of her case to come to a conclusion. However, because legislative bodies rarely write a statute to apply to one particular case, the language and purpose become ambiguous when the client's facts are applied. A lawyer's job, therefore, is to analyze the language of the statute to determine the intent of the legislature that wrote the particular statute—what did the lawmakers mean for the law to do when they wrote it? A good lawyer applies a number of steps in statutory interpretation.

1. Step 1: Finding an Applicable Statute

The first step in statutory interpretation is finding a statute that applies to your client. At times, there may be more than one statute that applies. Other times, there may be only common law available. Also, there may be a dispute as to whether a statute even applies. (For example, does an employment statute apply to independent contractors?)

2. Step 2: Reading the Whole Statute

Many law students who find a relevant statutory section online never realize there are a number of related statutory provisions that exist on the screen prior to and immediately after their particular provision. Therefore, many good lawyers prefer to read a statute in its printed format so they can look at a statute in the context of the entire act. Whether you read a statutory provision online or in the books, be aware that most statutes have many provisions or fall within a specific act. You should at least skim the whole act and look for some of the most important provisions for your particular statute, such as the following:

- The title of the act and the title of specific provisions
- The date of enactment (of the act or specific provisions)
- The date of any amendments
- A preamble or purpose section
- A definition section
- The language of the specific provisions that apply to your issue
- The language of provisions that appear in close proximity to your issue
- The remedy or relief provision of the act

3. Step 3: Breaking Down a Specific Provision into Its Elements

Once you begin to focus on the particular statutory provision you will apply, you need to break it down into its component parts. At times, the language will clearly lay out the structure for you (e.g., the plaintiff must prove a, b, and c). However, often you will need to analyze and break down the structure yourself. One trick to do this is to draw brackets around different language so that each bracketed section becomes one element that needs to be proven. Opposing lawyers will often break down the elements differently. Judges, in their case decisions, often will try to clarify the structure of a statute.

4.   Step 4: Reading Signaling Words Carefully

Particular words and punctuation can change the meaning of a statute. Therefore, you need to dissect specific statutory provisions very carefully. Here are some key words and their meanings:

- *And* = must prove all items in the list to meet statutory provision
- *Or* = must prove only one in the list to meet statutory provision
- *Including* = implies an exclusive list
- *Including but not limited to* = implies list is not exclusive
- *And any other factors* = states that previous list is not exclusive
- *Must* = required
- *Shall* = required
- *May* = not required

B.   *Statutory Interpretation Techniques*

Once you have dissected a statute and broken it down into its component parts, you can begin to interpret the meaning within each element. However, the language of the statute is usually ambiguous, and the lawyer uses a variety of techniques to interpret the statute. The main goal of statutory interpretation is to determine the legislature's intent when creating the law.

By reading the complete case, you will see the arguments analyzed here in context, which will further help you to understand them and apply them effectively in your own writing.

A good example to illustrate statutory interpretation techniques is <u>Smith v. United States</u>, 508 U.S. 223 (1993), in which the Supreme Court examined language in 18 U.S.C. § 924(c)(1), "uses or carries a firearm," to determine if Congress intended that language to include using a firearm as barter for drugs. Both Justice O'Connor's opinion and Justice Scalia's dissent use statutory interpretation techniques to determine the intent of Congress. Those typical techniques are explored below.

1.   Plain Language

The **plain language** of a statute means how a term of a statute is usually used in the English language. A court will usually start interpreting a statute by looking at the plain meaning of the text. If the court can determine a statute's meaning using the plain language of the statute, it might not look to other forms of statutory interpretation.

Plain Language

O'Connor Opinion

When a word is not defined by statute, we normally construe it in accord with its ordinary or natural meaning. See Perrin v. United States, 444 U.S. 37, 42, 100 S. Ct. 311, 314, 62 L. Ed. 2d 199 (1979) (words not defined in statute should be given ordinary or common meaning). Accord, post, at 2061 ("In the search for statutory meaning, we give nontechnical words and phrases their ordinary meaning"). Surely petitioner's treatment of his MAC-10 can be described as "use" within the everyday meaning of that term. Petitioner "used" his MAC-10 in an attempt to obtain drugs by offering to trade it for cocaine.

Scalia Dissent

In the search for statutory meaning, we give nontechnical words and phrases their ordinary meaning. See Chapman v. United States, 500 U.S. 453, 462, 111 S. Ct. 1919, 1925, 114 L. Ed. 2d 524 (1991); Perrin v. United States, 444 U.S. 37, 42, 100 S. Ct. 311, 314, 62 L. Ed. 2d 199 (1979); Minor v. Mechanics Bank of Alexandria, 1 Pet. 46, 64, 7 L. Ed. 47 (1828). To use an instrumentality ordinarily means to use it for its intended purpose. When someone asks, "Do you use a cane?," he is not inquiring whether you have your grandfather's silver-handled walking stick on display in the hall; he wants to know whether you walk with a cane. Similarly, to speak of "using a firearm" is to speak of using it for its distinctive purpose, i.e., as a weapon. To be sure, "one can use a firearm in a number of ways," ante, at 2055, including as an article of exchange, just as one can "use" a cane as a hall decoration—but that is not the ordinary meaning of "using" the one or the other.[1] The Court does not appear to grasp the distinction between how a word can be used and how it ordinarily is used. It would, indeed, be "both reasonable and normal to say that petitioner 'used' his MAC-10 in his drug trafficking offense by trading it for cocaine." Ibid. It would also be reasonable and normal to say that he "used" it to scratch his head. When one wishes to describe the action of employing the instrument of a firearm for such unusual purposes, "use" is assuredly a *243 verb one could select. But that says nothing about whether the ordinary meaning of the phrase "uses a firearm" embraces such extraordinary employments. It is unquestionably not reasonable and normal, I think, to say simply "do not use firearms" when one means to prohibit selling or scratching with them.

---

1. The Court asserts that the "significant flaw" in this argument is that "to say that the ordinary meaning of 'uses a firearm' includes using a firearm as a weapon" is quite different from saying that the ordinary meaning "also excludes any other use." Ante, at 2055. The two are indeed different—but it is precisely the latter that I assert to be true: The ordinary meaning of "uses a firearm" does not include using it as an article of commerce. I think it perfectly obvious, for example, that the objective falsity requirement for a perjury conviction would not be satisfied if a witness answered "no" to a prosecutor's inquiry whether he had ever "used a firearm," even though he had once sold his grandfather's Enfield rifle to a collector.

2. Definitions

Often lawmakers provide a **definition** section, which usually appears in the beginning of the code section. You should always look for a definition section in a statute because it provides key definitions to certain provisions. If no definitions exist, lawyers often look to other sources, such as definitions from other statutes, definitions from Black's Law Dictionary or other dictionaries, or definitions from scholars or judges.

Definitions

O'Connor Opinion

Webster's *229 defines "to use" as "[t]o convert to one's service" or "to employ." Webster's New International Dictionary 2806 (2d ed. 1939). Black's Law Dictionary contains a similar definition: "[t]o make use of; to convert to one's service; to employ; to avail oneself of; to utilize; to carry out a purpose or action by means of." Black's Law Dictionary 1541 (6th ed. 1990). Indeed, over 100 years ago we gave the word "use" the same gloss, indicating that it means "'to employ'" or "'to derive service from.'" Astor v. Merritt, 111 U.S. 202, 213, 4 S. Ct. 413, 419, 28 L. Ed. 401 (1884). Petitioner's handling of the MAC-10 in this case falls squarely within those definitions. By attempting to trade his MAC-10 for the drugs, he "used" or "employed" it as an item of barter to obtain cocaine; he "derived service" from it because it was going to bring him the very drugs he sought.

Scalia Dissent

"...use," whose meanings range all the way *242 from "to partake of" (as in "he uses tobacco") to "to be wont or accustomed" (as in "he used to smoke tobacco"). See Webster's New International Dictionary 2806 (2d ed. 1939).

---

3. Context

Lawyers look to see the **context** of the language, that is, where the terms of art appear in the statute, what words appear near those terms, and what terms appear nowhere in the statute to access the meanings of the terms.

Context

O'Connor Opinion

In petitioner's view, § 924(c)(1) should require proof not only that the defendant used the firearm, but also that he used it as a weapon. But the words "as a weapon" appear nowhere in the statute. Rather, § 924(c)(1)'s language sweeps broadly, punishing any "us[e]" of a firearm, so long as the use is "during and in relation to" a drug trafficking offense. See United States v. Long, 284 U.S. App. D.C. 405, 409-10, 905 F.2d 1572, 1576-77 (Thomas, J.) (although not without limits, the word "use" is "expansive" and extends even to situations where the gun is not actively employed), cert. denied, 498 U.S. 948, 111 S. Ct. 365, 112 L. Ed. 2d 328 (1990). Had Congress intended the narrow construction petitioner urges, it could have so indicated. It did not, and we decline to introduce that additional requirement on our own.

Language, of course, cannot be interpreted apart from context. The meaning of a word that appears ambiguous if viewed in isolation may become clear when the word is analyzed in light of the terms that surround it. Recognizing this, petitioner and the dissent argue that the word "uses" has a somewhat reduced scope in § 924(c)(1) because it appears alongside the word "firearm." Specifically, they contend that the average person on the street would not think ***230** immediately of a guns-for-drugs trade as an example of "us[ing] a firearm." Rather, that phrase normally evokes an image of the most familiar use to which a firearm is put—use as a weapon. Petitioner and the dissent therefore argue that the statute excludes uses where the weapon is not fired or otherwise employed for its destructive capacity. See post, at 2061-62. Indeed, relying on that argument—and without citation to authority—the dissent announces its own, restrictive definition of "use." "To use an instrumentality," the dissent argues, "ordinarily means to ****2055** use it for its intended purpose." Post, at 2060-61.

There is a significant flaw to this argument. It is one thing to say that the ordinary meaning of "uses a firearm" includes using a firearm as a weapon, since that is the intended purpose of a firearm and the example of "use" that most immediately comes to mind. But it is quite another to conclude that, as a result, the phrase also excludes any other use. Certainly that conclusion does not follow from the phrase "uses ... a firearm" itself….

Scalia Dissent

2062 *244 Given our rule that ordinary meaning governs, and given the ordinary meaning of "uses a firearm," it seems to me inconsequential that "the words 'as a weapon' appear nowhere in the statute," ante, at 2054; they are reasonably implicit. Petitioner is not, I think, seeking to introduce an "additional requirement" into the text, ibid., but is simply construing the text according to its normal import…. We are dealing here not with a technical word or an "artfully defined" legal term, ***245** cf. Dewsnup v. Timm, 502 U.S. 410, 423, 112 S. Ct. 773, 781, 116 L. Ed. 2d 903 (1992) (Scalia, J., dissenting), but with common words that are, as I have suggested, inordinately sensitive to context. Just as adding the direct object "a firearm" to the verb "use" narrows the meaning of that verb (it can no longer mean "partake of"), so also adding the modifier "in the offense of transferring, selling, or transporting firearms" to the phrase "use a firearm" expands the meaning of that phrase (it then includes, as it previously would not, nonweapon use). But neither the narrowing nor the expansion should logically be thought to apply to all appearances of the affected word or phrase. Just as every appearance of the word "use" in the statute need not be given the narrow meaning that word acquires in the phrase "use a firearm," so also every appearance of the phrase "use a firearm" need not be given the expansive connotation that phrase acquires in the broader context "use a firearm in crimes such as unlawful sale of firearms." When, for example, the statute provides that its prohibition on certain transactions in firearms "shall not apply to the loan or rental of a firearm to any person for temporary use for lawful sporting purposes," 18 U.S.C. §§ 922(a)(5)(B), (b)(3)(B), I have no doubt that the "use" referred to is only use as a sporting weapon, and not the use of pawning the firearm to pay for a ski trip. Likewise when, in § 924(c)(1), the phrase "uses ... a firearm" is not employed in a context that necessarily envisions the unusual "use" of a firearm as a commodity, the normally understood meaning of the phrase should prevail.

4.   Case Law

Lawyers use case law to determine the way in which other courts have interpreted the meaning of the statute (see below). Employing case analysis techniques, lawyers use cases as binding precedent in statutory interpretation. Annotated statutes provide references to cases that have interpreted the statutes. You should research these cases because judges' opinions will provide interpretations, definitions, and important policy arguments that may apply to your case. If a court interprets a statute incorrectly, the legislature can rewrite the statute.

Case Law

O'Connor Opinion

No court of appeals ever has held that using a gun to pistol-whip a victim is anything but the "use" of a firearm; nor has any court ever held that trading a firearm for drugs falls short of being the "use" thereof. But cf. Phelps, 877 F.2d at 30 (holding that trading a gun for drugs is not use "in relation to" a drug trafficking offense).

---

5.   Legislative History

Use legislative history to discover what the lawmakers said when they wrote, debated, and discussed the statute. To find legislative history, a lawyer would research committee reports, floor debates, and speeches. Legislative history is also useful to determine congressional intent if the statute has been amended. Some judges (Justice Scalia, for instance) do not believe legislative history is helpful when interpreting statutory language.

Legislative History

O'Connor Opinion

Finally, it is argued that § 924(c)(1) originally dealt with use of a firearm during crimes of violence; the provision concerning use of a firearm during and in relation to drug trafficking offenses was added later. Post, at 2063. From this, the dissent infers that "use" originally was limited to use of a gun "as a weapon." That the statute in its current form employs the term "use" more broadly is unimportant, the dissent contends, because the addition of the words "'drug trafficking crime' would have been a peculiar way to expand its meaning." Ibid. Even if we assume that Congress had intended the term "use" to have a more limited scope when it passed the original version of § 924(c) in 1968, but see supra, at 2054-56, we believe it clear from the face of the statute that the Congress that amended § 924(c) in 1986 did not. Rather, the 1986 Congress employed the term "use" expansively, covering both use as a weapon, as the dissent admits, and use as an item of trade or barter, as an examination of § 924(d) demonstrates. Because the phrase "uses ... a firearm" is broad enough in ordinary usage to cover use of a ***237** firearm as an item of barter or commerce, Congress was free in 1986 so to employ it. The language and structure of § 924 indicates that Congress did just that. Accordingly, we conclude that using a firearm in a guns-for-drugs trade may constitute "us[ing] a firearm" within the meaning of § 924(c)(1).

Scalia Dissent

Finally, although the present prosecution was brought under the portion of § 924(c)(1) pertaining to use of a firearm "during and in relation to any ... drug trafficking crime," I think it significant that that portion is affiliated with the pre-existing provision pertaining to use of a firearm "during and in relation to any crime of violence," rather than with the firearm trafficking offenses defined in § 922 and referenced in § 924(d). The word "use" in the "crime of violence" context has the unmistakable import of use as a weapon, and that import carries over, in my view, to the subsequently added phrase "or drug trafficking crime." Surely the word "use" means the same thing as to both, and surely the 1986 addition of "drug trafficking crime" would have been a peculiar way to expand its meaning (beyond "use as a weapon") for crimes of violence. Even if the reader does not consider the issue to be as clear as I do, he must at least acknowledge, I think, that it is eminently debatable—and that is enough, under the rule of lenity, to require finding for the petitioner here. "At the very least, it may be said that the issue is subject to some doubt. Under these circumstances, we adhere to the familiar rule that, 'where there is ambiguity in a criminal statute, doubts are resolved in favor of the defendant.'" Adamo ***247** Wrecking Co. v. United States, 434 U.S. 275, 284-85, 98 S. Ct. 566, 572-73, 54 L.Ed. 2d 538 (1978), quoting United States v. Bass, 404 U.S. 336, 348, 92 S. Ct. 515, 523, 30 L. Ed.2d 488 (1971).

6. Policy

Explore any policy arguments that could have determined the legislature's intent. Often a statute contains a policy or purpose section. Therefore, you should always check your statute for such a section. If there is no policy section, lawyers often employ various policy arguments to interpret the statute such as determining particular policy issues at the time the statute was enacted. See the sections on policy arguments (pages 40-41) and jurisprudence (see pages 10-14) for specific ideas.

Policy

O'Connor Opinion

When Congress enacted the current version of § 924(c)(1), it was no doubt aware that drugs and guns are a dangerous combination. In 1989, 56 percent of all murders in New York City were drug related; during the same period, the figure for the Nation's Capital was as high as 80 percent. The American Enterprise 100 (Jan.-Feb. 1991). The fact that a gun is treated momentarily as an item of commerce does not render it inert or deprive it of destructive capacity. Rather, as experience demonstrates, it can be converted instantaneously from currency to cannon. See supra, at 2059. We therefore see no reason why Congress would have intended courts and juries applying § 924(c)(1) to draw a fine metaphysical distinction between a gun's role in a drug offense as a weapon and its role as an item of barter; it creates a grave possibility of violence and death in either capacity. We have observed that the rule of lenity "cannot dictate an implausible interpretation of a statute, nor one at odds with the generally accepted contemporary meaning of a term." Taylor v. United States, 495 U.S. 575, 596, 110 S. Ct. 2143, 2157, 109L. Ed. 2d 607 (1990). That observation controls this case.

---

7. Canons of Construction

Canons of construction are commonly accepted ways to interpret particular provisions or phrases. Examples of canons of construction, some of which use Latin names, include the following:

- Read the statute as a whole.
- When no exception exists, none should be applied.
- Different statutes on the same issue should be interpreted consistently.
- A later provision takes precedence over an earlier one.
- *In pari materia* ("upon the same matter"): statutes on similar subjects are to be construed similarly.
- *Ejusdem generis* ("of the same genus"): when a statute contains a list followed by a catchall phrase, the catchall phrase includes only items similar to the ones on the list.
- *Expression unius* ("expression of one excludes another"): if a statute expressly includes something, then it excludes what is not mentioned.

Be careful when using canons. Some of the canons contradict each other, and many courts do not rely on them.

Canons of Construction

O'Connor Opinion

Finally, the dissent and petitioner invoke the rule of lenity. Post, at 2063. The mere possibility of articulating a narrower construction, however, does not by itself make the rule of lenity applicable. Instead, that venerable rule is reserved for cases where, "[a]fter 'seiz[ing] everything from which aid can be derived,'" the Court is "left with an ambiguous statute."

Scalia Dissent

Even if the reader does not consider the issue to be as clear as I do, he must at least acknowledge, I think, that it is eminently debatable—and that is enough, under the rule of lenity, to require finding for the petitioner here. "At the very least, it may be said that the issue is subject to some doubt. Under these circumstances, we adhere to the familiar rule that, 'where there is ambiguity in a criminal statute, doubts are resolved in favor of the defendant.'"

V. COMMON LAW ANALYSIS

A. Understanding Common Law

Common law is the body of law that develops through case precedent. Before you begin using cases in your analysis, it is important to understand the organization and function of the courts as well as the precedential weight of each case.

1. Function and Organization of the Courts

The American court system actually has two different kinds of courts: federal and state. The federal courts generally have jurisdiction over cases where the U.S. Constitution or federal law applies or where there is diversity of citizenship. Most of the other cases are heard in state courts.

a. The Federal Court System

The federal courts are broken down geographically by "circuits." There are thirteen circuits, the First through the Eleventh Circuits, as well as the D.C. Circuit (which hears D.C. federal cases) and the Federal Circuit (which hears specialized federal cases such as patent cases). The map on the next page shows all of the U.S. circuits. For more information on each, consult each circuit's website, listed in Table 1.2 (see pages 25-27).

Each circuit has a court of appeals; when you speak of a "circuit court," you are referring to the court of appeals in that circuit (so, for example, the First Circuit would be the U.S. Court of Appeals for the First Circuit). Each circuit is further subdivided into districts. Each state has at least one federal district, and many have more. The courts sitting in the district are the federal trial courts

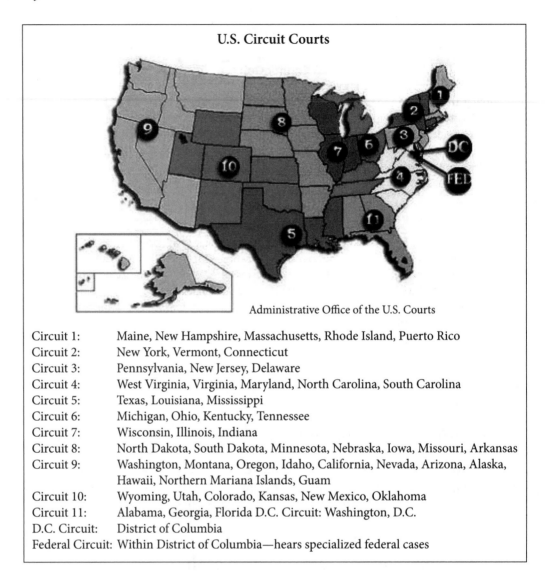

U.S. Circuit Courts

Administrative Office of the U.S. Courts

Circuit 1:   Maine, New Hampshire, Massachusetts, Rhode Island, Puerto Rico
Circuit 2:   New York, Vermont, Connecticut
Circuit 3:   Pennsylvania, New Jersey, Delaware
Circuit 4:   West Virginia, Virginia, Maryland, North Carolina, South Carolina
Circuit 5:   Texas, Louisiana, Mississippi
Circuit 6:   Michigan, Ohio, Kentucky, Tennessee
Circuit 7:   Wisconsin, Illinois, Indiana
Circuit 8:   North Dakota, South Dakota, Minnesota, Nebraska, Iowa, Missouri, Arkansas
Circuit 9:   Washington, Montana, Oregon, Idaho, California, Nevada, Arizona, Alaska,
                Hawaii, Northern Mariana Islands, Guam
Circuit 10:   Wyoming, Utah, Colorado, Kansas, New Mexico, Oklahoma
Circuit 11:   Alabama, Georgia, Florida D.C. Circuit: Washington, D.C.
D.C. Circuit: District of Columbia
Federal Circuit: Within District of Columbia—hears specialized federal cases

(so, for instance, the District Court of Maine is a federal trial court within the First Circuit). Table 1.2 lists the district courts, with their web addresses, for each circuit.

If you bring a case in the federal system, it will start in the district court in the appropriate circuit. If it is appealed, it will go to the court of appeals in that circuit. If appealed further, it might be heard in the U.S. Supreme Court.

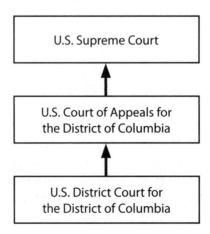

Table 1.2. Circuit Courts and District Courts of the United States

First Circuit
Court of Appeals: http://www.ca1.uscourts.gov
Maine District Court: http://www.med.uscourts.gov
Massachusetts District Court: http://www.mad.uscourts.gov
New Hampshire District Court: http://www.nhd.uscourts.gov
Rhode Island District Court: http://www.rid.uscourts.gov
Puerto Rico District Court: http://www.prd.uscourts.gov

Second Circuit
Court of Appeals: http://www.ca2.uscourts.gov
Connecticut District Court: http://www.ctd.uscourts.gov
New York Eastern District Court: http://www.nyed.uscourts.gov
New York Northern District Court: http://www.nynd.uscourts.gov
New York Southern District Court: http://www.nysd.uscourts.gov
New York Western District Court: http://www.nywd.uscourts.gov
Vermont District Court: http://www.vtd.uscourts.gov

Third Circuit
Court of Appeals: http://www.ca3.uscourts.gov
Delaware District Court: http://www.ded.uscourts.gov
New Jersey District Court: http://www.njd.uscourts.gov
Pennsylvania Eastern District Court: http://www.paed.uscourts.gov
Pennsylvania Middle District Court: http://www.pamd.uscourts.gov
Pennsylvania Western District Court: http://www.pawd.uscourts.gov
Virgin Islands District Court: http://www.vid.uscourts.gov

Fourth Circuit
Court of Appeals: http://www.ca4.uscourts.gov
Maryland District Court: http://www.mdd.uscourts.gov
North Carolina Eastern District Court: http://www.nced.uscourts.gov
North Carolina Middle District Court: http://www.ncmd.uscourts.gov
North Carolina Western District Court: http://www.ncwd.uscourts.gov
South Carolina District Court: http://www.scd.uscourts.gov
Virginia Eastern District Court: http://www.vaed.uscourts.gov
Virginia Western District Court: http://www.vawd.uscourts.gov
West Virginia Northern District Court: http://www.wvnd.uscourts.gov
West Virginia Southern District Court: http://www.wvsd.uscourts.gov

Fifth Circuit
Court of Appeals: http://www.ca5.uscourts.gov
Louisiana Eastern District Court: http://www.laed.uscourts.gov
Louisiana Middle District Court: http://www.lamd.uscourts.gov
Louisiana Western District Court: http://www.lawd.uscourts.gov
Mississippi Northern District Court: http://www.msnd.uscourts.gov
Mississippi Southern District Court: http://www.mssd.uscourts.gov
Texas Eastern District Court: http://www.txed.uscourts.gov
Texas Northern District Court: http://www.txnd.uscourts.gov
Texas Southern District/Bankruptcy Courts: http://www.txsd.uscourts.gov
Texas Western District Court: http://www.txwd.uscourts.gov

Sixth Circuit
Court of Appeals: http://www.ca6.uscourts.gov
Kentucky Eastern District Court: http://www.kyed.uscourts.gov
Kentucky Western District Court: http://www.kywd.uscourts.gov
Michigan Eastern District Court: http://www.mied.uscourts.gov
Michigan Western District Court: http://www.miwd.uscourts.gov
Ohio Northern District Court: http://www.ohnd.uscourts.gov
Ohio Southern District Court: http://www.ohsd.uscourts.gov
Tennessee Eastern District Court: http://www.tned.uscourts.gov
Tennessee Middle District Court: http://www.tnmd.uscourts.gov
Tennessee Western District Court: http://www.tnwd.uscourts.gov

Seventh Circuit
Court of Appeals: http://www.ca7.uscourts.gov
Illinois Central District Court: http://www.ilcd.uscourts.gov
Illinois Northern District Court: http://www.ilnd.uscourts.gov
Illinois Southern District Court: http://www.ilsd.uscourts.gov
Indiana Northern District Court: http://www.innd.uscourts.gov
Indiana Southern District Court: http://www.insd.uscourts.gov
Wisconsin Eastern District Court: http://www.wied.uscourts.gov
Wisconsin Western District Court: http://www.wiwd.uscourts.gov

Eighth Circuit
Court of Appeals: http://www.ca8.uscourts.gov
Arkansas Eastern District Court: http://www.ared.uscourts.gov
Arkansas Western District Court: http://www.arwd.uscourts.gov
Iowa Northern District Court: http://www.iand.uscourts.gov
Iowa Southern District Court: http://www.iasd.uscourts.gov
Minnesota District Court: http://www.mnd.uscourts.gov
Missouri Eastern District Court: http://www.moed.uscourts.gov
Missouri Western District Court: http://www.mowd.uscourts.gov
Nebraska District Court: http://www.ned.uscourts.gov
North Dakota District Court: http://www.ndd.uscourts.gov
South Dakota District Court: http://www.sdd.uscourts.gov

Ninth Circuit
Court of Appeals: http://www.ca9.uscourts.gov
Alaska District Court: http://www.akd.uscourts.gov
Arizona District Court: http://www.azd.uscourts.gov
California Central District Court: http://www.cacd.uscourts.gov
California Eastern District Court: http://www.caed.uscourts.gov
California Northern District Court: http://www.cand.uscourts.gov
California Southern District Court: http://www.casd.uscourts.gov
Guam District Court: http://www.gud.uscourts.gov
Hawaii District Court: http://www.hid.uscourts.gov
Idaho Bankruptcy/District Court: http://www.id.uscourts.gov
Montana District Court: http://www.mtd.uscourts.gov
Nevada District Court: http://www.nvd.uscourts.gov
Northern Mariana Islands District Court: http://www.nmid.uscourts.gov
Oregon District Court: http://www.ord.uscourts.gov
Washington Eastern District Court: http://www.waed.uscourts.gov
Washington Western District Court: http://www.wawd.uscourts.gov

Tenth Circuit
Court of Appeals: http://www.ca10.uscourts.gov
Colorado District Court: http://www.cod.uscourts.gov
Kansas District Court: http://www.ksd.uscourts.gov
New Mexico District Court: http://www.nmd.uscourts.gov
Oklahoma Eastern District Court: http://www.oked.uscourts.gov
Oklahoma Northern District Court: http://www.oknd.uscourts.gov
Oklahoma Western District Court: http://www.okwd.uscourts.gov
Utah District Court: http://www.utd.uscourts.gov
Wyoming District Court: http://www.wyd.uscourts.gov

Eleventh Circuit
Court of Appeals: http://www.ca11.uscourts.gov
Alabama Middle District Court: http://www.almd.uscourts.gov
Alabama Northern District Court: http://www.alnd.uscourts.gov
Alabama Southern District Court: http://www.alsd.uscourts.gov
Florida Middle District Court: http://www.flmd.uscourts.gov
Florida Northern District Court: http://www.flnd.uscourts.gov
Florida Southern District Court: http://www.flsd.uscourts.gov
Georgia Middle District Court: http://www.gamd.uscourts.gov
Georgia Northern District Court: http://www.gand.uscourts.gov
Georgia Southern District Court: http://www.gasd.uscourts.gov

D.C. Circuit
Court of Appeals: http://www.cadc.uscourts.gov
District Court for the District of Columbia: http://www.dcd.uscourts.gov/dcd
D.C. Bankruptcy Court: http://www.dcb.uscourts.gov
Federal Public Defender: http://www. www.dcfpd.org

Federal Circuit Court
U.S. Court of Appeals for the Federal Circuit: http://www.cafc.uscourts.gov

b. The State Court System

Each state has its own system, and many of those mirror the federal system with a trial court, an intermediate appellate court, and an appellate court. Some jurisdictions do not have an intermediate court, while other states have intermediate courts with multiple divisions. Each state has different names for the various courts (for example, in New York, the Supreme Court is the trial court and the Court of Appeals is the highest court).

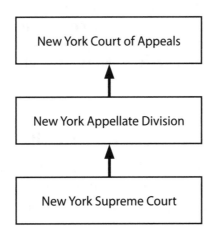

Each state's court system is represented through various sources online. For each state and for a number of territories, Table 1.3, on page 29, lists websites you can check for more information.

c.   The Function of the Courts

The trial courts and appellate courts have different functions. The trial court consists of a judge who sits on the bench and listens to both legal arguments and evidence. Therefore, the trial judge has an opportunity to observe witnesses and judge credibility. During the process at the trial level, the judge decides both questions of law and questions of fact (if it is a jury trial, most factual questions are decided by the jury). The appellate court serves a much different function; it does not simply sit in the trial court's shoes. An appellate panel usually consists of three judges who listen to arguments from lawyers about the specific errors made by the court below. Therefore, the appellate court reviews limited decisions of the trial court, using different levels of deference, or standards of review (see pages 168-169). Usually, when you read judicial opinions, you are reading appellate cases—either from the highest court of appeal or the intermediate court of appeal in your jurisdiction.

2.   Stare Decisis

Stare decisis is a core concept of the American legal system. It means that current cases are treated consistently with past precedent. Stare decisis has a number of benefits to litigants. First, it permits them to predict the outcome of a legal issue or dispute. Often, clients ask lawyers for advice as to whether they are permitted to perform a certain action; lawyers look to past cases to determine whether the requested action is permitted under the law. Clients can then rely on the prior cases, through the doctrine of stare decisis, to determine whether to perform the particular action. Second, lawyers look to prior decisions to determine whether to bring lawsuits and to determine how best to defend lawsuits. Third, stare decisis provides parties with fair treatment under the law. Each party is treated similarly, based on case precedent.

Stare decisis, while a core concept of the American legal system, operates with some flexibility. Because no one case is exactly like a prior case, courts can still follow precedent but massage the law to fit the current facts. Thus, case law develops over time, often by adding new elements to a rule or applying exceptions to existing rules. At times, however, courts do overtly overrule previous decisions. When they do so, the courts often justify these rulings based on changes in circumstances or societal values.

3.   Binding vs. Persuasive Authority

Stare decisis has both vertical and horizontal limitations. On a horizontal level, a court is bound only by decisions of other courts within its jurisdiction. These cases are therefore considered to be binding or mandatory. However,

Table 1.3. Websites for Courts in U.S. States and Territories

ALABAMA	http://judicial.alabama.gov
ALASKA	www.state.ak.us/courts
AMERICAN SAMOA	www.justice.gov/jmd/ls/americansamoa
ARIZONA	www.azcourts.gov
ARKANSAS	http://courts.state.ar.us
CALIFORNIA	www.courtinfo.ca.gov
COLORADO	www.courts.state.co.us
CONNECTICUT	www.jud.ct.gov
DELAWARE	http://courts.delaware.gov
DISTRICT OF COLUMBIA	www.dccourts.gov
FEDERATED STATES OF MICRONESIA	www.paclii.org/fm/courts.html
FLORIDA	www.flcourts.org
GEORGIA	www.georgiacourts.org
GUAM	www.guamsupremecourt.com
HAWAII	www.courts.state.hi.us
IDAHO	www.isc.idaho.gov
ILLINOIS	www.state.il.us/court
INDIANA	www.in.gov/judiciary
IOWA	www.iowacourts.state.ia.us
KANSAS	www.kscourts.org
KENTUCKY	http://courts.ky.gov
LOUISIANA	www.louisiana.gov/Government/Judicial_Branch/
MAINE	www.courts.state.me.us
MARSHALL ISLANDS	www.paclii.org
MARYLAND	www.courts.state.md.us
MASSACHUSETTS	www.mass.gov/courts
MICHIGAN	www.courts.michigan.gov
MINNESOTA	www.courts.state.mn.us
MISSISSIPPI	www.mssc.state.ms.us
MISSOURI	www.courts.mo.gov
MONTANA	http://courts.mt.gov
NEBRASKA	http://court.nol.org
NEVADA	www.nevadajudiciary.us
NEW HAMPSHIRE	www.courts.state.nh.us
NEW JERSEY	www.judiciary.state.nj.us
NEW MEXICO	www.nmcourts.com
NEW YORK	www.courts.state.ny.us
NORTH CAROLINA	www.nccourts.org
NORTH DAKOTA	www.ndcourts.com/court/courts.htm
NORTHERN MARIANA ISLANDS	www.cnmilaw.org
OHIO	www.sconet.state.oh.us
OKLAHOMA	www.oscn.net
OREGON	www.oregon.gov/OJD/courts
PENNSYLVANIA	www.courts.state.pa.us
PUERTO RICO	www.ramajudicial.pr
RHODE ISLAND	www.courts.ri.gov
SOUTH CAROLINA	www.judicial.state.sc.us
SOUTH DAKOTA	www.sdjudicial.com
TENNESSEE	www.tsc.state.tn.us
TEXAS	www.courts.state.tx.us
UTAH	www.utcourts.gov
VERMONT	www.vermontjudiciary.org
VIRGIN ISLANDS	www.visupremecourt.org
VIRGINIA	www.courts.state.va.us
WASHINGTON	www.courts.wa.gov
WEST VIRGINIA	www.state.wv.us/wvsca/wvsystem.htm
WISCONSIN	www.wicourts.gov
WYOMING	www.courts.state.wy.us

some cases are only persuasive. For example, the state of New Jersey is not bound by cases from North Dakota. Likewise, except in certain situations, state courts are not bound by cases from federal courts nor are federal courts bound by state courts opinions. These cases are considered to be persuasive.

On a vertical level, courts are bound only by decisions from courts from a higher level. Thus, trial courts are bound by appellate court decisions within that jurisdiction, but appellate courts are not bound by decisions from their trial courts.

Thus, a persuasive case is one from the same level court or a lower court within a jurisdiction or from a different jurisdiction altogether. If you look at the court systems diagram on page 27, the New York Court of Appeals is binding on the New York Appellate Division. If you are writing a brief to be filed in the New York Appellate Division, you would rely heavily on New York Court of Appeals cases. However, New York Appellate Division cases (even from that specific division) would be only persuasive. In addition, a case from the federal court, even the Court of Appeals from the Second Circuit, would be only persuasive in the New York Appellate Division because the case is from a different jurisdiction.

Most students are surprised to discover that federal courts usually do not bind state courts. In fact, the state's highest court (the New York Court of Appeals above) is binding not only on the rest of that state's courts, but also on federal courts applying that state's law. (So, the Second Circuit must follow the New York Court of Appeals decisions on matters of state law.) The U.S. Supreme Court does bind all state courts on matters of federal constitutional law, but states may still impose more rights under their own constitutions or laws.

4.   Precedential Weight of Cases

The concept of stare decisis becomes more nuanced when deciding which case to apply to your issue. When deciding how much precedential value to give to a case, it is important to consider both the organization and the function of the courts. Although an appellate case will have more authority than a trial court case, other distinctions also come into play.

a.   *Holding vs. Dicta*

When relying on judicial opinions, it is important to realize that only the case holding is binding—not the dicta. The holding is that part of the case that resolves the issue in dispute. Other statements the court makes in explaining its holding is called dicta. Only the holding is binding on other courts.

b.   *Majority Opinions vs. Dissents*

The majority opinion is the decision of the court that binds other courts. The dissent is not binding. Concurring decisions are also only persuasive.

c. Other Traits Affecting the Weight of Cases

There are a number of other traits that affect the weight of cases. Whether a decision is binding or persuasive, it will carry more weight depending on these factors:

- **Date:** A recent decision carries a lot of weight. Trial judges do not like being reversed. Therefore, when they write their opinions, trial judges are often wondering what the appellate court is thinking. A recent case will answer that question. On the flip side, a case that has been around for a while and has been followed consistently also carries a lot of weight.

- **Number and Names of Judges:** Most appellate courts use three-judge panels. However, at times, the full appellate court will hear a case in an en banc hearing. En banc decisions carry more weight because they are issued from the whole bench, not just a three-judge panel. Also, look for the name of the judge writing the decision. Often cases from well-known judges (such as Judge Posner) carry more weight.

- **The Court Itself:** Certain courts carry more weight than others, even when they are only persuasive authority. The U.S. Supreme Court is the most prestigious court, but other courts, such as the Second Circuit, also carry a lot of weight. Also, state courts often look to the decisions of their federal circuits for guidance (so, for example, the New York state courts might look to the Second Circuit). Also, state courts often look to neighboring states for guidance (the District of Columbia, for instance, might look to Maryland courts). In addition, some courts have reputations based on their past rulings. For example, the Ninth Circuit is considered to be a liberal court, whereas the Fourth Circuit is considered to be conservative.

- **The Treatment of the Case:** A case will carry more precedential value if other courts have followed its ruling. Updating the case is very important to discover not only how often a case has been cited but also by which courts. If other jurisdictions have followed suit, the case gains even more precedential value.

Now that you understand the organization and function of the courts as well as the relative weight of authorities, you are ready to use the concept of stare decisis to begin using case analysis in your legal reasoning.

B. Case Analysis

Case analysis is the use of cases to make legal arguments. Courts look to past decisions when making law so that citizens are treated fairly, predictably, and consistently. Case analysis is one of the hardest concepts for students to master, but one of the techniques most often used by lawyers to make arguments in the United States.

Case analysis is used in many situations:

1. **Interpreting statutes using cases:** When a statute or regulation exists on point, lawyers and courts look to past decisions to determine how a term or phrase or policy of a statute or regulation has been applied in the past. This technique uses deductive, rule-based reasoning and is discussed earlier in the section on statutory interpretation (see pages 12-13).
2. **Case synthesis:** When there is no statute on point, common law is used to determine the rule of law. Often, a body of cases will clearly enunciate a rule of law. However, when there is no clear rule, the lawyer needs to create the rule using a number of cases pieced together to form a coherent rule. Case synthesis, discussed in detail below, is used to articulate both general rules of law as well as specific rules and definitions within those rules.
3. **Case comparisons:** Once the rule of law is established, cases are used as comparison to apply the same law to different situations using case analogies and distinctions. Case comparisons are discussed in detail below.

1.   Case Synthesis

Case synthesis is the weaving together of cases to create a clearly enunciated rule. Lawyers use case synthesis to create a rule when there is no statute or regulation on point (for example, to articulate the elements of intentional infliction of emotional distress) or to create a specific rule or definition for a particular element in an already enunciated rule (for example, to define the outrageous element within intentional infliction of emotional distress).

Case synthesis can be tricky. While courts make decisions on similar points of law, each case is based on a specific set of facts, so no two decisions are exactly alike. A court can base its holding on specific facts or certain reasoning or policies. As a result, when a lawyer tries to synthesize a whole body of case law on a specific point, there might not be a lucid rule. If there is a clear rule, it is usually readily apparent as a court will state a rule and follow it; this rule then will often be cited in most subsequent cases on point. However, when no clear rule exists, a lawyer will need to synthesize the rule by combining the rulings from the prior cases. This task is usually difficult as the lawyer needs to determine if the court's rulings were based on reasoning, facts, or policies.

Many law students incorrectly believe they have "synthesized" a rule by simply describing a list of cases in a book report fashion. However, a synthesis involves pulling together similar threads from cases and weaving them into a coherent picture—not merely listing them in chronological order. Good lawyers can synthesize the law from cases into a number of viable rules and then choose the one that works best for the client's issue.

While there is no one way to synthesize a rule from a group of cases, there are some guidelines:

1. **Compile all the cases on point.** Here, you will need to thoroughly research your issue in order to find the relevant cases on point. Focus

first on binding cases within your jurisdiction. If you need to rely on persuasive cases, you may do so, but keep in mind that they might not fit consistently with the synthesis nor will a court be bound by persuasive decisions.

2. **Read all the relevant cases carefully.** Here, you are not just trying to pick out relevant quotations for the reader. A typical novice writer will mistakenly rely on language taken out of context and mislead the reader. Instead, be sure that you understand the whole case before you rely on one specific piece of it.

3. **Group cases according to explicit rules.** When a case sets out an explicit rule, try to find another case with a similar explicit rule. Sometimes the language will be exactly the same; other times the language will differ. In either instance, pull out the important rule that the court applied and group the cases according to that rule.

4. **Group cases according to implicit rules.** Often courts will make rulings without explicitly identifying the reasoning. However, you can imply the reasoning from the facts or from policy arguments within the opinion.

5. **Fit the pieces together.** Combine the explicit rules cases with the implicit rules cases to create a cohesive and consistent rule on the issue. By definition, this synthesized rule will not be articulated by any one case. However, the rule should be consistent with all the relevant cases on point. If a binding case in your jurisdiction contradicts the rule, then your synthesized rule will not be an accurate reflection of the law.

Case Synthesis Samples

Three separate cases have the following holdings:

1. Police may base re-entrance into a residence on a valid search warrant used thirty minutes prior to the re-entrance.
2. Police may not reenter a home the day after a valid search has been completed on a residence unless they first get a new search warrant.
3. To get a search warrant, police must have probable cause.

Some possible synthesized rules for these three cases:

- To search a residence for a second time, police must have probable cause and apply for a new search warrant if the second search is not performed in a timely fashion.

  Or

- Probable cause is not the only prerequisite to search a residence; police must also have a valid search warrant, and that warrant cannot be used again to make subsequent searches unless close in time to the initial search.

  Or

- Police may reenter a residence using a valid search warrant based on probable cause, even if the warrant has been used to justify a recent search of the same residence.

Watch out for these typical mistakes when synthesizing cases:

1. **Synthesizing in chronological order.** At times, it might make sense to create a synthesis based on the historical, chronological development of the law in your jurisdiction because cases often build on each other as the law develops. However, the law often develops in fits and starts so that one part of the rule may be enunciated and not revisited again for 10 or 20 years. Therefore, create your synthesis based on different facets of the law as opposed to a chronological arrangement.

2. **Confusing different terms of art that apply to the same part of the rule.** Some courts might create the same rule but use different terms of art to do so. Here, a novice writer might mistakenly use the different terms of art to articulate two different parts of a rule when, in fact, they are identifying the same part of the rule. Here, you will need to be flexible and craft a piece of the rule that incorporates both terms.

3. **Using quotations out of context.** Do not rely on quotations taken out of context to mislead the reader. Instead, you need to understand the case holistically to ensure that the piece you have isolated is still consistent with the holding and reasoning of the case.

4. **Avoiding rules articulated only by one court.** In synthesizing rules, you will be looking at an array of rules that come from various courts. While one part of the rule might come from multiple decisions, another part might come from just one court's ruling. Therefore, if a binding court in your jurisdiction adds another element to an already-existing rule, you cannot avoid that case—unless, of course, that case is older and all of the current cases that synthesize the rule ignore the case.

Once you have synthesized a rule, you apply the rule to the client's facts. Here, you can use rule-based reasoning (deductive reasoning (see pages 12-13) whereby you move from the general rule, apply your particular client's facts, and reach a conclusion), analogical reasoning (see case comparisons below), or policy arguments (see pages 40-41).

2. Case Comparisons

When a rule is clearly delineated, whether through statute or case synthesis, previous cases are used to compare and distinguish the current case. This method of analogical reasoning is based on the doctrine of stare decisis—that like cases should be treated similarly. If a prior court (hopefully in the same jurisdiction) has struggled with a similar issue and come to a conclusion, then this court should follow that decision. Here, the lawyer uses inductive reasoning (see pages 13-14) to create case comparisons.

When searching for cases effective for comparisons, a lawyer should look for cases addressing similar issues. So, if you are in a custody battle, look for cases involving custody disputes. Second, look for cases where the facts of the prior case are similar to your client's facts or where the reasoning of the prior case can be used in your case. Third, determine if the holding of the prior case is similar to the predicted or preferred outcome in your case. If the outcome is the same, you will be creating case analogies. If the outcome is different, you will be distinguishing cases.

a. *Analogizing Cases*

Analogizing a case is usually the strongest kind of case comparison because it allows a lawyer to argue that a prior case with a favorable holding is similar to his or her case, so that it should be followed. However, a prior case need not be exactly the same as your case for it to be analogous. In fact, it will be rare if you ever find a case during your career that is exactly on point. Therefore, you will need to determine if the similarities between your case and the prior case are legally significant to make it analogous. Do not worry if the facts are not the same; oftentimes it is the reasoning that is most significant.

b. *Distinguishing Cases*

On the other hand, at times you will find only cases where the holdings run contrary to your preferred outcome. In these situations, you will distinguish the unfavorable case by arguing that the rule doesn't apply at all or that it should be applied differently. While distinguishing cases can make you feel as if you are on the defensive, this technique can help you produce very effective legal arguments. However, do not feel as if you have to distinguish a case merely because it is different. All cases are different from one other. The question is whether the differences are legally significant.

Sample of Effective Case Analogy and Distinction

[Defendant was not subjected to any physical restraints throughout the course of the interview.] [In <u>Resper</u>, the court held the defendant was not in custody because he knew he was not under arrest, he voluntarily went to the police station, and he agreed to speak to a police officer. <u>Resper</u>, 793 A.2d at 456.] [Similarly, defendant in the present case knew he was not under formal arrest and voluntarily agreed to attend the meeting.] [However, the facts of the present case are far less extreme than Resper in a number of important ways. First, the meeting in this case occurred in the principal's office at the principal's request, not in the police station as in Resper. Second, the defendant in this case was not questioned by the police. In addition, the advance warning defendant had about the meeting and its purpose mitigate any possible apprehension.] [Therefore, the defendant was not physically restrained because he agreed to speak to the principal in the principal's office.]

This topic sentence clearly introduces the subelement of physical restraints.

This sentence provides the facts, reasoning, and holding of a prior case.

This sentence compares our case to the prior case in an analogy.

These sentences distinguish our case from the prior case.

This sentence finishes the comparison by concluding that the defendant was not physically retrained—the subelement addressed in this paragraph.

c.   *Crafting Effective Case Comparisons*

The creative aspect of crafting effective case comparisons is deciding what is important to compare. It might be the facts or the reasoning. You might argue that one particular fact is most important while your opposing counsel will focus on a different fact. You will have to show why your focus is more compelling.

While there is no formula for creating a case comparison, there are some helpful ingredients to consider:

- **Holding:** Be sure to include the holding of the prior case. The judge needs to know which way the other court decided. Remember that a holding is very specific to the particular case. A holding does not include dicta or policy arguments.
- **Facts:** You should also explain the important, relevant facts of the prior case. Because you are comparing the prior case to your case, be sure to show what facts are applicable. In addition, you need to illustrate how your case is similar or different from the prior case. Be specific for the reader so that he understands how the two are tied together.
- **Reasoning:** You should also explain the reasoning the prior court used to justify the holding. Because you are comparing the prior case to your case, you should show what reasoning is applicable to your case and why by relating back to the facts or to a policy argument. Be specific so that the reader understands how the reasoning from the prior case relates to your case.

While most effective case comparisons include a comparison of the facts, reasoning, and holding of the prior case to your case, there is no magic formula. Do not try to fit the same ingredients into every comparison, and do not attempt to do so in the same order every time. Instead, be creative and remember that your goal is to compare the two cases to show why the result should be the same or different.

d.   *Comparing One Case*

Most law students start with using just one prior case for comparison. In these situations, it is helpful if you provide the reader with the legal context, such as a rule or definition, before launching into a case comparison that applies that rule. To begin the actual comparison, consider starting with the prior case so that the reader understands the legal precedent first. Explain the relevant facts, reasoning, and holding, but be careful to provide only the information that is necessary to make your point clear. There is no need to provide all the facts from the prior case; you will only overload the reader with irrelevant information. Next, compare the prior case to your case and explicitly tie the relevant facts or reasoning together. Show why the cases are similar or different. Do not force the reader to flip back to your fact section to understand your case comparison. Consider counterarguments as well when appropriate. Be sure to provide a conclusion on the legal element so that the reader understands the outcome of the comparison.

e. Comparing Multiple Cases

While comparing one case to your case can be effective, it is often too simplistic or might not thoroughly and accurately reflect the law. Usually, multiple cases exist for each rule of law. Therefore, the judge will need to determine which prior cases are more on point and which are closer to the facts and issues presented by your client's case. By providing multiple cases for comparison, you present a broad view of the law and explain where your client's situation fits into that law.

Comparing multiple cases is similar but a bit more complicated than comparing just one case. While you still want to provide a rule up front for context when one is available, the comparison can take many forms. For example, you might start by explaining the facts, reasoning, and holding of the prior cases and explain the similar thread of these cases before applying them to your case. In fact, the thread might be the rule you provide up front for context. Or you might explain one case, compare it to your case, and then move on to a comparison of the second and third case. Yet another formulation would be to present two cases and then explain why one case is similar to your case and the other is different. No one formula is correct, and you should determine how to craft comparisons so that they are both clear and concise.

Sample of Effective Multiple-Case Comparison

[Defendant was not subjected to any physical restraints throughout the course of the interview.] [In Resper v. United States, 793 A.2d 450 (D.C. 2002), the suspect was not in custody despite being apprehended from his vehicle by officers with drawn weapons, because he was not handcuffed or subjected to any bodily restraints either at the time of apprehension or during his ride to the police station for questioning.] [Similarly, in Morris, 823 A.2d 236 (D.C. 2003), the defendant was not in custody when he rode unrestrained in the front seat of a police car to the police station for questioning, and during the interview, defendant was not handcuffed.] [Lance Harbor, on the other hand, was not subjected to similar physical restraints. He was never approached by officers with drawn weapons as in Resper nor was he placed in a moving police car as in Morris.] [Instead, when Lance Harbor confessed to distributing drugs, he sat in a principal's office in his high school with his parents and his friend without any physical restraints to hold him "in custody."]

This topic sentence clearly introduces the subelement of physical restraints.

This sentence provides the facts, reasoning, and holding of one prior case.

This sentence provides the facts, reasoning, and holding of a second prior case.

These sentences specifically compare the prior two cases to the facts of this case through case distinction.

This sentence finishes the comparison by providing more facts from the current case to prove why the defendant was not physically retrained—the subelement addressed in this paragraph.

<table>
<tr><td>This sentence introduces the element.</td><td rowspan="5">

Sample of Sliding Scale Argument

[McManus's identification of the defendant two months after the crime is unreliable.] [The acceptable length of time between the crime and the identification has varied widely. <u>Compare</u> Judd, 402 So. 2d at 1280 (identification one week after crime unreliable), <u>with</u> Simmons, 934 So. 2d at 1120 (identification one year after crime reliable). Ultimately, accuracy, degree of attention, opportunity to view, and certainty weigh heavily in determining reliability. <u>Judd</u>, 402 So. 2d at 1282.] [In <u>Simmons</u>, identification one year after the crime was reliable because of adequate opportunity to view, high degree of attention, and the extremely detailed and accurate description. 934 So. 2d at 1120. Similarly, in <u>Billue</u>, the identification was reliable a few days after the crime because witnesses looked directly at the defendant, had ample opportunity to view the defendant, directed their attention at him during the crime, and provided accurate descriptions. 497 So. 2d at 714.] [Unlike the witnesses in these cases, McManus's identification proves unreliable two months after the crime because he provided an extremely general, inaccurate description, did not focus his attention on the suspect, could not adequately view the suspect's face, and could not root his certainty in the robber's facial characteristics.] Ultimately, McManus's identification was unreliable under the totality of the circumstances.

</td></tr>
<tr><td>These sentences set out the sliding scale.</td></tr>
<tr><td></td></tr>
<tr><td>These sentences apply cases on the sliding scale.</td></tr>
<tr><td>This sentence applies the sliding scale to the facts of the case.</td></tr>
</table>

f. Using Multiple Cases to Set Out Legal Parameters or a Sliding Scale Argument

At times, you will find multiple cases that, when combined together, set out a legal parameter or a sliding scale of the law. Your job will be to use these cases to first set out the sliding scale for the judge and then to argue where your case falls on that scale.

For example, assume you are analyzing the reliability of a witness identification in a criminal case where you represent the defendant. One of the factors determining reliability of the witness identification is the time between the crime and the identification by the witness. You find a case that holds that the identification was reliable because there was only one day between the crime and the identification. You find another case that holds that a six-month delay was unreliable. In your case, there was a three-month delay between the crime and the identification of your client. To argue this particular factor, you would use these cases to set out the sliding scale for the judge, such as "one day is reliable, but six months is unreliable." Next, you would need to compare your case to these cases and argue where your case falls on the sliding scale: Three months is closer to the six months that was found unreliable. You would need to look at the reasoning or policy from the prior cases to argue the appropriate outcome.

Sliding Scale:

One Day		Six Months

? ← ← Three Months (your case) → → ?

Or consider adding even more cases to the scenario:

One Day	One Week	Four Months	Six Months

? ← ← Three Months (your case) → → ?

Here, you could incorporate all four of the cases into your analysis to determine whether three months would be too much delay between the crime and a reliable identification. See Sample of Sliding Scale Argument on page 38.

g. *Typical Problems with Case Comparisons*

Typical problems with case comparisons include the following:

1. **Using quotations from cases instead of analysis.** Often new lawyers rely on quotations, assuming that the author of the opinion will carry more weight and articulate the analogy better. This assumption is often wrong in case analogies. By definition, analogies compare a prior case to the present one. If a lawyer simply relies on language from the prior case, then the comparison itself is lost. While quotations are often useful, especially when enunciating a rule of law, do not over rely on them for analogies. Block quotations are especially cumbersome, and readers often skip over them.

2. **Using only facts of your case and omitting case precedent.** Grounding your arguments in the law is the key to case comparisons. A typical mistake of new lawyers is to provide a rule and then use only facts from the client's situation to show why the rule applies or doesn't apply. Instead, a lawyer should try to use prior cases to show how that rule has been applied (or not) in the past and then show why the facts of the case are similar (or not) to case precedent.

3. **Omitting the holding of the precedent.** A case is not going to be useful for analogies if the reader does not know which way the court held. Be sure to include the court's ruling in your analogy.

4. **Using too much of the prior case.** Use only the relevant facts and reasoning of the prior case to make your point. Do not inundate the reader with extraneous parts of the case because these will only cause confusion with the current case.

5. **Omitting the facts of the current case.** Relying solely on case precedent is not enough for a comparison. You should also supply enough of the facts of your case to show why the prior case is similar or not.

6. **Omitting the tie between the prior case and the current case.** Don't forget to show why the prior case is similar or different from your case. Here, facts, reasoning, and policy are often used for support.
7. **Ignoring the other side's argument.** Case analogies are stronger if they anticipate the other side's argument and show why that argument will fail.

VI. POLICY ARGUMENTS

When lawyers make policy arguments, they focus on broad social goals that will be affected by the outcome of the case. Policy arguments are made in a number of contexts. First, as discussed in the section on statutory interpretation above, lawyers make policy arguments when they interpret the legislature's purpose in writing the statute. Second, lawyers also make policy arguments when no clear rule exists; the lawyers will then argue what the rule should be based on a particular policy. This type of situation is called a case of first impression. Third, lawyers make policy arguments in addition to other legal arguments in constructing their legal analysis (see pages 41-45). In all of these instances, the lawyers will argue why the interpretation or creation of a particular law is consistent or inconsistent with the policy of the jurisdiction or society in general. Some possible policy arguments include the following:

- **Moral values.** Policy arguments based on moral values argue that a particular law will offend or perpetuate a moral value. For example, "Teenagers should be required to get parental approval for an abortion." Here, the moral issue is teen abortion and the argument would focus on the moral implications of killing a fetus or the protection of a teenager's right to choose. Oftentimes, these arguments are viewed as political, and it can be helpful to know your audience before you advance these arguments.
- **Social justice.** Policy arguments based on social justice are similar to those based on moral values except that the focus is on society in general instead of on a personal basis. For example, "The death penalty should not exist for minors." Here, arguments would be made by looking at the way society currently views the death penalty. Again, these arguments are often viewed as political, so it is helpful to know your audience.
- **Fairness.** Fairness arguments are based on fairness of the justice system specifically. For example, "Minors should not be held accountable as adults." Here, the arguments would revolve around the implications on the criminal justice system.
- **Economics.** Economic arguments focus on the effect the law will have on economic principles, such as allocation of sources or efficiency arguments. Here, lawyers argue how much rulings will cost society or particular organizations. For example, "Corporations should not be required to reduce greenhouse gases." Here, the focus would be on the cost benefit analysis of such a requirement.

- **Institutional roles and the administration of justice.** Here, the arguments are based on the role the court should play in society as well as whether the court can or should administer a particular rule. For example, a lawyer may argue that the court's role is not to legislate this particular issue or that the rule will lead to a "slippery slope" in the law or a plethora of unwanted litigation.

As a lawyer, you can be very creative with these policy arguments. Brainstorm many different policy reasons for your desired outcome and then choose the one or two that are most compelling. Consider whether other courts have used the same policy arguments to support their reasoning. If you can cite to other opinions, your policy arguments will be stronger.

Lawyers sometimes weave policy arguments throughout their documents in a fashion similar to a theory of the case. Amicus briefs filed in the U.S. Supreme Court often use policy arguments and reflect the beliefs of the organization filing the brief.

Some lawyers will argue the law first and then delineate a separate section in a document to craft policy arguments. In these situations, lawyers either argue in the alternative or use the policy arguments to show why their interpretation of the legal rule is correct. See **jurisprudence,** pages 10-14.

VII. CONSTRUCTING LEGAL ANALYSIS

Once you have a basic understanding of the various basic tools of legal analysis (see statutory interpretation, pages 14-23; case synthesis, pages 32-34; case analogies, page 35, and policy arguments, pages 40-41), you need to use them all to create a cohesive legal argument. This skill is usually the most challenging to learn and to teach. Students often complain that they receive no guidance until after they have written and submitted a document, and then they are "only told what they have done wrong." Students wish they could have been told "exactly what to do before writing." On the other hand, professors resist providing a "perfect" example or a formula for writing analysis because there are truly an infinite number of ways to write each document, and professors want the students to think about their choices instead of simply following one model or formula.

The following section provides a number of different "formulas" to use as guides when you first begin writing legal analysis. First, however, a warning: Do not follow the formulas blindly; instead, treat them as guides to begin the thinking process. Consider the formulas as myths; do not take them literally, but let them serve as legal compasses to focus you in the right direction and force you to ask the right questions. You need to understand the purpose of each part of the formula so that you can consider varying the formula or choose to ignore it altogether when your creativity allows for better choices.

A.   *The Formulas*

1.   IRAC

IRAC (pronounced "eye-rack") is the formula that most professors use to teach legal analysis.

I   *Issue.* Present the issue in the beginning of your analysis.
R *Rule.* Explain the legal rule. (This rule might come from a statute, a case, or a regulation.)
A *Application.* Apply the legal rule to the facts of your case.
C *Conclusion.* Conclude on the issue.

2.   CRAC

This formula is a variation of IRAC; it basically replaces the "issue" with "conclusion" so that the conclusion appears both in the beginning and the end of the analysis.

C *Conclusion.* Present your issue in a conclusive manner.
R *Rule.* Explain the legal rule. (This rule might come from a statute, a case, a regulation.)
A *Application.* Apply the legal rule to the facts of your case.
C *Conclusion.* Conclude on the issue.

3.   CRuPAC

This is simply a variation of CRAC, but with a bit more detail.

C   *Conclusion.* Present your issue in a conclusive manner.
Ru *Rule.* Explain the legal rule.
P   *Proof of rule.* Citation to the authority to prove the rule exists.
A   *Application.* Apply the legal rule to the facts of your case.
C   *Conclusion.* Conclude on the issue.

B.   *Unraveling the Myth of the Formulas*

The formulas are often very helpful when writing law school exams, essays on the bar exam, and simple legal writing. For example, when writing a paragraph on the term *outrageous* in an intentional infliction of emotional distress exam question or on a first-year memo assignment, a student might do the following within the formulaic structures:

1. *Issue:* Start with a topic sentence that tells the reader that the plaintiff must prove that the conduct was outrageous. (Or, if using CRAC, state that the conduct was or was not outrageous.)

2. *Rule and Proof:* Provide a definition of outrageous and provide a citation.
3. *Application:* Use a case to compare its reasoning, holding, and facts to the client's facts.
4. *Conclusion:* Conclude on the issue (the conduct was or was not outrageous).

This formula works fine for such a simple analysis. However, what if the analysis is more complicated? What if the rule comes from many sources? What if the rule is not clear? What exactly does *application* mean? Where should a counter-argument go? How does a policy argument fit into these formulas? Students who don't ask these questions and rely on the formulas alone often write legal analysis that is too simple for the existing law. In addition, many students incorrectly assume these formulas must always fit within one paragraph, whereby the topic sentence provides the issue or conclusion, the final sentence of the paragraph is the conclusion, and everything in between is the rule and the application. These paragraphs often span pages and pages of a memo, creating too much information within one paragraph for the reader to digest.

So what should you do when writing complicated legal analysis? First, if you choose to use a formula, understand its purpose and limitations and why each part of the formula exists. Understand how legal readers think and what they expect. Second, you should rely on your own creativity in legal analysis. Do not assume that there is only one way to interpret, analyze, or apply the law.

1. Issue or Conclusion

The issue, as used in this context, is not the issue statement or the whole issue for the underlying case. Instead, *issue* here is used to describe a specific issue or element within the law (such as the meaning of *outrageous* within intentional infliction of emotional distress). Keep in mind that legal readers want to understand the issue, but they are almost always in a rush. Therefore, the issue should be easy to find. Most busy readers skim documents by reading topic sentences. Thus, by placing your issues in topic sentences, they will be prominent for the skimming reader.

2. The Rule

The legal reader usually wants to understand the law before it is applied. Therefore, it makes sense to provide the legal context, or rule, before the application. However, this context can be a policy argument, a term of art, a definition, a rule from a case, or from many other sources. Many students mistakenly place a long quote from a case to explain the rule. While quotations are sometimes helpful, they are often too complicated when trying to explain a simple rule. Oftentimes, the term of art from the quotation is enough or a synthesis from a number of cases is necessary. Another mistake here is that students often forget to cite to the source of the rule. A legal reader wants to be assured that the writer did not simply make up the rule. It must come from some authority. Therefore, the authority needs to be cited. If the rule comes from multiple authorities, cite to all of them in a string cite.

3.   Application

Application of the law can be accomplished through case comparisons (see pages 34-40), case synthesis (see pages 32-35), statutory interpretation techniques (see pages 14-23), policy arguments (see pages 40-41), or any combination of these sources, and more. As a legal writer, you need to understand the purpose of legal application. The legal reader will want to know not only **if** the law applies to your client but why and how the law does or does not apply. Because your reader will be a doubting audience, you need to prove all your points. You will use the law and your facts in doing so. The trick here is to give the reader enough information so that she does not have to look elsewhere for information. So, you should have enough of your facts in the analysis so she does not have to flip back to your facts section. You should have enough law so that she does not have to read a case or look to the statute separately to make sure you are correct. Do not make your reader do your work for you. Provide all the information she needs within the analysis itself. On the other hand, do not provide information the reader does not need. For example, if you are analyzing the element of outrageous conduct in an intentional infliction of emotional distress memo, you do not need to discuss facts or law that discuss the intentional requirement. Wait for the analysis of that issue.

4.   Counterarguments

When reading your application, a legal reader should mentally ask questions and then find your answers to those questions within the analysis. For this reason, you should also address counterarguments in your application. Deciding which counterarguments to put in and where to place them will require some thinking on your part, and your decisions will often depend on the purpose of your document. For example, in briefs, you should address only those counterarguments that you think the other side will address; otherwise, you run the risk of creating arguments that your opposing counsel did not consider. In memos, you will include more counterarguments, but do not address counterarguments that don't pass the laugh test. In addition, in briefs, counterarguments are usually best placed after your own argument. Downplay them by arranging them within a paragraph instead of at the beginning or end of a paragraph. They should not get more "air time" in your document than your own arguments. In addition, they are usually most effective when they do not begin with "the other side will argue" or "the defense has claimed." These opening clauses only highlight the other side's argument and create a defensive tone in the brief. In memos, however, you might want to emphasize the strength of the counterargument by placing those arguments in the beginning of your application section, giving them priority in your writing, or using a defensive tone.

5. Conclusion

Finally, the reader wants a conclusion on your particular issue. Here, you should provide not only the ultimate conclusion but also the main reason for your conclusion. That way, the skimming reader will have an answer to the issue as well as a legal reason.

C. *Creativity in Legal Analysis*

If you simply follow the same formula over and over within your document, your writing will be very simple, boring, and not very effective. In addition, the formula might not make sense in every situation. Here are some other options and questions to consider:

- In persuasive writing, you might want to present your client's facts before you provide the rule, especially if the facts are compelling and the law is not very beneficial.
- What if the policy behind the rule helps your client more than the rule itself? You might want to start with an application of the policy before you present the rule.
- What about counterarguments? Sometimes it makes sense to address them within your analysis of the issue; other times, it might make more sense to address them separately as their own issues in a point-counterpoint organization.
- At times, you might abandon starting with an issue altogether; you might start with the party and analyze the law around each party's main arguments.
- When the law is very complicated or a rule is not clear, you might address multiple scenarios or various possible rule structures before you begin to apply each one separately.
- When you have separate issues, you may decide to combine issues instead of applying each one separately within the formula.
- You might organize persuasive analysis by themes instead of by issue.

Once you understand the reasoning behind the formulas, you can choose to abandon the formulas and apply the law creatively and effectively. Remember to think about your various choices and make your decisions according to your specific purpose and audience.

VIII. STUDY AIDS—LEGAL ANALYSIS

A. *Quick References and Checklists*

1. Legal Analysis Generally: Checklist

Collecting the Facts

✓ Collect the facts. Typical sources include:
- The client
- Other witnesses
- Documentation and tangible evidence
- Experts
- A site visit (e.g., accident scene)

✓ Prepare questions before you investigate, interview, or depose.
- Ask questions to help you understand the background to the case.
- Ask questions to help you find the relevant law.

✓ Utilize questions organized by editor's categories:
- Parties
- Places, Objects, Things
- Basis or Issue
- Defense
- Relief Sought
- Persons
- Places
- Acts
- Things

✓ Be flexible because facts often change, and you may need to retrace your steps.

Analyzing the Law

✓ Identify legal issues.
- Analyze the client's facts.
- Look for issues in your opponent's counterclaims and defenses.

✓ Find controlling law for each issue.
- Argue ambiguous terms.

✓ Understand the relationship among the various legal branches.
- If a statute is the controlling law, consider:
  - Is it constitutional?
  - What interpretation have the courts adopted?
  - Has the legislature amended the statute?
  - Is there consistent common law that predates the statute?

✓ Apply legal reasoning techniques to create sound legal arguments.
- Rule-based reasoning
  - Break the legal rule down into its elements.
  - Apply each element to your client's facts.
  - Conclude.

- Analogy-based reasoning
  - Compare client's case to cases already decided.
- Policy arguments
  - Make when case of first impression, when existing rules are ambiguous, and to bolster other legal arguments.
  - Show why an interpretation of the law is consistent or inconsistent with goals of the rule or society in general.

Understanding Legal Rules

✓ Determine what type of rule you are applying.
- Elements test
  - Must meet all the elements.
- Balancing of factors test
  - Sets out two or more considerations that must be weighed against each other.
- Totality test
  - Some factors may be more important than others. Not all factors need be met.
- Exceptions test
  - To argue rule does not apply, argue an exception applies.
  - To argue rule does apply, argue that exception does not apply.
- Combination of tests

✓ Look at terms within the rule you are applying.
- Be familiar with terms that always carry specific meaning.
  - *And v. Or*
  - *Shall v. May*
- Determine what terms are in dispute.

✓ Organize the rule into its elements or subcategories.
✓ Analyze each term within the rule.

---

 2. Statutory Interpretation: Checklist

Statutory Interpretation Generally

✓ Find the applicable statute.
✓ Read the whole statute, or at least skim for the following:
- The title of the act and provision titles
- Date of enactment
- Date of amendments
- Preamble or purpose section
- Definition section
- Language of specific provisions that apply to your issue
- Language of provisions in close proximity to your issue
- Remedy or relief provision of the act

✓ Break down your specific provision into its elements.
✓ Read signaling words carefully and pay attention to punctuation.
- *And*—must prove all the items in the list

- *Or*—must prove only one item in the list
- *Including*—implies exclusive list
- *Including* but not limited to—implies list is not exclusive
- *And any other factors*—states that previous list is not exclusive
- *Must*—required
- *Shall*—required
- *May*—not required

Statutory Interpretation Techniques

Overarching goal is to determine the legislature's intent.

✓ Plain Language
  - How is a term of the statute typically used in English language?
✓ Definitions
  - Is there a definition section in statute?
  - If not, look to other sources such as Black's Law Dictionary.
✓ Context
  - Where do terms of art appear in statute?
  - What words appear next to those terms of art?
  - What terms appear nowhere in the statute?
✓ Case Law
  - Use cases as binding precedent in statutory interpretation.
  - Use annotated statutes to find binding precedent.
✓ Legislative History
  - Research committee reports, floor debates, and speeches.
✓ Policy
  - Did you check your statute for a policy or purpose section?
  - Did you consider policy issues being debated at time statute was enacted?
✓ Canons of Construction
  - *Note: Canons can contradict each other, and many courts do not rely on them.*
  - Common canons of construction:
    - Read the statute as a whole.
    - When no exception exists, none should be implied.
    - *In pari material*—different statutes on the same issue should be interpreted consistently. A later provision takes precedent over an earlier one.
    - *Ejudsem generis*—when a statute contains list followed by a catchall phrase, the catchall phrase includes only items similar to the ones on the list.
    - *Expression unius*—if a statute expressly includes something, then it excludes what is not mentioned.

📓 3. Statutory Interpretation: Quick Reference

The following statutory interpretation techniques are used to help determine the legislature's intent when writing a particular statute.

1. **Plain language:** How a word or phrase is usually used in the English language.

2. **Definitions:** Often lawmakers provide a definition section, which usually appears in the beginning of the code section. If no definitions exist, lawyers look to other sources, such as definitions from other statutes, definitions from Black's Law Dictionary or other dictionaries, or definitions from judges or scholars.

3. **Context of the language:** Lawyers look to see where the terms of art appear in the statute, what words appear near those terms, and what terms appear nowhere in the statute to assess the meaning of the terms.

4. **Case law:** Judges write opinions that interpret the meaning of the statute. These cases then act as binding precedent in statutory interpretation.

5. **Legislative history:** When writing a statute, lawmakers discuss, debate, and write about the proposed statute. These pieces of legislative history can provide insight into the legislature's purpose in passing the statute. To find legislative history, a lawyer would research committee reports, floor debates, and speeches. Legislative history is also useful to determine congressional intent if the statute has been amended.

6. **Policy arguments:** Lawyers often make policy arguments to show why a particular statute was passed. Oftentimes the statute itself contains a policy or purpose section.

📋 4. **Statutory Interpretation: Note-Taking Chart: Quick Reference**

Use this note-taking chart to organize your arguments for your statute.

Code § Elements (breakdown of law)	Plain Language and Definitions	Purpose / Policy	Legislative History	Case Law	Context

 5. **Case Analysis: Checklist**

Understanding Common Law

✓ Function and Organization of the Courts
   • The federal court system
      • Jurisdiction over cases where U.S. Constitution or federal law applies or where diversity of citizenship
      • Thirteen circuits, each with a court of appeals
      • Each circuit is subdivided into districts, and each state has at least one federal district

- The district courts are the federal trial courts
- District Court → Court of Appeals → U.S. Supreme Court
- The state court system
  - Each state has its own system.
- The function of the courts
  - Trial judges listen to legal arguments and evidence and so decide both questions of law and fact.
  - Appellate judges review limited decisions of trial court, using different levels of deference.

✓ Precedential Weight of Cases
- Primary v. secondary sources
  - All case law and statutes are primary law.
- Binding v. persuasive authority
  - Binding cases—higher court, same jurisdiction—must be followed.
  - Persuasive cases—lower court, or different jurisdiction—need not be followed.
- Holding v. dicta
  - The case holding is binding.
  - Dicta is not binding.
- Majority opinions v. dissents
  - Majority opinions are binding.
  - Dissenting and concurring opinions are not binding.
- Other traits affecting the weight of the cases
  - More recent cases carry more weight.
  - En banc decisions carry more weight.
  - Court reputation bears on the weight a case carries.
  - Cases that have been followed by other courts carry more weight.

Analyzing Cases

✓ Use case analysis when
- Interpreting statutes.
- Synthesizing cases.
- Comparing cases.

✓ Case synthesis weaves together cases to create a clearly enunciated rule.
- Compile the cases on point.
- Read all the relevant cases carefully.
- Determine if the court's rulings were based on reasoning, facts, or policies.
- Group cases according to explicit rules.
- Group cases according to implicit rules.
- Fit the pieces together.
- When there are a number of viable rules, choose the one that best works for your client's issue.

✓ *When synthesizing cases, watch out for these typical mistakes:*
- Synthesizing in chronological order
- Confusing different terms of art that apply to the same part of the rule
- Using quotations out of context
- Avoiding rules articulated by only one court

✓ Case comparisons use inductive reasoning to predict the outcome of the current case.
- Look for cases addressing issues similar to the issues of your case.
- Look for cases where the facts are similar to your client's facts.
- Look for cases that employ reasoning that can be used in your case.
- Determine if the holding of the prior case is similar to your predicted or preferred outcome.
  - If yes, create case analogies.
    - Use legally significant similarities.
  - If no, distinguish the cases.
    - Use legally significant differences.
- To craft effective case comparisons:
  - Include the holding of the prior case.
  - Explain the important, relevant facts of the prior case.
  - Explain the reasoning the prior court used to justify the holding.
  - Compare multiple cases.
    - Explain the similar thread.
    - Set out the legal parameters.
    - Make a sliding scale argument.

✓ *When comparing cases, watch out for these typical mistakes:*
- Using quotations from cases instead of analysis
- Using only facts of your case and omitting case precedent
- Omitting the holding of precedent
- Using too much of the prior case
- Omitting the facts of the current case
- Omitting the tie between the prior case and the current case
- Ignoring the other side's argument

---

 6.   Case Comparisons: Quick Reference

Do's of Case Comparisons

1. **Do include enough of both your case and the prior case.** You must provide enough information on both your case and the prior case for the reader to understand the analogy.
2. **Do make the tie between your case and the prior case clear.** You cannot assume that the reader will be able to see the connection herself; make the tie clear with specific language.
3. **Do be creative.** Case comparisons do not always need to follow the same format. In fact, you may lose the reader's attention if yours do.

The typical IRAC (issue, rule, analysis, conclusion) format does not work for every piece of analysis and can become boring and redundant even when effective.

4. **Do use complicated case analysis.** Using more than one prior case in a case comparison can often be a powerful form of analysis, particularly if the synthesized rule from the prior cases is applicable to your case.

5. **Do remember that your argument should be based on case comparisons, not simply long quotes or abstract rules.** Simply stating the law or quoting a prior case is not helpful to your case analysis if the reader cannot see how it applies to your case. While quotations and rules are often necessary, be sure to take your analysis one step further and show the reader how the quote or rule applies to your particular facts.

Don'ts of Case Comparisons

1. **Don't use quotations from cases instead of analysis.** Analogies are, by definition, comparing a prior case to the present one. If a lawyer simply relies on language from the prior case, then the comparison itself is lost. While quotations are often useful, especially when enunciating a rule, do not over rely on them for analogies. Block quotes are especially cumbersome, and readers often skip over them.

2. **Don't use only the facts from your case and omit case precedent.** Grounding your arguments in the law is the key to case comparisons. A typical mistake is to provide a rule and then use only facts from the client's situation to show why the rule applies or doesn't apply. Instead, when available, use prior cases to show how that rule has been applied (or not) in the past, and show why the facts of the case are similar (or not) to case precedent.

3. **Don't omit the holding of the precedent.** A case is not useful for analogies if the reader does not know the court's holding.

4. **Don't use too much of the prior case.** Use only enough facts and reasoning from the prior case to make your point. Do not inundate the reader with extraneous parts of the case as it only confuses the reader.

5. **Don't omit the facts of the current case.** Relying solely on case precedent is not enough for a comparison. You should also supply enough of the facts of your case to show why the prior case is similar or not.

6. **Don't omit the tie between the prior case and the current case.** Don't forget to show *why* the prior case is similar or different from your case. Here, facts, reasoning, and policy are often used for support.

📋   7.   Case Comparisons: Note-Taking Chart: Quick Reference

Use this note-taking chart to organize your cases and arguments within each element of the law.

Note-Taking Chart

Relevant Issue	Case Name (citation)	Facts	Reasoning	Holding	Tie to Our Case

8. Policy Arguments: Checklist

✓ Choose the most compelling policy arguments.
✓ Be creative.
✓ Weave policy arguments throughout your document or create a separate section for policy arguments.
✓ Cite to other opinions to strengthen your policy arguments.
✓ Consider:
  • Moral values
  • Social justice
  • Fairness
  • Economics
  • Institutional roles in the administration of justice

---

 9. Jurisprudence and Classical Rhetoric: Checklist

Jurisprudence

✓ Natural Law
  • Make arguments based on reasonableness, equity, and fairness.
✓ Formalism or Positivism
  • Enumerate the applicable legal rules and apply with legal precedent.
✓ Realism
  • Make policy arguments to influence the judge.
✓ Critical Legal Studies
  • Make arguments based on helping underprivileged members of society.
✓ Law and Economics Theory
  • Present economic justifications for judge to rule in your favor.

Classical Rhetoric: Deduction vs. Induction

✓ Use deductive reasoning to create arguments and poke holes in your opponent's arguments.
  • A=B, B=C, A=C
  • Ensure your syllogisms contain valid and logical premises.
  • Use your syllogisms to reach an absolute conclusion.
✓ Use inductive reasoning to show why a case is more likely to be decided one way instead of another.
  • Use analogies and case comparisons.
  • Determine what characteristics are more important in your comparisons.
  • Show the judge why the characteristics you chose are the most compelling.

10.   Constructing Legal Analysis: Checklist

Do not follow formulas blindly; instead, treat them as a guide in the thinking process.

✓ IRAC
> I—present the *issue* at the beginning of your analysis
> R—explain the legal *rule*
> A—*apply* the legal rule to the facts of your case
> C—*conclude* on the issue

✓ CRAC
> C—present your issue in a *conclusive* manner
> R—explain the legal *rule*
> A—*apply* the legal rule to the facts of your case
> C—*conclude* on the issue

✓ CRuPAC
> C—present your issue in a *conclusive* manner
> Ru—explain the legal *rule*
> P—cite to other authority to *prove* the rule exists
> A—*apply* the legal rule to the facts of your case
> C—*conclude* on the issue

If you choose to follow a formula, you should understand its purpose and its limitations.

✓ Issue or conclusion
  - Specific issue or element within the law
  - Place in topic sentences for busy reader

✓ Rule
  - Legal context in form of policy argument, term of art, definition, rule from case, etc.
  - Include citation

✓ Application
  - Convince the doubting legal audience with case comparisons, case synthesis, statutory interpretation techniques, and policy arguments.
  - Provide enough information that the reader does not have to look elsewhere.
  - Address counterarguments.
  - Conclude on the particular issues and include your reasoning.

Do not let formulas stifle your creativity; rather, craft your legal analysis to suit your specific purpose and audience.

✓ In persuasive writing, consider presenting compelling client facts before providing the rule.
✓ Present especially helpful policy arguments before law that is not very beneficial.

✓ Present counterarguments separately as their own issues.
✓ Abandon starting with an issue, and analyze the law around each party's main arguments.
✓ When the law is complicated, address possible rule structures before analyzing the issue.
✓ Combine issues instead of analyzing each issue separately under a formula.
✓ Organize persuasive analysis by themes instead of issues.

B. Quizzes

⚙? 1. Legal Analysis in General: Quiz

Instructions: Mark each of the following statements regarding legal analysis either true or false. If you answer false, try to articulate why the statement is false before moving to the next question. If you have difficulty answering any of the questions on legal analysis, refer to the chapter text and to Legal Analysis Checklists for assistance.

1. An attorney should prepare questions before conducting a deposition, interview, or investigation. **True or False?**

2. Facts do not change. **True or False?**

3. Your opponent's counterclaims and defenses may raise additional legal issues you must analyze. **True or False?**

4. If a statute provides the controlling law, common law that predates the statute is inapplicable. **True or False?**

5. Effective and thorough legal arguments combine rule-based reasoning, analogy-based reasoning, and policy arguments. **True or False?**

6. Rule-based reasoning requires you to break down the legal rule into its elements, apply each element to your client's facts, and conclude on the element. **True or False?**

7. Analogy-based reasoning requires you to compare your client's case to cases already decided. **True or False?**

8. Make policy arguments only if existing rules are ambiguous. **True or False?**

9. In both an *elements test* and a *totality test,* all the elements of the legal rule must be met. **True or False?**

10. The *balancing of factors test* sets out two or more considerations that must be weighed against each other. **True or False?**

11. Analyze only ambiguous terms within a rule. **True or False?**

12. Natural law advocates formulate arguments based on reasonableness, equity, and fairness. **True or False?**

13. A proponent of positivism makes policy arguments to influence the judge. **True or False?**

14. A=B, B=C, A=C represents a syllogism, used in deductive reasoning. **True or False?**

15. Inductive reasoning is used to reach an absolute conclusion. **True or False?**

16. Once you find the applicable statute for your case, you should read (or at least skim) the whole statute. **True or False?**

17. The overarching goal of statutory interpretation is to win the case for your client. **True or False?**

18. You should always look for a definition section in the statute. **True or False?**

19. Annotated statutes may direct you to binding precedent that can be used in statutory interpretation. **True or False?**

20. Legislative history is not a good statutory interpretation technique because so many judges disfavor it. **True or False?**

21. If your statute lacks a policy or purpose section, you can consider policy issues being debated at the time the statute was enacted. **True or False?**

22. Canons of construction may contradict each other, and many courts do not rely on them. **True or False?**

23. Circuit courts are the federal trial courts. **True or False?**

24. Trial judges may decide both questions of fact and law because they hear both evidence and legal arguments. **True or False?**

25. Case holdings, majority opinions, and primary law are binding on all courts in the same jurisdiction. **True or False?**

26. In case comparisons, you should not use prior cases with holdings different from your predicted or preferred outcome. **True or False?**

27. Sophisticated case comparisons use multiple cases to set out the legal parameters of an issue and to make sliding scale arguments. **True or False?**

28. You can never include too much of a prior case—the "Euro"—in case comparisons. **True or False?**

29. Effective case comparisons tie the current case to the prior cases. **True or False?**

30. Citing to other opinions will strengthen your policy arguments. **True or False?**

31. You should always follow one of the legal writing formulas—IRAC, CRAC, CRuPAC—to ensure sound legal analysis. **True or False?**

Answer Key on page 513

🗣? 2. Binding vs. Persuasive: Quiz

1. You are clerking for a judge in the United States District Court for the Eastern District of Virginia. He asks you to research cases interpreting a particular provision of the federal Endangered Species Act. Your research uncovers a prior decision authored by a judge on the same court. That decision is:

    A. Binding, because it is a federal court decision interpreting a federal statute.
    B. Binding, because it was decided by the same United States District Court.
    C. Persuasive, because federal judges are not bound by precedent when interpreting federal statutes.
    D. Persuasive, because it was decided by the same United States District Court.
    E. None of the above.

2. Your law firm has been retained to represent a manufacturer for injuries caused by a defective soda bottle; the case is before the California Court of Appeal. A senior partner has asked you to find cases construing California product liability law. Which of the following authorities is the most binding?

    A. Johnson v. Kwik-Dry, Inc., 143 F.2d 548 (C.D. Ca. 2001)
    B. Hatfield v. McCoy International, 264 P.3d 703 (Cal. 2000)
    C. Potter v. Diagon Alley Broom Co., 188 F.2d 341 (9 th Cir. 2004)
    D. Matthews v. Orange Fizz Co., 280 P.3d 557 (Cal. Supr. 2005)
    E. McNee v. Calif. Mopeds, Inc., 242 P.3d 819 (Cal. App. 2003)

3. You sue for breach of contract in Texas state court. A decision by the United States District Court for the Southern District of Texas applying Texas contract law is:

    A. Binding, because federal court decisions always bind state courts.
    B. Binding, because it is a federal court decision construing state law.
    C. Persuasive, because it is a federal court decision construing state law.
    D. Persuasive, because federal courts have the final say on questions of state law.
    E. None of the above.

4-5: A sues B in for an alleged violation of the federal Americans with Disabilities Act (ADA) in the United States District Court for the District of Colorado.

4. A 12-year-old decision by the United States Court of Appeals for the Seventh Circuit interpreting the ADA is:

    A. Persuasive, because the United States Court of Appeals for the Seventh Circuit is not a higher court with direct appellate jurisdiction.
    B. Persuasive, because only Supreme Court decisions on matters of federal law have the power to bind other federal courts.
    C. Binding, because the United States Court of Appeals for the Seventh Circuit is a higher level federal court with direct appellate jurisdiction.

D. Binding, because the Seventh Circuit decision has stood for 12 years without being overturned.

E. None of the above.

5. A two-week old decision by the United States Court of Appeals for the Tenth Circuit interpreting the ADA is:

A. Persuasive, because the United States Court of Appeals for the Tenth Circuit is not a higher court with direct appellate jurisdiction.

B. Persuasive, because only Supreme Court decisions on matters of federal law have the power to bind other federal courts.

C. Persuasive, because it is only two weeks old and has not withstood the test of time.

D. Binding, because the decisions by a United States Court of Appeals bind all federal courts.

E. Binding, because the United States Court of Appeals for the Tenth Circuit is a higher court with direct appellate jurisdiction.

Answer Key on page 514

CHAPTER 2

WRITING & REWRITING

The Writing Process

In this section, you will learn legal writing techniques to help the reader follow and understand your analysis. This section will focus on the writing process rather than particular legal documents (for more on legal documents, see chapter 3). This section is broken into four parts. The first two parts, Introduction to the Writing Process and Writing, will provide general techniques for an efficient and effective writing process. The Rewriting section will provide specific techniques that will help you in both writing and rewriting your documents. The section on Persuasive Writing will provide techniques specific to briefs and motions.

I. INTRODUCTION TO THE WRITING PROCESS

Legal writing is different from any other writing you have done before. Whether you have been an undergraduate student, a business executive, or a paralegal, you are still a novice legal writer. As a novice, you will need to adjust your writing to meet your new audience, the legal reader, and to reach the goals of your writing in the legal community.

A. *The Legal Reader*

The legal reader has many traits specific to the legal discourse community. As you enter this new community, you will need to understand these nuances and adjust your writing to meet your audience. Below are common traits of the legal reader as well as suggested tips to assist the reader in understanding your writing.

Trait #1: The legal reader is a doubting audience. As he reads your writing, he will expect you to prove everything you say with legal authority and analysis.

> **Tip #1:** To help the doubting reader, you need to cite to legal authority and use concrete legal analysis to prove your arguments. Thus, whenever you write a proposition, back it up with a citation to a legal authority. (Most of these citations will appear within the text, not as footnotes.)

Trait #2: The legal reader talks to himself. As he reads your document, he will ask questions and expect answers immediately within your writing.

> **Tip #2:** Answer all possible relevant questions when writing. This does not mean that you should write questions within your document and then answer them. Instead, it means that you should show both sides of the legal issue and respond to all possible issues presented by the facts and the law.

Trait #3: The legal reader is reading for an answer to a specific question. Whether it is a supervising attorney who has asked you to write about a legal issue or a judge who is going to decide a case, he is looking for the answer to a particular issue or set of issues.

> **Tip #3:** Answer the question up front. Do not make the reader wait for the answer. Use the rest of your document to prove the answer.

Trait #4: The legal reader is in a rush. He often skims documents and wants a solid understanding of the law through a quick read. Assume his attention span is weakest mid-paragraph and mid-document.

> **Tip #4:** Use roadmaps and strong topic sentences. The reader should be able to skim the document reading only the roadmaps and topic sentences and be able to understand the basic structure of the law. The roadmap should present the law in an organized fashion, and the topic sentences should use the terms of the specific elements of the law.

Trait #5: The legal reader does not want to be bothered with too much detail or tangential information. The reader is looking for a specific answer to a specific question. However, when you research the issue, you might stumble across other issues as well that might affect the outcome of the case. Often, the supervising attorney has already considered these issues or has asked someone else to research them.

> **Tip #5:** Be sure to focus on the issue assigned. Ask the reader ahead of time, when possible, about other avenues or legal theories before you go on and on about them for wasted pages. On the other hand, it is a good idea to bring important issues to the reader's attention, whether in the particular document or in some other form of communication such as a conversation or an email.

Trait #6: You, as the writer, know more than the reader. You have spent the time researching, studying, and analyzing the issue. The reader has asked you to do so to teach him about the law and its application.

> **Tip #6:** Be specific. Do not assume the reader understands either the law or the facts. You know the issues, the facts, and the law better than the reader, so you need to spell out your analysis. Avoid holes in your arguments, and do not assume that the reader knows what you mean without making your point explicit.

B. The Goals of Legal Writing

Although the purpose of each legal document will be different, there are common goals and expectations within the legal writing community that differ from other writing communities. Below are some common goals in legal writing.

1. **Legal documents rely on legal precedent, not on your personal opinions.** In your undergraduate studies, you might have written papers to show your new ideas or perspectives on a certain subject. In legal writing, however, your opinions do not have the same value. Legal precedent is valued, not your personal opinions or beliefs. This does not mean that you cannot be creative or use your ideas to craft legal arguments—you can. However, the law will be your starting point, you

will rely on and cite to legal authority, and you should omit "I believe" and "I think" from your vocabulary.

2. **Legal writing has an effect on others.** If you are representing a client, your writing may help win or lose the case. If you are a judge (or a clerk), your writing not only will decide the particular case, but it also will affect cases in the future. If you are writing a contract, your writing will bind the parties for years to come. Your writing will also have an effect on yourself. Your reputation as a lawyer often rests on your writing abilities. A good legal writer usually makes a very marketable lawyer.

3. **Legal writing comes with responsibility.** When you write to a client, you must be accurate and thorough. If you are wrong, you could be liable for malpractice. When you write to the court, you must also be accurate and ethical (see "Ethics" on page 77). Failure to do so can lead to disbarment.

4. **Legal writing should be concise.** In undergraduate studies, long papers were often rewarded. In legal writing, long documents are discouraged. Instead, clear and concise writing is rewarded and appreciated.

5. **Legal writing should be well organized.** Because the law is often complex, legal writing needs to be well organized so that the reader can follow the legal arguments and analysis. A strong organizational scheme helps lead the legal reader through the complicated arguments.

6. **Legal writing should follow assigned formats.** Courts (and often law offices) have stringent rules for filing legal documents. If you fail to follow a simple formatting rule, courts often reject the document. Therefore, it is important to research your local court rules and follow them word for word.

Although legal documents share similar general audiences and overall goals, each document is written for a specific audience and has specific goals. A memo written to one partner in a law firm differs from one written to a different partner in the same firm. A brief to an appellate judge differs from a motion to a trial court. Before you begin to write any legal document, first consider purpose, audience, scope, and view. Descriptions of each of these appears in this book at the introduction to each new document in chapter 3, Legal Documents.

C. *Creating Your Own Effective Writing Process*

Writing is a personal matter. For some it comes naturally; for others it is a chore. Many writers, especially in the undergraduate setting, do not think about their process; they simply sit down to write. While this method might have been successful for you in the past, it will not be an efficient or effective process for legal writing.

As a legal writer, you will need to develop a writing process that works for you. Consciously developing an efficient and effective process now will save you time and money later. When thinking about your process, consider breaking it down into these manageable categories:

1. **Prewriting:** Researching, reading, and organizing the law before you begin your draft. Outlining may or may not be a part of your prewriting strategy. Researching is addressed in the corresponding research book *Experiential Legal Research: Sources, Strategies, and Citation* (Wolters Kluwer Law & Business, 2011). In this book, outlining is addressed in this section.
2. **Writing:** Writing the first draft of the legal document. In this book, writing is addressed in this section.
3. **Rewriting:** Reworking the draft, time and again, focusing on large-scale issues such as content, large-scale organization, analysis, and conciseness. A well-written legal document is often rewritten more than ten times. In this book, rewriting is addressed in the next part of this section.
4. **Editing and Citation:** Editing for syntax, sentence structure, and grammar; polishing for typos and citation. In this book, these areas are addressed in chapters 4 and 5.

When creating your own process, determine which category is your weakest and allot more time for it. Keep in mind that the process is not linear. Once you begin writing, you will often need to revisit the prewriting category for more research.

1.   Prewriting Tips

Prewriting takes a significant amount of time as legal research can be all consuming.

Here are a few tips:

1. A good research strategy will help make you become more efficient.[1]
2. Note-taking will also be important to keep track of the law as well as your research sources.
3. Maintain folders or piles for your notes. Oftentimes, the law will break down into different elements or arguments. It is helpful to organize your law accordingly. Here are some suggestions:
   a. Files of cases and other sources for each element
   b. Files or folders on the computer for each element
   c. Charts and graphs to categorize the law
4. Many people also write outlines to help them organize the research and the law. An outline can be detailed or just a few lines on a piece of paper—or anything in between. Some people prefer not to write outlines at all. You need to decide on your best method.

---

1. For guidance in conducting legal research, ask your law school reference librarian for help or consult the companion text to this volume, *Experiential Legal Research: Sources, Strategies, and Citation,* by Diana Donahoe (Wolters Kluwer Law & Business, 2011).

2.   Writing Tips

Some people are able to write a whole document in one sitting; for others, it can take days or weeks. Remember that this part of the process marks just the beginning of your writing. This is not the final draft.

A few tips:

1.   Write in a place where you are comfortable.
2.   Write in a place where you are not easily distracted (turn off the cell phone).
3.   Set aside a large amount of time so that you do not waste time later remembering what you thought you were going to write.
4.   Take breaks, but don't get sidetracked.
5.   If it's not working, take a long break or wait until the next day.
6.   Don't try to write it perfectly the first time.
7.   Do not attempt all-nighters and expect a final document; it might have worked in college, but it does not work with legal documents.

3.   Rewriting Tips

Below are a few tips on rewriting. More more information, see the section "Rewriting," beginning on page 78.

1.   Focus on one aspect of rewriting at a time (e.g., rewrite a new draft focusing solely on large-scale organization).
2.   Take a day or two away from your writing before rewriting, when possible.
3.   Start with the weakest parts of your writing, as they usually require the longest time.
4.   Do not progress from start to finish; the end of the document will usually not get enough of your time. Instead, progress from one aspect of your writing (e.g., content) to another (e.g., conciseness).
5.   Spend most of your time on rewriting, not on writing.
6.   Assume you will need multiple drafts.

4.   Editing and Citation Tips

Editing is focusing on the smaller scale items in your writing, such as syntax, sentence structure, and grammar. It makes sense to address these items after rewriting, as you do not need to focus on a particular sentence if you have decided to omit the whole paragraph.

Here are some editing tips:

1.   Focus on one part of editing at a time.
2.   Determine your weaknesses (see the Editing Self-Assessment in chapter 4).
3.   Focus on your weaknesses first to give yourself enough time to fix them.

4. Read your document from end to beginning to focus on spelling and grammar as opposed to content.
5. Read your document out loud.

Proper citation is necessary to reference your authority. Here are some citation tips:

1. Consult the Bluebook (or ALWD) often.
2. Use the Bluepages of the Bluebook. (The tables are very helpful.)
3. Do not rely on the citation format you find cited by other courts or Lexis or Westlaw.
4. Use jump cites whenever possible so that your reader can find your specific reference efficiently.

D.   *Managing Your Time*

Lawyers typically encounter rigid deadlines, either court-imposed or specified by a supervisor. Often, as a deadline approaches, another project implodes or a client is arrested and needs immediate attention. Therefore, time management, especially of written products, is important for lawyers to master. The best lawyers are often those that remain on schedule.

Here are a few tricks for effectively managing your time:

1. **Create a false deadline.** Instead of writing the supervisor's due date on your calendar, mark the due date a few days earlier.
2. **Self-impose a schedule.** Create dates for each step of the writing process. Come up with dates, for example, for finishing the first draft, the large-scale organization of the first draft, and the rewritten analysis of the revised draft. Make these dates realistic so you can stick to your schedule.
3. **Create incentives.** Give yourself a reward when you have finished a particular section.
4. **Set aside time to walk away from your document.** You will need time away from your document to begin to hear the reader's voice instead of your writer's voice. Allot time to spend on other projects before you come back to your document.
5. **Set aside time for unpredictable disasters.** Your computer will always crash hours before an assignment is due. Therefore, make sure your assignment is complete in enough time to deal with the computer or other problems that are bound to occur. An extra day on the calendar relieves a lot of anxiety, which may then contribute to writer's block.

The timeline below illustrates the adjustment many students need to make from an "all-nighter" writing process, in which the draft is written and rewritten in one sitting, to a paced writing process, in which the first draft is written with plenty of time for rewriting subsequent drafts and taking time away from the document. The key is adjusting your "draft" due date from the end of the timeline to the middle.

Timeline #1:
Possible Process in Undergrad Writing

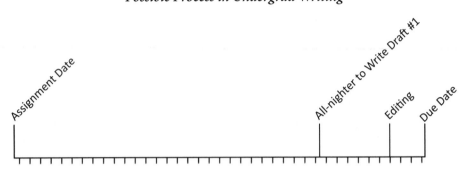

Timeline #2:
Preferred Process in Legal Writing

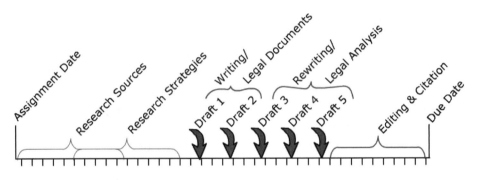

E.   Overcoming Writer's Block

Lawyers typically encounter writer's block either when (1) their task seems too daunting, or (2) they expect to write a perfect draft at the first sitting.

If your task seems daunting: If a project seems too complicated or large, break it up into small manageable chunks. Set small goals and realistic deadlines for each chunk. Envision the project as a group of smaller projects and then set out to accomplish one small project at a time.

If you expect to write a perfect draft: For some, writer's block stems from a seemingly incurable need to write the document perfectly the first time. For these legal writers, the draft is the final product. A writer with such a conviction will surely suffer as the law is such a malleable mess. Typically, the legal writer learns more about the law as she writes about it than she learned as she researched it. Therefore, the lawyer who assumes she can write about the law once and have a complete document will become frustrated. Instead, a legal writer should assume that writing is a learning process and that multiple drafts will be necessary to massage the law into a form that will be logical and readable. A legal writer should embrace the idea that the first draft is a starting point. Once that mindset is established, writer's block will fade as the writer begins her learning process in her draft.

II. WRITING

Legal writing is time consuming, yet rewarding. It is the craft of the lawyer. It is difficult to learn and harder to master. However, because it is an essential tool of the trade, it is extremely important that you take the time to learn to write effectively and efficiently. Your first-year legal research and writing course will teach you the basics of the craft. However, you should consider writing as often as possible throughout your law school career to continue to learn and practice legal writing. Upper class writing courses, law journals, and clinics will expose you to a variety of writing opportunities; this book will help you navigate those experiences as well.

This section of the book will expose you to the writing process, focusing on strategies and considerations as you sit down to write the first draft of your legal documents. The process of writing will help you learn the law, the strengths and weaknesses of your arguments, and the holes in your legal research. Keep in mind that you will probably spend more time rewriting multiple drafts than writing your first draft.

Considerations that will be addressed in this section:

Writing Creatively, immediately below.
Organizing Before You Write, page 72.
Plagiarism and Ethics, page 76.
Writing Process Testimonials, page 77.

A. *Writing Creatively*

Creativity is the key to effective legal writing. As a legal writer you must first develop creative arguments and then present them in a manner most likely to inform and sometimes persuade your audience. Legal writing should not feel or sound formulaic or staid. Use legal writing conventions as a method of understanding your audience, not as a way to stifle your creativity.

Here are some ways to write creatively:

1. Develop a unique theory for your case.
2. Use the facts of your case to tell a compelling story.
3. Create a novel argument.
4. Use case law creatively in a traditional argument.
5. Anticipate the other side's arguments and distinguish them.
6. Reorganize your document in a nontraditional manner.
7. Look at judge's opinions not only for what is there, but also what is not.
8. Create policy arguments.
9. Vary your sentence structure.
10. Do not be trapped into the IRAC (issue, rule, analysis, and conclusion) box.
11. In general, think outside the box.

B. *Organizing Before You Write*

Before you begin writing, it is a good idea to get organized. For some, this simply means getting all the research materials together in a coherent fashion. For others, it also means creating an outline of the document before writing the draft.

1. Getting Research Materials Together

Once you have researched the law, you will most likely have a pile of materials ready to include in your document. However, first, you need to organize these materials. Second, you must decide which materials are relevant—do not assume they will all be included in your document simply because you found them when doing your legal research.

Organizing the materials can be done in a variety of ways, depending on your comfort level and needs. Some writers prefer to print out all research (even if found online) and then organize it into piles. These piles are usually based on legal elements or issues. For those who are more comfortable on the computer, research can be organized by folders and files without the need for printing. Keep in mind that some materials can be copied and pasted (or physically piled) into numerous folders. So, a case on one issue might also discuss another issue; therefore, it would be placed in the both folders, but for different reasons. For example, a case on intentional infliction of emotional distress might be placed in a folder for the element of "intentional"; if it also discusses damages, it would be placed in the "damages" folder as well. (This is where using the computer is especially helpful.) WestlawNext and Lexis Advance now have folders within their platforms to help organize your research.

Determining what materials are relevant is a bit trickier. At times, it will take outlining the document to make this determination. Other times, it will take the actual drafting of the document to determine relevancy. And, even further along in the process, you might decide on relevancy during the rewriting stage of your process. Therefore, it makes the most sense to be over-inclusive in your outline, as it is usually easier to delete material than it is to add it later.

When your research involves a long list of cases, consider creating a note-taking chart to keep track of all the material.

Note-Taking Chart: Example

Name	Facts	Holding	Reasoning
Jones v. U.S. 779 A.2d 277 2001	A. After observing Jones drop two baggies on the ground, three officers approached Jones and picked up the bags, which contained a substance that later proved to be crack cocaine. B. The officers asked Jones "for his ID, if he had ID at that time, or if he didn't have his ID what is his name, address, where he lives, things like that." C. After these questions were posed to him, Jones stated that "he was holding for those two guys." D. At the time that he made these comments, Jones had not been advised of his rights under Miranda.	Not an interrogation; appellate court didn't address issue of custody	A. "Interrogation" is not only express questioning but also words or actions on the part of police that the police should know are reasonably likely to elicit an incriminating response from the suspect. B. Given the lack of the slightest logical nexus between the officer's question and the defendant's statement, it is difficult to understand how the judge could reasonably have found anything other than the statements were voluntary and spontaneous.
Dancy v. U.S. 745 A.2d 259 2000	A. Officer came to defendant's hospital room, where he saw him alone. B. Officer told D that he had an arrest warrant for him, about the police investigation (including what the police had found of defendant's role), and the penalty in the event of conviction. C. D responded by asking if "the girl" (person who drove Ds to the murder scene) was being charged and whether "Mike" (another D) was "finished. D. Officer asked D if he would be willing to talk about his involvement. E. D said that he wanted to speak to his lawyer, at which point officer read him his Miranda rights.	D was "interrogated" for Miranda purposes.	A. Officer should have known that his words were reasonably likely to elicit incriminating evidence. B. There were no other circumstances to indicate that the officer's words had any purpose other than getting the D to incriminate himself. C. Officer in this case also admitted that he made statements in an effort to get D to talk about his involvement.

2. Outlining Your Document

Some writers prefer to begin writing right away without creating an outline. This process is fine if it works for you. However, just because this process worked for you in undergraduate school, do not assume it will work for you in law school or your future legal writing career. It might, but it might not. Because organization is so important in legal writing, try creating a writer's outline before writing at least one legal document in law school. That way, you can determine if the process works for you before you begin representing real clients.

Creating an outline is a very personal process and can be done in a variety of ways. The following section provides some tips for writing an outline for a typical legal document where you apply a particular rule of law to a set of facts. However, do not assume this is the only way to create an outline; there are an infinite number of ways to write effective outlines, and there are an infinite number of documents you might write. Tailor your outline to the needs of the document. The overall goal is to create organization out of chaos.

As with your legal document, your outline should revolve around the rule of law. Therefore, your starting point and the foundation of your outline should be the actual legal rule you are going to apply. Rules come in many forms (see Understanding Legal Rules, page 6), and you should begin your outline by writing out the legal rule.

Once you have written the rule, you should separate it out into its component parts or subelements. That way, you will have space to begin adding your research within each part.

Now, pore through your research, file by file or pile by pile, and start filling in information under each element. Is there a definition? Where does it come from (it might come from multiple sources)? Are there cases that analyze that element? If so, what are the holdings, reasoning, and facts from each case? List each case separately under each issue. One case might appear under one element as well as under a different element (although you might include different facts and reasoning). This process will take some time as you are both rereading the law and deciding where each source fits within the analysis.

Now that your outline contains the rule of law and some of the definitions and applicable cases under each element, you can begin to add your facts from your own case. It is at this stage that you will begin to make some clear-cut relevancy determinations as your facts might differ substantially from other cases. If another case is factually very different from your own, it might not be useful for a case comparison (although it might have a useful definition or policy argument). As you fill in your facts, you can start writing notes about how the remaining cases might be compared to your facts.

By the end of this process, you might have produced a very long document. Some outlines are thinner than others, but some can be longer than the final document itself. The process is very personal, so you need to determine what works best for you. Keep in mind that the outline is to help you get started and to serve as a guide for writing. Do not let it confine you or stifle your creative thinking. Oftentimes, your outline will not be the best organizational scheme as it is your first attempt to organize the analysis. Feel free to keep reworking the organization and the law as you write, or consider writing multiple outlines before you even begin writing.

Some lawyers use charts instead of traditional outlines to keep track of the law.

Outlining Chart

Legal Elements	Plain Language and Definitions	Purpose or Policy	Case Law (facts, holding, reasoning)

3. Typical Questions About Outlines

1. **What if there is more than one issue?** Often, there is more than one issue. You might create separate outlines for each issue or create one outline with multiple issues. It is up to you, and it will depend on how you decide to write the document as a whole.

2. **How do I know what kind of test I am applying?** There are numerous types of tests in the law. For typical breakdowns, see Understanding Legal Rules (page 6). The test itself will be found in a statute, in a regulation, or within cases. Oftentimes, the same rule is repeated by various legal sources.

3. **What if one element of the test is easily met (or not met)?** In objective writing, you should still analyze the element in case your determination is wrong (unless it is absolutely certain: for example, "The victim is deceased"). In persuasive writing, you will make determinations based on different persuasive tactics (for advice on writing persuasively, see page 97).

4. **How do I show the relationship between elements?** Remember to include connectors such as and, or, may, and shall in your outline so that the relationship is clear in your organization.

5. **Do I need Roman numerals?** Labeling or numbering your outline is a personal choice. It works for some people and not for others. Be

careful if you do use numbers to be flexible. You might determine that your first argument is not your best once you fill in the outline.

6. **Can I use the outlining feature in my word processing software?** Yes, but you don't have to. It works well for some people, but not for others. Also consider using a table or a spread sheet for your outlining.

7. **Do I need to address elements in the same order as they appear in the rule?** For persuasive writing, you should address elements in the most persuasive order, which is often not the same order as the rule itself. At times, it might make sense to address the elements that are easily met first and then the others afterwards. The best advice is to start with the order as it appears in the rule, but digress from that order if you have good reasons to do so and if the writer can still follow the rule clearly and logically.

8. **Do I start an outline by following the formal requirements of the document, such as the question presented in the memo?** You can do that, but the best starting point for an outline is with the law, which basically begins in the discussion section of a memo or the argument section of a brief. It often makes more sense to start here, with the analysis, and then fill in the question presented, facts, and so on later, once you understand the law better.

Although there is no one set way to compile your research materials or to outline your document, you should find some way to organize the law before you begin writing. The process of culling, organizing, and writing an outline often helps you understand the basics and some of the intricacies of the law before you begin writing the document. Oftentimes, writing an outline saves a lot of time later in the writing and rewriting process.

C. *Plagiarism and Ethics*

1. Plagiarism

Plagiarism is the act of using someone else's words or ideas without giving credit to the author. To avoid plagiarizing, use quotation marks and citations and try to avoid frequent use of the "cut and paste" feature on your computer.

Most schools have plagiarism statements to help students avoid plagiarizing and to provide them with notice of the possible penalties. If caught plagiarizing in law school, penalties are usually stiff; you might be expelled or your transcript might reflect the plagiarism. Often, plagiarism occurs as students write notes for their journals or papers for seminar classes. Here, they often lift ideas verbatim from other law review articles. Avoid this urge. Instead, quote the author and then create your own novel ideas for your issue.

It is harder to plagiarize in practice as lawyers within a firm often exchange work product so as not to reinvent the wheel. In addition, when drafting briefs, lawyers often use arguments that have been successful in prior similar cases without giving credit to the lawyers who made the earlier arguments. While this method is accepted in practice—especially with lawyers working within the same firm—it is not acceptable while in law school.

2.   Ethics

As a lawyer admitted to the bar, you will be an officer of the court. Therefore, you will be bound to certain ethical rules. Become familiar with your specific jurisdictional rules and pay close attention in your professional responsibility course. Below are some basic ethical rules:

1. **You cannot knowingly make a false statement to the court.** Therefore, when writing your briefs or motions, be sure that your information—both about the law and the facts—is accurate.
2. **If there is authority within your jurisdiction that is directly adverse to your argument, you must bring it to the judge's attention.** This means that you might be ethically compelled to include an adverse opinion within your brief.
3. **You may not bring a frivolous suit or make an argument that is considered to be frivolous under existing law.** Therefore, when writing your briefs, do not make an argument that is unwinnable under any scenario.
4. **You may not make an ex parte communication to the judge unless permitted by law.** An ex parte communication is one where you communicate with the judge without the other party being present and without notifying the other party.

D.   *Writing Process Testimonials*

For videos of students talking to other students about their various techniques and processes for writing legal documents, see the link to "Writing Process Testimonials" on the text web site, accessed through http://www.aspenlawschool.com/books/donahoe.

III.   REWRITING

Rewriting, for the legal writer, is the process of reworking the large-scale facets of the document. Do not confuse this section with editing for grammar (for editing guidelines, see page 349).

It is important in the rewriting process to remember that you—the writer—have lived with this law for an extended period of time and have learned the nuances and intricacies of the analysis. The reader, however, is about to experience the law for the first time through your document. Therefore, one of the tricks to rewriting is to step into your reader's shoes by assuming you know nothing about the law or the client's situation.

A.   *Tips for Stepping into the Reader's Shoes*

1. **Take time away from your document.** Take a week, a day, an hour. The longer you are away from your document, the easier it will be to hear your reader's voice instead of your writer's voice.
2. **Read your document out loud.** A "read aloud"—done by yourself or by a colleague or friend—allows you to hear the words that have floated inside your brain for a while. The difference between what you hear orally and what you "hear" in your mind is striking.
3. **Create a reader-based outline.** Outline your first draft by reading only the topic sentences. The outline you create will simulate the busy reader's impression of your major points as she skims your document. If your reader-based outline mirrors the writer-based outline you may have created in the prewriting process, then your arguments will be clearly organized. See page 83.
4. **Use a focused rewriting process.** Develop a rewriting process in which you focus on one aspect of the writing at a time. If you try to rewrite everything at once, you will become overwhelmed and will not rewrite very effectively. Instead, focus on each of the following categories separately, spending days or hours on each one:

   - Content, immediately below.
   - Large-Scale Organization, page 79.
   - Paragraph Organization and Legal Analysis, page 86.
   - Small-Scale Organization—Sentence Structure, page 92.
   - Conciseness, page 94.

B.   *Content*

When rewriting, make sure that your content is accurate. To do this, reread the actual law relied on in the document. Reread the whole case or statute. Often, writers take notes when reading the law and then transfer those notes into the document. However, it is important to go back to the law—especially when it is case law—to ensure that you are accurately referencing the law. Oftentimes, you will find nuances within a case that further bolster your argument or find that you are misrepresenting a case or taking it out of context, which will hurt your credibility with your reader.

Some techniques for making sure your law is accurate include:

1. Reread in its entirety the law you have cited to make sure your characterizations are accurate.
2. Read a secondary source on your issue to make sure you have not omitted any important concepts and to ensure that you have accurately reflected the law.
3. Reread each piece of the law separately and compare it to the way you use it in your document.
4. Find any quotation and be sure you are using it properly and within context to ensure your credibility.
5. Be sure you are **citing** (see chapter 5) the law accurately, including pinpoint cites, so your reader can easily find your authorities.

In addition, make sure your facts are accurate. Review your notes from client interviews, look over relevant documents in the file, and talk to your client or witnesses to ensure accuracy. For your writing class in law school, you may simply need to re-read the fact pattern provided by your professor. However, in the real world, facts often change over time as you gather more information, and new or different facts could affect your legal analysis. Therefore, you should ensure that all the facts relied upon in your document are still accurate when you finalize your document.

C. *Large-Scale Organization*

Because the law is often complicated and dense, good organization is critical for the legal reader. To help the reader navigate your document, you should not only clearly identify the issues and outline the breakdown of the law, but you should also provide hand-holding techniques to help your reader understand those issues and legal elements.

1. Identifying Issues and Breaking Down the Law

One of the first things you will do in writing and rewriting is focus on your document's large-scale organization—the organization of the document as a whole. You need to decide how to break down the issues and how to present them in a manageable package for the reader. Although you will have a lot of discrepancy and room for creativity in your documents, your large-scale organization usually will be dictated by the issues and the legal rule.

First, you need to decide the issues you will address. As a law student, often you will address just one issue, usually dictated by your professor (e.g., you will write a memo on the issue of intentional infliction of emotional distress).

However, as a lawyer, you will need to decide the relevant issues and the order in which to address them. You should address each issue separately and, to help your reader, identify those issues up front.

Think of your document as an inverted triangle. The top part of the triangle should be a broad identification of the issues for your reader. As you work your way down the triangle, your writing becomes more and more focused.

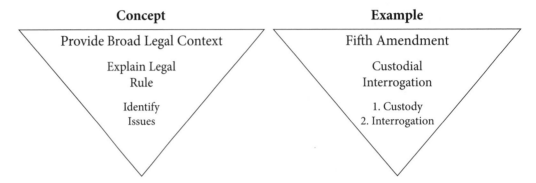

Second, organize each issue around the relevant legal rule. Whether they come from statutes, cases, regulations, or a combination, most legal rules are easily identified. Typical types of legal rules include a balancing test, a totality test, a multi-factored test, and a test with multiple exceptions. See Understanding Legal Rules (page 6). Regardless of the type of rule, break down the law into its subelements. Similar to the issues themselves, address each subelement separately and, to help your reader, identify those subelements at the beginning of each issue section.

Think of each issue as an inverted triangle. Start off your discussion of that issue broadly by providing the context for the reader as well as the breakdown of the subelements. Then, as your triangle becomes more narrow, your document focuses on the specific issues.

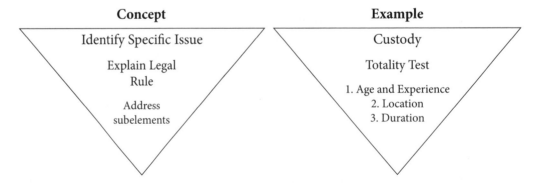

Third, each subelement should be clearly organized by identifying the subelement, providing the legal context for the reader, and applying the law to the facts. The organization of the legal application (see Constructing Legal Analysis, beginning on page 41) is complex. Here, many legal writers provide the legal definition for the subelement before they start applying the facts to that rule in a formula often called *IRAC* (see page 42). While this organizational scheme often makes sense, do not be tempted to fit your analysis into it all the time. First, the formula is too simplistic. Rules are sometimes much more complicated than the IRAC system allows for and cannot be easily defined. Second, the facts may provide a better starting point for context, especially in persuasive writing. Third, formulaic writing leads to boring writing. As a legal writer, you want to keep your reader's attention to inform or persuade. Don't get caught up in a formula when addressing each issue. Instead, follow the general principle of the inverted triangle: Begin broadly with context and focus your analysis more specifically as you work your way through the issue.

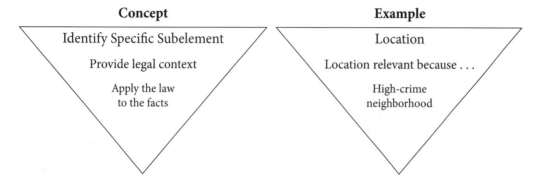

Keep in mind that there are a number of different, effective ways to organize your document. The above example shows an organizational scheme that revolves around legal elements. However, you can create any organizational scheme within the law that works for the purpose of your document. For example, in persuasive writing, you might choose to organize around a particular theory. When writing a memo to a partner or a letter to a client, you might decide to arrange the document around each party's arguments (we say/they say). You may choose to argue policy instead of the law, especially if you are arguing a case of first impression or you ever get a chance to argue in front of the Supreme Court. In addition, when multiple issues need to be addressed, you will have to determine which issues to discuss first and how the issues relate to each other.

2. Techniques to Help Guide the Legal Reader Through Your Document

Once you have decided on your issues, found the relevant law, and broken down the law into its subelements, you should use techniques to help guide the legal reader through the document. Legal readers are busy. They like to read documents quickly, often hoping to skim them for meaning. Therefore, you should craft documents that are easy to understand when skimmed. The following chart will help guide the legal reader through the organization of the document.

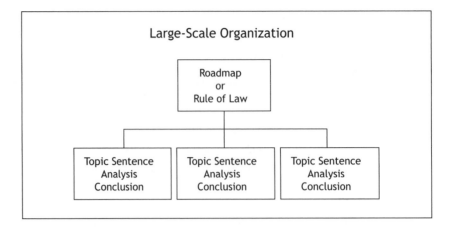

a. *Roadmaps*

Law students are desperate to understand the black-letter law of a problem as quickly as possible. The legal reader is no different. Therefore, a document that references the law at the front of the document is beneficial. "Fronting the law" or providing a "roadmap" usually helps the reader understand the writer's organization and the layout of the law. A roadmap is a signal to the reader that the document is organized around the law provided up front. The better legal documents provide a clear roadmap, which is dictated by the organization of the law, and then follow that organization throughout the document, using consistent legal terms. A roadmap may be one sentence, one paragraph, or longer, depending on the complexity of the law. A roadmap can identify issues or the law that defines each issue.

Roadmap Samples

1. A restrictive covenant in an employment contract is enforceable only if it passes every prong of a five-prong test:
    a. "is reasonably necessary for the protection of the employer;
    b. provides a reasonable time restriction;
    c. provides a reasonable territorial limit;
    d. is reasonable as to the employee; and
    e. is reasonable as to the general public."
       <u>Fields Found. Ltd. v. Christensen</u>, 309 N.W.2d 125, 128 (Wis. Ct. App. 1981).

OR

2. To show the contract is enforceable, the employer must prove the restrictive covenant provides reasonable time and territory restrictions, is reasonably necessary for the protection of the employer, and is reasonable as to the employee and to the general public. <u>Fields Found. Ltd. v. Christensen</u>, 309 N.W.2d 125, 128 (Wis. Ct. App. 1981).

Mini-roadmaps are another technique to help guide the reader through a complicated piece of the law. Just as a roadmap fronts the law of the whole document, a mini-roadmap provides a guide to a subsection of the document or one part of the analysis already laid out in the major roadmap. You may need a mini-roadmap to each subsection of the law or none at all.

Mini-Roadmap Sample

First, to determine if the covenant is reasonably necessary for the protection of the clinic, the court can consider three elements: confidential business information gained during her employment, her customer contact, and the level of competition she could give the clinic if she founded her own clinic.

---

b. Topic Sentences

Once a roadmap is provided, the document should use clear topic sentences that mirror the language and structure of the roadmap. Do not vary terms of art; words, after all, are what make up the law. In addition, transitional words such as *first, second,* and *finally* help hold the reader's hand and move him from one element of the roadmap to the next.

Topic Sentences

1. The main purpose of enforcing a restrictive covenant, to protect an employer from dissemination of its confidential business information, could be achieved by this covenant.

2. Second, the doctor's customer contacts at the clinic may amount to the clinic's protectible interest in making the covenant enforceable.

3. Finally, the covenant may be unenforceable because the doctor could not give the clinic more competition than an ordinary stranger.

---

c. Reader-Based Outlines

To ensure that your reader understands your large-scale organization, you should step into the reader's shoes by creating a "reader-based outline." A reader-based outline is not the same as the outline you might use in prewriting to organize your document (see page 73) before you write (a writer-based outline). Instead, a reader-based outline is created after you have written a full draft.

To create your reader-based outline, you should start at the analysis section of your document (the discussion section of a memo or the argument section of a brief). First, find and label your roadmap. Next, read *only* the topic sentences and try to create an outline—either in the margin or on a separate paper—using one or two words that describe the legal element or point made.

Here are additional tips:

- If you cannot label the topic sentences with a one- or two-word description of the legal element, your reader will not be able to understand your organization.
- If your labels resemble case names, your reader will not have a sense of the organization of the law itself because case names mean very little to a reader who is unfamiliar with the law.
- If your labels mirror your writer-based outline, then you have successfully conveyed your ideas to the skimming reader. If your reader-based outline does not mirror your writer-based outline, you still may want to keep your organization since it may have improved on your original design.

The Reader-Based outline appears in the margins below

Reader-Based Outline Sample

Following is a sample of a document in which a writer has created a reader-based outline.

Roadmap

[A restrictive covenant in an employment contract is enforceable only if it passes every prong of a five-prong test:

1. "is reasonably necessary for the protection of the employer . . . ;
2. provides a reasonable time restriction;
3. provides a reasonable territorial limit;
4. is reasonable as to the employee; and
5. is reasonable as to the general public."
    See Friends Foundation Limited v. Christensen, 309 N.W.2d 125, 128 (Wis. Ct. App. 1981); Chuck Wagon Catering v. Ruduege, 277 N.W.2d 787, 792 (Wis. 1979).

If any portion of the restrictive covenant is unenforceable, the entire covenant is void, even if the remaining elements would be enforceable. See Wausau, 514 N.W.2d 34, 38; Wis. Stat. Ann. § 103.465 (West 1997). Although Dr. Appleby's covenant is unreasonable because it fails the remaining prongs, and therefore, should not be enforced.]

1. Protection of Employer

Reasonably necessary for protection of clinic (also serves as mini-roadmap for this legal element)

[To determine if Dr. Appleby's covenant is reasonably necessary for the protection of the clinic, the court can consider three elements: confidential business information gained during her employment, her customer contacts, and the level of competition she could give the clinic if she founded her own clinic.] See Wausau, 514 N.W.2d 34, 39, Lakeside Oil Co. v. Slutsky, 98 N.W.2d 415, 419 (Wis. 1959). Under two of these three tests, the covenant may be reasonably necessary to protect the clinic.

Confidential business information (mirrors first part of mini roadmap above)

[The main purpose of enforcing a restrictive covenant, to protect an employer from dissemination of its confidential business information, could be achieved by Dr. Appleby's covenant.] See Wausau, 514 N.W.2d 34, 39. Considering this first element. Dr. Appleby's access to patient lists might be access to confidential business information, making the covenant reasonably necessary to protect the clinic. See Lakeside, 98 N.W.2d 415, 419; Pollack, 458 N.W.2d 591, 599. In Pollack, a restrictive covenant was enforced where a physician gained access to his employer's confidential patient lists. The employer spent considerable time, money and effort developing the lists, making them worthy of protection. See Pollack, 458 N.W.2d 591, 599. Similarly, Dr. Appleby had access to confidential patient lists through her dealings with the HMOs. As in Pollack, the clinic likely spent substantial time, effort and money on Dr. Appleby's development of the HMO affiliations and resulting patient lists. See id. Therefore, the covenant may be enforceable because Dr. Appleby had access to patient lists which could be the clinic's confidential and protectible business information.

[Second, Dr. Appleby's customer contacts at the clinic may amount to the clinic's protectible interest making the covenant enforceable.] See Wausau, 514 N.W.2d 34, 39-40. In Wausau, a clinic did not develop a protectible interest in customer contacts gained by a surgeon because the surgeon was only at the clinic for four months, and therefore, the covenant was not reasonably necessary for the protection of the clinic. See id.; contra Pollack, 458 N.W.2d 591, 599 (covenant necessary to protect an employer which invested considerable time, effort and advertising to generate customers for its sole physician). Dr. Appleby gained patient and HMO contacts throughout her seven years at the clinic, during which she affiliated the clinic with HMOs and gained a 25% share of the clinic's patients (400/1200 patients). In contrast to Wausau, Dr. Appleby may have gained significant customer contacts amounting to the clinic's protectible interest. See Wausau, 514 S.W.2d 34, 39-40. Therefore, the covenant may be enforced as reasonably necessary to protect the clinic.

— Customer contacts (mirrors second part of mini roadmap)

[Considering the final element, Dr. Appleby's covenant may be unenforceable because she could not give the clinic more competition than an ordinary stranger could.] See id.; Lakeside, 98 N.W.2d 415, 419. Upon termination of a surgeon's employment in Wausau, only one-half of one percent of his previous patients followed him to his new employer. Wausau, 514 N.W.2d 34, 40. That level of patient following was so minimal as to be the same type of competition that a stranger could give, and therefore, the covenant could not be enforced. See id. Dr. Appleby's relationships with decision-makers at the HMOs could give her a competitive edge if she sought alliance with them. However, Dr. Appleby believes that at least two of the three HMOs wold not leave the clinic for her practice. The one HMO that might follow her comprises a maximum of only four percent of the clinic's patients (50/1200 patients). Even if that HMO would affiliate with Dr. Appleby, there is no guarantee that the patients would chose Appleby fro the HMO's list of dentists. As in Wausau, there is a minimal amount of patient following and this low level of competition is the same type that a stranger could give. See id. Therefore, it is unlikely that Dr. Appleby is enough of a competitive threat to require enforcement of her covenant.

— Competition (mirrors third part of mini roadmap)

[Although the competition that would result if Dr. Appleby founded her own practice would be insignificant, her covenant may be reasonably necessary to protect the clinic because she gained confidential business information and customer contacts during her employment.]

— Mini-conclusion

2. Reasonable Time Limit

[To determine reasonableness of the covenant's time restriction, the court could examine both the total time period and the frequency of contacts within that period.] See Pollack, 458 N.W.2d 591; Lakeside, 98 N.W.2d 415, 420. Dr. Appleby's covenant fails the reasonableness test under either analysis.

— Time restriction (also serves as mini-roadmap to this legal element)

[Examining the total time period, five years is an unreasonably long period which makes Dr. Appleby's covenant unenforceable. See Pollack, 458 N.W.2d 591. In Pollack, a one-year restriction on a physician's business transactions coupled with a two year restriction on his patient contact was reasonable.] See id.; see also Chuck Wagon, 277 N.W.2d 787, 793 (a two year time period is reasonable). Dr. Appleby's five-year restriction is unreasonably long in comparison to the one and two year restrictions in Pollack, and therefore, the covenant should be unenforceable. See id.

— Time period (mirrors first part of mini roadmap above)

d.   *Mini-Conclusions*

At the end of the discussion of a legal element or issue, the document should provide a conclusion to that element or issue. This mini-conclusion should mirror the relevant terms of art in the roadmap and the applicable topic sentence, and it should provide the most important reasons for your conclusion.

Mini-Conclusion Sample

Therefore, the covenant may be enforceable because Dr. Appleby had access to patient lists which could be the clinic's confidential and protectable business information.

D.   *Paragraph Organization and Legal Analysis*

Once you have addressed large-scale organization, you need to focus on the organization within each paragraph as well as legal analysis (see chapter 1).

1.   Paragraph Organization

A paragraph usually discusses one idea, thesis, or element of the law. Each paragraph should be a discrete unit; it should contain only enough information to analyze that particular idea or element. An effective paragraph usually starts with a clear topic sentence, identifying the issue, idea, or theme to be discussed. The paragraph should then focus on that idea without digressing into other issues or tangential matters. Novice legal writers often spend time in their paragraphs discussing issues that are irrelevant or ideas that belong in different paragraphs. The internal consistency of a legal paragraph is especially important in complicated legal analysis.

Paragraphs that focus on legal application (see Constructing Legal Analysis on page 41) are often problematic for novice legal writers. Here, novices mistakenly may throw in as much law and as many legal quotations as possible to explain a legal concept. Better writers simplify the law for the reader by synthesizing it into a clear, concise package. An effective legal analysis paragraph sets forth a rule and applies it to the facts at hand. However, sometimes it takes more than one paragraph to accomplish a complete analysis of an issue. You need not address each issue in one full paragraph. A paragraph that is one double-spaced page is too long for your reader to digest; break it down into smaller pieces.

While each paragraph should stand adequately on its own, all your paragraphs should work together to create a cohesive, logical argument. If you believe your reader may become lost either within one paragraph or when moving from one paragraph to the next, reconsider the organization and the content of your paragraphs. In addition, use transitions to help the reader move from one paragraph to the next and to understand your ordering of the paragraphs.

Sample Transitions

Transitions help hold your reader's hand from one paragraph to the next. You can help your reader by providing transitions that explain the relationship from one paragraph to the next.

Transitions for a List or Sequence

- First
- Second
- Third
- Last
- Finally

Transitions for Comparison

- Similarly
- Likewise
- Like the defendant in _____, . . .
- As in _____, . . .
- In comparison

Transitions to Show Conclusions

- Thus
- Therefore
- In sum
- As a result

Transitions for Distinguishing

- On the other hand
- However
- In contrast
- Instead
- Although

Transitions to Show Time

- Previously
- Earlier
- Later
- Recently
- Now

---

2. The Analysis Within the Paragraph

When organizing analysis within each paragraph, start with the broad context of the law and work your way to the more specific application. Generally, you will present a rule and apply it to the facts of the case.

a. Presenting the Rules

When presenting the rule, you might use a definition from a statute or case, a policy statement, or a proposition you have created using case synthesis. Simplify the rule for the reader. Long quotations are usually not very helpful. While most lawyers try to present the rule in the beginning of the paragraph to provide a legal context for the reader, there will be times, especially in persuasive writing (page 97), when a lawyer might start with compelling facts or policy arguments instead of the legal rule.

b. Rule Application

When applying the rule to your facts, you will use case comparisons, policy arguments, statutory interpretation techniques, and other arguments discussed in legal analysis. As you apply the law to the facts, show how the rule has been applied in the past and how it should therefore be applied in this case. Rule application is extremely complicated. Therefore, various methods of rule application are discussed in depth in the following sections:

- Statutory Interpretation, page 14.
- Case Analysis, page 31.
- Policy Arguments, page 40.
- Constructing Legal Analysis, page 41.

The application of the law to the facts is often complex and difficult to explain to the reader. Remember that you have read and organized the law before you drafted the document; therefore, you are intimately involved with its nuances. Assume the reader has no such knowledge of the law. To provide clear analysis for your reader, scrutinize your document for holes in logic, omissions in the presentation of the prior law, and mistaken assumptions that the reader understands the facts of your case as well as you do.

Penny–Euro Cent Analogy

An analogy is helpful when rewriting your case comparisons. First, try to draw a penny—both sides—from memory. Go ahead. It will only take a minute, and it will illustrate an important point.

Now that you have drawn the penny, take a look at the images below.

The Familiar Lincoln Penny

The French Twenty-Cent Euro

How many of the details did you miss? If you are like most people, you have missed many of the fine details of the penny, an item you live with every day. Now, look at your drawing (not the real penny) and try to compare your penny to a French twenty-cent Euro coin. Your reaction should be confusion. This will be the reaction of your reader if you are not explicit with the prior law and the facts of your case.

Here is the analogy. The penny is similar to the facts of your case. Do not assume that your reader is familiar with them just because you have placed them in your statement of the facts. Instead, you need to keep taking them out of your pocket as you analyze the law and compare it to your facts. Be specific with those facts.

The French coin is the prior law. Assume your reader has not gone to France or read the prior cases. Even if she has gone to France, she probably does not remember all the details of her visit, let alone the coinage. Similarly, if she has read the prior case to which you are referring, she probably does not remember it with any detail. Therefore, you need to provide specifics. When referring to the prior case, it is often helpful to provide the facts, reasoning, and holding to help the reader understand its significance.

In addition, you should tie the penny to the Euro coin. For example, under the analogy, the penny presents a stoic bust of Lincoln; the French coin has a flowing picture of Marianne flitting across the sand under a burning sun. The penny writes out the number "one," whereas the French piece uses the numeral "20." These "ties" are helpful to compare the two coins. Similarly, you should compare the prior case to your facts to illustrate the logical connection for the reader. Be explicit.

3. Typical Analysis Mistakes

Legal writers make typical mistakes when performing case comparisons. First, when synthesizing the law, the novice legal writer often tries to explain all the case law up front before applying it to the case at hand. This is different from fronting the law or providing a roadmap (page 82) as mentioned earlier. Instead, the novice often spends pages laying out all the law she has read; then, pages later, she attempts to apply the client's facts to the law. The result is that the reader is required to constantly flip back to the prior pages to understand the prior law as it is being applied. This approach also leads to lengthy documents. Instead, provide a quick statement of the law and then address each element of that law with a layout of that element and simultaneous application of the facts to that element before moving on to the next facet of law. That way, the legal reader understands the law and its application to the facts at the same time. Each issue or element is addressed in full before moving on to the next.

Second, when performing case comparisons and actually showing how the prior case is similar or different from your case (see penny-Euro cent analogy above), novice writers typically omit either the penny or the Euro. Here are three typical problems with annotated samples.

a. The Lazy Analogy

Here, the writer takes the easy way out and provides block quotes or parentheticals instead of full analysis. Block quotes are usually difficult for the reader to digest and make the document painful to read. Often, the writer can rewrite the quote, utilizing only the most relevant language. Parentheticals are useful for secondary information but should not be used to make the actual case comparison. The writer should take the information out of the parenthetical and place it directly in the text with an explicit tie to the present case.

Lazy Analogy (Improper Use of Parentheticals)

Here, the important legal information appears in parentheticals instead of in the main text.

> Dr. Appleby's customer contacts at the clinic amount to the clinic's protectible interest making the covenant enforceable. If an employer invests a substantial amount of time, effort, and advertising to generate customers for its physician, the interest is protectible. See Simbolian, 543 N.W.2d at 223 (1998) (three months not enough for customer contacts); Wausau, 514 N.W.2d at 39 (1992) (four months not enough time to develop significant customer contacts); Pollack, 458 N.W.2d at 599 (1983) (only doctor in clinic so he was solely responsible for advertising). Dr. Appleby's seven years at the clinic where she associated the clinic with HMOs has given her substantial contacts with her patients.

b.   The Case-Study Method

Here, the writer provides brief descriptions of one case and continues with descriptions of other cases without actually applying these cases to the facts at hand. While this method might be appropriate for case briefs for a law class or case summaries if requested by a lawyer, they do not perform the function of analyzing the law and how it applies to the facts.

Case-Study Method

Here, the writer provides brief summaries of each case but does not synthesize a rule or apply the cases to the facts.

> Customer contact is another factor to determine if the covenant is reasonably necessary to protect the employer. In Wausau, Dr. William Wausau was a surgeon who was employed for four months. He was one of many surgeons in a large practice. In that case, there was not a threat under the customer contact theory. 514 N.W.2d at 39. In Simbolian, a doctor was with a practice for only three months; the court found he did not establish customer contacts. 543 N.W.2d at 223. In Pollack, the defendant was the only doctor in the abortion clinic. That doctor gained access to patient lists, and the clinic spent a lot of time advertising. 458 N.W.2d at 599. The court found that there was a threat under the customer contact theory. Our case is more similar to Pollack, and therefore, there is a protectible interest for the clinic.

c.   The One-Sided Approach

Some legal novices, especially when writing memos to supervising attorneys, forget to provide a full, objective analysis in an attempt to please the partner and the client. However, if cases exist that are not very helpful to the client's position, the writer should address and explain them. Even in a persuasive document, the writer should use the opportunity to distinguish these cases for the reader instead of ignoring them.

One-Sided Approach

Dr. Appleby's customer contacts at the clinic may amount to the clinic's protectible interest making the covenant enforceable. In <u>Wausau Medical Center v. Asplund</u>, 514 N.W.2d 34 (Wis. Ct. App. 1992), a clinic did not develop a protectible interest in customer contacts gained by a surgeon because the surgeon was at the clinic for only four months, and therefore, the covenant was not reasonably necessary for the protection of the clinic. In contrast, Dr. Appleby gained patient and HMO contacts throughout her seven years at the clinic, during which time she affiliated the clinic with HMOs and gained one-quarter of the clinic's patients. Unlike the four months in <u>Wausau</u>, seven years should have allowed Appleby significant customer contacts; these contacts probably amount to a protectible interest for the clinic.

> This analysis fails to address the relevant case, <u>Pollack</u>, found in other sample pages.

4. Effective Use of Signals in Your Analysis

Citation signals, such as *see, cf.,* and *but see* (see pages 406 and 460) can add depth to your analysis without distracting the reader. A signal is typically used in legal writing for two different reasons: (1) to inform the reader of the authority for the point made; and (2) to provide additional information to the reader. The latter is useful in adding depth to your analysis. For instance, if you have provided a case comparison to illustrate a point of law and another case illustrates the same point, you can provide a signal (<u>see also</u>) with a parenthetical to that case to show the reader that there is even more case law to back up the proposition without providing redundant analysis. In addition, at times a full case comparison is not necessary, and a signal will make your point concisely.

Appropriate Use of Signals: A four-hour interrogation is enough for a suspect to be in custody. <u>See, e.g.,</u> <u>Smith v. United States</u>, 542 U.S. 366 (1982) (4 hours, 20 minutes, enough for custody); <u>United States v. Jones</u>, 252 U.S. 543 (1975) (3 hours, 30 minutes, enough for finding of custody).

The key to using signals to add depth to analysis is to remember that signals provide additional or secondary information; they should not provide the actual analysis. If you are using signals and parentheticals to provide the actual analysis, you are making the Lazy Analogy mistake discussed earlier.

Signals in Analysis

This sample is an effective use of signals. The main analysis is provided in text through Wausau. The other cases are used to provide supplemental information.

Under the "customer contact theory," a threat is posed by the employee if she has enough control or influence over the customers that she would be able to take the customers away from the employer. The amount of time a doctor has worked for a clinic is especially relevant. For example, in <u>Wausau Medical Center v. Asplund</u>, 514 N.W.2d 34 (Wis. Ct. App. 1992), a surgeon was found not to have control or influence over his patients because he was one of many physicians at the clinic and was employed for only four months. <u>See also</u> <u>Simbolian</u>, 543 N.W.2d at 223 (three months not enough time for customer contact); <u>Pollack</u>, 458 N.W.2d at 599 (although amount of time not mentioned in case, control and influence were found where defendant was only doctor in abortion clinic and provided all clinic's advertising). Dr. Appleby has been with the three-doctor clinic for seven years as opposed to only four months in <u>Wausau</u> and is therefore likely to have control or influence over her patients.

E. Small-Scale Organization—Sentence Structure

Small-scale organization refers to the way in which you organize each sentence. Legalese and lengthy sentences, though often used in judicial opinions, are not very helpful to the busy legal reader. Instead, strive for simple, concise, clear sentences.

Here are some general rules to help with sentence structure in legal writing.

1. Use Strong Subject-Verb Combinations and Avoid Annoying Clauses

English readers like to know the subject and verb as quickly as possible, so create strong subject-verb combinations and place them in the beginning of the sentence. Because readers often get lost when you separate the subject from the verb, place modifying clauses and qualifiers after the subject and verb or in a separate sentence. As a result, you will avoid long sentences with annoying clauses.

Poor sentence structure: The victim of the assault, who was only sixteen at the time of the assault and photo array but now eighteen sitting in the courtroom, testified that she recognized the defendant from a photo array.

Better sentence structure: The eighteen-year-old victim testified she recognized the defendant from a photo array. She was only sixteen when assaulted.

Avoid beginning sentences with phrases such as *There was, It is,* and *There were.* Instead, start with a strong subject-verb combination.

Poor sentence structure: There were multiple defendants entering the courtroom when the judge took the bench.

Better sentence structure: Multiple defendants entered the courtroom when the judge took the bench.

---

2. Do Not Vary Terms of Art

In legal writing, the words create the law. Varying words or phrases can change the whole meaning of the law. Therefore, do not vary terms of art as you may have in undergraduate studies.

3. Avoid Long Quotations

Readers' eyes often skip over long quotations, especially block quotes. Consider writing part of the language in your own words and quoting only the necessary phrases.

4. Use Parallel Structure

When writing sentences that have lists or multiple rules, use consistent grammatical form. Parallel structure makes it easier for the reader to understand your ideas.

Poor sentence structure: The jury considered the evidence, the testimony, and what the judge had to say during jury instructions.

Better sentence structure: The jury considered the evidence, the testimony, and the judge's instructions.

---

5. Be Consistent in the Use of Titles

When referring to a person by name, be consistent so as not to confuse the reader. In addition, when referring to multiple people in a document, be consistent in how you refer to them. For example, if you use "Mr. Jones," do not use "Edith Jones" to refer to his wife; refer to her as "Mrs. Jones" or "Ms. Jones." Unless you have a specific reason, use *Ms.* instead of *Mrs.*

Use a parenthetical to explain a name only when it is necessary to clarify for the reader.

Poor use of parenthetical: The defendant, Mr. John Jones (Jones), ...

Better use of parenthetical: The employer, American Foundation for Better Learning (AFBL), ...

---

6. Write Short, Simple Sentences

Do not assume that you need to write long, complicated sentences to sound lawyerly. Instead, short, simple sentences will help you write clearly and apply the law logically. In persuasive writing, short sentences pack the most punch.

For more information, see Conciseness (below) and Grammar and Legal Usage Rules (page 349).

F. *Conciseness*

Legal readers are in a rush. They do not want to be bothered with long documents or excessive words. Short documents are often most effective and hold the readers' attention. Clear large-scale organization (page 79) and analysis (page 86) should help cure some wordiness issues. In addition, when rewriting, you can make your document more concise by editing for relevancy and redundancy, and remembering some word choice tricks.

Following are three tricks to eliminate wordiness.

1. Relevancy

What makes a fact relevant enough to place in your fact section? If you use a fact in your analysis, it is relevant and should appear in your fact section. What makes legal application relevant? If you use law to advance your argument, it is relevant. If it does not advance a point or help illuminate a breadth of caseload supporting your point, omit it. You should not include law just to show you have completed a lot of research.

2. Redundancy

Some redundancy is helpful for clarity. For example, topic sentences might seem redundant with headings and roadmaps, but they help guide the reader. In addition, consistent terms of art are conducive to good legal writing because the terms of art are constantly being interpreted. Therefore, do not vary terms of art. However, if certain words reappear within the same sentence or two, consider combining sentences to avoid redundancy. Never, though, sacrifice clarity for conciseness.

Redundant Words

Dr. Appleby is employed as a dentist by the Madison Dental Clinic. Seven years ago, she began her employment by signing an employment contract....

> *Comment: Notice the word* employ *or* employment *appearing three times. Consider omitting one or two of these redundancies.*

Sample Rewrite

Dr. Appleby is a dentist with the Madison Dental Clinic. Seven years ago, she signed a contract ...

---

3. Word Choice Tricks

Word choice is the art of legal writing. It gives the document meaning and voice. Concise word choice is preferred in most legal writing. By using the following word choice tricks, you can omit many extraneous words.

a. Omit "Glue Words"

One author, Richard Wydick, distinguishes words into two categories in each sentence: working words and glue words. The goal is to eliminate as many glue words as possible to make the documents less sticky.

Glue Words

A <u>claim</u> that the <u>restrictive covenant</u> is <u>unreasonable</u> may be brought by <u>Dr. Appleby</u>.

> *Comment: Four to five working words are underlined, leaving eight glue words remaining.*

Sample Rewrite

<u>Dr. Appleby</u> may <u>claim</u> the <u>restrictive covenant</u> is <u>unreasonable</u>.

> *Comment: Three glue words remain.*

---

b. Avoid Passive Voice If Unnecessary

Active voice, when the subject of your sentence is the actor, is usually preferred language because it is more concise. However, if you want to downplay the actor, passive voice might be the better option.

Passive Voice

Active voice: The defendant allegedly beat Ms. Jones.

Passive voice: Ms. Jones was allegedly beaten by the defendant.

> *Comment: The first sentence is shorter and therefore usually preferred in legal writing. However, although the second sentence is longer, it might be a better choice for a defense attorney.*

---

c. Avoid Legalese

Words that sound lawyerly are often long-winded and unnecessary. Avoid words such as *wherein, whereon, inasmuch, insofar, herein,* and *aforementioned* whenever possible.

d. Avoid Unnecessary Phrases

Lawyers often use twice the amount of words necessary in an attempt to seem lawyerly. Avoid this temptation. Aim for conciseness. Consider replacing the terms in the left column below with the more concise equivalents in the right column whenever you find them or others similar to them in your writing.

As a consequence of	→	Because
At this point in time	→	Currently or Now
Be able to	→	Can
Begin to develop	→	Develop
By means of	→	By
Despite the fact	→	Although
Distance of 100 miles	→	One hundred miles
Due to the fact that	→	Because
Employ	→	Use
Endeavor	→	Try
For the purpose of	→	For
In the event that	→	If
In order to	→	To
Period of five years	→	Five years
Void and unenforceable	→	Enforceable
Was aware of the fact	→	Knew

---

e. Create Strong Subject-Verb Combinations

Shorter sentences usually begin with a subject-verb combination. Sentences that begin with *There is, There was, It is,* or *It was* place their subjects and verbs midsentence, making it harder for readers to immediately grasp the meaning. To make these sentences more concise, omit *There is* or *It was* and begin with a subject-verb combination.

Strong Subject-Verb Combinations

There is a possibility that one HMO might affiliate with Dr. Appleby. That HMO represents a total of fifty patients. It is obvious that not all of these patients would go with Dr. Appleby.

Sample Rewrite

One HMO might affiliate with Dr. Appleby, but all patients would not go with her.

f. *Avoid Unnecessary Commentary*

Lawyers sometimes like to extend their personal thoughts into their writing. Avoid making this mistake as such commentaries are likely to distract from the merits of the case or provide unprofessional personal attacks against the other side's counsel.

Examples of Unnecessary Commentary

"We believe the defense incorrectly argues . . ."

"I think the law is unclear because . . ."

g. *Avoid Nominalizations*

A nominalization makes a verb into a noun. Leave the word as a verb. The following phrases illustrate some examples.

Give consideration to	→	Consider
Make a contribution to	→	Contribute
Have an understanding of	→	Understand
Gain knowledge from	→	Learn

IV.   PERSUASIVE WRITING

Persuasive writing is the art of convincing another that you are right. In most legal writing, whenever you are writing a persuasive document, someone on the other side is trying to persuade the reader that you are wrong. As a result, when learning to write persuasively, you need to consider the techniques for legal writing in general as well as additional techniques to make your argument more compelling than that of your opposing counsel.

This section introduces you to the following techniques used in persuasive writing to highlight your side while downplaying the other:

Specific forms of persuasion, such as oral argument (page 232), briefs (page 161), and motions (page 256), are discussed in chapter 3, Legal Documents.

A. Moving from Objective to Persuasive Writing

Some legal documents are written to show both sides of the argument and therefore present the information and analysis objectively. Memos, client letters, and other work product usually present information in an objective manner so that the attorney and client can make informed decisions.

Other documents are written persuasively—to win. Although the writer discusses the other side's argument, she does so in a light most favorable to her client. By distinguishing cases used by opposing counsel or illuminating gaps in reasoning, the legal writer can present persuasive documents that subtly persuade while informing about law on both sides. Trial briefs, motions, pleadings, and appellate briefs are among the typical persuasive documents; the opposing side is privy to these documents, and service is usually required.

This section illustrates some of the differences between objective and persuasive writing. However, keep in mind that most legal documents combine objective and persuasive writing. For example, briefs are considered to be persuasive, but they usually persuade the reader more effectively if they sound objective. On the other hand, legal memos are considered objective because they illustrate both sides of the argument; however, the writer usually tries to find every possible creative and viable argument for his client, so there are some persuasive undertones.

1. Objective Writing

In objective writing, such as legal memoranda (page 130), the writer's goal is to inform the reader of both sides of the argument so that the reader can make an informed decision. Thorough analysis of the arguments and counterarguments are required, and the writer should make a prediction as to the legal outcome.

Often, an objective document suggests that the client refrain from engaging in a particular activity or inform the client that she has performed some illegal act. The basic goal of an objective document is to thoroughly inform the reader, for better or worse. A typical mistake made in objective writing is to tell the reader what she wants to hear instead of presenting the facts and the law objectively.

2. Persuasive Writing

In persuasive writing, such as briefs (page 161) and motions (page 256), the writer's goal is to inform and persuade. Persuasion does not mean informing the reader of just one side of the argument. The best persuasive documents address the other side's arguments, but downplay or distinguish them. One of the biggest mistakes in persuasive writing is to hit the reader over the head with persuasion so that the arguments sounds hyperbolic or become personal attacks against the other side. Therefore, subtle persuasion is the trick in persuasive writing.

Many students enjoy writing persuasively. Not only is there a degree of competition involved, but the writer need not decide how the law should come out, as is the case with most objective writing. Instead, your position is dictated by the side you represent, and your goal is to choose the best strategy to win. As a lawyer, there may be times when you do not like the side you represent. However, your goal is to zealously represent your client and to do your best to win regardless of your distaste for the client or the position you are forced to argue.

B. *Designing the Theory of the Case*

1. What Is the Theory of Your Case?

Each persuasive document should contain a subtle theory. This is not a legal theory; instead, it is a simple, factual theory that will help your reader empathize with your client. For example, in a bus accident case, a legal theory might be negligence, but the theory of your case might be "the bus driver was in a rush." Such a simple theory is easy to understand and goes hand in hand with the legal theory. Thus, as you develop the law of negligence in your persuasive document, you can also use facts to enhance your theory of the case, such as the speed of the bus or the bus driver not paying careful attention. By using a subtle theory that is simple and easy to understand, the reader can sympathize with your client before she even understands the law. The theory of the case should be evident throughout your document, from the fact section to the argument section.

Opening Paragraphs of Opposing Briefs in the Supreme Court Case of <u>Clinton v. Jones</u>: Each Presents a Very Different Theory of the Case

OPENING OF PETITIONER'S STATEMENT	OPENING OF RESPONDENT'S STATEMENT
Petitioner William Jefferson Clinton is President of the United States. On May 6, 1994, respondent Paula Corbin Jones filed this civil damages action against the President in the United States District Court for the Eastern District of Arkansas. The complaint was based principally on conduct alleged to have occurred three years earlier, before the President took office. The complaint included two claims arising under federal civil rights statutes and two arising under state tort law, and sought $175,000 in actual and punitive damages for each of the four counts.	In Arkansas on May 8, 1991, respondent Paula Corbin Jones was a $6.35-an-hour state employee, and petitioner William Jefferson Clinton was the Governor. The complaint alleges that both were at the Excelsior Hotel in Little Rock that day for the Governor's Quality Management conference. While working at the conference registration desk, Mrs. Jones (Miss Corbin at that time) and a coworker were approached by Danny Ferguson, a state trooper assigned to Governor Clinton's security detail. Trooper Ferguson told Mrs. Jones that "[t]he Governor would like to meet with you" in a suite hotel, and gave her a piece of paper with the suite number written on it. When Mrs. Jones wondered what the Governor wanted, Trooper Ferguson responded, "It's okay, we do this all the time for the Governor." Trooper Ferguson then escorted Mrs. Jones to the Governor's floor. Complaint 6-13.

2. How to Develop a Theory of the Case

When you first begin to research and prewrite your document, you should brainstorm a number of potential theories for your case. Do not settle on one theory until you have had time to really think about the advantages and disadvantages of each one. Consider your audience: Which theory will best influence your particular judge? Look at the facts and the law: Which theory will be easier to prove? Consider the large-scale organization: Which theory will help your organizational scheme become stronger and more persuasive? Think about the other side: What will the other side choose for a theory? (You may already know your opponent's theory if, for example, you are writing an appellee's brief or opposition to a motion.)

3. Checklist for an Effective Theory

1. **Is the theory simple?** If you can't explain your theory in one or two sentences, it is too complex. In addition, be sure to stick to one theory. While you may argue the legal arguments in the alternative, you should have one overarching theory for your whole case.

2. **Is the theory subtle?** If you have to explain your theory over and over, it is not subtle. In fact, in persuasive writing, the best theories are those that are not written; instead, when the judge puts down the document after reading it, he should state your theory out loud. For example, if your theory is that the defendant, a grandmother and breast-cancer survivor, is lying, you probably should not write out in your brief that she is lying. Instead, you should lay out the facts in so

persuasive a manner that when the judge finishes reading he exclaims, "That grandmother is lying!"

3. **Does your theory take the high ground?** Make your client "the good guy" so that the judge wants to find for your side. You might provide a theory that makes the other side seem like the "bad guy," motivating the judge to punish her.

4. **Does your theory make sense within your factual framework?** Your theory must work not only within your own factual background, but also within all the facts that are not in dispute. If your theory also works within the other side's facts, it will be even more effective.

5. **Does your theory make sense within your legal framework?** Although your theory of the case is different from your legal argument, it still must fit within the legal framework. For example, arguing that your client is a wonderful teacher of new doctors in a hospital might not be a good enough theory to defend him against a medical malpractice case.

6. **Does your theory explain the "why" of the case?** Your facts will explain what happened. Your law will explain the legal implications of what happened. The theory should explain why it happened.

7. **Does your theory pull at the reader's heart strings?** While not all theories are emotional, some of the best theories force the judge to rule in your favor because of the emotional pull of the theory.

C. Crafting the Fact Section

The fact section of a persuasive document is your first opportunity to tell the story from your client's perspective. A chronological presentation is usually most effective because it is easily followed. A number of techniques help make fact sections more persuasive:

1. **Theory:** Although the theory of the case is woven throughout your whole brief, the fact section is the first opportunity to tell the full story from your client's perspective. The theory should be subtly embedded throughout the fact section so the reader feels for your client as the story unfolds.

2. **Starting Point:** Choosing a starting point for your facts is crucial as it provides a focal point for your theory of the case. For example, while a prosecutor might begin a fact section with the gruesome crime, the defense brief might start with the defendant's arrest. Whatever your starting point, it should be an opportunity for the judge to crawl into your client's perspective.

3. **Word Choice:** Word choice throughout the fact section is also important. The prosecutor might use the term *defendant* to highlight the fact that the other side stands accused. On the other hand, the defendant's brief would use the client's full, formal name: for example, Mr. Anthony Jones or Dr. Smith (first names alone, however, are usually too informal for a brief to a court). By personalizing your client, you

increase the chances that the judge will become familiar and comfortable with him.

4. **The Facts:** The fact section of a brief should be thorough and honest. Do not avoid harmful facts. If you do, the judge will read about them in the other side's brief and assume you are attempting to hide them. As a result, not only do you look distrustful, but also you lose an opportunity to distinguish and downplay the harmful facts. You can downplay them by discussing them in a light most favorable to your client. Some techniques to downplay facts are to explain them away or to place them in between more favorable facts for a less dramatic impact on the reader's impression of the client.

For an example of a Statement of Facts from a Supreme Court brief, see the section Statement of the Case on pages 170-174.

D. *Drafting the Argument Section*

The argument section uses legal analysis (see chapter 1)—the application of the law to the facts—to show why you should win. You should make informed decisions about the order in which you place the issues, the way in which you formulate the rule, and the way in which you handle adverse authority. In addition, avoid sounding defensive or attacking the other side personally.

1. Ordering of Issues

General legal wisdom is to present your best arguments first, initially using your strongest cases and other law to prove your point. The reasoning here is that you hold your reader's attention most carefully in the beginning of your document and at the beginning of each paragraph. Sometimes, however, ordering your arguments chronologically or in another order that best introduce your theory of the case makes more sense. A typical legal writer will order and reorder a persuasive document many times before filing. However, do not let the other side's brief dictate your ordering of issues. One of the biggest mistakes in writing oppositions is to follow the organizational scheme set out by the opposing side. Instead, you should choose the scheme that works best for your side and theory. In addition, keep in mind how much "air time" you give your arguments compared to the time you take addressing the other side's arguments. Your arguments should have the highest priority and so should take up the most space on the paper. While a complex counterargument may need a number of pages to cover the nuances, be wary of the subtle message that you send by spending too much time on a particular issue.

Pointheadings and subheadings (page 164) are also useful tools in persuasive writing. Sometimes they serve as a scoreboard: The more subheadings for your side, the more good arguments you have. However, do not just write as many subheadings as you can to have the most in your brief. Instead, craft your point headings and subheadings carefully. Choose terms of art and facts that are favorable for your side. Do not create subheadings or pointheadings for unfavorable issues or using unfavorable facts. Instead, address these adverse issues and facts within other subheadings.

2. The Legal Rules

Often, the rule of law that applies can be interpreted in multiple ways. The trick it to choose the interpretation that best fits within your theory of the case and is most persuasive for your side. Do not assume that the other side's interpretation is correct, especially when writing an opposition to a strong brief. To formulate the rule in a light most favorable to your client, look for key terms of art that are easy to prove (or disprove) and strong cases within your interpretation.

3. Adverse Authority

You will often find cases in your research that do not help your client. You will need to decide what to do with them. (See ethics, page 77.) If you decide to leave them out of your persuasive writing, you run the risk that the other side will rely on them, and you will then have lost an opportunity to distinguish them. Instead, consider addressing them head on and distinguishing them yourself.

You can use a number of strategies in dealing with adverse cases.

1. **Distinguish the facts:** Show the court that the facts of the case are so different from your facts that the case does not apply.
2. **Distinguish the reasoning or the policy:** Show the court that the reasoning or the policy of the case is so different from the reasoning or policy in your situation that the case does not apply.
3. **Find a better case:** Show how a more recent case or a case with more binding authority applies in a different fashion than the adverse case. Then rely on the better case.
4. **Downplay the case:** Address the case within a discussion of other cases so that the other cases seem more important (even if they are not).
5. **Overrule authority:** As a last resort (but not recommended), ask the court to overrule previous authority. Be aware, however, that judges, especially trial judges, rarely do so as they run the risk of being overruled by an appellate court.

4. Do Not Sound Defensive

Many poor persuasive documents sound defensive. As mentioned above, an opposition to a motion might use the opponent's motion as a model for organization and counter each argument in the same order. This technique is not effective for two reasons: (1) The writer loses the opportunity to make organizational decisions to help prove his argument. Instead, he accepts the carefully designed organizational decisions of his opponent. (2) The document consistently argues the negative, and the tone of the document is "did not"—a very whiny approach to legal writing. Therefore, watch for topic sentences that begin with "The opposing side argues" or "The defendant incorrectly states." There is no need to present the other side's argument again for him as repetition helps the reader remember. Instead, present your arguments affirmatively and in the order in which you decide is best for your theory of the case.

Samples of Defensive Writing

The following defensive topic sentences are from a plaintiff's opposition brief:

1. Defendants contend that they were not liable because ...
2. Defendant's reliance on <u>Jones v. Brown</u> is misplaced because ...
3. Then, unable to rebut the issue of jurisdiction, the Defendants propose ...
4. Finally, and most remarkably, Defendants argue that ...

---

5. Do Not Personally Attack the Other Side

Often, lawyers let arguments become personal. Avoid this urge. Instead, make sure that your document addresses issues and does not attack the other side personally. Judges do not appreciate personal gripes between lawyers, and usually your credibility suffers when you use such tactics.

Samples of Personal Attacks

The following unnecessary personal attacks are from defendants' briefs:

1. Remarkably, Plaintiffs disingenuously mislead this Court into believing that all discovery demands were met.
2. The Plaintiff's counsel continues to play fast and loose with this Court's requirements.
3. Plaintiff's overreaching and unethical behavior ...
4. Courts recognize, but Plaintiffs intentionally overlook, that ...

---

6. Do Not Overstate Your Case

Your credibility is your best tool in persuasive writing. Do not lose it. If you overstate your case or a particular fact, you lose credibility with the court. If you misstate a rule of law or present reasoning from a case out of context, you lose credibility. On the other hand, if you always sound reasoned and rational and admit any weaknesses in your case (preferably those that do not matter), your arguments will have more credibility and therefore will be more persuasive.

E. Using Effective Sentence Structure and Word Choice

If persuasive writing is the art of convincing another that you are right, then the sentences and words are the tools of the art form. The following rules can help make your sentences and words more persuasive:

1. **Short sentences have more punch.** Novice writers often try to pack their sentences with as much material as possible in hopes of providing the reader with all the necessary information. However, a reader who cannot understand a sentence or who does not have time to decipher all the clauses will not be persuaded. Shorter sentences are usually more persuasive and more easily digested by the reader.

2. **Affirmative language is more effective than negative language.** Here, tone comes into play as well as sentence structure. It is simply easier to understand an affirmative sentence, and a negative tone may come off as defensive or whiny.

3. **Vary the sentence structure.** Formulaic writing is boring. When you vary the sentence structure, the reader stays engaged longer. Shorter sentences pack a punch; use them wisely.

4. **Avoid passive voice.** Sentences are easier to read and more persuasive when the actor is doing the acting. Therefore, you should generally avoid the passive voice. However, if you want to downplay an actor's involvement, use the passive voice. ("The victim was allegedly shot by my client" is better than "My client allegedly shot the victim.")

5. **Avoid unnecessary dependent clauses.** Dependent clauses often get in the reader's way. Use them for facts or law that you want to downplay. Highlight helpful facts and law within the main clause of a sentence.

6. **Put key points in the beginnings of sentences and paragraphs.** Because a reader's attention wanes easily, put the important information up front—at the beginning of sentences and at the beginning of paragraphs.

7. **Avoid "clearly" and "really." Language that overstates your case is not helpful.** Empty words such as really, clearly, and obviously add nothing to your argument and make you sound as if you are stretching to make your points.

8. **Use Plain English.** Do not use flowery language or try to impress your reader with obscure words. Instead, use Plain English so that the reader can easily follow your arguments and rule in your favor.

9. **Selective word choice.** The words you choose can make a big impact on your persuasive writing. For example, a defendant might write that the police "burst" into a room while the prosecution will state the police "entered" the room. Likewise, a drug defendant might want to call his vehicle "the car," while the prosecution would be more specific

and refer to it as "the Porsche." Subtle choices like these can impact the reader.

F. *Taking Advantage of Technology*

People retain more information and remember it for a longer time if it is provided visually. As readers, we take the words we read and make mental images. Including images within a brief, then, can help to persuade your reader. As the number of courts requiring e-filing increases, so does the number of multimedia tools available that integrate images into your briefs. The trick with using such visuals, however, is to learn how to use them to help persuade, not just to provide a "wow" factor. As a writer, you should use technology within your briefs to create a simulated environment where the reader actually steps into the client's shoes.

Here are some ideas for embedding multimedia within briefs:

1. **Pictures.** If a picture paints a thousand words, then pictures can make our briefs a lot shorter. Consider embedding a picture in a brief if it will show the crime scene, bring the victim or her injuries to life, or personalize your client.
2. **Animations.** An animation can help to show how something works—especially in patent cases—or to show how a part of the body functions (such as blood running through a vessel).
3. **Simulations.** A simulation can be very effective to show your side of the facts. A simulation can make your reader feel as if he is a part of the action. He can then hold the visual image in his mind when reading the law.
4. **Video.** Videos can help show a day in the life of your client or can show a crime scene in a three-dimensional fashion such as a walk-through of a house.
5. **Diagrams and maps.** Diagrams often use very little technology and are already used as visuals within briefs. Maps can be downloaded from the Web and embedded within briefs to give the reader a sense of direction and distance.
6. **Scanned documents.** Documents that would have been attachments to briefs can now be embedded within the brief in an appropriate place within the writing so that the reader does not need to flip back and forth to understand the text about the scanned document.
7. **Links.** E-briefs can link directly to the law and other sources for the reader to easily locate and read referenced sources.

Make careful choices when using technology within your briefs. Develop a strategy for using multimedia that persuades the reader, for instance, by inviting her into your client's home or life. Do not simply throw technology into your brief without thinking about why and where. If you do, chances are you will not only miss the opportunity to persuade and inform, but you also might confuse and distract your reader.

V. STUDY AIDS—THE WRITING PROCESS

A. Quick References and Checklists

☑ 1. Writing in General: Checklist

The Legal Reader

Legal readers share some common traits. Here are some tips to adjust your writing to meet this audience.

- ✓ The legal reader is a doubting audience.
  - Cite to legal authority.
  - Use concrete legal analysis.
- ✓ The legal reader will ask questions and expect answers within your writing.
  - Show both sides of a legal issue.
  - Respond to all possible issues presented by the law and facts.
- ✓ The legal reader is looking for the answer to a particular issue or set of issues.
  - Answer the question up front.
  - Use the rest of the document to prove the answer.
- ✓ The legal reader is in a rush.
  - Use roadmaps and strong topic sentences.
- ✓ The legal reader does not want too much detail or tangential information.
  - Focus on the issue assigned.
  - Let the reader know if there are other issues that warrant investigation.
- ✓ The legal reader expects you to teach him or her about the law and its application.
  - Be specific.
  - Do not leave any holes in your argument.
  - Do not assume the reader understands either the law or the facts.

Goals of Legal Writing

The purpose of each legal document will be different, but this list explores common goals and expectations within the legal writing community.

- ✓ Legal precedent, not your personal opinion, is valued in court documents.
  - Be creative, but ground your writing in the law.
- ✓ Legal writing affects others as well as your own reputation.
- ✓ Legal writing should be concise.
- ✓ Legal writing should follow assigned formats.
  - Always research your local court rules.
- ✓ Before you begin to write a legal document, consider
  - Purpose
  - Audience

- Scope
- View

---

2. Writing: Checklist

Writing Process

✓ Consider breaking your writing down into manageable categories.
- Prewriting
    - Research, read, and organize the law.
    - Make an outline.
- Writing
    - Write a draft.
- Rewriting
    - Do multiple rewrites.
    - Focus on large-scale organization, analysis, and conciseness.
- Editing and citation
    - Edit for syntax, sentence structure, and grammar.
    - Polish for typos and citation.

✓ Effectively manage your time.
- Create a false deadline.
- Self-impose a realistic schedule.
- Set aside time to walk away from your document.
- Set aside time for unpredictable disasters.

✓ Overcome writer's block.
- Break up large and complicated tasks into small manageable chunks.
- Assume that writing is a learning process, meaning that multiple drafts are a necessary part of the process.

Writing Creatively

Develop creative arguments and present them using legal writing conventions.

✓ Develop a unique theory for your case.
✓ Use the facts of your case to tell a compelling story.
✓ Create a novel argument.
✓ Use case law creatively in a traditional argument.
✓ Anticipate the other side's arguments and distinguish them.
✓ Reorganize your document in a nontraditional manner.
✓ Look at the judge's opinion both for what is there and what is not there.
✓ Create policy arguments.
✓ Vary your sentence structure.
✓ Do not be trapped in the IRAC box.
✓ In general, think outside the box.

Organizing Before You Write

✓ Organize your research materials.
- By legal elements or issues
- In printed paper piles or in electronic folders

✓ Decide which materials are relevant.
- May require outlining
- May require an actual draft
- May be reconsidered during rewriting
- Verge on being overinclusive, especially early on

Outlining Your Document

When reading the tips that follow, remember that there are an infinite number of ways to write effective outlines. Do what works for you.

✓ The actual legal rule you are going to apply should be the foundation of your outline.
- Begin your outline by writing the actual legal rule.
- Separate the rule into its elements or component parts.
- If there are multiple issues, create one outline with multiple issues or create separate outlines for each issue.
- Use connectors—*and, or, may,* and *shall*—to show the relationship between elements.
- Address elements in the order they appear in the rule unless you have good reasons to digress from that order (for example, persuasive writing).

✓ Pore through your research and fill in information under each element.
- List each case separately under each issue.
- Include holdings, reasoning, and facts.
- A single case may appear under multiple elements.
- If one element is easily met, you should still analyze the element.

✓ Add facts from your own case.
- Write notes comparing your case to the other cases under each element.

✓ Do not let the outline stifle your creativity.

✓ Consider writing multiple outlines before you write your first draft.

---

 3. Rewriting: Checklist

Rewriting Generally

✓ The process of reworking large-scale components of the document.

✓ Step into your reader's shoes.
- Assume you know nothing about the law or the facts.
- Take time away from your document.
- Read your document out loud.

- Create a reader-based outline.
  - Outline only the topic sentences.
- Focus on only one aspect of the writing at a time:
  - Content
  - Large-scale organization
  - Paragraph organization and legal analysis
  - Small-scale organization—sentence structure
  - Conciseness

Content

✓ Is your content accurate? Reread the actual law in its entirety.
✓ Did you check your content against a secondary source?
✓ Are all quotations used within context?
✓ Did you cite the law accurately, including pinpoint cites?

Large-Scale Organization

✓ *First,* did you provide the broad legal context for the reader?
✓ *Second,* did you explain the legal rule?
  - Break the rule down into its elements.
✓ *Third,* did you organize each issue around the relevant legal rule?
  - Identify specific issue.
  - Explain the legal rule.
  - Address subelements.
    - Identify specific subelement.
    - Provide legal context.
    - Apply the law to the facts.
✓ *Fourth,* did you use techniques to guide the legal reader?
  - Roadmap:
    - Identifies issues of the law that defines each issue.
    - "Fronts" the law.
  - Mini-roadmaps:
    - Provides a guide to subsections of the law.
  - Topic sentences:
    - Mirror language and structure of roadmap.
    - Use signals and transitional words.
    - Can you label your topic sentence with a one- or two-word description of the legal element that mirrors your reader-based outline?

Paragraph Organization and Legal Analysis

✓ *Paragraph organization*
  - Does each paragraph contain only enough information to analyze a single idea or element?
    - Sets for the rule
    - Applies the facts at hand

- Is internally consistent
- Less than one double-spaced page
- Do your paragraphs work together to create a cohesive, logical argument?
  - Provide transitions to move the reader between paragraphs.

✓ *Analysis within the paragraph:*
- Present the rule in simplified form.
- Apply the rule to your facts.
- Use case comparisons, policy arguments, and statutory interpretation techniques.
  - Do you avoid the lazy analogy?
  - Do you avoid the case-study method?
  - Do you avoid a one-sided approach?
- Show how the rule has been applied in the past.
- Show how the rule should be applied in your case.
- Use citation signals to add depth to your analysis.

Small-Scale Organization: Sentence Structure

Strive for simple, concise, clear sentences.

✓ Use strong subject-verb combinations.
✓ Avoid annoying clauses.
✓ Do not vary terms of art.
✓ Avoid long quotations.
✓ Use parallel structure.
✓ Be consistent in the use of titles.
✓ Write short, simple sentences.

Conciseness

✓ Edit for relevancy and redundancy, and remember some word choice tricks.
✓ Relevancy:
  - Omit law that does not advance your point.
✓ Redundancy:
  - If words reappear within the same sentence or two, consider combining the sentences.
    - Do not sacrifice clarity for conciseness.
✓ Word choice tricks:
  - Omit "glue words."
  - Avoid passive voice if unnecessary.
  - Avoid legalese.
  - Avoid unnecessary phrases.
  - Create strong subject-verb combinations.
  - Avoid unnecessary commentary.
  - Avoid nominalizations.

4. Persuasive Writing: Checklist

Moving from Objective to Persuasive Writing

Keep in mind that most legal documents combine objective and persuasive writing.

- ✓ Objective writing is used to thoroughly inform the reader, for better or worse.
- ✓ Persuasive writing is used to inform and persuade.
  - Use subtle persuasion.
  - Address counterarguments, but downplay or distinguish them.

Designing the Theory of the Case

- ✓ Do you present a factual theory that will help the reader empathize with your client?
  - Is it evident from the fact section to the argument section?
- ✓ Brainstorm possible theories, and then weigh advantages and disadvantages.
  - Which theory will best influence your particular judge?
  - Which theory will be easier to prove?
  - Which theory strengthens your organizational scheme?
  - What will opposing counsel choose for a theory?
  - Is the theory simple?
  - Is the theory subtle?
  - Does your theory take the high ground?
  - Does your theory make sense within your factual framework?
  - Does your theory explain the "why" of the case?
  - Does your theory pull on the reader's heart strings?

Crafting the Fact Section

- ✓ Subtly embed your theory of the case.
- ✓ Start with the facts that best support your theory.
- ✓ Focus on word choice.
- ✓ Be brief and honest.
- ✓ Do not avoid harmful facts; rather, distinguish and downplay harmful facts
  - Explain them away.
  - Discuss them in a light most favorable to your client.
  - Place them between more favorable facts.

Drafting the Argument Section

- ✓ Apply the law to the facts to show why you should win.
- ✓ Consider in what order to place issues.
  - Present your best arguments first or choose the scheme that best works for your side and theory.
  - Give your arguments priority over counterarguments.
  - Craft pointheadings and subheadings carefully.

✓ Choose an interpretation of the rules that best fits with your theory of the case.
  - Look for key terms of art that are easy to prove (or disprove).
  - Look for strong cases with your interpretation.
✓ Consider addressing adverse cases head on and distinguishing them.
  - Distinguish the facts.
  - Distinguish the reasoning or policy.
  - Find a better case.
  - Downplay the case.
  - Overrule authority.
✓ Avoid sounding defensive or repeating your opponent's arguments.
  - Do not personally attack the other side.
  - Do not overstate your case.

Using Effective Sentence Structure and Word Choice

✓ Short sentences are high impact.
✓ Affirmative language is more effective than negative language.
✓ Vary sentence structure.
✓ Avoid passive voice.
✓ Avoid unnecessary dependent clauses.
✓ Put key points at the beginning of the sentences and paragraphs.
✓ Avoid words like really, clearly, and obviously.
✓ Use plain English.

Taking Advantage of Technology

✓ Embed multimedia within your brief to create a simulated environment where the reader actually steps into the client's shoes.
  - Use pictures.
  - Use animation.
  - Use simulations.
  - Use video.
  - Use diagrams and maps.
  - Use scanned documents.
  - Provide links to referenced sources.
✓ Make careful choices when embedding multimedia; you want to persuade the reader, not confuse or distract her.

Considering Plagiarism and Ethics

✓ Do not plagiarize someone else's work.
  - Use quotation marks and citations.
  - Avoid frequent use of your computer's cut and paste feature.
✓ Become familiar with your specific jurisdiction's ethics rules.
  - Do not make a false statement to the court.
  - Bring adverse authority to the attention of your judge.
  - Do not make an argument that is unwinnable under any scenario.
  - Do not make an ex parte communication to the judge unless permitted by law.

5.   Persuasive Techniques: Quick Reference

Develop a Subtle Theory of Your Case

This is not a legal theory; instead, it is a simple, factual theory that will help your reader empathize with your client. The theory of the case should be woven throughout your document, from the fact section to the argument section.

Write a Persuasive Fact Section

The fact section is an opportunity to tell the story from your client's perspective. Choosing a starting point is important, as it provides a focal point for your theory of the case. Word choice is also crucial: the prosecutor might use the term *defendant*, while the defendant's brief would use the client's name. The fact section should not avoid harmful facts; instead, it should downplay them by discussing them in a light most favorable to the client.

Write a Persuasive Argument Section

The argument section includes facts and law to persuade the judge that you win. Here, you should make informed decisions about the order you place your issues, legal points, and primary authority. General legal wisdom is to present your best arguments first, using the strongest cases to prove your point. The reasoning here is that you hold your reader's attention most carefully in the beginning of your document and at the beginning of each paragraph. Sometimes, however, ordering your arguments chronologically or in another order that best introduces your theory of the case makes more sense.

Avoid Sounding Defensive

Don't use your opponent's motion or brief as a model for your organization. This strategy is ineffective because you lose the opportunity to make organizational decisions to help prove your own argument and because you will be consistently arguing the negative. Watch out for topic sentences that begin with, "The opposing side argues . . . ." Don't present the other side's argument again, as the repetition will help your reader remember. Instead, present your arguments affirmatively and in the order in which you decide is best for your theory of the case.

Don't Personally Attack the Other Side

Don't let the argument become personal. Instead, make sure that your document addresses issues and does not attack the other side personally.

☑ **6.   Self-Evaluation Form for Memos: Checklist**

When evaluating your writing, do not try to "fix" everything at once. Instead, focus your attention on one aspect of the memo at a time. Start with the rewriting issues before moving on to editing issues. For example, looking for grammar problems in a paragraph that might be substantively irrelevant would be a waste of time. Answer each question as fully as possible, writing on both this checklist and your memo.

Large-Scale Organization

✓ Have you started your discussion section with a statement of the law that applies to your client's problem? Where is that "roadmap"? (Either circle on your memo or state where it is located.) _____

✓ Create a "reader-based outline" by reading only your topic sentences and writing a one- or two-word description of the point of each topic sentence. (You can make the outline on the margins to your memo or on this Quick Reference.)

   • Does your reader-based outline parallel the structure of your road-map? Why or why not? Do you use the same legal terms in your topic sentences as you use in your roadmap? _____
_____

   • Does your reader-based outline convey the major legal points you thought you made in your memo? Why or why not? (If you write an outline before you begin writing, how does your reader-based outline differ from your writer-based outline?) _____
_____

✓ Read the substance of each paragraph. Either here or in the margin of your paper, give a one- or two-word issue or sub-issue discussed in each paragraph. Does the paragraph actually discuss the issue and only the issue that your topic sentence addresses? Why or why not? _____
_____

✓ Do you provide a conclusion at the end of each element (1) to let the reader know that you have completed the discussion of that element, and (2) to tell the reader your reasons for the outcome of that element?
_____

Legal Analysis

✓ Is there an applicable statute for your memo? If so, what statutory inter-pretation techniques did you use in this paper, and what statutory tech-niques did you choose not to address? (Explain in detail the techniques you used, e.g., plain meaning, context, purpose, definitions, cases, legislative history. Explain where you used or did not use them.) _____
_____

✓ Do you support your legal conclusions with specific facts and/or legal authority? Point out a conclusion and your specific facts and legal authority that support that conclusion. Point out a conclusion that is not supported by facts or authority. _____
_____

Purpose

✓ Do you present arguments for both sides of each element you address? Where could you have been more objective? _____

_____

✓ Do you answer the question for the lawyer? Where in the memo did you put the answer? Is your final answer consistent with an answer you might have placed earlier in the memo? _____

_____

Citation

✓ Did you cite the statute correctly? What ALWD or Bluebook rules did you consult to cite the statute? _____

_____

Strengths and Weaknesses

List three strengths and three weakness in this memo.

1. _____   1. _____
2. _____   2. _____
3. _____   3. _____

☑ 7. Peer-Evaluation Form for Memos: Checklist

One of the goals of this book is to help you become your own editor. This Quick Reference is designed to help you continue developing your evaluation process. By evaluating a peer's memo, you become another set of eyes for that peer and begin reevaluating your own memo.

When evaluating your peer's writing, do not comment on everything at once. Instead, focus your attention on one aspect of the memo at a time. Start with the rewriting issues before moving on to revising issues. While it is important to give positive feedback, focus on places where the writer needs improvement so that every writer gets ample opportunity for helpful criticism. Answer each question as fully as possible, writing on both this form and your peer's paper, before moving on to the next question.

After evaluating the memo, meet with your peer to discuss your evaluation.

Formal Format

✓ **Question Presented:** Does the QP provide the reader with the jurisdiction, the specific legal question, and the most legally significant facts in a coherent and objective manner? Why or why not? Can you read the whole QP aloud in one breath? _____

_____

• How does this writer's QP differ from your own? _____

_____

✓ **Brief Answer:** Does the BA provide an answer to the QP? In addition, does the BA use the legal buzz words from the law to provide the main reasons for the conclusion? _____

- How does this writer's BA differ from your own? _____

_____

✓ **Conclusion:** Does the conclusion fill in the main facts and reasons from the Brief Answer? _____

- How does this conclusion differ from your own? _____

_____

✓ **Statement of Facts:** Does the statement of facts tell a clear and concise story, providing the legally significant facts from your case? Put square brackets around those facts that you believe are not legally significant.

_____

- How does this statement of facts differ from your own? _____

_____

Large-Scale Organization

✓ Has the writer started the discussion section with a statement of the law that applies to the client's problem? Where is that "roadmap"? (Either circle on the memo or state where it is located.) _____

_____

- How is that roadmap different from your own? _____

_____

✓ Create a "reader-based outline" by reading only the topic sentences and writing a one- or two-word description of the point of each topic sentence. (You can make the outline on the margins to the memo or on this form.)

- Does the reader-based outline parallel the structure of the roadmap? Why or why not? Does the writer use the same legal terms in the topic sentences as in the roadmap? _____

_____

- How does the writer's organizational scheme differ from your own?

_____

✓ Read the substance of each paragraph. Either here or in the margin of the paper, give a one- or two-word issue or sub-issue discussed in each paragraph. Does the paragraph actually discuss the issue and only the issue that the topic sentence addresses? Why or why not? _____

_____

✓ Does the writer provide a conclusion at the end of each element (1) to let the reader know that she has completed the discussion of that element, and (2) to tell the reader the prediction for the outcome of that element? Which mini-conclusions are effective? _____

_____

- Do you come out differently from the writer on each element? If so, where and why? _____

_____

Legal Analysis

✓ What statutory interpretation techniques did the writer use in this paper?

_____

✓ Did the writer effectively use cases to support the legal arguments? Where? Which cases are different from the ones you chose? _____

_____

✓ Look at the case analogies. For each analogy, does the writer use the facts, reasoning, and holding from the prior case and compare them to the specific facts of your case to predict an outcome for the client? Be specific in your answer. _____

- Which is the best case comparison? The worst? Why? _____

_____

- How might you now change your own case analysis techniques to make the comparisons clear and specific? _____

_____

Purpose

✓ Does the writer present arguments for both sides of each element addressed? Where could the writer have been more objective?
✓ Compare the writer's objectivity to that in your paper. What arguments might you make that you did not previously consider?

Editing

✓ Did you find any patterns of grammar problems? Where?
✓ Did you find any of your own grammar problems in this memo? Where?

📋 8. Self-Evaluation Form for Briefs: Checklist

When evaluating your writing, do not try to comment on everything at once. Instead, focus your attention on one aspect of the brief at a time. Start with the rewriting issues before moving on to revising issues. Answer each question as fully as possible, writing on both this form and your document, before moving on to the next question.

Brief in General

✓ **General Format:** Do you provide a title page, a table of contents with clear pointheadings and page numbers, and table of authorities? _____

_____

✓ **Statement of the Issue(s) Presented:** Does the issue statement provide the reader with the specific legal question, written in a persuasive manner? Why or why not? Can you read the whole issue statement aloud in one breath? _____

_____

✓ **Statement of the Case:** Does the statement of the case tell a clear and concise story? Does it provide the legally significant facts from the case? Is it written persuasively? _____

_____

- What is the theory of the case? _____

_____

- What specific word choices do you use that make the statement of the case persuasive? _____

_____

Argument Section

Large-Scale Organization

✓ Do you start the argument section with a statement of the law that applies to the client's problem? Where is that "roadmap"? (Either circle on the brief or state where it is located.) _____

_____

✓ Create a "reader-based outline" by reading only the topic sentences and writing a one- or two-word description of the point of each topic sentence. (You can make the outline on the margins to the brief or on this form.)

- Does the reader-based outline parallel the structure of the roadmap? Why or why not? Do you use the same legal terms in the topic sentences as in the roadmap? _____

_____

✓ Read the substance of each paragraph. Either here or in the margin of the paper, give a one- or two-word issue or sub-issue discussed in each paragraph. Does the paragraph actually discuss the issue and only the issue that the topic sentence addresses? Why or why not? _____

_____

✓ Do you provide a mini-conclusion at the end of each element (1) to let the reader know that you have completed the discussion of that element, and (2) to reiterate your position on that element? Which mini-conclusions are effective? _____

Legal Analysis

✓ Do you use legal authority to back up your arguments? Where?
✓ Look at the case analogies. For each analogy, do you use the facts, reasoning, and holding from the prior case and compare them to the specific facts of your case to prove your point? Do you use more complicated comparisons by referencing more than one case at a time? Be specific in your answer. _____

_____

✓ Which is the best case comparison? The worst? Why? _____

_____

✓ What other techniques do you use to make your arguments? Which are effective and which are not? _____

_____

Persuasive Techniques

✓ Can you tell what the theory of the case is in the argument section? If yes, what it is? Is it consistent with the theory of the case in the statement of the case? _____

✓ Is the roadmap written persuasively? Are the topic sentences written persuasively?_____

✓ Be specific. _____

✓ What specific word choices do you use that help with the persuasion? _____

✓ What other techniques do you use to make the document persuasive? _____

Editing and Polishing

✓ Do you find any patterns of grammar problems? Where? _____

_____

✓ Are there any citation problems in this brief? Where? _____

_____

☑️ 9.　Peer-Evaluation Form for Briefs: Checklist

One of the goals of this book is to help you become your own editor. This Quick Reference is designed to help you continue developing your evaluation process. By evaluating a peer's brief, you become another set of eyes for that peer and begin reevaluating your own brief.

When evaluating your peer's writing, do not comment on everything at once. Instead, focus your attention on one aspect of the brief at a time. Start with the rewriting issues before moving on to revising issues. While it is important to give positive feedback, focus on places where the writer needs improvement so that every writer gets ample opportunity for helpful criticism. Answer each question as fully as possible, writing on both this form and your peer's paper, before moving on to the next question.

After evaluating the brief, you should meet with your peer to discuss your evaluation.

Brief in General

✓ **General Format:** Does the writer provide a title page, table of contents with clear pointheadings and page numbers, and a table of authorities? _____

✓ **Statement of the Issue(s) Presented:** Does the issue statement provide the reader with the specific legal question, written in a persuasive manner? Why or why not? Can you read the whole issue statement aloud in one breath? _____

_____

- How does this writer's issue statement(s) differ from your own? _____
_____

✓ **Statement of the Case**: Does the statement of the case tell a clear and concise story, providing the legally significant facts from the case? Is it written persuasively? _____

_____

- What is the theory of the case? _____
_____

- What specific word choices does the writer use that make the statement of the case persuasive? Where could it be more persuasive? _____

_____

- How does this statement of the case differ from your own? _____
_____

Argument Section

Large-Scale Organization

✓ Has the writer started the argument section with a statement of the law that applies to the client's problem? Where is that "roadmap"? (Either circle on the brief or state where it is located.) _____

_____

- How is that roadmap different from your own? _____
_____

✓ Create a "reader-based outline" by reading only the topic sentences and writing a one- or two-word description of the point of each topic sentence. (You can make the outline on the margins to the brief or on this form.)
  - Does the reader-based outline parallel the structure of the roadmap? Why or why not? Does the writer use the same legal terms in the topic sentences as in the roadmap? _____

_____

  - How does the writer's organizational scheme differ from your own? _____

✓ Read the substance of each paragraph. Either here or in the margin of the paper, give a one- or two-word issue or sub-issue discussed in each paragraph. Does the paragraph actually discuss the issue and only the issue that the topic sentence addresses? Why or why not? _____

_____

✓ Does the writer provide a mini-conclusion at the end of each element (1) to let the reader know that she has completed the discussion of that element, and (2) to reiterate her position on that element? Which mini-conclusions are effective? _____

Legal Analysis

✓ Does the writer use legal authority to back up his arguments? Where? Where can the writer cite to more authority? _____

_____

✓ Look at the case analogies. For each analogy, does the writer use the facts, reasoning, and holding from the prior case and compare them to the specific facts of your case to prove his point? Does the writer use more complicated comparisons by referencing more than one case at a time? Be specific in your answer. _____

_____

✓ Which is the best case comparison? The worst? Why? _____

_____

✓ What other techniques does the writer use to make the brief's arguments? Which are effective and which are not? _____

_____

Persuasive Techniques

✓ Can you tell what the theory of the case is in the argument section of the brief? If yes, what it is? Is it consistent with the theory of the case in the statement of the case? _____

_____

✓ Is the roadmap written persuasively? Are the topic sentences written persuasively? Be specific. _____

_____

✓ What specific word choices does the writer use that help with the persuasion? _____

_____

✓ What other techniques does the writer use to make the document persuasive? _____

_____

Editing and Polishing

✓ Do you find any patterns of grammar problems? Where?
✓ Do you find any of your own grammar problems in this brief? Where?
✓ Are there any citation problems in this brief? Where?

B. Quiz

⚇? 1. Writing and Rewriting in General: Quiz

Instructions: Mark each of the following statements regarding writing and rewriting, either true or false. If you answer false, articulate why the statement is false before moving to the next question. If you have difficulty answering any of the questions on writing and rewriting, refer to the chapter text and to the Writing and Rewriting Checklists for assistance.

1. Creativity is undesirable in legal reading because only legal precedent is valued. **True or False?**

2. Before you begin to write a legal document, you should consider purpose, audience, scope, and view. **True or False?**

3. Effective legal writers accept that writing is a learning process and that multiple drafts will be necessary. **True or False?**

4. There are an infinite number of ways to write effective outlines, but a legal rule will often be the foundation of your outline. **True or False?**

5. When outlining, always address the elements of your legal rule in the order they appear in the rule. **True or False?**

6. Rewriting is the process of reworking large-scale components of your document, including content, large-scale organization, paragraph organization and legal analysis, sentence structure, and conciseness. **True or False?**

7. Busy associates writing legal documents do not have time to step away from their writing and should focus on editing and polishing instead of rewriting. **True or False?**

8. If the content of your legal writing is not accurate, you risk violating rules of professional ethics and damaging your credibility. **True or False?**

9. Your topic sentences should not mirror the language and structure of your roadmap because this will bore the legal reader. **True or False?**

10. The analysis of a single element should never span multiple paragraphs. **True or False?**

11. An effective paragraph in legal writing sets the rule, applies the facts at hand, is internally consistent, and is less than one double-spaced page. **True or False?**

12. Citation parentheticals provide effective and sufficient legal analysis. **True or False?**

13. Citations and citation parentheticals can provide depth to your legal analysis. **True or False?**

14. Effective sentences use strong subject-verb combinations. **True or False?**

15. When rewriting for conciseness, omit law that does not advance your point. **True or False?**

16. When rewriting, do not sacrifice clarity for conciseness. **True or False?**

17. Most legal documents combine objective and persuasive writing. **True or False?**

18. When choosing a theory for your case, do not be influenced by how easy or difficult a particular theory is to prove. **True or False?**

19. Burying harmful facts between more favorable facts violates professional ethics rules. **True or False?**

20. In persuasive writing, the fact section should be brief, honest, and subtly embedded with your theory of the case. **True or False?**

21. The ordering of issues within your brief should be dictated by the ordering of issues within your opponent's brief. **True or False?**

22. There is only one way to interpret any given legal rule. **True or False?**

23. In persuasive writing, you should address adverse cases head on and distinguish or downplay them. **True or False?**

24. You should avoid words like clearly and obviously, which tend to overstate your case. **True or False?**

25. Multimedia should be avoided because it has the potential to confuse and distract the reader. **True or False?**

26. Ethics rules require that you bring adverse authority to the attention of your judge. **True or False?**

Answer Key on page 514

CHAPTER 3

Legal Documents

In this chapter, you will learn about legal documents and oral arguments. First, you will learn how to consider purpose, audience, scope, and view before you begin writing legal documents. Second, you will learn the formal requirements for each type of legal document. Third, you can review annotated samples of each type of legal document.

I. Memorandums of Law
   A. Purpose, Audience, Scope, and View
   B. Formal Requirements
      1. Heading
      2. Question Presented
      3. Brief Answer
      4. Statement of Facts
      5. Discussion
         a. Discussion: Organization
         b. Discussion: Legal Analysis
      6. Conclusion
   C. Annotated Sample Memo 1
   D. Annotated Sample Memo 2
   E. Annotated Sample Memo 3
II. Briefs
   A. Purpose, Audience, Scope, and View
   B. Formal Requirements
      1. Title Page
      2. Table of Contents, Pointheadings, and Subheadings
      3. Table of Authorities
      4. Jurisdiction
      5. Standard of Review
      6. Statement of the Issues Presented for Review
      7. Statement of the Case (Facts)
      8. Summary of the Argument
      9. Argument
         a. Argument: Content
         b. Argument: Organization
         c. Argument: Legal Analysis
      10. Conclusion
      11. Signature and Certificate of Service

I.   MEMORANDUMS OF LAW

A memorandum of law, or memo, is a document written to a lawyer addressing a particular legal issue. Usually, it is written by an associate to a supervising attorney with a client's specific interest at issue. Memos are often the first type of documents written by young associates.

A.   *Purpose, Audience, Scope, and View*

- **Purpose:** A memo informs the supervising attorney of the relevant law and how it applies to the client's issue. It should be objective and show both sides of an issue so that the attorney can make an informed decision about the client's interests.
- **Audience:** A memo is written for a lawyer, usually a supervising attorney. Assume that the attorney will be busy and expect you to apply the law to the facts of the case to analyze the issue. Legal conventions, such as proper citation format and an understanding of legal interpretation and analysis, are presumed. Legalese, however, is not recommended.
- **Scope:** A memo can vary in scope; therefore, the associate should inquire about the amount of time, money, and attention required on each memo. The associate should focus only on the particular issue that she is asked to address rather than go beyond the scope of the problem.
- **View:** The point of view of a memo can vary greatly. Most are very formal, but the writer should consider tone. For example, some clients might read these memos, so an associate should watch for any condescending or accusatory language.
- For sample memos, see pages 143, 150, and 156.

B.   *Formal Requirements*

The following are the formal requirements of a legal memo. However, many attorneys do not require all of them. For example, some prefer an introduction to replace the traditional question presented and brief answer. Therefore, before you begin writing, you should inquire as to your supervising attorney's preferences or your office's requirements in general.

For more information about the formal elements of a memo, including samples, see the following pages:

- Heading, page 131.
- Question Presented, page 131.
- Brief Answer, page 133.
- Statement of Facts, page 134.
- Discussion, page 136.
- Conclusion, page 141.

Writing a memo is a recursive process. Most legal writers understand the law more when they are forced to write about it. They learn what they know, what they still need to research, and what facts they need to discover. They might not make a decision or form an opinion about the outcome until they have finished writing the analysis portion of the memo. As a result, many legal writers begin writing the discussion section instead of starting with the question presented, brief answer, or facts section. As a novice legal writer, you might be asked to write the question presented or brief answer first. This process will help you focus your analysis. However, once you are finished writing the discussion section, you should go back and rewrite the other sections of the memo to ensure they are consistent with your analysis.

1. Heading

As in any memo, "to," "from," subject, and date lines are expected. A legal memo's subject line should include more than just a client name or number, however, because many memos likely will be written for the same client file. Include in the subject line the specific legal issue you are addressing.

Sample Heading

TO: Partner

FROM: Associate

DATE: September 12, 2006

RE: <u>Dawson v. Dawson</u>: Possibility of Protective Order for Andrea Dawson

---

2. Question Presented

The question presented is one sentence that provides the reader with a quick summary of the issue addressed in the memo. It should contain (1) the jurisdiction and applicable law, (2) the legal issue presented, and (3) the most legally significant facts that are necessary to answer the question. Many legal writers use the "under-did-when" convention to ensure that the three parts of the question presented are included.

- **Jurisdiction (under):** The jurisdiction and applicable law is covered in a simple few words that let the reader know what law applies. For example, "Under New Jersey law" might be sufficient. "Under New Jersey common law" is more specific if the writer determines that specificity is preferred. A code provision or a case name is usually too specific, as the reader probably knows very little about the law. (However, "<u>Roe v. Wade</u>" or "Chapter 11 bankruptcy" would be appropriate, as a lawyer would gain meaning from either of these phrases.)

Sample 1

Jurisdiction. Here, the writer includes the full name of the applicable New Jersey statute.

Legal issue. Here, the writer identifies the issue as "retaliatory action" and identifies the parties as "Andy Ross"—to personalize his client—and "his employer" to show the legal relationship.

Legally significant facts. Here the writer includes a number of facts that he then uses in the discussion section.

Sample 2

Jurisdiction. Here the writer simply identifies New Jersey as the jurisdiction without specifying the actual law.

Legal issue. The writer here uses the term "CEPA claim" to identify the issue. However, the reader might not know what "CEPA" means at this early point of the memo.

Legally significant facts. Although the facts are legally significant, the last phrase "informed a customer" is unclear as the reader might not know if the writer is referring to the employer or Andy Ross.

Sample 3

Jurisdiction. Here, the writer includes the full name of the applicable New Jersey statute.

Legal issue. Here the writer focuses on the employer first and provides both the name of the employer and employee.

Legally significant facts. Here the writer effectively includes a number of facts that he then uses in the discussion section.

Sample 4

Legal issue. This writer chose the "whether" format. Therefore, he starts with the legal issue itself.

Jurisdiction. The writer chose to place the jurisdiction in the middle of the sentence. Using the whether format, the jurisdiction could also be placed at the end of the sentence.

Legally significant facts. Although the writer includes legally significant facts, he uses passive voice—which makes the sentence too wordy—and he assumes a conclusion ("as a result of his refusal to conceal parental warning labels"). This argument should be made in the discussion section, not in the question presented.

Sample Questions Presented for CEPA Memo

Sample 1

[Under New Jersey's Conscientious Employee Protection Act (CEPA),] [does Andy Ross have a sustainable claim against his employer for retaliatory action,] [when his working hours were substantially cut after his refusal to conceal parental warning labels on compact discs?]

Sample 2

[Under New Jersey law,] [does Andy Ross have a CEPA claim against his employer] [who reduced his hours and moved him to inventory after he refused to place sale stickers over parental advisory labels and informed a customer of the covered label?]

Sample 3

[Under New Jersey's Conscientious Employee Protection Act (CEPA),] [did employer Power Records unlawfully retaliate against employee Andy Ross] [when it reduced his work hours and reassigned his duties after he refused to cover up parental warning labels?]

Sample 4

[Whether Andy Ross can bring a retaliatory action claim against his employer] [under New Jersey's Conscientious Employee Protection Act] [when his hours were decreased and his duties were reassigned as a result of his refusal to conceal parental warning labels on CDs.]

- **Legal issue (did or can or will):** The legal issue presented defines the legal scope of the memo. For example, "Did Mr. Jones assault Mr. Smith?" or "Can Mr. Jones prove libel?" Here, you need to be careful to avoid making your issue too broad and generic (Can he be convicted?) or too narrow and detailed (Can Robert Austin, a well-known actor, prove that Gail Lain, his ex-girlfriend, made false and misleading statements regarding his three illicit affairs to The Hollywood Star Magazine . . .?).
- **Legally significant facts (when):** The legally significant facts are those that apply to the client and are most likely to affect the outcome of this particular issue. Here, the writer needs to choose only those facts that are most significant so that the sentence is readable. A simple "breath test"—reading the question aloud—works to determine wordiness. Also, the writer should be careful not to be one-sided in addressing these facts; often the best questions presented include facts from both sides of the argument so that the reader has a more objective viewpoint.

Some legal writers prefer to use the word "whether" to begin the question presented. This structure is an accepted legal convention, even though it creates a sentence fragment. Because this convention is used as a shorthand for the phrase "the question is whether," the sentence ends with a period instead of a question mark.

If the memo addresses more than one issue, you should include more than one question presented. Include the questions in the same order that you address them in the memo. Each question presented should have a corresponding brief answer.

3. Brief Answer

The purpose of the brief answer is to inform the reader how you think the issue will be resolved. You are predicting an outcome of a legal issue—not providing a guarantee on how the judge will decide the case. However, do not include phrases such as "I think" or "I believe."

The brief answer typically contains two parts:

- **Short Answer:** First, the brief answer quickly answers the question presented with a simple "yes," "no," "probably," or "probably not."
- **Terms of Art:** Next, using no more than a few sentences, the brief answer uses the terms of from the applicable law to answer the question presented. Although you will use many of the same terms here as in your roadmap (see page 82), your brief answer does not substitute for a roadmap.
- **Legally Significant Facts:** The brief answer uses legal terms of art embedded within significant facts to answer the question. Keep in mind, however, that the brief answer will be read in conjunction with the question presented, so repetition of the same facts is usually not necessary. Likewise, citations usually are not necessary in a brief answer.

A brief answer should be brief. It should not analyze each element of the law. In the **conclusion** (see page 141), you will provide the reader with more

Sample 1

Short answer.

While this answer is "brief" and focuses the reader on the two key legal elements (clear mandate of public policy and reasonable belief), it could benefit from a few facts to give the reader some context for the answer.

Sample 2

Short answer.

The writer does not need to repeat the jurisdiction as it is already provided in the question presented.

Here the writer provides the main legal elements (reasonable belief and clear mandate of public policy) as well as some of the key facts.

Sample 3

Short answer.

The writer provides the main legal elements and some of the key facts. However, the writer introduces "Siller" for the first time but incorrectly assumes the reader knows Siller's role in the action.

Sample 4

Short answer.

This writer uses the main legal elements and key facts to briefly and effectively answer the question.

Sample Brief Answers for CEPA Memo

Sample 1

[No.] Ross does not have a sustainable claim because he fails to prove a violation of a "clear mandate of public policy," and he cannot show objective support that he reasonably believed such a violation occurred.

Sample 2

[Yes.] Andy Ross has a viable cause of action under [New Jersey's CEPA] because his employer took retaliatory action against him by demoting him and reducing his hours after he refused to cover the parental advisory labels because he reasonably believed that act to be against a clear mandate of public policy.

Sample 3

[Yes.] Power Records did unlawfully retaliate against Andy Ross by reducing his hours and reassigning his duties after Ross refused to cover up parental warning labels as directed by Siller because Ross reasonably believed that covering parental warning labels violated a clear mandate of public policy.

Sample 4

[Yes.] Ross reasonably believed that covering the parental warning labels violated a clear mandate of public policy and Power Records retaliated against Ross by demoting him and reducing his hours.

---

specific reasons for your answer and you will fully analyze the law in the discussion section (see page 136) of the memo.

If you provide more than one question presented, you should provide the same number of correlating brief answers.

4.   Statement of Facts

The statement of facts presents the facts to the reader in a clear, concise, and objective manner. Although the supervising attorney may have provided you with the facts originally, you do not simply repeat verbatim the facts as given to you by the supervising attorney. Instead, craft a concise and objective story using the legally significant facts and background facts. In addition, do not

---

Sample Statement of Facts for CEPA Memo

[Andy Ross works at Power Music.] [Recently,] new management took over the store and changed it from a family place to a store that markets controversial music. When [the store manager, Tim Sillers,] instructed Ross to place sales stickers over the parental advisory warning labels on the CDs, Ross refused [and was subsequently sent] to the back of the store to do inventory. Ross, once back up front, informed a customer of the covered warning label. The following week his hours were reduced from forty to ten hours a week. Ross was not the only employee to have his hours reduced; [however, the other employees needed part-time hours as they were returning to school.] Ross still needed all of his hours, and his hours were reduced the most out of all the employees. Power Records is a member of the National Association of Recording Merchandisers (NARM). NARM supports the voluntary system of parental advisory warning labels and works with the Recording Industry Association of America (RIAA), which creates the labels and the guidelines for their use.

A short, clear introductory sentence helps provide the reader with context. Telling the reader that Andy Ross is our client might have been helpful.

Specific dates might be more helpful as the memo will go in a file and be read over the course of time—perhaps many years.

Here the writer provides a clear introduction to a key player in the litigation.

Passive voice. It might be helpful to the reader to find out who sent Ross to the back of the store.

Objective writing—this information might not be helpful to the client's case, but the reader will want to know about it because it will be used by opposing counsel.

This statement of facts is concisely written and tells an objective story.

---

assume your reader remembers the facts. Your supervisor might have hundreds of clients; as a result, he or she will rely on your fact statement to refresh his or her memory about the case. Also, facts change. Unlike fact patterns provided in your legal writing class, in real cases, lawyers discover facts as the case proceeds. Therefore, by writing a fact statement, you are creating a record on which you are relying to answer the legal question. If the facts change (and they often do), then your opinion may change as well.

An effective statement of facts should include the following:

- **Legally Significant Facts:** Your statement of facts should focus mainly on legally significant facts. A fact is legally significant if it is considered when applying the law. Therefore, if you use a fact in your discussion section, it is legally significant. One trick to writing the statement of facts is to write it after writing the discussion section to ensure that all facts in the discussion section are included in the fact section.

- **Background Facts that Tell a Clear and Concise Story:** Your statement of facts should tell a story. Therefore, you will need to include background facts to tie the legally significant facts together. Do not use bullet points. Instead, consider the best organizational schema for presenting the facts to the reader. Chronological organizations usually work well, but there may be circumstances when you will organize your facts by topic, by client, or by causes of action.

- **Objective Writing:** The fact section should be written objectively. Do not omit facts that might not be helpful to your client. Remember that a legal memo is confidential; the opposing side and the court do not have access to it. The supervising attorney is relying on the facts to make decisions about how to proceed with the case. Therefore, you should strive to be as accurate and honest as possible when presenting the facts. At times, you might include emotional facts because they may affect the way a judge or jury will decide the case. However, do not make arguments in the fact section and avoid partisan or qualifying language.

Do not create new facts or make assumptions in your fact section. Your opinion in the memo is based on the facts as you know them at the time. When in doubt, indicate that more facts are necessary.

5. Discussion

The discussion section is the meat of the memo. Here, the writer presents the law in an organized fashion and applies it to the client's situation. The purpose of the discussion section is to show the reader the application of the law to the facts to prove the predicted outcome. There are many other sections of this book that discuss the process of writing the discussion section as well as organizing and analyzing the law. References are provided below.

a. Discussion: Organization

The organizational schema of the discussion section should be based on the organization of the law itself. Thus, the beginning of the discussion section should set out the law for the reader with a clear roadmap (see page 82). The rest of the discussion section follows the organization of the roadmap with strong topic sentences (see page 83).

Typical Mistakes:

1. **Do not vary the terms of art in your discussion section.** Instead, legal terms remain consistent as you analyze their meaning within the law. So, terms in your topic sentences should be consistent with the terms in your roadmap.
2. **Do not feel compelled to provide a history of the law.** The legal reader wants to know what the law is today. Unless the history is significant for some reason, there is no need to provide the history of the law for the reader.
3. **Do not forget to cite the roadmap.** The roadmap will be based on the law. Therefore, you need to cite to the appropriate legal authority in your roadmap.

b. Discussion: Legal Analysis

The reader expects a thorough application of the law to the facts in the discussion section. Here is where you will use primary law and create policy arguments to show why you think the issue will come out the way you predict.

Typical Mistakes:

1. **Not enough law.** Many novice writers argue the facts but fail to prove their conclusions using the law.
2. **Not enough facts.** Do not force the reader to flip back to your fact section. Include the legally significant facts within the analysis.
3. **Too many quotations.** If you find yourself quoting the law instead of applying it, you are not writing an effective discussion section.
4. **Failure to conclude.** Many novice writers are afraid to conclude on an issue or element of the law. Remember that you are providing an opinion—not a guarantee. Provide the reader with enough of the logical reasoning so that he or she can disagree with your position.
5. **Failure to provide counter-arguments.** Because your discussion section should be objective, you need to anticipate the other side's arguments.

For more information on writing and rewriting an effective discussion, including additional samples, see the following pages in the Writing Process chapter.

Large-Scale Organization, page 79.
Paragraph Organization and Legal Analysis, page 86.
Conciseness, page 94.
Writing Process, page 64.

Sample Discussion

[Three elements must be satisfied to bring a successful cause of action under CEPA: (1) there needs to be a retaliatory action; (2) that action must be causally connected to the employee's objection to or refusal to participate in an activity; (3) the employee must reasonably believe that this activity is incompatible with a clear mandate of public policy. N.J. Stat. Ann. § 34:19-3 (West 2002).]

Roadmap. Here, the writer clearly lays out the organization of the discussion section.

[The first element is demonstrating that there was a retaliatory action taken against the employee by the employer. N.J. Stat. Ann. § 34:19-3 (West 2000).] [New Jersey law defines "retaliatory action" as "discharge, suspension, or demotion of an employee or other adverse employment action taken against an employee in the terms and conditions of employment." N.J. Stat. Ann. § 34:19-2 (West 2002). In <u>Higgins</u>, the plaintiff alleged a CEPA violation against her employer after she was temporarily transferred, had her work

Topic sentence. This topic sentence effectively uses the same term of art—"retaliatory action"—from the roadmap.

Legal analysis. The writer uses a statutory definition and a case to apply the law to the facts of the case.

hours reduced, and was denied a promotion after she reported the misconduct of two colleagues to her supervisor. Higgins v. Pasack Valley Hosp., 703 A.2d 327, 329 (N.J. 1999). The court found for the plaintiff holding that the employer's actions constituted adverse employment actions and were therefore retaliatory acts. Id. The actions taken against Ross also meet this definition. Like the employee in Higgins, Ross suffered from adverse employment actions when Sillers temporarily transferred him to inventory and reduced his hours.] Thus, Sillers's actions against Ross were retaliatory acts.

Topic sentence. By using the term "retaliatory action," the writer clearly tells the reader that he is still discussing this element of the law.

[The phrase "taken against an employee" implies that the adverse action necessary to prove a retaliatory action is one taken against an individual rather than a group. N.J. Stat. Ann. § 34:19-2 (West 2002).] [See Estate of Roach v. TRW, 163 A.2d 598, 607-08 (2000). In Roach, the plaintiff brought CEPA actions against his employers when he was fired for reporting a colleague's unethical behavior. Id. The employers claimed that his dismissal was the result of a poor employment review. Nevertheless, the court found that the fact that of the thirty-seven individuals being reviewed only the plaintiff was fired sufficient evidence to prove a retaliatory action. Id. As in Roach, Ross was singled out by his employer. The other employees were students and needed to reduce their hours as school was about to begin. Ross did not need or want his hours to be scaled back; yet, his hours were reduced the most drastically.] [Therefore, Ross meets the first required element of bringing a CEPA cause of action because he suffered a retaliatory act when he was transferred to inventory, had his hours reduced, and was singled out to receive the most drastic hour reduction.]

Legal analysis. Here the writer applies a prior case to our facts.

Mini-conclusion. Here the writer concludes on this element and provides the main reasons for that conclusion.

Topic sentence. Here, the writer uses a topic sentence to let the reader know he is moving on to the second part of the roadmap.

[The second element is that the detrimental action taken against the employee is causally connected to his refusal to participate in or objection to an activity. N.J. Stat. Ann. § 34:19-3 (West 2002).] [To establish a causal connection, the plaintiff must demonstrate by a preponderance of evidence that the action taken against him was linked to his refusal. See Donofry v. Autotote Sys., Inc. 759 A.2d 260, 271 (N.J. Super. Ct. App. Div. 2001). See also Estate of Roach v. TRW, Inc. 164 A.2d 598 (N.J. Super. Ct. App. Div. 2000). An important piece of proving that more likely than not there is a casual connection is discounting other potential explanations.]

Legal analysis. The writer provides a clear rule. While he provides legal authority for the first part of the rule, he should have also provided authority for the second part.

Topic sentence. While this sentence introduces the reader to the test, it is wordy. The writer should consider omitting the phrase: "In Donofry, the court stated that."

[In Donofry, the court stated that the test to prove a causal connection is whether or not by the use of circumstantial evidence there is a preponderance of evidence that retaliation made a difference in the decision. Donofry, 759 A.2d at 271.] [The plaintiff alleged CEPA violations when he was fired after reporting that there were unlicensed technicians in the tote room of the Casino in which he worked. Id. The court held that the plaintiff met this test because he was more likely than not fired in retaliation for his report because of the circumstantial evidence: He was the only employee fired, and the temporal proximity between his report and his discharge was close. Id. Ross also has circumstantial evidence creating a casual connection. Like the employee in <u>Donofry</u>, Ross was singled out to receive a retaliatory act, and the time between his refusal and the retaliatory act was short. Only a week after he had refused to cover the labels, Sillers cut Ross's hours.] Therefore, it seems more likely than not that Ross's hours were reduced because of his objections to the covering of the labels; however, the test is not yet fully satisfied.

[To prove by a preponderance of evidence that there is a causal connection, other possible explanations for the retaliatory act need to be considered.] [In <u>McLelland</u>, the plaintiff brought suit against the police department alleging a violation of CEPA. <u>McLelland v. Moore</u>, 779 A.2d 463 (N.J. Super. Ct. App. Div. 2001). The plaintiff had a history of insubordinate acts and disagreements with his superiors, and so the court dismissed the claim. Id. at 599. Ross also shares a negative personal history with his employer. He was angry with the new management because of the new controversial music being sold in the store. In turn, Sillers did not think much of Ross and chastised and mocked him for his beliefs. Nonetheless, Ross's situation is distinguishable from <u>McLelland</u>. In <u>McLelland</u>, the court decided against the plaintiff because there was no circumstantial evidence to prove that the action taken against the plaintiff was anything more than a routine disciplinary action. In the case of Ross, circumstantial demonstrates that Sillers's actions were not routine. Ross's negative personal relationship with Sillers loses its relevance when coupled with the fact that he was singled out to suffer an adverse employment action shortly after he refused to cover the labels.] [The combination of all these factors establishes a preponderance of evidence that Sillers's retaliatory acts were causally connected to Ross's refusal to cover the labels.]

[The third element is that the employee must reasonably believe that there was a clear mandate of public policy against the activity he refused to be a part of. N.J. Stat. Ann. § 34:13-3(c) (West 2002).] [This element has two sub-elements: (a) the employee has a reasonable belief that this activity is against public policy; (b) there is a clear mandate of public policy against the activity.]

[The first sub-element is that the employee refused to participate in a given activity because he reasonably believed that there was a mandate of public policy prohibiting such actions. N.J. Stat. Ann. § 34:19-3(c) (West 2002).] [In <u>Mehlman</u>, the plaintiff brought a CEPA action alleging that he was fired for objecting to the high levels of benzene in the gasoline produced and sold in Japan. <u>Mehlman v. Mobil Oil Corp.</u>, 707 A.2d 1000 (N.J. 1998). The court held that even though the plaintiff did not have "specific knowledge of the precise source of public policy," he did have a reasonable belief that one existed because he knew the chemical was dangerous and that rules were in place regulating its use. Like <u>Mehlman</u>, Ross knew that covering the labels was harmful and that there were guidelines in the industry about their use. He knew of parents who did not want their children to listen to such music and of the store's membership in NARM, an organization supporting

---

Legal analysis. Here, the writer uses a case to compare to our facts.

Topic sentence. Here, the writer provides a clear topic sentence notifying the reader that he is still discussing the element of causal connection.

Legal analysis. Here the writer distinguishes our facts from a case.

Mini-conclusion. Here the writer concludes on this element.

Here the writer provides a topic sentence informing the reader that he is moving on to the third element. However, the sentence structure could be improved so that the sentence does not end with "of."

Here the writer provides a clear mini-roadmap to this element.

Topic sentence. Here, the writer provides a clear topic sentence using the same language from the mini-roadmap.

Legal analysis. Again, the writer uses a prior case to compare to our facts. This analysis is effective, but he should consider using more than one case where available.

Mini-conclusion. Here the writer concludes on the issue and provides reasons for that conclusion.

Topic sentence. This clear topic sentence also parallels the mini-roadmap.

Counterargument. Here, the writer provides a counterargument to address the other side's position.

Here, the writer continues with the counterargument and discusses it.

Topic sentence. Here the writer lets the reader know that he is still discussing [the] clear mandate of public policy.

Legal analysis. Here the writer distinguishes the facts from a prior case.

Mini-conclusion. Here the writer provides a mini-conclusion on this element.

the parental advisory program.] [Therefore, Ross had a reasonable belief that covering the labels was against a mandate of public policy because he knew that it was harmful to the public and was aware of the existence of organizations regulating the labels' use.]

[The second sub-element is that a clear mandate of public policy must exist. N.J. Stat. Ann. § 34:19-3(c)(3) (West 2002).] [A strong argument can be made that there is no clear mandate about parental advisory labels. Many courts state that the definition of a clear mandate of public policy does not include "a vague, controversial, unsettled, or otherwise problematic public policy." E.g., Mehlman, 707 A.2d 1000 at 1010; Smith-Bozarth v. Coalition Against Rape & Abuse, Inc., 747 A.2d 322, 326 (N.J. Super. Ct. App. Div. 2000); MacDougall v. Weichert, 677 A.2d 162, 168 (N.J. 1996).] [Courts have defined "vague" and "unsettled" as lacking a base in law. For example, in Pierce, a doctor brought suit against a pharmaceutical company alleging retaliatory action because of her opposition to continued research on a certain drug. Pierce v. Ortho Pharmaceutical Corp., 417 A.2d 505 (N.J. 1980). The court held that she did not have a cause of action because "as a matter of law, there is no public policy against conducting research on drugs that may be controversial." Id. at 513. Like controversial drugs, controversial music is not censored by law. There is not a law enforcing the use of parental advisory warning labels. However, this argument can be overcome by invoking the full definition of clear mandate used by the courts. "The sources of public policy include legislation; administrative rules, regulations, or decisions; and judicial decisions. In certain instances, a professional code of ethics may contain an expression of public policy." Mehlman, 707 A.2d 1000 at 1009; see also Regan, 702 A.2d 523 at 529; Smith-Bozarth, 747 A.2d at 325.]

[Accordingly, the definition of a clear mandate of public policy can be met by a professional code of ethics.] [In Smith-Bozarth, the plaintiff brought action under CEPA alleging the she was fired for refusing to hand over confidential files to her supervisor. Smith-Bozarth, 747 A.2d 322. The court held that there was no violation of a clear mandate of public policy because CARA's own internal policy was for staff to share files; the plaintiff was the one violating the professional code of ethics. Unlike the employee in Smith-Bozarth, Ross had authority to refuse to follow his employer's orders. Power Records, as a member of NARM, is a member of an organization that actively supports the parental advisory labels. NARM works closely with the RIAA, which creates the labels and the guidelines for their use. One of these guidelines is that the label is to be clearly displayed. By intentionally covering the labels, Power Records was violating not only a guideline to which they subscribed, but was also its own professional code of ethics.] [Therefore, Power Records was violating a clear mandate of public policy when it covered the warning labels with sales stickers because it was violating its own professional code of ethics.]

6. Conclusion

The conclusion answers the particular question but with more detail than the brief answer (see page 133). An effective conclusion usually breaks down the component parts of the law and uses specific client facts and legal reasoning to show why that element of the law is either favorable or unfavorable for the client. It should not include references to specific authorities such as statutes or cases; these specifics belong in the discussion section.

A busy reader should be able to read your question presented, brief answer, and conclusion together to have a complete summary of the issue, the law, and the effect on the client. Make sure that they are all consistent.

If you have multiple questions presented and brief answers you should have multiple corresponding conclusions.

If you believe that more investigation is necessary or that another issue should be addressed, you should consider including a separate paragraph in your conclusion addressing your concerns.

Sample Conclusions for CEPA Memo

Sample 1

CONCLUSION

[Andy Ross does not have a sustainable CEPA claim because he cannot satisfy two of the five elements of the prima facie case.] [He cannot establish that his employer was in violation of a clear mandate of public policy because the sources of that policy do not satisfy two subelements.] First, the RIAA warning label guidelines are voluntary, subject to retailers' discretion, and are therefore not binding. Second, this source represents a policy of self-censorship that is both vague and controversial. The second prima facie element is also probably not satisfied because Ross's extensive experience in the music industry indicates that he cannot claim a reasonable belief that his employer was in violation of a clear mandate of public policy. The third and fourth elements—refusal to participate in the activity and an adverse employment action—can successfully be established. Ross explicitly refused to cooperate with his employer's instructions, and his working conditions worsened severely. Finally, Ross will be able to establish the fifth element, causality, because the temporal immediacy of the employment action meets the threshold requirement that his refusal to participate in concealing the labels "made a difference" in his employer's retaliatory action. [Having satisfied only three of the five required elements of the prima facie case, however, Ross does not have a sustainable course of action and would be best advised to pursue alternative employment options rather than a legal remedy.]

Here the writer provides a clear conclusion right up front for the reader.

Next the writer explains that the reason the claim will fail is based on two elements. The writer then goes on to explain those two elements.

The writer explains the outcome of the remaining elements as well.

The writer clearly explains his conclusion.

The writer provides his conclusion up front. He then lays out his reasons under each element using clear signals (first, second, third).

These transitions help the reader move from one element to the next.

The writer helps the reader distinguish between legal elements.

The writer signals he is moving on to the third element.

Sample 2

CONCLUSION

[Ross does have a viable CEPA cause of action under New Jersey law.] [First,] his employer took a retaliatory action against him when he singled Ross out, drastically reduced his hours, and transferred him to inventory. [Second,] the fact that Ross was singled out and that this occurred so soon after he refused to cover the labels shows by a preponderance of evidence that his employer's adverse action was causally connected to Ross's refusal to partake in such activity. [Third,] Ross reasonably believed that covering the advisory labels was against public policy because of the store's membership in NARM, and the covering of the labels was in fact a violation of a clear mandate of public policy because Power Records infringed on its own professional code of ethics.

C.   Annotated Sample Memo 1

TO: Diana Donahoe
FROM: Associate
DATE: October 15, 2006
RE: Wrongful discharge claim for Andy Ross

QUESTION PRESENTED

Under New Jersey's Conscientious Employee Protection Act (CEPA), does Andy Ross have a sustainable claim against his employer for retaliatory action resulting in a [worsening of his employment situation,] when his working hours were substantially cut [relative to other employees] after his refusal to conceal parental warning labels on music CDs?

Conciseness; consider omitting.

BRIEF ANSWER

No. Ross does not have a sustainable claim because he fails to establish all of the necessary elements of the prima facie CEPA case, particularly the violation of a "clear mandate of public policy" and objective support that he reasonably believed such a violation had occurred. Other elements are successfully established, but without satisfying all of the required elements, his cause is not actionable.

Which elements? The brief answer should provide the conclusion to all of the elements using the legal language (without looking like a roadmap).

STATEMENT OF FACTS

In 1985, the Recording Industry Association of America (RIAA) instituted a self-regulating policy of displaying parental warning labels on music [that is] deemed inappropriate [to] minors. At http://www.riaa.com/issues/parents/advisory.asp. This has been implemented in coordination with the National Association of Recording Merchandisers (NARM), an organization of retailers that established guidelines for marketing and selling music that has the advisory labels. At http://www.narm.com/. While this policy has been followed with interest by Congress and state legislatures, it remains a voluntary program of industry self-regulation.

Conciseness; consider omitting.
for

Andy Ross worked for the past five years full time (40 hours[/]week) in a music store that came under new management last year. Ross's new employer recently began a sales campaign to market to teens. As part of this campaign, he instructed employees to use sales price stickers to conceal the RIAA parental advisory labels. Ross objected to the practice and refused to take part; shortly thereafter he was transferred from [retail] to inventory. [Recently] his hours were reduced from 40 to 10 hours per

per

Is this the right word?
Before or after the objection?

week, considerably less than any of his [colleagues, whose hours were also reduced]. [He has inquired whether he has any legal recourse under the circumstances.]

Conciseness; consider omitting.

This statement of facts works because it provides some of the legally significant facts. Some of these facts are not included in the discussion section: This may be a clue that they are not legally relevant.

RBO: CEPA

DISCUSSION

In 1986, the New Jersey Legislature passed the Conscientious Employee Protection Act (CEPA). N.J. Stat. Ann. § 34:19(1)-(8) (West 2002). Section 3 of this code establishes:

> An employer shall not take any retaliatory action against an employee because the employee does any of the following:
> …
> C. Objects to, or refuses to participate in any activity, policy or practice which the employee reasonably believes:
> …
> (3) is incompatible with a clear mandate of public policy concerning the public health, safety or welfare or
> protection of the environment." N.J. Stat. Ann. § 34:19-3 (West 2002).

The history, although interesting, might not be of too much use to the busy partner. Consider simply stating the elements established for a prima facie case.

[Subsequent case law in New Jersey applied this statute to a variety of circumstances and developed a prima facie case for establishing a CEPA claim consisting of five elements derived from the statutory language.] Kolb v. Burns, 727 A.2d 525, 531 (N.J. Super. Ct. App. Div. 1999); Falco v. Community Med. Ctr., 686 A.2d 1212, 1221-22 (N.J. Super. Ct. App. Div. 1997); Young v. Schering Corp., 645 A.2d 1238, 1244 (N.J. Super. Ct. App. Div. 1994). To maintain a cause of action under CEPA, the employee must establish the following:

1. The existence of a clear mandate of public policy that the employer's conduct has violated (for CEPA claims under N.J. Stat. Ann.§ 34:19-3(c)(3) only), Kolb, 727 A.2d at 530;
2. Employee's reasonable belief that employer's conduct was in violation;
3. Performance of a whistle-blowing activity;
4. That the employee has suffered an adverse employment action; and
5. A causal connection between the whistle-blowing activity and the adverse employment action.

Roadmap: This roadmap works because it clearly sets out the legal elements and the organization of the memo.

Cite for roadmap is needed.

RBO: Sources of public policy/CMPP

Sources not CMPP: It looks like establishing a source of CMPP is the actual issue. Can you make the roadmap parallel the language if this is indeed the structure? Otherwise, this topic sentence works because it introduces the element clearly and concisely.

Conciseness; consider omitting.

include

CLEAR MANDATE OF PUBLIC POLICY

[The sources of public policy that Ross relies on for his claim do not establish the existence of a clear mandate of public policy.] [The courts have identified the sources of public policy] [as] legislation; administrative rules, regulations, or decisions; common law; professional codes of ethics (in some instances); the N.J. Constitution; and federal law and policy, including the U.S. Constitution. See, e.g. D'Agostino v. Johnson & Johnson, Inc., 628 A.2d 305, 311-12 (N.J. 1993). This list has been expanded over time. In Abbamont, the court upheld a CEPA claim for a teacher who was refused tenure because of his complaints regarding improper ventilation in a school workshop. Abbamont v. Piscataway Twp. Bd. of Educ., 634 A.2d 538 (N.J. Super. Ct. App. Div. 1993), aff'd, 650 A.2d 958 (N.J. 1994). The court found that the New Jersey Industrial Arts Education Safety Guide was "specific and binding" and therefore was a valid source of public policy. Id. at 544. Ross's claim requires expanding this list of sources to include the RIAA and NARM regulations. However, where the source in Abbamont is similar to the other sources of public policy because it is "specific and binding," or, in the words of the statute, it provides a "clear mandate," [Ross's claim fails to identify a source of public policy that satisfies these two subelements: specific/clear in content and binding/mandatory.]

[To satisfy the first subelement of the "clear mandate of public policy," the source from which the public policy is derived must specifically and clearly define the policy in question.] MacDougall v. Weichert, 677 A.2d 162, 167 (N.J. 1994) ("A vague, controversial, unsettled, and otherwise problematic public policy does not constitute a clear mandate."); Pierce v. Ortho Pharmaceutical Corp., 417 A.2d 505 (N.J. 1980). In Pierce, the employee refused to perform research on a controversial drug. The employee argued that the drug was potentially dangerous, therefore its research violated the Hippocratic oath. The court dismissed the claim for failing to identify a clear mandate of public policy. In the absence of any specific source, the Hippocratic oath was insufficient to establish a public policy, and the research, though controversial, was not unlawful. Id. at 513. Similarly, Ross's claim is insufficient to support a cause of action because concealment of parental warning labels—like the drug research in Pierce—is controversial, but not unlawful. Although the RIAA guidelines are more explicit than the Hippocratic oath, they are general and subjective industry guidelines of [self-censorship] that do not clearly establish a public policy; no clear definition differentiates between offensive and inoffensive content. [This subelement is not satisfied because Ross's claim is not based on a clear and specific public policy, but rather one that is substantively controversial and unsettled.]

Good idea to begin with a legal rule to focus immediately on the law.

Why cite the facts, reasoning, and holding of Abbamont here? There is no real case comparison.... If you mean only to introduce "specific and binding," simply state the rule and cite it.

Where does mandatory come from? Don't feel you have to tie the subelements directly to words in the statute?

This is a mini-roadmap. It's a good idea to use it to help the reader know where the memo is going. It would help the reader even more if it were closer to the beginning. So, if you can get to the subelements faster, consider doing so.

RBO: CMPP—specifically + clearly define

Source specific/CMPP: This topic sentence works because it follows the language of the mini-roadmap and stays in the context of the element.

No need to bury this in a parenthetical.

Why was the Hippocratic Oath not a specific source?

How does this analysis fit under the subelement?

Right word?

It's unclear how this subelement works. Is it that the source needs to be detailed on what to do or not to do? The Hippocratic Oath is pretty clear about not harming patients. Its content is also arguably not controversial, only its application. Or does the issue behind the source have to be clear? Then, maybe it's not the source that's the real issue.

This mini-conclusion works because it concludes on the subelement using legal language and reasoning.

RBO: PP—binding mandatory nature

BINDING/SOURCE PP: This topic sentence works, again because it introduces the subelement and uses the legal language of the broad element to remind the reader of the context.

Cite needed.

Good idea to use the same language to tie the two cases.

This case comparison works because it provides the facts, reasoning, and holding from the prior case and ties the two together with a meaningful standard. Can you make the final connection by telling the reader exactly what this broad discretion means under the law?

This mini-conclusion works because it concludes using the language of the subelement.

This mini-conclusion works because it provides legal reasoning and concludes on the whole element.

RBO: Reasonable Belief

REASONABLE BELIEF: This topic sentence works because it introduces the legal element in the language of the law.

The description of this case works because it provides the relevant facts, reasoning, and holding.

This case comparison is effective because it provides relevant facts, reasoning and holding from the prior case, and makes a meaningful comparison to the current case. Can you use the same language from the prior case to make the tie even stronger?

[The second subelement that must be satisfied is the binding, mandatory nature of the source of public policy.] In Schechter v. N.J. Dept. of Law & Public Safety, Div. of Gaming Enforcement, an employee's CEPA claim was based on a dispute with his employer over the prioritization of casino "exclusion lists." The court found that there was no violation of a clear mandate of public policy because the employer—the Casino Control Commission—had "broad discretion" in enforcing its regulations. Schechter v. New Jersey Dept. of Law & Public Safety, Div. of Gaming Enforcement, 743 A.2d 872, 875 (N.J. Super. Ct. App. Div. 2000). Similarly, in Ross's claim, the RIAA regulation is voluntary and its application by NARM members is subject to the retailers' broad discretion. At http://www.riaa.com/issues/parents/advisory.asp (guidelines for the "voluntary parental advisory program"); at http://www.narm.com/ ("Some retailers choose not to interfere with parenting decisions and sell entertainment products without regard to age."). [This second subelement—establishing that the source of the public policy at issue is binding or mandatory—is not satisfied because the RIAA and NARM guidelines are voluntary.]

The sources of public policy upon which Ross's claim rests are neither specific and clear, nor binding and mandatory. The first element of the prima facie CEPA case is not established because it lacks these two subelements necessary to establish a "clear mandate of public policy."

REASONABLE BELIEF

[It is unlikely that Ross can satisfy the second element of the CEPA claim, establishing the employee's reasonable belief that the employer's conduct was in violation.] This reasonable belief is based on an objective standard. See, e.g., Regan v. City of New Brunswick, 702 A.2d 523, 530 (N.J. Super. Ct. App. Div. 1997). In McLelland v. Moore, the court denied a police officer's claim that he was retaliated against for objecting to his supervisor's allegedly improper issuance of two gun permits. McLelland v. Moore, 779 A.2d 463 (N.J. Super. Ct. App. Div. 2001). The court determined that there was no reasonable basis for believing this activity was illegal given the "knowledge, education and employment background of the plaintiff...." Id. at 473. Ross's claim, if judged by the same standard, is not likely to be accepted. Having worked forty hours a week for five years in the music industry, Ross is expected to have considerable knowledge about the industry standards, including the parental warning labels. Like the officer in McLelland, Ross should know to a greater degree if his employer was actually in violation of a clear mandate of public policy. It may, in fact, be true that he was not aware of the voluntary nature of the RIAA guidelines (in his preliminary interview he suggested that "there's got to be a law against this"), but the court will judge his position by an objective standard. [Given his considerable work experience in the music industry, Ross's claim that he reasonably believed that his employer's conduct was in violation of a clear mandate of public policy is not likely to be accepted.]

This mini-conclusion works because it provides the reasoning and conclusion, and the reader knows the analysis is complete.

WHISTLE-BLOWING ACTIVITY

RBO: Whistle blowing

[Though Ross's claim fails to satisfy the first two elements of the prima facie case, he can establish the third required element, the performance of a whistle-blowing activity.] In Young v. Schering Corp., the court rejected the employee's CEPA claim based on a refusal to research a controversial drug. Young v. Schering Corp., 645 A.2d 1238, 1244 (N.J. Super. Ct. App. Div. 1994). The court held that the CEPA statute was broader in its protection to employees than the common law had been prior to the statute's enactment, because while the common law required the employee to have reported the violation, the statute recognizes a claim for an employee who "objects to, or refuses to participate in" the activity. N.J. Stat. Ann. § 34:19-3(c) (West 2002); Young, 645 A.2d at 1245. The employee's claim in Young failed because of other prima facie elements, but his refusal to participate in the alleged violation did satisfy this particular element. Like the employee in Young, Ross informed his employer of his objection to the practice of concealing the warning labels and was the only employee to demonstrably not participate. Ross will be able to satisfy this element of the claim because although he did not perform a classic whistle-blowing activity of reporting his employer's activity to any other authority, he did openly object to it and refused to take part.

WHISTLE-BLOWING ACTIVITY: This topic sentence works because it introduces the third element and follows the roadmap.

Watch conflicting tenses if using "while."

This history is interesting, but can the partner use this information in the case?

Essentially, what you've done in this element is to summarize the statute's language into the term "whistle blowing" and then to use a case to dissect it again into "object to and refuse to participate." Is this the most efficient way to analyze the element?

ADVERSE EMPLOYMENT ACTION

RBO: Adverse employment action

[Ross can successfully establish the fourth prima facie element: that he has suffered from an adverse employment action.] His working hours were reduced from 40 to 10 hours a week. After years of working directly with customers in the retail area, Ross was assigned to inventory work in the back of the store. CEPA claims have been brought for analogous reasons other than termination of employment. Cf. Kolb, 727 A.2d at 531 (recognizing withholding of salary increment as basis of CEPA claim); Abbamont, 650 A.2d at 958 (upholding CEPA claim against school board for not rehiring nontenured teacher for tenure position); Regan v. City of New Brunswick, 702 A.2d 523, 530 (N.J. Super. Ct. App. Div. 1997) (accepting nonpromotion of police officer as adverse action for purposes of CEPA

ADVERSE EMPLOYMENT ACTION: This topic sentence works because it introduces the element. The signpost ("fourth") also helps the reader navigate.

Cite: Where does this legal language come from?

Can you spell out how these are analogous? A case comparison to at least one of those would make the point. Or, use multiple cases to find a trend and apply the trend to our case.

The reader may read the first of the parentheticals, but she'll probably gloss over the rest. If you are trying to show a trend, do so explicitly in the text.

claim). [According to Ross's account,] this change of circumstances was considerably more "severe" for Ross than for other employees, some of whom also had their hours reduced. The employer's claim that Ross was just one of several employees to have his hours reduced is therefore insufficient to disprove this element. [Ross can successfully establish that an adverse employment action was made against him when his employer reduced his working hours and transferred his responsibilities from retail to inventory.]

CAUSAL CONNECTION

[Ross can also satisfy the final element, establishing a causal connection between the whistle-blowing activity and the adverse employment action.] In Donofry, an employee's CEPA claim was upheld where he had informed his supervisor about illegal employment practices under [his] indirect management. Donofry v. Autotote Sys., Inc., 795 A.2d 260 (N.J. Super. Ct. App. Div. 2001). This report led to an investigation against the employer, and the employee was subsequently terminated. The employer argued that it had a legitimate reason for discharging the employee because the illegal employment had been in the department under his general management; the court nevertheless found that even in the face of "credible evidence of a lawful reason for the termination," there was still sufficient evidence to establish causality. Id. at 270-71. The court held that it is enough to prove that the employee's whistle-blowing activity "made a difference" in the employer's decision. Id. at 273 (citing Bergen Commercial Bank v. Sisler, 723 A.2d 944, 955 (N.J. 1999)). Ross's account meets the Donofry standard—his transfer to inventory and subsequent reduction in hours came immediately after his refusal to accept his employer's instructions and after his employer's open ridicule of Ross's objections; this dispute at least "made a difference" in his employer's decision. [Because his refusal to participate in the concealment of the warning labels played a role in his employer's subsequent decisions about his employment status, Ross will succeed in establishing this element.]

CONCLUSION

Andy Ross does not have a sustainable CEPA claim because he cannot satisfy two of the five elements of the prima facie case. He cannot establish that his employer was in violation of a clear mandate of public policy according to that phrase's two subelements. First, the controversial nature of the parental warning label program prevents it from being defined as either "clear" or "specific." Second, the RIAA recognition that this is a voluntary program denies it the status of "mandatory" or "binding." The

---

Margin notes (left column):

Tone: The client might read this too: make sure it's clear we believe him.

Does it matter whether other employees were affected? If so, explain. Doesn't this seem to go to causation?

Some of the legal reasoning would improve this mini-conclusion because the partner is looking for a brief recap of the important points of the element.

RBO: Causal connection

CAUSAL CONNECTION

Pronoun unclear.

How did the court determine whether it made a difference? Are there fact, reasoning, and holding relating to this aspect of the case?

How does the reader know that these factors satisfy the test? Were these factors present in Donofry?

Use the legal language.

It would help the reader if some of the legal language of the element (from the roadmap) were used in this mini-conclusion.

This recap of the first element works because it provides the legal reasoning using the roadmap and mini-roadmap language.

second prima facie element is also probably not satisfied, because Ross's extensive experience [working] in the music industry [makes it difficult to establish by an objective standard that he had] a reasonable belief that his employer was in violation of a clear mandate of public policy. The third and fourth elements—performance of a whistle-blowing activity and an adverse employment action—can successfully be established. Ross explicitly refused to cooperate with his employer's instructions, and his working conditions worsened even in relation to his colleagues. Finally, Ross will be able to establish the fifth element, causality, [because the circumstances of his claim support the threshold requirement that] his whistle-blowing activity "made a difference" in his employer's retaliatory action. Having satisfied only three of the five required elements of the prima facie case, however, Ross does not have a sustainable course of action and would be best advised to pursue alternative employment options rather than a legal remedy.

Conciseness: consider omitting.

Indicates that he does not have.

Conciseness: consider omitting.

If you can, be specific about the legal factors. "Circumstances" does not tell the reader much.

This conclusion works because it sets out the legal conclusions for each element and follows the roadmap. See suggestions for conciseness.

D.   Annotated Sample Memo 2

MEMORANDUM

TO: District Attorney
FROM: Assistant District Attorney
DATE: November 22, 2010
RE: State v. Dupree—potential charge of aggravated stalking

QUESTION PRESENTED

Under Missouri criminal law, did John Dupree commit aggravated stalking when he threatened to kill Don Richardson, blocked his car, and threw eggs at his windshield?

BRIEF ANSWER

Yes. Dupree committed aggravated stalking because his threat to kill Richardson was credible, and he purposefully harassed Richardson by blocking his car and throwing eggs at his windshield.

STATEMENT OF FACTS

On September 22, Don Richardson was leaving an Elks Club meeting when fellow member John Dupree approached him and asked if he was "Don Richardson, the Speaker of the House." Richardson replied "Yes, can I help you with something?" Dupree began yelling at Richardson, blaming him for a new law. "I'm going to kill you and crack your head open like a dozen eggs."

Richardson got into his car and began to drive away. Dupree stepped in front of Richardson's car and threw a carton of eggs at the windshield. Richardson stopped because he could not see. The entire incident lasted less than ten minutes. When Richardson returned to his car after the next Elks meeting on October 27, there were a dozen eggs splattered on his windshield. No one saw Dupree that night. Richardson did not call the police after either incident.

Dupree is twenty years older and forty pounds lighter than Richardson. Richardson is worried he will be constantly looking over his shoulder when he gets out of Elks meetings. The eggs on his car were annoying and humiliating. He has lost some sleep over the incident and is thinking about getting another car to avoid recognition. Richardson plans to continue attending Elks meetings.

This Question Presented includes the jurisdiction, legal issue, and legally significant facts.

Short answer.

This answer is brief and focuses the reader on the main elements discussed in the memo. However, it is not necessary to repeat facts from the Question Presented as the QP and BA work together.

The statement of facts concisely and objectively presents the facts of the case.

DISCUSSION

Dupree committed the crime of aggravated stalking if he (1) purposefully, through his course of conduct, (2) harassed or followed with the intent of harassing Richardson, and (3) made a credible threat. Mo. Ann. Stat. § 565.225(3) (West 2010).

(1) Purposeful Course of Conduct

First, Dupree's course of conduct must have been purposeful. Id. Dupree acted purposefully if he had a "specific purpose in mind," and was "deliberate." Black's Law Dictionary (9th ed. 2009, West 2010). In State v. Martin, the defendant made threatening calls to the victim and stated that he had a bullet for her. 940 S.W.2d 6 (Mo. Ct. App. 1997). The court held that defendant's language demonstrated a purposeful attempt to cause the victim substantial emotional distress. Id. Similarly, Dupree specifically threatened to crack Richardson's head open like a dozen eggs, and then deliberately threw eggs at his windshield. Thus, Dupree acted purposefully.

Dupree must also have engaged in the requisite course of conduct, defined as (a) a pattern of conduct composed of two or more acts, which may include (b) communication by any means, over a period of time, however short, evidencing a (c) continuity of purpose. Mo. Ann. Stat. § 565.225(1)(1) (West 2010).

(a) Pattern of Conduct of Two or More Acts

If Dupree is found responsible for the incident on October 27, there is a pattern of two or more acts. A defendant is not presumed to be responsible for similar incidents. In State v. Dawson, the court held that defendant's semen in co-worker's mug did not support reasonable inference that he was responsible for prior incidents involving semen on telephone and substance on victim's car and, thus, was insufficient to establish a pattern of two or more acts. 985 S.W.2d 941 (Mo. Ct. App. 1999). Similarly, there is no evidence that Dupree was responsible for the incident on October 27. No one saw Dupree that night. To reason from the first incident to the conclusion that Dupree also threw the eggs on October 27 is too speculative just as the court found it too speculative in Dawson. Therefore, the incident on September 22 must consist of two or more acts to satisfy the course of conduct requirement.

ROADMAP: This roadmap effectively sets out the elements necessary to prove the crime of aggravated stalking.

RBO: course of conduct must have been purposeful

This topic sentence clearly and concisely sets out the first element.

Because there is no definition in the statute or relevant cases, the writer refers to Black's Law.

ANALYSIS: Here, the writer concisely presents the facts, reasoning, and holding of a prior case and applies them to our case to conclude on this issue.

ORGANIZATION: Here, the writer provides a mini-roadmap for this subelement.

RBO: pattern of two or more acts

This topic sentence mirrors the language of the first prong of the mini-roadmap to make the organization clear for the reader.

This is a legal proposition so it should have a citation to authority.

ANALSYIS: Here, the writer provides the facts, reasoning, and holding of a prior case and compares them to our facts to come to a conclusion.

RBO: <u>State v. Baker</u>

Here, the writer focuses the topic sentence on a case name instead of a legal issue. As a result, the reader is confused as to the issue discussed in the paragraph.

In <u>State v. Baker</u>, the court held that following the victim, knocking on her door and intruding into her trailer was sufficient to support finding that defendant engaged in two or more acts. 40 S.W.3d. 392 (Mo. Ct. App. 2001). Dupree may argue that the incident on September 22 was one continuous act. However, the acts need not occur on separate dates. Threatening to kill Richardson, stepping in front of his car, and throwing eggs at his windshield would likely qualify as two or more acts under the <u>Baker</u> standard, therefore, Dupree is likely to satisfy this sub-element.

(b) Communication over Period of Time, However Short

RBO: communication

ANALSYIS: The writer effectively ties the facts of the prior case to our facts; however, the analysis would be stronger if the reasoning was also provided. Why is stepping in front of a car and throwing eggs similar to banging on a trailer and shining a light in a bedroom? How long did they last and what was their purpose?

In addition to the verbal threat to kill Richardson, either blocking his car or throwing eggs at his windshield must qualify as communication. Communication can be verbal or nonverbal. <u>See</u> <u>id.</u> Banging on the victim's trailer and shining a light in her bedroom constituted communication. <u>Id.</u> at 394. Stepping in front of Richardson's car and throwing eggs at his windshield are similar to banging on a trailer and shining a light in a bedroom in duration and purpose, thus constituting communication.

(c) Continuity of Purpose

RBO: continuity of purpose

Although the incident on September 22 lasted less than ten minutes, the acts show a continuity of purpose. Throwing eggs at Richardson's windshield was an act in furtherance of the threat, and performed with the intent to reinforce and heighten the message. The broken eggs on Richardson's window could be a symbolic representation of cracking Richardson's head open.

This topic sentence effectively focuses the reader on the element discussed.
ANALYSIS: Is there any case law that can be applied here?

ORGANIZATION: This paragraph provides a mini-conclusion to a complicated element.

Dupree intentionally engaged in two or more acts on September 22 when he threatened Richardson, blocked his car, and threw eggs at his windshield. Furthermore, his acts evidenced a continuity of purpose to harass. Therefore, Dupree satisfies the element of purposeful course of conduct.

(2) Harass or Follow with Intent to Harass

RBO: harasses

ORGANIZATION: Here, the writer provides a mini-roadmap to a complicated element and then follows that roadmap in the organization below.

A defendant "harasses" by (a) engaging in a course of conduct directed at a specific person, (b) that serves no legitimate purpose, and (c) would cause a reasonable person under the circumstances to be frightened, intimidated, or emotionally distressed. Mo. Ann. Stat. § 565.225(1)(3) (West 2010).

(a) Course of Conduct Directed at a Specific Person

Dupree's conduct was directed specifically at Richardson, because he verified the identity of Richardson before he threatened him and threw eggs at his car. Furthermore, Dupree's comments were directly related to Richardson's position as Speaker of the House. Dupree may argue that his comments were directed at Congress, generally, but his threat to kill Richardson contradicts this claim.

RBO: conduct directed specifically

ANALYSIS: Here, the writer makes a purely factual argument to prove the element. If there is relevant law on point, it would have been helpful to include it here for the reader to show how other cases have treated this element.

(b) Serves No Legitimate Purpose

As used in the context of the statute, the term "legitimate" means "complying with the laws; lawful." Black's Law Dictionary (9th ed. 2009, West 2010). Although it may have been lawful for Dupree to voice his opposition to the new law to an elected official, he exceeded legitimate means of expression when he threatened to kill Richardson and threw eggs at his windshield.

RBO: legitimate

(c) Cause a Reasonable Person to be Frightened, Intimidated, or Emotionally Distressed

The third sub-element is whether Dupree's conduct would cause a reasonable person under the circumstances to be frightened, intimidated, or emotionally distressed. In State v. Lasley, the court held that the tenor of the defendant's messages would cause the victim to reasonably fear for her safety, despite statements by the defendant in which he denied that he was going to kill her. 130 S.W.3d 15 (Mo. Ct. App. 2004). Unlike the defendant in Lasley, Dupree never denied his intention of killing. Id. Dupree may attempt to use his age and physical stature to establish a lack of reasonable fear. Dupree is twenty years older and forty pounds lighter than Richardson. However, Dupree's actual present ability to perform the threatened action is a not required. See State v. McCauley, 317 S.W.3d 132 (Mo. Ct. App. 2010). In McCauley, the court held that defendant's threats via phone were credible without proof that defendant was even in the State. Id.

RBO: reasonable person under circumstances to be frightened

This topic sentence effectively focuses the reader on the subelement discussed in the paragraph below.

COUNTERARGUMENT: Here, the writer effectively addresses a counterargument.

Dupree may claim that only a medical or psychological expert can accurately evaluate whether Richardson had reason to be frightened, intimidated, or emotionally distressed. However, expert testimony is not required to establish that defendant's conduct caused victim to experience substantial emotional distress. State v. Martin, 940 S.W.2d. 6 (Mo. Ct. App. 1997). In Martin, the defendant left numerous threatening messages for

RBO: medical or psychological expert

COUNTERARGUMENT: Again, the writer effectively addresses a counterargument to provide an objective memo.

the victim, resulting in loss of sleep and appetite. Furthermore, the victim relocated to avoid contact with the defendant, was afraid to go outside, and sought counseling. Id. at 9. Similarly, Richardson has lost some sleep over the incidents, and is considering purchasing a new car to avoid recognition by Dupree. Although Richardson plans to continue attending Elks meetings, he worries that he will be looking over his shoulder after Elks meetings.

ORGANIZATION: Here, the writer provides a mini-conclusion for a complicated element.

Dupree's conduct was directed specifically at Richardson, it did not serve a legitimate purpose, and would cause a reasonable person to be frightened, intimidated, or emotionally distressed. Therefore, Dupree satisfies the element of harassment.

(3) Credible Threat

RBO: credible threat

This topic sentence clearly and concisely tells the reader the element to be addressed and provides a statutory reference to the element.

The final element of the statute is the making of a credible threat. Mo. Ann. Stat. § 565.225(3)(1) (West 2010). Dupree must have made a threat to Richardson that was (a) communicated with the intent to cause Richardson to reasonably fear for his safety, or the safety of his family, household members, domestic animals or livestock, kept at his residence or on his property. Additionally, the threat must (b) be against the life of, or a threat to cause physical injury to, or the kidnapping of, Richardson, his family, household members, domestic animals or livestock, kept at his residence or on his property. Id.

ORGANIZATION: The writer provides a mini-roadmap for this element.

(a) Communicated with Intent to Cause Reasonable Fear for Safety

RBO: intent to cause victim to reasonably fear

A defendant's intent to cause a victim to reasonably fear for his or her safety does not depend upon the victim's later actions. See State v. Cartwright, 17 S.W.3d 149 (Mo. Ct. App. 2000). In Cartwright, the victim's failure to call the police after receiving specific threats of physical violence did not establish that the defendant lacked intent to cause her to fear for her safety. Similarly, Richardson did not call the police after either incident. Like in Cartwright, the specificity of Dupree's threat evidences intent to cause fear. Id.

(b) Threat to Physically Injure or Kill

RBO: certain words

This topic sentence is not very effective because it does not focus the reader on the element discussed—threat to physically injure or kill.

Certain words are associated with physical violence. See id. In Cartwright, the defendant was found to have made a credible threat because his communications with victim involved words like "kill" and "destroy" that are frequently associated with severe physical harm, and victim testified that she was afraid defendant was going to kill her, that she believed what defendant told her, and that she had trouble sleeping and eating. Id. at 153. Similarly, Dupree stated that he was going to kill Richardson, and crack his head open like a dozen eggs.

ANALYSIS: Here, the writer needs to apply the case to our facts. The reader is left asking—how is it similar?

Dupree intended to threaten the life of Richardson and cause him to reasonably fear for his safety; therefore, he made a credible threat.

CONCLUSION

Dupree committed aggravated stalking. First, Dupree identified Richardson, and directed his course of conduct at him. Moreover, he threatened Richardson and threw eggs at his car with the specific purpose of harassing him. Although the incident was short, it consisted of two or more acts. Second, he harassed Richardson by threatening to kill him, blocking his car, and throwing eggs at his windshield. Dupree's acts did not serve a legitimate purpose, and he intended to frighten, intimidate or cause Richardson emotional distress. Third, Dupree made a credible threat when he stated he was going to kill Richardson and crack his head open like a dozen eggs. Having satisfied all three of the required elements, Dupree can be charged with aggravated stalking.

This conclusion effectively addresses each of the elements and clearly concludes on the issues and overall question presented.

E.   Annotated Sample Memo 3

MEMORANDUM

To: Diana Donahoe, District Attorney
From: Jane Johnson, Assistant Attorney
Date: November 22, 2010
Re: State v. Dupree: Potential aggravated stalking charge

QUESTION PRESENTED

Under Missouri law, did John Dupree commit the crime of aggravated stalking when he said, "I'm going to kill you and crack your head open like a dozen eggs," threw eggs at Don Richardson's car, and a month later Richardson found eggs on his car?

BRIEF ANSWER

Yes. Although Dupree cannot be linked to the second set of eggs, he purposely engaged in a course of conduct when he made a credible threat, blocked, and threw eggs at Richardson's car. In addition, Dupree harassed Richardson because his conduct was unlawful and reasonably caused Richardson to experience ongoing nervousness.

STATEMENT OF FACTS

On September 22, 2010, Richardson attended an Elks meeting. When Richardson was leaving the meeting, Dupree, an eighty-year-old man, approached him and asked if he was the Speaker of the House. Richardson said yes. Dupree began yelling about spending a night in jail due to a new DWI law the Missouri General Assembly passed. Dupree yelled, "I am way too old to have spent a night in jail. It is all your fault. I'm going to kill you and crack your head open like a dozen eggs." Richardson felt nervous, entered his car, locked the door, and began to drive. Dupree blocked the front of and threw a dozen eggs at the car. Richardson waited until enough of the eggs cleared from his windshield, watched Dupree leave, drove home, and washed his car. Richardson did not call the police.

After the next Elk meeting on October 27th, Richardson found a dozen eggs splattered on his car. He did not see Dupree. No one saw Dupree at the meeting or in the area that night. Richardson went home, washed his car, and did not call the police. Richardson says he will not be intimidated;

Annotations (left margin):

This question presented effectively provides the jurisdiction, legal question, and legally significant facts.

Short Answer.

This Brief Answer effectively addresses each element of the crime in a conclusive and concise manner.

however, he worries he will constantly look over his shoulder at Elk meetings. The eggs on his car are humiliating. Richardson is taking over-the-counter sleeping pills.

This statement of facts clearly and concisely tells the story in an objective manner.

DISCUSSION

A person commits the crime of aggravated stalking when he (1) makes a credible threat and (2) purposely, (3) through his or her course of conduct, (4) harasses or (5) follows with the intent of harassing another person. Mo. Ann. Stat. §565.225(3) (West 2010).

ROADMAP: Here, the writer provides an effective roadmap for the discussion section.

Credible Threat

Dupree made a credible threat. He (a) communicated a threat with the intent to cause Richardson to reasonably fear for his safety. The threat was (b) against the life of and to cause physical injury to Richardson. See id. § 565.225(1)(2).

RBO: credible threat

ORGANIZATION: The writer provides a clear mini-roadmap to lay out the elements of this particular section on the element of "credible threat."

Dupree communicated a threat with the intent to cause Richardson to reasonably fear for his safety. Using words frequently associated with severe physical harm, like "kill," shows the defendant's intent to cause the plaintiff to reasonably fear for his or her safety. State v. Cartwright, 17 S.W.3d 149, 153 (Mo. Ct. App. 1997). Dupree said he was going to kill Richardson. Dupree intended to cause Richardson to reasonably fear for his safety.

RBO: communicated a threat

This topic sentence is effective; it parallels the language of the mini-roadmap and sets out the subelement to be discussed below.

Dupree's threat was against the life of and to cause physical injury to Richardson. In Lasley, the court held that saying, "I'm going to kill your nasty [ass]" is a credible threat. State v. Lasley, 130 S.W.3d 15, 17 (Mo. Ct. App. 2004). However, in Heather, "I'm getting ready to put the shammy on everybody you f-ing know" was not a credible threat because the meaning of "shammy" was too ambiguous and could not be considered a threat to kill. City of Kansas City v. Heather, 273 S.W.3d 592, 594 (Mo. Ct. App. 2009). Like the defendant in Lasley, Dupree's statement, "I'm going to kill you and crack your head open like a dozen eggs" was a threat against a life. Unlike Heather, Dupree's statement is not ambiguous because he threatened to kill and crack Richardson's head open. Thus, Dupree made a threat against the life of and to cause physical injury to Richardson.

RBO: threat was against life

This topic sentence effectively focuses the reader on the second prong of the mini-roadmap provided earlier.

ANALYSIS: Here, the writer provides two cases to illustrate opposite sides of the argument. The writer then compares those cases to our facts to come to a conclusion on this issue.

Purposely

Dupree acted purposely. Purposely means, "done with a specific objective, goal, or end." Blacks Law Dictionary 1356 (9th ed. 2009). Dupree

RBO: purposefully

This topic sentence effectively focuses the reader on the legal element to be discussed.

ANALYSIS: Here, the writer uses a simple definition (there was no definition in the statute or from case law) to apply to our facts.

RBO: course of conduct

ORGANIZATION: Here, the writer uses a mini-roadmap to set out the subelements that follow.

Here, the writer uses passive voice. Active voice would make the sentence more concise.

Again, the writer uses passive voice here unnecessarily.

ANALYSIS: Here, the writer compares and distinguishes the prior case from our facts. However, the reader is left wondering how our facts are unlike Dawson. Is it because the prosecution can prove three separate acts or is it just the difference between two and three acts that is important?

RBO: Communication by any means

RBO: period of time

identified Richardson as the Speaker of the House before yelling, "I am way too old to have spent a night in jail. It is all your fault. I'm going to kill you and crack your head open like a dozen eggs." Dupree's goal is retaliation for his night in jail; therefore, Dupree acted purposely.

Course of Conduct

Dupree engaged in a course of conduct. Course of conduct is (a) a pattern of conduct composed of two or more acts, which may include (b) communication by any means, (c) over a period of time, however short, evidencing a continuity of purpose. § 565.225(1)(1).

Dupree engaged in a pattern of conduct composed of two or more acts. In Dawson, it could not be proved that the sticky-substance on the plaintiff's phone and car was the same substance she drank: the defendant's semen. State v. Dawson, 985 S.W.2d 941, 944 (Mo. Ct. App. 1999). Dawson was not convicted of stalking because it could only be proved that he committed one act. Id. at 946; See also State v. Wayman, 926 S.W.2d 900, 903 (Mo. Ct. App 1996). Like Dawson, because Dupree was not seen on October 27th, he cannot be charged with throwing the second set of eggs found on Richardson's car. Unlike Dawson, Dupree committed three acts. He: 1) yelled a threat; 2) blocked a car; and 3) threw eggs. Therefore, Dupree engaged in a pattern of conduct composed of two or more acts.

Dupree's conduct involved communication by any means. Communication means "the expression or exchange of information by speech, writing, gestures, or conduct." Blacks Law Dictionary 316 (9th ed. 2009). In Magalif, the court considered blocking a car with another car communication. State v. Magalif, 131 S.W.3d 431, 433 (Mo. Ct. App. 2004). Like Magalif, Dupree blocked Richardson's car with his body. Dupree also made a verbal threat and a symbolic gesture by throwing eggs. Therefore, Dupree's conduct involved communication by any means.

Dupree's conduct took place over a period of time, however short, evidencing a continuity of purpose. In Lasley, the defendant was charged with one count of aggravated stalking for leaving hostile telephone messages for over a year. Lasley, 130 S.W.3d at 17. In McCauley, the defendant was convicted of three counts of aggravated stalking; one count for each day the defendant called over thirty times and made a credible threat. State v. McCauley, 317 S.W.3d 132, 136 (Mo. Ct. App. 2010).

Dupree made a threat, blocked, and threw eggs at Richardson's car in retaliation for his night in jail. Unlike Lasley, Dupree's conduct took ten minutes but, like McCauley, it occurred in one day. Given McCauley and the plain meaning of "however short", Dupree's conduct took place over a period of time, however short, evidencing a continuity of purpose.

Harass

Dupree harassed Richardson. Harass means (a) to engage in a course of conduct directed at a specific person that serves no legitimate purpose, (b) that would cause a reasonable person under the circumstances to be frightened, intimidated, or emotionally distressed. § 565.225(1)(3).

Dupree engaged in a course of conduct directed at a specific person that served no legitimate purpose. A legitimate purpose is a "lawful objective, goal, or end." Blacks Law Dictionary (ed. 9th 2010). In Magalif, the defendant engaged in a course of conduct directed at a kitchen manager because he did not like the restaurant's odor. Magalif, 131 S.W.3d at 433. The defendant was charged with aggravated stalking for threatening, making obscene gestures, and blocking and photographing the plaintiff and her car. Id. at 435. Like the defendant in Magalif, who focused on the kitchen manager, Dupree focused on Richardson, the Speaker of the House, because he spent a night in jail due to the new DWI bill. Dupree yelled at Richardson, "I'm going to kill you and crack your head open like a dozen eggs" and threw a dozen eggs at his car. Whether Dupree's goal was retaliation or protestation, credible threats and vandalism are unlawful acts. Therefore, Dupree engaged in a course of conduct directed at a specific person that served no legitimate purpose.

Dupree's conduct would cause a reasonable person under the circumstances to be frightened, intimidated, or emotionally distressed. Emotional distress means mental anguish such as ongoing fright, humiliation, nervousness or nausea. State v. Baker, 40 S.W.3d 392, 395. Before the 2008 revisions, the aggravated stalking statute required the defendant's conduct to reasonably cause and for the plaintiff to suffer substantial emotional distress. In Martin, the plaintiff moved to a women's shelter because of her physically abusive ex-boyfriend's credible threat. State v. Martin, 40 S.W.3d 392, 395 (Mo. Ct. App 2001). The court held that Martin's conduct reasonably caused substantial emo-

---

ANALYSIS: The writer effectively uses two cases to compare to our facts.

RBO: harass
Here the writer uses a short topic sentence to effectively focus the reader.

ORGANIZATION: The writer uses another mini-roadmap to help the reader understand the sub-elements.

RBO: course of conduct directed as specific person
Here the reader might be confused with the language, "course of conduct" because it was already discussed earlier. A quick reference to the earlier section may have been helpful so that the reader understood why the focus in this paragraph was only on the remaining elements: directed at a specific person and no legitimate purpose.

RBO: reasonable person to be frightened

ANALYSIS: Here the writer effectively uses a definition from a prior case.

tional distress. Id. at 9. Magalif's conduct reasonably caused substantial emotional distress because he repeatedly yelled and followed the plaintiff, which produced a fear of being alone and a need for sleeping pills. Magalif, 131 S.W.3d at 436. Unlike Martin, here Dupree does not have a physical abuse record and Richardson continued to attend Elks meetings. However, Dupree's conduct only would need to cause a reasonable person emotional distress to satisfy the current statutory language. An eighty-year-old with diabetes is still capable of acting out a credible threat and taking sleeping pills suggests ongoing symptoms of nervousness. Therefore, Dupree's conduct would cause a reasonable person to be frightened, intimidated, or emotionally distressed.

COUNTERARGUMENT: Here, the writer successfully address a counterargument.

Followed with the Intent to Harass

Dupree followed with the intent to harass Richardson. Intent means "the state of mind accompanying an act." Blacks Law Dictionary (9th ed. 2009). The defendant's intent to cause the victim to reasonably fear for his or her safety does not depend on the victim's later actions, such as calling the police. Cartwright, 17 S.W.3d at 153. In Baker, the plaintiff saw the defendant at her son's tennis practice, on her walk, in front of her car at Walmart, and at her trailer where the defendant shined a light in her face. Baker, 40 S.W.3d at 393. The court held that Baker followed with the intent to harass. Id. at 394. Both Dupree and Richardson regularly attend Elk meetings; therefore, unlike Baker, Dupree did not follow Richardson to the meeting. However, Dupree threw eggs, which is similar to shining a flashlight in the defendant's trailer, as in Baker. Furthermore, Dupree had eggs in his possession and his verbal threat, "I'm going to . . . crack your head open like a dozen eggs" contains an egg simile. Therefore, Dupree did not accidently run into Richardson but rather, followed him with the intent to harass.

RBO: follow with intent to harass

ANALYSIS: Here, the writer effectively provides a rule up front. The writer then applies that rule using a case comparison below.

ANALYSIS: How is throwing eggs similar to shining a flashlight?

The mini-conclusion effectively addresses each element of the crime to conclude on the issue presented in the question presented.

CONCLUSION

Dupree's actions meet all the elements of aggravated stalking. Dupree made a credible threat when he said, "I'm going to kill you and crack your head open like a dozen eggs." He acted purposely because the goal of his conduct was retaliation for his night in jail. Dupree's actions constitute a course of conduct, even though they occurred in less than ten minutes because he engaged in two or more acts, namely, making a credible threat, blocking, and throwing eggs at Richardson's car. Dupree harassed Richardson because his course of conduct involved unlawful acts, such as a credible threat and vandalism, which would reasonably cause ongoing emotional distress. Finally, the possession of eggs and the egg simile in the credible threat indicate that Dupree followed Richardson with the intent to harass.

The conclusion effectively summarizes all the elements and concludes on the issue.

II.   BRIEFS

Briefs are persuasive documents written for appellate and trial courts. This section will address appellate briefs. For information about trial briefs, see motions (page 256). For information about persuasive writing techniques, see chapter 2, page 97.

Appellate briefs are carefully crafted documents that attempt to persuade a panel of appellate judges to rule in the client's favor. Appellate briefs are not a rehashing of the trial. Instead, they focus on specific errors at the trial level. Therefore, appellate attorneys must carefully choose the issues they raise on appeal and focus the court on those issues. The appellant (or petitioner) files his or her brief first and the appellee (or respondent) must respond by filing his or her brief within a certain prescribed time. The appellant has an opportunity to file a reply brief (and some courts permit reply briefs from appellees). In some instances, amicus briefs may also be filed.

A.   Purpose, Audience, Scope, and View

- **Purpose:** The underlying purpose of a brief is to convince the judges to affirm, reverse, or remand the case to the lower court. Thus, an appellate brief should inform and persuade. It should be written to win a particular issue or a number of issues. The best briefs seem objective and reasonable, but are subtly persuasive so that the judges feel compelled to rule for the client. The least effective briefs attempt persuasion with incendiary passages that often attack the other side's position or present a defensive posture.
- **Audience:** The judge (or panel of judges) is the primary audience for an appellate brief. When you know which judges are assigned to your panel, you should research their prior opinions to understand their leanings and reasoning in previous decisions. Often this research will give you a much better sense of your audience. You can research state judges by consulting the table of state courts' websites on page 29, and you can find information on federal appellate judges by searching each circuit, shown in the map on page 24. You can find opinions they have written through Lexis and Westlaw. Keep in mind that the judges' clerks are also the audience; oftentimes they are the worst critics. Other secondary audiences

include opposing counsel, your client, the opposing client, and the public. Therefore, tactical considerations are also necessary.

- **Scope:** The scope of an appellate brief turns on the errors in the court below. In most instances, an appellate attorney may request the trial court only to reconsider issues already addressed at the trial level. Therefore, the appellate attorney must scour the trial record for error and decide which issues to raise on appeal. Many briefs raise multiple issues. Appellate courts have page or word number limits on briefs filed. You should always consult your court's rules before beginning a brief. You can find these rules through the state courts' websites, listed on page 29, or the websites of the circuit courts, listed on page 25.
- **View:** You should have a "theory of the case" or "core theory" underlying your brief. This is not the actual legal theory, but instead a writing theory that tugs at the emotions of the judges. The core theory can be based on policy arguments, emotional facts, fairness issues, logical analysis, or any creative argument that is easily understood. Think of the core theory as your "cocktail party answer" when a nonlawyer asks you about your case. For example, a bus accident case might have a legal theory of negligence, but the theory of the case for the brief might be: "The bus driver was in a rush." The theory should be subtle and interwoven throughout the brief itself, starting with the fact section and pervading every facet of the argument.
- For sample briefs, with annotations, see pages 183, 196, and 216.

B.   Formal Requirements

The following are the possible formal requirements of an appellate brief. Most courts do not require all of them. You should always consult the rules in your jurisdiction before beginning to write an appellate brief. These rules not only require specific formal requirements of a brief, but they also dictate page, font, and filing requirements. (To access your court's rules, see the state courts' websites or the circuit courts' websites.) Some professors create fictional rules or require a particular jurisdiction's rules, so be sure to follow your course requirements. For more information, with samples of the formal elements of a brief, consult the following pages:

- Title Page, below.
- Table of Contents, Pointheadings, and Subheadings, page 164.
- Table of Authorities, page 167.
- Jurisdiction, page 168.
- Standard of Review, page 168.
- Statement of the Issues Presented for Review, page 169.
- Statement of the Case, page 170.
- Summary of Argument, page 174.
- Argument, page 176.

- Conclusion, page 182.
- Signature and Certificate of Service, page 182.

Writing a brief is a recursive process. Don't expect to thoroughly understand all of your arguments until you begin writing them. During the writing process, you will discover gaps in your legal reasoning as well as strengths of your opponent's arguments. As a result, you will need to research the law again to address these concerns.

Most legal writers begin their briefs by writing the argument section or the summary of the argument section. Some prefer to outline the arguments first by writing the pointheadings and subheadings. Others prefer to draft an issue statement to focus on the main issues or to write the facts to help create the theory of the case. Regardless of your starting point, you will need to rewrite the specific sections once you have completed the argument. An issue statement will need fine-tuning once your arguments are detailed. A fact section will need to be rewritten to include all the legally significant facts in the argument. Pointheadings and subheadings will need to be rewritten to conform to the final organizational schema. Of course, you will need to rewrite your argument section as you discover nuances in the law and logical gaps in your analysis. For guidance on rewriting, see pages 78-97.

1. Title Page

Because a brief is filed in a court, it needs identification. Therefore, the title page contains the name of the court itself, the name of the case, the docket number and judge's name (if available), and the names and addresses of counsel. Some courts require different color pages for the title pages to distinguish appellants' briefs from appellees' briefs.

Sample Title Page

CRIMINAL ACTION NO. CR07-0288

FLORIDA FOURTH DISTRICT COURT OF APPEALS

STATE of Florida, Appellant

v.

ROGER KINT, Appellee

ON APPEAL FROM THE CIRCUIT COURT FOR THE SEVENTEENTH

JUDICIAL CIRCUIT, BROWARD COUNTY

BRIEF FOR APPELLANT

Diana R. Donahoe

600 New Jersey Avenue, N.W.

Washington, D.C. 20001

March 14, 2010

---

2.   Table of Contents, Pointheadings, and Subheadings

The **table of contents** (sometimes called the *index page*) refers the reader to page numbers for each section of the brief. Usually, page 1 begins with the statement of issues presented for review. Previous pages, such as the table of contents and the table of authorities, are usually referenced as i, ii, iii, and so on. The table of contents often takes a substantial amount of time to create.

Pointheadings and subheadings are also specifically referenced in the table of contents. Pointheadings serve as thesis statements for each part of the argument section. They illustrate the organization and arguments of the brief.

The pointheadings and subheadings appear in two places: (1) the table of contents and (2) the argument section. In the table of contents, the pointheadings and subheadings provide the reader with an understanding of your large-scale organization and your arguments. Therefore, it is important that they both inform and persuade the reader. In the argument section, the pointheadings and subheadings break your argument into readable sections and serve as signs for the reader that you are moving from one argument to the next. Strong pointheadings and subheadings do not substitute for strong topic sentences; your brief will need both.

Pointheadings are usually your main arguments and correlate with each issue statement. Each pointheading should be one sentence, written persuasively, and should contain the legal issue you will address in that section. Pointheadings might also reference some of your favorable facts or the standard of review. Each pointheading should answer the correlating issue statement.

Subheadings are used to break down the organization within each pointheading. They flesh out the arguments under each pointheading, providing facts and legal reasoning. You might have one subheading for each factor within a multi-factor test or you may combine a number of factors to create each subheading. At times, you might provide subheadings within subheadings, but rarely would you go beyond this third level of organization.

You can be very creative when designing your organizational schema. You need not provide the same number of subheadings under each pointheading. You might not have any subheadings at all under one particular pointheading. However, if you choose to write a subheading A, you should also include a subheading B. If you do not have separate sub-issues, there is no need for a subheading—just make your argument in the pointheading.

Novice writers tend to write excessively long pointheadings and subheadings. Instead, keep them readable by focusing the reader on the main point you are making. While they should be full sentences, short headings often are the most persuasive.

Briefs filed in different courts serve different purposes; your pointheadings and subheadings should mirror those purposes. If you file a brief in the United States Supreme Court, your pointheadings and subheadings might be more general and lay out policy arguments and reasons for changes in the law. However, most briefs apply already-existing law to the client's facts and the pointheadings and subheadings should specifically reference that law and the facts of the case.

Sample Table of Contents

TABLE OF CONTENTS

This pointheading focuses the reader on the main issue of the admissibility of the defendant's confession, and it is written conclusively.

This pointheading focuses the reader on the main issue of the identification and provides two reasons for its admissibility. The two subheadings below mirror those two reasons.

This subheading focuses the reader on "impermissibly suggestive" and is persuasive because it uses facts to lead the reader to the desired conclusion.

This subheading argues in the alternative and focuses the reader on the reliability issue. The writer then provides further subheadings below to flesh out the totality factors.

The writer provides sub-subheadings to address each factor of the totality test. These subheadings effectively combine the legal factors and the legally significant facts.

3. Table of Authorities

Sometimes called *authorities cited,* the table of authorities alphabetically lists the legal authorities cited within the brief with references to page numbers. The citations provided should be complete and conform to the citation format required by that court (usually the Bluebook or ALWD). Some jurisdictions require that seminal law be cited with an asterisk (*). Various types of legal authority (constitutions, cases, statutes, regulations) are often separated when listed.

Sample Table of Authorities

**Table of Authorities—Petitioner's Supreme Court Brief—
Yarborough v. Alvarado**

Cases

Berkemer v. McCarty, 468 U.S. 420 (1984) 28, 31-34, 35-37, 39

Butler v. McKellar, 494 U.S. 407 (1990) 13, 14, 22, 28

California v. Beheler, 463 U.S. 1121 (1983)................................ 25, 30, 32, 35

Caspari v. Bohlen, 510 U.S. 383 (1994)..14

Dickerson v. United States, 530 U.S. 428 (2000)........................ 28, 29, 38, 39

Lockyer v. Andrade, 583 U.S. 63 (2003) 12-14, 28

Miranda v. Arizona, 384 U.S. 436 (1966) 25, 29, 30, 37, 39, 40

Mitchell v. Esparza, No. 02-1369 (U.S. Nov. 3, 2003)...............................12

Moran v. Burbine, 475 U.S. 412 (1986)...

New York v. Quarles, 467 U.S. 649 (1984)...39

Northbrook Nat'l Ins. Co. v. Brewer, 493 U.S. 6 (1989)...........................24

Oregon v. Mathiason, 429 U.S. 492 (1977).................................. 25, 30, 31, 34

Orozco v. Texas, 394 U.S. 324 (1969) 34

Pennsylvania v. Bruder, 488 U.S. 9 (1988)..36

People v. P., 21 N.Y.2d 1, 233 N.E.2d 255 (1967)....................................32

Thompson v. Keohane, 516 U.S. 99 (1995)........................... 31, 33, 34, 39

Tyler v. Cain, 533 U.S. 656 (2001) 15, 16

United States v. Erving L., 147 F.3d 1240 (10th Cir. 1998)........................25

United States v. J.H.H., 22 F.3d 821 (8th Cir. 1994) 26, 28

United States v. Macklin, 900 F.2d 948 (6th Cir. 1990)..........................26

Yarborough v. Gentry, No. 02-1597 (U.S. Oct. 20, 2003) 22, 25

Constitutional Provisions

U.S. Const. amend. V 2, 23, 29

U.S. Const. amend. VIII...12

Statutes

28 U.S.C. § 1254(1)..1

28 U.S.C. § 2254 .... 2, 5, 11, 24

Other Authorities

141 Cong. Rec. S7845 (June 7, 1995) 13

Webster's Third New Int'l Dictionary 804 (2002) 19

4.   Jurisdiction

Not all courts require a jurisdiction section. When one is required, this section briefly states the jurisdictional basis for appeal by providing relevant facts and a specific legal foundation.

Sample Jurisdiction

Petitioner's Supreme Court Brief—<u>Yarborough v. Alvarado</u>

The judgment of the Court of Appeals granting habeas corpus relief was amended and entered on February 11, 2003. The Court of Appeals denied Warden Yarborough's petition for rehearing and suggestion for rehearing en banc on February 11, 2003. Pet. App. A5. The petition for writ of certiorari was filed on May 12, 2003, and was granted on September 30, 2003. The jurisdiction of this Court rests on 28 U.S.C. § 1254(1).

---

5.   Standard of Review

In appellate cases, the court must apply a certain standard of review over the trial court. This standard is analogous to the burden of proof in trial cases. The appellate court determines how much deference to give to the trial court because the appellate court does not sit in the same shoes as the trial judge.

First, the appellate court does not hear witnesses or judge credibility like the trial judge; therefore, the trial judge is given great deference in deciding questions of fact. Her ruling is overturned only if it was **"clearly erroneous"** as to the facts.

On the other hand, the appellate court needs to ensure that *stare decisis* is preserved so that laws are followed in an equitable manner; therefore, questions of law are reviewed independently, or ***de novo,*** with no deference given to the trial court.

For issues that present mixed questions of law and fact, the standard is not always clear. Courts themselves seem to be confused on the standard of review. Therefore, it is important to pay attention to what standard the court says it is using, but also look at what standard the court actually applies.

Another standard, **abuse of discretion,** applies for procedural and evidentiary issues where the trial court has discretion. On appeal, the appellate court will overrule a trial judge only if he has abused his discretion on that particular issue.

Some courts require a separate section for the standard of review, while others require that you include it in the statement of the case or the argument section. Consult your appellate court rules to ensure proper placement of the standard of review.

Sample Standard of Review

STANDARD OF REVIEW

Whether Defendant faced custodial interrogation absent Miranda warnings is a question of law, and the court must review the Superior Court's decision to grant Defendant's Motion to Suppress *de novo*. <u>Jones v. United States</u>, 779 A.2d 277, 281 (D.C. 2001).

Here, the standard of review is *de novo* and the writer has provided a citation to at least one authority that establishes the standard.

---

6. Statement of the Issues Presented for Review

The issue statements explain the precise legal issues the court will need to address. They should be written persuasively and contain both the legal issue and some of the most persuasive facts for your side. They are usually one sentence and should pass the breath test. Although not required, lawyers often include the standard of review within the issue statement.

Many briefs include multiple issue statements if the brief itself addresses more than one issue on appeal. Each issue statement should correlate to a main pointheading. If you argue in the alternative in a brief, your issue statements should reflect those specific arguments.

This section is similar to the question presented (see page 131) in a memo; however, it does not require a jurisdictional statement as one is usually provided in a separate section. Unlike a memo, the issue statement in a brief should be written persuasively so that the reader empathizes with your client. The answer should be implicit because a brief, unlike a memo, does not include a corresponding brief answer. However, be careful not to provide the actual conclusion in the issue statement.

This effective issue statement refers to the correctness of the court below, focuses the reader on the legal element (reasonable expectation of privacy), and is written persuasively (open sleeping bag and cot). It is clear that it is written by the defendant.

This effective issue statement focuses the reader on the legal issue-reasonable expectation of privacy—and is written persuasively (temporary shelter and hundreds of students). It is clear that it is written by the prosecution.

This issue statement is not effective because it is conclusory—the issue before the court is whether Kramer had a reasonable expectation of privacy. Also, it is not very persuasive; a defense attorney would not want to reveal the seizure of such a large quantity of cocaine in an issue statement.

Sample of Issues Presented for Review

ISSUES PRESENTED FOR REVIEW

1. Whether the Superior Court correctly found that Shelley Kramer had a reasonable expectation of privacy in items stored under her cot and covered by her open sleeping bag.

2. Whether Defendant had a reasonable expectation of privacy in a temporary shelter where Defendant was sharing a field house with hundreds of other evacuated students following a dormitory fire.

3. Whether the evidence should be suppressed because Shelley Kramer had a reasonable expectation of privacy in the 120 pounds of cocaine found under her cot in a field house that was temporarily used as a dorm.

---

7. Statement of the Case (Facts)

The statement of the case (also called the *statement of the facts*) presents the facts to the reader in a clear, concise, and persuasive manner. As an appellate attorney, you will probably receive the facts in the form of a record, which usually includes a lower court transcript and a variety of documents. Your job will be to cull through the record and pull out the most relevant facts to tell the client's story.

The statement of the case is your first opportunity to tell the story from the client's perspective. There are a number of persuasive techniques that you can use to make the statement of the case persuasive:

- **Provide emotional facts.** Unlike the objective fact section in a memo (see page 134), the statement of facts in a brief should provide the reader with emotional facts. These facts should tug at the heart strings of the reader so that the judge feels compelled to rule for your client—even before he or she understands the law.
- **Provide legally significant facts and background facts.** In addition to emotional facts, you will need to provide legally significant facts and use background facts to tie the significant facts to the emotional facts. Facts are legally significant if you use them in your argument section.
- **Tell a compelling story.** Here, you can use your creativity to tell your client's story. A chronological organization is often preferred, but it is not necessary. Consider whether you want to organize by claims, witnesses, crimes, or other schema.

- **Choose a starting point.** The starting point for your story is important. It should engage the reader from your client's point of view. For example, if you represent a client who has been arrested, you might start with the scene of the arrest. If you represent the prosecution in the same case, you might start with the crime from the victim's perspective.

- **Choose a theory of the case.** You need to decide on an overall theory of your case (see page 99). It will pervade your writing and should be an integral part of your fact section.

- **Highlight helpful facts.** Highlight those facts that are most helpful for your position. You can focus on them by placing them at the beginning of paragraphs and sentences. Use short sentences to highlight important points.

- **Do not avoid harmful facts.** You will lose credibility if you do not include facts that help the other side. (Remember that opposing counsel will include them in his brief.) When you include the harmful facts, you can downplay them by explaining them or including them mid-paragraph or mid-sentence.

- **Choose names and titles carefully.** You should personalize your client and be more generic with names of the opposing party. For example, refer to your client as Mr. Jones or Michael Jones. Refer to the other party with more generic terms such as the employer, the government, or the defendant.

- **Use subtle persuasion.** Your persuasion should be subtle. Avoid overly dramatic statements or Hollywood scripts. The key to a statement of facts is to sound objective while you subtly persuade.

Some jurisdictions distinguish between the terms "statement of the facts" and "statement of the case." In these jurisdictions, the statement of the facts is usually a general term that includes the whole fact section, while the statement of the case contains only the procedural history. Most courts have specific requirements for the procedural history sections of the statement of the case.

Sample Statement of the Case from Supreme Court Briefs in <u>Rhode Island v. Innis</u>

In these samples, compare where the writers begin their stories, how they refer to the parties, and how they highlight helpful facts and downplay harmful facts.

Prosecution's Statement of the Case

On January 16, 1975, the body of John Mulvaney, a cab driver, was found in a shallow grave in Coventry, Rhode Island (Aff. 5-6). The cab company dispatcher had last heard from Mulvaney at approximately 10:25 P.M. on January 12, 1975 (Aff. 7). Death had resulted from a shotgun blast to the back of the head (Aff. 6-7). The facts as elicited during the trial and the voir dire may be summarized as follows.

On January 16, 1975, shortly after midnight, the Providence police received a phone call from a cab driver, Gerald Aubin, who reported that he had been robbed by a man carrying a sawed-off shotgun and that he had dropped off this person in the vicinity of Rhode Island College (Aff. 64-66). A police cruiser responded, and Mr. Aubin was asked to follow the car to the Providence police station (Aff. 66). While Mr. Aubin was in the Providence police station waiting to give his statement, he happened to observe his assailant's, the respondent's, picture on a bulletin board (Aff. 66-67). He told this to a police officer. After giving his statement, Mr. Aubin picked the same individual's photograph out of a group of six photographs (Aff. 67-68). Shortly thereafter, the Providence police began a search of the Mount Pleasant area (Aff. 12, 42).

At approximately 4:30 A.M. on January 17, 1975, Patrolman Lovell apprehended the respondent, placed him under arrest, searched for weapons, and advised him of his Miranda rights (Aff. 12-14, 17-18, 27). Within minutes, Sergeant Sears arrived at the scene and again advised Innis of his constitutional rights (Aff. 19, 28-29). Immediately thereafter, Captain Leyden arrived and also advised Innis of his Miranda rights (Aff. 20-21, 34-36). In response to the captain's warnings, the respondent stated that he understood these rights and that he wanted an attorney (Aff. 35). The captain then directed three officers, Patrolmen Gleckman, McKenna, and Williams, to place the respondent in the rear of a caged four-door sedan and transport him to the central station (Aff. 35). They were also instructed by the captain not to question Innis or to intimidate or coerce him in any way (Aff. 46). Two of the officers sat in front; one sat in the back with Innis (Aff. 43, 50, 58).

While en route to the central station, Patrolman Gleckman, who had been on the force for only two years, began a conversation with Patrolman McKenna (Aff. 43-44). The respondent could hear this conversation (Aff. 46). Patrolman Gleckman stated:

"A. At this point, I was talking back and forth with Patrolman McKenna, stating that I frequent this area while on patrol and there's a lot of handicapped children running around in this area, and God forbid one of them might find a weapon with shells and they might hurt themselves.

"Q. Who were you talking to?

"A. Patrolman McKenna.

"Q. Did you say anything to the suspect Innis?

"A. No, I didn't.

"Q. Did he say anything to you prior to this? * * *

"A. No. * * *

"Q. And what happened next?

"A. At that point, as I was saying, there were kids running around there, as it is a handicapped school, and he says, you know, back and forth with Patrolman McKenna, he at this point said: 'Stop, turn around, I'll show you where it is.' At this point, Patrolman McKenna got on the mike and told the captain: 'We're returning to the scene of the crime, or where the weapon might be, and the subject is going to show us where it will be.'" (Aff. 43-44).

Patrolman McKenna radioed Captain Leyden and informed him that they were returning to the scene of the arrest to locate the weapon (Aff. 44, 50, 59). The car had traveled less than a mile at the time of this statement, and they returned to the arrest scene at Obadiah Brown Road within minutes of leaving (Aff. 22-23, 38).

The other two officers corroborated this sequence of events and the general scope of their "conversation," disagreeing only on the question of where each officer was seated in the car (Aff. 43, 46, 49-50, 52-53, 58-59). All three testified that no one spoke to or with Innis (Aff. 44, 46, 53-54, 58-59).

Upon returning to the scene, Innis alighted from the car, and Captain Leyden again advised him of his Miranda rights (Aff. 36, 38-39). Innis replied that he understood those rights, but wanted to show them where the gun was because of the school that was in the area and the "small kids around" (Aff. 36, 39). He was placed back in the car, and they all proceeded to a nearby field (Aff. 39-40). The respondent at first had trouble finding the weapon, finally locating it under some rocks along the side of Obadiah Brown Road (Aff. 14-15, 23-24).

The respondent elected not to testify at the voir dire and did not dispute these facts either at the trial or on appeal (Aff. 61). The trial judge found that the respondent had been "repeatedly and completely advised of his Miranda rights" and that his offer to locate the gun constituted a waiver (Aff. 62-63). The respondent's motion to suppress the gun was denied (Aff. 63).

* * * The trial proceeded, and exhibit 41, the gun, was identified by one witness as having been in Innis's possession on the morning of January 13, 1975 (A. 68). * * * The respondent was found guilty by the jury of murder, kidnapping, and robbery. The respondent then appealed to the Supreme Court of Rhode Island. * * *

Defendant's Statement of the Case

At approximately 4:30 A.M. on January 17, 1975, the respondent, Thomas Innis, was arrested at gunpoint by Officer Lovell of the Providence police (App. 11; R. 452). In rapid succession the respondent was handcuffed, searched, advised of his constitutional rights, and placed in a patrol car (App. 13, 17). Within minutes, approximately twelve other officers were on the scene, one of whom, Sergeant Sears, again advised the respondent of his constitutional rights while seated beside him in the rear of the car (App. 29, 31). When Captain Leyden arrived, the respondent was outside the vehicle, being held by Officer Lovell and Sergeant Sears and surrounded by a total of four officers (App. 37, 49). Captain Leyden advised him of his constitutional rights, and the respondent stated that he wanted an attorney (App. 35). Officers Gleckman, McKenna, and Williams all heard the respondent make this request (App. 42, 50, 58). Captain Leyden then directed that the respondent be placed in the "caged wagon," and that he be taken to the central station (App. 35). He was placed in the vehicle, and the doors were closed (App. 55). Captain Leyden ordered a third person, Officer Gleckman, to accompany Officers Williams and McKenna, who were assigned to the wagon (App. 55-56). Captain Leyden further directed that the officers were not to question the respondent or intimidate or coerce him in any way (App. 46). The three officers then entered the vehicle, and it departed.

The wagon proceeded in a westerly direction, going "out" of the city (App. 45, 52, 60). It traveled approximately a mile, the trip encompassing from three to five minutes (App. 45, 52, 59; R. 452). During this period, Officer Gleckman initiated a conversation with his fellow officers:

"A. At this point, I was talking back and forth with Patrolman McKenna stating that I frequent this area while on patrol and there's a lot of handicapped children running around this area, and God forbid one of them might find a weapon with shells and they might hurt themselves." (App. 43-44.)

Officer McKenna apparently shared his brother officer's apprehension:

"A. I more or less concurred with him [Gleckman] that it was a safety factor and that we should, you know, continue to search for the weapon and try to find it." (App. 53.)

While Officer Williams said nothing, he recalled with specificity certain details of the conversation:

"A. He [Gleckman] said it would be too bad if the little—I believe he said a girl— would pick up the gun, maybe kill herself." (App. 59.)

As the conversation proceeded, the respondent interrupted, exclaiming that he would show them where the gun was located (App. 58). Officer McKenna immediately radioed back to Captain Leyden that they were returning to the scene and that the respondent would show them where the gun was (App. 44, 50, 59).

At the scene the officers reiterated that the respondent "wanted to show them where the gun was because he didn't want anybody—any kids up there to get hurt" (App. 22). The respondent was again advised of his constitutional rights, to which he responded that "[h]e wanted to get the gun out of the way because of the kids in the area in the school" (App. 39).

The respondent was then placed back in the wagon, which then led a parade of police cars up the hill to where Mr. Innis had indicated the shotgun would be found (App. 23, 39). The respondent, still handcuffed and being held by Officer Gleckman, began searching for the weapon (App. 72). Captain Leyden ordered the numerous officers still present to position their vehicles so that the headlights could illuminate the area in which the respondent was searching (App. 39-40, 72). After a false start, the respondent located the weapon (App. 45).

8.   Summary of the Argument

The summary of the argument provides the court with a snapshot of your arguments. The summary should show the court which way it should decide on each issue referring to rules of law, application of the law to the facts, and any relevant policy issues. However, specific cites to cases are usually not required.

The summary of the argument is similar to the **conclusion** (see page 141) section of the memo in that it briefly summarizes the main legal points of the document, using key facts from the client's case. However, in a brief, this section is persuasive and designed to give a compelling overview for the very busy reader. Consider writing a paragraph or two per issue to summarize your main points for the reader; do not try to make every specific point in your summary.

Some lawyers choose to write summaries that refer only to the law while others write very fact-specific summaries, applying the law to the facts on each issue but only highlighting the most compelling arguments.

Not all jurisdictions require a summary of the argument; however, consider including this section if space permits.

Sample Summary of Argument

Summary of Argument

I. Police are required to perform a protective sweep to ensure no dangerous third parties are present during an arrest. Maryland v. Buie, 494 U.S. 325 (1990). Detective Dent conducted a protective sweep of those places in Defendant's house where a dangerous person could hide, including an ottoman where Detective Dent found evidence of a crime. Police had a reasonable, articulable suspicion that a dangerous third party was in the house because they had recently seen someone resembling the assailant's at-large accomplice there, heard suspicious noises inside the house, and knew the assailant was violent and involved in gang activity. Dent confined his search to the time necessary to dispel that suspicion.

II. Police are permitted to search incident to arrest the area around an arrestee for weapons that could be used against them. Chimel v. California, 395 U.S. 752 (1969). Detective Dent recovered a can of lye when he searched a cabinet toward which Defendant was moving. This search was contemporaneous with the arrest because Defendant never left the area around the lye. The lye was within Defendant's immediate control; it was accessible to him because police lacked physical control of the situation. Police had reason to fear that Defendant had a weapon because one was used in the assault and the arrival of an accomplice could provide an opportunity to use that weapon on the officers.

This summary of the argument is very fact specific and lays out the two issues in separate paragraphs.

The first sentence is written from the government's perspective and focuses the reader on the issue of protective sweep.

The writer uses a citation to support the assertion, although a citation is not always necessary in the summary of the argument.

Here, the writer focuses the reader on specific facts of the case to support the protective sweep argument.

Here, the writer focuses on the specific elements of protective sweep and uses facts to support his argument.

This sentence focuses the reader on the second issue of the brief, search incident to arrest, and is written persuasively for the government.

Here, the writer uses a citation to support the proposition, although a citation is not always necessary in the summary.

The writer persuasively applies legally significant facts to the legal elements of search incident to arrest. Therefore, the writer has set out the large-scale organization in a persuasive way.

9.   Argument

The argument section is the "meat of the brief," complete with pointheadings **and** subheadings (see page 164). Here, the writer presents the law and applies it to the client's situation in a persuasive manner, applying the theory of the case and other persuasive techniques to the writing. The purpose of the argument section is to prove your arguments to the court using sound legal analysis and persuasive techniques. There are many other sections of this book that discuss writing the argument section, writing persuasively, and organizing and analyzing the law. References are provided below.

a.   *Argument: Content*

First, you will need to decide which arguments to include and which to ignore. You might not make some of these decisions until you actually write the argument section and discover your weak points in the analysis. Most judges prefer to read only the most compelling arguments instead of the kitchen-sink approach where the lawyer includes every possible alternative argument.

b.   *Argument: Organization*

The argument section should be organized around the law in a persuasive fashion. This section usually starts with a persuasive roadmap (see page 82), which sets out the legal arguments for the court. The rest of the argument section follows the organization of the roadmap with clear pointheadings and subheadings and conclusive topic sentences. Here are some techniques to make your organization more persuasive:

1. Start with your strongest argument.
2. Combine a weak factor with a strong factor.
3. Organize your sentences with strong subject-verb combinations.
4. Create active topic sentences to focus the reader on your strong points.
5. Use passive voice to downplay an actor.

For more on organizing content, with samples, see the sections Large-Scale Organization, starting on page 79, Persuasive Writing, starting on page 97.

c.   *Argument: Legal Analysis*

The reader expects a thorough analysis of the law to the facts in the argument section. You should start with the law that is most favorable to your side. If the law is not favorable, start with the facts of your case. If neither the facts nor the law provide the basis for your best argument, consider beginning with a policy argument. As you create your legal arguments, you should combine all three when possible—law, facts, and policy arguments—to make a compelling case for the reader. Here are some techniques for persuasive analysis:

1. Present the rules in a light most favorable to your client.
2. Start with the most compelling cases for your client.
3. Don't ignore the other side's counterargument.
4. Downplay the other side's counterargument but don't highlight it. (You will highlight it if you state the other side's argument defensively— especially in a topic sentence.)
5. Use policy arguments to show the court why the law should apply in a certain way or why the law should be changed.

For more on constructing an argument in a brief, consult the following sections of this text:

- Persuasive Writing, page 97.
- Paragraph Organization and Legal Analysis, page 86.
- Conciseness, page 94.
- Writing Process, page 64.

Sample Argument

The detention of Swanson's luggage extended beyond the permissible scope of a valid investigative detention.

This sentence is written persuasively from the defendant's point of view and focuses the reader on the protection of the Fourth Amendment.

[The Fourth Amendment protects individuals from unreasonable government intrusions into their possessory interests, and thus prohibits warrantless seizures. U.S. Const. amend. IV,] [A brief investigative detention of property on the basis of reasonable articulable suspicion that it contains evidence of criminal activity is permitted only if the detention of the property does not extend beyond the limited scope of an investigative detention. Place, 462 U.S. at 702.] [The detention of Swanson's luggage was unreasonable because it extended beyond its limited scope.]

This sentence persuasively sets out the legal standard of a brief investigative detention of property and cites to the seminal Supreme Court case on point.

This sentence persuasively sets out the main argument of the brief.

[Dunne exceeded the limited scope of an investigative detention when he detained Swanson's luggage because (1) he detained the luggage for approximately seventy-five minutes, an unreasonable duration; (2) he and Officer Dale did not act diligently; and (3) he failed to inform Swanson of the detention's duration and location, and the method of returning the luggage after the investigation. See Peschel v. State, 770 P.2d 1144, 1150 (Alaska Ct. App. 1989). The intrusive circumstances of the detention were intensified by Swanson, as a traveler, having to elect between disrupting her travel and leaving her luggage behind. Id. Under the totality of the circumstances of the detention and the categorization of Swanson as a traveler, the seizure of her luggage went beyond the permissible scope of an investigative detention.]

This persuasive roadmap paragraph effectively uses the law to inform the reader of the large-scale organization of the brief.

A. Swanson's luggage was detained for an unreasonable duration.

This topic sentence mirrors the roadmap and persuasively addresses the duration issue.

[The approximately seventy-five-minute duration of the detention of Swanson's luggage was beyond the scope of a brief investigative detention.] The detention of a traveler's luggage that persisted for thirty minutes was unreasonable, Peschel, 770 P.2d at 1150, but in LeMense v. State, 754 P.2d 268, 273 (Alaska Ct. App. 1988), the detention for the same duration was found to be reasonable and not unduly intrusive. The distinguishing circumstance was that the traveler in Peschel had to elect between missing his flight and leaving his luggage with the officers, but the traveler in LeMense did not. The detention of Swanson's luggage was similar to the detention in Peschel because Swanson was forced to elect between disruption of her scheduled travel plans and separation from her luggage, and therefore, the seventy-five-minute detention of her luggage was overly intrusive and consequentially beyond the scope of an investigative detention.

Here, the writer uses two cases to compare to her case and to conclude on this factor.

B. Dunne did not diligently pursue the investigation, and thereby failed to minimize the intrusion on Swanson's possessory interests.

[Officer Dunne did not act diligently when he detained luggage in Swanson's custody and transported the luggage forty yards, as less intrusive investigative methods were available.] [An officer investigates diligently by using the least intrusive means possible to minimize inconvenience. Peschel, 770 P.2d at 1148.] [In Peschel, an officer who diligently administered a dog sniff in thirty minutes did not perform an investigative detention within the permissible scope because less intrusive methods of investigating were available that would have minimized the inconvenience to the traveler. Id. Similarly, Officer Dunne did not investigate diligently, as (1) the directed process of checking the bar codes was intrusive and (2) less intrusive methods which would have minimized the inconvenience to Swanson were available.]

1. The detention of Swanson's luggage was particularly intrusive, as it interfered with her actual possession and forced the luggage to move significantly.

[Dunne detained Swanson's luggage in a particularly intrusive manner.] [The factors considered in Chandler v. State support that] [the intrusiveness of the detention was increased because (a) Swanson had direct custody of her luggage when it was seized, and (b) Dunne transported the luggage. See Chandler, 830 P.2d 789, 792 (Alaska Ct. App. 1992).]

[Swanson had custody of the luggage when Dunne detained it for investigation, causing the intrusiveness of the detention to be greater than if Swanson had previously given control to a third party.] In Gibson v. State, the intrusion was minimal when officers picked up a package no longer in the defendant's control from an airline counter. 708 P.2d 708, 711 (Alaska 1985). On the other hand, the seizure was more intrusive when officers detained luggage in a defendant's direct custody for investigation. Chandler, 830 P.2d at 792. The seizure of property that was in a defendant's custody was more intrusive because the possessory interest of the individual was infringed upon; therefore, the person was inconvenienced or made to alter her agenda due to the detention of the luggage. Dunne inconvenienced Swanson when he detained luggage in her custody, and, as a result, the intrusion was significant.

[Dunne moved Swanson's luggage forty yards from the location where the luggage was originally detained, and in effect required Swanson to elect to either accompany her luggage or board the ferry without it.] [In circumstances where a traveler's luggage is moved from the point of seizure, the impact can restrain the traveler. Place, 462 U.S. at 708.] In Wright v. State, officers who immobilized the defendant's luggage and conducted a dog sniff at the point of seizure were minimally intrusive. 795 P.2d 812, 814 (Alaska Ct. App. 1990). In contrast, officers who detained luggage at the airport and moved the property to the police station were particularly intrusive because the luggage was moved a significant distance. Chandler, 830 P.2d at 792. Like the officers in Chandler, Dunne was intrusive because he moved Swanson's luggage forty yards to investigate the bar codes and, in effect, inconvenienced

---

This topic sentence is written persuasively and focuses the reader on the second element in the roadmap—diligence.

Here, the writer effectively sets out a rule for context before applying it to the facts of the case.

Here, the writer effectively uses a case comparison to apply the rule to her facts.

This topic sentence effectively informs and persuades the reader of the third element from the roadmap.

Consider omitting.

Here, the writer sets out a persuasive mini-roadmap to introduce the reader to the large-scale organization of this section.

This topic sentence effectively mirrors the mini-roadmap and sets out the argument for the reader.

Here, the writer uses two cases to compare to her facts to come to a conclusion on the first subelement of this section.

This topic sentence effectively focuses the reader on the second part of the mini-roadmap to this section. It uses facts to make the argument persuasive.

Here, the writer provides a rule for context before she applies that rule.

Here, the writer lays out two cases that explain the parameters of the rule.

Here, the writer attempts to
compare her case to the prior
cases; however, she could have
tied the cases together a bit more
specifically and referred to both
cases instead of just one.

This topic sentence persuasively
focuses the reader on the second
element of the argument.

Here, the writer sets out the rule
for the reader.

Here, the reader applies the rule
through case analysis.

This topic sentence persuasively
focuses the reader on the
alternative method available to
the police.

Here, the writer uses a Supreme
Court case to compare to her facts.

Swanson by forcing her to choose between accompanying her luggage and leaving without it.

2. Officers Dunne and Dale did not minimize the intrusion by using the least intrusive means of investigation available.

[Less intrusive means of checking the bar codes on Swanson's luggage against the bar codes of the missing bag were available, but Dunne and Dale failed to employ these alternatives.] [When the detention of luggage forced Swanson to choose between leaving her luggage and disrupting her travel plans, Dunne was obligated to use the least intrusive means possible in conducting the detention. See Peschel, 770 P.2d at 1148.]

Allowing Swanson's luggage to be checked through to Wrangdell and arranging for search upon arrival was a reasonable, less intrusive alternative which Dunne failed to utilize. See id. In Peschel, officers failed to use the least intrusive means possible to investigate the defendant's luggage; officers had twenty minutes to arrange to have luggage checked on the defendant's flight and searched at the final destination, but rather detained the luggage as the defendant prepared to board, creating a situation where he had to elect between leaving his luggage and missing his flight. Id. at 1149. Similarly, Dunne recognized the necessity to detain Swanson's bag over an hour before Swanson's ferry departed, but failed to arrange to have her bag checked on the ferry and detained by Wrangdell officers upon arrival. Instead, Dunne detained her bag in Sitka and forced her to elect between forgoing her spot on the ferry and leaving her luggage. The alternatives Dunne and the Peschel officers failed to employ were less intrusive because under the alternative methods, the luggage would have only momentarily been detained prior to departure, if at all, and thus, would not have disrupted or delayed Swanson's travel plans.

[Dunne also could have investigated the bar codes in a much more expeditious way that would have detained Swanson's luggage only momentarily, thus allowing Swanson to board the ferry early enough to obtain her desired seat.] In Florida v. Royer, officers moved a traveler to an office within the terminal to investigate the traveler's bag, although it would have been more expeditious and thus less intrusive to have used a dog sniff on the luggage while in control of the airline. 460 U.S. 491, 500 (1983). Similarly, Dunne could have investigated the bar codes more expeditiously by requesting the missing luggage's bar code at 3:15 p.m., when he was first notified of its use, and then had the bar code along with him when he approached Swanson in line. This alternative investigative technique would have allowed Swanson to keep possession of her luggage and, as in Royer, would have been more expeditious, thereby not requiring Swanson to choose between missing her ferry and leaving her luggage behind.

C. Swanson was not told accurate information about the detention of her luggage and was forced to elect between disrupting her travel plans and leaving without her luggage.

[Dunne did not tell Swanson accurate information about the detention of her luggage, and he ultimately forced Swanson to choose between leaving without her luggage and losing her preferred spot on the ferry.] Both the lack of information and the requirement to elect between leaving without her luggage and losing her spot on the ferry caused the prolonged detention to go beyond the permissible limits of an investigative detention. See Peschel, 770 P.2d at 1147. In United States v. Erwin, the defendant was accurately given information about the length of time for the sniff test, the location of the luggage, and the assurance that the luggage would be returned to him. Erwin was not forced to elect to miss a flight or leave his luggage; therefore, the forty-five-minute detention was within the permissible limits. 803 F.2d 1505, 1507 (9th Cir. 1986).

On the other hand, in Peschel, the defendant was forced to elect between disrupting his travel plans and leaving without his luggage. Peschel, 770 P.2d at 1147. The detention in Peschel was therefore beyond the permissible scope of investigative detentions. In Place, the defendant had already arrived at his destination and did not have to make a similar type of decision. 462 U.S. at 699. However, the detention in Place was outside the limited scope because the defendant was misinformed of relevant information. See Place, 462 U.S. at 710.

Dunne's detention of Swanson's luggage was characterized by a lack of information similar to the impermissible detention in Place, and by a requirement to choose between disrupting her travel plans and leaving without her luggage, as characterized by the impermissible detention in Peschel. Therefore, the seizure of her luggage was intrusive and beyond the permissible scope of an investigative detention.

This topic sentence effectively combines two elements to make a persuasive argument on the last factors.

The writer effectively sets out the law for the reader.

Here, the writer uses three cases to compare to her facts.

10. Conclusion

The conclusion in a brief differs from that in a memo. In a brief, the conclusion simply states the relief requested, usually in one sentence.

Sample Conclusion

The judgment of the Court of Appeals should be reversed.

---

11. Signature and Certificate of Service

The attorney's signature, name, bar number, and address are required at the end of every brief. In addition, the court requires a short statement indicating that the writer has provided a copy of the brief to opposing counsel (indicating whether service was hand-provided, emailed, or mailed). An attorney's signature is required after the certificate of service as well.

Sample Certificate of Service

CERTIFICATE OF SERVICE

I, Diana R. Donahoe, certify that a copy of this brief was hand-delivered to John Johnson, Counsel for the Prosecution, on Monday, February 23, 2009.

> Diana R. Donahoe
> D.C. Bar # *** ***
> Donahoe & Associates

C.   *Annotated Sample Brief 1*

Criminal No. 03-9051-F

DISTRICT OF COLUMBIA COURT OF APPEALS

UNITED STATES,

Appellant v.

Lance HARBOR, Appellee

ON APPEAL FROM THE SUPERIOR COURT FOR THE DISTRICT OF COLUMBIA BRIEF FOR APPELLANT—DRAFT

Richard Garson,

Counsel

600 New Jersey Avenue, N.W.

Washington, D.C. 20001

(202) 662-0000

Table of Contents

If your issue here is "custody," you might want to make that term explicit for the reader.

Persuasive use of terms here. Instead of calling it an "interrogation," you call it a routine discussion. Very effective.

This subheading does not make logical sense to the reader. Why does he have sufficient age and experience by witnessing a mother in uniform?

This pointheading clearly lays out your focus—interrogation—for the reader. In addition, it provides persuasive terms and facts to help the reader understand your position.

This subheading is short and to the point—very effective.

In general, your pointheadings clearly lay out the large-scale organization of your brief. In addition, they are written persuasively to start informing the reader of your position.

Table of Authorities

Are there more cases? The research looks thin. In addition, do you mention the Fifth Amendment? If so, you should reference it in your Table of Authorities. If not, you should consider doing so because this appeal is based upon a Fifth Amendment Suppression Motion.

Issue Statement

1. [Whether Mr. Harbor was in custody because he was subject to a restraint on freedom of movement of the degree associated with formal arrest when he voluntarily came to a routine information gathering meeting to discuss the use of deadly steroids, while his parents and another student were present?]

2. [Whether Mr. Harbor was interrogated because he was subject to the functional equivalent of questioning when Mrs. Moxon addressed to another mother a comment about her son's unfortunate situation at the conclusion of Principal Gulch's meeting?]

Statement of the Case

[This is an appeal from the Superior Court of the District of Columbia, which denied the admission of Lance Harbor's confession to distributing illegal steroids holding that Mr. Harbor was entitled to a <u>Miranda</u> reading because he was in custody and subject to interrogation.] The Superior Court for the District of Columbia improperly applied the rule of law in determining that Mr. Harbor was in custody and subject interrogation and its decision is therefore subject to *de novo* review. When the proper legal standard is applied, Mr. Harbor was not in custody nor was he interrogated.

Statement of the Facts

[To the surprise of Principal Gulch, Mr. Harbor's parents, Jonathan Moxon, and Jonathan's parents, Lance Harbor blurted out that he had distributed illegal steroids to his teammates.] (Tr. 32.) The confession occurred during a routine information-gathering session conducted by Principal Gulch after Gulch was notified that members of the school football team were using deadly steroids.

Gulch first learned that the steroid Vitapro was being used by some of his students when Mrs. Moxon, an officer on the West Canaan police force, called him to discuss her concerns after finding a bottle of Vitapro in her son Jonathan's possession. (Tr. 8.) A pill similar to Vitapro had recently caused the death of a football player at a neighboring high school. (Tr. 15.) Unsure of how to proceed, Principal Gulch spoke to the police chief, James Baylor. Chief Baylor suggested that Principal Gulch discuss the steroid

---

Margin notes:

This issue statement clearly lays out the basis of the law and some persuasive facts. Using "deadly steroids" is effective from a prosecutor's position because it makes the crime seem reprehensible. However, the last clause seems a bit out of place. Can you rewrite the sentence to make it less awkward?

This issue statement also has a good handle on the issues and the facts, but is a bit awkward grammatically.

Both issue statements seem to conclude that the defendant was in custody and was interrogated. Is that the impression you would like to start off with as the prosecutor? In addition, issue statements should not be conclusory.

Consider breaking this sentence into two in order to make it easier for the reader to understand.

Effective way to start out your facts—from the standpoint of the prosecution.

with the players on the football team. (Tr. 16.) Baylor also suggested that Mrs. Moxon might be able to help Principal Gulch with the interviews. (Tr. 16).

After learning of steroid use by school football players, Principal Gulch began interviewing every member of the school's football team to make sure that no student's life was in jeopardy. About one week after learning of the interviews, Mr. Harbor was asked to come to the principal's office. (Tr. 14.) Mr. Harbor expected to be called to the office because many of his teammates had related their discussion with Principal Gulch and [subsequent release.] (Tr. 28.). After arriving, Mr. Harbor remained outside the principal's office until his parents [were present.] During this time he spoke with Officer Brown, the school security officer stationed nearby at the school's main entrance. (Tr. 22.) [Mr. Harbor and Mr. Brown often spoke about football games, and Mr. Brown attempted to calm the slightly nervous Mr. Harbor. (Tr. 26.)]

Once Mr. Harbor's parents arrived, they accompanied Mr. Harbor into Principal Gulch's office. Principal Gulch informed the Harbors that he was trying to learn who had distributed steroids to team members. During the interview, Mr. Harbor's mother intervened on his behalf, adamantly denying his involvement. After thirty minutes, Principal Gulch asked the Harbors if Jonathan Moxon and his parents could enter the room. [Mr. and Mrs. Moxon were at the school to pick Jonathan up for a doctor's appointment to check for complications from the steroid use. (Tr. 17.). The Moxons asked Principal Gulch if he had any information they should know before they brought Jonathan to his appointment.] Principal Gulch had no information, but explained the procedure that would follow for testing all of the players and the possibility of canceling the football season. (Tr. 18.)

[The Harbors agreed without hesitation to Principal Gulch's question about the Moxons entering.] (Tr. 17.) Mr. Harbor's father adamantly announced that his son had nothing to hide. (Tr. 17.) Mr. Harbor had spoken with Mrs. Moxon earlier in the year about arranging a police escort for his team bus because he wanted to help out his team. While arranging the police escort, he mentioned that he liked to help out his teammates. Mr. Harbor also regularly witnessed Mrs. Moxon pick her son up from school while in full uniform after she finished work. (Tr. 27, 36.)

After learning of the suspensions that would result if no one admitted to distributing the steroids, Mrs. Moxon expressed to both boys that this steroid incident was causing many problems. (Tr. 18.) [As Principal Gulch

---

Margin notes:

The term "subsequent release" makes it seem as if they were held in custody.

arrived?

Good idea to nest this fact in the middle of this section.

Conciseness: Notice how you have the appointment in this sentence and in the previous sentence. Is there any way to condense and combine these two sentences to omit one reference to the appointment and cut down on the words?

Persuasive techniques. Effective choice of words.

Appointment?

Do you want to put this in quotes?

Then?

Your statement of facts tells a persuasive story. Work on tightening up the language to make it more concise. Also, work on making your theory of the case stronger—it is not clear to the reader exactly what your theory is from reading the facts.

RBO: Fifth Amendment

Persuasive technique: Effective way to address the Fifth Amendment. Don't forget to also cite to it.

Good uses of policy to persuade reader.

RBO: Lance Harbor not in custody or interrogated.

Do you need the roadmaps here, in the introduction to the argument? You do have them within the specific sections on custody and interrogation where the reader is more likely to need them.

spoke to his secretary about the next student and parents scheduled to discuss the steroids with him, Mrs. Moxon sought the sympathy of Mrs. Harbor.] Mrs. Moxon leaned over to Mrs. Harbor and mentioned that [it was a shame that players were letting her young son take all the heat.] She also mentioned that [she thought teammates looked out for the weaker players.] (Tr. 19, 32.)

[It was at this time that] Harbor blurted out that he had given the illegal and deadly steroid pills to Jonathan Moxon. (Tr. 32.) Hearing the confession, Mrs. Moxon quickly returned to her police officer duty and told Principal Gulch to call the police. (Tr. 19.) Previously, Mr. Harbor had been a confident academic and social leader. (Tr. 16.) In fact, he had been confident enough to walk out of a meeting with the athletic director and was a regular sight in the offices of upper-level school administration. (Tr. 33.)]

Argument

[The Fifth Amendment] does not require suppression of a confession when the suspect is not in custody or interrogated.] See Miranda v. Arizona, 384 U.S. 436 (1966). In Miranda, the Court was concerned with preventing coerced criminal confession in situations where the police used extreme psychological measures to extract confessions. Id. at 445. The Court's decision addressed situations such as the physical manhandling of a suspect that resulted in eight months of medical treatment, depriving a suspect of food until he confessed, and requiring a suspect to lie on a cold board and asking questions whenever the suspect looked tired. Id. at 446. However, the decision in Miranda was "not intended to hamper the traditional function of police officers in investigating crime." Id. at 476. Confessions remain a proper element in law enforcement. Id.

[Lance Harbor was not entitled to a Miranda reading because he was not in custody or interrogated.] First, Mr. Harbor should have known that his freedom was not restricted to the degree associated with formal arrest because [(1) he voluntarily attended the meeting and Mrs. Moxon did not tell him he could not leave the room, (2) he had information that he would be allowed to leave, (3) he had sufficient age and experience with Mrs. Moxon to know that his freedom of movement was not being restricted, and (4) he was not isolated or in a room with a police officer for a significant period of time.] Second, Mr. Harbor was not interrogated because

Mrs. Moxon should not have known that her comment would elicit an incriminating response from Mr. Harbor when (1) she had no knowledge of any susceptibility on his part and (2) she asked only one question and made one comment.

I. Mr. Harbor was not subject to formal arrest or a restraint on freedom of the degree associated with formal arrest when he voluntarily participated in a routine information gathering meeting in the principal's office accompanied by his parents.

[Mr. Harbor was not in custody because he should have known that he could leave the principal's office at any time.] The Supreme Court has held that custody is an objective test: whether under the totality of the circumstances a reasonable man in the suspect's position would believe he was subject to formal arrest or a restraint on freedom of the degree associated with formal arrest. <u>Stansbury v. California</u>, 511 U.S. 318 (1994); <u>Berkemer v. McCarty</u>, 468 U.S. 420 (1984). In weighing the totality of the circumstances, the Supreme Court has considered [(1) restraint on the suspect's freedom of movement through verbal direction or other means, (2) information the suspect has about his ability to leave, (3) the suspect's age and experience with the circumstances, and (4) whether the suspect was isolated and in a room with a police officer for a significant period of time.] <u>See</u> <u>Oregon v. Mathiason</u>, 429 U.S. 492 (1997); <u>Berkemer</u>, 468 U.S. 420. [Considering these circumstances, Mr. Harbor could not have reasonably believed he was in custody.]

A. There was no restraint on Mr. Harbor's freedom of movement because he came to the principal's office voluntarily and no one with the authority to arrest Mr. Harbor informed him that he could not leave.

[Courts have consistently found the absence of custody when the suspect, like Mr. Harbor, arrived voluntarily and was not informed by the police that he could not leave or subjected to physical restraints on his freedom of movement.] <u>See</u> <u>Berkemer</u>, 468 U.S. at 420; <u>Harris v. United States</u> 738 A.2d 269 (D.C. 1999); <u>United States v. Turner</u>, 761 A.2d 845 (D.C. 2000). [Just because a suspect is in a coercive environment does not mean he is in custody.] <u>Oregon v. Mathiason</u>, 429 U.S. 492 (1997). For example, in <u>Berkemer</u>, the defendant was pulled over for a traffic violation and asked questions for several minutes. The Supreme Court held that the suspect was not in custody because the officer did not inform the suspect that he could not leave. 468 U.S. at 438. Without a verbal or physical restriction on

RBO: Should have known could leave office.

You could make this roadmap much more persuasive. As a matter of fact, your roadmap located in the previous paragraph would be better placed here because it is persuasive and it sets up the analysis for custody in particular.

If your roadmap is persuasive, you should not need this sentence.

RBO: voluntary; not informed by police; physical restraints

Your topic sentence focuses the reader on the legal issues, but there are so many issues and the sentence structure makes it difficult to decipher. You could rewrite making it more concise or further break down the issues.

Good idea to set out the general rule of law. However, be careful—you sound a bit defensive here.

his freedom of movement, the suspect could not reasonably have believed that he was in custody. Id. Similarly in Harris, the defendant voluntarily accompanied the police to the police station without being told that he was under arrest or being placed in handcuffs. 738 A.2d at 272. The D.C. Court of Appeals, like the Court in Berkemer, held that defendant could not reasonably have believed that he was in custody without some explicit action by the police to restrict his freedom of movement. Id. at 275. Like the defendants in Berkemer and Harris, who had no restriction placed on their freedom of movement, Mr. Harbor was never told that he could not leave the room by Mrs. Moxon. To the contrary, Mrs. Moxon required Mr. Harbor's permission to enter the room. Moreover, Mrs. Moxon was leaving the conference shortly to take her son to the doctor. [Furthermore, like the defendant in Harris, Mr. Harbor voluntarily came to Principal Gulch's office.]

[If circumstances change,] a defendant who voluntarily comes to the police station might later be found to be in custody. [However, the circumstances never changed for Mr. Harbor.] In Turner, 761 A.2d at 845, the suspect had come to the station voluntarily. However, the court found that when the police executed a search warrant on the suspect his situation changed dramatically and he could reasonably have believed that he was now in custody. Id. [Unlike the defendant in Turner, who had a search warrant executed on him after his arrival, Mr. Harbor's situation did not change dramatically with the appearance of Mrs. Moxon because she requested permission to enter the room and focused her attention on her son's situation.] It would have been unreasonable for Mr. Harbor to believe that Mrs. Moxon was restricting his freedom to the degree associated with formal arrest because Mrs. Moxon did nothing more than walk into the room as a concerned mother.

B. Mr. Harbor could not have believed he was in custody when teammates had given him information that he would be allowed to leave after taking his turn in the routine discussion.

[Mr. Harbor could not have reasonably believed he was in custody because teammates had informed him that he would be allowed to leave after the discussion.] See Berkemer, 468 U.S. at 438; In re E.A.H., 612 A.2d 836 (D.C.1992). In Berkemer, defendant was stopped for a traffic violation and asked questions for several minutes. The Court held that the suspect was not in custody because the suspect should have known

---

Analysis: You do a good job of using two cases for case comparisons. You present the facts, reasoning, and holding of each case and then apply them to our case. This last sentence, however, seems to hang at the end without a concluding point to sum it all up for the reader.

RBO: changed circumstances

This is an effective way to deal with a counterargument. Short sentences, like this one, are often very persuasive.

Analysis: Here, again, you have a solid case comparison. The reader understands enough of the prior case and how it applies to Lance Harbor.

RBO: Informed he was allowed to leave.

This topic sentence clearly lays out the element to be discussed and does so persuasively.

that traffic stops are temporary and that typically suspects in his situation were released. 468 U.S. at 438. Similarly in E.A.H., a juvenile suspect was questioned after witnessing another suspect being questioned about the same event and subsequently released. 612 A.2d at 839. The court held that defendant could not have reasonably believed he was in custody after witnessing another suspect in the same situation be allowed to leave. Id. Like the defendant in Berkemer who should have known he could leave a traffic stop and the defendant in E.A.H. who had witnessed another suspect released after similar questioning, Mr. Harbor had information that he would be allowed to leave the meeting with Principal Gulch. Teammates who had already attended their meetings had told Mr. Harbor of their discussions with Principal Gulch and [subsequent release.] With this information about others in his situation who were allowed to leave, like the defendants in E.A.H. and Berkemer, Mr. Harbor could not reasonably have believed that he was in custody.

C. Football team captain Mr. Harbor had sufficient age and experience to know he was not in custody because he had witnessed Mrs. Moxon acting as Jonathan Moxon's mother in uniform.

[Mr. Harbor was a mature and confident seventeen-year-old who had interacted with Mrs. Moxon on numerous occasions so that his maturity, parental protection,] and experience should have made him adept at determining whether he was in custody. See E.A.H., 612 A.2d at 836; Haley v. Ohio, 332 U.S. 596 (1948). [First, Mr. Harbor's age and parental protection were sufficient to indicate he was free to leave.] In E.A.H., a fourteen-year-old boy was questioned in his bedroom by a police officer without his mother being present. The court held that being a boy of fourteen with no formal experience with the law was not sufficient for the juvenile to reasonably believe he was in custody. Id. Alternatively, in Haley, a fifteen-year-old boy was questioned for five hours in the middle of the night without his parents present. 332 U.S. at 599. [The Court held that because of the suspect's juvenile status he may have been awed by the situation when an adult would not have been. Id. The Supreme Court also pointed to the absence of the boy's parents as a reason that he may have believed he was in custody.] Id. In comparison, Mr. Harbor was at least two years older than the suspects in E.A.H. and Haley; in addition, he was at the top of his school class and consistently performed at athletic events in front of large audiences. [Unlike in E.A.H., where custody was still not found, Mr.

Be careful of your word choice. Subsequent release makes it sound like they were in custody at some point in time.

This case comparison makes your legal point clearly; however, you could probably tighten up the language to make it more concise.

RBO: 17-year old; maturity; parental protection; experience

Most of your word choice in this topic sentence is persuasive. However, there is a lot going on in this topic sentence. Consider breaking it down—maybe creating a mini-roadmap here for the reader. In addition, it is unclear to the reader what you mean by parental protection.

Your organization within this element is very helpful to the reader.

Here, you do a good job providing the law for the case comparison.

Harbor's parents were present and intervening on his behalf. His mother's adamant defense of her son should allay any of the Court's remaining fears that Mr. Harbor was a juvenile taken advantage of by the system. Mr. Harbor could not reasonably have believed he was in custody because he was a mature adult and his parents were by his side competently intervening on his behalf.]

Here, you are clearly tying the facts of our case to the prior cases.

[Second, Mr. Harbor had more [extensive experience] with the officers than the juveniles in E.A.H. and Haley, who had never met the officers who spoke with them.] [While] Mr. Harbor did not have experience with the legal system, he had many interactions with Mrs. Moxon in her officer status. He had spoken with Mrs. Moxon as a team representative and found her very friendly. Mr. Harbor had also witnessed Mrs. Moxon perform the motherly role that she was performing in Principal Gulch's office when she routinely picked Jonathan Moxon up from school in her uniform.

RBO: extensive experience

Again, good large-scale organization within this section.

"Although" is more appropriate than "while" because this sentence does not have to do with time.

[Finally, Mr. Harbor was confident in his dealing with upper-level school administration and was familiar with their offices.] [Mr. Harbor had gone so far as to walk out of the athletic director's office to express his disagreement with proposed disciplinary measures.] [Following E.A.H. and Haley, Mr. Harbor could not reasonably have believed he was in custody because of his maturity, parental protection, and experience with Mrs. Moxon.]

RBO: confident in dealing

This topic sentence does not focus the reader on a legal element.

Good start at this analysis. Are there any cases you can rely on to make your point?

Your mini-conclusion is a bit abrupt. Consider beefing up your argument in this paragraph before you conclude on this element.

D. Mr. Harbor was not isolated and questioned for a lengthy period of time because his parents were present and the discussion lasted less than an hour.

Mr. Harbor's confession did not occur in an isolated situation for a lengthy period of time because his parents were present and his discussion lasted less than one hour. See Berkemer, 468 U.S. at 438. [First, in Berkemer, the defendant was questioned at a traffic stop in public in full view of many people.] 468 U.S. at 438. The Supreme Court held that the suspect was not in custody because of the numerous people passing by. Id. Like the suspect questioned in public in Berkemer, rather than being isolated, Mr. Harbor was accompanied by his parents and another friend was in the room. Mr. Harbor's parents intervened on his behalf, and questions were not repeatedly directed at him but posed in a general manner.

Your organization within this element is very clear for the reader.

[Second, Mr. Harbor's less than thirty-minute discussion with Mrs. Moxon present was not of sufficient duration to lead a reasonable person to believe he was in custody.] See Oregon v. Mathiason, 429 U.S. 492 (1977);

RBO: 30-minute duration

Again, your organization is clear for the reader.

Beheler, 463 U.S. at 1123; <u>Turner</u>, 761 A.2d 845. [In <u>Mathiason</u>, the defendant was questioned for thirty minutes before confessing to a crime. 429 U.S. at 493. The Supreme Court held that the suspect was not in custody because thirty minutes of questioning was not a deprivation of freedom of action in any significant way.] <u>Id.</u> at 495. A similar thirty-minute discussion was held to be no restriction in freedom whatsoever in <u>Beheler</u>. 463 U.S. at 1123. In <u>Beheler</u>, the suspect was questioned by an officer at a police station for less than thirty minutes. <u>Id.</u> Finally, in <u>Turner</u>, the defendant was held to be in custody even though he was detained for only one hour. 761 A.2d at 848. The court's holding was not based on the duration of the detention but on the officer's execution of a search warrant that caused the suspect to believe he was restrained in his freedom of movement. <u>Id.</u>

Can you combine these two sentences to make it more concise?

RBO: length of time

[Like the [length of the suspect's time] in the police station in <u>Mathiason</u> and <u>Beheler</u>, Mr. Harbor was in a room with Mrs. Moxon for only thirty minutes. Furthermore, unlike the suspect in <u>Turner</u> who was detained for an hour, as discussed earlier, Mr. Harbor's situation did not change dramatically. Mr. Harbor could not have reasonably believed he was in custody, because he was in a room with Mrs. Moxon for less than thirty minutes and was not isolated because his parents were present and intervening on his behalf and a teammate was sharing in the discussion.]

Your case comparisons are effective because you provide facts, reasoning, and holdings from prior cases and compare them to our facts. You could tighten up the language to make this analysis more concise.

[Mr. Harbor was never told he could not leave the room, had knowledge that he would be allowed to leave, had sufficient maturity and experience to fully understand the situation, and was not isolated or in a room with an officer for a significant period of time. Mr. Harbor therefore could not reasonably have believed he was in custody.]

This mini-conclusion indicates to the reader that you are ending this section of the brief and it is written persuasively. Do you want to let the reader know that this is a totality of the circumstances standard?

II. Mr. Harbor was not interrogated because he was not subject to the functional equivalent of questioning when Mrs. Moxon should not have known that her comment about her son's unfortunate situation, addressed to another mother, would elicit an incriminating statement.

[Mr. Harbor was not interrogated because he was not subject to the functional equivalent of questioning by Mrs. Moxon.] <u>See</u> <u>Rhode Island v. Innis</u> 466 U.S. 291 (1980); <u>Stewart v. United States</u>, 668 A.2d 857 (D.C. 1995). [The Supreme Court has held that interrogation is any question or act that a police officer should have known would elicit a confession from the suspect.] Mr. Harbor was not subject to the functional equivalent of questioning because [(1) Mrs. Moxon had no knowledge of any susceptibility of Mr. Harbor, and (2) Mrs. Moxon's one broad question and one comment to Mrs. Harbor were not extensive or coercive.]

RBO: interrogation

You need a cite for this proposition.

This roadmap is effective because it provides the LSO for the analysis and is written persuasively. In addition, it is very concise.

Remember that the reader is not as familiar with the facts as you are. This topic sentence assumes the reader knows the facts and, therefore, is not as effective as it could be. It might help if you actually use the term "susceptibility" in your topic sentence to be specific.

This is a lot of information in one sentence for the reader to digest. Do you need it all or can you break it down into smaller sentences?

RBO: detective's encouraging words

Cite? Is this Stewart? The facts are unclear here; was he questioned in a jail cell? If this first sentence is from Stewart, it would help to combine it with the next sentence to make it more concise.

RBO: susceptibility

OK—if your point is to compare the "susceptibility" part of the cases, you don't need all the facts you have from the prior cases. Just focus on the susceptibility. Also, this is the first topic sentence in this subject where you finally use the term, "susceptibility."

This what? This sentence is unclear to the reader.

Can you tie any of these facts to the prior cases?

A. Mrs. Moxon did not have any knowledge of any susceptibility of Mr. Harbor.

[Mrs. Moxon should not have known that her comment would elicit Harbor's confession because she could not know that he would respond to a comment about looking out for weaker teammates.] See Innis 446 U.S. at 291; Stewart, 668 A.2d at 857. [In Innis, the defendant confessed to a crime after hearing a police officer mention to another police officer that the gun used in the murder defendant was suspected of committing could be found by one of the handicapped children at a nearby school.] Id. The Court held that defendant's confession, motivated by concern for the handicapped children's safety was not interrogation. Id. The suspect's confession was not the result of words or actions on the part of the police that they should have known were reasonably likely to elicit an incriminating response. The officers had no knowledge of the suspect's susceptibility to appeals to his conscience. Id. At 291.

[Following the same reasoning, the District of Columbia Court of Appeals held a [detective's encouraging words] to a suspect who had been questioned for hours and was held in a jail cell to be interrogation.] In Stewart, a detective spoke to a jailed suspect whom he had known from birth and who was in the same church. The court reasoned that, unlike the officers in Innis, the detective had knowledge of the suspect's susceptibility because the detective had an extensive relationship with the suspect since birth and because the defendant had already responded receptively to the detective's religious approach. 668 A.2d at 866.

[Like the officers in Innis, and unlike the detective in Stewart, Mrs. Moxon had no knowledge of any [susceptibility] of Mr. Harbor.] Mr. Harbor did not have the extensive, lifelong, relationship that the detective had with the defendant in Stewart. [While Mr. Harbor had mentioned that he liked to help out his teammates when he arranged a police escort to a game, this was not a comment Mrs. Moxon could relate to the situation in Principal Gulch's office.] [First, Mrs. Moxon could not reasonably extract from Mr. Harbor's offhand comment while helping his teammates arrive at a game in style that he would throw away his entire future and go to jail for a teammate. Second, Mrs. Moxon was in the office trying to gather information about her ill son; she was not concerned about Mr. Harbor. Acting as a concerned mother with no knowledge of any susceptibility of Mr. Harbor, Mrs. Moxon could not reasonably have known her comment would elicit an incriminating response.]

B. [Mr. Harbor was not asked a direct question or subject to extensive coercion when Mrs. Moxon asked one general question and made one comment to another mother.]

[Mr. Harbor was not interrogated because Mrs. Moxon did not ask Mr. Harbor a direct question or subject him to extensive coercion.] See Berkemer, 468 U.S. at 445; Innis, 446 U.S. at 291. The interrogations that Miranda addressed were those that lasted for fifteen hours or that did not end until the defendant made a confession. Miranda, 384 U.S. at 436. A modest number of questions by an officer is not interrogation. Berkemer, 468 U.S. at 445. Furthermore, in Innis, the Court held that there was no interrogation when police conducted a graphic discussion appealing to the defendant's conscience in the police car. Innis, 446 U.S. at 306. The Court reasoned that the brief conversation was not "a lengthy harangue in the presence of the suspect" that might have constituted interrogation. Id. at 303. Like the modest number of questions in Berkemer and the car conversation in Innis, Mrs. Moxon's comments were not extensive or coercive. Mrs. Moxon was pointing out only that the steroid problem could have drastic consequences, and she was appealing for comfort from another mother. Her comments could not have lasted for more than a few seconds, considerably less than the series of questions posed in Berkemer and most likely less than the graphic story conjured by the officer in Innis.

Furthermore, like the officer's comment in Innis, [Mrs. Moxon did not direct her comments to the defendant; they were directed to Mrs. Harbor.] If such general questions and comments made by a mother concerned only for her son are regarded as interrogation, any confession would be inadmissible if made after a police officer spoke.

[Mrs. Moxon should not have known that her comment would elicit Mr. Harbor's confession because, following Innis and Stewart, she had no knowledge of any susceptibility of Mr. Harbor and should not have been thinking of Mr. Harbor. Furthermore, following Innis and Berkemer, her comment was not extensive enough to constitute the functional equivalent of interrogation. Mr. Harbor was therefore not interrogated and did not require Miranda rights under the Fifth Amendment.]

Conclusion

The judgment of the Superior Court should be reversed.

Respectfully Submitted,

R.G.

Margin notes:

This argument seems stronger than the previous one. Consider discussing it first in this section.

RBO: No direct question or extensive coercion.

RBO: directed comments

This mini-conclusion effectively summarizes your arguments in this section.

D. Annotated Sample Brief 2: Draft Version with Comments

This sample has two parts: (1) a brief written as a draft with comments and (2) the same brief revised in its final form after incorporating the suggested comments from the draft.

Criminal No. 03-9051-F
DISTRICT OF COLUMBIA COURT OF APPEALS

UNITED STATES, Appellant

v.

Lance HARBOR, Appellee

ON APPEAL FROM THE SUPERIOR COURT FOR THE
DISTRICT OF COLUMBIA

BRIEF FOR APPELLANT—DRAFT
John Doe, Counsel
600 New Jersey Avenue, N.W.
Washington, D.C. 20001 (202) 662-0000

TABLE OF CONTENTS

Where's "B"? If you are going to have subheadings, you should have at least two. Otherwise, make your initial point heading broad enough to encompass what is under "A."

Again, where's "B"? Do you need subheading A? Doesn't it just repeat the idea presented in point heading II?

You do an effective job of conveying your point and including relevant facts in these 4 point headings. Could you reword point heading 2 to make it less awkward?

Can you avoid excess words like "thereof" in point heading III?

Also, is subheading 2 correct? Did defendant actually invite Moxon in, or simply indicate assent?

TABLE OF CASES

This is effective because you use facts to imply to the reader that the answer is "yes." However, the wording is awkward for the reader to get through—could you make it less entangling? Also, careful not to be conclusory in the issue statement.

STATEMENT OF THE ISSUES

[Whether the Superior Court erred in suppressing Defendant's confession of supplying illegal drugs to the high school football team when it found "custodial interrogation absent <u>Miranda</u> warnings" where the confession was voluntarily given during a meeting in the school principal's office during which defendant was free to leave and was asked no questions by the police?]

STATEMENT OF THE CASE

Does this need to be in the procedural history? Can this be conveyed in the facts?

[Lance Harbor, defendant, a student at West Canaan High School, confessed during a meeting with his parents, the parents of another student, and the school principal to supplying members of the school football team with an illegal steroid called Vitapro.] (Tr. 2, 19.) Defendant filed a pretrial motion to suppress his confession as a violation of his Fifth Amendment protection against self-incrimination, alleging that the confession was the result of custodial interrogation without <u>Miranda</u> warnings. (Tr. 2.) The Superior Court granted defendant's motion, and this appeal follows.

Facts

Good persuasive technique as a prosecutor to start out with the substance of the crime.

[On November 25, 2003, defendant confessed to supplying members of the West Canaan High School football team with Vitapro, an illegal steroid.] (Tr. 19.) Defendant's confession occurred in the school principal's office during a meeting with his parents and Robert Gulch, the school principal. (Tr. 15.) The meeting was called as part of Mr. Gulch's school disciplinary investigation about the source of the Vitapro found in another football player's equipment bag. (Tr. 10, 12.)

The school's investigation was initiated after Lea Moxon called Mr. Gulch on November 16, 2003, and reported finding a bottle of Vitapro in her son's football equipment bag. Her son told her "he got the bottle from a friend on the football team." (Tr. 10.) Mrs. Moxon was concerned because of recent reports about a star athlete at another high school being killed by harmful supplements. At Mr. Gulch's request, Mrs. Moxon brought the bottle to the school the next day. [Unsure of its contents and wanting to find out if it "was something that violated our school policy," Mr. Gulch called his "buddy" Jim Baylor, "who happens to be the chief

Do you want to downplay it this much? Throughout the course of events, Baylor acts in his official capacity as Chief of Police, so referring to him only as Mr. Baylor may be seen as ignoring some key points. Also, does it really help you to ignore his position? Does it hurt you to mention it?

of police," and asked Mr. Baylor if he knew of anything about steroid use in the area.] (Tr. 11.) Mr. Baylor provided no information, but offered to have the bottle tested to determine its contents. (Tr. 11.) [Mr. Baylor also suggested that Mr. Gulch start interviewing team members. Mr. Gulch was planning to interview team members already as part of his duties as school principal. (Tr. 11.)]

[Next, Mr. Gulch obtained a list of team members and began interviewing the players on November 18, but decided, after one interview, to wait until the contents of the pills had been identified to continue the player interviews. (Tr. 2, 13). On November 20, Mr. Baylor informed Mr. Gulch that the test results indicated the pills were illegal steroids. (Tr. 13.) At this point, the investigation became "a school disciplinary matter," and Mr. Gulch started scheduling appointments with team members and their parents. Mr. Gulch conducted numerous parent-student meetings the afternoon of November 20, all day on Friday the 21, and continuing on Monday and Tuesday. (Tr. 13-14.)]

Defendant and his parents were scheduled to meet on Tuesday, November 25, at 12:30. Defendant was called out of class at 12:30 and waited in the main office until his parents arrived. (Tr. 15.) While waiting, defendant talked with Wendell Brown, an officer stationed at the school's main entrance, near the principal's office. (Tr. 22, 29.) [Defendant was neither surprised at being called to the principal's office nor at the presence of his parents because he had been informed about the meetings by teammates and "didn't think it was any big deal."] (Tr. 28-29, 34-35.)

After defendant's parents arrived, Mr. Gulch apprised them about the serious situation and informed them that he "planned to talk to all the kids on the team to get to the bottom of it." (Tr. 15.) Defendant was never handcuffed, threatened with arrest, physically restrained from leaving, or told he could not leave; in addition, defendant never asked to leave. (Tr. 22, 24, 35.) [After about thirty minutes of "talking," Mrs. Moxon arrived at Mr. Gulch's office, with her husband and son. Mrs. Moxon is a police officer and was in her uniform when she arrived.] Mr. Baylor had told Mr. Gulch that he had asked Mrs. Moxon to participate in some of the interviews, [but the Moxons indicated they were there only to take their son to a doctor's appointment and wanted to ask Mr. Gulch a couple of questions.] Mr. Gulch asked and obtained the permission of defendant and his parents to allow the Moxons to join the discus-

---

Marginal notes:

Conciseness—could you condense these last two sentences?

Can you tighten up this paragraph to make it more concise?

This sentence is effective because it conveys part of your theory to the reader: the defendant knew what he was getting into.

This is an effective way to draw attention away from facts that work against you by hiding them in the middle of the paragraph.

Can you use language that is more formal?

sion. (Tr. 17.) Defendant knew Mrs. Moxon because she was the parent of his teammate and he was friendly with her, having previously asked her for a favor for the football team. (Tr. 27-28, 36.)

[Mrs. Moxon began asking Mr. Gulch numerous questions about the status of his investigation and requested a copy of the lab report. (Tr. 17.) Mrs. Moxon did not direct any questions to the defendant. (Tr. 35.) Mr. Gulch answered Mrs. Moxon's questions and announced that he was going to continue interviewing players and their parents until he found the source of the pills and the level of usage. In addition, Mr. Gulch stated that the team would be drug tested and any player with positive results would not be allowed to play. Further, Mr. Gulch indicated that if the matter was not resolved soon, the team would not be able to finish the season. (Tr. 18, 31-32.) At this point, Mrs. Moxon rhetorically asked her son and defendant, "Do you see what trouble this is causing?" (Tr. 18.)]

> Here again the reader sees more of your theory: the defendant was not forced against his will to remain in the presence of Mrs. Moxon, nor was he interrogated. Rather, he was in the room while a conversation was going on.

Between 1:30 and 1:45, Mr. Gulch's assistant called him to inform him the next student and set of parents were waiting, at which point Mrs. Moxon turned to defendant's mother and said, "If Mr. Gulch didn't find out who had given her son the pills, she was sure the police would find the player or players" and "it was a shame that players were letting her young son take all the heat." (Tr. 18-19, 32.) At this moment, defendant abruptly confessed: "Okay, okay, enough already. It was me, okay? I'm the one who gave Jonathan [Mrs. Moxon's son] the Vitapro." No one was speaking to defendant at the time, and neither Mr. Gulch nor Mrs. Moxon had asked him any question. (Tr. 19.) Upon hearing this, Mr. Gulch left the office, called the police, asked everyone to wait, and went outside to wait for the police. (Tr. 19.) At about 2:05, [Chief Baylor] arrived, arrested defendant, and issued a Miranda warning. (Tr. 6, 21.)

> Here you finally call him Chief Baylor. This can be confusing to the reader. Try to maintain consistency with your term usage.

> This is an effective statement of facts, albeit a bit long. You presented the facts completely yet persuasively, burying and choosing not to dwell on facts that work against your case. When you revise, you may want to tighten up the language a bit so that this section is more concise—leaving you more room for your analysis.

Standard of Review

Whether defendant was "subjected to custodial interrogation without the benefit of Miranda warnings is a question of law." Reid v. United States, 581 A.2d 359, 363 (D.C. 1990). Accordingly, the Court will "determine the ultimate question of law *de novo.*" Jones v. United States, 779 A.2d 277, 281 (D.C. 2001) (quoting In re E.A.H., 612 A.2d 836, 838 (D.C. 1992)).

Argument

[I. **THE SUPERIOR COURT ERRED IN RULING DEFENDANT'S CONFESSION INADMISSIBLE BECAUSE THE CONFESSION WAS NOT THE RESULT OF CUSTODIAL INTERROGATION ABSENT <u>MIRANDA</u> WARNINGS.**

    A. <u>Miranda applies only where there is both "custody" and "interrogation" at the same time.</u>

[In 1966, the Supreme Court outlined [the so-called] <u>Miranda</u> warnings as "concrete constitutional guidelines for law enforcement agencies and courts to follow" to adequately protect an individual's Fifth Amendment right against self-incrimination during "custodial interrogation." <u>Miranda v. Arizona</u>, 384 U.S. 436, 442, 444 (1966); U.S. Const. amend. V. A year later, the Court ruled that the Fifth Amendment protection and requisite <u>Miranda</u> warnings are equally applicable to juveniles. <u>In re Gault</u>, 387 U.S. 1, 55 (1967). However, as noted above, the "requirements of Miranda apply only if custodial interrogation has taken place; there must be both custody and 'interrogation' at the same time." [<u>See, e.g.</u> <u>Jones</u>,] 779 A.2d at 280.]

[An individual can be interrogated without <u>Miranda</u> warnings if he is not in custody, and, conversely, an individual may be taken into custody without <u>Miranda</u> warnings if he is not interrogated. The custodial interrogation requirement is conjunctive requiring both elements to be met in order for a <u>Miranda</u> warning to be required.] In the present case, defendant was neither in custody nor interrogated and, therefore, <u>Miranda</u> warnings were unnecessary and defendant's statement is admissible. The Superior Court erred in concluding otherwise.]

II. **DEFENDANT WAS NOT IN CUSTODY BECAUSE HE WAS NEITHER UNDER FORMAL ARREST NOR SIGNIFICANTLY DEPRIVED OF HIS FREEDOM OF ACTION, AND UNDER THE TOTALITY OF CIRCUMSTANCES, A REASONABLE PERSON WOULD NOT HAVE BELIEVED HE WAS SO DEPRIVED.**

A finding of custody requires a formal arrest or a "restraint on freedom of movement of the degree associated with formal arrest." <u>Resper v. United States</u>, 793 A.2d 450, 456 (D.C. 2000) (quoting <u>Stansbury v. California</u>, 511 U.S. 318, 322 (1994)). [In the present case, it is conceded that defendant was not under formal arrest, and the only question relevant

---

Margin annotations:

Avoid contentious language like this. You are not arguing that <u>Miranda</u> should be overturned.

Remember to check the Bluebook for correct punctuation of signals.

Can you be more concise in introducing the law? Is the history of <u>Miranda</u> important?

Do you need both these sentences? Don't they both say the same thing? Do you have a citation for this?

Do you need a separate point heading for this introduction? Your point heading indicates that you will be discussing why there was neither custody nor interrogation. However, you save that analysis for your later point headings.

This sentence need not be so wordy. Do you need the passive voice here?

A roadmap of the following subheadings (the factors you will be analyzing) would be helpful to the reader.

As per comments on table of contents, this heading A is not necessary—especially since you don't have a B. A roadmap here, instead, would provide the reader with the context before jumping into factors 1-4.

This topic sentence effectively introduces the topic of the analysis. Is there any way you can make it more persuasive?

Do you need to say this? Didn't you say all this above when you told the reader what the test was?

How does his capacity to commit a crime bear on the custody issue?

to custody is whether he was restrained to the degree associated with formal arrest.] Courts utilize an objective "totality of circumstances" test to make this determination, under which no reasonable person in defendant's place could have believed he was under formal arrest. Id. The defendant was not "physically deprived of his freedom of action in any significant way," and the circumstances could not lead "him to believe he [was] so deprived." Miley v. United States, 477 A.2d 720, 722 (D.C. 1984).

    A. Defendant was not in custody because a reasonable person, under the totality of circumstances, would not have understood the consensual meeting to constitute custody

        1. Defendant's age or inexperience do not create a presumption of custody because he was nearly an adult, of above average intelligence, familiar with the principal and all other involved parties, and in the company of his parents.

[There is no *per se* rule that a juvenile with no criminal history is automatically deemed to be in custody when being interviewed regarding illegal activity.] Defendant's age and experience "are but factors to be viewed in the totality of circumstances." Matter of W.B.W., 397 A.2d 143, 146 (D.C. 1979); see also In re M.A.C., 761 A.2d 32, 36 (D.C. 2000). While both W.B.W and M.A.C. concern a juvenile's ability to waive his Miranda rights, the totality of circumstances tests utilized by those courts can equally be applied to a determination of the relevant factors in deciding whether a juvenile was entitled to Miranda warnings. In M.A.C., the court considered the juvenile's "age, experience, education, background and intelligence, the circumstances under which the statement was given," as well as "the length of detention." M.A.C., 761 A.2d at 36. It is possible for particular factors indicating custody to be counterbalanced or mitigated by other factors indicating lack of custody. [It is a "totality" test.]

Under the totality of these factors, defendant's age and inexperience are inconsequential in determining custody. [First, defendant was 17, less than one year from majority, and is being tried as an adult, indicating that the courts believe defendant has the capacity of an adult to commit crime and necessitating an adult standard in criminal proceedings.] See, e.g., Gault, 387 U.S. at 50-51; In re D.H., 666 A.2d 462, 478 (D.C. 1995). Furthermore, defendant is of above average intelligence and participates in numerous "leadership" activities, which indicate a level of maturity and responsibility beyond that of an average juvenile. In addition, other circumstances surrounding the defendant's interview and confession further mitigate any misconceptions resulting from his age or inexperience and indicate that no reasonable person, of any age, could have believed he was in custody.]

> Could you make this analysis more effective by using case law to support your factual arguments? Are there any cases that speak to age or experience and its bearing on custody?

2. The meeting occurred in the school principal's office at the request of the principal, and defendant knew in advance the meeting was likely to occur, was aware of its purpose, attended voluntarily, and could have left at any time.

> Can you make this topic sentence sound (1) less defensive, and (2) less contentious (by not using words like "unreasonable")? Furthermore, the point heading indicates that voluntariness is not the only factor at issue in this analysis. How can your topic sentence effectively convey the entire topic of this analysis?

[It is unreasonable to hold that defendant believed his voluntary attendance at the meeting amounted to police custody.] The meeting was called by the principal, not the police, and occurred in the principal's office, not the police station. [While the courts of this jurisdiction have not ruled on "custody" within a school principal's office, [we contend] that the reasoning behind the Supreme Court's decision regarding search and seizure by school officials in New Jersey v. T.L.O., 469 U.S. 325 (1985), is equally applicable to questions of custody.] [In T.L.O., the Court ruled that school officials must have leeway in conducting internal, self-initiated investigations and are not constrained by the restrictions of the Fourth Amendment. T.L.O., 469 U.S. at 342. It is logical that the same leeway should be extended to the Miranda requirement in a school setting.] [In addition, the weight of persuasive authority from other jurisdictions explicitly states that school disciplinary or investigative meetings do not constitute custody.] [See, e.g., In re Navajo County Juvenile Action No. JV91000058, 901 P.2d 1247 (Ariz. Ct. App. 1995) (holding that student's meeting in the principal's office did not constitute custody, even if principal intended to report his findings to police).] [Furthermore, defendant was aware of the likelihood he would be asked to meet with the principal and knew the purpose of the meeting in advance.] Nothing in the facts indicates defendant believed the meeting was part of a police investigation or that he was required by the police to attend. The fact that the principal obtained defendant's permission prior to allowing Mrs. Moxon to join the meeting further confirms that the meeting was not under police control (discussed below). Finally, the principal testified that defendant was free to leave at any

> Would it be more effective to state the rule of law before discussing our facts in this section?

> What language can you use other than "we contend"? The court is not too concerned with what you think; rather, the court wants to know what the law is and should be.

> Why? These are two entirely different amendments. Is the court likely to draw from Fourth Amendment case law when Fifth Amendment case law is so extensive? The court enforces the rights of the two Amendments in different ways, and uses different theories to determine when the rights of each Amendment are activated.

> This argument is much stronger than the previous one, because it deals with the same legal issue that we are facing.

> This case seems to be very relevant. Therefore, it might be helpful to do a case comparison here.

> This appears to be your second legal factor, why isn't it in your topic sentence? Also, is there any law you can use to support the idea that this is a relevant legal factor?

Can you turn this into an effective case comparison? When you use a parenthetical, you are not effectively comparing it to our own case. Can you explain Johnson textually, and compare it to our own case?

1) This paragraph begins with a discussion of defendant's knowledge about the meeting, and then morphs into a discussion of whether or not defendant was told he could leave. What is the factor you are discussing? Are you discussing them both? Make sure this is clear to the reader. Also, you could use more case law in this argument. So far this is just a factual argument that incorporates a quotation from a case. Do any cases present the same rule of law you are arguing? Do any have fact patterns similar enough to our own such that you can draw a case comparison?

2) Can you make this sentence more persuasive? Try not to set up sentences in the format: "Even though A, we have B." It sounds as though you are conceding a weakness, and this is not the perception you want your reader to have, especially at the beginning of a paragraph. Although this sentence structure can work, here it doesn't sound as persuasive as it could.

Including the rule of law here would make the transition from your contention to the facts of Resper smoother. Further, the rule of law would give the reader a context in which to view the rest of this paragraph.

This is an effective argument because you interweave our facts with case law. This case comparison provides a basis for your application of the law to our fact pattern. Further, you managed to effectively include the arguments you made above (principal's office not as custodial as police office and defendant's advance knowledge of the meeting). Given that you have concisely included all the factors you mention in your point heading in this one paragraph, do you need the previous two paragraphs? With a case comparison in such good shape, you can now work on making it more concise by tightening up the language.

Is this in your fact section?

time, and defendant admits he was never handcuffed and that he never asked to leave. Although defendant was never told that he could leave, "neither was he told that he could not." Johnson v. United States, 616 A.2d 1216, 1229 (D.C. 1992) [(finding no custody when defendant was questioned for more than four hours at the police station).] In sum, the available facts demonstrate that defendant was never prevented from leaving, either physically or verbally, and was, therefore, not restrained to a degree associated with formal arrest.]

[Even assuming defendant erroneously believed the school principal was participating in a police investigation, the consensual nature of the meeting vitiates any notion of custody.] [In Resper, the court ruled that Resper was not in custody because he knew he was not under arrest and voluntarily went to the police station and agreed to speak to a police officer. Resper, 793 A.2d at 456. The court rejected the argument that Resper had no choice but to "agree" to go to the station because he knew he was not under formal arrest and no "reasonable person in his situation [would] have understood he was under arrest. Id. Similarly, defendant in the present case knew he was not under formal arrest and voluntarily agreed to attend the meeting. In addition, the only police presence, an off-duty police officer with whom defendant was familiar, occurred only after defendant's consent. The facts of the present case are far less extreme than Resper in that the meeting occurred in the principal's office at the principal's request and defendant was not questioned by the police. In addition, the advance warning defendant had about the meeting and its purpose mitigate any apprehension he may have had. The available facts when compared to those in the Resper case indicate it would be unreasonable to conclude that defendant was or thought he was in police custody.]

3. **Defendant's parents were present during the meeting and neither indicated concern about the legal status of defendant nor expressed indicated they thought the meeting was anything other than an internal school disciplinary meeting.**

The presence of defendant's parents is relevant in two respects. [First, defendant explicitly acknowledges that any restriction on his freedom to leave was the result of his parents' presence and not Mrs. Moxon's.] As such, any subjective belief harbored by defendant that he could not leave the meeting was not the result of police words or action and does not indicate defendant was in custody. [As stated in <u>Calaway v. United States</u>,] "what is determinative of custody is that the police have by word or conduct manifested to the suspect that he is not free to leave." 408 A.2d 1220, 1224 (D.C. 1979). [As noted above, the only perceived restriction on defendant's freedom was caused by the presence of his parents and Mr. Gulch, not the police. In admitting as much during in his testimony, defendant implicitly acknowledged that he was not in custody under the <u>Calaway</u> standard.]

[Second, defendant's parents also provided the defendant with a level of guidance and protection. Any intimidation allegedly felt by defendant as a result of Mr. Gulch or Mrs. Moxon's questions and statements, respectively, is likely to be mitigated by the presence of his parents. If defendant's age or inexperience reduced his capacity to determine the nature of the meeting, the presence of his parents serves to counteract this misconception.] [Defendant's parents gave no indication that they believed the principal was conducting a police investigation or that Mrs. Moxon was present as part of an investigation.] Absent any manifestation to the contrary, it must be assumed that defendant's parents believed the meeting was a normal part of a school investigation and that Mrs. Moxon's presence was coincidental and in the capacity of a parent. It is reasonable to hold that if defendant's parents did not believe defendant was in custody, their judgment, as defendant's guardians, is additional proof of the absence of custody.

4. **Mrs. Moxon entered the meeting, with the consent of defendant and his parents, and asked questions of the principal regarding her son and the school's investigation, as a concerned parent, not a police officer.**

[Although mentioned above, it is worth explicitly stating that Mrs. Moxon was not on official police business when she arrived at the principal's office.] Mrs. Moxon was acting in her capacity as a concerned parent, picking up her son from school, and asking for information and documents concerning her son's well-being. Defendant knew Mrs. Moxon as both a parent and a police officer, having talked to her and requested a favor from her for the football team in the past and, given this experience, is unlikely to have been intimidated by her. Furthermore, as noted above, any intimidation felt by defendant was likely to be

Conciseness: No need for this introductory clause. Start with the law and let the cite say where the quote came from.

It seems that the legal factor here is whether defendant felt free to leave (which you portray as a function of who is present in the room), not whether the parents were present. How can you convey this point to the reader before surprising her with it in the middle of the paragraph? Do you want to change your point heading and topic sentence? Do you want to make this point when you add a roadmap to the beginning of the Custody section?

These first three sentences seem to be part and parcel of the idea presented in the previous paragraph. Can you work them into that analysis?

Does the parents' perception matter? Isn't it from the point of view of the reasonable person? Why make this argument?

Avoid such an informal, conversational tone when writing court documents.

mitigated by the protective presence of his parents. Finally, Mr. Gulch asked the defendant's permission prior to Mrs. Moxon joining the meeting and Mrs. Moxon asked question directed at the principal only, indicating that the meeting was not under Mrs. Moxon's control and that her purpose in the office was not to question the defendant, which, when viewed in light of the other available information, indicates that it was unreasonable for defendant to believe that Mrs. Moxon exerted any custody over him or control over the situation.

[In light of the totality of circumstances, including the defendant's age, experience, the location and nature of the meeting, the presence of defendant's parents, and the coincidental presence of Mrs. Moxon acting in her parental capacity, no reasonable person could believed he was in police custody and any alleged restraint on defendant's liberty "did not approach a level comparable to that of a formal arrest."] [In re E.A.H., 612 A.2d 836, 839 (D.C.1992) (holding that police questioning of juvenile in his bedroom while conducting a search warrant did not constitute custody).]

III. DEFENDANT WAS NOT INTERROGATED BECAUSE THERE WAS NEITHER EXPRESS QUESTIONING BY THE POLICE NOR THE FUNCTIONAL EQUIVALENT THEREOF.

[We assert that because, as demonstrated in Part II, defendant was never in custody, an examination of interrogation is unnecessary. Nonetheless, it is worthwhile to further demonstrate that,] in addition to a lack of custody, there also was an absence of interrogation, leaving both prongs of the Miranda requirement unmet and rendering defendant's statement admissible.

Interrogation is defined as either express questioning by the police or "any words or actions on the part of the police "that the police should know are reasonably likely to elicit an incriminating response from the suspect." Rhode Island v. Innis, 446 U.S. 291, 301 (1980). The key component of either definition is role of the police. [Express questioning or its functional equivalent triggers a Miranda inquiry only when questioning (or its equivalent) is conducted by the police.] [In the present case, there was neither express questioning by the police nor the functional equivalent thereof.]

Margin annotations:

Can you use any law to support these factual arguments?

This mini-conclusion is effective. It might also work well in a roadmap paragraph earlier in this section.

You found E.A.H., do you think this case is relevant to your analysis of the defendant's status as a juvenile?

Conciseness: Is any of this necessary?

Do you need this sentence? The next sentence seems to convey the same point.

Can you roadmap A and B here for the reader?

A. [Defendant was not questioned by the police at all, but only by the school principal.]

1. **The school principal is neither an agent of the police nor acting in any police capacity, but only following normal procedure for investigating an internal school concern.**

[Mr. Gulch, the school principal, is not a police officer and was not acting in any police capacity.] Mr. Gulch was investigating a school safety and disciplinary concern on his own initiative. The fact that he asked Chief Baylor for advice and assistance does not indicate that he was acting at the police's behest or under police command. Mr. Gulch testified that he would have questioned the students regardless of Chief Baylor's suggestion to do so. [To put it simply, Mr. Gulch is not a police agent in any way.] [As such, any question or action attributed to him is irrelevant to an examination of interrogation.]

2. **Mrs. Moxon was not "on assignment" during the meeting, was known outside of her official capacity and invited into the room by defendant, and did nothing to indicate she was acting in her police capacity.**

[During the meeting with defendant, Mrs. Moxon was not "on assignment" and was not acting in her official capacity. Although she was asked to sit in on some of the principal's interviews with students, Mrs. Moxon was not assigned to participate in defendant's meeting specifically.] In fact, Mrs. Moxon's presence at defendant's meeting was a mere coincidence of timing in that defendant happened to be in the office when Mrs. Moxon came to pick up her son and obtain a lab report and other information from Mr. Gulch. Furthermore, the fact that Mr. Gulch asked defendant's permission before Mrs. Moxon joined the meeting indicates that Mrs. Moxon was neither required nor expected to be at the meeting.

The totality of circumstances indicates that Mrs. Moxon was neither acting as a police officer, nor viewed as one by defendant or his parents. [As noted in Part II,] defendant and his parents knew Mrs. Moxon previously, not because she was a police officer, but because she was the parent of defendant's teammate. Additionally, none of Mrs. Moxon's actions during the meeting indicated she was there as part of a police investigation. [For example, Mrs. Moxon asked Mr. Gulch for a copy of the lab results, something the police already had. In addition, she told defendant's mother that she was "sure the police would find the player,"

Margin notes:

Before you dive into the factors, consider providing the reader with some legal context and a roadmap to the factors within this subsection.

This is a strong, persuasive topic sentence.

This is redundant.

Is this analysis necessary? You have already stated that the express questioning or functional equivalent must be conducted by the police to constitute interrogation. Is there a case out there where interrogation was found when someone other than a police officer questioned the defendant? If so, you might want to bring that up and distinguish it, because right now it seems as though this section is unnecessary. If you do know of a case, you definitely want to mention it because even if the other side neglects to bring it up, the judge might and you don't want you argument to look incomplete.

You launch into a lot of facts here; however, the reader is left wondering if these facts are even legally relevant. What does the law say? It would help if you provide some legal context for your factual argument.

Surplus words.

Effective use of factual detail to make your argument.

You use the facts well to argue that Moxon was acting as a parent, not an officer. However, this argument could be much stronger if you had some case law to support it. Are there any cases you can analogize to? Do you think distinguishing from all those cases where police interrogation was found would help make your argument stronger?

Tone.

This is confusing. It sounds as though you're arguing that there is no police action, but even if there was, there was no direct questioning, and thus you must examine whether Moxon's statements were the functional equivalent of direct questioning. Do you think this would make more sense to the reader if you had a roadmap when you introduced the interrogation issue?

You could also use a roadmap here before you begin addressing the specific factors under B.

You?

Doesn't all this restate what was said above? The reader just read that part, you don't need to go into it again. Rather, stick to the issue raised in your point heading (and topic sentence).

LSO: This does not appear to be relevant to point heading 1. Point heading 1 makes the assertion that the confession was NOT the result of words or actions meant to elicit a statement. You don't appear to be arguing that point here. Rather, you are setting up the functional equivalent argument. Do you think this paragraph, followed by a roadmap detailing the factors you will be examining, would work better under point heading B?

Haven't you already argued that there was no direct questioning? Do you need to state it again? The same goes for your point heading. Also, does this topic sentence effectively convey the point you are going to make to the reader? How can you change it so that it does?

---

rather than stating "we will find the player," indicating that, at the time, she did not view herself as the police, but as a fellow mother. Finally, she did not arrest defendant after his confession but asked Mr. Gulch to call the police.] [In sum, all of Mrs. Moxon's actions indicate she was neither acting as a police agent nor trying to convince the defendant that she was. Mrs. Moxon was acting only as a parent, and, necessarily defendant's confession could not be the result of police interrogation.]

[For the above reasons, we are of the position that there was no police action whatsoever during defendant's interview.] [In the alternative, it is unequivocally established in the factual record that there was no express questioning of defendant by Mrs. Moxon, thus limiting the court's review to the consideration of whether Mrs. Moxon's general statements and questioning constituted the functional equivalent of express questioning.]

[B. <u>Defendant's statement was not the result of the functional equivalent of express questioning because it was not provoked by police actions that were reasonably likely to elicit an incriminating response.</u>]

1. **Defendant's confession was not the result of any words or action on the part of police that could objectively be considered reasonably likely to elicit an incriminating response.**

[As noted above, the principal's actions and questions are not at issue because he is not an agent of the police. Furthermore, we contend that Mrs. Moxon was not acting as a police agent and her actions are also excluded from [you.] [In the alternative, however, Mrs. Moxon's actions did not constitute the functional equivalent of express questioning because they were not reasonably likely to elicit an incriminating response.] Mrs. Moxon's intent is of secondary importance to a finding of interrogation, and the court must make "an objective evaluation of the normally foreseeable effect of [her] remarks viewed in context." <u>United States v. Brown</u>, 737 A.2d 1016, 1020 (D.C. 1999).]

2. **[Mrs. Moxon's statement to defendant's mother immediately preceding defendant's confession was neither a question nor the functional equivalent thereof as it was neither directed at defendant nor reasonably likely to elicit an incriminating response.**

[Defendant's confession was not preceded by any question or statement directed at him, but only by a statement by Mrs. Moxon to defendant's mother.] [Viewed objectively, the statement that she was "sure the police would find the player or players," that "it was a shame that players were letting her young son take all the heat," and that she "thought that teammates looked out for weaker players" cannot be deemed reasonably likely to elicit an incriminating response.] [First of all,] as noted above, Mrs. Moxon was not acting in a police capacity and D.C. courts have repeatedly held that juvenile responses to questions or statements from people other than the police are admissible.]

[For example, in Matter of C.P., this Court allowed a juvenile's confession given, after invoking his Miranda rights, in response to his mother's question to be admitted into evidence despite the fact that the police had expressly asked the mother to elicit a response from her son. 411 A.2d 643, 649 (1980).] [Similarly, in In re C.P.D., this Court held admissible a juvenile's confession made in response to a question by his stepfather.] [As noted above,] during the meeting, Mrs. Moxon was acting in the capacity of a concerned parent, not a police officer, as indicated by her purpose for being in the meeting [(to obtain information regarding her son)] and her assertion within the very statement in question that "the police," as opposed to "we," will find the player. [As such, the facts of this case can be easily compared to both C.P. and C.P.D., the only difference being that the defendant was not responding to a question from his own parent and the precipitating statement was not made at the police's request.] [These differences only lessen the likelihood that the Mrs. Moxon's statement was the functional equivalent of express questioning] and, therefore, was not interrogation.]

[Assuming for the moment that Mrs. Moxon was acting in her police capacity,] [the defense will likely argue that Mrs. Moxon was attempting to play on defendant's known susceptibilities stemming from his role as team captain and admission that it was his "job to help out the other players on the team."] However, such an argument is logically inconsistent. For Mrs. Moxon's statement to be reasonably likely to elicit an incriminating response, Mrs. Moxon would have had to suspect the defendant of supplying her son with drugs so as to have something to incriminate himself with. Yet, supplying a young player with drugs runs completely counter to defendant's alleged susceptibility toward helping out other players. Providing illegal and dangerous drugs to a young and naïve player cannot possibly be viewed as helping him. The

---

Margin annotations:

Are all of these statements in your fact section? If not, be sure to add them in.

Wordy: First?

Is there a second part to your argument? Citation? Preferably more than one case, as you have referenced D.C. courts in this sentence.

If you do a reader-based outline here, it will be difficult to come up with a word or two to describe this topic sentence. What is your point in this paragraph?

Citation?

Notice how you keep having to refer to "above." If you change your LSO so that the law is provided as a context first, you can then use the facts of our case just one time for comparison. There will be no need to "refer to above." This will make for better LSO, clearer analysis, and more concise writing.

If it is not important enough for the text, you probably don't need it at all. If it is important to make your point, take it out of the parenthetical.

This sentence is very wordy.

Why?

This specific argument seems to stem from your premise that Moxon was NOT acting as a police officer. Isn't everything under point heading B analyzing functional equivalent from the standpoint of Moxon as a police officer? Why do you choose to place this analysis under this point heading?

Isn't that what we're doing under this point heading?

Why even bring up the defense's argument in this manner? It is important to address opposing legal arguments, but can you address them in a more persuasive manner?

two aspects of the [statement-confession nexus] are mutually exclusive. Mrs. Moxon's statement is reasonably likely to elicit an incriminating response only if the defendant was particularly sensitive to the well-being of other players; [yet, providing drugs to teammates, the suspicion of which would have had to precede Mrs. Moxon's statement in order for an incriminating response to be likely, indicates a disregard for the well-being of teammates.]

Finally, Mrs. Moxon's statement to defendant's mother was wholly unrelated to the defendant. [Assuming Mrs. Moxon was acting in her police capacity, the statement can be likened to the dialogue between an officer and a third party to which defendant's response was "neither invited nor expected."] Spann v. United States, 551 A.2d 1347, 1349 (D.C. 1988). [In Spann, the police were conducting an interview within earshot of Spann, to which Spann responded with a confession.] It was not the intention of the police in Spann to provoke a response from the defendant, and the mere fact that he happened to overhear a private conversation does not make the police action's the functional equivalent of interrogation. Id. Similarly, Mrs. Moxon's remarks were made solely to defendant's mother and cannot be viewed as an interrogation of the defendant. [Mrs. Moxon purposefully leaned close to defendant's mother before making the statement and nothing indicates her remarks were intended to be heard by the defendant, and, therefore, Mrs. Moxon's statement cannot be deemed likely to elicit an incriminating response from the defendant.]

3.   Defendant's confession was entirely voluntary and not the result of police action likely to elicit an incriminating response and, accordingly, is not barred by the Fifth Amendment.

Defendant's confession was entirely [voluntary] and "volunteered statements of any kind are not barred by the Fifth Amendment." Miranda, 384 U.S. at 478. The confession was either entirely spontaneous, unrelated to any question or statement, or a voluntary response to a statement by Mrs. Moxon, in her parental capacity, to the defendant's mother. At worst, the confession occurred during a consensual encounter with the police and was a voluntary response to a statement by a police officer to defendant's mother that was not reasonably likely to elicit an incrimi-

---

Margin annotations:

What exactly is the statement-confession nexus? Is this just your term for "reasonably likely to elicit an incriminating response" or is this something else? If it is the former, try to continue using the court's language. Unless this is a relatively new legal issue, it is not a good idea to create your own legal terms.

Can you support this with law?

Before comparing to a case, do you think the reader would like you to state the relevant rule of law here?

Citation?

Can you shorten this sentence so that it is easier for the reader to understand? Also, a mini-conclusion would be very effective here.

This is the first time in your analysis under heading II that you use words like "voluntary." Is it a different issue/factor than the ones you discussed previously? If not, then do you want to use terms that you have used throughout your analysis so that the reader doesn't get confused with the introduction of a new one?

nating response. As this Court plainly stated in <u>Lewis v. United States</u>, "voluntary responses offered by someone during a consensual encounter with the police are admissible." 767 A.2d 219, 221 (2001). [In sum, defendant's voluntary confession was not the result of police interrogation and is admissible in the absence of <u>Miranda</u> warnings.]

This seems to be summarizing the points you made under point headings A and B. Do you think this should be under point heading C?

CONCLUSION

For the above stated reasons, the Superior Court's granting the motion to suppress defendant's confession should be reversed.

Respectfully Submitted,

_____

John Doe

_____

END COMMENTS

John,

The comments below and in the margins are meant to serve as a springboard for your rewriting and revising processes.

LARGE-SCALE ORGANIZATION

As in the memo, roadmap paragraphs serve to guide the reader through your analysis. Pointheadings and topic sentences function in the same way. Adding roadmap paragraphs to your analysis would be very helpful to the reader. For example, before actually going into your analysis of Interrogation (beginning p. 13), wouldn't it be helpful to include a roadmap of subheadings A and B before going into the analysis in subheading A? Similarly, mini-roadmaps underneath subheadings A and B would make the analysis underneath them easier to follow. It is important that your pointheadings and topic sentences accurately convey the discussion beneath them. Specifically, they should tell the reader what legal factor(s) you will be analyzing. In several places, your pointheadings/topic sentences do not match up with the subsequent analysis. As you revise, make a reader-based outline of your pointheadings and a separate reader-based outline of your topic sentences. Check to see that each outline matches up with the order and substance of your analysis, and that each outline matches up with the other; they should be pretty much parallel.

ANALYSIS

Generally, you need to add more support to your analysis through greater use of case law. You have a strong grasp on the facts of our case and are able to use the specific details to make strong factual arguments. However, without case law, these arguments are not as effective as they could be and will be hard-pressed to stand up to opposing counsel's arguments. When you do use case law, you must use law that addresses the legal issue we are addressing. This is very important. You should not use Fourth Amendment case law to argue a Fifth Amendment case without a very convincing reason. Similarly, you should not use a case regarding waiver of <u>Miranda</u> rights when we are addressing the issue of whether <u>Miranda</u> warnings were even necessary without explaining to the judge why that case should apply. Also, when you do use case comparisons, remember to include the general rule of law. The first thing the reader usually wants to know is the rule of law. Then, when you give the facts, holding, and reasoning, the reader can understand the context in which you are presenting and analyzing them.

PERSUASIVENESS

You maintain a persuasive stance throughout your brief. You effectively play up the facts that work in our favor, while drawing attention away from (but not ignoring) those facts that do not. Some of your topic sentences could be more persuasive, however. While you still want to address the major counterarguments that will be made against, you don't want to give weight to those arguments. This is not an objective memo where you need to weigh the arguments and then choose the winning side. Rather, you must convince the judge that your arguments are the winning arguments and that opposing counsel's arguments are not valid. On a related point, you must remember to keep your tone professional. In several places throughout your brief, you write in a very conversational manner. Remember, this is a judge you are addressing. Using colloquialisms and informal language is inappropriate. They also unnecessarily add words to your document. You also want to refrain from phrases such as "we contend"; this only waters down your argument. The court does not want to know what you and your co-counsel think. The court wants to know what it should do under the law.

CONCISENESS

As noted above, removing the conversational tone from your language should cut down on the number of words you are using. You also want to avoid unnecessarily repeating yourself, as you do in a few areas. Also, some of your analysis is repetitive. When you reread your brief, check for redundancies. Examine all of your arguments and see if they are actually new arguments or merely restating or extending what was already said. If it is a restatement, eliminate it. If it is an extension of the previous argument, you probably can condense the two. You also want to avoid reminding the reader what you said in the previous pointheading because of space constraints and because that's what pointheadings are for. If the reader wants to remind herself what your argument was about Moxon's status as a police officer vs. parent, the reader will revisit that pointheading.

POLISHING

You have a few minor grammatical and typographical errors that can be easily fixed through more careful proofreading. You also have some citation placement errors. My comments are not exhaustive, so you want to do a separate edit for these types of errors as you polish your document.

The above comments are meant to supplement, not substitute, the margin comments. Please refer to both when rewriting. I look forward to reading your final draft. As always, feel free to come to me if you have any questions.

E.   Annotated Sample Brief 2: Revised Final Version

Criminal No. 03-9051-F

DISTRICT OF COLUMBIA COURT OF APPEALS

UNITED STATES, Appellant
v.

Lance HARBOR, Appellee

ON APPEAL FROM THE SUPERIOR COURT FOR THE
DISTRICT OF COLUMBIA

BRIEF FOR APPELLANT

John Doe, Counsel for Appellant

600 New Jersey Avenue, N.W.

Washington, D.C. 20001

(202) 662-0000

TABLE OF CONTENTS

TABLE OF CASES

STATEMENT OF THE ISSUES

Whether the Superior Court erred in suppressing Defendant's confession to supplying illegal drugs to the high school football team when the confession was made during a meeting in the school principal's office during which Defendant was permitted to leave and was asked no questions by the police.

STATEMENT OF THE CASE

Defendant filed a pretrial motion to suppress his confession as a violation of his Fifth Amendment protection against self-incrimination, alleging that the confession was the result of custodial interrogation without <u>Miranda</u> warnings. (Tr. 2.) The Superior Court granted Defendant's motion, and this appeal follows.

FACTS

On November 25, 2003, Lance Harbor (Defendant) confessed to supplying members of the West Canaan High School football team with Vitapro, an illegal steroid. (Tr. 19.) Defendant's confession occurred in the school principal's office during a meeting with his parents and Robert Gulch, the school principal. (Tr. 15.) The meeting was called as part of Mr. Gulch's school disciplinary investigation about the source of Vitapro found in another football player's equipment bag. (Tr. 10, 12.)

The school's investigation was initiated after Lea Moxon called Mr. Gulch on November 16, 2003, and reported finding a bottle of Vitapro in her son's football bag. Her son told her "he got the bottle from a friend on the football team." (Tr. 10.) Unsure of the bottle's contents, and concerned because of the supplement-related death of a student at another local school, Mr. Gulch called Jim Baylor, the West Canaan chief of police, who offered to have the bottle tested to determine if it was something that violated "school policy." (Tr. 11.) Chief Baylor also suggested that Mr. Gulch start interviewing team members, which Mr. Gulch was planning to do already as part of his duties as school principal. (Tr. 11.)

On November 20, Mr. Baylor informed Mr. Gulch that the pills were illegal steroids. (Tr. 13.) At this point, the investigation became "a school disciplinary matter," and Mr. Gulch renewed his interviews with team members and their parents. (Tr. 13-14.) Defendant and his parents were scheduled to meet on November 25. Defendant was called out of class at 12:30 and waited in the main office until his parents arrived. (Tr. 15.) While waiting, Defendant talked with Wendell Brown, an officer stationed at the school's main entrance, near the principal's office. (Tr. 22, 29.) Defendant was neither surprised at being called to the principal's office nor at the presence of his parents because he had been informed about the meetings by teammates and "didn't think it was any big deal." (Tr. 28-29, 34-35.)

After Defendant's parents arrived at 12:45, Mr. Gulch apprised them of the serious situation and informed them that he planned to talk to all the kids on the team to get to the bottom of it. (Tr. 15.) Defendant was never handcuffed, threatened with arrest, physically restrained from leaving, or told he could not leave; in addition, Defendant never asked to leave and admits that any reluctance to leave was solely the result of the presence of his parents and Mr. Gulch. (Tr. 22, 24, 30, 35.) After about thirty minutes of "talking," Mrs. Moxon arrived at Mr. Gulch's office, with her husband and son. (Tr. 16.) Mrs. Moxon is a police officer and was in her uniform when she arrived. While Chief Baylor had told Mr. Gulch that he had asked Mrs. Moxon to participate in some of the interviews, Mrs. Moxon indicated she was there only to take her son to a doctor's appointment and ask Mr. Gulch some questions. (Tr. 16-17, 31.) Mr. Gulch asked and obtained the permission of Defendant and his parents to allow the Moxons to join the discussion. (Tr. 17.) Defendant was friendly with Mrs. Moxon because she was the parent of his teammate and he had previously asked her for a favor for the football team. (Tr. 27-28, 36.)

Mrs. Moxon began asking Mr. Gulch numerous questions about the status of his investigation and requested a copy of the lab report. (Tr. 17.) Mrs. Moxon did not direct any questions to the Defendant. (Tr. 35.) Mr. Gulch answered Mrs. Moxon's questions and announced that he was going to continue interviewing players and their parents until he found the source of the pills. In addition, Mr. Gulch stated that the team would be drug tested and indicated that if the matter was not resolved soon, the team would not be able to finish the season. (Tr. 18, 31-32.) At this point, Mrs. Moxon rhetorically asked her son and Defendant, "Do you see what trouble this is causing?" (Tr. 18.)

Between 1:30 and 1:45, Mr. Gulch's assistant called to inform Mr. Gulch that the next student and set of parents were waiting, at which point Mrs. Moxon turned to Defendant's mother and said, "If Mr. Gulch didn't find out who had given her son the pills, she was sure the police would find the player or players" and "it was a shame that players were letting her young son take all the heat." (Tr. 18-19, 32.) At this moment, Defendant abruptly confessed: "Okay, okay, enough already. It was me, okay? I'm the one who gave Jonathan [Mrs. Moxon's son] the Vitapro." No one was speaking to Defendant at the time, and neither Mr. Gulch nor Mrs. Moxon had asked him any question. (Tr. 19.) Upon hearing this, and at Mrs. Moxon's suggestion, Mr. Gulch left the office and called the police. (Tr. 19.) At about 2:05, Chief Baylor arrived, arrested Defendant, and issued a Miranda warning. (Tr. 6, 21.)

STANDARD OF REVIEW

Whether Defendant was "subjected to custodial interrogation without the benefit of Miranda warnings is a question of law." Reid v. United States, 581 A.2d 359, 363 (D.C. 1990). Accordingly, the Court will "determine the ultimate question of law de novo." Jones v. United States, 779 A.2d 277, 281 (D.C. 2001) (quoting In re E.A.H., 612 A.2d 836, 838 (D.C. 1992)).

ARGUMENT

In 1966, the Supreme Court outlined the <u>Miranda</u> warnings as "concrete constitutional guidelines for law enforcement agencies and courts to follow" in order to adequately protect an individual's Fifth Amendment right against self-incrimination during "custodial interrogation." <u>Miranda v. Arizona</u>, 384 U.S. 436, 442, 444 (1966); U.S. Const. amend. V. In order to trigger the <u>Miranda</u> requirements, "there must be both 'custody' and 'interrogation' at the same time." <u>Jones</u>, 779 A.2d at 280. In the present case, Defendant was neither in custody nor interrogated and, therefore, <u>Miranda</u> warnings were unnecessary and Defendant's confession is admissible. The Superior Court erred in concluding otherwise.

> **I. Defendant was not in custody because he was neither under formal arrest nor significantly deprived of his freedom of action, and, under the totality of circumstances, a reasonable person would not have believed he was so deprived.**

Defendant was not in police custody. A finding of custody requires a formal arrest or a "restraint on freedom of movement of the degree associated with formal arrest." <u>Resper v. United States</u>, 793 A.2d 450, 456 (D.C. 2000) (quoting <u>Stansbury v. California</u>, 511 U.S. 318, 322 (1994)). In the present case, Defendant concedes he was not under formal arrest, making the only relevant question whether he was restrained to the degree associated with formal arrest. Courts utilize an objective "totality of circumstances" test to make this determination. <u>Id.</u> In the present case, the totality of circumstances, including (1) the Defendant's age and experience, (2) the location and nature of the meeting, (3) the presence of Defendant's parents, and (4) the coincidental presence of Mrs. Moxon acting in her parental capacity, indicate that no reasonable person in Defendant's position could have believed he was in police custody because any alleged restraint on Defendant's liberty "did not approach a level comparable to that of a formal arrest." <u>E.A.H.</u>, 612 A.2d at 839.

> A. <u>Defendant's age or inexperience are but factors to be viewed in the totality of circumstances and do not create a presumption of custody.</u>

There is no *per se* rule that a juvenile with no criminal history is automatically deemed to be in custody when being interviewed regarding illegal activity. Defendant's age and experience "are but factors to be viewed in the totality of circumstances." <u>Matter of W.B.W.</u>, 397 A.2d 143, 146 (D.C. 1979); <u>see also</u> <u>E.A.H.</u>, 612 A.2d at 838-39. For example, in <u>E.A.H.</u>, this Court acknowledged that, in the case of juveniles, while courts may apply "a wider definition of custody," it is unnecessary to interject age into the objective reasonable person test for custody when other factors outweigh any effect of the defendant's age or inexperience. <u>Id.</u> at 839. The fourteen-year-old defendant in <u>E.A.H.</u> was questioned by police inside his home during the execution of a search warrant, while officers blocked the doorway, preventing him from leaving during the search. Despite this overt restriction on his freedom and the defendant's age, the court found that E.A.H. was not in custody because he was not handcuffed, no weapons were drawn, the questioning took place in a familiar environment "within earshot" of his family, and his stepbrother had been questioned previously and was not arrested. Id. Similarly, the Defendant in this case was not handcuffed and his family was "within earshot" of the conversation. Therefore, Defendant was not in custody despite his relative age and inexperience.

B. <u>A reasonable person, in Defendant's position, would have felt free to leave the meeting because it occurred in the principal's office, and Defendant knew of the meeting in advance, was aware of its purpose, and was not physically or verbally restrained from leaving.</u>

Given the location, purpose, and Defendant's advance knowledge of the meeting, as well as the lack of physical or verbal restraint, no reasonable person in Defendant's position could have believed the encounter constituted police custody or that he was not free to leave. The meeting was called by the principal, not the police, and occurred in the principal's office, not the police station. While the courts of this jurisdiction have not yet ruled on the question "custody" within a school principal's office, the Supreme Court has ruled that the rigid enforcement of constitutional requirements would hinder the ability of school officials to conduct internal disciplinary investigations. <u>New Jersey v. T.L.O.</u>, 469 U.S. 325, 342 (1985) (holding that warrantless searches by school officials do not violate the Fourth Amendment).

In addition, the weight of persuasive authority indicates that school disciplinary or investigative meetings do not constitute custody. <u>See, e.g.</u>, <u>In re Navajo County Juvenile Action No. JV91000058</u>, 901 P.2d 1247 (Ariz. Ct. App. 1995) (holding that student's meeting in the principal's office did not constitute custody, even if principal intended to report his findings to police); <u>In re Drolshagen</u>, 310 S.E.2d 927 (S.C. 1984) (holding that questioning of a student in a high school "principal's office, in the presence of police officers, did not render it a custodial interrogation"). In addition, Defendant was aware of the likelihood he would be asked to meet with the principal and knew the purpose of the meeting in advance. Nothing in the record indicates Defendant believed the meeting was part of a police investigation or that he was required by the police to attend.

Furthermore, the principal testified that Defendant was free to leave at any time, and Defendant admits he was never handcuffed or threatened with arrest and that he never asked to leave. In <u>Johnson v. United States</u>, the court held that the defendant was not in custody despite being questioned at the police station for four and one-half hours. 616 A.2d 1216, 1229 (D.C. 1992). The court reasoned that "although defendant was never told that he could leave, neither was he told that he could not." The suspect was not handcuffed or threatened with arrest, and never requested to leave, while the police never said anything to make him feel as though he was in custody. As such, the location and length of time of the questioning were insufficient justification to find custody. <u>Id.</u> Similarly, Defendant in the present case never asked to leave, was not handcuffed or threatened with arrest, and neither the principal nor Mrs. Moxon said anything to indicate he was not free to leave. Furthermore, Defendant's meeting was three and one-half hours *shorter* than that in Johnson and took place in the principal's office, a notably less coercive environment than a police station. In sum, the available facts demonstrate that Defendant was never prevented from leaving, either physically or verbally, and was, therefore, not restrained to a degree associated with formal arrest.

C.   The consensual nature of the meeting and the presence of Defendant's parents militate against a finding of custody.

Even assuming Defendant erroneously believed the school principal was participating in a police investigation, the consensual nature of the meeting vitiates any notion of custody. In Resper v. United States, the court ruled that Resper was not in custody because he knew he was not under arrest and voluntarily went to the police station and agreed to speak to a police officer. 793 A.2d at 456. The court rejected the argument that Resper had no choice but to "agree" to go to the station, despite the fact that the police had intimated that Resper's car had been identified at a murder scene, because no "reasonable person in his situation [would] have understood he was under arrest." Id.

Similarly, Defendant in the present case voluntarily agreed to attend the meeting and could not have reasonably believed he was under formal arrest. In addition, Defendant was not accused of involvement in any crime, as was the case in Resper, but was questioned only as part of a general investigation. Furthermore, the meeting occurred in the principal's office, at the principal's request, and the only police presence, an off-duty police officer with whom Defendant was familiar, occurred only after Defendant's consent. Finally, the advance warning Defendant had about the meeting and its purpose militate against any misapprehension he may have had. As such, Defendant was not in police custody because he was not under formal arrest and the meeting was wholly consensual.

Finally, the presence and impact of Defendant's parents during the meeting further indicate Defendant was not in police custody. First, the presence of Defendant's parents creates a presumption of protection from police coercion, further mitigating any particular susceptibility of Defendant due to his age or inexperience. Second, according to his testimony, the weight of parental authority made Defendant reluctant to leave the meeting. While this may explain why Defendant never asked to leave, despite being free to do so, it does not create a level of restraint of the degree associated with formal arrest. Determination of custody requires that "*the police* have by word or conduct manifested to the suspect that he is not free to leave." Calaway v. United States, 408 A.2d 1220, 1224 (D.C. 1979) (emphasis added). In Calaway, the court held that a suspect was not in custody when he was questioned at a police station because *the police* had not created an "atmosphere of significant restraint." Id. At 1224-25. In the present case, Defendant explicitly acknowledges that his reluctance to leave was the result of his parents' presence (in addition to Mr. Gulch), and not the police (Mrs. Moxon). As such, the erroneous belief harbored by Defendant that he could not leave the meeting was not the result of police words or action. In admitting as much during his testimony, Defendant implicitly acknowledged that he was not in custody under the Calaway standard. This admission, coupled with the consensual nature of the meeting, precludes a finding of custody.

> D. Mrs. Moxon entered the meeting, with the consent of Defendant and his parents, and asked questions of the principal regarding her son and the school's investigation, as a concerned parent, not a police officer.

Mrs. Moxon, the *only* police presence during the meeting, was not on official police business when she arrived at the principal's office. Rather, she was acting in her capacity as a concerned parent, explicitly stating that she was there to pick up her son from school, and request information and documents concerning her son's well-being. Defendant knew Mrs. Moxon as both a parent and a police officer, having talked to her and requested a favor from her for the football team in the past and, given this experience, is unlikely to have been intimidated by her. Furthermore, any intimidation felt by Defendant was likely to be mitigated by the protective presence of his parents. Additionally, Mr. Gulch asked the Defendant's permission prior to Mrs. Moxon joining the meeting, and Mrs. Moxon asked questions of the principal only, further indicating that the meeting was not under Mrs. Moxon's control. Finally, after Defendant's confession, Mrs. Moxon did not arrest Defendant herself, but suggested that the police be called, indicating she was not acting in an official capacity. While the courts of this jurisdiction have not had the opportunity to rule on the question of when an off-duty police officer is acting in her official capacity, it seems reasonable that the presence of an off-duty police officer who gives no "significant indicia of official power" should not be sufficient for a finding of police custody. See Commonwealth v. Tynes, 510 N.E.2d 244 (Mass. 1987).

When viewed in their totality, the circumstances surrounding Defendant's confession indicate he was not in police custody. Defendant's age, the presence of his parents, the benign location of the meeting, Defendant's advance knowledge of the meeting, the lack of physical or verbal restraint on his liberty, and the absence of official police presence, taken together, indicate that no reasonable person, in Defendant's position, could have believed he was under formal arrest. Because Defendant was not in police custody, the Miranda warning was not required, and Defendant's confession is admissible.

> II. Defendant was not interrogated because there was neither express questioning by the police nor its functional equivalent, and his confession was entirely voluntary

In addition to a lack of police custody, the present case demonstrates an absence of police interrogation, leaving both prongs of the Miranda requirement unproven and rendering Defendant's statement admissible. Interrogation is defined as either express questioning by the *police* or "any words or actions on the part of the *police* "that the *police* should know are reasonably likely to elicit an incriminating response from the suspect." <u>Rhode Island v. Innis</u>, 446 U.S. 291, 301 (1980) (emphasis added).

In the present case, there was neither express questioning by the police nor its functional equivalent. In fact, Defendant was not questioned by the police at all. Furthermore, even if it is determined that Mrs. Moxon was acting as a police officer, she never expressly questioned the Defendant, and the statements she made cannot be considered the functional equivalent of express questioning because they were not intended for the Defendant to hear and were not reasonably likely to elicit an incriminating response from him.

    A. <u>Defendant was not questioned by the police at all.</u>

The police did not question the Defendant. First, Mr. Gulch is not a police official. Second, Mrs. Moxon was not acting in her police capacity during the meeting.

    1. Mr. Gulch is not an agent of the police, and his actions are irrelevant to a determination of interrogation.

Mr. Gulch, the school principal, is not a police officer and was not acting in any police capacity. Rather, he was investigating "a school disciplinary matter" on his own initiative. The fact that he asked Chief Baylor for advice and assistance does not indicate that he was acting at the police's behest or under police command. Mr. Gulch testified that he would have questioned the students regardless of Chief Baylor's suggestion to do so. On the rare occasion where a court has found interrogation by non-police actors sufficient to trigger the <u>Miranda</u> warning, the reasoning has been based on the presence of aggravating coercive elements not found in the current case. For example, in <u>Robinson v. United States</u>, questioning by a prison psychologist was found to be interrogation for the purposes of <u>Miranda</u>, despite the fact that the interrogator was not a police agent. 439 F.2d 553, 562-63 (D.C. Cir. 1970). However, <u>Robinson</u> is distinguishable from the present case. In <u>Robinson</u>, the psychologist was expressly ordered by the police to interrogate the defendant. Furthermore, the interrogation took place while the defendant was in the coercive environment of prison, and the doctor used a psychological ploy of minimizing the offense to elicit a response. <u>Id.</u> None of these factors are present in the current case. Mr. Gulch was not ordered to question the Defendant by the police, the interview took place in a noncoercive environment, and Mr. Gulch did not use psychology to compel a confession. As such, any action attributed to Mr. Gulch is irrelevant to an examination of interrogation.

    2. Mrs. Moxon was not "on assignment" during the meeting, was known outside of her official capacity and invited into the room by Defendant, and did nothing to indicate she was acting in her police capacity.

During the meeting with Defendant, Mrs. Moxon was not "on assignment" and was not acting in her official capacity. Although she was asked by Chief Baylor to sit in on some of the principal's interviews with students, Mrs. Moxon was not assigned to participate in Defendant's meeting specifically. In fact, Mrs. Moxon's presence at Defendant's meeting was a mere coincidence of timing in that Defendant happened to be in the office when Mrs. Moxon came to pick up her son and obtain a lab report and other information from Mr. Gulch. Furthermore, the fact that Mr. Gulch asked Defendant's permission before Mrs. Moxon joined the meeting indicates that Mrs. Moxon was neither required nor expected to be at the meeting.

The totality of circumstances indicates that Mrs. Moxon was neither acting as a police officer nor viewed as one by Defendant. Defendant knew Mrs. Moxon previously, not because she was a police officer, but because she was the parent of his football teammate. Additionally, none of Mrs. Moxon's actions during the meeting indicated she was there as part of a police investigation. For example, Mrs. Moxon asked Mr. Gulch for a copy of the lab results, something the police already had. In addition, she told Defendant's mother that she was "sure *the police* would find the player," rather than stating "*we* will find the player," indicating that, at the time, she did not view herself as a police officer but as a fellow mother. Finally, she did not arrest Defendant after his confession but *suggested* that Mr. Gulch should call the police. In sum, all of Mrs. Moxon's actions indicate she was neither acting as a police agent nor trying to convince the Defendant that she was.

For more than twenty years, D.C. courts have consistently held that juvenile responses to statements made by nonpolice actors are admissible. <u>See, e.g.</u>, <u>Matter of C.P.</u>, 411 A.2d 643 (D.C. 1980); <u>In re C.P.D.</u>, 367 A.2d 133 (D.C. 1976). For example, in <u>C.P.</u>, this Court allowed a juvenile's confession given, after invoking his Miranda rights, in response to his mother's question to be admitted into evidence despite the fact that the police had expressly asked the mother to elicit a response from her son. 411 A.2d at 649. In <u>C.P.D.</u>, this Court held that a juvenile's confession made in response to a question by his stepfather was admissible. 367 A.2d at 134.

Similarly, Mrs. Moxon was acting in the capacity of a concerned parent when she made the statement immediately preceding Defendant's confession. The only facts that distinguish the present case from <u>C.P.</u> and <u>C.P.D.</u> are that the Defendant was not responding to a *question* from his own parent and the precipitating statement was not made at the police's request. These differences only lessen the likelihood that the Mrs. Moxon's statement was the functional equivalent of express questioning. A question from one's own parent is much more likely to command a response than a statement from a friend's parent. Furthermore, the fact that Mrs. Moxon's statement was not made at the behest of the police lessens the likelihood it was intended to be a coercive police tactic. As such, under the precedents of this Court, Mrs. Moxon's statement did not constitute interrogation.

B. <u>Defendant's statement was not the result of the functional equivalent of express questioning because it was entirely voluntary and not provoked by police actions that were reasonably likely to elicit an incriminating response.</u>

Mrs. Moxon's actions did not constitute the functional equivalent of express questioning because they were not reasonably likely to elicit an incriminating response. The Court must make "an objective evaluation of the normally foreseeable effect of [Mrs. Moxon's] remarks viewed in context." <u>United States v. Brown</u>, 737 A.2d 1016, 1020 (D.C. 1999). In evaluating a statement, courts will examine the intended audience and whether a response was invited or reasonably expected, the absence of trickery or psychological ploys, and the spontaneous and voluntary nature of any response.

> **1. Mrs. Moxon's statement to Defendant's mother, immediately preceding Defendant's confession, was neither a question nor the functional equivalent as it was neither directed at Defendant nor reasonably likely to elicit an incriminating response.**

Defendant's confession was not preceded by any question or statement directed at him, but only by a statement by Mrs. Moxon to Defendant's mother. Viewed objectively, the statement that she was "sure the police would find the player or players," that "it was a shame that players were letting her young son take all the heat," and that she "thought that teammates looked out for weaker players" cannot be deemed reasonable likely to elicit an incriminating response.

Mrs. Moxon's statement was made to Defendant's mother and was wholly unrelated to the Defendant. The statement can be likened to dialogue between a police officer and a third party to which Defendant's response was "neither invited nor expected." <u>Spann v. United States</u>, 551 A.2d 1347, 1349 (D.C. 1988). In <u>Spann</u>, the police were conducting an interview within earshot of Spann, to which Spann responded with a confession. <u>Id.</u> It was not the intention of the police in <u>Spann</u> to provoke a response from the defendant, and the mere fact that he happened to overhear a private conversation does not make the police's actions the functional equivalent of interrogation. <u>Id.</u> Similarly, Mrs. Moxon's remarks were made solely to Defendant's mother and cannot be viewed as an interrogation of the Defendant. Mrs. Moxon purposefully leaned close to Defendant's mother before making the statement and nothing indicates her remarks were intended to be heard by the Defendant, and, therefore, Mrs. Moxon's statement cannot be deemed likely to elicit an incriminating response from the Defendant.

Furthermore, Mrs. Moxon's statements cannot be viewed as an attempt to play on the particular susceptibilities of the Defendant in order to elicit an incriminating response. For Mrs. Moxon's statement to be reasonably likely to elicit an incriminating response, Mrs. Moxon would have had to suspect the Defendant of supplying her son with drugs so as to have something to incriminate himself with. Yet, supplying a young player with drugs runs completely counter to Defendant's alleged susceptibility toward helping out other players. Mrs. Moxon's statement is only reasonably likely to elicit an incriminating response if the Defendant was particularly sensitive to the well-being of other players; yet, providing drugs to teammates, the suspicion of which would have had to precede Mrs. Moxon's statement in order for an incriminating response to be likely, indicates a disregard for the well-being of teammates. As such, it is logically impossible for Mrs. Moxon's statement to be considered a psychological ploy to exploit Defendant's alleged susceptibilities and elicit an incriminating response.

In order to be the functional equivalent of express questioning, the words or actions of the police must be reasonably likely to elicit an incriminating response. In the present case, Mrs. Moxon's were directed at Defendant's mother and were not intended to elicit any response whatsoever from the Defendant. Furthermore, the actual statement was entirely innocuous and cannot be considered a psychological ploy to exploit the Defendant's weakness and was, therefore, not likely to elicit an incriminating response from the Defendant. Mrs. Moxon's words were a casual comment from one parent to another and nothing more.

2. **Defendant's confession was entirely voluntary and not the result of police action likely to elicit an incriminating response and, accordingly, is not barred by the absence of Miranda warnings.**

Defendant's confession was a spontaneous and voluntary outburst, unrelated to any specific words or actions on the part of Mrs. Moxon or anyone else. As such, the confession is admissible because "volunteered statements of any kind are not barred by the 5th Amendment." Miranda, 384 U.S. at 478. Defendant's confession was either entirely spontaneous, completely unrelated to any question or statement, or a voluntary response to a statement by Mrs. Moxon, in her parental capacity, to Defendant's mother. *At worst,* the confession was the result of a consensual encounter with the police and was a voluntary response to a statement by a police officer to Defendant's mother that was not reasonably likely to elicit an incriminating response. As this Court plainly stated in Lewis v. United States, "voluntary responses offered by someone during a consensual encounter with the police are admissible." 767 A.2d 219, 221 (D.C. 2001). In sum, Defendant's voluntary confession was not the result of police interrogation through express questioning or its functional equivalent and is, therefore, admissible in the absence of Miranda warnings.

III. CONCLUSION

For the above stated reasons, the Superior Court's granting the motion to suppress Defendant's confession should be reversed.

Respectfully Submitted,

_____

John Doe

_____

END COMMENTS

John,

First, I want to remind you that on this brief, I have included only end comments. These comments are meant to help you improve as a self-editor and find areas where you can work on improving your writing.

ANALYSIS

You have integrated more case law with your arguments, making your analysis even more effective. However, your analysis is still very fact based. In several areas of your analysis you devote a great deal of time on the facts, which lessens the impact of your case law analysis. For example, look at your analysis under subheading 2 on p. 13. You spend two full paragraphs just discussing facts. While it is okay to discuss the facts before going into a case comparison, particularly when the facts are salient, devoting so much space to facts might indicate to the judge that you do not have much case law backing you up.

There are still some areas where you have entirely factual arguments that could use legal support. As I've noted throughout the year, arguments that cannot be grounded in law or policy have a very difficult time convincing the reader of its weight. For example, on pp. 15-16, you make an argument that Mrs. Moxon was not playing on Defendant's particular susceptibilities. Is there no case law you can refer to? How does the reader know this is even a valid means of determining a psychological ploy?

In other areas, you still mention case law without providing a context for it or otherwise showing the reader its relevance. For example, under subheading D on pp. 10-11, you don't use any case law except for one case, which you mention in a citation sentence as indirect support.

Case comparisons are not the only way you can analyze case law. Recall how we used case synthesis last semester. You appear to have the beginnings of an effective case synthesis on p. 8 of your analysis, when you discuss custody in the context of school disciplinary meetings. While you extract the rules from relevant cases, you do not go the extra step of combining these rules to provide one synthesized rule that you can work with and apply. This would tie up your analysis and make it more effective.

PERSUASIVENESS

You have made your writing more effective by keeping your tone professional. You have also lost that defensive stance that was present in your first draft.

Your fact section remains persuasive, and it is even more cogent now that you have tightened up the language and made it more concise. Further, your pointheadings, topic sentences, and issue statement are all persuasive because you use specific facts.

Your roadmap paragraphs could still be more persuasive. While you tell the reader what factors/issues you will be analyzing and in what order, you do not use specific facts to explain why the factors/issues will turn out a certain way. This does not mean that your roadmap must be lengthy: You can make your roadmap more specific to our case while still keeping it concise.

LARGE-SCALE ORGANIZATION

Your pointheadings effectively convey the topic of your analysis to the reader. Remember that your topic sentences serve the same function. Recall the reader-based outline technique I explained in my last set of comments. Your reader wants to be able to determine what your analysis will focus on after reading your topic sentence. If you are discussing two different factors within one section of analysis, you want to mention both of those in your topic sentence. Under subheading C on p. 9, what does the reader think based only on reading your topic sentence? Does the reader know that you will be addressing both consent *and* parental presence?

Your organization under interrogation could be clearer. You seem to provide a roadmap of subheadings A and B, as well as the mini-roadmaps within those sections, under pointheading II. The reader expects the roadmap of A and B. However, in this particular section, your inclusion of mini-roadmaps is confusing because it is unclear how your analysis is structured and what the major and minor subdivisions are. This can be remedied by making your language clearer, or by merely having a roadmap of A and B in this particular paragraph, and then including mini-roadmaps at the beginning of your analyses under A and B.

CONCISENESS

Your brief is more effective because you have made it more concise. However, as noted above, you can still cut out some excess language. You refer to the facts extensively. Consider how much reference you actually need to make to the facts in your analysis. You give the reader a statement of fact for a reason. You want to refer to specific facts when they are relevant to your particular legal argument and when they add to the persuasiveness of that argument. However, do not repeat entire sections of your fact section. This is a question of degree, and you will often have to let your paper sit for a day before performing this type of edit.

REVISING/POLISHING

Careful, you have some minor typographical errors. These can be fixed through more careful proofreading. As a rule of thumb, perform a separate edit for citation placement and form as well as for typographical and grammatical errors.

This is not an exhaustive set of comments. I gave specific examples so you can understand how my comments apply to your entire brief. If you have any questions, feel free to ask.

To listen to examples of arguments before the Supreme Court, see http://www.oyez.org.

III. ORAL ARGUMENT

A. *What Is Oral Argument?*

If the brief is your first chance to persuade the appellate court, then oral argument is your last chance. In a typical appellate court oral argument, the two opposing counsel appear in front of a three-judge panel and argue their cases for approximately half an hour. The appellant argues first, then the appellee argues, and the appellant has a chance for rebuttal. During oral argument, the judges ask questions about the issues presented in the briefs. While the judges' levels of preparation differ, you should assume that your judges have not only read the briefs, but also done additional research. Oral argument provides you with an opportunity to answer questions the judges find important, stress issues and cases you find most compelling, and persuade the bench that you win.

1. Audience

You are answering questions for a panel of judges. Therefore, you must be respectful at all times, regardless of the judges' possible antagonistic tones, irrelevant questions, or apparent disregard for you or your client. Remain professional at all times; do not show your exasperation with a judge's barrage of irrelevant questions. On the other hand, do not inundate the court with unnecessary platitudes such as "As this masterful court has already decided" or "As I have read in your artfully worded opinion."

Answer questions directly, looking the judge in the eye: "Yes, Your Honor." or "No, Judge Schwelb." If a judge interrupts you, let her talk. Do not try to talk over a judge at any point in time and do not interrupt a judge on the bench. Do not tell a judge that she is wrong. Give deference to the bench at all times.

With a three-judge panel, you need to make sure two of the judges are on your side by the time the oral argument has finished. The best appellate attorney is the one who can assess which judges are for him during oral argument and win over those judges who are against him.

Your bench will usually be a "hot bench," peppering you with constant questions. Rarely will you encounter a "cool bench." Often, the cooler benches make for more difficult oral argument because it is hard to engage the judges and understand their concerns and questions if they ask very few questions.

2. Purpose

Oral argument is not a speech but a conversation with the court. The purpose of oral argument is to answer the judge's questions and to convince each judge on the panel that your client should win. Therefore, you should answer each question thoroughly—relying on facts, law, and policy arguments. Speak slowly, make eye contact, and avoid hand gestures or body movements that could distract from the argument.

Listen carefully to each judge's question and feel free to repeat the question if you are unsure of its meaning. Active listening is the most important tool during oral argument; you must be completely focused on the judge's question instead of thinking about your next sentence. Do not be afraid to take a moment to think about your argument before stating your answer.

3. Scope

Your oral argument should focus on the main, most compelling arguments of your brief. The judges might steer you into different areas of law or points made by the other side. While you need to answer these questions, you should try to steer the court back to your main arguments whenever possible. Framing the issue from your client's viewpoint is important in oral argument.

4. Stance

Tie your argument back to your theory of the case whenever possible. You want the judges walking off of the bench and repeating your theme to the other judges on the panel when they are deciding how to rule on the case.

B. How Should I Prepare?

To prepare for oral argument, you need to do much more than reread the briefs. While all attorneys have their own methods of preparation, a novice should prepare an outline of arguments. In addition, the law should be handy for reference. The outline and law should provide you with a flexible guideline to make sure you cover all important issues. Often, the judges will steer you away from your outline with their questions. A good attorney will be able to weave in points from the outline in answering the judges' questions.

In preparing, you should practice your argument in front of other attorneys in a "moot," or mock, oral argument. Discuss your answers and prepare better approaches to the tough questions. Also practice the level, tone, and speed of your voice. Arguments that are strong on substance can be weakened by poor delivery.

If possible, videotape yourself practicing oral argument. When you play back the video, you will notice your tone, speed, delivery, and distracting gestures. The use of a low-tech webcam can be very helpful for practicing oral arguments. Time yourself when practicing because time will go faster than you expect.

C. Are There Conventions for Oral Argument?

1. Introduction

Typically, before beginning to speak, you should ask permission from the court to do so by saying, "May it please the court." It is often helpful to introduce yourself (and your co-counsel if appropriate) and give an overview of the case. This overview is similar to the theory of your case in the brief. (This case is about a bus driver who was in too much of a rush.) You should memorize the introduction as judges rarely interrupt you during this short time frame.

Introduction

May it please the court. My name is Diana Donahoe. I represent the defendant in this case, Roger Kint. This case is about the illegal use of suggestive and unreliable identifications by police officers.

---

2. Facts

If you have compelling facts, you should tell them to the court. If the other side has already presented the facts, you should take the opportunity to present them from your client's perspective instead of relying on the recitation of the facts by the opposing counsel. If the facts are not very helpful and you would prefer to start with the law, you are free to do so. Often, counsel will ask the court if it wants a brief recitation of the fact; be prepared to do so or to answer factual questions from the bench.

3. Roadmap

You should provide the court with an oral roadmap. Typically, you will argue two or three main issues or provide a number of reasons why the court should rule in your favor. List those issues or arguments up front for the court. Start with your most compelling argument to be sure the court has heard it. If the judges want to hear one of your later arguments first, they will ask. Otherwise, begin with your first argument. At this point, judges might ask you what legal authority you are relying on and what relief you are seeking.

Sample Roadmap

The identification should be excluded because it was both suggestive and unreliable. Based on the totality test detailed in *Manson v. Braithwaite*, the unreliability stems from three main factors: first, the witness did not have an opportunity to view the assailant during the crime; second, the witness was not certain of his identification; and third, the witness was persuaded by the police that my client was the assailant.

4. Main Argument and Types of Questions to Expect

After the introduction, facts, and roadmap, you will spend the rest of your time arguing your case and answering the judges' questions.

You will be asked a range of questions from the panel. Typical questions include the following.

a. Softball Questions

Here, one judge will try to help you make the argument to the rest of the panel. Take these questions as a sign that at least one judge is already willing to rule in your favor. Help this judge convince his or her colleagues that your position is correct. Also, listen to this judge's questions and arguments; they will provide you with insights as to which of your arguments are compelling.

b. Hypothetical Questions

Judges' decisions affect not only your client but also cases that arise in the future. Therefore, judges will ask you how far you think the rule should be stretched. Here, you need to sound reasonable or you will lose credibility with the court.

c. Factual Questions

The judges might ask you about the facts of your case or pose questions regarding possible factual scenarios. Do not tell the judge that "those are not the facts of this case." You can distinguish the facts or clarify them if necessary.

d. Legal Questions

Here the judges might ask for authority to support your argument or ask about a specific case. You need to be extremely familiar with the details of the law; know the facts, reasoning, and holding of the cases so that you can refer directly to these cases and distinguish them if necessary. If you don't know the case the judge is referencing, do not make up an answer. Instead, be honest and tell the court you are not familiar with the case. Often, a judge will fill you in on the details of the case so that you can provide an intelligent answer to the question. At times, the judge might ask you to file a supplemental brief to address the case.

5. Conclusion

At the end of the argument, conclude with a brief summary of the points you made and a request for relief (for example, the reversal of the lower court's holding). In most cases, however, you will run out of time, so try to do so gracefully. If you are in the middle of answering a question when time runs out, pause and ask the court for permission to briefly answer the question and wrap up. You should never continue speaking after your time is up without the leave of the court.

D.   *What Should I Do When Opposing Counsel Is Speaking?*

When opposing counsel stands up to give his presentation, pay attention and take notes. The best arguments respond directly to points raised by opposing counsel. Reviewing the opposing brief beforehand can give you a preview of opposing counsel's arguments, but you must always listen to what he actually says so that you can effectively rebut him, either as the appellee in your main argument or as the appellant on rebuttal.

E.   *What Is Rebuttal?*

Rebuttal should not be a rehashing of your arguments. Instead, you should address only one or two points usually as a counterpoint to one of opposing counsel's best arguments. For example, if the opposing counsel mentions a case that seems compelling, be sure to distinguish the case in your rebuttal. If you have a chance for rebuttal, you should always take the opportunity to be the last speaker.

Examples of oral argument are available on video at http://www.aspen-lawschool.com/books/donahoe. To listen to Supreme Court oral arguments, go to http://www.oyez.org.

Dos and Don'ts of Oral Argument

Do	*Don't*
• Answer judges' questions	• Put off judges' questions
• Have a flexible outline	• Strictly adhere to your outline
• Have a conversation with the judges	• Make a speech
• Rely on authority	• Pretend to know a case you have not read
• Listen carefully and ask for clarification of questions	• Think about your next point while judge is asking a question
• Keep constant respect for court	• Get frustrated or angry with judges
• Keep a positive and professional tone	• Become defensive or attack other attorney personally
• Dress and act professionally	• Fidget, slouch, chew gum, or otherwise act unprofessionally

---

IV. PLEADINGS AND MOTIONS

Pleadings are the documents used to initiate lawsuits. They include complaints, answers, and interrogatories. Together, the complaint and answer focus the issues of the lawsuit. The interrogatories begin the discovery process. In drafting pleadings, attorneys must investigate the facts, research the law, and make tactical decisions regarding the case. Often, young associates are asked to draft pleadings without much guidance. Therefore, this section will discuss the basics of drafting complaints, answers, and interrogatories.

Motions are legal documents requesting the court to rule on a particular legal or procedural issue during litigation. They come in many forms and are also called trial briefs. This following sections will focus on the formal requirements of filing motions of various types, but they should be read in conjunction with the earlier section on appellate briefs (see page 161) and persuasive writing (see page 97). Each of these types of document are treated in full below:

- Complaints, immediately below.
- Answers, page 247.
- Interrogatories, page 253.
- Motions, page 256.

A. Complaints

1. Purpose, Audience, Scope, and View

- **Purpose:** The complaint commences the legal action. It also provides notice to the defendants and stops the running of the statute of limitations on the action.
- **Audience:** The complaint is written and served on the defendant. However, it is basically written for the legal audience as it is also filed with the court and read by the eventual counsel for the defense.
- **Scope:** The complaint actually sets the scope of the lawsuit by alleging particular legal claims against the defense. Some complaints are only a page or two; others can be particularly lengthy if they set out a plethora of claims.
- **View:** A complaint is a very formal document. It is usually written in bullet point form with numbered allegations.

For a sample complaint, see page 244.

2. Formal Requirements of a Complaint

Before drafting a complaint, you should do the following:

1. Research the rules for filing complaints in your jurisdiction.
2. Research the substantive law of your case.
3. Investigate the facts for your client.

First, each jurisdiction has rules governing the content of a complaint and the procedures for filing them. Check the civil procedure rules for your jurisdiction as well as the local rules. These rules set out the appearance, content, and filing requirements for the complaint. For an example of filing requirements for a complaint, see those for the District of Columbia Superior Court at http://www.dccourts.gov/dccourts/docs/civil_actions_handbook.pdf.

Second, you will need to research the law to determine (1) the legal causes of actions you will assert, and (2) the elements necessary to prove those causes of action. It will take some time and tactical care to determine which causes of action you will allege. For complicated cases, the causes of action can be numerous and tedious.

Third, the specific facts of the case are essential to determine if you can meet a particular cause of action. Therefore, you will need to investigate the facts before you draft your complaint. Depending on the type of case, factual investigation can include interviewing the client and potential witnesses, locating police reports, copying medical records, observing the client, and investigating the scene of an accident.

Once you are ready to draft your complaint, you should consider looking at complaints already filed by your firm or form complaints. While forms and samples are helpful, they are not end points for drafting a complaint or substitutes for researching the procedural requirements, law, or facts for your case. They should help only to determine the formal requirements of a complaint. Each complaint should be drafted for your particular client's situation as no case is exactly the same as another.

For information on each of the elements usually included in a complaint, see the following pages:

- Caption, immediately below.
- Commencement, page 239.
- Body or Charging Part, page 239.
- Prayer or Demand for Judgment, page 240.
- Signature and Verification, page 241.

a. Caption

The caption contains the name of the court and jurisdiction as well as the names of the parties. It also identifies the document as the complaint.

Caption Sample

SUPERIOR COURT FOR THE DISTRICT OF COLUMBIA CIVIL DIVISION

DAVID BRINK,   :

Defendant   :

v.   :   Civil Action No. _____

DR. ROBERT TAYLOR,   :

Plaintiff   :

COMPLAINT

---

b. Commencement

The commencement introduces the complaint, usually using some form of legalese. However, legalese is not necessary.

Commencement Samples

- Now comes David Brink by his attorney, Diana Donahoe, and herein alleges
- Comes now plaintiff, David Brink, by his attorney, Diana Donahoe
- Comes now plaintiff, David Brink, for cause of actions allege and complaint against Dr. Robert Taylor, herein alleges
- Plaintiff, David Brink, makes the following allegations against Defendant, Robert Taylor

---

c. Body or Charging Part

This is the meat of the complaint and is comprised of numbered paragraphs. Some courts require immediate allegations of jurisdiction; for example, if filing in federal court, you must allege subject matter jurisdiction, personal jurisdiction, and venue. Afterward, the initial paragraphs often state the parties' names and addresses. The following paragraphs give notice of the legal causes of action and allege each element of those actions. You may organize these allegations by "counts," by providing headings for Count I, Count II, etc. While you need to allege sufficient facts to support those allegations, you need not include all of your evidence. Tactical considerations come into play here as you decide how much of your case you want to display. At the least, you need enough to survive a motion to dismiss. If you are requesting a jury trial, some jurisdictions require that the jury demand be made in the charging portion of the complaint or in a separate section labeled "jury demand." The last paragraphs of a complaint usually describe the plaintiff's injuries and damages.

Sample Body or Charging Portion

1. David Brink, the plaintiff, an eighteen-year-old, resides at 2211 North Capital St., N.W., Washington, D.C. 20001.
2. Dr. Robert Taylor, the defendant, an adult, resides at 432 Nebraska Ave., N.W., Washington, D.C., 20003.
3. On or about August 8, 2000, the vehicle operated by the defendant, Dr. Robert Taylor, struck the vehicle owned and operated by the plaintiff, David Brink.
4. The defendant, Robert Taylor, was operating the vehicle in a negligent and careless manner in violation of traffic laws then and there in full force.
5. As a direct cause and proximate cause of the negligence, the defendant's vehicle collided with the plaintiff's vehicle.

---

d. Prayer or Demand for Judgment

Here, the plaintiff lists the relief requested, such as specific performance, special damages, punitive damages, and equitable relief. The demand for judgment is not numbered; it usually begins with "WHEREFORE" and ends with a catchall phrase requesting all other relief appropriate. You may place the demand for judgment at the end of the complaint or at the end of each cause of action if different relief is appropriate for different counts. In some courts, specific amounts must be pleaded, while in others, specific amounts may not be pleaded. Again, be sure to check your local rules.

Sample Prayer or Demand for Judgment

- WHEREFORE, the plaintiff demands judgment against the defendant in the sum of five hundred thousand dollars. ($500,000)
- WHEREFORE, the plaintiff requests that this court:
  - declare the defendant in breach of contract;
  - award the plaintiff damages plus interest;
  - award the plaintiff costs and attorneys' fees;
  - award the plaintiff any other relief the court deems appropriate.

e. *Signature and Verification*

The attorney's signature, bar number, and address are required at the end of the complaint. (If the plaintiff is filing *pro se*, he must sign his own name and provide an address.) Your signature states you have read the document and believe it is not a frivolous claim. Federal rules and some state rules require verification of the complaint by the party or an affidavit accompanying the complaint. In the verification clause, the party swears under oath that the allegations are believed to be true.

Signature and Verification Sample

By: _____ Diana R. Donahoe Bar # 111-111
     Donahoe & Associates, L.L.P.
     600 New Jersey Ave., N.W.
     Washington, D.C. 20001

Attorney for Plaintiff

On March 30, 2010, David Brink, being duly sworn, claims he is the plaintiff in the above action and that the facts set forth above are true except for those statements made upon information and belief, which he believes to be true.

_____
Plaintiff's signature   date

_____
Notary's signature   date

Form Complaint for Negligence Action

Rev. 6-95   SUPERIOR COURT CIVIL PRACTICE 25-25

Exhibit A

Superior Court of the District of Columbia
Civil Division

XXXXXXXXXXXXXX)	
XXXXXXXXXXXXXX)	
XXXXXXXXXXXXXXXXXXX)	
Plaintiff)	
v.)	
)	C.A. No. _____
XXXXXXXXXXXXXXXXXXX)	
XXXXXXXXXXXXX)	
XXXXXXXXXXXXX)	
XXXXXXXXXXXXXXXXXX)	
Defendant)	

Complaint
(Automobile Negligence)

1. Jurisdiction of this Court is founded on D.C. Code (1981 Edition). Section 11-921.

2. On or about December 16, 1986, the plaintiff was operating his vehicle southbound on 26th Street, N.W. near Irving St., N.W. in the District of Columbia when the plaintiff's car stopped for a red light. At that time and place, the vehicle owned and operated by the defendant struck and collided with the rear of the plaintiff's vehicle.

3. The striking and colliding was due to the violations of law and negligence of the defendant, including but not limited to failure to pay full attention, following too closely, excessive speed under the circumstances, and failure to maintain control.

4. As a result, the plaintiff was seriously and permanently injured, incurred and will in the future incur medical expenses, and was prevented from pursuing his employment and other ordinary activities. The plaintiff also incurred property damage to his vehicle.

-2-

WHEREFORE, the plaintiff demands judgment against the defendant in the sum of TWENTY-FIVE THOUSAND ($25,000.00) DOLLARS, plus costs

_____
XXXXXXXXXXXXXXXX
Attorney for Plaintiff
XXXXXXXXX
XXXXXXXXXXXXX
XXXXXXXX

JURY DEMAND

Plaintiff demands trial by jury.

_____
XXXXXXXXXXX

3. Sample Complaint

Caption

SUPERIOR COURT OF THE DISTRICT OF
COLUMBIA
Civil Division

RICHARD P. HOLLINGS   :
1787 R Street, N.W.
Washington, D.C. 20009   :

    Plaintiff,   :

    v.   :   Civil Action No.: _____

STEPHANIE HARPER   :
600 N. 14th Street,
Arlington, Virginia 22202   :

    and   :

STATE FARM INSURANCE CO.   :
  Serve: Shawna Howard
      20 Broad Drive   :
      Silver Spring, MD 20904

    Defendants

COMPLAINT FOR NEGLIGENCE
(Automobile)

1. General jurisdiction is founded in D.C. Code § 11-921 as the cause of the action arose in the District of Columbia.

2. Plaintiff Richard P. Hollings is a resident of the District of Columbia. At the time of the occurrence upon which this Complaint is based, plaintiff was an adult resident of the District of Columbia.

3. Defendant Stephanie Harper (hereinafter "Harper") is, and at the time of the occurrence upon which this Complaint is based, was a resident of the State of Virginia.

4. Defendant State Farm was a District of Columbia corporation licensed to provide insurance services to residents of the District of Columbia.

FACTS

5. On January 12, 2004, at approximately 7:00 p.m., the plaintiff, on foot, was crossing the intersection of 14th Street & Madison in the District of Columbia. As the plaintiff proceeded east on Madison into the intersection, he had a green light.

Caption

Body or Charging Part

6. Defendant Harper, while driving an SUV, traveling South on 14th Street went through the red light and proceeded to hit the plaintiff with the above-mentioned vehicle.

COUNT I
(Negligence)

7. Plaintiff incorporates by reference paragraphs 1 through 6 and further alleges as follows:

8. The collision was the direct and proximate result of the negligence of defendant Harper.

9. At the same time and place, it was the duty of defendant Harper to use ordinary and reasonable care to keep the vehicle she was operating under proper control, to pay full time and attention to the operation of said vehicle, to obey traffic laws, including speed limits, and/or to drive said vehicle in a reasonable, careful, and prudent manner with due regard for the safety of others.

10. Notwithstanding said duties, defendant Harper did carelessly and negligently cause the collision. Defendant Harper's negligent acts and/or omissions include, but are not limited to, the following:

    (a) failure to follow the posted speed limit; and/or

    (b) failure to maintain a proper lookout; and/or

    (c) failure to pay full time and attention to the operation of the motor vehicle; and/or

    (d) failure to maintain control of her motor vehicle; and/or

    (e) failure to avoid the collision; and/or

    (f) failure to operate said vehicle in a reasonable, careful, and prudent manner; and/or

    (g) otherwise failing to comply with the applicable District of Columbia traffic and Motor Vehicle Regulations then and there in effect.

11. As a direct and proximate result of the negligence of defendant Harper, plaintiff sustained serious injuries to various parts of his body, including, but not limited to, his shoulder, finger, bruises, a torn rotator cuff, some or all of which are permanent.

12. As a further direct and proximate result of defendant's negligence, plaintiff has incurred, and will continue to incur, substantial expenses for medical care and attention, a loss of earnings and wage-earning capacity and has suffered, and continues to suffer, considerable physical pain and mental anguish.

WHEREFORE, plaintiff Richard P. Hollings demands judgment, against defendant Harper, in the full and just amount of $1,000,000.00, plus interest and costs.

COUNT II
(Underinsured Motorist Benefits)

13. Plaintiff incorporates by reference paragraphs 1 through 12 and further alleges as follows:

Charging Portion with Specific Counts

14. State Farm provided underinsured motorist benefits, by contract, for injuries suffered by plaintiff as a result of a defendant with insufficient insurance coverage.

Demand for Judgment

15. Upon information and belief the defendant Harper may have insufficient insurance coverage. WHEREFORE, plaintiff Richard P. Hollings demands judgment, against defendant State Farm, in the full and just amount of $100,000.00, plus interest and costs.

Respectfully submitted,

DONAHOE & ASSOCIATES

By: _____

Diana R. Donahoe # 111-111
200 New Jersey Ave. N.W.
Washington, D.C. 20006
(202) 659-5500

Attorney for Plaintiff

Demand for Jury Trial

JURY TRIAL DEMANDED:

_____

Diana R. Donahoe

B. Answers

1. Purpose, Audience, Scope, and View

- **Purpose:** The answer responds to the complaint by indicating whether the defendant admits, denies, or is unable to answer each allegation.
- **Audience:** The answer is written for the plaintiff, but its primary audience is the plaintiff's attorney and the court.
- **Scope:** The scope of the answer is related to the scope of the complaint as the answer must admit or deny each of the plaintiff's allegations.
- **View:** An answer is a formal document. It usually follows the numbered paragraphs in the complaint and adds additional numbered paragraphs for affirmative defenses and counterclaims.
- For a sample answer, see page 251.

2. Formal Requirements of an Answer

An answer responds to the complaint by indicating which of the plaintiff's allegations the defendant admits, denies, or is unable to answer due to insufficient information. An answer also raises affirmative defenses and possible counterclaims. You should consult the rules in your jurisdiction for affirmative defenses as well as for procedural filing requirements. For an example of filing requirements for an answer, see those for the District of Columbia Superior Court at www.dccourts.gov/dccourts/docs/civil_actions_handbook.pdf.

For information on each of the elements usually included in an answer, see the following pages:

- Caption and Introductory Sentence, immediately below.
- Admissions in Answer, page 248.
- Denials in Answer, page 248.
- Affirmative Defenses, page 249.
- Affirmative Claims and Demand for Judgment, page 249.
- Signature and Verification, page 249.

a. Caption and Introductory Sentence

The caption is identical to the one in the complaint except that it is labeled "Answer." An introductory sentence can be used before the answer.

Caption and Introductory Sentence Sample

SUPERIOR COURT FOR THE DISTRICT OF COLUMBIA CIVIL DIVISION

DAVID BRINK,   :

Defendant   :

v.   :   Civil Action No. _____

DR. ROBERT TAYLOR,   :

Plaintiff   :

<u>Answer</u>

In response to the plaintiff's allegations, defendant states the following:

---

b. Admissions in Answer

Some rules require defendants to admit portions of the complaint that are true so that the attorneys are acting in good faith. In addition, by admitting portions of the complaint, the defendants help to narrow the issues. You can admit specific paragraphs individually, group admissions together, or admit only parts of paragraphs.

Admissions in Answer Samples

- Defendant admits allegations in paragraph 1.
- Defendant admits allegations in paragraph 2.
- Defendant admits allegations in paragraphs 3, 5, 7, and 10.
- Defendant admits that she owned and operated a vehicle on September 21, 2000, but denies that she was operating it negligently.

---

c. Denials in Answer

The defendant may make a general denial, which denies the whole complaint, or a special denial, which denies only certain paragraphs or parts of paragraphs. In addition, the defendant may state that there is insufficient evidence to deny or admit certain parts of a complaint, which, in effect, acts as a denial.

Denials in Answer Samples

Sample General Denial:
- The defendant denies each allegation in the plaintiff's complaint.

Sample Special Denial:
- The defendant denies paragraph 1.
- The defendant denies paragraph 2.
- The defendant denies the allegations in paragraphs 11, 12, 14-21, and 23.
- The defendant denies the allegations in paragraph 5 except to state that he does own a 1999 Honda Accord.
- The defendant is without sufficient information to admit or deny the allegations in paragraph 15.

---

d. Affirmative Defenses

Some jurisdictions require certain affirmative defenses to be raised in an answer or they are waived. For example, the federal rules require the following affirmative defenses to be raised in an answer: lack of personal jurisdiction, improper venue, insufficient process or insufficient service. When writing affirmative defenses, you can separate them by headings or by count.

Affirmative Defenses Samples

- The complaint fails to state a cause of action upon which relief can be granted.
- First Affirmative Defense: The plaintiff's claims are barred for lack of personal jurisdiction.
- Affirmative Defenses to Count II: The plaintiff's claims are barred by his assumption of the risk.

---

e. Affirmative Claims and Demands for Judgment

Counterclaims, cross-claims, and third-party claims are made in the same form as the complaint (see page 237), using numbered paragraphs with separate headings to label each claim. If a defendant alleges a claim, he should also include a demand for judgment.

f. Signature and Verification

Similar to the complaint, a signature and verification are usually required in an answer.

Signature and Verification Sample

By: _____

       Diana R. Donahoe Bar # 111-111

       Donahoe & Associates, L.L.P.

       200 New Jersey Ave. N.W.

       Washington, D.C. 20001

       Attorney for Defendant

On March 30, 2010, Robert Taylor, being duly sworn, claims he is the defendant in the above action and that the facts set forth above are true except for those statements made upon information and belief, which he believes to be true.

_____

Defendant's signature   date

_____

Notary's signature   date

3. Sample Answer

Caption and introduction to Answer

SUPERIOR COURT OF THE DISTRICT OF COLUMBIA
CIVIL DIVISION

David Brink	:	
Plaintiff	:	
vs.	:	Civil No. 91-CA15834
Dr. Robert Taylor	:	
Defendant	:	

VERIFIED ANSWER

Comes Now the defendant, Dr. Robert Taylor, by and through his attorneys, Esquire, and in Answer to the Complaint filed by the plaintiff herein states as follows:

FIRST DEFENSE

Affirmative Defenses

That the Complaint fails to state a cause of action upon which relief can be granted.

SECOND DEFENSE

That the plaintiff's claims are barred by his contributory negligence.

THIRD DEFENSE

That the plaintiff's Complaint is barred by his assumption of the risk.

FOURTH DEFENSE

That the plaintiff's injuries, if any, are the result of acts of omissions of others for which this defendant cannot be held responsible.

FIFTH DEFENSE

That the cause of this accident was the speed of plaintiff's vehicle which was traveling excessively fast for the conditions then and there existing, without any fault or negligence on defendant's part contributing thereto.

SIXTH DEFENSE

That with respect to the specific averments in plaintiff's Complaint, defendant responds:

Admissions and Denials

1. Defendant neither admits nor denies the allegations contained in paragraph 1 of plaintiff's Complaint insofar as it states a legal conclusion which does not require admission or denial.

2. With respect to paragraph 2 of plaintiff's complaint, defendant admits that an accident took place on or about August 8, 1990 at or about Michigan Avenue and South Dakota Avenue but denies the remainder of the averments.

3. Defendant denies the averments of paragraph 3 of the Complaint.

4. Defendant denies the averments of paragraph 4 of the Complaint.

5. Defendant denies the averments of paragraph 5 of the Complaint.

6. Defendant denies the averments of paragraph 6 of the Complaint.

Demand for Judgment

WHEREFORE, the above premises considered, it is respectfully requested that the plaintiff's Complaint be dismissed with prejudice.

McCarthy & McCarthy

By: _____

Attorneys for Defendant

VERIFICATION

The undersigned swears and affirms that I verily believe the facts stated in the above pleading to be true.

_____
Dr. Robert Taylor

JURY DEMAND

The defendant, Dr. Robert Taylor demands a trial by jury of twelve (12) persons as to all issues raised herein.

_____

CERTIFICATE OF SERVICE

I HEREBY CERTIFY, that a copy of the aforegoing Answer was mailed, first-class, postage prepaid this 27th day of March, 2010, to:

_____

C. *Interrogatories*

1. Purpose, Audience, Scope, and View

- **Purpose:** Interrogatories are used in the discovery process to ask questions of the other side. They should not be used to overwhelm opposing counsel or to overload the litigation process.
- **Audience:** Interrogatories are written for a layperson and a lawyer. Typically, the lawyer will ask the layperson, or client, to answer the interrogatories. Then, the lawyer will review the interrogatories and the answers with the client.
- **Scope:** Many jurisdictions limit the amount of interrogatories permitted. While some jurisdictions impose number limits, others prohibit certain types of interrogatories, such as those that cause "annoyance, embarrassment, oppression, or undue burden or expense."
- **View:** Interrogatories should be written clearly and precisely. They are numbered and often arranged by subject matter.

2. Formal Requirements of an Interrogatory

Interrogatories are the questions posed by one party to another during the discovery process. They are usually used early in the litigation process to begin discovery and to prepare for depositions. However, they can also be used to fill in gaps from depositions or obtain information later in the process. Interrogatories are served on opposing counsel and also filed with the court. They must be answered within a proscribed amount of time, depending on your jurisdiction's procedural rules.

Before you begin drafting interrogatories, you should research the procedural rules controlling interrogatories in your jurisdiction as well as the substantive law on the legal issues involved. First, the procedural rules will notify you of any limits on number or types of interrogatories permitted. For example, the Federal Rules of Civil Procedure permit only 25 interrogatories, see Fed. R. Civ. P. 33, while the trial court in the District of Columbia limits parties to 40 interrogatories, including subparts. See Super. Ct. Civ. R. 33. The procedural rules also control answering interrogatories, such as format, filing, and objecting to certain questions. Second, the substantive law will help you draft your interrogatories to gain factual information regarding the elements of the cause of action and possible defenses.

When drafting interrogatories, you may review forms or previously filed interrogatories. However, because each case is factually different, you should draft interrogatories for your specific case.

For information on each of the elements usually included in interrogatories, see the following pages:

- Preface, page 254.
- Definitions, page 254.
- Preliminary Questions, page 254.

- Substantive Questions, page 255.
- Concluding Questions, page 255.

a. Preface

The preface usually serves as the instructions for the interrogatories; it often states the duties of the parties, the time limit for answering, and the rule under which the interrogatories are propounded.

Preface Samples

- These interrogatories are propounded under Rule 33 of the Federal Rules of Civil Procedure. You must answer them, under oath, within thirty days.
- You are requested to answer the following interrogatories pursuant to Superior Court Rule 33. These interrogatories are continuing in nature so as to require you to file supplemental answers if you obtain further or different information before trial.

---

b. Definitions

A definition section in a set of interrogatories helps to clearly identify certain terms so that there can be no confusion later in litigation. This section, while often written last, usually appears toward the beginning of the interrogatories.

Definitions Samples

- "You" refers to the Defendant to whom these interrogatories are addressed as well as your predecessors and successors, attorneys, and all others acting or purporting to act on the behalf of the Defendant.
- "Person" refers to any individual, association, partnership, corporation, governmental entity, or business entity.

---

c. Preliminary Questions

These questions usually ask for background information about the parties. Depending on your jurisdiction, they may not count as one of the permitted interrogatories. However, if they are part of the limit, you will want to keep these types of questions to a minimum.

Preliminary Questions Samples

- 1. State your full name, age, address, marital status, social security number, and date of birth.
- 2. State all places of residence for the past five years, including addresses and dates.
- 3. By whom were you employed, and what were your duties and wages, at the time of the occurrence?

---

d. Substantive Questions

These questions are the meat of the interrogatories and provide the factual information you will need for litigation. The questions may be general or specific. Consider organizing your interrogatories based on subject matter and remember to number them.

Substantive Questions Samples

- General Questions:
  - 14. Give a concise statement of the facts as to how you contend that the occurrence took place.
  - 21. Describe your injuries.
- Specific Questions:
  - 22. List the dates you were able to do the following for the first time after your injury: 1. move your leg; 2. put pressure on your leg; 3. walk with a cane; 4. walk on your own; 5. participate in sports (please list specific sports).

---

e. Concluding Questions

These questions are usually catch-all questions to ask for information regarding other people who might provide information or to ask for the party's narrative of the facts. If you are in a jurisdiction with limits on the number of interrogatories, you will use these types of interrogatories sparingly.

Concluding Questions Samples

- 36. Identify all documents related to this case.
- 37. Identify all persons with knowledge of this case.
- 38. State in detail your version of how the accident occurred.
- List all relevant details you have obtained about the case from other sources.

D. Motions (or Pretrial Briefs)

Motions are persuasive documents written at the trial level. They can be categorized as pretrial motions, trial motions, and post-trial motions. They are similar to appellate briefs in that they inform and persuade. However, unlike appellate briefs, motions raise issues as they arise in the litigation. Therefore, while appellate briefs rely on the record below, most motions are written without the benefit of admitted evidence. As a result, tactics differ as the writer needs to consider how much information to put in the motion without giving away too much of his trial strategy.

In a motions practice, the party requesting the court for particular relief files a motion. The opposing party then has time to file an opposition to the motion. Some courts permit the moving party to file a reply to the opposition. Rarely, courts will also permit the opposing party to submit a surreply.

This section addresses the format for motions, oppositions, and replies (all generically referred to as motions). While most motions do not require the stringent formal elements of an appellate brief, you should read this section in coordination with the section on briefs (starting on page 161) and chapter 2, The Writing Process (Persuasive Writing, starting on p. 97).

1. Purpose, Audience, Scope, and View

- **Purpose:** A motion is a persuasive document that requests a trial court for certain relief. Therefore, a motion should inform and persuade. It should be written to win a particular issue. The best motions seem objective and reasonable, but are subtly persuasive so that the judge wants to rule for the client. The poorest motions attempt persuasion with incendiary language that either attacks the other side's position or develops a defensive posture. Motions should not be written to harangue opposing counsel, burden the court, or improperly delay litigation.
- **Audience:** The trial judge is the primary audience for a motion. Therefore, the writing should conform to the legal standards of your jurisdiction. However, secondary audiences include opposing counsel, your client, the opposing client, and the public. Therefore, tactical considerations are also necessary.
- **Scope:** Unlike appellate briefs, which usually cover multiple issues from the trial litigation, motions usually only address one particular issue for the court's consideration. Similar to appellate briefs, motions are often controlled by page limits set by each court's procedural rules.
- **View:** Your motion should be subtly persuasive. It should contain a subtle theory of the case and persuade the judge to rule for you. Because many motions are filed pretrial, you must consider how much of your case to reveal in your motion. Tactical considerations are, therefore, essential.

For sample motions, see the Forms and Orders page of the District of Columbia Superior Court at http://www.dccourts.gov/dccourts/superior/civil/forms.jsp.

2. Formal Requirements of a Motion

If you are involved in a motions practice, you will be writing motions as well as oppositions to motions. Both of these are similar in form and content. Before you begin to draft a motion or opposition, you should consult your jurisdiction's filing requirements. In addition to format, these rules control the timing of filing, page limits, and requirements for gaining consent from opposing counsel for the motion before filing.

For an example of filing requirements for a motion, see those for the District of Columbia Superior Court at http://www.dccourts.gov/dccourts/docs/civil_actions_handbook.pdf.

In addition, you should look for form motions. Most jurisdictions have forms on their courts' websites and most firms have sample forms for associates. Consulting these forms is a good idea to get started; however, do not blindly follow any form as each motion you file will have its own issues and tactical implications. Try to find multiple forms for each motion and consider the purpose, audience, scope, and view of your particular motion.

There are a variety of motions filed with trial courts. Some examples include the following:

Pretrial Motions:

Motion to Dismiss: requests court to dismiss a particular claim or all claims

Motion for Continuances: requests court for more time

Motion in Limine: requests court to admit, deny, or limit admission of certain evidence in trial

Motion to Suppress Evidence: requests court to suppress evidence in criminal cases based on constitutional violations

Motion for Summary Judgment: requests court to dismiss claims based on the law because there is "no genuine issue of material fact"

Motion to Compel Discovery: requests court to compel other side to produce discoverable evidence

Trial Motions:

Motion for Judgment Notwithstanding the Verdict: requests court to render verdict despite jury's verdict—these motions are made at the end of the plaintifif's case as well as after the verdict.

Post-Trial Motions:

Motion for New Trial: requests court to retry case

Motion for Remittitur: requests court to lower monetary award given by jury

A typical trial court requires the following formal requirements for any of these motions:

- A Notice of the Motion
- The Memorandum of Points and Authorities

- A Certificate of Service
- An Affidavit (at times if appropriate)
- An Order

a. *Notice of Motion or The Motion*

While some courts simply term this document "the Motion," the Notice of Motion serves the purpose of putting the court and the other party on notice of a particular motion being filed with the court. Parts of the notice include:

The Caption—which typically contains the name of the court, names of the parties, docket number, and judge's name;

The Heading—which states what type of motion such as "Motion to Dismiss";

The Body of the Notice—which includes an introduction stating the precise relief sought and supporting grounds for the motion that are often listed in numbered paragraphs;

Your Signature—including your bar number;

The Date; and

The Name and Address of the Opposing Party

Notice of Motion
    Caption
    Heading
    Body
    Your Signature
    Date
    Name and Address of Opposing Counsel

For an example of the form for a notice of motion, see www.dccourts.gov/dccourts/docs/civil_actions_handbook.pdf.

When motions are unopposed, often the Notice of Motion is all that is required. However, a statement is necessary indicating that opposing counsel consents to the motion. Motions for a continuance or more time to file a motion or opposition are often unopposed by the other party.

Sample Consent Motion

**IN THE SUPERIOR COURT OF THE DISTRICT OF COLUMBIA
CIVIL DIVISION**

CHARLIE SANDERS	)	
	)	
Plaintiff,	)	
	)	
v.	)	Civil Action No. 2008 CA 000888 M
	)	Calendar 11 – J. Fellow
ST LUKE'S HOSPITAL	)	
	)	
Defendant.	)	

**CONSENT MOTION FOR
ENLARGEMENT OF DISCOVERY DEADLINES**

COMES NOW the plaintiff, by and through undersigned counsel, and respectfully moves this Court pursuant to Rule 6 of the Superior Court Rules of Civil Procedure for an enlargement of the discovery deadlines in the above-captioned case. In support thereof, the parties state as follows:

1. This case is not currently set for trial.

2. This is a complex case involving allegations of medical negligence regarding the care and management of a patient with kidney disease.

3. Despite the cooperative efforts of the parties, the progression of discovery has been delayed due to difficulties encountered in obtaining and organizing the voluminous medical records and locating and deposing the relevant material fact witnesses.

4. Despite the cooperative efforts of all parties, additional time is needed to complete discovery of the necessary fact medical witnesses and obtain relevant medical records. The parties have jointly cooperated in an effort to obtain these records and locate the necessary witnesses and the process in ongoing.

5. This extension will not prejudice any of the parties.

6. All parties consent to this request.

WHEREFORE, the parties respectfully request that the Court grant the requested enlargement of the discovery deadlines in the above-captioned case in accordance with the Superior Court of the District of Columbia Rules of Civil Procedure, Rules 6, 12-I and 26.

Respectfully submitted,

DIANA R DONAHOE

By: _____

Diana R. Donahoe, Bar # XXXXX
600 New Jersey Avenue N.W.
Washington, DC 20001
(202) XXX - XXX

Attorney for Plaintiff

CERTIFICATE OF SERVICE

I HEREBY CERTIFY that a copy of the foregoing CONSENT MOTION FOR ENLARGEMENT OF DISCOVERY DEADLINES, POINTS AND AUTHORITIES, and ORDER were served via the court's electronic filing system, on January 1, 2011 to:

Drew Hanson
121 K Street, N.W.
Suite 200
Washington, D.C. 20002

_____
Diana R. Donahoe

b. *The Memorandum of Points and Authorities*

This is the document that provides the meat of your argument. It should contain the facts as well as the legal analysis to support your motion. Motions for a continuance are going to be short and contain no legal analysis; however, motions for summary judgment or other substantive motions will be filled with legal analysis and factual support. A memorandum of points and authorities is filed either in support of a motion or in opposition to a motion. Either way, the document is basically a trial brief and is very similar to an appellate brief, but without many of the formal requirements. The memorandum will start with a caption and a heading and will end with a signature and address. In addition, it may petition the court for a hearing on the matter. If a hearing is not granted or requested, the court will decide the matter on the pleadings. Therefore, the memorandum of points and authorities may be your only chance to inform and persuade the court.

Some courts have rules that dictate the form of memorandum of points and authorities; however, these rules are usually not nearly as specific as the format for briefs and allow for more flexibility in formatting. Usually, a table of contents and table of authorities is not required. However, in complicated motions, you may consider including a table of contents if it will help the court understand your arguments. Typically, a memorandum of points and authorities includes the following:

Caption and Heading
Introduction
Facts
Argument
Conclusion
Signature

For an example of the form for points and authorities, see www.dccourts. gov/dccourts/docs/civil_actions_handbook.pdf.

Caption and Heading: These mirror the caption and heading in the Notice of Motion. The only difference is that the heading will read: "Memorandum of Points and Authorities in Support of Motion to Dismiss" or "Memorandum of Points and Authorities in Opposition to Motion to Dismiss."

Introduction: Although it need not be labeled, the introduction serves the purpose of identifying the party filing the motion, explaining the main reasons for the motion and the underlying issues. It should be written persuasively and concisely so that the court immediately understands the party's position. Many memorandum include a sentence before the introduction that repeats the information in the heading, setting out the type of motion filed as well as the names of the parties.

Sample Sentence Before Introduction in an Opposition

The plaintiff, by and through undersigned counsel, respectfully requests that this Court deny defendant's untimely motion to compel experimental testing of the minor plaintiff in the above-captioned case.

Facts: The fact section should inform the court of the background facts of the case as well as the facts relevant to the motion. Some motions present the facts in numbered paragraphs while others use traditional paragraphs. Either way, the facts should be written to persuade the court to grant the motion. Remember that for most motions, you will present the facts as you predict they will be proven at trial. Tactical decisions are important here—in addition to the judge, opposing counsel reads your motion so you may not want to provide all relevant information in pretrial motions.

Argument: The argument is the meat of the memorandum. It provides the application of your facts to the law to prove your client's particular position is correct. It should be written persuasively to inform the court why the motion should be granted or denied. It may include pointheadings and should be well-organized and thoroughly analyzed. See pointheadings on page 164, large-scale organization on page 79 (chapter 2), persuasive techniques on page 97 (chapter 2), and chapter 1, Legal Analysis.

Conclusion: The conclusion should provide the relief requested from the court—usually asking that the court either grant or deny the motion.

Sample Conclusion

As the defendant's motion was made after the close of discovery, is unlikely to clarify any issues at trial, and will result in significant prejudice and delay, the plaintiff respectfully requests that the Court deny defendant's untimely request to compel the minor plaintiff to submit to experimental testing in the above-captioned case.

Signature: You must provide your signature and your bar number.

c. Certificate of Service

This sentence appears after the attorney's signature in both a Notice of Motion and the Memorandum of Points and Authorities and certifies that the attorney has served a copy of the motion on opposing counsel. It can be served in person, by mail, or by email and should specify delivery.

Sample Certificate of Service

I, Diana R. Donahoe, certify that a copy of this brief was emailed to John Johnson, Counsel for the Prosecution, on Monday, February 23, 2010.

_____
Diana R. Donahoe
D.C. Bar # *** ***
Donahoe & Associates
200 New Jersey Ave. N.W.
Washington, D.C. 00000

Counsel for Defendant

---

d. Affidavit

An affidavit is a sworn statement. It is often appendixed to motions to show factual support. It will begin with a caption and an introductory paragraph; the meat of the affidavit is written in numbered paragraphs and signed by the affiant. For an example of the form for an affidavit, see www.dccourts.gov/dccourts/docs/civil_actions_handbook.pdf.

e. Order

The order is the actual document you are asking the court to sign. It should specify that the judge is granting (or denying) the motion and should have a signature and date line for the judge.

Sample Order

IN THE SUPERIOR COURT OF THE DISTRICT OF COLUMBIA
CIVIL DIVISION

CHARLIE SANDERS	)	
	)	
Plaintiff,	)	
	)	
v.	)	Civil Action No. 2008 CA 000888
	)	Calendar 11 – J. Fellow
ST LUKE'S HOSPITAL	)	
	)	
Defendant.	)	

ORDER GRANTING JOINT CONSENT MOTION FOR
ENLARGEMENT OF DISCOVERY DEADLINES

UPON CONSIDERATION of the Consent Motion For Enlargement of Discovery Deadlines, and for the reasons stated therein, it is this _____ day of _____, 2011, hereby **ORDERED,** that the Motion be and hereby is GRANTED

_____

The Honorable Judge Fellow

Copies to:

Drew Hanson
121 K Street, N.W.
Suite 200
Washington, D.C. 20002

Diana R. Donahoe,
600 New Jersey Ave. N.W.
Washington, D.C. 20001

For an example of the form for an order, see www.dccourts.gov/dccourts/ docs/civil_actions_handbook.pdf.

3. Annotated Sample Pretrial Brief (or Memorandum of Points and Authorities)

IN THE UNITED STATES DISTRICT COURT
FOR THE DISTRICT OF MAINE

Betsy King, d/b/a	)
New England Salvage Co.,	) Case No: 01-4653
Plaintiff,	)
	)
	)
v.	) Judge STEPHENS
	)
The Shipwrecked Vessel, Known as	)
the Harbor Belle,	) [MEMORANDUM OF POINTS AND
Defendant.	) AUTHORITIES IN OPPOSITION TO
	) PLAINTIFF'S MOTION FOR A
	) PRELIMINARY INJUNCTION

_____]

This portion is the caption and title. The title of the document can go within the caption or centered and underlined just below the caption.

TABLE OF CONTENTS

The Table of Contents is not necessary in a Motion, but it can help persuade and inform the court.

TABLE OF AUTHORITIES

A Table of Authorities is usually not required in a trial brief but it can be helpful to the court.

The writer has included the procedural aspects in the Introduction, identified the parties, succinctly explained why the court should rule in its favor, and stated what action it wants the court to take. The procedural facts could have been included in the Facts instead.

Effective opening paragraph because it draws the reader into the narrative.

Notice the citations to the record throughout the Statement of Facts.

INTRODUCTION

[In its underlying in rem action, New England Salvage moved to acquire title to the shipwrecked vessel, Harbor Belle, a ship owned by Metropolitan Insurance Co. (Metropolitan), and, pursuant to Fed. R. Civ. P. 65, petitioned the Court to grant a preliminary injunction designed to keep Metropolitan from its property. Metropolitan, as Claimant/Intervenor, submits this memorandum in opposition to Plaintiff's motion since New England Salvage will be unable to establish any of the four factors used in the First Circuit to grant preliminary injunctions: It will not win its case on the merits; the harm it alleges is not irreparable; the hardship to Metropolitan, on balance, would be extreme if the injunction is granted; and public policy, which favors the rights of property owners, strongly supports Metropolitan's position. Therefore, Plaintiff's request should be denied.]

FACTUAL ALLEGATIONS

[On August 13, 1910, during a voyage from Portland, Maine, to Boston, Massachusetts, the passenger ship, Harbor Belle, was lost at sea due to a tragic explosion of unknown origins. (King Aff. ¶¶ 4, 5, 7, 8, 12, Nov. 5, 2006.) The ship went down about 50 miles off the coast of Maine, in approximately 4000 feet of water. (V. Compl. ¶ 6, Nov. 5, 2006.) Rescue efforts were undertaken immediately but failed to find any trace of the ship, crew, passengers, or cargo. (King Aff. ¶¶ 9, 10.)]

[Metropolitan insured the Harbor Belle, her contents, and her cargo in 1910. (V. Countercl. Claimant/Intervenor Metro. Ins. Co. ¶ 4, Nov. 12, 2001.) After the unsuccessful search for the missing ship, and acting in good faith on behalf of its clients, Metropolitan declared the ship a total loss in 1911 and promptly paid claimants the full amount of their policies. (Id. ¶¶ 6, 8.) Having paid the claim in full, Metropolitan claims all rights of ownership to the Harbor Belle, through subrogation. (Id. ¶ 6.)]

Within a short time, Metropolitan began a series of attempts to salvage the Harbor Belle. (Id. ¶¶ 8, 9.) Metropolitan made its first attempt in 1915 and was unsuccessful. (Id. ¶ 8.) With determination to find and recover its property, Metropolitan contracted with a professional salvor for a second attempt, in 1918, which was also unsuccessful. (Id. ¶ 9.) Since 1911, Metropolitan has retained the original insurance policy on the Harbor Belle, with a copy of the settlement document and other correspondence, in its files. (Id. ¶¶ 5, 6.)

With knowledge of Metropolitan's linkage to the Harbor Belle, provided by historical documents in its possession, Plaintiff began its activity to locate her and now claims to have done so on July 15, 2006. (King Aff. ¶¶ 13, 14.)

If, in fact, it has found the Harbor Belle, it has done so using new and highly advanced underwater technology not available to Metropolitan at the time of its earlier searches and not generally available today. (Id. ¶ 15.)

New England Salvage has failed to make any contact with Metropolitan concerning this issue. (V. Countercl. ¶ 10.) Instead, it made a business decision, independent of Metropolitan, to speculate in its venture and claims to have spent over $2 million. (King Aff. ¶¶ 16, 17.) Metropolitan became aware of New England Salvage's operation only when a book publisher inadvertently leaked information about the company's activities. (V. Countercl. ¶ 11.) New England Salvage has kept its activities secret from Metropolitan and has already begun to remove Metropolitan's property from the ship and presumably continues to do so. (King Aff. ¶ 17.) Plaintiff alleges that the presence of any other vessel in the area of the Harbor Belle would be a "hazard and an encumbrance" to its efforts to continue salvage operations. (V. Compl. ¶ 16.) Plaintiff petitioned the court to grant a preliminary injunction ordering all parties, including Metropolitan, to refrain from approaching the Harbor Belle within 10 square miles. (Mot. TRO & Prelim. Inj., Nov. 5, 2006.)

[Metropolitan has and continues to assert its ownership status and rights to the Harbor Belle. (V. Countercl. ¶ 12.) Metropolitan, via its counterclaim, has requested that the court deny Plaintiff's claim and enter an Order that grants Metropolitan the exclusive rights to conduct salvage and retrieval operations over its ship, the Harbor Belle, and to enjoin any further presence by New England Salvage or its agents at or near the site of its property. (Id.)]

> Notice the effective use of persuasive techniques to introduce the opposing party's role in the Facts. The writer has made effective use of placement and word choice.

> Notice the strong ending to the facts. The writer reasserts its claim for relief and uses positions of emphasis very well.

ARGUMENT

[Plaintiff's application for a preliminary injunction, under Fed. R. Civ. P. 65, should be denied because the claim on which it is based will not pass the four-part test used in the First Circuit for injunctive relief. Water Keeper Alliance v. U.S. Dept. of Def., 271 F.3d 21, 25 (1st Cir. 2001). To prevail on the first factor, Plaintiff must prove the likelihood that its request to keep Metropolitan from its property will succeed on the merits of the claim. Id. To prevail on the next two factors, Plaintiff must show first that it would be harmed irreparably if the injunction is denied and second, if its request is denied, the hardship to it, on balance, would be relatively greater than the hardship to Metropolitan if its request is upheld. Id. At 25. Last, Plaintiff must show that a ruling that denies Metropolitan its fundamental rights to its property would benefit public interest. Id. Plaintiff is unable to establish, with assurance, any of the four factors required for a preliminary injunction, and therefore, its application should be denied.]

> Opening thesis paragraph. It begins with an assertion and sets out a roadmap for the argument to come.

I.   [PLAINTIFF'S APPLICATION FOR PRELIMINARY INJUNCTION
      SHOULD BE DENIED BECAUSE IT WILL FAIL ON THE MERITS
      SINCE IT RELIES ON THE LAW OF FINDS, WHICH IS NOT
      FAVORED BY ADMIRALTY COURTS, AND IS BASED ON A FALSE
      ALLEGATION THAT METROPOLITAN ABANDONED THE HARBOR
      BELLE.]

[The court should deny Plaintiff's motion for a preliminary injunction because it will fail on the merits. Metropolitan has continuously asserted its rights of ownership over the Harbor Belle; therefore, Plaintiff's reliance on the law of finds is inappropriate because it requires a clear showing that Metropolitan abandoned the Harbor Belle. Depending on the circumstances, courts use two very different legal theories to resolve matters that pertain to shipwrecked vessels, the law of finds and the law of salvage. Moyer v. Wrecked & Abandoned Vessel, 836 F. Supp. 1099, 1104 (D.N.J. 1993). Particularly when sunken ships or their cargo are discovered and claimed by parties other than the owners, "courts favor the law of salvage over the law of finds." Columbus-Am. Discovery Group v. Atl. Mut. Ins. Co., 974 F.2d 450, 464 (4th Cir. 1992). The law of finds is only applicable when there is a finding that the owner abandoned the shipwrecked vessel. Moyer, 836 F. Supp. at 1105. The court should use the preferred law of salvage because Plaintiff will be unable to prove, with assurance, that Metropolitan has either explicitly or implicitly abandoned the Harbor Belle. Therefore, Plaintiff will not be able to establish the first factor needed to secure a preliminary injunction.]

A.   [The law of salvage is preferred by admiralty courts over the law of finds when the original owner is identified because it is viewed as more equitable for all parties.]

[Admiralty courts prefer the law of salvage over the law of finds when the original owner is identified because it is more equitable for all parties. When sunken ships are discovered by those other than the true owners, "courts favor applying the law of salvage over the law of finds." Columbus-Am., 974 F.2d at 464. Salvage law is more harmonious with the needs of maritime activity because it fosters cooperation among parties and allocates compensation in an equitable manner. Id. at 460. Traditionally, the law of finds was applied only to maritime property, "which had never been owned by anybody, such as ambergris, whales, and fish." Id. at 459, 460. The law of finds is "disfavored in admiralty courts because of its aims, its assumptions, and its rules." Id. At 460. In recent years, courts have been forced to resort to the law of finds in only a "handful of cases," where no owner came forward to claim the property. Id. at 462. If, however, the owner learns of the discovery and appears in court to claim the property and the owner has never expressly repudiated his ownership rights, "the law of salvage must be applied." Id. at 461.]

Marginal annotations:

Major pointheading. This pointheading follows the structure of the roadmap by focusing clearly on the first issue.

This is a mini-roadmap where the writer persuasively sets out the two subarguments in this section.

This is the subheading for the first issue and parallels the mini-roadmap.

In this paragraph, the writer provides a clear topic sentence, the rule on the issue, and the underlying law and policy regarding the issue. The writer could have considered splitting this paragraph into two paragraphs to make the issue easier for the reader to digest.

[In Columbus-Am., the insurance company owner appeared in court to claim its property after it had been lost at sea for 130 years. Id. at 459. [Despite a lower court ruling based on circumstantial evidence of abandonment,] the appellate court found [that the court "clearly erred when] it found abandonment and applied the law of finds." Id. at 468.]

Conciseness: consider omitting these two phrases as the procedural history is not important."

[As in Columbus-Am., a ship was lost at sea for many years but eventually discovered, and the owner has appeared in court to assert its ownership rights. (V. Countercl. ¶¶ 6, 7,12.) Given the court's preference for the law of salvage, Metropolitan's assertion of its ownership rights, and the lack of any express or implied declaration of abandonment, the court will use the law of salvage to resolve ownership of the Harbor Belle. Plaintiff's claim will fail on the merits, and therefore, its request for a preliminary injunction should be denied.]

Here, the writer applies a prior case to our facts. However, instead of focusing the reader on the case name in the topic sentences, the writer would have been more effective if the focus was on the legal issue instead.

B. Metropolitan has neither explicitly nor implicitly abandoned the Harbor Belle, and Plaintiff's allegation to the contrary is not supported by the facts.

Metropolitan has neither explicitly nor implicitly abandoned the Harbor Belle. Abandonment has been defined as a "voluntary act" that clearly and unmistakably indicates the intent to "repudiate ownership." Columbus-Am., 974 F.2d at 461. There are two ways to indicate the intent to abandon: expressed abandonment, where a party publicly disclaims ownership rights in a property, and implied abandonment, where circumstances give a clear and unmistakable indication of intent to cede ownership rights. Id. In the case of implied abandonment, admiralty courts "recognize a presumption against finding abandonment." Fairport Intl. Exploration v. Shipwrecked Vessel, 177 F.3d 491, 498 (6th Cir. 1999) ("Fairport III"). Metropolitan has neither expressly stated nor implicitly indicated the intent to abandon the Harbor Belle. (V. Countercl. ¶ 7.) Since Plaintiff's allegation to the contrary is not supported by the facts, it will be unable to establish the first factor needed for a preliminary injunction.

This paragraph provides a clear topic sentence, focuses the reader on the legal issue, and concludes with a mini-roadmap that sets out the organization for the two subelements.

1. Metropolitan has explicitly avowed its ownership rights to the Harbor Belle and has neither expressly stated nor affirmatively acted to repudiate ownership.

[Metropolitan has never expressly abandoned its ownership rights to the Harbor Belle. Express abandonment is a voluntary, affirmative act that clearly and unmistakably repudiates ownership. Columbus-Am., 974 F.2d at 461. It requires strong proof, like an "owner's express declaration abandoning title." Id. In Columbus-Am., there was evidence of an affirmative declaration to retain ownership in a correspondence with a potential salvager. Id. at 467. Also, because the insurance company owner negotiated with salvors to rescue its property, its actions were viewed as strong evidence of expressed ownership. Id. at 468. In a similar case, an underwriter owner was able to produce a mere business letter from 1860, which instructed a company agent not to abandon the shipwrecked vessel in question. Zych v. Unidentified, Wrecked & Abandoned Vessel, 755 F. Supp. 213, 215 (N.D. Ill. 1991). The letter was accepted as strong and adequate evidence of its intent to maintain ownership. Id. at 216.]

[[Similar to the owners in Columbus-Am. and Zych,] Metropolitan has never made an express declaration of abandonment of the Harbor Belle, nor has plaintiff alleged one. (See King Aff.) As in both Columbus-Am. and Zych, Metropolitan can produce historical documents from its files to support its claim that it is the owner of the Harbor Belle, through subrogation. (V. Countercl. ¶ 6.) Like the underwriter owner in Columbus-Am., Metropolitan negotiated with an independent salvor for a second attempt to rescue its property eight years after the loss in 1918. (Id. ¶ 9.) Last, by appearing to assert its ownership rights upon learning that New England Salvage was challenging those rights, Metropolitan has firmly made another clear statement of ownership. Metropolitan has consistently avowed its ownership rights to the Harbor Belle and has never made an express declaration of abandonment.]

2. Metropolitan has implicitly established its intent to retain ownership rights to the Harbor Belle by promptly paying claimants in full, by mounting salvage operations, and by preserving key documents.

[Metropolitan has performed, over time, in such manner to support its ownership rights to the Harbor Belle and has given no clear and convincing implication of an intent to abandon her. When an owner of a sunken vessel has not expressly abandoned its ship, courts have allowed the inference of abandonment to be determined from circumstances. Columbus-Am., 974 F.2d at 461. Circumstantial evidence may be inferred from various factors, such as lapse of time and nonuse, the place of the shipwreck, and the overall actions and conduct of the owners. Moyer, 836 F. Supp. at 1104. None of these factors, standing alone, is adequate to establish enough evidence to prove abandonment but must be considered in combination with all the factors. Fairport Intl. Exploration v. Shipwrecked Vessel, 72 F. Supp. 2d 795, 797 (W.D. Mich. 1999) ("Fairport IV"). But the circumstantial evidence must be clear and convincing and meet an intentionally "elevated, relatively stringent evidentiary standard." Fairport III, 177 F.3d at 500, 501. Particularly in situations where a vessel was lost at sea against the will of the owners, courts have imposed an "exacting burden of proof" on plaintiffs who argue by inference that the owners abandoned their property. Id. at 499, 500. The burden can be met by a material affirmative act by the owner, such as the intentional

---

Margin notes:

Notice how the writer uses two cases to illustrate the point and then compares these cases to the facts below.

Conciseness: consider omitting.

Notice how in the application, the writer makes the connections with the precedents explicit.

This topic sentence successfully focuses the reader on the second argument. This point of law was the strongest for the opposing side. Notice how the writer "buried" this argument. The writer earns the court's respect by addressing opposing arguments and authority in this analysis, but forcefully showing that the facts in this case are distinguishable.

destruction of pertinent documents, to show, by inference, the intent to abandon future claims. Zych, 755 F. Supp. at 216. The lack of such affirmative acts, on the other hand, is clear evidence that the intent to abandon should not be inferred. Id.]

In Columbus-Am., attempts to salvage the lost vessel were undertaken immediately, without success, and no further attempts were launched for over 125 years. Columbus-Am., 974 F.2d at 457. The plaintiff argued that the lapse of time involved, during which the owner was inactive in attempting to find and salvage the ship, was clear evidence of the intent to abandon. Id. at 465. The court ruled that the mere cessation of attempts to recover a lost ship, even for 125 years, was not conclusive of the intent to abandon. Id. at 464.

In Zych, a prospective salvor mounted a successful, technology-based campaign to locate a ship lost in the Great Lakes for 130 years. Zych, 755 F. Supp. at 215. He claimed, by law of finds, that the owner had abandoned the vessel through the lapse of time, nonuse, and failure to take steps toward recovering the ship. Id. The court found for the insurance company owner because the technology needed to find the ship was unavailable throughout the years and the lapse of time was understandable. Id. at 216. The court also found that an owner is not required to attempt salvage efforts over the years that a have minimal chance of success using the available technology of the day. Id.

[Another factor that can be used to infer abandonment is the place of the shipwreck, where available technology may also refute implied abandonment.] In Columbus-Am., the ship was lost in 8000 feet of water, 160 miles off the coast of South Carolina. Columbus-Am., 974 F.2d at 455. The discoverers employed a proprietary "high-tech" submersible robot they invented for such exploration of the ocean floor. Id. at 458. Similarly in Zych, the salvors used newly available technology to locate a ship lost in unknown and deep water. Zych, 755 F. Supp. at 215. The court held that, without advanced and rare technology, the chance of locating a ship in such place during the years was minimal and the fact it remained lost was not supportive of an inference of abandonment. Id. at 216. On the other hand, in Moyer, the location of the ship was specifically and widely known and immediately accessible, as divers were able to reach her the next day. Moyer, 836 F. Supp. at 1102. These factors contributed to a finding of implied abandonment. Id. at 1104.

[The overall conduct and general lack of action by the owners of the ship in Moyer added weight to the inference of abandonment. Id. The insurance company, which owned the ship through subrogation, made no effort to conduct salvage operations, nor did it contest the removal of valuable items from the ship by salvors during open and notorious operations. Id. at 1103. Similarly, in Fairport IV, the owner knew where the vessel went down, technology was available to salvage her, the conditions were difficult but salvage was possible, yet no attempt to salvage the ship was made over an extensive time

> This topic sentence is more effective than the previous two topic sentences. Where the two previous topic sentences focus on case names, this topic sentence focuses the reader on the legal factor addressed in the paragraph.

Unfavorable law in these rule illustrations, but the writer is including details that later are distinguished in the analysis.

The writer goes back to favorable authorities to finish the legal analysis.

This is an example of analysis that anticipates and forcefully repudiates the counterargument.

frame. Fairport IV, 72 F. Supp. 2d at 798, 799. The overall actions and conduct of the owner combined to support the inference of abandonment. Id. at 800.]

On the other hand, the insurance company owners in Columbus-Am. began negotiating with salvors within weeks of the shipwreck and mounted two unsuccessful salvage attempts. Columbus-Am., 974 F.2d at 457. Additionally, the underwriter was able to produce several original documents that described its attempts and established its ownership through subrogation. Id. at 465. Preserving the records for 130 years was viewed as significant, after an expert witness testified that insurance companies today routinely purge their inactive files after five years. Id. at 466. The underwriter's failed salvage attempts, combined with the historic documents, were adequate to establish that there was no implied intent to abandon the lost ship. Id. at 468. In Zych, the underwriter owner similarly was able to show early attempts to salvage the lost ship. Zych, 755 F. Supp. at 215. But it was able to produce only a few business letters written in 1860, which indicated merely that it was the owner through subrogation and that it asserted its ownership rights. Id. [Along with other factors, the conduct of the underwriter to preserve these scarce few documents was adequate for the court to find no inference of abandonment. Id. at 216.]

[Like the owners in Columbus-Am. and Zych, but unlike the owners in Fairport IV and Moyer, Metropolitan launched an unsuccessful salvage expedition in 1915, five years after the ship was lost. (V. Countercl. ¶ 8.) Undeterred and committed to recover its property, it contracted with an independent salvor in a second unsuccessful attempt in 1918. (Id. ¶ 9.) Like the owners in Columbus-Am. and Zych, it is reasonable to infer that Metropolitan rightly concluded that, given the technology of the day, the depth of water where the Harbor Belle went down, and the lack of specific coordinates, further salvage attempts had no real chance of success. Also, like the prospective salvors in both Columbus-Am. and Zych, New England Salvage employed "newly available state-of-the-art technology, including the Sea Marc side-scanning sonar and undersea robot" not widely available to other salvors and specifically not available to Metropolitan, to locate the Harbor Belle. (King Aff. ¶ 15.) The fact that it required advanced equipment of that sophistication to locate the Harbor Belle is strong evidence that Metropolitan's decisions over the years to refrain from pointless salvage attempts, which would have used then current technology, were prudent and could not be considered the intent to abandon.]

Metropolitan's early attempts at salvage also contrast with the lack of effort by the owners in Moyer and Fairport III, where the ships were in shallower water, the locations were specifically known to the owners, and the ships were salvageable using the technology of the day. Similar to the underwriters in <u>Columbus-Am.</u> and <u>Zych</u>, but to a markedly greater extent, Metropolitan protected and maintained key documents pertaining to the Harbor Belle for nearly a century. (V. Countercl. ¶¶ 5, 6.) Unlike the mere business letters and rather meager documents that the court viewed as dispositive evidence to negate an inference of abandonment in those cases, Metropolitan has maintained the original insurance policy on the Harbor Belle, the settlement document used to pay claims on the ship and establish ownership through subrogation, and copies of a letter from the period. (<u>Id.</u>) Also, Plaintiff has indicated that it has additional historical documents related to the Harbor Belle. (King Aff. ¶ 13.) As in <u>Columbus-Am.</u>, for a company in the insurance industry, where inactive documents are purged after five years, preserving documents on the Harbor Belle for nearly a century is clear and convincing evidence that Metropolitan has never implied the intent to abandon her. Metropolitan has not given any implication of an intent to abandon through lapse of time, or the place of the shipwreck, or by its overall conduct.

Therefore, Plaintiff should be denied its motion for a preliminary injunction because it will fail on the merits as Metropolitan has neither expressly nor implicitly abandoned the Harbor Belle and the court should use the law of salvage, which will affirm Metropolitan's ownership rights.

II. [PLAINTIFF'S APPLICATION FOR PRELIMINARY INJUNCTION SHOULD BE DENIED BECAUSE ANY HARM IT ALLEGES WILL BE MITIGATED BY ITS REWARD UNDER THE LAW OF SALVAGE AND, ON BALANCE, THE HARDSHIP TO METROPOLITAN WILL BE EXTREME IF THE INJUNCTION IS APPROVED.]

Notice how the writer decided to combine two of the factors under one major heading.

New England Salvage will be unable to establish the second and third factors required to receive a preliminary injunction because a finding for Metropolitan would not constitute irreparable harm to Plaintiff and to the contrary, a finding for Plaintiff would cause extreme hardship to Metropolitan. Under the law of salvage, New England Salvage, as discoverer of the Harbor Belle, is entitled to compensation in an amount deemed appropriate given the level of service to the owner and to the extent that a finder of fact believes it deserves such compensation. <u>See</u> <u>Columbus-Am.</u>, 974 F.2d at 461. Such compensation will more than mitigate any alleged harm to Plaintiff. However, on balance, a finding for Plaintiff would deny Metropolitan's fundamental rights to access and secure its property and would allow Plaintiff to continue to take Metropolitan's property from the Harbor Belle, clearly constituting an extreme hardship to Metropolitan. For these reasons, the balance of equity favors Metropolitan, and Plaintiff will be unable to establish the second and third factors needed for a preliminary injunction.

A. Plaintiff's request for preliminary injunction should be denied because its alleged harm is not irreparable, since it will be mitigated by Plaintiff's reward under salvage law.

New England Salvage's request for preliminary injunction should be denied because its alleged harm is not irreparable since it will be mitigated by its reward under salvage law. Plaintiff must clearly demonstrate that it will suffer irreparable harm if its request for a preliminary injunction is denied. Water Keeper, 271 F.3d at 27. In Water Keeper, the plaintiff attempted to show irreparable harm by offering nonspecific, general claims that the defendant's activities threatened a number of endangered species. Id. Its request was denied, in part, for vagueness of complaint and inability to clearly demonstrate irreparable harm. Id. at 28, 29. New England Salvage's claim mentions the inconvenience of having other ships in the general area of the Harbor Belle and the increased need for extra safety precautions as reasons to grant a preliminary injunction. (V. Compl. ¶¶ 16, 17.)

Like the inherent vagueness in Water Keeper, Plaintiff's nonspecific claim of harm from the mere presence of another ship in the general area of the Harbor Belle and the obvious need for appropriate safety precautions to avoid any hazardous conditions certainly do not rise to the level of irreparable harm. While not clear, Plaintiff's main concern appears to be financial, however, claiming to have spent over $2 million in its venture. (King Aff. ¶ 16.) Under the law of salvage, New England Salvage, as discoverer of the Harbor Belle, is entitled to compensation in an amount deemed appropriate given the level of service to the owner and to the extent that a finder of fact believes it deserves such compensation. Given that Plaintiff has speculated to the level it claims, it is reasonable to infer that it believes the potential value of the Harbor Belle to be worth many times its expense to date. In the end, its salvage award will more than adequately compensate it for its effort. Therefore, Plaintiff has not demonstrated with clarity and assurance that it will suffer irreparable harm, and its motion for a preliminary injunction should be denied.

B. Plaintiff's request for preliminary injunction should be denied because on balance, the hardship to Metropolitan will be extreme if the injunction is approved.

The harm to Metropolitan will be extreme if Plaintiff's request for preliminary injunction is approved because, during the injunction period, New England Salvage will continue to remove Metropolitan's property from the Harbor Belle. To establish the third factor needed for a preliminary injunction, Plaintiff must show, on balance, that the hardship to New England Salvage is greater if the injunction is denied than it is to Metropolitan if it is upheld. Water Keeper, 271 F.3d at 25. In Water Keeper, the court described the appropriate and positive balance given to the national policy of supporting

---

Instead of using the exact same language from the subheading, this topic sentence would have been more effective by stating the same proposition, but in a different way.

military readiness in favor of mere economic harm claimed by a plaintiff. Id. at 28.

Similar to the plaintiff described in <u>Water Keeper</u>, New England Salvage is ostensibly asserting inconvenience and economic impact against the extreme and severe hardship to Metropolitan if it is denied its fundamental right to access and secure its property. Plaintiff has stated that it has conducted two salvage operations and has already taken an unspecified amount of gold and passenger jewelry from the Harbor Belle. (King Aff. ¶ 17.) If Plaintiff's request is not denied, Metropolitan would be placed in a position to lose, forever, an immeasurable quantity of its property, until its rights are affirmed in full court. New England Salvage has failed to adequately describe any hardship that could compare to the potential loss by Metropolitan. Therefore, Plaintiff's request should be denied because, on balance, the hardship to Metropolitan will be extreme if the preliminary injunction is granted.

III. PLAINTIFF'S APPLICATION FOR PRELIMINARY INJUNCTION SHOULD BE DENIED BECAUSE THE PUBLIC'S INTEREST IN PRESERVING AN ORIGINAL OWNER'S PROPERTY RIGHTS IN SHIPWRECKED VESSELS IS STRONG.

[New England Salvage's application for preliminary injunction should be denied because the public's interest in preserving an original owner's property rights in shipwrecked vessels is strong. To establish the fourth factor needed for a preliminary injunction, Plaintiff must demonstrate that granting its application serves the public's interest better than would a denial. <u>Water Keeper</u>, 271 F.3d at 25. Public interest is documented in longstanding admiralty laws, which protect the property rights of owners, to the point that they uphold a presumption against finding that a shipwrecked vessel was abandoned. <u>Zych</u>, 755 F. Supp. At 498. Admiralty law preserves an owner's property rights, and courts have long adhered to the tenet that property that was lost at sea was taken involuntarily from the owner and must rightly be restored should the owner appear to claim it. <u>Columbus-Am.</u>, 974 F.2d at 460, 461. Metropolitan has appeared to firmly assert its property ownership rights to the Harbor Belle and to proclaim that it has acted, in all ways, clearly and convincingly consistent with that fact. (V. Countercl. ¶¶ 6-9, 12.) Public policy, as documented and reflected in admiralty law, strongly favors Metropolitan's fundamental right to access and secure its property, the Harbor Belle. Therefore, Plaintiff's request for a preliminary injunction, which is intended to keep Metropolitan from its property, should be denied.]

Notice how the writer is able to complete the analysis here in just one paragraph. This was a good choice for this issue. However, one paragraph will usually not be enough space to address most issues.

CONCLUSION

Plaintiff's request for a preliminary injunction should be denied since it is unable to establish any of the four factors required by the First Circuit to grant such request. It will not win on the merits. It has not established any irreparable harm. On balance, if its request is upheld, the relative hardship to Metropolitan is extreme. Last, public policy favors upholding Metropolitan's assertion of its property rights. Therefore, Metropolitan respectfully requests that the Court deny Plaintiff's Motion for Preliminary Injunction.

Respectfully Submitted,

Associate # XXX

V.   CLIENT LETTERS

Lawyers write a variety of letters including cover letters, demand letters, and letters to opposing counsel. This section focuses on letters written to clients. Client letters are written to provide the client with a legal opinion and advice. They should answer the client's questions in clear, concise, and easy-to-understand language. Client letters are similar in purpose to the memorandum of law (see page 130) in that they provide objective analysis of a legal issue; they differ, however, in audience, scope, and view.

A.   *Purpose, Audience, Scope, and View*

- **Purpose:** A client letter informs the client of her options under the law. It provides answers to the client's questions and explains the reasoning for those answers. A letter to a client also provides a paper trail for the lawyer—oftentimes to memorialize the lawyer's opinion and the facts of the case at the time.
- **Audience:** The client is the primary audience for this type of letter. However, clients can vary enormously in background, education, and knowledge. Therefore, keep in mind your particular audience for each letter; a letter written to a CEO of a large business will differ greatly from one written to an incarcerated drug offender. Your audience will determine if you use legal terms, discuss cases, provide citations, and reveal all of your research.
- **Scope:** The client letter should answer the question whether to, and provide advice on how, the client should proceed. It should also clarify the limitations of the letter for the client; for example, it should inform the client that if the facts change, the lawyer's opinion might change as well. In addition, a lawyer should keep in mind clarity and costs when writing a client letter. A long letter might be too cumbersome to read and might indicate that the lawyer has spent a lot of money in its preparation.
- **View:** The view of a client letter can vary greatly, depending on the audience. The reasoning may be cursory or in-depth; the tone can be conversational, friendly, or formal. However, client letters should always be professional; avoid slang and flippant remarks.

See page 282 for an annotated sample client letter.

B.   *Formal Requirements*

Before writing a client letter, you should gather the facts from your client, research the legal issue, and clarify the client's question. The requirements of a letter vary greatly depending on the audience, the particular purpose, and the scope of the letter. The traditional requirements, listed below, are similar to the formal requirements of a memorandum. However, you need not provide headings labeling each requirement. For more information on each, see the pages indicated.

- Date and Salutation, immediately below.
- Opening Paragraph, below.
- Facts Section, below.
- Analysis Section, page 281.
- Closing, page 281.

1.   Date and Salutation

The date on the letter memorializes when you have given your opinion. If facts or law changes after that date, your opinion may no longer be valid. The salutation sets the tone of the letter; therefore, determine if you want to use a first name or a title and last name. When in doubt, choose formality over informality.

2.   Opening Paragraph

The opening paragraph usually provides the context for the letter and restates the issue. Often, it will provide an answer, especially if the answer is one the client would like to hear right away. This paragraph serves a function similar to the question presented (see page 131) and brief answer (see page 133) of a memorandum of law.

Sample Opening Paragraph

On November 12, 2004, we discussed the trial tactic of requesting a jury instruction of the lesser-included offense of voluntary manslaughter in your murder trial. As I explain below, I believe the trial judge will include a voluntary manslaughter instruction; however, I am not certain whether the jury will find you guilty of murder or voluntary manslaughter.

---

3.   Facts Section

The facts section provides background information as well as legally significant facts. This section should be written objectively. The facts may be based on documents you have reviewed, client or witness interviews, or your own investigation. Consider noting the source for some of your facts in complicated cases. In addition, ask the client to review the facts and make any necessary additions or corrections. The facts you present in your client letter memorialize those facts as of that date.

Sample Facts Section

I have based my opinion on the facts below. Please read them carefully and inform me of any changes, corrections, or additions as these might alter my legal opinion.

On September 13, 2004, you were riding in a rental car in Memphis, Tennessee ...

---

4. Analysis Section

The analysis section of a client letter is similar to the discussion section (see page 136) of a memorandum of law. It should be organized around the law itself with clear topic sentences and explanations for your conclusions. This section should be written objectively, providing counterarguments where appropriate so that the client understands both sides of the issue. This section differs from a discussion section in a memo in the form of the analysis. A client wants to understand how the law applies to her problem, but she might not want to know the details, citations, or intricacies of the law itself. Here, you must determine how much detail you will provide regarding the cases, statutory definitions, and policy behind the law. If you must use detailed case descriptions or legal terms of art, consider providing an explanation for the reader.

5. Closing

The closing of a client letter is similar to the conclusion (see page 141) of a memorandum of law. It provides a conclusion and your advice. Provide enough information so that your client understands the next steps she should take. In addition, consider mentioning other issues that might be pursued in the future.

Closing Sample

I believe the judge will grant our motion to include a jury instruction on self-defense; however, I am concerned about the jury's willingness to find you guilty of voluntary manslaughter as opposed to murder. Therefore, I suggest you come in at your earliest convenience to discuss the voluntary manslaughter instruction. The sooner we discuss this lesser-included offense, the easier it will be to prepare for trial. In addition, we might consider other lesser-included offenses that might apply to your situation. When you come in to meet with me, please bring the names and phone numbers of any witnesses to this accident.

C.   *Annotated Sample Client Letter*

September 15, 2005

Mr. Andy Ross
1313 Whistleblower Drive
Red Bank, New Jersey 00202

Re: Wrongful discharge claim

Dear Mr. Ross,

[On September 8, 2005, we discussed the possibility of filing a wrongful discharge claim against your former employer under New Jersey's Conscientious Employee Protection Act (CEPA). Because you are unlikely to establish at least one of the five elements necessary to sustain such a claim, I would recommend an alternative course of action.]

[My conclusions are based on the facts set forth below. Please review them carefully and inform me of any changes, corrections, or additions you deem necessary, as such considerations may affect my legal opinion.]

From 1999-2005, you worked 40 hours per week at Krazy Karl's Music Emporium in Toms River, NJ. After a management change in June 2005, your new employer began a marketing campaign aimed toward teenage customers. As part of that campaign, he directed you to use price stickers to conceal parental advisory labels on compact discs and other products. The parental advisory labels were affixed to the merchandise as part of a voluntary self-regulation program jointly implemented by the Recording Industry Association of America (RIAA) and the National Association of Recording Merchandisers (NARM). The goal of the program is to apprise parents of music containing lyrics that may be inappropriate for minors. Because you objected to the practice of purposefully concealing parental advisory labels, you declined to obey your employer's instructions. You were then reassigned from the retail department to inventory and your hours were reduced from 40 to 10 per week. Although several of your colleagues' hours were also reduced, your reduction was considerably more severe.

Margin annotations:

This opening paragraph successfully lays out the issue and the answer right up front for the client. Careful—the client might not want to wait for the last paragraph to discover the "alternative course of action."

This paragraph sets up the fact section of the letter and informs the client that the lawyer's advice is based on these facts.

This fact section presents legally significant facts as well as background facts and is written objectively for the client.

[To maintain a cause of action for [wrongful discharge], we must prove all of the following legal elements: [(1) the existence of a clear mandate of public policy that has been violated by the employer's conduct; (2) a reasonable belief that the employer's conduct was in violation of such mandate; (3) the performance of a whistleblowing activity; (4) the employee has suffered adverse employment action; and (5) a causal connection existed between the adverse employment action and the whistleblowing activity.] Although we can prove some of these elements, we cannot prove the first and second element. [I address each of these elements below.]

> RBO: wrongful discharge

> This roadmap sets out the elements clearly for the reader.

> This sentence helps the client understand the organization of the letter; however, it would not be necessary in a legal memo as a lawyer would assume the writer would address each one of the elements in turn.

[We will be unsuccessful in establishing a [clear mandate of public policy], the first required element of a prima facie case under CEPA. A clear mandate of public policy can be established only by sources that are [(1) specific and (2) binding.] To qualify as specific, a source must clearly define the policy in question. The RIAA/NARM regulation passes this test because it is aimed at achieving the clear goal of informing parents that certain musical selections may be inappropriate for children. [Although the regulation fails to provide comprehensive criteria for determining which material is inappropriate, a court will likely conclude that it clearly sets forth a method of informing parents that certain material may be objectionable.] [It is therefore probable that we can establish the first sub-element of the required clear mandate of public policy.]

> RBO: clear mandate of public policy

> This mini-roadmap clearly lays out the two sub-elements to be addressed. However, it is written in passive voice and can be more concise if changed to active voice.

> A reader may ask, "Why?" here. Whenever possible, explain your reasoning.

> This mini-conclusion does conclude on the issue. However, it can be written more concisely (i.e., we can probably prove…).

[However, the RIAA/NARM regulation does not qualify as [binding]. A binding source of public policy places mandatory restrictions or obligations on those it governs; the regulation at issue here serves no such function, as it is implemented on an entirely voluntary basis. We will be unable to show that the RIAA/NARM regulation is a binding source and our argument on this first element—and therefore the whole claim—will fail.]

> RBO: binding

> This mini-conclusion effectively concludes on this element and informs the client why the claim will not succeed.

[In addition, we might not be able to prove the [second element] of the claim.] The second element of a cognizable CEPA claim is the employee must prove he had a reasonable belief that the employer's action violated a clear mandate of public policy. In determining whether such a belief exists, New Jersey courts employ an objective standard, which will take into account your knowledge, education, and employment back-

> RBO: second element

> This topic sentence is not very helpful to the reader. Instead, consider combining this sentence with the next sentences so the reader understands the element to be discussed.

Avoid legalese. ————————

Conciseness. "It remains debatable" is a cumbersome way to begin a sentence. Instead, start with strong subject-verb combinations (i.e., Your employer will argue that...).

Conciseness. Try to avoid starting sentences with "It is" or "There are." Instead, use strong subject-verb combinations.

RBO: whistle-blowing activity ————

This mini-conclusion effectively concludes on the element and tells the client the reason for your conclusion. ————

RBO: adverse employment action ————

This topic sentence could be more concise. ——

This mini-conclusion effectively concludes on the element and tells the client the reason for your conclusion. ————

RBO: adverse employment action ————

This topic sentence clearly informs the reader of the element to be addressed in the paragraph.

This analysis is probably enough for a client letter; however, if you were writing a memo, you would need to address "substantial factor" in more detail so that the lawyer would understand what has been considered to be substantial in prior cases. ————

ground as an employee. Given your experience in the music industry, we can show that you are familiar with industry standards and guidelines, including the use of parental warning labels. [Notwithstanding this assumption,] [it remains debatable] whether a reasonable employee in your situation would know that the RIAA/NARM policy is voluntary. This question would likely turn on testimony from similarly situated employees. [It is therefore uncertain whether] you can establish that you reasonably believed your employer was violating a clear mandate of public policy when he instructed you to cover the parental advisory labels with price stickers.

[Third, although you did not report your employer's actions, you will be able to show that you performed a [whistleblowing activity], the third required element of a successful claim under CEPA. CEPA has been interpreted to protect employees who object to or refuse to participate in conduct that they reasonably believe violates a clear mandate of public policy. Because you refused to obey your employer's instructions to conceal the parental warning label, we can successfully establish that you performed a whistleblowing activity.]

[Turning to the fourth required element of a CEPA claim, we can adduce proof that you suffered an [adverse employment action.]] After five years of working in retail, you were abruptly transferred to inventory where you were no longer able to interact with customers and represent the Krazy Karl's sales team. In addition, your hours were reduced from 40 to 10 per week. Because you were transferred to a position you found less desirable and because your hours were reduced against your wishes, we will be able to establish an adverse employment action.]

[Finally, we can also establish a causal connection between [the adverse employment action] and your whistleblowing activity.] We need only show that the whistleblowing activity was a substantial factor in your employer's decision to take adverse action. Here, we will show that your reduction in hours was considerably more drastic than that of the other employees. Moreover, the facts set forth above indicate that you were the only employee subjected to a departmental transfer. Because this evidence indicates that your reluctance to conceal parental warning labels was a [substantial factor] in your employer's later decisions, you are likely to succeed in establishing the required causal connection between whistleblowing activity and adverse employment action.]

This mini-conclusion effectively concludes on the element and tells the client the reason for your conclusion.

[In sum, a wrongful discharge claim on your behalf is likely to fail as we will be unable to establish at least one—and possibly two—required elements of the claim. Because the RIAA/NARM parental warning policy is strictly voluntary, we cannot show a clear mandate of public policy. Depending on witness testimony, we may also be unable to establish a reasonable belief that your employer's order to cover parental warning labels violated such a policy mandate. Although we are likely to establish the remaining three elements of a successful claim, we need to prove all five elements to prevail. Therefore, I would advise against pursuing a legal remedy under CEPA. However, I would be more than happy to help you mediate this problem with your employer to try to restore your position and your hours. Please call me if you would like to pursue this less litigious avenue.]

This closing paragraph is effective because it answers the client's question and provides guidance for the client's next step.

Sincerely,

Peter J. Martin
Donahoe & Associates
243 River Road
Edison, New Jersey 08916

VI.   SCHOLARLY WRITING

While the other sections of this book address writing in legal practice, this section focuses on writing to criticize the law or propose new ideas within the legal scholarly community. Scholarly writing takes on many forms. Professors usually write law review articles; students often write seminar papers, law review notes, and law review competition papers.

A.   *Purpose, Audience, Scope, and View*

- **Purpose:** All forms of scholarly writing are written to provide a particular point of view. They usually criticize a particular body of law, specific case, or traditional principles. In addition, they should propose original ideas and novel theories. The best scholarly papers have clear thesis statements and consistently focus on those thesis statements. Most students struggle with focusing on a specific purpose and proposing novel ideas.
- **Audience:** The primary audience is other scholars—law professors and students. However, oftentimes the secondary audience is the practicing lawyer and judge focusing on a particular issue as law review articles are often cited when judges create new law. Lawyers specializing in specific areas of practice are also familiar with scholarly articles on their subjects. The biggest mistake students make is assuming that the primary audience is the professor in the seminar course. While the professor is the actual audience, the student should assume the professor is reading the paper as a scholar in the field.
- **Scope:** The scope of any scholarly paper should be narrow. The best papers remain focused on one specific thesis. The biggest mistake students make is to address multiple issues on a superficial basis instead of providing an in-depth analysis of one issue.
- **View:** The point of view of the author is crucial in scholarly writing; the reader is expecting to hear what the author thinks and why. Therefore, the author's voice, personal opinions, and novel ideas are expected to be heard throughout the article. Use of the first person (e.g., "I will address the following ideas ...") is expected.

For more on writing seminar papers and law review notes, see the section immediately below. Law review write-on competition papers are covered in the section beginning on page 290.

B.   *Seminar Papers and Law Review Notes*

Seminar papers and law review notes are very similar. One is written as a requirement for a class; the other is written as a requirement for law review. Often, seminar papers are published as law review notes. Therefore, this section will focus on the process of creating either a seminar paper or law review note:

- Selecting a Topic, immediately below.
- Performing a Preemption Check, below.
- Researching the Issue, page 288.
- Writing and Rewriting a Scholarly Piece, page 288.
- Cite-Checking, page 289.
- Getting Published, page 289.

For a sample law review article, see http://www.law.georgetown.edu/faculty/donahoe/.

1. Selecting a Topic

Selecting a topic is the most critical step in the seminar paper process. Be sure you set aside enough time for this decision.

First, the topic should be relevant to the seminar or to your law review (many law reviews address particular areas of law such as international environmental law or ethics). Often, professors provide lists of possible subject matters. However, don't rely solely on these lists to decide what interests you most; instead, look at the readings, consider the discussions in class, and follow the news. Helpful sources for legal news and current trends include The United States Law Week and the "new developments" sections of Westlaw and Lexis. Choose a topic that will keep you interested; writing about a boring subject makes for boring writing.

Second, the topic should be narrow; it should focus on a specific issue—not just a broad area of law. Write an issue statement to focus your topic on a particular question within your field.

Third, try to answer that issue statement. In doing so, you will create your proposed thesis for the paper. That thesis might change as you start researching and writing, but it will help you focus at this stage of the process.

Fourth, be sure your issue is novel. The purpose of a scholarly paper is not to summarize the law on a particular issue, but to create original ideas about that issue. Therefore, your paper will need to say something different from other papers. Your topic can, therefore, be on a totally new issue or it can be a different spin on an old issue.

2. Performing a Preemption Check

Because your paper is expected to propose novel ideas, you must check to make sure that no one else has written on the same subject with the same issue and thesis. Therefore, you will need to do a preemption check—a search through other law reviews and journal literature to determine what has been written on your subject. As you perform your preemption check, take note of helpful articles that might assist in your future research.

To perform a preemption check, search the indexes and databases of law review articles.

3. Researching the Issue

Scholarly research has two phases: background research and specific issue research. First, you want to understand the general field of law you have chosen to write about. You need to know where your topic fits into the broader picture. Therefore, a secondary source, such as a treatise or hornbook, law review articles, and looseleafs can prove helpful to educate yourself at this stage of the process. As you read, take notes of citations throughout the readings that you think might prove useful.

Second, you want to narrow your research to articles and primary law that focus directly on your thesis. Your starting point for this research can be your list of relevant citations you found doing your background research. It is at this point in the process that you will begin to take notes on the substance of the topic. Of course, you are bound to find more articles cited within these sources. Be sure to research current articles first; these will help you find some of the older sources as well as provide recent ideas on the topic. In addition, consider asking other scholars in the field. Often the professor of the seminar is the best research source.

4. Writing and Rewriting a Scholarly Piece

The same techniques described in chapter 2, The Writing Process, apply for scholarly writing. Your article should be well organized, thoroughly analyzed, and concise.

When writing the scholarly article, provide the following:

An introduction that gives some context for the topic and specifically tells the reader where the paper will lead. Typically, roadmaps are included at the end of the introduction section and are written in the first person: "I will first address ..."; "Next, I will discuss ..."; "Finally, I will propose new ideas ...."

A section of the article that informs the reader of the current state of the law in that topic. Most readers need some background information before they can appreciate your new ideas on your topic.

A section where you propose novel ideas and areas of reform. Here is where your original thought should shine. Creativity, thoughtfulness, and logical analysis are the ingredients to good writing in this section.

Provide a conclusion so that the reader can understand a summary of your thesis. Make sure your thesis is consistent here with the introduction.

When rewriting the scholarly article, consider the following:

- **Purpose:** Have you provided a clear, focused thesis? Is your thesis consistent throughout your article?
- **Audience:** Have you addressed a particular audience for this paper? Who is that audience? Have you answered the audience's concerns? Be sure

that you have not tried to address multiple audiences; this problem often leads to a paper that is not focused.
- **Scope:** What was your particular thesis? Have you gone beyond the scope of that thesis? On the flip side, have you provided enough depth to address your issue and prove your thesis?
- **View:** Your point of view should shine throughout your article. Your voice, opinions, and theories should stand out and be heard.

5. Cite-Checking

Cite-checking is a two-part process. First, you need to check the substance of your citations. Does each article you cite really say what you purport it to say? You must find each source and read it to perform this part of the cite-check. Second, you need to make sure that the citation format is correct. If you are using Bluebook format, refer to the front inside cover of the Bluebook where you will find a quick summary of law review article citation. If you are using ALWD format, see ALWD Rule 23 and the Fast Formats section under that rule. Remember that the Bluebook rules are written primarily for law review articles; the practitioner's notes (the Bluepages in the beginning of the Bluebook) modify the rules for legal documents filed in court and legal memoranda. Be careful, though: Most first-year students are taught citation as practitioners, not as cite-checkers for law reviews. Therefore, consult the rules of the Bluebook (see page 455) or ALWD (see page 401) as you cite-check.

6. Getting Published

Be sure your paper is in the best possible shape before you submit it to be published. Have other colleagues read it and discuss it with you before submission.

If you have written a seminar paper, you should consider trying to publish your paper. Although it might seem like an unnecessary "hassle" to you as a busy student, it will be well worth your time in the future. If you have written a law review note, you will submit it to your law review. The law review editors will then decide whether it is a note that is worthy of publication in the journal. If your law review decides not to publish it, consider sending it to other journals.

Here's how to publish your note or paper:

a. Find Appropriate Law Journals

To publish a note or seminar paper, first create a list of appropriate law reviews—journals that publish articles on your topic. Your seminar professor will have some good ideas for appropriate journals. There are directories of law journals that you can consult as well: Directory of Law Reviews, Current Law Index, and Index to Legal Periodicals and Books. For an excellent online submission site, see Expresso at http://law.bepress.com/expresso/.

b.   *Consider Timing*

General folklore suggests that you should avoid sending out articles (unless they are time sensitive) from October through February. Because most editorial boards start in March, that is usually a good month to submit articles. And because August is the month that editorial boards come back from summer break, August and early September are also good times to submit articles.

c.   *Write a Cover Letter*

The purpose of the cover letter is to make the editor interested in your article. Therefore, provide a concise summary of the paper and show why it is novel and important in the field. A one-page cover letter should be sufficient.

C.   *Law Review Write-On Competition Papers*

To join a law review, most first-year students are invited to participate in a "write-on competition." The competition, which usually occurs at the end of the first year or during spring break, requires students to write a paper during a limited amount of time. The students receive (or purchase) a closed packet of materials (no outside research is required), and the instructions in the packet lay out the rules and issues for the competition. Usually, students are required to write a "case note" for the competition.

This section discusses the following considerations for law review write-on competition papers.

- Should I Participate? (immediately below)
- What Is a Case Note? (page 291)
- Writing a Case Note (page 291)
- Citation (page 292)

1.   Should I Participate?

When deciding whether to participate in the write-on competition, you should ask yourself:

1. Do I want to join a law review (also called a journal)?
2. Do I want to write the competition paper?

First, you should consider whether you want to join a law review. Typically, second-year students spend time on their law reviews cite-checking other authors' articles and notes to make sure they are substantively correct (i.e., the source actually says what the author claims) and in the correct citation format (most schools still use the Bluebook for this task; others use ALWD). During your third year in law school, you might become an editor on your law review, editing the substance of the article as opposed to checking the citations. In addition, you might write your own note for publication in your law review. While the law review experience is not always glamorous, it will help you improve your writing and editing skills. In addition, many judges prefer that their clerks have law review experience.

Even if you do not want to join a journal or if you are undecided, you still might want to participate in the write-on competition. The experience of writing a scholarly paper is worthwhile. It will force you to critically analyze a particular legal subject and help improve your writing process. If you plan to take a writing seminar during your second or third year in law school, the writing competition will provide a transition from the first-year practical writing course to upper-class scholarly seminar papers. In addition, the challenge of writing a concise paper in an abbreviated amount of time, while daunting, is extremely rewarding when accomplished.

If you decide not to participate in the write-on competition, make sure you have a good reason. That reason should never be that you do not think you will qualify for a law review or that you are not a good enough writer.

2. What Is a Case Note?

A case note, or case comment, is a critique of a judicial opinion. It differs from a law review note, which is an article written by a student and published in a law journal. Case comments are also published in law journals, but they focus on a specific case opinion and can be written by students or professors. Typically, the write-on packet will contain the opinion as well as background information on the legal issue. The author of a case note will comment on the court's decision and its reasoning. The author can agree, disagree, or both (agree on one part and disagree on another). However, a good case note should not simply repeat the court's (or the dissent's) reasoning; instead, it should go beyond the opinion itself using the background materials and novel ideas to present clear, logical legal reasoning to show why the court was correct or incorrect.

3. Writing a Case Note

Writing a case note is similar to the process of writing any legal document. You should research the issue, take a stance on the issue, write a first draft, rewrite, and then polish.

a. Research

The good news is that usually in a write-on competition no outside research is permitted. Instead, all you need to do is read the materials provided in the packet. However, this reading may take some time, and you should consider reading the packet through once for an overview before you read it over and over to take notes and become familiar with the material.

b.   Take a Stance

You need to decide on your stance. Will you agree with the court or disagree (or both)? Try not to spend too much time deciding on your stance as the law review judges do not care which way you come out on the issue; instead, they are judging you on your reasoning and how you prove your stance.

c.   Write a First Draft

Write a draft as soon as feasible. You want to save as much time as possible for rewriting and editing. If you have organizational problems, consider creating an outline before you begin drafting. Remember to consider audience (upper-class students on law review), purpose (to critique an opinion), scope (stick to issue and page limit), and stance (let your voice be heard).

d.   Rewrite

You want to spend as much time as possible on rewriting. Here, you should refer to the chapter The Writing Process (beginning on page 61), Large-Scale Organization (see page 79), Paragraph Organization and Legal Analysis (see page 86), and Conciseness (see page 94).

e.   Polish

You will also need to spend an enormous amount of time on your polishing—especially citation. While your grammar should be excellent (see chapter on Editing), your citation needs to be perfect. See the next page for more information on law review citation.

4.   Citation

Proper citation is one of the most important pieces in the write-on competition because most law reviews require their members to "Bluebook" as their first assignments. Therefore, the judges want you to prove that you can properly cite to authority. Here are a few tips:

a.   Provide Citations for Scholarly Writing

In your first-year class, you most likely learned to cite in legal documents. Now, you need to shift gears and provide citations for law reviews. This shift is not very difficult; follow all the same rules but without the practitioner's notes or Bluepages of the Bluebook.

b.   Use the Inside Front Cover of the Bluebook

The inside cover page of the Bluebook provides a quick summary for law review citation. In your first-year class, you probably referred to the back inside cover of the Bluebook, which summarizes citation style for legal documents. For law review citation style, refer to the Bluebook's inside cover page.

c.   Cite to All Authority in Footnotes or Endnotes

In your first-year class, you probably cited to authority right in the text. For law review articles, you need to provide the citations in the endnotes or footnotes (look at the packet rules). Remember to cite to authority whenever you write a legal proposition, quote, or paraphrase. Cite to authority often in law review articles.

d.   Use Basic Citation as Well as Complicated Citation

You should prove that you can follow basic citation rules perfectly. In addition, you should provide some complicated citations so that the judges will recognize your ability to succeed when Bluebooking complicated citations.

See chapter on Citation on page 395.

VII. STUDY AIDS—LEGAL DOCUMENTS

A. *Quick References and Checklists*

Memos

 1. Memo Format: Quick Reference

Heading

A legal memo, like any other memo, should have a heading with lines for sender, recipient, date, and subject. However, the subject line should contain more than just the client name and file number; it should also include a brief description of the specific issue discussed in the memo.

Question Presented

The question presented is one sentence that provides the reader with a quick summary of the issue addressed by the memo. It should include three major elements:

1. *Jurisdiction:* A question presented should include a brief statement of the jurisdiction and applicable law. A statement such as "under New Jersey law" may be sufficient, but the statement can be more specific, such as "under New Jersey common law," if the author deems it necessary. Reference to a specific code provision or case name is usually too specific, unless it is well known and conveys meaning, such as "Roe v. Wade."
2. *Legal issue:* The legal issue presented defines the legal scope of the memo. For example, "Did Mr. Jones assault Mr. Smith?" or "Can Ms. Brown prove libel?"
3. *Legally significant facts:* The legally significant facts are the facts that apply to the client that will most likely affect the outcome of this particular issue. Here, the writer needs to choose only those facts that are most significant so that the sentence is readable. The writer should also be careful to include facts from both sides of the argument to present the most objective view to the reader.

> The basic format of a question is as follows:
>
> Under [jurisdiction], did/can/will [legal issue]
> when [legally significant facts]?

Brief Answer

The brief answer quickly answers the question presented with a simple "yes," "no," "probably," or "probably not." Next, using no more than a few sentences, the brief answer uses the terms of art from the applicable law to answer the question presented. A repetition of facts stated in the question presented is not necessary, nor are citations.

Statement of Facts

The statement of facts presents the facts to the reader in a clear, concise, and objective manner. Only legally significant facts and background facts are necessary in a memo fact section. If a particular fact is not referred to later in the memo, it probably isn't necessary to put in the statement of facts unless it is important background information. In this section, the writer should avoid argument and persuasive tactics.

Discussion

The discussion section is the meat of the memo. Here, the writer presents the law and applies it to the client's situation. Legal analysis is required, as is citation to all authority so that the lawyer can refer to the actual law. This section should be well organized, clearly analyzed, and concisely written.

Conclusion

The conclusion answers the particular question, but with more detail than the brief answer. An effective conclusion usually breaks down the component parts of the law and uses specific client facts to show why that element of the law is either favorable or unfavorable for the client. A busy reader should be able to read your question presented, brief answer, and conclusion to have a complete summary of the issue, the law, and the effect on the client.

---

2. Memos Generally: Checklist

✓ Consider your audience, often a busy supervising attorney.
  • Apply the law to the facts of the case. Anticipate counterarguments.
  • Use proper legal conventions, but avoid legalese.
  • Focus on organization so a busy reader can understand the main points.
✓ Remember that the purpose of the memo is to help your supervising attorney make an informed decision about the client's interests.
  • Explain how relevant law applies to the client's issue.
  • Be objective and show both sides of the issue.
✓ Consider the memo's scope.
  • Inquire about amount of time, money, and attention required.
  • Focus only on particular issues assigned by supervising attorney.
✓ Consider point of view and tone.
  • Memos should be formally written.
  • Clients may read memos, so avoid condescending or accusatory language.

> *Memo Formal Requirements*
>
> - Heading
> - Question Presented
> - Brief Answer
> - Statement of Facts
> - Discussion
> - Conclusion

 ## 3.　Memos: Question Presented: Checklist

✓ Does it provide a quick, one-sentence summary of the issue addressed?
  - Does it pass the breath test?

✓ Does it use either the "under-did-when" or "whether" format?

✓ Does it provide the jurisdiction and applicable law? ("under")
  - Avoid case names and code provisions unless widely known.

✓ Does it provide the legal issue? ("did" or "can" or "will")
  - Is the issue too broad and generic?
  - Is the issue too narrow and detailed?

✓ Does it provide the legally significant facts? ("when")
  - Choose only facts likely to affect the outcome of the particular case.
  - Avoid being one-sided.

✓ Do you include a question presented for each issue addressed in the memo?
  - Include questions presented in the same order addressed in the memo.
  - Include a corresponding brief answer for each question presented.

 ## 4.　Memos: Brief Answer: Checklist

✓ Does it provide a quick answer to how the issue will likely be resolved?
  - Yes, No, Probably, Probably Not
  - Try not to use more than a few sentences.

✓ Does it use the key terms of art to answer the question?
  - Remember, the brief answer is not a substitute for a roadmap.

✓ Does it incorporate some of the significant facts from the case?
  - Repetition of the facts cited in the question presented is not necessary.
  - Citations are generally not necessary.

✓ Is it brief?

✓ Does it work in conjunction with the question presented?
  - Treat the brief answer as a response to the question presented.
  - Provide a brief answer for every question presented.

5. Memos: Statement of Facts: Checklist

✓ Does it tell a clear and concise story?
   • Do not repeat verbatim the facts provided by the supervising attorney.
   • Do not use bullet points.
   • Develop an organizational schema for presenting your facts.
      • Chronological
      • By topic
      • By client
      • By causes of action
✓ Does it provide legally significant facts?
   • A fact is legally significant if considered when applying the law.
   • If you use a fact in your discussion section, it is legally significant.
   • Be sure to include all facts included in your discussion section.
✓ Does it provide background facts?
   • Weave your background facts with legally significant facts to tell a story.
✓ Is it written objectively?
   • Do not omit facts harmful to your client.
   • Be accurate and honest.
   • Include emotional facts if they will bear on the decision of judge or jury.
   • Do not make arguments in the statement of facts.
   • Avoid partisan or qualifying language.
   • Do not create facts or make assumptions.
   • If in doubt, indicate that more facts are necessary.

---

 6. Memos: Discussion: Checklist

✓ Remember the discussion's purpose is to show the reader the application of the law to the facts to prove the predicted outcome.
✓ *Organization:*
   • Is the organization based on the law itself?
      • Does it provide a clear roadmap to set out the law for the reader?
      • Does the roadmap include citations as necessary?
   • Does it provide topic sentences that parallel the organization and terms of art from the roadmap?
      • Does it avoid a historical overview of the law?
      • Does it tell the reader the state of the current law?
✓ *Analysis:*
   • Does it ground arguments in the law?
      • Do you use primary law?
      • Do you create policy arguments to support the outcome you predict?
      • Do you use enough law to prove your prediction?

- Does it use the facts of the case and apply them to the law?
  - Do not force the reader to flip back to the statement of facts.
- Does it provide clear conclusions using sound reasoning?
  - Conclude on an issue or element.
  - Provide enough logical reasoning so the reader can agree or disagree.
- Does it apply the law instead of simply quoting it?
- Does it provide counterarguments?
- Is it written objectively?
- It is thorough?
- Is it concise?
- Does it include proper citations?

7.   Memos: Conclusion: Checklist

✓ Does it answer the question presented?
✓ Do you provide a conclusion for each question presented?
✓ Does it provide reasons, including specific client facts, regarding each element of the law?
✓ Is it consistent with the corresponding brief answer?
✓ Does it provide more information than the brief answer?
✓ Does it avoid providing citations?
✓ If necessary, include a separate paragraph addressing your concern that more investigation is required or that another issue should be addressed.

Briefs

8.   Brief Format: Quick Reference

The following are the possible formal elements of an appellate brief. Not all courts require all these elements. You should always consult the rules in your jurisdiction before beginning to write an appellate brief. These rules not only require specific elements of a brief, but they also dictate page, font, and filing requirements.

Title Page

Because a brief is filed in a court, it needs identification. Therefore, the title page contains the name of the court itself, the name of the case, the docket number and judge's name (if available), the type of brief, and the names and addresses of counsel.

Table of Contents

This page refers the reader to page numbers for certain sections. Usually page 1 begins with the statement of the issue presented for review and the previous pages, including the table of contents, referenced as i, ii, iii, etc. Pointheadings are specifically referenced in the table of contents; if they are effectively written, they allow the reader to understand your organization from a quick glance at the table of contents. Pointheadings are essentially thesis statements for each part of the argument, using a mixture of law and facts to persuasively inform the reader of your client's point of view.

Table of Authorities

This page alphabetically lists the legal authority cited within the brief with references to page numbers. The most heavily relied-on law is often cited with an * asterisk. Various types of legal authority (e.g., constitutions, cases, statutes, regulations) are often separated when listed.

Jurisdiction

Not all courts require a jurisdiction section. When one is required, this section briefly states the jurisdictional basis for appeal by providing relevant facts and a specific legal foundation.

Standard of Review

In appellate cases, the court must apply a certain standard of review over the trial court, which is similar to the burden of proof in trial cases. Standard of review essentially has to do with how much deference the appellate court will give to the trial court. For questions of fact, the very deferential "clearly erronenous" standard applies. For questions of law, the nondeferential "de novo" standard applies. For mixed questions of law and fact, the middle-ground "abuse of discretion" standard applies. Briefs should include a statement of the applicable standard of review.

Statement of the Issue Presented for Review

This is similar to the question presented section of a memo, but it should not include a jurisdictional statement, as this is provided elsewhere. The issue statement in a brief should be written persuasively, and the answer should be implicit. A brief may include several issue statements if it deals with several issues.

Statement of Facts

The statement of facts presents the facts to the reader in a clear, concise, and persuasive manner. Legally significant facts, background facts, and emotional facts are necessary in a brief's fact section. This section is a significant opportunity for the writer to tell the story in such a way that allows the reader to see the client's perspective. The writer should be persuasive, developing and working in a subtle theory of the case. The writer should not avoid facts that are harmful to the case, but, instead, should downplay or distinguish them.

Summary of the Argument

The summary of the argument briefly summarizes the main legal points of the document, using key facts from the client's case. However, in a brief, this section is persuasive and designed to give a compelling overview for the very busy reader. This section may or may not include citations.

Argument

The argument section is the meat of the brief, complete with pointheadings and subheadings. Here, the writer presents the law and applies it to the client's situation in a persuasive manner, applying the theory of the case and other persuasive techniques to the writing. The theory of the case should be woven throughout the argument, and this section should be well organized, clearly analyzed, and concisely written.

Conclusion

The conclusion in a brief differs from that in a memo. In a brief, the conclusion simply states the relief requested, usually in one sentence. It does not summarize the argument.

Example: For the aforementioned reasons, this Court should reverse the trial court and remand for new trial.

Signature and Certificate of Service

The attorney's signature, name, bar number, and address are required at the end of every brief. In addition, the court requires a short statement indicating that the writer has provided a copy of the brief to opposing counsel, indicating whether service was hand-delivered or mailed. An attorney's signature is required after the certificate of service as well.

 ## 9.   Briefs Generally: Checklist

✓ The purpose of the brief is to convince the court to affirm, reverse, or remand the case.
- The brief should be informative.
- The brief should be subtly persuasive.
- The brief should be written to win a particular issue or a number of issues.
- Avoid writing defensively.
- Avoid attacking the opposing party.
- Avoid incendiary language.

✓ Consider the audience.
- Judges are your primary audience.
  - Try to find out which judges are assigned to your panel.
  - Research the judges' prior cases and understand their leanings and reasoning.

- Remember that the judges' clerks are also the audience.
- Opposing counsel, your client, the opposing client, and the public are your secondary audience.
    - Make tactical considerations accordingly.
✓ Remember that the scope of your brief is defined by the errors in the court below.
    - Always consult your court's rules for page and word limits; this may affect how many issues you appeal.
✓ Consider point of view and tone.
    - Did you weave your theory of the case throughout the brief?

Formal Requirements

Formal requirements will vary based on your court rules.

- Title Page
- Table of Contents, Including Pointheadings and Subheadings
- Table of Authorities
- Jurisdiction
- Standard of Review
- Statement of the Issues Presented for Review
- Statement of the Case
- Summary of the Argument
- Argument
- Conclusion
- Signature and Certificate of Service

---

 10. Briefs: Title Page: Checklist

✓ Did you consult your jurisdiction's rules for formatting requirements?
✓ Did you include the name of the case?
✓ Did you include the name of the court?
✓ Did you include the docket number?
✓ Did you include the names and addresses of counsel?
✓ Did you indicate the type of brief you are submitting?

---

 11. Briefs: Table of Contents and Pointheadings: Checklist

✓ Do you begin page 1 with the Statement of Issues Presented for Review, and reference preceding pages (including Table of Contents and Authorities) with small Roman numerals?
✓ Do you proceed to reference page numbers for each section of the brief?
✓ Do you specifically reference pointheadings and subheadings? (Pointheadings and subheadings will reappear in your argument section.)

Pointheadings and Subheadings

Pointheadings

✓ Do your pointheadings inform the legal reader of the main issue you will address?

✓ Do your pointheadings persuade the reader that you have a winning argument on that issue?

✓ Do you use subtle persuasion?

Subheadings

✓ Do your subheadings inform the legal reader of the sub-issues for each main issue?

✓ Do your subheadings show the reader, using specific facts, why you win on each sub-issue?

✓ Do you use subtle persuasion?

---

12. Briefs: Table of Authorities (Authorities Cited): Checklist

✓ Did you consult your jurisdiction's rules for formatting requirements?
  • In your jurisdiction, do you need to cite seminal law with an asterisk?
  • In your jurisdiction, do you need to separate different types of legal authority (constitutions, cases, etc.)?
✓ Did you order all cited authorities alphabetically?
✓ Did you reference the page numbers where each cited authority is found?

---

13.   Briefs: Jurisdiction: Checklist

✓ Did you consult your jurisdiction's rules to determine if your brief should include a jurisdiction section?
✓ If a jurisdiction section is required, briefly state the jurisdictional basis for appeal.
  • Did you provide a specific legal foundation?
  • Did you provide the relevant facts of your case?

---

14. Statement of the Issue(s) Presented for Review: Checklist

✓ Do your issue statements clearly present the issues to be addressed to the court?
✓ Do your issue statements present the issues in a light most favorable to your client?
✓ Did you keep your issue statements brief?

✓ Did you write your issue statements persuasively so the reader empathizes with your client?

✓ Did you include an issue statement for each issue on appeal?

 ## 15. Briefs: Statement of the Case: Checklist

✓ Did you present the facts in a clear and precise manner?

✓ Did you present the facts in a persuasive manner, shaping the case in a light most favorable to your client?

- Did you begin with facts that help the reader view the case from your client's perspective?
- Did you pay close attention to word choice?
- Did you use short sentences to create high impact?
- Did you develop a theory for your case and subtly weave it into your facts?
- Did you downplay or distinguish facts harmful to your case?

✓ Did you include the procedural history in your facts?

✓ Did you include relevant background facts for the legal reader?

✓ Did you include legally significant facts for the legal reader?

✓ Did you include emotional facts to persuade the legal reader?

 ## 16. Briefs: Summary of the Argument: Checklist

✓ Did you provide a brief and compelling overview of the argument for the busy legal reader?

✓ Did you include all main legal points from your brief?

✓ Did you write persuasively?

---

17. Briefs: Argument: Checklist

✓ Organization:
- Did you use roadmaps to guide the reader and enhance the clarity of your argument?
- Did you use pointheadings and subheadings, written in complete sentences, to advance your arguments?
- Did you use persuasive topic sentences that parallel your roadmap, pointheadings, and subheadings?
- Did you use mini-conclusions to show the reader you have concluded on a particular element?

✓ Analysis:
- Did you use legal analysis to create reasoned, logical arguments?
  - Did you effectively use rule-based reasoning by deducing the general legal rule and applying it to the facts of your case?
  - Did you use analogies to compare your client's case with controlling precedent?

- Did you make policy arguments to bolster your other legal arguments?
  - Were you thorough yet concise in your legal analysis?
- Did you anticipate and address counterarguments?
  - Did you present your arguments in a persuasive manner?
    - Did you apply your theory of the case?
    - Did you present your strongest arguments first?
✓ Did you check your citations to ensure they are in proper Bluebook or ALWD format?

---

 18. Briefs: Conclusion, Signature, and Certificate of Service: Checklist

Conclusion

✓ Did you use one sentence to simply state the relief requested?
✓ Do NOT summarize the argument.

Signature and Certificate of Service

✓ Did you include your (the attorney's) signature?
✓ Did you include your (the attorney's) bar number?
✓ Did you include your (the attorney's) address?
✓ Did you include a short statement indicating that you provided a copy of the brief to opposing counsel and indicate whether service was hand-delivered, emailed, or mailed?
✓ Did you (the attorney) sign the certificate of service?

---

 19. Oral Argument: Quick Reference

What Is Oral Argument?

An oral argument is more of a conversation with the court than a speech. It is an opportunity for the judges to ask questions of each side to clarify the significant points of law, and it is an opportunity for counsel to stress the important aspects of the case and persuade the court. A judge may often use her questions as a way to convince the other judges of her position, or she may ask antagonistic and challenging questions to draw out the weaknesses in the attorney's case. Successful attorneys at oral argument are good listeners, respond well to questions, and can convince judges to change their original positions to side with them.

Preparation for Oral Argument

Novices should prepare an outline of their arguments. The law should also be handy for reference during the argument. The outline and law should provide you with a general guideline for what to discuss, but be prepared to be flexible. "Mooting" your argument in front of other attorneys beforehand is a helpful way to prepare for the unexpected and to get more comfortable with your presentation. Also work on the level, tone, and speed of your voice. Arguments that are strong on substance can be weakened by poor delivery.

Conventions of Oral Argument

Typically, before beginning to speak, you should ask permission from the court to do so by saying "May it please the court" and introduce yourself. It is often helpful to give a brief introduction to your argument that lays out your major points for the court. After this introduction, you will spend the rest of your time arguing your case and answering the judge's questions. At the end of the argument, you should conclude with a brief summary of the points you made and a request for relief. In most cases, however, you will run out of time. If you are in the middle of answering a question when time runs out, ask the court for permission to briefly answer the question and wrap up.

When Opposing Counsel Is Speaking

When opposing counsel stands up to give his or her presentation, you should be paying attention and taking notes. The best arguments respond directly to points raised by opposing counsel.

Rebuttal

Rebuttal should not be a rehashing of your arguments. Instead, plan to address one or two compelling points, usually counterpoints to opposing counsel's best arguments. If opposing counsel brings up a case that seems compelling, make sure to distinguish it in your rebuttal.

Do's and Don'ts During Oral Argument

Do's	Don't
Answer judges' questions	Put off judges' questions
Have a flexible outline	Strictly adhere to your outline
Have a conversation with the judges	Make a speech
Rely on authority	Pretend to know a case you have not read
Listen carefully and ask for clarification of questions	Think about your next point while the judge is asking a question
Keep constant respect for court	Get frustrated or angry with the judges
Keep a positive and professional tone	Become defensive or attack the other attorney personally
Dress and act professionally	Fidget, slouch, chew gum, or otherwise act unprofessionally

Client Letters

20.   Client Letters: Checklist

Purpose

✓ The purpose of a client letter is to provide the client with a legal opinion and advice.
  • It should inform the client of her options under the law.
  • It should answer client questions and explain those answers.
✓ A second purpose of a client letter is to create a paper trail for the lawyer.

Audience

✓ Your audience is the particular client to whom you are writing.
  • Consider your client's background, education, and knowledge.
  • Determine whether to use legal terms, discuss cases, provide citations, reveal research.
✓ Advise the client whether or not to proceed and, if so, how to proceed.

Scope

✓ Clarify limitations of the letter.
  • Inform the client that if facts change, your legal opinion may change as well.
✓ Focus on conciseness; a long client letter may be too cumbersome to read.
✓ Remember costs when preparing a client letter.

View

✓ The view of a client letter may vary greatly, but it must always be professional.
  • A client letter may be cursory or in depth.
  • A client letter may be conversational, friendly, or formal.
  • Client letters should always avoid using slang or flippant-sounding remarks.

Prewriting

✓ Gather the facts from your client.
✓ Research the legal issue.
✓ Clarify the client's question.

Formal Requirements

✓ Date and Salutation
✓ Opening Paragraph
✓ Facts Section
✓ Analysis Section
✓ Closing

Date and Salutation

✓ Include the date to memorialize when you have given your opinion.
- Remember, your opinion may change if the facts change.

✓ Set the tone of the letter with your salutation.
- Do you want to use the client's first or last name?
- If in doubt, choose formality over informality.

Opening Paragraph

✓ Use the opening paragraph to *provide the context* of the letter and *restate the issue*.

✓ Common practice is to provide an answer in the opening paragraph.

Facts Section

✓ Provide both background and legally significant facts.

✓ Write objectively.

✓ Base your facts on
- documents you have reviewed.
- client or witness interviews.
- your own investigation.

✓ In complicated cases, consider citing the source of your facts.

✓ Ask the client to review the facts, and make additions or corrections as necessary.
- "I have based my opinion on the facts below. Please read them carefully and inform me of any changes, corrections, or additions as these might alter my legal opinion."

Analysis Section

✓ The analysis section is similar to the discussion section in a legal memo.
- Organize your analysis around the law.
- Write clear topic sentences.
- Provide clear explanations for your conclusions.
- Write objectively.
- Provide counterarguments to help the client understand both sides of the issue.

✓ Tailor your analysis to your client's needs.
- Consider how much detail is necessary for your client to understand how the law applies to her problem.
- If detail is necessary, provide explanation.

Closing

✓ Advise your client whether or not to proceed.

✓ Explain how your client should proceed.

✓ Consider mentioning other issues that might be pursued in the future.

📋 21. Client Letter vs. Memo vs. Brief: Quick Reference

Client Letter (Objective)	Memo (Objective)	Brief (Persuasive)
Date and Salutation	*Heading*	*Title Page*
Memorializes date on which your opinion is given and sets tone for the letter.	Includes lines for sender, recipient, date, and subject. In addition to the client name and file number, the subject line should also include a brief description of the specific issue discussed in the memo.	Serves as a means of identification; contains the name of the court, the name of the case, the docket number and judge's name (if available), the type of brief, and the names and addresses of counsel.
		Table of Contents
		Refers the reader to page numbers for each section of the brief. Includes individual pointheadings and subheadings from argument section, forming an outline of the author's argument.
		Table of Authorities
		Lists, in alphabetical order, each legal authority cited within the brief, with references to page numbers. Different types of legal authorities (e.g., constitutions, cases, statutes, regulations) are cited separately.
		Jurisdiction
		When required, this section consists of a brief statement of the jurisdictional basis for appeal, including relevant facts and a specific legal foundation.
		Standard of Review
		Dictates the level of deference given to the trial court. Questions of fact are reviewed under the deferential "clearly erroneous" standard, while questions of law are subjected to nondeferential "de novo" review.

Client Letter (Objective)	Memo (Objective)	Brief (Persuasive)
Opening Paragraph	*Question Presented*	*Statement of the Issue*
Provides context for the client, restates the legal issue presented, and often offers a brief statement summarizing the author's conclusion (similar to the brief answer in a legal memo).	Provides the reader with a brief summary of the issue addressed in the memo. It contains three elements: 1) Jurisdiction: consists of a brief statement of the jurisdiction and applicable law (e.g., "Under New Jersey law …"). 2) Legal issue: defines the scope of the memo (e.g., "Did Mr. Jones assault Mr. Smith?"). 3) Legally significant facts: these include those facts (and only those facts) that are most likely to affect the outcome of the legal issue presented. As a legal memo is an objective document, facts from both sides should be included.	Provides the reader with a brief summary of the issue(s) addressed in the brief. An issue statement in a brief does not contain a jurisdictional component; jurisdiction is addressed elsewhere in the document. Issue statements contained in briefs are written persuasively, implying a specific answer or conclusion.
	Brief Answer	*Pointheadings and Subheadings*
	Provides a short response to the question presented (e.g., yes, no, probably, probably not), followed by a short explanation, employing applicable legal terms of art to support the answer. It is unnecessary to include citations or to repeat facts included in the question presented.	The pointheadings and subheadings, when read together, provide the arguments supporting the answer to the issue statement.
Facts Section	*Statement of Facts*	*Statement of Facts*
Provides the client with background and legally significant facts in an objective manner; memorializes the facts as they currently stand. Writer should provide client opportunity to make necessary corrections or additions.	Presents the facts to the reader in a clear, concise, and objective manner. Only legally significant facts should be included.	Presents the facts to the reader in a clear, concise and persuasive manner. Legally significant facts, background facts, and emotional facts should all be included. The author should state the facts from the perspective of his client and subtly develop her theory of the case. Facts that are detrimental to that theory should be downplayed or distinguished, but not avoided.
		Summary of Argument
		Provides a short, persuasive statement of the main legal points advanced by the argument, including any legally significant facts.

Client Letter (Objective)	Memo (Objective)	Brief (Persuasive)
Analysis Section	*Discussion*	*Argument*
Should be organized around the law itself and provide the client with an understanding of how the law applies to the facts of her particular case. Citations, statutory definitions, and substantial analyses of prior case law are usually unnecessary for this audience. Should be written objectively.	The meat of the memo; here the author presents the law and applies it to the facts of her client's case in an objective manner. Citation to legal authorities is required. Large-scale organization (e.g., roadmaps, subheadings, topic sentences, and mini-conclusions), conciseness, and clear legal analysis are particularly important in this section.	Here the author presents the law and applies it to the facts of her client's case in a persuasive manner, providing legal support for the theory of the case established in the statement of the facts. Pointheadings and subheadings should be included to structure the presentation of significant legal points. As with the discussion section of a legal memo, large-scale organization, conciseness, and clear legal analysis are important.
Closing	*Conclusion*	*Conclusion*
	Provides a more detailed response to the question presented than the brief answer; breaks the law into separate elements and uses specific facts to illustrate why each element of the law either favors or does not favor the client.	Does not summarize the argument. Unlike a conclusion in a legal memo, a conclusion contained in a brief simply states the relief requested, usually in one sentence.
		Signature and Certificate of Service
		Required at the end of every brief; includes the attorney's name, bar number, address, signature, and a short statement indicating that the document has been served on opposing counsel.

Function	Client Letter (objective)	Memo (objective)	Brief (persuasive)
Purpose	Should inform the client of what the law is and how it applies to the facts of her particular case; provides a paper trail for the lawyer.	Should inform the supervising attorney of what the law is and objectively analyze how it applies to the client's case.	Should inform and persuade, showing both sides of an issue while subtly framing both the issue and the analysis in the way that most benefits the client.
Audience	The client; letters should be tailored to the background, education, and knowledge of each client.	Supervising attorney. Proper Bluebook format is necessary, contractions are inappropriate, and legalese should be avoided.	The appellate judge (or panel of judges). Secondary audience includes opposing counsel, your client, and the public.
Scope	Should advise the client on how to proceed; limitations should be clarified, as changes in facts can alter legal conclusions.	Should focus on the particular issue the attorney is asked to address. Stick to the issue!	Should focus on errors committed by the trial court; appellate courts review only issues raised at the trial level. Brief must conform to court-imposed page limit.
View	Varies according to audience; letters should always be professional and avoid flippant remarks.	Tone is generally very formal; the author should avoid accusatory or condescending language.	Tone is generally very formal; author should persuade by incorporating theory of the case throughout the document.

Motions and Pleadings

 ### 22.   Complaints Format: Quick Reference

What Is a Complaint?

The complaint is the document that commences the legal action. It also provides notice to the defendants and stops the running of the statute of limitations on the action. It is written to and served on the defendant, but it is basically written for the legal audience as it is also filed with the court and read by the eventual counsel for the defense. The complaint actually sets the scope of the lawsuit by alleging particular legal claims against the defense. This is a very formal document and is usually written with numbered allegations.

How Do You Write a Complaint?

Before drafting a complaint, a lawyer must (1) research the rules for filing in the particular jurisdiction, (2) research the substantive law of the case to determine the legal causes of action to assert and their elements, and (3) research the facts of the case to determine if it meets the cause of action.

Each jurisdiction will have rules governing the content of a complaint and the procedures for filing them. You should check the civil procedure rules for your jurisdiction as well as the local rules. These rules will set out the appearance, content, and filing requirements for the complaint.

A complaint usually contains the following elements:

- *Caption*, which contains the name of the court, jurisdiction, and the names of the parties.
- *Commencement*, which introduces the complaint.
- *Body, or charging part*, which is the meat of the complaint and is comprised of numbered paragraphs. Initial paragraphs often state the parties' names and addresses. The following paragraphs give notice of the legal causes of action and allege each element of those actions. If you are requesting a jury trial, some jurisdictions require that the jury demand be made in the charging portion of the complaint or in a separate section labeled "jury demand." The last paragraphs of a complaint usually describe the plaintiff's injuries and damages.
- *Prayer or demand for judgment*, which lists the relief requested, such as specific performance, special damages, punitive damages, and equitable relief. The demand for judgment is not numbered, usually begins with "WHEREFORE," and usually ends with a catchall phrase requesting all other relief appropriate.
- *Signature and verification*, which includes the attorney's name, bar number, signature, and address and appears at the end of the complaint. In the verification clause, the party swears under oath that the allegations are believed to be true.

✅ 23.　Complaints: Checklist

Complaints commence legal action, provide notice to defendants, and stop the running of statute of limitations.

Complaints Generally

✓ Served on the defendant, but written for a legal audience
✓ Defines the scope of the lawsuit
✓ Very formal document
- Written in bullet point form with numbered allegations

Formal Requirements

✓ Caption
- Check your court's local rules
- Name of court
- Full names of all plaintiffs
- Full names of all defendants
- Title of document [complaint]
- Civil action number will be assigned by the court

✓ Statement of the Court's Jurisdiction and Venue
  • Jurisdiction—first paragraph
  • Venue—second paragraph
✓ Parties
  • List of plaintiffs
  • List of defendants
✓ Facts
  • Allege enough facts to meet all the elements of your claim.
    • Do this for each defendant if multiple defendants.
  • If you do not personally know a fact to be true, write: "upon information and belief."
✓ Statement of Legal Claims
  • The first numbered paragraph in this section should read: "Plaintiffs allege and incorporate by reference paragraphs 1-X" [X being however many paragraphs precede the Statement of Legal Claims].
  • Each legal claim is addressed in a separate paragraph.
✓ Demand for Judgment
  • State what you are asking the court to do.
✓ Signature
  • Signature
  • Date
  • Address
✓ Verification [optional]

 ## 24. Answers Format: Quick Reference

What Is an Answer?

The answer responds to each allegation in the complaint by indicating whether the defendant admits, denies, or is unable to answer. The scope of the answer is related to the scope of the complaint, as the answer must admit or deny each of the plaintiff's allegations.

Elements of an Answer

A complaint can contain the following elements:

• **Caption and introductory sentence:** The caption is identical to the one in the complaint, except that it is labeled "Answer." Introductory sentences are used before the answer.
• **Admissions in answers:** Some rules require defendants to admit portions of the complaint that are true so that attorneys are acting "in good faith." In addition, by admitting portions of the complaint, the defendants help to narrow the issues. You can admit specific paragraphs individually, group admissions together, or admit only parts of paragraphs.
• **Denials in answers:** The defendant may make a general denial, which denies the whole complaint, or a special denial, which denies only certain

paragraphs or parts of paragraphs. In addition, the defendant may state that there is insufficient evidence to deny or admit certain parts of a complaint, which, in effect, acts as a denial.

- *Example general denial:* "The Defendant denies each allegation in the Plaintiff's complaint."
- *Example specific denial:* "The defendant denies the allegations in paragraphs 11, 12, 14-21, and 23."
- **Affirmative defenses:** Some jurisdictions require certain affirmative defenses to be raised in an answer or they are waived. When writing affirmative defenses, you can separate them by headings or by count.
- **Affirmative claims and demand for judgment:** Counterclaims, cross-claims, and third-party claims are made in the same form as the complaint, using numbered paragraphs with separate headings to label each claim. If a defendant alleges a claim, he should also include a demand for judgment.
- **Signature and verification:** Similar to the complaint, an answer typically requires a signature and verification.

---

25. Interrogatories: Checklist

Interrogatories Generally

✓ Used to ask questions of the other side
✓ Written for layperson and lawyer
✓ Many jurisdictions limit interrogatories
  - Limit by number or by prohibiting certain types of interrogatories
✓ Written clearly and precisely
✓ Arranged by subject matter

Formal Requirements

✓ Preface
✓ Definitions
✓ Preliminary Questions
✓ Substantive Questions
✓ Concluding Questions

---

26. Motions: Checklist

Motions Generally

✓ Persuasive documents written to raise issues as they arise in the litigation
  - Pretrial motions
    - Motion for continuance
    - Motion in limine
    - Motion to suppress evidence
    - Motion to exclude evidence

- Motion for summary judgment
- Motion to compel discovery
- Trial motions
  - Motion for judgment notwithstanding the verdict
- Post-trial motions
  - Motion for new trial
  - Motion for remittitur

✓ Used to request the court for specific relief
✓ Trial judge is the primary audience
  - But tactical considerations are important because your client, opposing counsel, opposing client, and the public are a secondary audience
✓ Each motion should address one particular issue

Formal Requirements

✓ Notice of the motion (or "The Motion")
  - Puts court and opposing party on notice a particular motion will be filed with the court
✓ The Memorandum of Points and Authorities
  - Caption and Heading
  - Introduction
  - Facts
  - Argument
  - Conclusion
  - Signature and Address
  - May petition the court for a hearing
✓ A Certificate of Service
  - Certifies opposing counsel was served with copy of motion
  - Indicates whether service was in person or by mail
✓ Affidavit (sometimes)
✓ An Order
  - Actual document you are asking court to sign
  - Specifies that judge granting (or denying) motion
  - Line for judge's signature and date

Seminar Papers and Law Review Notes

 ## 27. Seminar Papers and Law Review Notes: Checklist

Seminar Papers and Law Review Notes Generally

✓ Present a particular point of view such as criticizing existing law, principles, and decisions coupled with proposals of new ideas and theories.
✓ Develop a clear thesis statement and consistently focus on this thesis statement.

✓ Your primary audience will be other scholars, but judges and practicing attorneys will also read your writing.

✓ Provide in-depth analysis of one specific issue, rather than superficial analysis of multiple issues.

✓ Use the first person voice.

✓ Ensure the reader hears your voice, opinions, and novel ideas throughout the article.

Seminar Papers and Law Review Notes—Generally

Seminar papers and law review notes are very similar, and the following apply to both.

✓ Select a topic.
✓ Perform a preemption check.
✓ Research the issue.
✓ Write.
✓ Rewrite.
✓ Cite-check.
✓ Get published.

Selecting a Topic

✓ Set plenty of time aside for this decision.

✓ Choose a topic relevant to your seminar or to your law review that interests you.

- Consider class discussions, class readings, the news.
- Refer to United States Law Week or the new developments sections of Westlaw and Lexis.

✓ Narrow your topic to focus on one specific issue by writing an issue statement.

✓ Create a proposed thesis for your paper by answering the issue statement.

✓ Be sure your issue is novel.

Performing a Preemption Check

✓ Search the indexes and databases of law review articles to ensure no one else has written on the same subject with the same issue and thesis.

✓ While searching, take note of helpful articles.

Researching the Issue

✓ First, conduct background research to understand the general field of law.

- Use secondary sources such as treatises, hornbooks, law review articles, and looseleafs.
- Note citations that might prove useful.

✓ Second, conduct research focused directly on your thesis.

- Take notes.
- Begin with the citations you noted during background research.

- Research current articles first.
- Ask other scholars in the field, especially your seminar professor.

Writing and Rewriting a Scholarly Piece

✓ When writing the scholarly article, provide:
- An introduction
  - Context for the topic
  - A roadmap for the paper
- The current state of the law
- Novel ideas and ideas for reform
- A conclusion summarizing your thesis

✓ When rewriting the scholarly article, consider:
- Whether your thesis is focused and consistent throughout the article
- Whether you addressed a particular audience, answering its concerns
- Whether the scope of your thesis is narrow
- Whether you provided in-depth analysis
- Whether your voice, opinions, and theories stand out

Cite Checking

✓ First, check the substance of your citations.
- Find and read each source, asking: does the article say what you purport it to say?

✓ Second, check your citation format.
- Format should be for law review articles.
  - Bluebook formatting: refer to inside cover.
  - ALWD formatting: refer to Parts 3 and 4, Fast Formats.

Getting Published

✓ Consider publishing seminar papers.

✓ If your law review does not publish your note, consider sending it to other journals.

✓ Be sure your paper is in the best possible shape before submitting it to a publisher.

✓ *First,* create a list of journals that publish articles on your topic.
- Consult your seminar professor.
- Consult directories of law journals.
  - Directory of Law Reviews
  - Current Law Index
  - Index to Legal Periodicals and Books

✓ *Second,* consider submitting papers in March, August, or early September.

✓ *Third,* write a concise cover letter summarizing your paper and its importance.
- One page should suffice.

28. Law Review Write-On Competition Papers: Checklist

Law Review Write-On Competition Papers Generally

✓ Present a particular point of view such as criticizing existing law, principles and decisions coupled with proposals of new ideas and theories.

✓ Develop a clear thesis statement and consistently focus on this thesis statement.

✓ Your primary audience will be other scholars, but judges and practicing attorneys will also read your writing.

✓ Provide in-depth analysis of one specific issue, rather than superficial analysis of multiple issues.

✓ Use the first person voice.

✓ Ensure the reader hears your voice, opinions, and novel ideas throughout the article.

Should I Participate?

✓ *Ask:* Do I want to join a law review?
  • Second-year students on law review cite-check other author's articles and notes.
    • Check that citations are substantively correct.
    • Check that citations are in proper format.
  • Third-year students may become editors or write their own notes.
  • Judges prefer that clerks have law review experience.

✓ *Ask:* Do I want to write the competition paper?
  • Experience provides transition between practical writing and scholarly writing.
  • Writing a competition paper is rewarding.

What Is a Case Note?

✓ A case note is a critique of a judicial opinion.
  • Agree, disagree, or both (agree in part; disagree in part).
  • Use clear, logical legal reasoning.
  • Present novel ideas.

Writing the Case Note

✓ Research the issue.
  • Generally, no outside research is allowed.
  • Familiarize yourself with the write-on packet materials.

✓ Take a stance on the issue.
  • You will be judged on your reasoning and ideas, not on the stance (agree, disagree, both) you take.

✓ Write a draft.
  • Write a first draft as soon as possible.
  • Consider creating an outline to organize your draft.

- Consider *audience*—upper-class students on law review.
- Consider *purpose*—to critique an opinion.
- Consider *scope*—stick to the issue and page limit.
- Consider *stance*—let your voice be heard.
✓ Rewrite the case note. Consider:
  - Large-scale organization
    - Analysis
    - Conciseness
✓ Polish the case note.
  - Use excellent grammar.
  - Use perfect citations.

Citations

✓ Provide citations for scholarly writing.
  - Refer to inside cover of Bluebook.
✓ Cite to all authority in endnotes or footnotes.
✓ Use basic and complicated citations.

B. *Quizzes*

⚇? 1. Memos: Quiz

Instructions: For each of the following statements regarding legal memos, choose either true or false. If you answer false, articulate why the statement is false before moving to the next question. If you have difficulty answering any of the questions on legal memos, refer to the chapter and the Memos Checklists for assistance.

1. When writing a legal memo, the primary audience is usually a judge. **True or False?**

2. An effective memo will explain how relevant law applies to the client's issue, anticipate counterarguments, and use proper legal conventions. **True or False?**

3. Legalese is desirable because supervising attorneys are accustomed to it. **True or False?**

4. Organization is essential because it allows a busy reader to understand the main points of the memo. **True or False?**

5. Generally, the purpose of a legal memo is to help a supervising attorney make an informed decision about a client's interests. **True or False?**

6. An effective memo should illustrate how the client will win the case. **True or False?**

7. An effective memo is objective and shows both sides of the issue. **True or False?**

8. It is inappropriate for an associate to inquire about the amount of money to be allocated toward a particular memo. **True or False?**

9. Memos are shared between attorneys working on the same case, so formal writing is not required. **True or False?**

10. Clients will never be allowed to read memos prepared by an associate attorney. **True or False?**

11. The only formal requirements of a memo are the heading, questions presented, brief answer, statement of facts, and discussion. **True or False?**

12. For purposes of clarity, only the client's name should appear in the subject line of a memo heading. **True or False?**

13. A date line is not appropriate in a memo heading because memos must be continually updated as new facts are discovered and new issues explored. **True or False?**

14. A question presented may be more than one sentence, as long as each sentence passes the breath test. **True or False?**

15. For questions presented, the "under-did-when" format is preferred because most attorneys disdain how the "whether" format creates a sentence fragment. **True or False?**

16. A question presented will not always provide the jurisdiction and applicable law. **True or False?**

17. When using the "under-did-when" format, "under" should refer to the jurisdiction and applicable law. **True or False?**

18. A question presented should address a single legal issue; if there are multiple legal issues, multiple questions presented should be used. **True or False?**

19. When using the "under-did-when" format, "did" (or can or will) should refer to the legal issue being analyzed. **True or False?**

20. Subtly persuasive facts are appropriate in a question presented because a question presented should imply its answer. **True or False?**

21. Legally significant facts are facts that affect the outcome of a case. **True or False?**

22. When using the "under-did-when" format, "when" should refer to the legally significant facts. **True or False?**

23. Brief answers should avoid being inconclusive and should answer yes or no. **True or False?**

24. The purpose of the brief answer is to provide a quick answer to how the issue will likely be resolved. **True or False?**

25. Acceptable answers in a brief answer include yes, no, probably, probably not. **True or False?**

26. The brief answer may substitute for a roadmap. **True or False?**

27. The brief answer should use key terms of art to answer the question presented. **True or False?**

28. For emphasis, the brief answer should repeat facts cited in the question presented. **True or False?**

29. A brief answer should incorporate some significant facts from the case. **True or False?**

30. A brief answer should always include citations. **True or False?**

31. To be effective and to assist a busy legal writer, the brief answer should analyze every element of the law. **True or False?**

32. The brief answer should work in conjunction with the question presented. **True or False?**

33. If there are multiple questions presented, there should be multiple brief answers. **True or False?**

34. The statement of facts should tell a clear and concise story. **True or False?**

35. When writing the statement of facts, you should assume that the reader remembers the facts already provided in the question presented and brief answer. **True or False?**

36. To ensure accuracy, an associate attorney should repeat verbatim the facts provided by the supervising attorney. **True or False?**

37. It is important to develop an organizational schema for presenting your facts. **True or False?**

38. Acceptable organizational schemas for the statement of facts section are limited to chronological, by topic, by causes of action. **True or False?**

39. The statement of fact should include all legally significant facts. **True or False?**

40. If you use a fact in your discussion section, it is legally significant. **True or False?**

41. After writing the discussion section, you should return to the statement of facts and ensure that it includes all discussion section facts. **True or False?**

42. Only legally significant facts need to be included in the statement of fact. **True or False?**

43. The statement of facts section in a memo should be subtly persuasive, promoting the interest of your client. **True or False?**

44. Facts harmful to your client should be omitted from the statement of facts in a memo. **True or False?**

45. Emotional facts should be included in the statement of facts in a memo if they will bear on the decision of a judge or jury. **True or False?**

46. It is not appropriate to make arguments in the statement of facts. **True or False?**

47. If necessary, you should make assumptions in your statement of facts. **True or False?**

48. If in doubt, you should indicate that more facts are necessary. **True or False?**

49. The purpose of the discussion section in a memo is to show the reader why your client will win the case. **True or False?**

50. The discussion section should be organized based on the law itself. **True or False?**

51. The discussion section should include a clear roadmap to set out the law for the reader, unless the brief answer already lays out the law for the reader. **True or False?**

52. If necessary, the roadmap should include citations. **True or False?**

53. Topic sentences in the discussion section should parallel the terms of art from the roadmap. **True or False?**

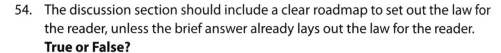

54. The discussion section should include a clear roadmap to set out the law for the reader, unless the brief answer already lays out the law for the reader. **True or False?**

55. The writer of a legal memo should ground his or her arguments in the law, but also develop policy arguments to support his or her predicted outcome. **True or False?**

56. It is not necessary to include a lot of facts in the discussion section because the reader can flip back to the statement of facts. **True or False?**

57. An effective memo concludes on each issue or element and provides enough logical reasoning that a reader can agree or disagree. **True or False?**

58. Quoting the law is effective because then the supervising attorney knows exactly what the state of the law is. **True or False?**

59. The discussion section should anticipate and address counterarguments. **True or False?**

60. The discussion should be written objectively. **True or False?**

61. An effective discussion section includes proper legal citations. **True or False?**

62. The conclusion section should answer the question presented. **True or False?**

63. The conclusion section does not need to address each element of the law. **True or False?**

64. The conclusion may not be consistent with the brief answer if, after writing the discussion, the writer has changed his or her reasoning or predicted outcome. **True or False?**

65. The conclusion should provide more information than the brief answer, including specific client facts regarding each important element of the law. **True or False?**

66. If necessary, the writer should include a separate paragraph addressing his or her concern that more investigation is required or that another issue should be addressed. **True or False?**

Answer Key on page 515

2. Briefs: Quiz

Instructions: For each of the following statements regarding legal briefs, choose either true or false. If you answer false, articulate why the statement is false before moving to the next question. If you have difficulty answering any of the questions on briefs, refer to the chapter text and the Briefs Checklists for assistance.

1. The purpose of the brief is to convince the court to affirm, reverse, or remand the case. **True or False?**

2. Subtle persuasion may include defensive writing or attacks on the opposing party. **True or False?**

3. When writing a brief, a busy supervising attorney is your primary audience. **True or False?**

4. It is inappropriate to try to discover which judges are assigned to your panel. **True or False?**

5. The judges' clerks are also the audience for the brief. **True or False?**

6. Opposing counsel, your client, the opposing client, and the public compose the secondary audience for your legal brief; you should make tactical considerations accordingly. **True or False?**

7. The scope of your brief is defined by the errors in the court below. **True or False?**

8. You should weave your theory of the case throughout the brief. **True or False?**

9. Every jurisdiction requires that seminal cases be noted with an asterisk (*). **True or False?**

10. The formal requirements for all briefs include title page, table of contents, table of authorities, jurisdiction, standard of review, statement of issues presented for review, statement of the case, summary of the argument, argument, conclusion, signature, and certificate of service. **True or False?**

11. In some jurisdictions, the table of contents is referred to as the index page. **True or False?**

12. Pointheadings and subheadings cited in the table of contents must reappear in the argument section. **True or False?**

13. Pointheadings inform the legal reader of the sub-issues you address in the brief. **True or False?**

14. Subheadings inform the legal reader of sub-issues you address in the brief. **True or False?**

15. Pointheadings are designed to be informative and should be written objectively rather than persuasively. **True or False?**

16. Effective subheadings use specific facts to show the reader why you win on each sub-issue. **True or False?**

17. In some jurisdictions, the table of authorities is called authorities cited. **True or False?**

18. The table of authorities formatting rules do not vary by jurisdiction because all jurisdictions follow the Bluebook. **True or False?**

19. Authorities presented in the table of authorities should be organized alphabetically. **True or False?**

20. The table of authorities references only the first page where each cited authority is found. **True or False?**

21. Different types of legal authority must be separated within the table of authorities. **True or False?**

22. If an authority appears in your brief only as part of a string cite, it need not be included in the table of authorities. **True or False?**

23. Every brief requires a jurisdiction section. **True or False?**

24. An effective jurisdiction section briefly states the jurisdictional basis for appeal by providing a specific legal foundation and the relevant facts of the case. **True or False?**

25. Standard of review is appropriate only in appellate briefs. **True or False?**

26. Questions of law are reviewed de novo, and questions of fact are reviewed for abuse of discretion. **True or False?**

27. The statement of the issue presented for review is also called an issue statement. **True or False?**

28. An effective issue statement clearly presents the issues to be addressed by the court, in a light most favorable to your client. **True or False?**

29. An issue statement is presented in a light most favorable to your client if it leads the reader to empathize with your client. **True or False?**

30. The issue statement does not imply an answer because that is the function of the brief answer. **True or False?**

31. The standard of review must be included within each issue statement. **True or False?**

32. Each issue on appeal requires an issue statement. **True or False?**

33. An effective statement of the case presents the facts in a clear, precise, persuasive manner. **True or False?**

34. The statement of the case should always present the facts chronologically. **True or False?**

35. Because an effective statement of the case is persuasive, word choice is important. **True or False?**

36. Short sentences create high impact and should be used strategically. **True or False?**

37. Your theory of the case should be woven into your statement of the case. **True or False?**

38. An effective statement of the case avoids harmful facts. **True or False?**

39. An effective statement of the case weaves background facts, legally significant facts, and emotional facts together to persuade the legal reader. **True or False?**

40. Use the summary of the argument to provide busy legal readers with a brief and compelling overview of your argument. **True or False?**

41. Your summary of the argument should introduce your theory of the case and be written persuasively. **True or False?**

42. When writing the argument section, focus on both organization and analysis. **True or False?**

43. In a brief, pointheadings and subheadings substitute for a roadmap. **True or False?**

44. Pointheadings and subheadings should be written in complete sentences and should advance your argument. **True or False?**

45. In your argument section, use persuasive topic sentences that parallel your roadmap, pointheadings, and subheadings. **True or False?**

46. An effective argument section provides a historical overview of the law. **True or False?**

47. When writing your argument section, use legal analysis to develop reasoned and logical arguments. **True or False?**

48. Effective legal analysis combines rule-based reasoning and legal analogies, but avoids policy arguments that are not grounded in the law. **True or False?**

49. Rule-based reasoning requires deducing the general legal rule and applying it to the facts of your case. **True or False?**

50. Legal analogies compare your client's case with controlling precedent. **True or False?**

51. Avoid policy arguments because they signal to the court that your client's case is without sufficient support in the law. **True or False?**

52. The argument section should anticipate and address counterarguments. **True or False?**

53. An effective argument section is thorough yet concise. **True or False?**

54. A persuasive argument section presents the strongest arguments first and weaves in the theory of the case. **True or False?**

55. Proper legal citations are required throughout the argument section. **True or False?**

56. The conclusion should persuasively and concisely conclude on each legal issue addressed in the brief. **True or False?**

57. A proper signature and certificate of service includes your signature, bar number, and address. **True or False?**

Answer Key on page 516

⚇? 3.   Persuasive Techniques: Quiz

Instructions: For each of the following statements regarding persuasive techniques, choose either true or false. If you answer false, articulate why the statement is false before moving to the next question. If you have difficulty answering any of the questions on persuasive techniques, refer to the chapter text and the Briefs Checklists for assistance.

1. An effective theory of the case uses subtle persuasion to help the reader empathize with your client. **True or False?**

2. Your theory of the case should be evident throughout your brief. **True or False?**

3. Arguing in the negative and attacking your opponent are high-impact persuasive techniques and should be used strategically. **True or False?**

4. You should never use the passive voice in legal writing. **True or False?**

5. Using points of emphasis in your sentences and using active voice to highlight the subject of your sentences are effective persuasive techniques. **True or False?**

6. You can downplay points made by the other side by placing those points in independent clauses. **True or False?**

7. Burying weaker arguments mid-paragraph may weaken your credibility with the court. **True or False?**

8. Short sentences are not as persuasive as longer, fact-filled sentences. **True or False?**

Answer Key on page 516

⚇? 4.   Oral Argument: Quiz

Instructions: For each of the following statements regarding oral argument, choose either true or false. If you answer false, articulate why the statement is false before moving to the next question. If you have difficulty answering any of the questions on oral argument, refer to the chapter text and the Oral Argument Checklists for assistance.

1. It is unprofessional to refer to notes or reference sheets during oral argument. **True or False?**

2. Conducting moot or mock arguments will improve your oral arguments. **True or False?**

3. Thorough preparation for oral argument includes anticipating counterarguments and hypotheticals and preparing your approach to these tough questions. **True or False?**

4. Do not devote limited oral argument time to introductions or to a recitation of the facts; the judges will know this information already. **True or False?**

5. If you have strong arguments and solid legal support for your position, you should not reserve time for rebuttal. **True or False?**

6. An effective oral advocate delivers a brief introduction to her argument to provide the court with a roadmap. **True or False?**

7. An effective oral advocate will end his argument by summarizing the points he made and request relief. **True or False?**

8. An effective oral advocate listens to a judge's question, identifies the judge's concern, and then addresses that concern thoroughly. **True or False?**

9. Oral arguments are formal and should not be thought of as a conversation with the court. **True or False?**

Answer Key on page 516

❓ 5.   Client Letters: Quiz

Instructions: For each of the following statements regarding client letters, choose either true or false. If you answer false, articulate why the statement is false before moving to the next question. If you have difficulty answering any of the questions on client letters, refer to the chapter text and the Client Letter Checklist for assistance.

1. The sole purpose of a client letter is to provide the client with a legal opinion and advice on how to proceed. **True or False?**

2. The depth and formality of a client letter will vary based on the client's background, education, knowledge, and needs. **True or False?**

3. It is inappropriate to consider costs when preparing a client letter. **True or False?**

4. Legal opinions are fact-driven. If the facts of your client's case change, your opinion may also change, and it is your professional obligation to inform the client of this possibility. **True or False?**

5. Even informal client letters should avoid slang and flippant-sounding remarks. **True or False?**

6. Before beginning a client letter, you should gather the facts, research the legal issue, and clarify the client's question. **True or False?**

7. There are no formal requirements for a client letter because many client letters are informal. **True or False?**

8. The salutation you choose sets the tone for the letter; when in doubt, choose formality over informality. **True or False?**

9. The opening paragraph should not include any conclusions. **True or False?**

10. It is proper to ask that your client review the facts section of your letter and inform you of any changes or corrections. **True or False?**

11. You should avoid citing fact sources in a client letter because citations make the letter more cumbersome to read. **True or False?**

12. Like the discussion section of a legal memo, the analysis section of a client letter should include citations and legal terms of art. **True or False?**

13. In concluding a client letter, it is appropriate to mention other issues that might be pursued in the future. **True or False?**

Answer Key on page 517

⛊? 6. Pleadings and Motions: Quiz

Instructions: For each of the following statements regarding pleadings and motions, choose either true or false. If you answer false, articulate why the statement is false before moving to the next question. If you have difficulty answering any of the questions on pleadings and motions, refer to the chapter text and the Pleadings & Motions Checklists for assistance.

1. Pleadings—including complaints, answers, and interrogatories—are the documents used to initiate lawsuits. True or False?

2. Associate attorneys will never be asked to draft pleadings without guidance from supervising attorneys. **True or False?**

3. The defendant is the primary audience for the complaint. **True or False?**

4. The complaint is a formal document that defines the scope of the lawsuit. **True or False?**

5. The complaint must allege enough facts to meet all the elements of your claim. **True or False?**

6. The answer must indicate whether the defendant admits or denies each allegation made in the complaint. **True or False?**

7. Affirmative defenses and counterclaims must be raised in the answer. **True or False?**

8. Interrogatories are written for a legal audience. **True or False?**

9. Motions are persuasive documents used to request specific relief from the court. **True or False?**

10. Tactical considerations are important when drafting motions. **True or False?**

Answer Key on page 517

❓ 7.   Write-On Competition Papers: Quiz

Instructions: For each of the following statements regarding write-on competition papers, choose either true or false. If you answer false, articulate why the statement is false before moving to the next question. If you have difficulty answering any of the questions on write-on competition papers, refer to the chapter text and the Law Review Competition Checklists for assistance.

1. Many judges prefer that their clerks have law review experience because the experience improves writing and editing skills. **True or False?**

2. A good case note may simply repeat the court's (or the dissent's) opinion. **True or False?**

3. You should spend an enormous amount of time on rewriting and polishing your case note. **True or False?**

4. It is not necessary to use complicated citations, as long as you do your basic citations well. **True or False?**

Answer Key on page 517

C. Self-Assessment

🔳? 1.   Rewriting a Legal Memo—Self-Assessment

INSTRUCTIONS: This self-assessment is designed to test your knowledge of writing legal memos. Read through the document, taking note of the numbered and highlighted passages. Each number and highlighted passage represents a question about which you should decide whether the material is **effective** or **ineffective.** Write your response to each question. When you are finished, check your work against the answer key on page 517. The answer key also indicates why the material is effective or ineffective. This review will help you to assess your understanding of legal memos and to more quickly and accurately write and rewrite your own.

To: Partner Diana Donahoe
From: Associate
Date: November 21, 2005
RE: Possible Stalking Charge against Nick Castle

QUESTION PRESENTED

#1 Under Georgia criminal law, did Nick Castle stalk his former girlfriend, Jessica Sandstone, when he posted three unwanted messages to her on a blog that he knew Sandstone frequented?

#1 Effective/Ineffective

BRIEF ANSWER

#2 Probably not. Castle did not follow Sandstone because he was never in close proximity to her. He contacted her at a place by posting public messages on the site he knew she visited; however, this contact may have been consensual, and was not unquestionably for the purpose of harassing and intimidating Sandstone because the messages may not have been specifically directed at her.

#2 Effective/Ineffective

STATEMENT OF THE FACTS

Nick Castle and Jessica Sandstone dated for four years in college in Massachusetts. #3 Castle was typically "polite and pleasant," but after Sandstone ended the relationship, he became jealous and upset. Sandstone has ignored Castle's messages, but since the breakup she has developed migraine headaches requiring medication.

#3 Effective/Ineffective

On October 15, Sandstone moved to Atlanta to get away from Castle and to live and work with her sister. Castle found out about Sandstone's move from mutual friends.

Sandstone often accessed a public blog, Badacts, from her sister's home computer. Anyone could post, read, and comment on the blog. Sandstone and Castle had often read it together, and Castle would sometimes post poems to Sandstone on the blog.

On October 25, Sandstone found an entry from Castle. It was entitled "Today's Love Note," included a picture of the couple, and concluded with a warning. #4 After reading this, Sandstone began to experience migraines.

She accessed Badacts again on October 31 and found another "Love Note" from Castle, which also included a picture and a warning. Sandstone experienced a severe migraine after reading this entry, but continued to access the blog daily.

On November 5, Sandstone found another note from Castle. It read:

I'm finally on my way,
Cause I can't wait another day,
Even if you don't want me,
Both of us need to be free.
CAUTION: Romantics beware—it's all over.

A picture of Castle at the "Welcome to Georgia" sign was included. Sandstone called the police, but they declined to act.

DISCUSSION

#5 A person is guilty of stalking if he (1) follows another person or (2) contacts her (3) at a place (4) without her consent (5) for the purpose of harassing and intimidating her. Ga. Code Ann. § 16-5-90(a)(1) (2003 & Supp. 2005). #6 Castle did not follow Sandstone. He was never in close proximity to her. #7 In Adkins v. State, the defendant would appear at his sister's friend's workplace on a regular basis. He also broke into her car. Adkins v. State, 471 S.E.2d 896, 897 (Ga. Ct. App. 1996). Unlike Adkins, Castle was never at any location Sandstone frequented. He merely entered the same state. There was a much greater distance between Castle and Sandstone than existed in Adkins. See also Hooper v. State, 478 S.E.2d 606, 608 (Ga. Ct. App. 1996) (stalker would appear wherever victim went). #8 Castle did not come close enough to Sandstone to follow her.

Because he did not follow Sandstone, Castle must have contacted her to be found guilty of stalking. #9 Contact is defined as "any communication including without being limited to communication in person." Ga. Code Ann. § 16-5-90(a)(1). Methods of communication include "computer network." Id. Castle posted his messages on the Badacts site, which is part of a computer network. See Ga. Code Ann. § 16-9-92(2) (2003).

Castle will argue that he did not communicate with Sandstone because he did not know if she was reading the blog entries. The existence of communication is determined by common understanding. #10 In Wright v. State, the stalker contacted his victims by slowly driving down their street. This action was contact because "people of ordinary intelligence would understand" it as communication. Wright v.

(margin annotations)
#4 Effective/Ineffective
#5 Effective/Ineffective
#6 Effective/Ineffective
#7 Effective/Ineffective
#8 Effective/Ineffective
#9 Effective/Ineffective
#10 Effective/Ineffective

State, 502 S.E.2d 756, 757 (Ga. Ct. App. 1998). Wright knew his victims would be on their street. Similarly, Castle knew Sandstone visited Badacts on a regular basis when he posted messages due to the couple's history of browsing together. In addition, writing is a more common understanding of communication than driving. Therefore, Castle contacted Sandstone through his Badacts posts because ordinary people would understand this writing to be communication.

#11 Contact between Castle and Sandstone occurred at a place. A place is "any public or private property occupied by the victim other than the residence of the defendant." § 16-5-90. Computer-based contact occurs where it is received. Id. Sandstone received Castle's messages in her sister's apartment, which is private property. Castle does not reside there. According to the statutory definition, Castle contacted Sandstone at a place.

#11 Effective/Ineffective

Castle must lack Sandstone's consent to this contact. Lack of consent can be implied, or "inferred from one's conduct." Black's Law Dictionary 323 (8th ed. 2004). In Adkins v. State, a man stalked his sister's friend by sending sexually explicit letters. Lack of consent was implied because the victim avoided situations where she might encounter her stalker. She did not respond to his letters, stayed away from him, and stopped socializing with his sister. Adkins, 471 S.E.2d at 897. Sandstone, like the victim in Adkins, put distance between herself and Castle when she moved to Atlanta. Her behavior was also similar to the Adkins victim's in that she failed to answer Castle's messages. #12 Therefore, Sandstone's actions may constitute implied lack of consent.

#12 Effective/Ineffective

However, it is equally plausible that her actions implied consent. Unlike the victim in Adkins, who stopped going where she knew her stalker would be, Sandstone continued to access Badacts although she knew Castle posted there. Sandstone's choice to visit Badacts and read Castle's entries may imply consent. However, the newness of Internet stalking makes the validity of this implied consent uncertain. #13 There are strong arguments that Sandstone's conduct implies consent; however, it may also imply lack of consent.

#13 Effective/Ineffective

Contact must be "for the purpose of harassing and intimidating" the victim. Ga. Code Ann. § 16-5-90(a)(1). #14 To meet this element, the contact must (1) be knowing and willful, (2) be directed at a specific victim, (3) cause emotional distress, (4) cause reasonable fear for safety, (5) establish a pattern of behavior, and (6) serve no legitimate purpose. Id.

#14 Effective/Ineffective

Castle's contact with Sandstone was knowing and willful. "Knowing" means deliberate and conscious; "willful" means voluntary and intentional. Black's, supra, at 888, 1630. The rhyme scheme of each note indicates that Castle took time to craft each message, writing consciously and deliberately. There is no indication he was coerced into making these postings or posted accidentally. Castle posted the messages knowingly and willfully.

#15 The messages were not definitely specifically directed at Sandstone. Badacts is a public website; its messages are accessible to everyone. The entries were not sent to Sandstone alone. Furthermore, each of the warnings was plural, urging, "Romantics

#15 Effective/Ineffective

Beware." If the only intended target was Sandstone, this is illogical. Additionally, none of the messages specified the identity of the "you" mentioned in the poems. A reader could infer that "you" was the woman in the pictures, especially if he knew Castle had posted messages for Sandstone before. However, Sandstone's presence in the pictures does not mean the messages were directed at her. They could have been posted for all visitors to appreciate. Although it is reasonable to infer that the messages were specifically directed at Sandstone, it is also plausible to conclude that they were not.

Castle's messages caused Sandstone emotional distress. She began to experience migraines after reading the first post and had a more severe migraine after reading the second. Sandstone's migraines are usually controllable with medication; their recurrence indicates that she was unusually distressed. Sandstone's decision to call the police also demonstrates her distress. #16 People typically do not involve the police unless they are extremely upset. See Johnson v. State, 592 S.E.2d 507, 509 (Ga. Ct. App. 2003). Sandstone experienced emotional distress, manifested in migraines and calls for help, due to Castle's postings.

#17 Castle's blog entries caused Sandstone to reasonably fear for her safety. Her fear need not arise from an overt threat of death or bodily injury. Ga. Code Ann. § 16-5-90. In Adkins v. State, where the victim was stalked by her friend's brother, one of the letters she received stated, "I hope we have talked before you get this or you may find me waiting on your doorstep one day." Adkins, 471 S.E.2d at 897. The victim's fear was reasonable because the stalker's "threats and hints of violence were only thinly veiled and laced with declarations of love and selfless concern." Id. #18 Subtle threats are sufficient to cause reasonable fear.

#19 Castle's notes, like Adkins's, contain an implication that he is approaching. Adkins says he might be waiting on his victim's doorstep, while Castle says he is "on [his] way." The inference is clearer in Sandstone's case because Castle has included a picture of himself at the Georgia state line. While Adkins uses hypothetical language, Castle speaks categorically and includes evidence that he is nearing Sandstone's residence. The threat of proximity contributes to the reasonableness of Sandstone's fear.

Sandstone's fear for her safety may be less reasonable than the Adkins victim's due to Castle's "polite and pleasant" personality. However, the Adkins victim "always got along fine" with her stalker, who was convicted. Id. Warnings of increased proximity and veiled threats of violence make Sandstone's fear for her safety reasonable.

#20 Castle's three messages probably do not establish a pattern of harassing and intimidating behavior. #21 All Georgia stalking cases involve more than three incidents. See, e.g., Hall v. State, 487 S.E.2d 41, 42 (Ga. Ct. App. 1997); Hooper v. State, 478 S.E.2d 606, 608 (Ga. Ct. App. 1996). However, in Jerusheba v. State, the defendant was convicted of stalking after he sent five sexually explicit letters. Jerusheba v. State, 487 S.E.2d 465, 465 (Ga. Ct. App. 1997). #22 The difference between three notes and five may be negligible. While Castle's messages would not traditionally be numerous enough to establish a pattern, the term could be interpreted broadly.

#16 Effective/Ineffective

#17 Effective/Ineffective

#18 Effective/Ineffective
#19 Effective/Ineffective

#20 Effective/Ineffective
#21 Effective/Ineffective

#22 Effective/Ineffective

Castle's blog entries could probably be construed as serving a legitimate purpose. #23 The restriction of First Amendment freedoms should not be undertaken lightly. Therefore, any plausibly legitimate purpose for his postings, such as sharing photographs or grieving, is persuasive. However, if Castle's messages are harassing and intimidating, the entries cannot be legitimate. Such conduct is not constitutionally protected. <u>Johnson v. State</u>, 449 S.E.2d 94, 96 (Ga. 1994). Castle's writing probably served a legitimate purpose, unless it satisfied the other sub-elements of harassment and intimidation.

#23 Effective/Ineffective

CONCLUSION

#24 A stalking charge could probably not be brought against Castle because all elements cannot be conclusively established. First, while Castle did not follow Sandstone, he contacted her by posting messages on the website because ordinary people would understand this writing as communication. In addition, Sandstone received Castle's messages in her sister's private apartment, so contact occurred at a place.

#24 Effective/Ineffective

#25 However, questions remain about Sandstone's consent to contact. Lack of consent could be implied from her moving away and not responding to Castle's messages. However, Sandstone may have given implied consent by continuing to access Badacts.

#25 Effective/Ineffective

The prosecution will not be able to prove that Castle's conduct was harassing and intimidating. Although Castle's postings (1) were knowing and willful because they were not accidental or coerced; (2) caused Sandstone's emotional distress, manifested in migraine headaches and a call to the police; and (3) made Sandstone's fear for her safety reasonable, the prosecution will not be able to prove the remaining sub-elements. First, Castle's notes were not specifically directed at Sandstone because they were posted on a public blog and phrased in the plural. In addition, three incidents are not enough to establish a pattern of behavior.

Answer Key on page 517

？ 2.   Rewriting a Legal Brief—Self-Assessment

INSTRUCTIONS: This self-assessment is designed to test your knowledge of writing legal briefs. Read through the document, taking note of the numbered and highlighted passages. Each number and highlighted passage represents a question about which you should decide whether the material is **effective** or **ineffective.** Write your response to each question. When you are finished, check your work against the answer key on page 519. The answer key also indicates why the material is effective or ineffective. This review will help you to assess your understanding of legal briefs and to more quickly and accurately write and rewrite your own.

DISTRICT OF COLUMBIA COURT OF APPEALS

Criminal No. 03-9051-F

UNITED STATES, Appellant

v.

LANCE HARBOR, Appellee

APPEAL FROM THE SUPERIOR COURT FOR THE DISTRICT OF COLUMBIA

BRIEF OF THE APPELLEE

Counsel for Appellee

TABLE OF CONTENTS

#1 Effective/Ineffective

#2 Effective/Ineffective

Legal Documents—Study Aid Material

TABLE OF CITATIONS

Cases

Constitution

STATEMENTS OF THE ISSUE

#3 I. Whether the Superior Court for the District of Columbia was correct in finding that 17-year-old Lance Harbor was subject to interrogation in violation of his fifth amendment rights when he was questioned by the principal in his office and a police officer made statements to him in the presence of his parents and Harbor answered a question which led to his arrest?

#3 Effective/Ineffective

 #4 II. Whether the Superior Court was correct in finding that Lance Harbor was in custody when Harbor was summoned to the principal's office, detained there for over and hour, and questioned in the presence of a uniformed police officer?

#4 Effective/Ineffective

STATEMENT OF THE CASE

The case was brought by the United States against Lance Harbor in the Superior Court for the District of Columbia. Lance Harbor filed a motion to suppress an incriminating statement. The Superior Court granted the motion to suppress after finding that Lance was interrogated while in police custody in violation of <u>Miranda v. Arizona</u> and the Fifth Amendment of the U.S. Constitution. The case reaches this court on appeal from the Superior Court's decision.

STATEMENT OF THE FACTS

#5 Lance Harbor, a seventeen-year-old high school senior, is the captain of the football team, a sprinter on the track team, and a member of several clubs including Students Against Drunk Driving. (T. 25, 26) As captain of the football team, Lance's priority was to watch out for younger players on the football team. (T. 27) Lance Harbor never had any interaction with criminal justice system nor had he had any disciplinary problems in the past. (21, 25, 26)

#5 Effective/Ineffective

 On November 25 th, Lance Harbor was called out of his #6 Honors Calculus class and told to report directly to the principal's office. (T. 29) Students from the football team had been called into the principal's office in order to be questioned about the use and distribution of a supplement purchased on the internet prior to this incident. (T. 13, 28) Lance waited outside the principal's office until his parents arrived, in the presence of Officer Brown, an armed guard posted next to the principal's office. (T. 15, 22, 29)

#6 Effective/Ineffective

 The principal informed Lance and Mr. and Mrs. Harbor that some of the boys on the football team had been taking a supplement supplied by someone else on the team. (T. 15) Throughout the meeting, the principal did not inform Lance that he was free to leave the meeting. (T. 22) Officer Moxon, Mr. Moxon, and Jonathan Moxon arrived at the principal's office to ask the principal a few questions at which time the principal permitted the Moxons to sit in on the discussion with the Harbors. (T. 17) Lance Harbor had met Officer Moxon on a previous occasion during which Officer Moxon thanked Lance for being kind to young players on the team, including her son, to which Lance responded that it was his job to help the young players. (T. 27, 28)

Officer Moxon, wearing her police uniform, proceeded to ask questions and said to Lance and Jonathan, "Do you see what trouble this is causing?" (T. 18) Lance remained quiet. (T. 18) While the principal took a phone call, Officer Moxon told the Harbors that "it was a shame that players were letting her young son take all the heat. She thought that teammates looked out for the weaker players." (T. 32) Immediately after hearings Office Moxon's statement, Lance stated that he have given the supplement to Jonathan Moxon. (T. 32) The police were then called, and Lance was subsequently arrested. (T. 20, 33)

STANDARD OF REVIEW

The Court will defer to findings of evidentiary fact by the Superior Court for the District of Columbia, but the question of law will be reviewed *de novo* by the Court. Jones v. United States, 779 A.2d 277, 281 (D.C. 2001). Determining custodial interrogation without the benefit of Miranda warnings is a question of law. Reid v. United States, 581 A.2d 359, 363 (D.C. 1990). The record must also be reviewed in the light most favorable to the party who prevailed in the lower court. Jones, 779 A.2d at 281.

ARGUMENT

#7 Effective/Ineffective

#7 The Fifth Amendment of the U.S. Constitution protects people from compelled self-incrimination and abuse of police power. The Fifth Amendment specifically states, "No person... shall be compelled in ay criminal case to be a witness against himself, nor be deprived of life, liberty, or property, without due process of law." In Miranda v. Arizona, the Court created further safeguards from police abuse known as the Miranda warnings. Miranda v. Arizona, 384 U.S. 436, 439 (1966). Protection from police coercion tactics is of such high importance given that such tactics lead to a high risk that a suspect's Fifth Amendment rights would be violated. Miranda, 384 U.S. at 439. Evidence obtained during custodial interrogation is only admissible if a suspect was advised of his rights accorded to him or her by law. Miranda,

#8 Effective/Ineffective

384 U.S. at 439. #8 In order for Miranda warnings to be required the suspect must be subject to interrogation and be in custody. California v. Beheler, 463 U.S. 1121, 1123-25 (1983).

#9 Effective/Ineffective

#9 The questions asked and statements made by Officer Moxon to the Harbors and Lance and Jonathan Moxon constitute interrogation. When determining the existence of interrogation, courts consider whether the police knew or should have known that their statement would likely elicit a response. Rhode Island v. Innis, 446 U.S. 291, 300-01 (1980). The Superior Court for the District of Columbia found that given the totality of the circumstances, Lance Harbor was interrogated by Officer Moxon.

A. Officer Moxon was aware Lance's concern about fellow teammates and knew or should have known that her statements would likely elicit a response from Lance.

#10 Officer Moxon was aware of Lance's susceptibility and desire to look out for younger teammates; therefore she knew or should have known that her statements would elicit a response. Officer Moxon stated that "it was a shame that letting her young son take all the heat" and that "she thought that teammates looked out for the weaker players." Interrogation includes express questioning as well as any words or actions on the part of the police that they know or should know are reasonably likely to elicit an incriminating response from a suspect. Innis, 446 U.S. at 300-01. The important focus in analyzing this factor is looking at the perceptions of the suspect rather than the intent of the police. Innis, 446 U.S. at 301.

Officer Moxon was not making statements to the defendant but her statements are the functional equivalent of questioning. #11 In Innis, the respondent was not interrogated for Miranda purposes because he was neither expressly questioned nor subject to the functional equivalent of questioning. Id. There was nothing in the record indicating that the officers were aware of the respondent's particular concern for handicapped children. Innis, 446 U.S. at 302-03. As a result the officers should not have known that the conversation between themselves about a handicapped child finding the gun would reasonably elicit an incriminating response from the respondent. Innis, 446 U.S. at 303. In this case, Officer Moxon did expressly question both Lance Harbor and Jonathan when stating, "Do you see what trouble this is causing?" Even if this cannot be considered express questioning, Lance Harbor was subject to the functional equivalent of questioning, because Officer Moxon should have known that her statements about looking out for younger players and taking the heat off her son were reasonably likely to elicit an incriminating response from Lance. Officer Moxon knew of Lance's particular susceptibility to an appeal to his conscience to look out for younger players on the team this, because she had thanked Lance for looking out for younger players on the team including her son on a previous occasion.

#12 In Stewart, the Court determined that words of encouragement from a detective who was a fellow church member of the suspect constituted interrogation for Miranda purposes. Stewart v. United States, 668 A.2d 857, 865-866 (D.C. 1995). The detective was aware that the suspect was religious and the detective's comments minimizing the serious of the offense were meant to encourage the suspect. Stewart, 668 A.2d at 865. The court determined that any knowledge the police may have had concerning any unusual susceptibility of a defendant to a given type of persuasion is an important factor in determining whether the police should have known that their words or action were reasonably likely to elicit an incriminating response from a suspect. Stewart, 668 A.2d at 865-66. The Court also determined that the conversation could not be labeled as causal or personal, because no conversation concerning a criminal investigation between an experienced officer and a suspect can be considered purely personal. Stewart, 668 A.2d at 866. Similarly, Officer Moxon cannot

#10   Effective/Ineffective

#11   Effective/Ineffective

#12   Effective/Ineffective

claim that she was acting purely in the capacity of a concerned mother. Officer Moxon is an experienced lieutenant in the crime prevention unit and aware of the supplement problem on the football team. As a result Officer Moxon's conversation with Harbors concerning a criminal investigation cannot be purely personal. Given that Officer Moxon had prior knowledge of Lance's susceptibility and that she was an experienced lieutenant, Officer Moxon knew that her statements would reasonably elicit an incriminating response from Lance.

B. Lance Harbor did not initiate a conversation with Officer Moxon, rather Officer Moxon directed statements at Lance Harbor while he remained quiet.

Lance Harbor did not voluntarily make the incriminating statement nor initiate a conversation with Officer Moxon. In order for a person to be interrogated for Miranda purposes, the questioning or functional equivalent of questioning must be initiated by law enforcement officers. <u>Miranda</u>, 384 U.S. at 344. #13 The issue of custody will be discussed in subsequent sections of this brief. This section concerns only whether the questioning was initiated by the police.

#14 In <u>Gilmore</u>, the Court held that the defendant was not subject to interrogation because the defendant voluntarily initiated the discussion with the detective about the matters surrounding his charges and the detective did not question the defendant about the matters with which he was charged. <u>Gilmore v. United States</u>, 742 A.2d 862, 869 (D.C. 1999). The Court stated that police must have asked a question that was probing or likely to elicit an incriminating response in order to constitute interrogation for Miranda purposes. <u>Gilmore</u>, 742 A.2d at 869.

Unlike the defendant in <u>Gilmore</u>, Lance did not voluntarily make an incriminating statement and the questioning leading Lance's statement was initiated by Officer Moxon. Lance was called into the principal's office and asked a few question by the principal. Once Officer Moxon entered the principal's office she proceeded to make statements directed at Harbors. When she asked Lance Harbor and her son Jonathan, "do you see what trouble you are causing?," Lance remained quiet. Lance did not make his incriminating statement until Officer Moxon made her statement which she knew would likely elicit an incriminating response from Lance.

II. LANCE HARBOR WAS IN CUSTODY BECAUSE HE WAS QUESTIONED IN THE PRINCIPAL'S OFFICE IN THE PRESENCE OF A UNIFORMED POLICE OFFICER AND HE WAS NOT REASONABLY FREE TO LEAVE.

#15 Lance Harbor was in custody for <u>Miranda</u> purposes when he was interrogated by Officer Moxon. The test for determining whether a person is in custody is objective. <u>Berkemer v. McCarty</u>, 468 U.S. 420, 421 (1984). It focuses on how a reasonable person would act in the suspect's position and how a reasonable person would have understood his or her position. <u>Berkemer</u>, 468 U.S. at 421. In order to determine custody, the court must look at the totality of the circumstances. <u>See</u> <u>Patton v. United States</u>, 633 A.2d 800, 814 (D.C. 1993). Several of the factors to be considered to

#13   Effective/Ineffective

#14   Effective/Ineffective

#15   Effective/Ineffective

include location, whether the suspect was told that he was free to leave, whether a reasonable person in those circumstances would have felt that his or her freedom was restricted, the age of the suspect, and if the suspect had prior experience with the criminal process. The Superior Court for the District of Columbia found that Lance Harbor was in custody for Miranda purposes upon looking at the totality of the circumstances.

A. Lance Harbor was in custody despite the fact that he was in a principal's office rather than a police station because his freedom of action was deprived.

#16 Although Lance Harbor was interrogated in the somewhat familiar environment of the principal's office, he was in custody for Miranda purposes because he was not free to leave. #17 The Supreme Court has not focused on the distinction between familiar and unfamiliar places, but rather the distinction of whether or not the person is free to leave. For example, in <u>Orzoco v. Texas</u>, 394 U.S. 324, 326-27 (1969), the Supreme Court held that the defendant was in custody for Miranda purposes despite the fact that he was in his bed when he was interrogated, because he freedom was restrained and he was not free to leave. The principal's office was even less familiar to Harbor than the bedroom in <u>Orozco</u>. In addition, like the defendant in <u>Orozco</u>, Harbor was not free to leave and his freedom was restrained the minute that Officer Moxon walked in the office and began asking questions and making comments. Therefore, Harbor's freedom of action was restrained in the school principal's office.

    #18 The situation which took place in the principal's office was dominated by the police, and this is a major concern when determining custody. In <u>Turner</u>, the court stated that what is of chief concern when making distinctions as to what location is proper for custody is whether the questioning is dominated by police. <u>Turner</u>, 761 A.2d at 852. Once Officer Moxon arrived at the principal's office she dominated the conversation by questioning the principal, the Harbors, and directing statements and questions at Lance and Jonathan Moxon.

B. A reasonable person in Lance's position would have believed that his or her freedom was restricted given that the questioning took place in front of his parents, the principal, and a uniformed police officer and that there was an armed guard stationed outside the principal's office.

#19 A reasonable person would have also felt that his or her freedom was restricted to a degree associated with a formal arrest. #20 Courts have not developed a hard and fast rule setting forth what constitutes restriction of freedom but a few different factors that courts have considered include restraints such as handcuffs, being placed under arrest, and whether weapons were drawn.

    Lance Harbor was at no time notified that he was free to leave the principal's office. In several instances where the courts have found that the suspect is not in custody, it has been determined that the suspect was informed that he or she was free

#16 Effective/Ineffective

#17 Effective/Ineffective

#18 Effective/Ineffective

#19 Effective/Ineffective
#20 Effective/Ineffective

#21 Effective/Ineffective

to leave or that he or she was not under arrest. See In re E.A.H., 612 A.2d 836, 837 (D.C. 1992); United States v. Gayden, 492 A.2d 868, 873 (D.C. 1985). #21 In E.A.H., the juvenile was informed that he was not under arrest before being interrogated. In re E.A.H., 612 A.2d at 837. Similarly in Gayden, the suspect was informed that he was free to leave at any time; however, the Court ultimately determined that he was in custody because his situation has changed so he was no longer free to go. Gayden, 492 A.2d at 873. Unlike E.A.H. and Gayden, Lance was never informed that he was free to leave the office; therefore it is unlikely that a reasonable person in such circumstances would believe that he or she was permitted to leave.

Even if Lance Harbor was not initially in custody when entering the principal's office, once Officer Moxon entered the room and began making statements and asking questions, Lance was in custody because circumstances had changed so significantly that he was no longer free to go. The court in Turner determined that despite the fact that the suspect was informed that he would be released at the end of the conversation and that he was familiar with the police questioning process, once he was compelled to submit to a procedure to obtain bodily fluids, he was no longer free to leave. Turner, 761 A.2d at 852. The circumstances had changed dramatically so that he was probably not free to leave. Turner, 761 A.2d at 852. Similarly in Gayden, the suspect was initially told that he was free to leave at any time, but then he was confronted by officers who claimed that his statements were contradictory, the court held that the suspect's situation had changed so significantly that he was no longer free to go. Gayden, 492 A.2d at 873.

In the case at hand, Lance Harbor 's position changed significantly from the time he entered the principal's office until the time he made the incriminating statement. Initially Lance entered the principal's office under the notion that he would be answering the questions of the principal in front of his parents. He was not aware that a police officer would be part of the process and the use of Officer Moxon's interrogation tactics changed the situation so significantly that Lance was not free to go and a reasonable person under such circumstances would also feel that his or her freedom was restricted to a degree associated with a formal arrest.

While Lance Harbor was not physically restrained, he was not allowed to leave the principal's office unhindered. He was arrested after making an incriminating statement. Upon determining that Lance Harbor was in a police dominated location and situation with an armed security guard at his usual post outside the principal's office and that the circumstances drastically changed for Lance while being questioned in the principal's office, the totality of circumstances show that Lance Harbor was in custody for Miranda purposes.

C. The fact that Lance Harbor is a juvenile and has not had any prior experience is an important consideration in determining custody.

#22 Effective/Ineffective

#22 Two additional interrelated factors that the court should consider when determining custody are age and experience with the criminal process. Lance Harbor is a juvenile and while a custody determination requires an objective reasonable test, courts have recognized that juveniles should not be treated exactly the same as adults. In re E.A.H., 612 A.2d at 839. In E.A.H., the court recognized that juveniles are not simply young adults and that it is reasonable for courts to apply a wide definition of custody for Miranda purposes in the case of juvenile. Id. Statements and confessions made by juveniles require special caution. In re Gault, 387 U.S. 1, 45 (1967). As a result that fact that Lance is a juvenile must be considered when determining whether or not he is in custody for Miranda purposes.

#23 Lance has had no previous experience with the criminal system or any other disciplinary system and has been described by the principal of the school as an outgoing kid. The Court has taken experience with the criminal system into account when determining whether or not a Miranda waiver is valid. The Court in M.A.C. determined that the juvenile's experience in the criminal system was an important factor in determining a valid Miranda waiver. See In re M.A.C., 761 A.2d at 38. The juvenile was familiar with the streets, treated well by the police and as such was aware of the way the system worked. In re M.A.C., 761 A.2d at 38. Similarly in F.D.P., the court used experience with criminal process as an important factor when determining that the juvenile waived his Miranda rights knowingly given that the juvenile had been arrested two or three times previously and spent time in custody at a juvenile detention center. In re F.D.P., 352 A.2d 378, 380 (D.C. 1976).

While the case at hand does not concern valid waiver of Miranda rights, this same analysis should be used to determining whether or not custody is present for Miranda purposes. Both cases are concerned with protecting the Fifth Amendment rights of a person. In particular Lance Harbor is juvenile and special care must be taken when determining the validity of a statement or confession of a minor. Experience with the criminal process is a valid factor to consider when trying to determine the totality of the circumstances. Unlike M.A.C. and F.D.P., Lance Harbor has never had any experience with the criminal process. His youth and his naivety with the process must be considered in order to properly make a determination about the totality of the circumstances. Given Lance's youth, inexperience with the criminal process, reasonable belief that he was not free to leave, and the police dominated location of the interrogation, it can be determined that the Superior Court for the District of Columbia was correct in determining that Lance was in custody for Miranda purposes.

CONCLUSION

#24 For the above stated reasons, the motion to suppress granted by the Superior Court of the District of Columbia should be affirmed.

#23 Effective/Ineffective

#24 Effective/Ineffective

Answer Key on page 519

Legal Documents—Study Aid Material

CHAPTER 4

Editing

EDITING &
CITATION

This chapter covers editing for both grammatical correctness and effective legal usage. In it, you will find legal usage and grammar rules as well as editing strategies.

I. Strategies for Editing
II. Grammar and Legal Usage Rules
  - Active vs. Passive Voice
  - Affect vs. Effect
  - Although vs. While
  - Apostrophes
  - Because vs. Since
  - Capitalization
  - Clearly or Obviously (Avoid Using)
  - Colons and Semicolons
  - Commas
  - Comparisons
  - Conciseness
  - Contractions
  - Dangling and Misplaced Modifiers (Avoid Using)
  - Due To
  - Effect vs. Affect
  - Farther vs. Further
  - Hyphens
  - Italics
  - Legalese (Avoid Using)
  - Misplaced and Dangling Modifiers (Avoid Using)
  - Nominalizations (Avoid Using)
  - Numbers and Quantities
  - Obviously or Clearly (Avoid Using)
  - Parallel Structure
  - Passive vs. Active Voice
  - Pronouns
  - Quantities and Numbers
  - Quotation Marks
  - Redundancy (Avoid Using)
  - Semicolons and Colons
  - Sentence Fragments (Avoid Using)
  - Sexist Language (Avoid Using)

- Short Sentences
- Since vs. Because
- Split Infinitives (Avoid Using)
- Strong Subject-Verb Combinations
- Subject-Verb Agreement
- Terms of Art (Avoid Varying)
- That vs. Which
- Verb Tense
- Which vs. That
- While vs. Although
- Who, Whom, and Whose

III. Study Aids—Editing
   A. Quick Reference
      1. Grammar and Legal Usage Strategies: Quick References 🗒️
      2. Grammar and Legal Usage Rules: Checklist ☑️
   B. Quizzes
- Active vs. Passive Voice: Quiz 👤?
- Affect vs. Effect: Quiz 👤?
- Although vs. While: Quiz 👤?
- Apostrophes: Quiz 👤?
- Because vs. Since: Quiz 👤?
- Capitalization: Quiz 👤?
- Commas: Quiz 👤?
- Due To: Quiz 👤?
- Farther vs. Further: Quiz 👤?
- Sentence Fragments: Quiz 👤?
- Grammar: Quiz 👤?
- Hyphens: Quiz 👤?
- Indefinite Pronouns: Quiz 👤?
- Legalese: Quiz 👤?
- Modifiers: Quiz 👤?
- Nominalizations: Quiz 👤?
- Numbers and Quantities: Quizzes 👤?
- Parallel Structure: Quiz 👤?
- Quotation Marks: Quiz 👤?
- Semicolons and Colons: Quiz 👤?
- That vs. Which: Quiz 👤?
- Verb Tense: Quiz 👤?
- Who, Whom, and Whose: Quizzes 👤?

   C. Self-Assessment
      1. Editing (Grammar) Self-Assessment 👤?

I.   STRATEGIES FOR EDITING

This chapter is designed to help you learn to edit at the sentence and word choice levels. It will be most useful to you after you have revised your document for content, large-scale organization, analysis, and conciseness. Editing a sentence is a waste of time if you later decide to delete the whole paragraph or argument. (For advice on writing and rewriting your document, see chapter 2.)

There are many strategies for editing your sentence structure, syntax, and word choice:

1. **Read the whole document out loud.** A "read aloud" helps you hear the words and understand how they might affect the reader. If you are breathless in your reading, your sentences are too long. If you sound choppy in your reading, your sentences are too short. Mix them up.

2. **Determine your grammar and usage weaknesses and look for them in your document one at a time.** To determine your weaknesses, take the editing self-assessment at the end of this chapter. Next, focus on one weakness at a time in your document. For example, if you know you have a problem with your modifiers, read all your sentences, find the clauses, and make sure that your modifiers are correctly positioned. You will actually save time using this method as your focus will make you more efficient.

3. **Read one paragraph at a time and look for all grammar and usage problems paragraph by paragraph.** Take a break after a couple of paragraphs to ensure you remain focused.

4. **Read your document backward,** either word by word, to make sure there are no typos, or starting with the last sentence or last paragraph first. The purpose of reading backward is to distance yourself from the substance of the document. If you are reading in the correct order, from start to finish, you will tend to read for content instead of usage. If you read the last paragraph first, you will be more able to concentrate on the words and sentence structure. In addition, you tend to lose steam at the end of your editing process, and, as a result, the end of the document is usually not as well polished as the beginning. If one of your strategies is to edit from end to start, your whole document should be well polished.

II.   GRAMMAR AND LEGAL USAGE RULES

Active vs. Passive Voice

In active voice, the subject is doing the acting:

The judge ruled.

In passive voice, the subject of the sentence is not the actor; instead, the subject is being acted on:

> The ruling was made by the judge.

Usually in legal writing, active voice is preferred because it makes for more concise writing. However, passive voice is sometimes appropriate, especially when the writer wants to downplay the actor:

> The gun was possessed by my client.

Affect vs. Effect

Generally, *effect* is a noun and *affect* is a verb:

> The effect of the medication was severe: It affected Plaintiff's ability to stay awake while driving.

The exception is *effect* when it is used to mean "to cause to come into being" or "to effectuate":

> Defendant effected the transaction only after Plaintiff's consent.

Although vs. While

Although should be used to introduce a counterargument or for a causal relationship:

> Although Defendant opened the door to his apartment, he did not consent to the search.

While should be used for temporal circumstances:

> While the police were in the apartment, they seized the contraband in plain view.

Apostrophes

- Because legal writers avoid contractions (see page 355), apostrophes are generally used only for the possessive.
- Do not use an apostrophe for possessive pronouns such as *hers, its, theirs, ours, yours,* and *whose.*
- *Its* is the possessive of *it. It's* means "it is."
- Because legal writing is generally formal writing, avoid using contractions such as *he's, we're,* or *didn't.*

Because vs. Since

Because should be used for causation:

> I am going to study because my exam will be difficult.

Since should be used for temporal circumstances:

> I have been studying since 9:00 a.m.

Capitalization

The Bluebook and ALWD, the standard citation guides for legal writers, provide a number of capitalization rules.

A. **Court:** In memos and briefs, the Bluebook and ALWD require capitalization of the word *court* in the following examples:

1. When naming any court in full:

> The U.S. Court of Appeals for the Fifth Circuit held ...

2. When referring to the U.S. Supreme Court:

> The Supreme Court held ...

3. When referring to the court reading the document:

> This Court should find ...

ALWD includes a fourth rule for capitalizing the word *court* in memos and briefs:

4. When referring to the highest court in *any* jurisdiction after it has been fully identified:

> The Oklahoma Supreme Court held ...
>
> In its ruling, the Court outlined ...

B. **Constitutional Amendments:** Capitalize the amendments of the U.S. Constitution in text:

> The First Amendment protects ...

C. **Party's Names:** In memos and briefs, when referring to the actual parties involved in the matter being discussed, capitalize party designations:

> Plaintiff, Defendant, Appellant, Appellee

D. **Titles:**

1. Capitalize civil, professional, military, and religious titles only when they directly precede a personal name:

> Judge Alexander, the judge
>
> Secretary of State Rogers, the secretary of state

2. Two exceptions to the preceding rule apply. Both the Bluebook and ALWD capitalize the titles of U.S. Supreme Court Justices, even when used without proper names:

> Chief Justice Roberts, the Chief Justice
>
> Justice Ginsburg, the Justice

3. ALWD also capitalizes titles of honor when they substitute for a person's name:

> Secretary of State Rogers addressed the United Nations...
>
> In his speech, the Secretary of State...

Clearly or Obviously (Avoid Using)

Usually, when a legal writer uses the words *clearly* or *obviously,* the argument is neither clear nor obvious. Avoid using these words because they usually substitute for the logical reasoning that will make the argument clear and obvious. Similar terms to avoid are *plainly* and *certainly.*

Colons and Semicolons

The following are the most popular uses of a semicolon:

1. To separate items in a list when the items themselves have commas;
2. To join two independent (but related) clauses without a coordinating conjunction; and
3. To separate items in a series when the items are separate, as in a statute.

The following are the most popular uses of a colon:

1. To join two related independent clauses; and
2. To introduce a block quotation, a numbered list, or a list that further explains the object of the sentence.

If the phrase following the colon is not a complete sentence, do not capitalize the first word following the colon (unless it is a proper noun).

Commas

Use a comma for the following purposes.

1. To separate items in a list:

> The prosecution introduced the murder weapon, the victim's diary, and photographs of the scene of the crime.

2. To offset an introductory phrase (optional for short introductory phrases):

> Because the police did not comply with the Fifth Amendment, the confession is inadmissible.
>
> In December 2002, the plaintiff moved for summary judgment.

3. To join two independent clauses with *and, or, nor, for, so, but,* or *yet* (coordinating conjunctions):

> The defendant confessed to the crime, but the confession was not voluntary.

Independent clauses are complete thoughts; they can stand alone as complete sentences.

4. To offset a phrase that could be omitted without changing the meaning of the sentence:

> The defendant, who had been a close friend of the victim, had a key to the apartment.

5. To offset a dependent clause preceding an independent clause:

> Because she was tired, Lisa took a nap.

However, if the dependent clause follows the independent clause, no comma is necessary:

> Lisa took a nap because she was tired.

Comparisons

In comparisons, the items compared should be of the same type. Cases can be like other cases, defendants can be like other defendants, and evidence can be like other evidence. Cases cannot be like evidence.

> Like the baton in *Goya*, the car in the present case was used as a weapon.
>
> *OR*
>
> As in *Goya*, the evidence here was used as a weapon.
>
> *BUT NOT*
>
> Like *Goya*, the car in the present case was used as a weapon.

Conciseness

Legal readers prefer documents that are concise, not wordy. Therefore, omit redundancy and irrelevancy.

In addition, avoid using phrases that can be replaced with a single word:

By way of, By means of → By
For the purpose of → To (unless *purpose* is a term of art)
In the event that → If
Begin to develop → Develop
Void and unenforceable → Unenforceable
Period of five years → Five years
Distance of 100 miles → 100 miles *(unless at the beginning of a sentence; see the entry "Numbers and Quantities")*
Due to the fact that → Because
In the event that → If
At this point in time → Now
Be able to → Can
Was aware of the fact → Knew
Despite the fact → Although
As a consequence of → Because
In order to → To

See The Writing Process: Conciseness on page 94.

Contractions

Because legal writing is generally formal writing, you should avoid using contractions such as *he's, we're,* or *didn't* unless you are quoting passages in which contractions are used.

Dangling and Misplaced Modifiers (Avoid Using)

A modifier is misplaced when it modifies a term that the author does not intend. Moving the modifier cures a misplaced modifier.

Misplaced modifier: Sitting on a flagpole, I saw three birds. [According to this sentence, "I" am the one sitting on the flagpole.]

Write instead: I saw three birds sitting on a flagpole.

A modifier is dangling if it does not modify anything in the sentence. Rewriting the sentence to insert the modified object cures a dangling modifier.

Dangling modifier: To collect damages, three elements must be met.

Write instead: To collect damages, a plaintiff must meet three elements.

Due To

The phrase *due to* should be used only in rare circumstances. It must follow a linking verb (for example, *is* or *seems*) and precede the phrase modifying the subject.

> The contract's termination was due to rescission.

Effect vs. Affect

See the entry "Affect vs. Effect."

Farther vs. Further

Farther refers to spacial distances:

> He ran farther than he had ever run.

Further refers to nonspatial distances:

> He went further in proving Fermat's theorem than any mathematician before him.

Hyphens

You can use a hyphen to join together related modifiers:

> The tax-deductible expense was not included on the return.
>
> The two-year-old child did not take the witness stand.

However, do not use a hyphen to join proper names or if the modifiers follow a linking verb:

> The expense is tax deductible.
>
> The child is two years old.

Italics

Italics may be used in the following situations:

1. To add emphasis to quotations;
2. To mark foreign language words; and
3. For certain Bluebook and ALWD citations.

Do not use italics to emphasize your own points. Instead, rewrite the sentence so the emphasis is clear without italics.

Legalese (Avoid Using)

Language like *herein, aforementioned,* and *heretoformentioned* often make legal documents difficult to read. Instead, consider substituting for these terms with simpler ones: *here* or *above.*

You might need to use legal language and terms of art because the analysis calls for them, but do not insert legal-sounding terms simply because they strike you as more lawyerly.

Misplaced and Dangling Modifiers (Avoid Using)

See the entry "Dangling and Misplaced Modifiers."

Nominalizations (Avoid Using)

A nominalization occurs when the writer makes a verb or an adjective into a noun. Although grammatically correct, nominalizations decrease sentence clarity and persuasiveness. Consider omitting nominalizations in your legal writing whenever possible.

Enforcement, a noun, is a nominalization of *enforce,* a verb.

So, instead of ...

The statute neglected to provide a means of enforcement for the ordinance.

Write ...

The statute neglected to provide the means to enforce the ordinance.

For the nominalization *justification,* a noun, use *justify,* a verb.

For the nominalization *specificity,* a noun, use the verb *specify* or the noun specific, depending on the context.

Numbers and Quantities

- According to Bluebook Rule 6.2 and ALWD Rule 4.2, spell out the numbers zero through ninety-nine. Use numerals for any numbers higher than ninety-nine.

They were locked up for fourteen days.

They were locked up for 144 days.

There are a number of exceptions to the above rule, including (but not limited to) the following:

1. Spell out numbers that begin a sentence.
2. Do not spell out numbers in a series in which at least one number is 100 or greater.
3. Do not spell out numbers if used repeatedly for percentages or dollar amounts.
4. Use numerals for section numbers.

Two defendants entered the courtroom.

Three hundred people were called in for jury duty.

The people killed in Iraq on three subsequent days were 25, 122, and 6.

He received a score of 96% on one test and 84% on another.

The fee was $223.

- Use the words *number, fewer,* and *many* to discuss multiple things that can be counted. Use the words *amount, less,* and *much* to discuss singular things that cannot be counted.

The defense listed a number of objections to the prosecution's line of questioning.

The plaintiff received a large amount of mail.

OR

The plaintiff received a large number of letters.

- Use between to refer to two items; use among to refer to more than two.

> He had to choose between juror #212 and juror #21.
>
> He had to choose among juror #45, juror #567, and juror # 14.

Obviously or Clearly (Avoid Using)

See the entry "Clearly or Obviously."

Parallel Structure

Strive to use parallel structure when writing lists or rules with multiple elements.

> The judge ruled based on the following: the attorneys' briefs, oral arguments, and the sentencing guidelines.
>
> *Not* …
>
> The judge based her ruling on the following: the attorneys' briefs, the way in which they conducted oral argument, and her need to follow the sentencing guidelines.

Passive vs. Active Voice

See the entry "Active vs. Passive Voice."

Pronouns

When using a pronoun, make sure that the word the pronoun refers to is clear. If it isn't, avoid using the pronoun and spell out the full term instead.

The following indefinite pronouns are singular: *another, each, either, every, neither, nobody, no one, nothing, one,* and *other.*

> Neither of the parties is willing to settle.

The following pronouns can be singular or plural, depending on what follows: *all, any, more, most, none,* and *some.*

All of the money is in my wallet. [*Money* is a singular, noncountable noun.]

All of the dollar bills are in my wallet. [*Bills* is a plural, countable noun.]

Quantities and Numbers

See the entry "Numbers and Quantities."

Quotation Marks

Periods and commas go inside quotation marks:

Defendant said, "I will be there."

Semicolons and colons go outside quotation marks:

Defendant said, "I will be there"; Plaintiff said, "I will not."

Question marks go inside quotation marks only if the question mark was part of the original quoted material:

Defendant asked Plaintiffs, "Will you be there at noon?" Smith responded, "Maybe," and Jones responded, "Doubtful": Defendant decided not to attend.

Quotations of fifty or more words should be indented on the left and right, without quotation marks. [See Bluebook Rule 5.1 and ALWD Rule 47.5.]

Redundancy (Avoid Using)

Watch out for words that do not add any meaning but are redundant:

any and all
first and foremost
null and void

Semicolons and Colons

See the entry "Colons and Semicolons."

Sentence Fragments (Avoid Using)

Sentence fragments are phrases that are not complete sentences. They are grammatically incorrect because they lack a subject or verb or begin with a subordinating conjunction. One way to check for sentence fragments is to read each sentence out loud.

Sentence fragment: Whether she should come or go.

Sexist Language

- Avoid language that can be construed as sexist:

  Firefighter *not* fireman
  Police officer or officer *not* policeman

- Avoid using awkward constructions such as *he or she* or *s/he*. Instead, choose the gender that applies to your client or specific situation.

An employee can feel uncomfortable if she is asked to perform menial tasks; Ms. Jones felt uncomfortable when asked to get Mr. Smith's shirts from the cleaners.

Short Sentences

Writing short sentences helps with clarity and conciseness.
Shorter sentences can also make your writing more persuasive; usually a short sentence has more "bang for the buck."

Since vs. Because

See the entry "Because vs. Since."

Split Infinitives (Avoid Using)

A split infinitive is when a word (often an adverb) appears between "to" and the verb. Usually writing teachers suggest avoiding the split infinitive because it distracts from the action. Avoid split infinitives when the word can be moved without changing the meaning or reducing the clarity of the phrase. However, if splitting an infinitive leads to clarity in legal usage, you may split it.

- When the clarity and meaning of the phrase can be preserved, avoid split infinitives by re-arranging the sentence.

> The short memo is used to express the client's potential claim more concisely.
>
> *NOT*
>
> The short memo is used to more concisely express the client's potential claim.

- Split infinitives that lead to clarity in legal usage.

> The attorney tried to affirmatively establish a motion for summary judgment.
>
> The defendant's failure to timely answer extensive interrogatories resulted in the plaintiff filing the Motion to Compel Discovery.

Strong Subject-Verb Combinations

English readers expect a subject and a verb and then an object, in that order. When your writing interjects many words between the subject and the verb, the reader tends to become distracted and confused.

Although not all of your sentences need to follow a formulaic *subject-verb-object* order, be wary of the sentences that interject too many words between the subject and the verb.

See Conciseness at page 355.

Subject-Verb Agreement

Keep the subject and verb of a sentence in agreement. Here are some tips:

- When the subject of the sentence is plural (uses *and*), use a plural verb:

> The attorney and her client were in agreement.
>
> *Not*
>
> The attorney and her client was in agreement.

- When the subject of the sentence is singular (uses *or* or *nor*), use a singular verb:

> Neither the attorney nor the client was ready for the verdict.
>
> *Not*
>
> Neither the attorney nor the client were ready for the verdict.

- When the subject uses *each* or *every,* use a singular verb:

> Each of the defendants was ready for the verdict.
>
> *Not*
>
> Each of the defendants were ready for the verdict.

When the subject and verb of a sentence are not close together, it is sometimes difficult to ensure that they agree. To avoid this problem, see the entries "Strong Subject-Verb Combinations" and "Short Sentences" above. Also problematic are indefinite pronouns (see the entry "Pronouns" above).

Terms of Art (Avoid Varying)

In legal writing, terms of art are important; they are defined, analyzed, and argued. Therefore, when writing, you should keep the terms of art consistent. Do not vary them as you might have been taught in undergraduate studies.

That vs. Which

That and *which* are not interchangeable in legal writing. *That* incorporates a limiting phrase, meaning it narrows the field of objects to the one being discussed:

> The case that the defense cited on page 127 of its brief has been overruled.

Which incorporates a descriptive phrase or a phrase that could be eliminated without changing the meaning of the object:

> The Smith case, which has been overruled, would have been helpful to the defense.

Use a comma before *which,* but not before *that.*

Verb Tense

Use present tense in legal writing to refer to legal rules still in effect.

<u>Miranda</u> requires officers to read suspects their rights before an arrest.

Use past tense to describe facts, reasoning, and holdings of prior case law. Also use past tense to describe any facts in your case that are complete as of the time of the writing.

Plaintiff is a seventy-five-year-old woman who brought this action after she was terminated.

Whenever possible, maintain consistent tenses throughout a text.

Which vs. That

See the entry "That vs. Which."

While vs. Although

See the entry "Although vs. While."

Who, Whom, and Whose

Who is a subject. *Whom* is an object.

That is the man who was in the lineup.

That is the man whom the witness identified.

- *Whose* is the possessive of *who,* not to be confused with *who's* (a contraction for "who is").

III. STUDY AIDS—EDITING

A. Quick References and Checklists

 ### 1. Grammar and Legal Usage Strategies: Quick Reference

Strategies for Editing Grammar and Legal Usage

Focusing on sentence structure, syntax, and word choice, try the following strategies:

- Read your document out loud. If you are breathless, your sentences are too long.
- If your reading sounds choppy, your sentences are too short.
- Identify your grammar and usage weaknesses, and look for them in your document. (See below for common weaknesses.)
- Edit one paragraph at a time, and take breaks so you stay focused.
- Read your document backwards word by word to find typos.

 ### 2. Grammar and Legal Usage Rules: Checklist

✓ *Active vs. Passive Voice*

- With active voice, the subject is doing the work.
  - Preferred in legal writing
  - Makes for concise writing
- With passive voice, the subject is being acted on.
  - Can be helpful in persuasive writing
  - Helps the writer downplay an actor

✓ *Affect vs. Effect*

- Generally, *effect* is a noun.
  Exception: when it is used to mean "to bring into being."
- Affect is a verb.

✓ *Although vs. While*

- *Although* is used to introduce a counterargument or for a causal relationship.
- *While* is used for temporal circumstances.

✓ *Apostrophes*

- Avoid using contractions.
- Use apostrophes to show possession.
  Exceptions: possessive pronouns such as *hers, its, theirs, ours, yours,* and *whose.* Its is the possessive form.

✓ *Because vs. Since*

- *Because* is used to show causation.
- *Since* is used for temporal circumstances.

✓ *Capitalization*

Bluebook and ALWD follow the same rules.
- Capitalize the word court in memos and briefs when:
  - referring to a court by its full name.
  - referring to the U.S. Supreme Court.
  - referring to the court reading the document.
  - referring to the highest court in any jurisdiction after it has been fully identified. *(ALWD only)*
- Capitalize party designations in a legal memo or brief when referring to the actual parties involved in the matter.
- Capitalize civil, professional, military, and religious titles only when they directly precede a personal name. BUT:
  - Capitalize titles of U.S. Supreme Court Justices, even when used without proper names. *(Bluebook and ALWD)*
  - Capitalize titles of honor when they substitute for a person's name. *(ALWD only)*

✓ *Clearly or Obviously*

Avoid using.

✓ *Colons and Semicolons*

- Use a semicolon to
  - separate items in a list when the items themselves have commas.
  - join independent clauses without a coordinating conjunction.
  - separate items in a series when the items are separate.
- Use a colon to
  - join related independent clauses.
  - introduce a block quotation, numbered list, or list that further explains the subject of the sentence.

Note: If the phrase following a colon is not a complete sentence, do not capitalize the first word following the colon. (*Exception:* proper nouns)

✓ *Commas*

- Use a comma to
  - separate items in a list.
  - offset an introductory phrase (optional for short introductory phrases).
  - join two independent clauses with *and, or, nor, for, so, but,* or *yet.*
    Note: Independent clauses can stand alone as complete sentences.
  - offset a phrase that could be omitted without changing the meaning of the sentence.
  - offset a dependent clause preceding an independent clause.

✓ *Comparisons*

The items compared should be of the same type.

✓ *Conciseness*

- Omit redundancy and irrelevancy.
- Avoid phrases replaceable with a single word.
  - *By way of, By means of*—Use *by*
  - *For the purpose of*—Use *to* (unless *purpose* is a term of art)
  - *In the event that*—Use *if*
  - *Begin to develop*—Use *develop*
  - *Void and unenforceable*—Use *unenforceable*
  - *Period of five years*—Use *five years*
  - *Distance of 100 miles*—Use *100 miles*
  - *Due to the fact that*—Use *because*
  - *In the event that*—Use *if*
  - *At this point in time*—Use *now*
  - *Be able to*—Use *can*
  - *Was aware of the fact*—Use *knew*
  - *Despite the fact*—Use *although*
  - *As a consequence of*—Use *because*
  - *In order to*—Use *to*

✓ *Contractions*

Avoid using contractions. *Exception:* quoting passages in which contractions are used.

✓ *Due to*

- Should only be used in rare circumstances.
- Must follow a linking verb and precede the phrase modifying the subject.

✓ *Farther vs. Further*

- *Farther* refers to measurable distances.
- *Further* refers to nonmeasurable distances.

✓ *Hyphens*

- Use to join together related modifiers.
  Exceptions: Do not use a hyphen to join proper names. Do not use a hyphen if the modifiers follow a linking verb.

✓ *Italics*

- Use to add emphasis to quotations.
- Use to mark foreign-language words.
- Use for certain Bluebook and ALWD citations
- Do not use italics to emphasize your own points.

✓ *Legalese*

Avoid using legalese.

✓ *Misplaced and Dangling Modifiers*

- A modifier is misplaced if it modifies a term you did not intend.
  Solution: Move the modifier.
- A modifier is dangling if it does not modify anything in the sentence.
  Solution: Rewrite the sentence and insert the modified subject.

✓ *Nominalizations*

Avoid making a verb or an adjective into a noun.

✓ *Numbers and Quantities*

- Spell out the numbers zero through ninety-nine.
- Use numerals for any numbers higher than ninety-nine.

Exceptions include but are not limited to the following:

- Spell out numbers that begin a sentence.
- Do not spell out numbers in a series where at least one number is 100 or greater.
- Do not spell out numbers if used repeatedly for percentages or dollar amounts.
- Use numerals for section numbers.
- Use the words *number, fewer,* and *many* to discuss multiple things that can be counted.
- Use the words *amount, less,* and *much* to discuss singular things that cannot be counted.
- Use *between* to refer to two items; use *among* to refer to more than two items.

✓ *Parallel Structure*

Use parallel structure when writing lists or rules with multiple elements.

✓ *Pronouns*

- Use a pronoun only when the word the pronoun refers to is clear.
- Singular indefinite pronouns include *another, each, either, every, neither, nobody, no one, nothing, one, other.*
- Some pronouns may be singular or plural, depending on what follows: *all, any, more, most, none, some.*

✓ *Quotations*

- Periods and commas go inside quotation marks.
- Semicolons and colons go outside quotation marks.
- Question marks go inside quotation marks only if the question mark was part of the original quoted material.
- Quotations of fifty or more words should be indented on the left and right, without quotation marks.

✓ *Redundancy*

Avoid words that do not add any meaning.

✓ *Sentence Fragments*

- Avoid sentence fragments.
- Check for sentence fragments by reading each sentence out loud.

✓ *Sexist Language*

- Avoid language that can be construed as sexist.
- Avoid awkward constructions; instead choose the gender that applies to your specific situation.

✓ *Short Sentences*

- Use short sentences to help with clarity and conciseness.
- In persuasive writing, use short sentences for big impact.

✓ *Split Infinitives*

Generally, avoid split infinitives.
> *Note:* But if splitting an infinite leads to clarity in legal usage, you may split it.

✓ *Strong Subject-Verb Combinations*

Avoid placing too many words between the subject and the verb.

✓ *Subject-Verb Agreement*

- When the subject of the sentence is plural (uses *and*), use a plural verb.
- When the subject of the sentence is singular (uses *or* or *nor*), use a singular verb.
- When the subject uses *each* or *every,* use a singular verb.

✓ *Terms of Art*

Keep terms of art consistent.

✓ *That vs. Which*

- *That* narrows the field of objects to the one being discussed.
- *Which* incorporates a descriptive phrase or a phrase that could be eliminated without changing the meaning of the object. *Note:* Use a comma before which.

✓ *Verb Tense*

- Use *present tense* to refer to legal rules still in effect.
- Use *past tense* to describe facts, reasoning, and holdings of prior case law.
- Use *past tense* to describe any facts in your case that are complete as of the time of the writing.
- If possible, maintain consistent tenses throughout a text.

✓ *Who, Whom, Whose*

- *Who* is a subject.
- *Whom* is an object.
- *Whose* is the possessive of who.

B. Quizzes

⊗? 1. Active vs. Passive Voice: Quiz

For each of the following sentence pairs, choose which is the better sentence, <u>sentence A</u> or <u>sentence B</u>.

1. A. The neo-Socratic method is used by many modern legal professors so that legal reasoning can be practiced in class.

    B. Many modern legal professors use the neo-Socratic method so that their students can practice legal reasoning in class.

2. A. Because the Enron accountants, lawyers, and executives behaved unethically, Congress enacted the Sarbanes-Oxley Act.

    B. Because of the unethical behavior practiced by the Enron accountants, lawyers, and executives, the Sarbanes-Oxley Act was enacted.

3. A. Congress enacted campaign finance reform to prevent candidates from being significantly influenced by campaign contributions.

    B. Campaign finance reform was enacted by Congress to prevent candidates from being significantly influenced by campaign contributions.

4. A. The court will be presented with evidence by the prosecuting attorney.

    B. The prosecuting attorney will present evidence to the court.

5. A. The judge is reminded of his high-profile case by the evening news.

    B. The evening news reminds the judge of his high-profile case.

6. A. The police have interviewed witnesses since early this morning.

    B. Witnesses have been interviewed by the police since early this morning.

Answer Key on page 521

⊗? 2. Affect vs. Effect: Quiz

For each sentence below, choose the correct word: <u>affect</u> or <u>effect</u>.

1. Whether the plaintiff has claimed previous damages does not _____ this court's decision; we hold for the defendant.

2. The allocation of the tax deduction to the partner's capital account is legitimate because the allocation has substantial economic _____.

3. A contract exists even before the parties _____ the transaction.

4. Before coming to a conclusion, we must consider the cause and _____ that led to this situation.

5. The severe weather will have an _____ on the way people choose to travel to work today.

6. The severe weather will _____ the way that people choose to travel to work today.

Answer Key on page 521

⊙? 3. Although vs. While: Quiz

For each sentence below, choose the correct word: <u>although</u> or <u>while</u>.

1. _____ the court in <u>Brown</u> allowed the evidence, it had no bearing on the verdict.

2. The defendant allegedly entered through the back door _____ her room-mate was asleep.

3. _____ the evidence was only circumstantial, the jury found it sufficient for a conviction.

4. _____ the judge did not believe the evidence was sufficient for the case to succeed, he allowed it to go forward because the plaintiff presented enough evidence to support a trial.

5. The police found a weapon and a pair of gloves _____ they searched the crime scene.

6. _____ the expert witness was testifying, the defendant looked uneasy.

Answer Key on page 522

⊙? 4. Apostrophes: Quiz

For each sentence below, choose the correct form:

1. The _____ office is across the hall from the elevators.

   A) professors
   B) professor's

2. _____ Bluebook is this?

   A) Whose
   B) Who's

3. _____ up to the prosecutor to determine if a plea bargain is appropriate.

    A) It's
    B) Its

4. The Supreme Court used _____ power to declare the law unconstitutional.

    A) it's
    B) its

5. This Court _____ hold the defendant responsible for this crime; he is innocent.

    A) shouldn't
    B) should not

6. The _____ conference luncheon was catered by an excellent Italian restaurant.

    A) teachers
    B) teachers'

7. I visited a friend _____ house is in Georgetown.

    A) whose
    B) who's

8. _____ cat, CC, eats from a crystal bowl.

    A) Brian's
    B) Brians

Answer Key on page 522

8? 5.   Because vs. Since: Quiz

For each sentence below choose the correct word: <u>because</u> or <u>since</u>.

1. _____ the time of the defendant's arrest, no incidents of arson have occurred in the neighborhood.

2. The neighborhood is safer _____ a serial arsonist is behind bars.

3. Dana went to the store _____ she needed refreshments for her party.

4. The Eagles have scored three times _____ the beginning of the second half.

Answer Key on page 522

⚇? 6. Capitalization: Quiz

For each of the following questions, pick the response showing any necessary corrections in capitalization.

1. Because police actions violated his fifth amendment rights, the defendant respectfully requests that this court exclude the confession.

    A. "fifth amendment" only
    B. "fifth amendment," and "defendant"
    C. "fifth amendment," "defendant," and "court"
    D. "defendant," and "court"

2. The supreme court opinion in <u>miranda</u> was a landmark decision because the court introduced a new protection for criminal defendants.

    A. "miranda" only
    B. "supreme court," "miranda," and "court"
    C. "supreme court" and "miranda"
    D. "supreme court," "miranda," and "defendants"

3. To summarize this pleading, the plaintiff respectfully requests the court to affirm the district court decision. The following words should be capitalized:

    A. "plaintiff" and "court"
    B. "plaintiff," "court," and "district court"
    C. "plaintiff" only
    D. "district court" only

4. The judge rejected the plaintiff's claims of a fifth amendment violation.

    A. "plaintiff" only
    B. "plaintiff" and "fifth amendment"
    C. "fifth amendment" only
    D. None of the above

5. The court ruled on the matter, but the defendant intends to appeal to seek review from the court of appeals.

    A. "court" only
    B. "court" and "defendant"
    C. "court," "defendant," and "court of appeals"
    D. "court of appeals" only

6. The U.S. court of appeals for the third circuit ruled on the matter, but the supreme court did not agree.

    A. "court of appeals" only
    B. "court of appeals" and "third circuit"
    C. "court of appeals," "third circuit," and "supreme court"
    D. "third circuit" only

Answer Key on page 522

○? 7. Commas: Quiz

After each sentence, choose the correct answer.

1. A janitor several firefighters and a few neighbors were called as witnesses in the related arson case.

   A. No commas are needed.
   B. A comma is needed after "janitor" only.
   C. A comma is needed after "janitor" and "firefighters."

2. Considering the volume of evidence and testimony in the defendant's favor the jury returned a verdict of not guilty.

   A. No commas are needed.
   B. A comma is needed after "favor."
   C. A comma is optional after "favor."

3. On Friday the jury deliberated for only thirty minutes and returned a guilty verdict.

   A. A comma after "Friday" is required, and no other commas are needed.
   B. A comma after "Friday" is optional, and no other commas are needed.
   C. A comma may be placed after "Friday," and a comma is needed before "and."
   D. Any commas placed in this sentence would be incorrect.

4. The house which was located on Long Island was unoccupied at the time of the crime and the defendant knew that the owners had left for the summer.

   A. No commas are needed.
   B. A comma is needed only after "crime."
   C. Commas are needed after "house" and "Island" only.
   D. Commas are needed after "house," "Island," and "crime."

5. Despite the evidence against him the defendant was not convicted of voluntary manslaughter.

   A. No commas are needed.
   B. A comma is needed after "convicted."
   C. A comma is needed after "him."

6. The judge after her walk in the park returned to her chambers to continue her work.

   A. No commas are needed.
   B. A comma is needed after "judge."
   C. A comma is needed after "judge" and "park."

Answer Key on page 522

8. Due to: Quiz

Determine whether each of the following sentences is a proper or improper use of the expression <u>due to</u>.

1. Due to Defendant's negligence, Plaintiff broke her leg. **Proper or improper?**

2. Plaintiff's injury is due to Defendant's negligence. **Proper or improper?**

3. Plaintiff broke her leg due to the fact that the ladder manufactured by the defendant had a defect. **Proper or improper?**

Answer Key on page 522

9. Farther vs. Further: Quiz

For each of the following sentences, choose the correct word: <u>farther</u> or <u>further</u>.

1. If this legal principle is taken _____, then the result will be contrary to Congress's intent.

2. The house arrest sentence allows the defendant to go no _____ than his home.

3. The _____ away he roams, the harder it will be to find him.

4. The child roamed _____ into the woods than he ever has before.

5. The preliminary discussions did not proceed _____.

Answer Key on page 522

10. Sentence Fragments: Quiz

Mark whether each sentence below is a complete sentence or a sentence fragment.

1. The option to accept the plea bargain or to go to trial. **Complete or fragment?**

2. The defendant considered his options carefully before deciding. **Complete or fragment?**

3. The case continued indefinitely. **Complete or fragment?**

4. The Restatement of Property, which contains a wealth of information but is not accepted by all, or even most, courts. **Complete or fragment?**

5. Regardless of what the judge says. **Complete or fragment?**

6. It is a new type of legislation. **Complete or fragment?**

7. The attorney interviews the client. **Complete or fragment?**

Answer Key on page 523

⚇? 11. Grammar: Quiz

Instructions: Mark each of the following statements regarding editing and citation either true or false. If you answer false, articulate why the statement is false before moving to the next question. If you have difficulty answering any of the questions on editing and citation, refer to the Grammar and Legal Usage Rules in the chapter text and to the Editing Quick Reference for assistance.

1. You should identify your grammar and usage weaknesses and look for them in your document. **True or False?**

2. Passive voice is preferred in legal writing because it makes for concise writing and prevents the writer from overstating her case. **True or False?**

3. Effect is always a noun. **True or False?**

4. When referring to temporal circumstances, use while instead of although. **True or False?**

5. Apostrophes are never appropriate in legal writing because legal writing is formal. **True or False?**

6. Legal writing uses because and since interchangeably. **True or False?**

7. Both the Bluebook and ALWD require you to capitalize the word court in legal memos and briefs. **True or False?**

8. The words clearly and obviously overstate your case, and you should usually avoid using these words in legal writing. **True or False?**

9. Never capitalize the first word following a colon. **True or False?**

10. Using a comma to offset a short introductory phrase is optional. **True or False?**

11. Make your legal writing more concise by avoiding phrases that can be replaced with a single word. **True or False?**

12. The words further and farther are interchangeable in legal writing. **True or False?**

13. Always join related modifiers with a hyphen. **True or False?**

14. A dangling modifier modifies a term the author did not intend to modify in the sentence. **True or False?**

15. Using nominalizations makes for more concise writing. **True or False?**

16. You should always spell out the numbers zero through ninety-nine and use numerals for any numbers higher than ninety-nine. **True or False?**

17. Use among to refer to two or more items. **True or False?**

18. Every is a plural indefinite pronoun, and each is a singular indefinite pronoun. **True or False?**

19. Periods, commas, and question marks always go inside quotation marks. **True or False?**

20. Avoid awkward gender constructions in your writing, such as s/he, by choosing the gender that applies to your specific situation. **True or False?**

21. You should always avoid split infinitives in legal writing. **True or False?**

22. Use a comma before which, but not before that. **True or False?**

23. You should vary terms of art to prevent the reader from becoming bored. **True or False?**

24. Whose is the possessive of who. **True or False?**

Answer Key on page 523

12. Hyphens: Quiz

For each exercise below, choose the sentence showing the correct use of hyphens.

1. A. The plaintiff's decision was ill advised.
   B. The plaintiff's decision was ill-advised.
   C. *Both sentences are correct.*
   D. *Neither sentence is correct.*

2. A. This ill-conceived plan can never work.
   B. This plan was ill conceived from the beginning.
   C. *Both sentences are correct.*
   D. *Neither sentence is correct.*

Answer Key on page 523

⚇? 13.   Indefinite Pronouns: Quiz

For each exercise below, choose the sentence showing the correct use of indefinite pronouns.

1. A. Either of the defendants are able to accept the plea bargain.
    B. Either of the defendants is able to accept the plea bargain.
    C. *Both sentences are correct.*

2. A. Another one of these options is available to indigent defendants.
    B. Another one of these options are available to indigent defendants.
    C. *Both sentences are correct.*

3. A. Most of the publicity is relating to a single case.
    B. Most of the news articles and reports are relating to a single case.
    C. *Both sentences are correct.*

4. A. No one in the crowd is leaving before the end of the game.
    B. No one in the crowd are leaving before the end of the game.
    C. *Both sentences are correct.*

5. A. Some of the students are going home for vacation.
    B. Some of the audience is getting frustrated.
    C. *Both sentences are correct.*

6. A. They are going to support the politician's positions no matter what it is.
    B. They are going to support the politician's positions no matter what they are.
    C. *Both sentences are correct.*

Answer Key on page 523

⚇? 14.   Legalese: Quiz

For each exercise below, choose the sentence showing the successful avoidance of legalese.

1. A. According to the aforementioned guidelines, the corporation must obtain shareholder approval before taking action.
    B. According to the guidelines discussed above, the corporation must obtain shareholder approval before taking action.

2. A. The court held, among other things, that the plaintiff was reckless.
    B. The court held, inter alia, that the plaintiff was reckless.

Answer Key on page 523

⚇? 15.   Modifiers: Quiz

For each exercise below, choose the sentence showing the correct use of modifiers.

1. A. To prove a tort, there must be a duty, breach, causation, and damages.
    B. To prove a tort, a plaintiff must show duty, breach, causation, and damages.

2. A. The car swerved because the driver, acting negligently, had been drinking earlier that night.
    B. Acting negligently, the car swerved because the driver had been drinking earlier that night.

3. A. Having completed the work, the television was turned on.
    B. Having completed the work, Michelle turned on the television.

4. A. The loaf of bread was removed from the oven, having been cooked thoroughly.
    B. The loaf of bread, having been cooked thoroughly, was removed from the oven.

5. A. When shopping for a computer, the wide variety of choices can confuse most people.
    B. The wide variety of choices can confuse most people when shopping for a computer.

6. A. After seeing the demonstration, the new security system was installed in all the entrepreneur's buildings.
    B. After seeing the demonstration, the entrepreneur had the new security system installed in all of his buildings.

Answer Key on page 523

⚇? 16.   Nominalizations: Quiz

For each exercise below, choose the sentence that best avoids the use of nominalizations.

1. A. The court applied the business-judgment rule.
    B. The court's ruling was an application of the business-judgment rule.

2. A. The corporation is required to receive approval before acting.
    B. Receipt of approval is a requirement for the corporation's action.

3. A. Enforcement of the traffic laws is a patrol officer's main duty.
    B. A patrol officer's main duty is to enforce the traffic laws.

4. A. A court must make a determination on the outcome of the case.
    B. A court must determine the outcome of this case.

5. A. There is an investigation being conducted into this matter.
    B. This matter is being investigated.

6. A. The attorney conducted a cross-examination of the defense witness.
    B. The attorney cross-examined the defense witness.

Answer Key on page 524

17.   Numbers and Quantities: Quizzes

Numbers and Quantities: Quiz

For each of the following sentences, choose the correct word: <u>less</u> or <u>fewer</u>.

1. Since the arrest, the defendant has had _____ opportunities to treat her medical condition.

2. The evidence shows that _____ water has reached the plaintiff's farm than in previous years.

3. The new FDA guidelines encourage consumers to choose foods with _____ calories.

Many vs. Much: Quiz

For each of the following sentences, choose the correct word: <u>many</u> or <u>much</u>.

4. The defendant has had _____ correspondence with prison officials about getting treatment for her illness.

5. She has written _____ letters and placed a number of phone calls.

Numbers in Sentences: Quiz

For each of the following sentences, choose the correct form: <u>15</u> or <u>fifteen</u>.

6. The defendant visited the health center _____ times in the first week of March alone.

7. _____ police officers were called to the scene of the bank robbery.

8. The winning lottery numbers for the "Pick 3" game were 7, _____, and 125.

Answer Key on page 524

⚇? 18.   Parallel Structure: Quiz

Is each sentence correctly written in parallel structure?

1. A tort requires a duty, a breach of duty, causation by the defendant, and damages to the plaintiff. **Parallel or not parallel?**

2. Defendant's motion to dismiss should be granted because (1) the evidence was obtained illegally, (2) the defendant was not read his Miranda rights while in custody, and (3) the police brutality involved in the arrest. **Parallel or not parallel?**

3. When he could get away from his demanding job, the judge enjoyed hiking, swimming, and boating. **Parallel or not parallel?**

4. The attorney said she prefers litigation because she enjoys debate, likes thinking quickly, and her briefs are well written. **Parallel or not parallel?**

5. A good student goes to school, does his homework, and finds time to relax. **Parallel or not parallel?**

6. Legal encyclopedias are used to find out how a law is generally applied, as a starting point for research, and to find a few seminal cases in various jurisdictions. **Parallel or not parallel?**

Answer Key on page 524

⚇? 19.   Quotation Marks: Quiz

For each exercise below, choose the sentence that correctly uses quotation marks.

1. A. The attorney said, "Justice demands that the lower court's opinion be reversed."
   B. The attorney said, "Justice demands that the lower court's opinion be reversed".

2. A. Is it true that the witness exclaimed in court, "He is the killer"?
   B. Is it true that the witness exclaimed in court, "He is the killer?"
   C. *Both sentences are correct.*

3. A. The witness said in court, "He is the killer, right"?
   B. The witness said in court, "He is the killer, right?"

4. A. The witness said, "He is the killer"; the jury agreed.
   B. The witness said, "He is the killer;" the jury agreed.

Answer Key on page 524

8? 20.   Semicolons and Colons: Quiz

For exercises 1, 2, and 3 below, choose the response from those offered that will correctly fill the indicated space with the correct punctuation.

1. The professor is holding office hours today __ students can meet with her between 3 and 5 p.m. **A. semicolon, B. colon, C. comma, or D. no punctuation?**

2. We request the following documents __ employment records, pay stubs, and health insurance records. **A. semicolon, B. colon, C. comma, or D. no punctuation?**

3. I am considering several different color schemes for this room _a_ red, white, and blue _b_ purple, gold, and white _c_ and blue, red, and yellow.

    3a. **A. semicolon, B. colon, C. comma, or D. no punctuation?**
    3b. **A. semicolon, B. colon, C. comma, or D. no punctuation?**
    3c. **A. semicolon, B. colon, C. comma, or D. no punctuation?**

4. *Choose the sentence with no punctuation errors.*

    A. The Supreme Court has sought to fix problems of segregation in schools, public facilities, and private companies, has exercised its power in new and creative ways, and has addressed new and complicated questions in the past 75 years.
    B. The Supreme Court has sought to fix problems of segregation in schools, public facilities, and private companies; has exercised its power in new and creative ways; and has addressed new and complicated questions in the past 75 years.
    C. The Supreme Court has sought to fix problems of segregation in schools, public facilities, and private companies; has exercised its power in new and creative ways, and has addressed new and complicated questions in the past 75 years.

Answer Key on page 524

8? 21.   That vs. Which: Quiz

For each of the sentences below, choose the correct word: that or which.

1. The defendant's gold Rolex watch, _____ was found at the crime scene, is inadmissible evidence.

2. The evidence _____ was seized at the crime scene included a watch, a dollar bill, and a note.

3. A watch _____ allegedly belonged to the defendant was purchased at a department store across town.

4. The DNA sample _____ the police found at the victim's home cannot be linked to the defendant.

5. The car, _____ was the fastest last week, did not win this week's race.

6. The bedroom was particularly hot because the fan _____ was placed in the window was broken.

Answer Key on page 524

---

22. Verb Tense: Quiz

For each of the sentences below, choose the correct word: is or was.

1. The defendant, who _____ a student at the time of the crime, is charged today with larceny.

2. The plaintiff, who _____ a teacher in the D.C. public schools last year, is suing the school system for wrongful termination.

3. The former teacher _____ suing to recover lost pay and punitive damages.

Answer Key on page 524

---

23. Who, Whom, Whose: Quizzes

Who vs. Whom: Quiz

For each of the sentences below, choose the correct word: who or whom.

1. The defendant, _____ the police had arrested at the scene of the crime, immediately requested an attorney.

2. The plaintiff, a friend of _____ is the defense's star witness, will be unlikely to prevail.

3. The eyewitness, _____ will take the stand tomorrow, is expected to add dramatically to the case.

4. To _____ was the plea bargain offered?

5. _____ are the police questioning concerning the recent murder?

6. The appellate judge, _____ answers only to the Supreme Court, understands the impact of his decisions.

7. The appellate judge, over _____ only the Supreme Court has authority, understands the impact of his decisions.

Answer Key on page 524

Whose vs. Who's: Quiz

For each of the sentences below, choose the correct word: <u>whose</u> or <u>who's</u>.

8. The neighbor, _____ dog is responsible for the damage, must pay restitution.

9. The neighbor, _____ out of the country at the moment, cannot appear in court.

Answer Key on page 524

C. Self-Assessment

⚇? 1. Editing (Grammar) Self-Assessment

INSTRUCTIONS: This self-assessment is designed to test your knowledge of the basic grammar and usage rules covered in this chapter. Read through the document, taking note of the numbered and highlighted passages. Each number and highlighted passage represents a point on which you should decide whether the phrasing is correct and should be kept as is or if a change is needed. If a change is needed, please make the required correction. When you are finished, check your work against the answer key on page 525. The answer key also indicates for each item the applicable grammar or usage rule. This review will help you to assess your understanding of the grammar and usage rules that apply to legal writing so you can more quickly and accurately review and correct your own documents.

Civil Action No. 02-2332

UNITED STATES COURT OF APPEALS FOR THE ELEVENTH CIRCUIT

DR. CHARLES OSSINING, Appellant, v.

HARRISON BRUBAKER, ET AL., APPELLEES

ON APPEAL FROM UNITED STATES DISTRICT COURT FOR THE SOUTHERN DISTRICT OF ALABAMA

BRIEF OF RESPONDENT

STATEMENT OF ISSUES PRESENTED FOR REVIEW

    I. Whether an inmate, who exhibits no medical symptoms warranting special treatment and receives care for all documented symptoms, has an Eighth Amendment claim when, with only the inmate's self-diagnosis of a rare condition, the prison declined his request for a special diet and further testing.

    II. Whether the trial court was correct in finding an inmate's rights under the #1 first amendment were not violated after the #2 prison Warden had reviewed and subsequently denied certain publications addressed to the inmate based upon established prison regulations in response to the unreasonable burden placed upon the prison's resources by the inmate receiving such publication?

#1 Change/Keep as is

#2 Change/Keep as is

STATEMENT OF THE CASE

Nature of the Case

    This is an appeal of summary judgment in a prisoner's rights case. Wellville requests that summary judgment be affirmed because there are no genuine issues of fact in dispute. Wellville also requests that Ossining's complaint be dismissed because treatment did not violate the #3 prisoners' constitutional rights.

Procedural History

Ossining alleges violations of his #4 first and eighth amendment rights by the prison. The United States District Court for the Southern District of Alabama granted the defendant's motion for summary judgment. The #5 District Court #6 has concluded that Plaintiff's publications caused unreasonable burdens on the resources of the prison and that #7 they were not deliberately indifferent to any serious medical need of Plaintiff.

STATEMENT OF FACTS

The prisoner, Dr. Charles Ossining, was convicted of #8 Medicare fraud, mail fraud and making false claims to the government. At the time of Ossining's incarceration in January 2002, a routine medical examination confirmed that he was in good health. (Brubaker Aff. 7.) After his arrival, Ossining received a considerable #9 amount of medical journals and newsletters pertaining to allergies. (Brubaker Aff. 8.) Ossining intentionally ordered additional brochures #10 for the purpose of disseminating allergy information to other prisoners. (Ossining Aff. 4.) By the end of March, the infirmary reported a significant increase in prisoner visits #11: #12 15% more visits than in the same quarter a year before, and 100% more requests for allergy testing.

More than half of these requests were declined, as these prisoners showed no symptoms warranting testing. Many of the inmates who requested allergy testing indicated that Ossining had suggested they be tested for various allergies. (Brubaker Aff. 9.)

The medical staff could not accommodate all incoming requests for allergy testing, leading to prisoner agitation and strain on medical resources. (Brubaker Aff. 9, 10.) Additionally, the prison cafeteria received an influx of complaints as well as special requests and disorderly conduct. To calm the disorder, the prison hired two more security guards. (Brubaker Aff. 11.) Based on these events, Brubaker, the #13 long time warden of the prison, rejected certain medical publications addressed to Ossining, identifying them as detrimental to the security and resources of the prison. The rejection procedure is authorized by 28 C.F.R. §540.71(b). (Brubaker Aff. 8, 12.)

#14 Concerned with his condition, a blood test in March revealed Ossining was borderline anemic. The infirmary doctor prescribed iron supplements to relieve the anemia. (Ossining Aff. 12.) In April, Ossining #15 self-diagnosed himself with celiac disease, a rare infection, and claimed he needed an endoscopy to confirm his diagnosis. (Flowers Aff. 6.) #16 In reviewing Ossining's blood test results, Dr. Gerta

Margin notes:

#3 Change/Keep as is

#4 Change/Keep as is

#5 Change/Keep as is
#6 Change/Keep as is
#7 Change/Keep as is

#8 Change/Keep as is

#9 Change/Keep as is
#10 Change/Keep as is

#11 Change/Keep as is
#12 Change/Keep as is

#13 Change/Keep as is

#14 Change/Keep as is

#15 Change/Keep as is

#16 Change/Keep as is

Flowers, a specialist in internal medicine and resident physician at the prison, determined that Ossining did not exhibit severe enough symptoms to warrant further investigation, and she rejected his request for an endoscopy. (Flowers Aff. 7.) In July, Ossining requested a gluten-free diet, claiming only this diet could treat celiac disease. (Ossining Aff. 21.) Dr. Flowers informed the prison that sufficient alternatives in the prison cafeteria were available to Ossining should he prefer to eat a gluten-free diet. (Flowers Aff. 8.) #17 Dr. Flowers promised that should Ossining present severe symptoms in the future, she would treat him appropriately. (Brubaker Aff. 15.)

#17 Change/Keep as is

STANDARD OF REVIEW

The issue before this Court is whether the trial court properly applied the law to the facts in granting summary judgment. Review of the district court's ruling on a motion for summary judgment is #18 *de novo.* <u>Pope v. Hightower</u>, 101 F.3d 1382, 1383 (11th Cir. 1996).

#18 Change/Keep as is

SUMMARY OF ARGUMENT

#19 Based on the established facts in the record, it would seem his First and Eighth Amendment claims fail. #20 As to the Eighth Amendment claim, Ossining showed no evidence of a serious medical need, his treatment by the prison did not violate contemporary standards of decency, and the medical staff was not deliberately indifferent to his condition. As to the First Amendment claim, because Ossining's assertion of his rights posed a threat to the security of the prison and created an unreasonable burden on prison resources, #21 Warden Brubaker's rejection of particular publications was justified.

#19 Change/Keep as is
#20 Change/Keep as is

#21 Change/Keep as is

ARGUMENT

Dr. Charles Ossining, a prisoner, is currently serving a #22 five-year sentence. #23 His crime being fraud of the federal government. Ossining alleges the prison violated his First Amendment right by denying him access to professional journals and by denying him a gluten-free diet and further testing for a rare, self-diagnosed disease. #24 While detainees are accorded protections of the Constitution, prisoners' rights are inherently restricted, and some constitutional violations may be acceptable in the event that they serve "legitimate penological interests #25 ", such as order, security, and safety. <u>See Thornburgh v. Abbott</u>, 490 U.S. 401, 407-408 (1989). Moreover, as operation of a prison falls under the province of the legislative and executive branches of government, deference should be paid by the #26 Courts to appropriate prison authorities regulating this delicate balance between prison security and legitimate rights of prisoners. <u>Turner v. Safley</u>, 482 U.S. 78, 84-85 (1987).

#22 Change/Keep as is
#23 Change/Keep as is

#24 Change/Keep as is

#25 Change/Keep as is

#26 Change/Keep as is

I. PLAINTIFF'S EIGHTH AMENDMENT CLAIM OF CRUEL AND UNUSUAL PUNISHMENT IS WITHOUT MERIT BECAUSE THE PRISONER EXHIBITED NO MEDICAL CONDITION WARRANTING SPECIAL TREATMENT

#27 Change/Keep as is
#28 Change/Keep as is

#15 Change/Keep as is
#16 Change/Keep as is

#27 There is no sufficient evidence of a serious medical problem related to #28 being denied a gluten-free diet, and there is no evidence that the prison was "deliberately indifferent" to Ossining's symptoms, as required for claims under the Eighth Amendment. See Helling v. McKinney, 509 U.S. 25, 29 (1993). In Helling, the #29 Supreme Court established a #30 two prong test for proving Eighth Amendment violations. Under the subjective prong, the prisoner must show deliberate indifference by the prison toward a serious risk posed to the prisoner. Under the objective prong, the prisoner must show the unreasonable risk of harm he faces is contrary to contemporary standards of decency. Id. at 35-36. Because Ossining received adequate treatment for his ailments and exhibited no medical condition warranting special treatment, he fails both prongs of the Eighth Amendment test.

A. The prison was not deliberately indifferent to prisoner's medical condition when the prison physician reviewed prisoner's blood test results to find no severe symptoms of celiac disease warranting further treatment and the prison menu offered adequate gluten-free alternatives

#31 Change/Keep as is

Under the subjective prong, the prisoner must show #31: 1) the prison had knowledge of a serious risk of harm to him and 2) deliberate indifference by the prison toward this risk. Id. at 35.

1. The prison had no subjective knowledge of any serious risk of harm to the prisoner in denying him a gluten-free diet or in rejecting his request for an endoscopy to further test for celiac disease

#32 Change/Keep as is
#33 Change/Keep as is

#34 Change/Keep as is

#35 Change/Keep as is

Ossining #32 clearly fails to demonstrate prison officials knew of and disregarded "an excessive risk to his health or safety #33 ." See Farmer v. Brennan, 511 U.S. 825, 837 (1994). As serious complications from celiac disease are rare, and as Dr. Flowers determined the prisoner did not present such severe symptoms to warrant further investigation, Ossining fails to show the prison's subjective knowledge of a serious risk of harm when denying him a gluten-free diet and further testing. #34 In Campbell v. Sikes, the plaintiff inmate alleged cruel and unusual punishment when the defendant prison psychiatrist misdiagnosed her with poly-substance abuse disorder when in fact she had a bipolar disorder, a diagnosis unreported in jail records or prior hospitalization records. #35 Summary judgment was granted by the court for the prison because there was no evidence that the psychiatrist knew he misdiagnosed her or that he knew of a substantial risk of serious harm to the inmate as a result of his treatment. Campbell v. Sikes, 169 F.3d 1353, 1366-1368 (11th Cir. 1999). Similarly, Ossining fails to present evidence from which a reasonable jury could infer that prison officials knew he had celiac disease, the prison officials know they were misdiagnosing him, or that they understand their treatment was grossly inadequate but proceeded with the treatment anyway. #36 Like Campbell, Ossining's medical records did not indicate a prior history of celiac disease and a professional review of his blood did not give medical professionals reason for concern. Therefore, Ossining fails the first part of the subjective prong of the Helling test #37 since the prison exhibits no subjective knowledge of his mistreatment.

#36 Change/Keep as is

#37 Change/Keep as is

2. The prison was not deliberately indifferent toward the medical concerns of the prisoner

To show deliberate indifference, Ossining must demonstrate his medical treatment by the prison constituted the "unnecessary and wanton infliction of pain." Gregg v. Georgia, 428 U.S. 153, 173 (1976). In Estelle, the prisoner injured his back while engaged in prison work, claiming deliberate indifference by the prison for failure to perform an X-ray to treat him. The court held that questions concerning forms of treatment are matters of medical judgment, and that failure by prison medical staff to use additional diagnostic techniques beyond ordinary treatment #38 doesn't constitute deliberate indifference or cruel and usual punishment. Estelle v. Gamble, 429 U.S. 97, 107 (1976). Similarly, Dr. Flowers was not deliberately indifferent to Ossining's medical needs when she refused to order an endoscopy #39 to simply confirm Ossining's self-diagnosis of celiac disease following her professional review of his blood test results. Regarding his claims against the staff, Ossining offers no evidence that prison medical staff failed to meet appropriate professional standards in determining that his symptoms did not warrant further testing. Moreover, Ossining's difference in opinion from prison officials concerning diagnosis and recommended treatment does not constitute cruel and unusual punishment. See Harris v. Thigpen, 941 F.2d 1495, 1505 (11th Cir. 1991). Although an endoscopy may have led to an appropriate diagnosis and treatment for his condition, Ossining fails to demonstrate deliberate indifference because medical decisions concerning forms of treatment beyond ordinary care do not constitute cruel and unusual punishment. See Estelle, 429 U.S. at 107.

#38 Change/Keep as is

#39 Change/Keep as is

Denial of Ossining's request for a special #40 gluten-free diet does not constitute #41 intentional indifference because the prisoner lacks convincing symptoms requiring special treatment. In McElligot, an inmate with a history of stomach problems was treated by prison doctors with #42 tylenol, pepto-bismol, and an anti-gas medication when experiencing severe intestinal pains, even after it was evident these treatments were not responding to his deteriorating condition. The court held that although prison doctors could not be held liable for failing to diagnose the inmate's colon cancer, the failure to diagnose #43 further and treat severe pain experienced by a prisoner was evidence of deliberate indifference. McElligot v. Foley, 182 F.3d 1248, 1256-1258 (1999). Unlike the plaintiff in McElligot, Ossining exhibits no severe symptoms of celiac disease. The prison staff examined Ossining, conducted a blood test, proscribed him iron supplements to overcome his weight loss and psychological depression, and professionally reviewed his blood work to conclude there

#40 Change/Keep as is
#41 Change/Keep as is

#42 Change/Keep as is

#43 Change/Keep as is

was nothing seriously wrong with him. Therefore, as the prison exercised professional standards of care in evaluating his health, and as the inmate exhibits no severe symptoms warranting special treatment, Ossining fails to show deliberate indifference to his medical needs.

B. The prison's denial of prisoner's requests for a special gluten-free diet and additional testing for a rare disease do not violate contemporary standards of decency

#44 Change/Keep as is

#44 Under the objective prong, exposure to an unreasonable risk of harm contrary to "contemporary standards of decency" failed to be shown. Helling, 509 U.S. at 36. The objective standard requires showing treatment rising to the level of "serious" deprivation. Campbell, 169 F.3d at 1363. In Rhodes, the Court held confin-

#45 Change/Keep as is

ing two inmates to a single cell #45 did not constitute the "unnecessary and wanton infliction of pain" that violates the Eighth Amendment because inmates suffered only minor deprivations of privileges, not necessities such as essential food, medical care, or sanitation. Only when these "minimal civilized measure of life's necessities" are denied is there basis for an Eighth Amendment violation. Rhodes v. Chapman, 452 U.S. 337, 346, 349 (1981). Similarly, Wellville's denial of additional testing and special diet to Ossining when trained medical professionals failed to recognize symp-

#42 Change/Keep as is

toms requiring such treatment #46 does not constitute deprivation of life's minimal necessities. Ossining was not denied adequate medical care when he was examined by prison medical staff, had his blood tested and reviewed by Dr. Flowers, and was proscribed adequate iron supplements to combat weight loss and fatigue. Moreover, Ossining was never denied essential food as adequate alternatives remained available in the cafeteria should Ossining prefer a gluten-free diet. Therefore, life's minimal necessities were not denied, and a claim may be brought against Ossining

#43 Change/Keep as is

for failing the #47 aforementioned objective standard because his treatment did not violate contemporary standards of decency.

II. PRISONER'S FIRST AMENDMENT CLAIM IS WITHOUT MERIT BECAUSE WARDEN BRUBAKER REVIEWED AND DENIED PRISONER'S PUBLICATIONS IN RESPONSE TO THE UNREASONABLE BURDEN PLACED UPON THE PRISON'S RESOURCES AS AUTHORIZED UNDER 28 C.F.R. § 540.71

As authorized under 28 C.F.R. § 540.71 (b), Warden Brubaker legitimately restricted Ossining's right to receive publications deemed "detrimental to the secu-

#48 Change/Keep as is
#49 Change/Keep as is

rity, good order, or discipline of the institution #48 ..." 28 C.F.R. § 540.71 (2002). #49 Exercise of constitutional rights within the prison must pay due regard to the order and security of the prison environment. See Turner, 482 U.S. at 84-85. Ossining fails to show Wellville's restrictions on his First Amendment rights were not "reasonably related to legitimate penological interests" as required under the four-part <u>Turner-Thornburgh</u> test. <u>See id.</u> at 89; <u>See</u> <u>Thornburgh</u>, 490 U.S. at 401. Under Turner-Thornburgh, the court must #50 give consideration to the following factors: A) the impact that accommodation of the asserted constitutional right will have on others in the prison; B) whether the government objective underlying the regulations at issue is legitimate and neutral, and whether the regulations are rationally related to that objective #51 ; C) whether the regulation represents an exaggerated response to prison concerns; and D) whether there are alternative means of exercising the right that remain open to prison inmates at *de minimis* cost to penological interests. <u>Owen v. Wille</u>, 117 F.3d 1235 (11th Cir. 1997). Whereas Ossining's exercise of his First Amendment right created an unreasonable burden on resources of the prison and put prison security in jeopardy, restricting his access to medical publications was constitutional because it was reasonably related to a legitimate penological interest.

#50 Change/Keep as is

#51 Change/Keep as is

<u>A. Accommodation of prisoner's asserted First Amendment right would be detrimental to the order and security of the prison, placing an unreasonable burden on the resources of the prison medical facility and cafeteria</u>

The Court should be particularly deferential to the informed discretion of Warden Brubaker's given interests in security when Ossining's assertion of his constitutional right created a "ripple effect" among fellow inmates and prison staff. <u>See</u> <u>Turner</u>, 482 U.S. at 90. #52 In Turner, a class of inmates challenged prison regulations restricting correspondence between inmates as violations of their First Amendment rights. The court deferred to judgment of correction officials and upheld the regulation as reasonably related to legitimate security interests given the potential for coordinating criminal activity #53 by means of inmate-to-inmate correspondence, and given the probability of material circulating within the prison in a ripple #54 affect. <u>See Id.</u> at 91.

#52 Change/Keep as is

#53 Change/Keep as is
#54 Change/Keep as is

Like the warden in <u>Turner</u>, Warden Brubaker determined that Ossining created a #55 "ripple effect;" he threatened the order and security of the prison while placing an unreasonable burden on prison resources by circulating publications among prisoners to encourage them to believe they were sick. According to Brubaker, the temporal relationship between Ossining's receipt of medical publications and increased inmate complaints indicates a correlation between the assertion of his constitutional rights and the #56 riling up of prisoners, over taxing of prison personnel, and additional expenditure of prison resources. Dramatic increases in infirmary visits and requests for allergy testing among inmates, many of #57 which showed no symptoms warranting testing, support Brubaker's hypothesis. Given the threat to order and cost of additional resources required to accommodate Ossining's assertion of his rights, deference should be given to Brubaker's informed discretion in rejecting these publications.

#55 Change/Keep as is

#56 Change/Keep as is

#57 Change/Keep as is

B. Governmental objective in maintaining prison security is legitimate and neutral, and prison regulations governing the availability of publications to inmates rationally relate to this objective by reducing frivolous medical complaints and special requests

Under the second factor of the Turner-Thornburgh test, the Court must determine whether 1) the governmental objective underlying the regulation at issue is legitimate and neutral, and whether 2) the regulation is rationally related to that objective. Thornburgh, 490 U.S. at 414.

1. Protecting prison security is a legitimate and neutral governmental objective

In rejecting Ossining's publications, Warden Brubaker acted pursuant to 28 C.F.R. § 540.71, **#58** whose underlying objective of protecting prison security is undoubtedly legitimate and is neutral with regard to the content of the expression regulated." See Thornburgh, 490 U.S. at 402. In Thornburgh, inmates filed a class action against the prison challenging regulations excluding incoming sexually explicit publications. **#59** The Court upheld the regulations because maintenance of prison order and security is a legitimate governmental purpose, and because the prison's bank on sexually explicit material was neutrally based on security interests. See Id. at 414-415. Like Thornburgh, Ossining's publications were rejected **#60** as a consequence of their creating obstacles to the legitimate governmental objective of maintaining prison security. Warden Brubaker rejected only those publications deemed a threat to prison security, remaining "neutral" to the legitimate governmental interest in maintaining security and order. Therefore, Brubaker's exercise of authority under 28 C.F.R. § 540.71 was consistent with the legitimate and neutral objectives underlying the regulation.

2. Application of prison regulation governing the availability of publications to inmates is rationally related to the governmental objective

There is a "valid, rational connection" between the rejection of various publications addressed to Ossining and the legitimate government interests in security and preservation of resources. See Turner, 482 U.S. at 89. In Onishea, inmates with HIV brought a class action challenging the prison's segregation of recreational, religious, and educational programs based on prisoners' HIV status. The prison justified **#61** it's actions claiming the cost of hiring additional guards to monitor the threat of "high-risk" behavior in integrated programs would create an undue financial burden on resources. The Court upheld the segregated programs as rationally related to government objectives as

> **#62** "Penological concerns such as security and cost are legitimate, and the evidence in this case shows that these are in fact the concerns behind the program requirements that participating prisoners neither create a threat of disorder or

#58 Change/Keep as is

#59 Change/Keep as is

#60 Change/Keep as is

#61 Change/Keep as is

#62 Change/Keep as is

unreasonable costs. Thus, even if the district court's importation of the Turner standards into the Rehabilitation Act was no precisely correct as a matter of legal theory, determining whether penological concerns impose requirements for program participation is not error."

Onishea v. Hopper, 171 F.3d 1289, 1300 (11th Cir. 1999). Similarly, Brubaker's rejection of certain items addressed to Ossining #63 was rationally related to legitimate governmental interests because of the Warden's concern that these publications created threat of disorder and unreasonable costs for the prison. #64 By rejecting these publications, Warden Brubaker intended to remove obstacles to maintaining security by reducing the agitation of prisoners, easing the burden placed on the prison medical staff, and removing the need for additional guards to maintain order in the cafeteria. #65 Therefore, as security was the underlying concern behind Brubaker's actions, his rejection of Ossining's publications was rationally related to legitimate governmental objectives.

#63   Change/Keep as is

#64   Change/Keep as is

#65   Change/Keep as is

C. The prison regulation is not an exaggerated response to prison concerns because alternatives accommodating prisoner's rights at de minimus cost to penological interests are not immediately obvious or feasible

Brubaker's rejection of prisoner's publications is not an exaggerated response to the threat these items posed to prison resources and security because there are no "obvious, easy alternatives." Turner, 482 U.S. at 90. In Spellman, inmates challenged the prison's blanket ban on publications sent to prisoners in administrative segregation #66 on the grounds that the regulation was an exaggerated response to security and safety concerns. The Court held the prison's actions unconstitutional because of recognized alternatives to the blanket ban #67 , such as placing reasonable limits on the quantity of publications permitted in confinement, #68 which still address the concerns of security, fire, and sanitation. See Spellman v. Hopper, 95 F. Supp.2d 1267, 1286 (M.D. Ala. 1999).

#66   Change/Keep as is

#67   Change/Keep as is
#68   Change/Keep as is

Unlike Spellman, Brubaker did not ban all publications sent to Ossining #69 : Brubaker only restricted items deemed a threat to prison security. Moreover, unlike Spellman, less restrictive alternatives can be rejected because of reasonably grounded fears they will lead to greater harm or administrative inconvenience. See Thornburgh, 490 U.S. at 419. The resources required to read through every allergy magazine received to eliminate publications deemed a threat would be too expansive as prisoners have complained of a wide variety of allergies. Also, allowing Ossining to read magazines while in confinement would not come at a de minimus cost to the prison #70 due to the fact that additional resources would be required to fund such an arrangement. Thus, as less restrictive alternatives are not readily available or feasible, the Warden's actions do not represent an exaggerated response to legitimate penological concerns.

#69   Change/Keep as is

#70   Change/Keep as is

D. The prison restrictions on prisoner's receipt of publications are reasonable as prisoner has alternative means of exercising his First Amendment rights to keep up with developments in his field of work

#71 Change/Keep as is

#72 Change/Keep as is

#73 Change/Keep as is

#74 Change/Keep as is

#75 Change/Keep as is

#76 Change/Keep as is

　　#71 The fourth factor of the Turner-Thornburgh test: other means of expression available to the prisoner despite imposition of prison regulations restricting his access to certain publications. See Thornburgh, 490 U.S. at 417. In Turner, the prison restricted inmate-to-inmate correspondence #72 among prisons to prevent future criminal behavior, a legitimate security concern. The Court held the fourth factor satisfied #73 in the event that any other means of expression remained open to the prisoners, not necessarily other means of communicating with inmates in other prisons. Turner, 482 U.S. at 90, 92. Similarly, Brubaker's application of the regulation merely prohibits publications of particular kind #74 , and does not deprive the prisoner of all means of expression. The prison is not prohibiting Ossining from gaining access to allergy information because he can still receive phone calls and visits from colleagues #75 who can keep him up to date. Moreover, the prisoner is still free to receive a variety of other publications. Alternative means of exercising his #76 First Amendment rights are still available to the prisoner, and therefore, Ossining fails to satisfy the fourth factor.

CONCLUSION

For the above stated reasons, the judgment of the District Court should be affirmed.

Respectfully submitted,

_____

Student
Attorney for Respondents

CERTIFICATE OF SERVICE
I, _____, swear on this day, the 28th of February, 2003, that I have served Respondent's brief on Appellant's counsel.

_____

Attorney for Respondents

Answer Key on page 525

CHAPTER 5

Citation

This chapter covers the essentials of citation, addressing the two most used authorities: the ALWD citation manual and the Bluebook.

3. Basic Structure and Signals: Checklist ☑
4. Signals: Checklist ☑
5. Subdivisions and Pinpoint Cites: Checklist ☑
6. Short Form Citations: Checklist ☑
7. Abbreviations: Checklist ☑
8. Cases: Checklist ☑
9. Constitutions: Checklist ☑
10. Statutes: Checklist ☑
11. Administrative and Executive Materials: Checklist ☑
12. Books, Reports and Other Nonperiodic Materials: Checklist ☑
13. Periodicals: Checklist ☑
14. Electronic Media: Checklist ☑

B. ALWD Quizzes
1. Typefaces: Quiz 👤?
2. Basic Structure and Signals: Quiz 👤?
3. Signals: Quiz 👤?
4. Order and Punctuation of Signals and Citations: Quiz 👤?
5. Subdivisions and Pinpoint Cites: Quiz 👤?
6. Short Form Citations: Quiz 👤?
7. Abbreviations: Quiz 👤?
8. Cases: Quiz 👤?
9. Constitutions: Quiz 👤?
10. Statutes: Quiz 👤?
11. Administrative and Executive Materials: Quiz 👤?
12. Books, Reports and Other Nonperiodic Materials: Quiz 👤?
13. Periodicals: Quiz 👤?
14. Electronic Media: Quiz 👤?

C. ALWD Self-Assessment
1. ALWD Citation Self-Assessment 👤?

IV. Strategies for Using the Bluebook
A. The Purpose of Bluebook Citation
B. Design, Layout, and Basic Citation Rules of the Bluebook
1. Bluebook Design
2. Bluebook Layout
3. Bluebook Basic Citation Rules
a. Cases
b. Constitutions
c. Statutes
d. Rules and Regulations
e. Books
f. Periodicals
C. Often-Used Bluebook Rules
• Typefaces
• Basic Structure and Signals
• Subdivisions and Pinpoint Cites
• Short Citations
• Abbreviations

- Cases
- Constitutions
- Statutes
- Administrative and Executive Materials
- Books, Reports, and Other Nonperiodic Materials
- Periodical Materials
- Electronic Media

V. Study Aids—Bluebook Citation
  A. Bluebook Quick References and Checklists
     1. The Bluebook in General: Quick Reference 🗒
     2. Typefaces: Checklist ☑
     3. Basic Structure and Signals: Checklist ☑
     4. Signals: Checklist ☑
     5. Subdivisions and Pinpoint Cites: Checklist ☑
     6. Short Form Citations: Checklist ☑
     7. Abbreviations: Checklist ☑
     8. Cases: Checklist ☑
     9. Constitutions: Checklist ☑
     10. Statutes: Checklist ☑
     11. Administrative and Executive Materials: Checklist ☑
     12. Books, Reports and Other Nonperiodic Materials
     13. Periodicals: Checklist ☑
     14. Electronic Media: Checklist ☑
  B. Bluebook Quizzes
     1. Typefaces: Quiz ⚇?
     2. Basic Structures and Signals: Quiz ⚇?
     3. Citation Signals: Quiz ⚇?
     4. Order and Punctuation of Signals and Citations: Quiz ⚇?
     5. Subdivisions and Pinpoint Cites: Quiz ⚇?
     6. Short Form Citations: Quiz ⚇?
     7. Abbreviations: Quiz ⚇?
     8. Cases: Quiz ⚇?
     9. Constitutions: Quiz ⚇?
     10. Statutes: Quiz ⚇?
     11. Administrative and Executive Materials: Quiz ⚇?
     12. Books, Reports and Other Nonperiodic Materials: Quiz ⚇?
     13. Periodicals: Quiz ⚇?
     14. Electronic Media: Quiz ⚇?
  C. Bluebook Self-Assessment
     1. Bluebook Citation Self-Assessment ⚇?

I.   ALWD AND THE BLUEBOOK

What follows is not intended to substitute for The Bluebook or ALWD Citation Manual but is only a guide to their use.

Finding the authority referenced in a legal document is so important to the legal reader that rules have developed to standardize citation. Although most law students and practicing attorneys dislike citation rules, they are necessary to allow the reader to access the materials referenced. If a legal authority is improperly cited, the reader will have a difficult time finding the law. In addition, the legal reader might not trust the substance of the document; if the writer's citation is inadequate, then perhaps the research and writing are similarly inadequate or improper. Thus, citations for the legal reader are not only helpful for finding law, but they also have become a tool to measure the writer's credibility. Currently, there are two widely accepted citation reference manuals: the more recent ALWD (Association of Legal Writing Directors) and the more traditional Bluebook.

This book covers citation using both ALWD (starting on page 399) and the Bluebook (Starting on page 453), although you will probably learn only one of these citation reference manuals in your class.

A.   *ALWD*

In 1997, the board of directors of the Association of Legal Writing Directors decided to create a citation manual to fulfill three primary goals: to simplify legal citation rules, to create one set of rules for all forms of legal writing, and to present these rules in a format that judges, lawyers, instructors, and students would find easy to use. The result was the *ALWD Citation Manual: A Professional System of Citation,* written primarily by Dean Darby Dickerson of Stetson University College of Law. Known as ALWD, this manual is now in its fourth edition, published in 2010 by Wolters Kluwer Law & Business.

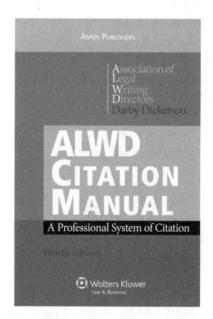

B.   *The Bluebook*

The first and most widely recognized citation standardization manual, titled *The Bluebook: A Uniform System of Citation,* was developed in the 1920s by a Harvard law student and is still published by the Harvard Law Review. The Bluebook is the traditional citation manual used by courts, lawyers, and law schools, despite complaints by some that the book is difficult to use and inconsistent in places. The Bluebook is currently in its nineteenth edition (2010), and it is now available online.[1]

II.   STRATEGIES FOR USING ALWD

The trick for using ALWD is to learn these three things:

1.   The purpose of citation
2.   The design, layout, and basic citation rules of ALWD
3.   Some of the often-used rules

A.   *The Purpose of Citation*

Lawyers use citation to provide authority in legal documents and to find the law referenced in legal documents. The *ALWD Citation Manual: A Professional System of Citation* (or ALWD for short) is designed to provide a uniform system of citation rules so that lawyers can easily find and reference legal sources. Eventually, when electronic filings are required with links to each cited source, citation might become obsolete. But until that time, lawyers are required to use citation that permits other lawyers easy access to their references. ALWD

---

1. http://www.legalbluebook.com/.

and the Bluebook are the most commonly used citation systems. Using correct citation adds credibility to your writing; if a judge can trust your citations, she can also trust your analysis.

B.   Design, Layout, and Basic Citation Rules of the ALWD Citation Manual

1.   ALWD Design

Unlike the Bluebook, the ALWD Citation Manual does not have separate citation formats for scholarly writing and legal documents. Thus, a citation based on ALWD style appears the same, regardless of the type of document you are writing.

2.   ALWD Layout

ALWD is divided into seven parts:

Part 1: Introductory Material. This section summarizes the organization of the manual, discusses common citation problems that word processors may cause, and provides information regarding local citation formats.

Part 2: Citation Basics. This section contains the basic rules for citing a source, including typeface, abbreviations, spelling, capitalization, numbers, page numbers, citing particular sections or divisions of a source, internal cross-references, and short citation formats. A careful review of these fundamental rules is necessary before using ALWD to cite a source.

Part 3: Citing Specific Print Sources. This section focuses on print sources, both primary and secondary, and is divided into subsections by source type. At the beginning of each subsection, a "Fast Formats" table provides quick examples of correct citations for several commonly used sources.

Part 4: Electronic Sources. This section discusses the proper citation for electronic resources from LexisNexis, Westlaw, e-mail, and the Internet. It also provides information regarding the citation of sources available both in print and electronic formats.

Part 5: Incorporating Citations into Documents. This section explains how to place and use citations, how to use signals, how to order cited authorities, and when and how to include explanatory parentheticals.

Part 6: Quotations. This section discusses use of quotations, alteration of quoted material, and omission within quoted material.

Part 7: Appendices. The appendices contain more information about primary sources by jurisdiction, local court citation rules, abbreviations, federal taxation materials, federal administrative publications, and a sample legal memorandum showing proper citation placement.

ALWD also has a detailed table of contents and an index.

Throughout the manual, green triangles (▲) are used to designate spaces in citation formats, and green circles (●) are used to separate components of citations. On the inside front cover is a "Fast Format Locator" that gives the page numbers for the Fast Formats tables throughout the manual. On the inside back cover is a "Short-Citation Locator for Commonly Used Sources" that lists rule numbers for many short citation formats.

3. ALWD Basic Citation Rules

a. Cases (Rule 12)

Citation of a U.S. Supreme Court Case:

Lakeside v. Oregon, 435 U.S. 333, 345 (1978).

> Lakeside = plaintiff
> Oregon = defendant
> 435 = reporter volume #
> U.S. = reporter abbreviation
> 333 = first page
> 345 = specific page
> (1978) = date case decided

NOTE: Be sure to include both the first page of the cited case and a specific page if one is referenced.

Citation of a case decided by the U.S. Court of Appeals for the Eleventh Circuit:

Campbell v. Sikes, 169 F.3d 1353, 1366-67 (11th Cir. 1999).

> Campbell = plaintiff
> Sikes = defendant
> 169 = reporter volume #
> F.3d = reporter abbreviation
> 1353 = first page
> 1366-67 = specific pages
> 11th Cir. = court—this is necessary if it's not clear from reporter abbreviation
> 1999 = date case decided

Short form for cases:

Campbell, 169 F.3d at 1369.

> Campbell = plaintiff; use defendant's name in short cite if plaintiff's name is a
>   common litigant (i.e., United States)
> 169 = reporter volume #
> F.3d = reporter abbreviation
> 1369 = specific pages

b. Constitutions (Rule 13)

Citation of Section 2 of the Eighteenth Amendment to the U.S. Constitution:

U.S. Const. amend. XVIII, § 2.

U.S. Const. = abbreviation of Constitution
amend. = abbreviation of amendment
XVIII = # of amendment
§ 2 = # of section if applicable

Citation of a state constitution:

N.C. Const. art. III, § 1.

N.C. Const. = abbreviation of Constitution
art. = abbreviation of article
III = # of article
§ 1 = # of section if applicable

c. Statutes (Rule 14)

Citation of an entire statue, as codified in the United States Code:

Federal Trademark Dilution Act, 15 U.S.C. § 1125 (2000).

Federal Trademark Dilution Act = official name
15 = title #
U.S.C. = abbreviation of code
§ 1125 = section #
2000 = date of code edition

Citation of an individual provision of the United States Code:

15 U.S.C. § 1125 (2000).

15 = title #
U.S.C. = abbreviation of code
§ 1125 = section #
2000 = date of code edition

Short citation of provision of the United States Code:

Id. at § 1125 (where appropriate) or 15 U.S.C. § 1125.

Id. at § 1125—use when referring to the immediately preceding authority

d.   *Federal Administrative and Executive Materials (Rule 19)*

Citation of a particular provision of a regulation in the Code of Federal Regulations:

49 C.F.R. § 172.101 (2005).

> 49 = title #
> C.F.R. = abbreviation of regulations
> § 172.101 = section #
> 2005 = date of C.F.R. edition

NOTE: Cite all final federal administrative rules and regulations to the C.F.R.

Short citation of particular provision of a regulation in the C.F.R.:

Id. at § 172.101 (where appropriate) or 49 C.F.R. at § 172.101.

> Id. at § 172.101 (where appropriate)—use when referring to the immediately
>   preceding authority
> 49 = title #
> C.F.R. = abbreviation of regulations
> at § 172.101 = section #

e.   *Books, Treatises, and Other Nonperiodic Materials (Rule 22)*

Citation of a treatise:

William L. Prosser & W. Page Keeton, <u>Prosser and Keeton on the Law of Torts</u> § 3.65
(5th ed., West 1984).

> William L. Prosser & W. Page Keeton = full name of 1st and 2nd authors
> Prosser and Keeton on the Law of Torts = title of treatise
> § 3.65 = section #
> 5th ed. West, 1984—edition—if there is more than one—publisher, and date of
>   edition

Short citation of a treatise:

Prosser & Keeton, <u>Prosser and Keeton on the Law of Torts</u> at § 3.65.

> Prosser & Keeton = last name of 1st and 2nd authors
> Prosser and Keeton on the Law of Torts = title of treatise
> at § 3.65 = section #

NOTE: If using footnotes, use the following form.

Prosser & Keeton, <u>supra</u> n. 7, at § 3.65.

> Prosser & Keeton = last name of 1st and 2nd authors
> supra n. 7 = word supra & note number where full cite appears
> at § 3.65 = section #

Citation of a particular page in a novel:

J. K. Rowling, <u>Harry Potter and the Sorcerer's Stone</u> 125 (Scholastic 1997).

> J.K. Rowling—use full name of author unless author uses initials only
> Harry Potter and the Sorcerer's Stone = title of book
> 125 = section or page #
> Scholastic = publisher's name
> 1997 = year published

f. Legal and Other Periodicals (Rule 23)

Citation of particular pages within a law review article:

Mustave Hurt, <u>Unimaginable Pain</u>, 742 Geo L.J. 801, 831-32 (2003).

> Mustave Hurt = full name of author
> Unimaginable Pain = title of article
> 742 = journal volume #
> Geo. L.J. = abbreviation of journal
> 801 = first page of article
> 831-32 = specific pages
> 2003 = year published

Citation of a magazine article:

J. Madeleine Nash, <u>Fertile Minds</u>, Time 18 (Feb. 3, 1997).

> J. Madeline Nash = author's full name
> Fertile Minds = title of article
> Time = name of magazine
> 18 = first page
> Feb. 3, 1997 = cover date

Citation of a newspaper article:

Adam Gourna, <u>Celiac Disease: A Killer</u>, N.Y. Times F3 (Dec. 12, 1994).

> Adam Gourna = author's full name
> Celiac Disease: A Killer = headline
> N.Y. Times = abbreviation of newspaper
> F3 = page #
> Dec. 12, 1994 = date

C.   Often-Used ALWD Rules

The following are some of the most often-used rules in citation from the ALWD Citation Manual.

ALWD Typefaces (Rule 1)

ALWD RULE	KEY POINTS
Rule 1.1: Typeface Choices	• Most material should be presented in ordinary type. • Italics may be presented either with *slanted type* or <u>underlining</u>. • Periods are typically part of the citation component that they follow and should be underlined. • Commas are not typically part of the citation component and so should not be underlined. • Note that citations in law journals and book publishers that do not use the ALWD Citation Manual have different typeface conventions.
Rule 1.3: When to Use Italics in Citations	Italicize only the following: • Introductory signals • Internal cross-references • Case names, both in full and short citation formats • Phrases indicating subsequent or prior history • Titles of most documents • Topics or titles in legal encyclopedia entries • Names of Internet sites • The short forms <u>id.</u> and <u>supra</u>.
Rule 1.8: Italicizing Foreign Words	Generally italicize foreign words that have not been incorporated into normal English. Do not italicize words, such as ad hoc, amicus curiae, and habeus corpus, that have been incorporated into normal English. Consult Rule 1.8 or <u>Black's Law Dictionary</u> if you are unsure about a particular word.

ALWD Spelling and Capitalization (Rule 3)

ALWD RULE	KEY POINTS
Rule 3.1: Words in Titles	• Retain the spelling of the title of a source, such as a book or law review article, from the original source. • Change capitalization to conform to the following rules: • Capitalize the first word in the title. • Capitalize the first word in any subtitle. • Capitalize the first word after a colon or dash. • Capitalize all other words except articles, prepositions, the word "to" when used as part of an infinitive, and coordinating conjunctions. • Rule 3.1(c) contains special rules for capitalizing hyphenated words.
Rule 3.2: General Rules	Generally capitalize the following: • Professional titles and titles of honor or respect • Organization names • Proper nouns • Adjectives formed from proper nouns • Holidays, events, and epochs • Defined terms in a document
Rule 3.3: Capitalizing Specific Words	Certain words, such as "Act," "Board," and "Circuit," have special capitalization rules. Consult Rule 3.3 for the full list and accompanying rules.

ALWD Basic Structure and Signals (Rules 10, 43, and 44)

ALWD RULE	KEY POINTS
Rule 10: Internal Cross-References	• Internal cross-references may be used to reference text, footnotes, appendices, or any other internal material to avoid repeating text or to help readers. They may not be used to reference outside sources that have been cited elsewhere in the document. For those, use the appropriate short citation forms (see Rule 11). • To refer to material that appears earlier in the document, use <u>supra</u>. • To refer to material that will appear later in the document, use <u>infra</u>.
Rule 43: Citation Placement and Use Rule 43.1: Placement Options	• When a source relates to the whole sentence in the text, include the citation to that source in a separate citation sentence, beginning with a capital letter and ending with a period. • When a source relates to only part of a sentence in the text, include the citation as a clause within the sentence, immediately after the text it concerns, and set the clause off with commas. • Rule 43.1(e) discusses the use of footnotes in legal documents.

Rule 43.2: Frequency of Citation	Include a citation immediately after any sentence or portion thereof that contains a legal principle, legal authority, or thoughts borrowed from other sources.

Rule 44: Signals	• Signals are words or terms that inform readers about the type and degree of support (or contradiction) that the cited authority provides.
	• Use no signal if the cited authority directly supports the statement, identifies the source of a quotation, or merely identifies authority referred to in the text.
	• Signals that indicate support include:
	   • See
	   • Accord
	   • See also
	   • Cf.
	• Signals that indicate contradiction include:
	   • Contra
	   • But See
	   • But cf.
	• Other signals indicate background material, See generally, indicate an example, See e.g., or draw a comparison, Compare … with ….
	• Signals should be capitalized if they begin a citation sentence, but not otherwise. Signals should be separated from the rest of the citation with one space, but no punctuation. Italicize or underline each introductory signal, unless it is used as a verb within the citation sentence.
	• Consult Rules 44.7 through 44.8 for specifics regarding the use of multiple signals or the same signal for multiple citations.

Rule 44.8: Order of Signals	• Signals of the same basic type are strung together within one citation sentence and are separated from each other by semicolons. • Signals of different types must be grouped in separate citation sentences. • Consult Rule 44.3 (Support, Comparison, Contradiction, and Background).
Rule 45.4: Order of Authorities Within Each Signal	• Constitutions; statutes; rules of evidence and procedure; treaties and international agreements; cases; case-related material; administrative and executive material; materials from intergovernmental organizations • Consult Rule 45 for more specifics.
Rule 46: Explanatory Parentheticals and Related Authority	• Parenthetical information explains the relevance of a particular authority to proposition given in the text. • If explanatory parenthetical information includes one or more full sentences, it should start with a capital letter and end with correct punctuation. • If the parenthetical information includes one or more full sentences, it should start with a capital letter and end with the correct punctuation. • Explanatory parenthetical phrases come before any citations concerning subsequent history or other related authority.

ALWD Subdivisions and Pinpoint Cites (Rules 5, 6, and 7)

ALWD RULE	KEY POINTS
Rule 5.1: Initial Pages	When citing a source with page numbers that is contained within a larger source (for example, a law review article), always include the initial page number of the source being cited.
Rule 5.2: Pinpoint Pages	• When citing specific material from a source, include a pinpoint page reference that provides the exact page on which the cited material is located. This rule applies both to material that is directly quoted and to specific information, such as a case holding, from a source. • Consult Rules 5.3 and 5.4 for details on how to cite consecutive pages or multiple pages within a source. • Consult Rule 5.5 for the format for star pagination. • Give page numbers or numbers before the date parenthetical, without any introductory abbreviation. • Use ", at" if a pinpoint page might be confused with the title. • If you are referring specifically to material on the first page of a source, repeat the page number. • When citing material within a concurring or dissenting opinion, give only the initial page of the case and the page on which the specific material appears. See Rule 12.5(d). • When citing material that spans more than one page, give the inclusive page numbers separated by the en dash (–) or the word "to." See Rule 5.3. • Cite nonconsecutive pages by giving the individual page numbers separated by a comma and a space (Rule 5.4).
Rule 6: Citing Sections and Paragraphs	If a source is divided into sections or paragraphs, cite the relevant subdivision using the section (§) and paragraph (¶) symbols, with a space between the symbol and the following number.
Rule 6.4: Subsections and Subparagraphs	Cite to the smallest subdivision possible when citing a section or paragraph. Use the original source punctuation to denote subsections. If the original source does not use punctuation to denote subsections, place subdivisions in parentheses, without inserting a space between the main and section and subdivision. Example: Fed. R. Civ. P. 26(a)(1)(D). Rules 6.6 through 6.10 address citation of multiple sections, subsections, paragraphs, and subparagraphs.
Rule 7: Citing Footnotes and Endnotes	• When citing a footnote or endnote, include the page on which the note begins and give the note number. • One note is abbreviated as "n."; multiple notes are abbreviated as "nn." Place one space between the abbreviation and the note number(s).

ALWD Short Citations (Rule 11)

ALWD RULE	KEY POINTS
Rule 11.2: Short Citation Format	• Only use short citation format after an authority has been cited once in full citation format and when the reader will not be confused as to which source is being referenced. • Rules for each specific type of source should be consulted to find the short citation format for that source. • For short form citations to cases, refer to Rule 12.20. • For short form citations for federal and state statutes, refer to Rule 14.6.
Rule 11.3: Id. as a Short Citation	• Id. generally replaces whatever portion of the immediately preceding citation is identical with the current citation. For example, if a full citation is provided for a law review article with pinpoint citation after one textual sentence, the citation for the next textual sentence may substitute "id." for all the details regarding the article name, source name, and so on, and include only the new pinpoint page number: • Example: "And so it goes in Bankruptcy Court these days." Susan Dinero, The Three Bs: Bankruptcy and Baby Boomers, 105 Harv. L. Rev. 233, 245 (2002). Dinero adds, "And so it should." Id. at 246. • Id. may be used only to refer to the immediately preceding authority. In a paper with footnotes, if the preceding footnote has more than one citation, id. may not be used to refer because it would be unclear to the reader which citation is being referred to. • Italicize id. (if you use underlining to represent italics, underline the period in id. also). • Capitalize id. only if it begins a sentence.
Rule 11.4: Supra as a Short Citation	• Supra can be used to cross-reference a full citation provided previously in the document. • Supra is typically used for sources that are cited by author name, such as books and law review articles. Do not use supra as a short citation for cases, statutes, session laws, ordinances, legislative materials (other than hearings), constitutions, and administrative regulations. • Example: Baker, supra n. 3, at 55. *This citation provides the author name, the location of the original citation in the document, and a pinpoint citation to the page number in the original source.* • Rule 11.4(b)(2) states that legal writers should not use the supra format in documents that do not have footnotes or endnotes. • Rule 11.4(d) discusses the use of "hereinafter" to shorten supra citations or other short citations where a source has a particularly long title.

ALWD Abbreviations (Rule 2)

ALWD RULE	KEY POINTS
Rule 2: Abbreviations	• Abbreviations are often used in legal citation for common sources, such as legal periodicals and case names, and also for other less common words and phrases. • Consult Appendices 3, 4, and 5 for tables of standard abbreviations. Note that certain contractions may now be used as abbreviations. For example, Appendix 3 permits both "Govt." or "Gov't" as abbreviations for government. Once you choose the abbreviation, be consistent within your document. • Appendix 3 lists words, such as "commonwealth" or "insurance," that should be abbreviated in citations. Appendix 4 lists court abbreviations for both state and federal courts. • Appendix 5 lists abbreviations for legal periodicals, such as law reviews, including well-known law journals in some other English-language jurisdictions. • Appendix 5 also clarifies that commas should not be included in periodical abbreviations.

ALWD Numbers (Rule 4)

ALWD RULE	KEY POINTS
Rule 4: Numbers	• Numbers within citations should be presented as numerals unless the number appears in a title. If a number does appear in a title, present it as it is presented in the original. • Numbers within textual material may be presented as either numerals or words, but whichever you use, remain consistent. The convention in law is to present numbers zero to ninety-nine as words, and numbers above 100 as numerals. • Rule 4.3 addresses special rules for ordinal numbers (such as "first").

ALWD Quotations (Rules 47, 48, and 49)

ALWD RULE	KEY POINTS
Rule 47.4: Short Quotations	• If a quotation is fewer than fifty words, or runs fewer than four lines of typed text, simply enclose it in double quotation marks (" "). • Place the citation for the quoted material after the sentence containing the quoted material. In a footnoted document, place the note reference number immediately after the closing quotation mark, even if it is in the middle of the sentence. However, if a single textual sentence includes multiple quoted phrases from the same source and pinpoint reference, place the note reference number at the end of the sentence to reference all the quoted phrases.

Rule 47.4(d): Punctuation	Periods and commas should generally be placed inside quotations marks, regardless of whether they are part of the original quotation. Other punctuation, such as semicolons and question marks, should generally be placed outside the quotation marks unless they are part of the original quoted material.
Rule 47.5: Longer Quotations	If a quotation is fifty words or more, or exceeds four lines of typed text, present it as a block of type by single-spacing it and indenting it by one tab on both the right and left. Do not use quotation marks at the beginning or end of the block quotation. Separate the block quotation from the surrounding text by one blank line above and below.
Rule 47.7: Quotations within Quotations	• Within a short quotation, set off quotations with single quotation marks (' '). • Within a block quotation, set off quotations with double quotation marks (" ").
Rule 48: Altering Quoted Material Rule 48.1: Altering the Case of a Letter	When changing a letter from uppercase to lowercase, or vice versa, within a quotation, enclose the altered letter in brackets (for example, "[B]asketball" or "[f]ootball").
Rule 48.2: Adding, Changing, or Deleting One or More Letters	When adding, changing, or deleting letters from a quoted word, enclose the added, changed, or deleted material in brackets (indicate omitted or deleted material with empty brackets—[ ]).
Rule 48.4: Substituting or Adding Words	When substituting or adding words to a quotation, such as to clarify a detail for the reader, enclose those words in brackets.
Rule 48.5: Altering Typeface	When altering the typeface of quoted material, such as by adding or deleting italics for emphasis, describe the alteration in a parenthetical following the citation.
Rule 48.6: Mistakes within Original Quoted Material	When quoting material that contains mistakes, either correct the mistake and enclose changes in brackets as discussed above, or denote the mistake with "[sic]." Do not italicize or underline "[sic]."
Rule 49: Omissions within Quoted Material	• Use ellipsis to indicate omission of one or more words. An ellipsis consists of three periods with one space between each (. . .). Insert one space before and after the ellipsis as well. • Rule 49 contains many additional, more specific rules regarding the use of ellipses, particularly specifying spacing and punctuation.

ALWD Cases (Rule 12)

ALWD RULE	KEY POINTS
Rule 12.1: Full Citation Format	The general citation form for cases includes: Case Name, reporter volume number + reporter abbreviations + first page of case, page number (deciding court + date of decision). • Example: <u>N.Y. Times Co. v. Sullivan</u>, 144 So. 2d 25, 40-41 (Ala. 1962), <u>rev'd</u>, 376 U.S. 254 (1964).
Rule 12.2: Case Name	• Italicize or underline the case name, but not the comma following it. • If a caption on a case lists more than one case, cite only the first case listed. If a single case has two different names, use the one listed first. • Cite only the first-listed party on each side of the case, and do not use "et al." or other terms to denote any omitted parties. • If the party is an individual, use only the last name. If the party is an organization, include the organization's full name, but omit abbreviations such as "d/b/a" and any material following. Usually omit "The" when it appears as the first word in a party's name. • Generally, omit given names or initials of individuals, but not in names or businesses of firms. See Rule 12.2(e)(2). • Use the abbreviations listed in Appendix 3 to abbreviate listed words in case names pursuant to Rule 12.2(e)(3), unless doing so would create confusion for the reader. • Omit business firm designations such as "Inc." if the name of the firm also contains a word that clearly indicates the status of a business firm, such as "Ass'n." See Rule 12.2(e)(8). • Rule 12(g) now permits the use of "U.S." or "United States" when referring to the United States as a party in a case citation. • Omit "State of," "Commonwealth of," and "People of" unless citing decisions of the courts of that state, in which case only "State," "Commonwealth," or "People" should be retained. See Rule 12.2(h)(1). • Bankruptcy cases with two names follow Rule 12.2(p)(2). • If a case is unreported but available on electronic media, cite according to Rules 12.12, 12.13, 12.2. • Other more specific rules regarding the presentation of a case name in a citation sentence are provided in Rule 12.2.
Rule 12.4: Reporter Abbreviation	• After the volume number, include the abbreviation for the reporter in which the case appears. Abbreviations for reporters are found in Appendix 1. • When submitting a document to a state court, check the local rules for that court (see Appendix 2) to determine which reporter to cite to. Remember that some states require parallel citation (citation of both official and unofficial reporters). • When submitting a document to federal court, check the local rules for that court (see Appendix 2). • For U.S. Supreme Court cases, typically cite to only one reporter, preferably the United States Reports (abbreviated "U.S."), or to other reporters listed in Rule 12.4(c) if a "U.S." cite is not yet available.

Rule 12.6: Court Abbreviation	• Include the appropriate abbreviation for the court that decided the case in the parentheses following the page number, just before the year the case was decided. Check Appendices 1 and 4 for abbreviations of courts. • No court abbreviation is required for U.S. Supreme Court cases because the name of the reporter indicates that the case is a U.S. Supreme Court case. Simply include the year the case was decided in the parentheses.
Rule 12.8: Subsequent History	• Subsequent history should be included in a citation if the action is listed in Rule 12.8(a). Also indicate when a judgment in a cited case has been overruled. • Consult the rules in Rule 12.8 directly for formatting and other details.
Rule 12.9: Prior History	• Prior history may be included, but is never mandatory and should be used sparingly. • Prior history should be presented in the same manner as subsequent history.

Rule 12.20: Short Citation Format	• If <u>id.</u> is appropriate, use it as the preferred short citation for cases.
	• If all or part of a case name is not included in the textual sentence, include some portion of the case name in the short citation to identify it for the reader.
	
	   • Example: The judge thought otherwise and ruled against the defendant. <u>Seel</u>, 971 P.2d at 924.
	
	• If the case name, or part of it, is included in the textual sentence, simply include in the short citation the volume number, reporter abbreviation, the word "at," and then the pinpoint reference.
	
	   • Example: The judge in <u>Seel</u> thought otherwise and ruled against the defendant. 971 P.2d at 924.

ALWD Constitutions (Rule 13)

ALWD RULE	KEY POINTS
Rule 13.2: Full Citation Format for Constitutions Currently in Force	• A citation to a constitution currently in force should include the name of the constitution and a pinpoint reference. • Example: U.S. Const. amend. XIV, § 2. • Check Appendix 3C for appropriate abbreviations of article (art.), amendment (amend.), section (§), and clause (cl.). • Abbreviate United States (U.S.) if referring to the federal Constitution, or refer to Appendix 3A for the appropriate abbreviation if citing a state constitution (Rule 13.2 (a)). • Be as specific as possible with pinpoint references.
Rule 13.3: Full Citation Format for Constitutions No Longer in Force	For constitutions no longer in force, use the same citation format given in Rule 13.2, but use a parenthetical to explain why it is no longer in force and include the year in which it lost effect. • Example: U.S. Const. amend. XVIII (repealed 1933 by U.S. Const. amend. XXI).
Rule 13.4: Short Citation Format	If appropriate, use <u>id.</u> as the short-form citation for constitutional provisions.

ALWD Statutes (Rule 14)

ALWD RULE	KEY POINTS
Rule 14.2: Full Citation, Print Format for Federal Statutes Currently in Force	• Example: 18 U.S.C. § 1965 (2000). The official code for federal statutes is the United States Code, abbreviated "U.S.C." Do not include a publisher for U.S.C. • Make sure that the abbreviations of code names are properly formatted. There should be periods and no spaces between the letters of "U.S.C." See Appendix 1 to determine the proper abbreviation formats for state codes. • Use "§" to denote the section number of the code that you are citing. Leave a space between "§" and the section number, and use "§§" if you are citing multiple sections (Rule 14.2(c)). • Include the date of the code edition cited in a parenthetical following the section number (Rules 14.2(f)(1) and 14.2(f)(2)). • If citing to a code that is published, edited, or compiled by someone other than state officials, give the name of the publisher, editor, or compiler in the parenthetical phrase (14.2(e)). For example: (West 2006). • If the statute is commonly cited using a different name or is known by a popular name, give that name and the original section number preceding the normal citation format (14.2(g)).
Rule 14.3: Full Citation, Print Format for Federal Statutes No Longer in Force	Cite as described in Rule 14.2, but include a statement that the statute was repealed or superseded, with the year in which the statute ceased to be in force. • Example: 26 U.S.C. § 1071(a) (repealed 1995).

Rule 14.4: Full Citation, Print Format for State Statutes	Abbreviations and formats for state codes are included in Appendix 1.
Rule 14.6: Short Citation, Print Format for Federal and State Statutes	Use <u>id.</u>, if appropriate. Otherwise, use all required components of the full citation, but omit the date. • Example: The full citation "42 U.S.C. § 12101 (2000)" may be cited in short form as "42 U.S.C. § 12101."

ALWD Administrative and Executive Materials (Rule 19, Appendix 7(C))

ALWD RULE	KEY POINTS

Rule 19.1: Full Citation Format for Code of Federal Regulations	Whenever possible, cite all federal rules and regulations to the Code of Federal Regulations (C.F.R.) by title, section or part, and year.
	
	    • Example: 28 C.F.R. § 540.71 (2003).
	    • Example: 31 C.F.R. pt. 730 (2005).
	
	• Be sure to cite the most recent edition of C.F.R., according to Rule 19.1(d).
	• Do not leave spaces between the letters of "C.F.R."
	• Cite to arbitrations and administrative adjudications using Rule 19.5.
	• Advisory opinions from the United States Attorney general or Office of Legal Counsel are cited according to Rule 19.7 (full citation format) and Rule 19.8 (short citation format).
	• Presidential executive orders are found in title 3 of C.F.R. and should be cited to C.F.R. according to Rule 19.9, with a parallel citation to the United States Code if therein. However, if an executive order is not found in C.F.R., cite according to the federal Register. Examples of each citation format can be found in Rule 19.9.

Rule 19.2: Short Citation Format for Code of Federal Regulations	If <u>id.</u> is appropriate, use it as the preferred short citation for rules and regulations cited in the C.F.R. If <u>id.</u> is not appropriate, repeat all elements in the full citation except the date. • Example: 28 C.F.R. at § 540.90.
Rule 19.3: Full Citation Format for Federal Register	Cite final rules and regulations not yet entered in the C.F.R., proposed federal rules and regulations, and notices to the Federal Register. Include a pinpoint cite if appropriate, and use a full date. • Example: 70 Fed. Reg. 10868, 10870 (Mar. 5, 2005).
Rule 19.4: Short Citation Format for Federal Register	If <u>id.</u> is appropriate, use it as the preferred short citation for rules and regulations cited in the Federal Register. If <u>id.</u> is not appropriate, repeat all elements in the full citation except the date. • Example: 70 Fed. Reg. at 10875.
Appendix 7(C): Administrative Materials	See Appendix 7(C) for help in citing Treasury regulations and other federal taxation materials.

ALWD Books, Reports, and Other Nonperiodic Materials (Rule 22)

ALWD RULE	KEY POINTS
Rule 22.1: Full Citation Format	Cite books, treatises, reports, or other nonperiodic materials by author, title (italicized or underlined), pinpoint reference (if appropriate), edition (if any), publisher, and year.
	• Example: Joshua Dressler, <u>Understanding Criminal Law</u> §10.04 (3d ed., Lexis 2001).
	• When citing a publication for the first time, give the author's full name as it appears on the publication. However, do not include designations indicating academic degrees such as "Dr."
	• For works with two authors, give their names in the order in which they are listed on the title page, separated by "&" (Rule 22.1(a)(2)(a) and Rule 22.1(a)(2)(b)).
	• Give the full name of the editor in a parenthetical as it appears in the publication. In the same parenthetical, after the full name of the editor, indicate the editor's title with "ed.," the name of the publisher (if other than the original publisher), and the year of publication (Rule 22.1(d)).
	• For specifics on works with translators, refer to Rule 22.1(e).
	• For works that have been published in only one edition, give the year of publication in parentheses (Rule 22.1(j)).
	• For works that have been published in multiple editions, cite the latest edition (Rule 22.1(f)(3)).
Rule 22.2: Short Citation Format for Works Other Than Those in a Collection	If <u>id.</u> is appropriate, use it as the preferred short citation for books. If <u>id.</u> is not appropriate, the format of the short citation varies.
	• Example (document without footnotes): Dressler, <u>Understanding Criminal Law</u>, at § 12.08.
	• Example (document with footnotes): Dressler, <u>supra</u> n. [note number], at § 12.08.

ALWD Periodicals (Rule 23)

ALWD RULE	KEY POINTS
Rule 23.1: Full Citation Format	• Cite to articles in law reviews, journals, newspapers, magazines, and other periodicals by author, title (italicized or underlined), volume number (if any), periodical abbreviation, first page, pinpoint reference (if appropriate), and date. Use Appendix 5 to abbreviate periodical names and to determine whether the journal you are citing is consecutively or nonconsecutively paginated.
	• Example (consecutively paginated periodical): Howard F. Chang, <u>Risk Regulation, Endogenous Public Concerns, and the Hormones Dispute: Nothing to Fear but Fear Itself?</u> 77 S. Cal. L. Rev. 743, 751 (2004).
	• Example (nonconsecutively paginated periodical): Linda Buckley, <u>A Hole in the Safety Net</u>, Newsweek 40 (May 13, 2002).

Rule 23.2: Short Citation Format	If id. is appropriate, use it as the preferred short citation for periodicals. If id. is not appropriate, the format of the short citation varies. • Example (document without footnotes): Chang, 77 S. Cal. L. Rev. at 752. • Example (document with footnotes): Chang, supra n. [note number], at 752.

ALWD Electronic Media (Rules 12, 14, and Part 4)

Rule 12.12: Cases Published Only on LexisNexis or Westlaw	Include the case name (italicized or underlined), the database identifier, the name of the database (either LEXIS or WL) plus a unique document number, and a parenthetical containing the court abbreviation and a full date. • Example: Goodyear Tire & Rubber Co. v. Moore, 2005 WL 1611323 (Va. App. July 12, 2005). Rule 12.12(d) explains how to format a docket number and when and how to include a docket number in a case citation. See below under "Rule 4" for information on citing Westlaw and Lexis formats, web sites, emails, CD-ROMs, and E-Readers.
Rule 14.5: Statutes Available on Electronic Databases	Cite statutes according to Rules 14.2 and 14.4. In addition, include in the date parenthetical the name of the database provider and information about the currency of the database. • Example: Ga. Code Ann. § 7-1-841 (Westlaw current through 2004 1st Spec. Sess.).
Part 4: Electronic Sources Rule 38: General Information About Online and Electronic Citation Formats	Cite only to print sources unless the material would be difficult for most readers to find or the source is more widely available in electronic form. In that case, include the electronic source information in a parenthetical. If a source is available in print, you may add a parenthetical with the electronic cite if it will help the reader access the source more easily. • Example: U.S. Census Bureau, Statistical Abstract of the United States 119 (121st ed. 2001) (available at http://www.census.gov/prod/2002pubs/01statab/stat-ab01.html).
Rule 39: Addresses Citation formats for documents found on commercial electronic databases such as LexisNexis or Westlaw.	• Unreported cases that are available on widely used electronic database such as LexisNexis or Westlaw can be cited to that database according to Rule 12.3. • If citing to a specific page of an opinion, place "at" after the database identifier and indicate the page number preceded by an asterisk. See Rule 12.12(b). • Cite statutes according to Rules 14.2 and 14.4. In addition, include in the date parenthetical the name of the database provider and information about the currency of the database (Rule 14.5).
Rules 38-42	For more about citing electronic sources, see Rules 38 through 42, which cover Westlaw and Lexis formats, web sites, email, CD-ROMs, and E-Readers.

III. STUDY AIDS—ALWD CITATION

A. *ALWD Quick References and Checklists*

📓 1. ALWD in General: Quick Reference

To use ALWD effectively, you should understand the following:

- The purpose of citation
- The design, layout, and basic citation rules of ALWD
- Some often-used rules of ALWD

Purpose of Citation

The purpose of citation is to allow lawyers to easily find and reference legal sources.

Design, Layout, and Basic ALWD Citation Rules

- ALWD citation formats are the same for scholarly writing and legal documents.
- ALWD layout:
  - Part 1—Introductory Material
  - Part 2—Citation Basics
  - Part 3—Citing Specific Print Sources
  - "Fast Formats"—examples of citations for commonly used sources
  - Part 4—Electronic Sources
  - Part 5—Incorporating Citations into Documents
  - Part 6—Quotations
  - Part 7—Appendices
  - Detailed table of contents and an index
  - Green triangles (▲) designate spaces in citation formats.
  - Green circles (●) separate components of citations.
  - "Fast Format Locator" on inside front cover gives page numbers for Fast Format tables.
  - "Short Citation Locator for Commonly Used Sources" on inside back cover lists rule numbers for short citation formats.
- Basic ALWD Citation Rules
  - Legal and Other Periodicals: Rule 23

Often-Used Citation Rules in ALWD

- Typefaces: Rule 1
- Spelling and Capitalization: Rule 3
- Basic Structure and Signals: Rules 10, 43, and 44
- Subdivisions and Pinpoint Cites: Rules 5, 6, 7
- Short Citations: Rule 11
- Abbreviations: Rule 2

- Statutes: Rule 14
- Administrative and Executive Materials: Rule 19, Appendix 7C
- Books, Treaties, and Other Nonperiodic Materials: Rule 22
- Legal and Other Periodicals: Rule 23
- Electronic Media: Rules 12, 14, and Part 4

 ## 2.   ALWD Typeface Conventions: Checklist

✓ Rule 1 addresses typeface conventions for court documents. In court documents, underline (or italicize) the following:
  - Introductory signals
  - Internal cross-references
  - Case names, in both full and short citation formats
  - Phrases indicating subsequent or prior history
  - Titles of most documents
  - Topics or titles in legal encyclopedia entries
  - Names of Internet sites
  - The short forms <u>id.</u> and <u>supra</u>

✓ Note that citations in law journals and book publishers that do not use the ALWD Citation Manual have different typeface conventions.

 ## 3.   Basic Structures and Signals for ALWD Citations: Checklist

✓ Internal Cross-References: See Rule 10. Internal cross-references may be used to reference text, footnotes, appendices, or any other internal material to avoid repeating text or to help readers. They may not be used to reference outside sources that have been cited elsewhere in the document. For those, use the appropriate short citation forms (see Rule 11). Use <u>supra.</u> to refer to material that appears earlier in the document and <u>infra.</u> to refer to material that appears later in the document.

✓ Citation Placement and Use and Placement Options: See Rule 43. When a source relates to the whole sentence in the text, include the citation to that source in a separate citation sentence, beginning with a capital letter and ending with a period. When a source relates to only part of a sentence in the text, include the citation as a clause within the sentence, immediately after the text it concerns, and set the clause off with commas.

✓ Frequency of Citation: See Rule 43.2. Include a citation immediately after any sentence or portion thereof that contains a legal principle, legal authority, or thoughts borrowed from other sources.

✓ Categories of Signals: See Rule 44.3
  - Signals that show support: <u>See</u>, <u>Accord</u>, <u>See also</u>, <u>Cf.</u>
  - Signal that draws a comparison: <u>Compare</u> ... <u>with</u> ...
  - Signals that indicate contradiction: <u>Contra</u>, <u>But see</u>, <u>But cf.</u>

- Signal that indicates background material: <u>See generally</u>
- Signal that indicates an example: <u>E.g.</u>

✓ Order of Signals: See Rule 44.8. Signals of the same basic type are strung together within one citation sentence and are separated from each other by semicolons. If there are signals of different types then they must be grouped in separate citation sentences. Follow order in Rule 44.3 (Support, Comparison, Contradiction, and Background).

✓ Order of Authorities Within Each Signal: See Rule 45 generally for more details within each category. Constitutions; statutes; rules of evidence and procedure; treaties and international agreements; cases; case-related material; administrative and executive material; materials from intergovernmental organizations.

✓ Parenthetical Information explains the relevance of a particular authority to proposition given in the text. See Rule 46.

- Explanatory parenthetical phrases that do not directly quote the authority usually begin with a present participle and usually do not begin with a capital letter.
- If the parenthetical information includes one or more full sentences, it should start with a capital letter and end with the correct punctuation.
- Explanatory parenthetical phrases come before any citations concerning subsequent history or other related authority.

4.   ALWD Citation Signals: Checklist

Signals in Text	Proposition	Cited Authority and Meaning
SUPPORT		
[No signal]		Directly states, identifies, or <u>supports</u> the proposition.
<u>See</u>; <u>see also</u>		Clearly supports; contains dicta that supports the proposition.
<u>Cf.</u>		Analogous proposition.
<u>E.g.</u>; <u>see, e.g.</u>,		Multiple authorities clearly <u>state</u> the proposition.
CONTRADICTION		
<u>Contra</u>		Directly <u>states</u> contrary proposition.
BACKGROUND		
<u>See generally</u>		Helpful, related background material.
COMPARISON		
<u>Compare</u> … <u>with</u> …		Comparison of cited authorities supports proposition.

5. ALWD Rules for Citing Subdivisions and Pinpoint Cites: Checklist

✓ Rule 5.2 addresses the proper format for citations to specific page numbers:

    a. Give page number or numbers before the date parenthetical, without any introductory abbreviation.

    b. Use ", at" if a pinpoint page might be confused with the title.

    c. If you are referring specifically to material on the first page of a source, repeat the page number.

    d. When citing material within a concurring or dissenting opinion, give only the initial page of the case and the page on which the specific material appears. See Rule 12.5(d).

    e. When citing material that spans more than one page, give the inclusive page numbers separated by the en dash (–) or the word "to." See Rule 5.3.

    f. Cite nonconsecutive pages by giving the individual page numbers separated by a comma and a space (Rule 5.4).

---

 6. ALWD Rules for Short Form Citations: Checklist

✓ According to Rule 11.2(a), once you have provided one full citation to an authority, you are free to use a "short form" in later citations to the same authority. Use a short citation when:

- it will be clear to the reader from the short form what is being referenced,
- the earlier full citation falls in the same general discussion, and
- the reader will have little more trouble quickly locating the full citation. General rule: Avoid confusion.

✓ For short form citations to cases, refer to Rule 12.20. Use first party's name, the volume number, reporter designation, and page number.

- Example: Youngstown, 343 U.S. at 585.
- Party Name: When using only one party name in a short form citation, use the name of the first party, unless that party is a geographical or governmental unit or other common litigant.

✓ Rule 14.6 gives the short form citation rules for federal and state statutes.

✓ Id.: Use to refer to the immediately preceding authority (Rule 11.3).

- The "i" in "id." is capitalized only when it begins a citation sentence.
- To refer to a different page within the immediately preceding authority, add "at" and the new pinpoint cite.
- Id. may be used only when the preceding citation cites to only one source.

✓ Supra: See Rule 11.4. Once a work in a periodical, book, legislative hearing, report, unpublished work, or nonprint resource has been fully cited, use "id." to refer to material cited in the immediately preceding citation. Otherwise, use <u>supra</u> for legislative hearings, reports, unpublished materials, nonprint resources, periodicals, regulations, etc. that have previously been cited fully. <u>Supra</u> form generally consists of the last name of the author of the work (or the title if the author is not available), followed by a comma and the word "<u>supra</u> n.", the note number, "at" and the page number. (Rule 11.4(c)).

- Example: Reich, <u>supra</u> n. 18, at 6.

---

 7. ALWD Abbreviations: Checklist

✓ Rule 2.1 is the general rule on abbreviations. Appendices at the end of ALWD contain lists of specific abbreviations:
  - General Abbreviations: Appendix 3
  - Court Abbreviations: Appendix 4
  - Abbreviations for Legal Periodicals: Appendix 5
✓ Spacing: Generally, close up adjacent single capitals (e.g., N.W.), but do not close up single capitals with longer abbreviations (e.g., D. Mass.). See Rule 2.2.

---

 8. ALWD Rules for Citing Cases: Checklist

✓ According to Rule 12.1, the general citation form for cases includes: Case Name, reporter volume number + reporter abbreviations + first page of case, page # (deciding court + date of decision).
✓ Case Names: Rule 12.2
  a. For case names that appear in textual sentences, refer to Rule 12.2:
    - Italicize or underline the case name (Rule 12.2(a)), but not the comma following it.
    - If a caption on a case lists more than one case, cite only the first case listed. If a single case has two different names, use the one listed first (Rule 12.2(b)). Bankruptcy cases with two names follow Rule 12.2(p)(2).
    - Cite only the first-listed party on each side of the case, and do not use "et al." or other terms to denote any omitted parties (Rule 12.2(c)). If the party is an individual, use only the last name (Rule 12.2(d)). If the party is an organization, include the organization's full name, but omit abbreviations such as "d/b/a" and any material following (Rule 12.2(e)). Usually omit "The" when it appears as the first word in a party's name (Rule 12.2(e) and Rule 12.2(q)).
    - Use the abbreviations listed in Appendix 3 to abbreviate listed words in case names pursuant to Rule 12.2(e)(3), unless doing so would create confusion for the reader.
    - Omit "State of," "Commonwealth of," and "People of" unless citing decisions of the courts of that state, in which case only

"State," "Commonwealth," or "People" should be retained. See Rule 12.2(h)(1).

- Generally, omit given names or initials of individuals, but not in names or businesses of firms. See Rule 12.2(e)(2).
- Omit business firm designations such as "Inc." if the name of the firm also contains a word that clearly indicates its status as a business firm, such as "Ass'n." See Rule 12.2(e)(8).

b. For case names that appear in citations, refer to Rule 12. Note that case names in citations generally follow the rules in Rule 12.2, with the following modification:

- You may abbreviate any word in a party's name and any state, country, and geographic unit that appear in Appendix 3.

✓ Reporters: See Rule 12.3, 12.4, Chart 12.1, Appendix 1 and Appendix 2. Include the volume number of the reporter, followed by the abbreviated name of the reporter as found in Chart 12.1 and Appendix 1.

✓ Appropriate short form citations for cases are listed in Rule 12.20.

 ## 9. ALWD Rules for Citing Constitutions: Checklist

✓ Abbreviate United States (U.S.) if referring to the federal Constitution, or refer to Appendix 3A for the appropriate abbreviation if citing a state constitution (Rule 13.2(a)).

✓ Abbreviate "Constitution" as "Const." (Rule 13.2(a)).

✓ Refer to Appendix 3C for the appropriate abbreviations of article (art.), amendment (amend.), section (§), and clause (cl.).

✓ If the constitutional provision has been repealed, amended, or superseded, refer to Rule 13.3 for the appropriate citation format.

✓ Id. is the only acceptable format for short citations to constitutions (Rule 13.4).

 ## 10. ALWD Rules for Citing Statutes: Checklist

✓ Cite to the official federal and state codes whenever possible. The official federal code is the United States Code, "U.S.C." To determine the official code for a particular state, see Appendix 1 (Rule 14.1).

✓ Make sure that the abbreviations of code names are properly formatted. There should be periods and no spaces between the letters "U.S.C." See Appendix 1 to determine the proper abbreviation formats for state codes.

✓ Use "§" to denote the section number of the code that you are citing. Leave a space between "§" and the section number, and use "§§" if you are citing multiple sections (Rule 14.2(c)).

✓ Include the date of the code edition cited in a parenthetical following the section number (Rules 14.2(f)(1) and 14.2(f)(2)). If citing to a code that is published, edited, or compiled by someone other than state officials, give the name of the publisher, editor, or compiler in the parenthetical phrase (Rule 14.2(e)). For example: (West 2006).

✓ According to Rule 14.2(g), if the statute is commonly cited using a different name or is known by a popular name, give that name and the original section number preceding the normal citation format.

✓ If a statute appears in a supplement or pocket part, cite the statute according to Rule 8.1.

✓ If a statute has been invalidated, repealed, or amended, cite it in accordance with Rule 14.3. When citing a current version of a statute that has prior history, you may give the prior history in an explanatory parenthetical phrase according to Rule 14.2(h) and Rule 14.7(i).

✓ If a statute is previously cited, you may use a short form of the statute according to Rule 14.6. Use <u>id.</u>, if appropriate.

 ## 11. ALWD Citations for Administrative and Executive Materials: Checklist

✓ Whenever possible, cite all federal rules and regulations to the Code of Federal Regulations (C.F.R.) by title, section or part, and year using the format specified in Rule 19.

    a. Be sure to cite the most recent edition of C.F.R., according to Rule 19.1(d).

    b. Do not leave spaces between the letters of "C.F.R."

✓ According to Rule 19.3, if a rule or regulation has not yet been published in C.F.R., cite to the Federal Register. Administrative notices should also be cited to the Federal Register.

✓ To use a short citation to identify a rule or regulation, use one of the formats listed in Rule 19.2 for C.F.R. or Rule 19.4 for Federal Register.

✓ Cite to arbitrations and administrative adjudications using Rule 19.5.

✓ Advisory opinions from the United States Attorney General or Office of Legal Counsel are cited according to Rule 19.7 (full citation format) and Rule 19.8 (short citation format).

✓ See Appendix 7(C) for help in citing Treasury regulations and other federal taxation materials.

✓ Presidential executive orders are found in title 3 of C.F.R. and should be cited to C.F.R. according to Rule 19.9, with a parallel citation to the United States Code if therein. However, if an executive order is not found in C.F.R., cite according to the Federal Register. Examples of each citation format can be found in Rule 19.9.

✓ Patents should be cited according to the patent number and the date the patent was filed, using the format specified in Rule 19.13.

---

12. ALWD Citations for Books, Reports, and Other Nonperiodic Materials: Checklist

✓ According to Rule 22.1(a), when citing a publication for the first time, give the author's full name as it appears on the publication. However, do not include designations indicating academic degrees such as "Dr." For works with two authors, give their names in the order in which they are listed on the title page, separated by "&" (Rule 22.1(a)(2)(a) and Rule 22.1(a)(2)(b)).

✓ Rule 22.1(d) specifies the format for works with editors and Rule 22.1(e) specifies the format for works with translators. Give the full name of the editor in a parenthetical as it appears in the publication. In the same parenthetical, after the full name of the editor, indicate the editor's title with "ed.," the name of the publisher (if other than the original publisher), and the year of publication.

✓ For works that have been published in only one edition, give the year of publication in parentheses (Rule 22.1(j)). For works that have been published in multiple editions, cite the latest edition according to Rule 22.1(f)(3)).

 ## 13. ALWD Rules for Citing Periodical Materials: Checklist

✓ For consecutively paginated articles in law reviews, journals, newspapers, magazines, and other periodicals (Rule 23.1):
  a. Cite the author's full name as it appears in the publication according to Rule 22.1(a).
  b. Cite the full title of the article according to Rule 23.1(b).
  c. Cite the volume number, followed by the abbreviation for the periodical according to Appendix 5, and the page number on which the cited material begins.
  d. Indicate the date of publication in a parenthetical.
  e. If the piece you are citing is student-written, follow Rule 23.1(a)(2) and consult Sidebar 23.1.
  f. For book reviews reference Rule 23.1(b)(2).

 ## 14. ALWD Rules for Citing Electronic Media: Checklist

✓ Rule 39 addresses citation formats for documents found on commercial electronic databases such as LexisNexis or Westlaw.
  a. Unreported cases that are available on a widely used electronic database such as LexisNexis or Westlaw can be cited to that database according to Rule 12.13.

b. If citing to a specific page of an opinion, place "at" after the database identifier and indicate the page number preceded by an asterisk. See Rule 12.12(b).

c. Cite statutes according to Rules 14.2 and 14.4. In addition, include in the date parenthetical the name of the database provider and information about the currency of the database (Rule 14.5).

✓ Cite only to print sources unless the material would be difficult for most readers to find or the source is more widely available in electronic form. In that case, include the electronic source information in a parenthetical (Rule 38).

a. See Rule 40.1(d) for URL citation formats.

b. Personal e-mail correspondence may be cited according to Rule 32, but insert the designation "Email from" (Rule 41.1(a)). The e-mail addresses of the sender and recipient of the e-mail are not required. Include information that will assist the reader in finding a copy of the message (Rule 41.1(d)).

B. ALWD Quizzes

🗄? 1. ALWD Typeface Conventions: Quiz

Assume the following citations appear in court documents.

1. Choose the correct citation for Missouri v. Holland.

   A. <u>Missouri v. Holland, 252 U.S. 416</u> (1922).
   B. <u>Missouri v. Holland</u>, 252 U.S. 416 (1922).
   C. <u>Missouri v. Holland,</u> 252 U.S. 416 (1922).
   D. Missouri v. Holland, 252 U.S. 416 (1922).

2. Which citation does NOT have an error?

   A. See <u>Brown v. Board of Education</u>, 347 U.S. 438 (1954).
   B. <u>Brown</u>, 347 U.S. at 440.
   C. <u>Clark v. Davis,</u> 533 U.S. 678, 719 (2001) (citing <u>Evanson v. United States,</u> 345 U.S. 206 (1953)).
   D. Matt Corney, Red House (Oxford ed., Penguin Books 1979) (1899).

3. Which citation does NOT have an error?

   A. See <u>id.</u> at 348.
   B. <u>Id. at 348.</u>
   C. See <u>id.</u> at 348.
   D. See <u>id.</u> at 348.

4. Which citation does NOT have an error?

   A. Gretel C. Kovach, Use of False Hiring Data Found in Dallas Schools, N.Y. Times, Nov. 15, 2 A10.

   B. Greg Gelpi, Attorney Still Loves Fighting for Little Guys, Augusta Chron., Dec. 8, 2008, at B.

   C. David Rudovsky, Police Abuse: Can the Violence Be Contained?, 27 Harv. C.R.-C.L. L. Rev 500 (1992).

   D. Andrew Rosenthal, Medicine and the Law, N.Y. Times A1 (June 15, 1990).

5. Which citation does NOT have an error?

   A. Sciolino v. City of Newport News, 480 F.3d 642, 647 (4th Cir. 2007) (Wilkinson, J., dissenting.

   B. Id. at 735.

   C. Codd v. Velger, 429 U.S. 624, 627 (1977).

   D. U.S. Const. amend XIV, § 1.

Answer Key on page 528

2. Basic Structure and Signals for ALWD Citations: Quiz

Assume the following citations appear in court documents.

1. Choose the string citation without an error.

   A. See Edwards v. Arizona, 451 U.S. 477 (1981). But see Berkemer v. MacCarty, 468 U.S. 420 Compare Orozco v. Texas, 394 U.S. 324 (1969).

   B. See Edwards v. Arizona, 451 U.S. 477 (1981); but see Berkemer v. McCarty, 468 U.S. 420 (1984).

   C. Edwards v. Arizona, 451 U.S. 466 (1981). See Berkemer v. McCarty, 468 U.S. 420 (1984).

   D. See Edwards v. Arizona, 451 U.S. 477 (1981); But see Berkemer v. MacCarty, 468 U.S. 420 (1984).

2. Choose the string citation without an error.

   A. See Edwards v. Arizona, 451 U.S. 477 (1981); State v. Bradshaw, 457 S.E.2d 456 (W. Va. 2 Orozco v. Texas, 394 U.S. 324 (1969).

   B. See Edwards v. Arizona, 451 U.S. 477 (1981); Orozco v. Texas, 394 U.S. 324 (1969).

   C. See State v. Bradshaw, 457 S.E.2d 456 (W. Va. 1995); State v. Singleton, 624 S.E.2d 527 (2005).

   D. See Edwards v. Arizona, 451 U.S. 477 (1981); U.S. Const. amend V.

3. Choose the string citation without an error.

   A. See Greg Gelpi, Attorney Still Loves Fighting for Little Guys, Augusta Chron., Dec. 8, 2008, a Swilley v. Alexander, 629 F.2d 1018, 1020 (5th Cir. 1980).

B. See 42 U.S.C.A. § 1983 (2009); <u>Swilley v. Alexander</u>, 629 F.2d 1018, 1020 (5th Cir. 1980).

C. See 42 U.S.C.A. § 1983 (2009); U.S. Const. amend XIV, § 1.

D. See <u>Cox v. Roskelley</u>, 359 F.3d 1105, 1110 (9th Cir. 2002); <u>Codd v. Velger</u>, 429 U.S. 624, 62 (1977).

4. Choose the citation without an error.

A. <u>Cox v. Roskelley</u>, 359 F.3d 1105, 1110 (9th Cir. 2002) (holding once stigmatizing information placed into Cox's personnel file, it became public record under Washington law).

B. ("Nor shall any State deprive person of life, liberty, or property, without due process of the law Const. amend XIV, §1.

C. Gretel C. Kovach, <u>Use of False Hiring Data Found in Dallas Schools</u> (newspaper ran article after obtaining report, marked highly confidential, through a records request), N.Y. Times, Nov. 15, A10.

D. U.S. Const. ("Nor shall any State deprive person of life, liberty, or property, without due process law") amend XIV, § 1.

5. Choose the string citation without an error.

A. <u>See also</u> <u>Miranda v. Arizona</u>, 384 U.S. 436 (1966); <u>see</u> <u>Edwards v. Arizona</u>, 451 U.S. 477 (1981).

B. <u>See</u> S.C. Const. art. I, § 12; U.S. Const. art. IV, § 1.

C. <u>See</u> <u>Miranda v. Arizona</u>, 384 U.S. 436 (1966); <u>see</u> <u>Edwards v. Arizona</u>, 451 U.S. 477 (1981)

D. <u>See</u> <u>State v. Jameson</u>, 461 S.E.2d 67 (W. Va. 1995); <u>but see</u> <u>State v. Green</u>, 260 S.E.2d 257 (W. Va. 1979).

Answer Key on page 528

⚇? 3. ALWD Citation Signals: Quiz

You are researching a state water quality issue for a partner at your firm, and you have uncovered a number of authorities that support, contradict, or supplement the following excerpt from a Maryland statute: Factories may not dispose of hazardous materials in the Chesapeake Bay. What signal would you use to best cite each authority described below?

1. A case decided by the Maryland Court of Appeals (the highest court in Maryland) that holds that factories cannot dispose of hazardous materials in Maryland rivers.

A. No signal

B. <u>But see</u>

C. <u>See e.g.</u>

D. <u>Cf.</u>

E. <u>Contra</u>

2. A law review article that discusses hazardous waste disposal laws in several states on the eastern seaboard, including Maryland.

    A. No signal
    B. See generally
    C. See
    D. Cf.
    E. Contra

3. A Delaware statute that prohibits dumping of hazardous materials in the Chesapeake Bay.

    A. No signal
    B. See generally
    C. Accord
    D. Cf.
    E. See

4. One of several Maryland cases holding that factories may not dispose of hazardous waste in Maryland waters.

    A. No signal
    B. See e.g.
    C. See
    D. See generally
    E. Compare … with …

5. A Maryland Court of Appeals case holding that factories may not dispose of hazardous materials in the Chesapeake Bay.

    A. No signal
    B. See
    C. But see
    D. Contra
    E. Cf.

6. A Maryland Court of Appeals case holding that no individual or organization may dispose of polluting materials in the bays or other marshland areas of the state of Maryland.

    A. No signal
    B. Cf.
    C. See
    D. But see
    E. See e.g.

Answer Key on page 529

⚷? 4.   ALWD Order and Punctuation of Signals and Citations: Quiz

1. Select the correct citation sentence.

   A. See Matthews v. Potter, 19 P.2d 368 (Cal. 1999). See also Morrison v. Perkins, 56 P.2d 247 (Cal. 2000). But see Smith v. Jennings, 85 P.2d 465 (Cal. 2001).

   B. See Matthews v. Potter, 19 P.2d 368 (Cal. 1999); see also Morrison v. Perkins, 56 P.2d 247 (Cal. 2000); but see Smith v. Jennings, 85 P.2d 465 (Cal. 2001).

   C. See also Morrison v. Perkins, 56 P.2d 247 (Cal. 2000); see Matthews v. Potter, 19 P.2d 368 (Cal. 1999). But see Smith v. Jennings, 85 P.2d 465 (Cal. 2001).

   D. See Matthews v. Potter, 19 P.2d 368 (Cal. 1999); see also Morrison v. Perkins, 56 P.2d 247 (Cal. 2000). But see Smith v. Jennings, 85 P.2d 465 (Cal. 2001).

2. Which of the following is the correct order and punctuation of signals when more than one signal is used?

   A. See; cf.; but see; see generally.
   B. See; cf. But see. See generally.
   C. See. But see. Cf. See generally.
   D. See; cf. But see; see generally.
   E. See. Cf. But see. See generally.

3. A partner at your firm has asked you to revise a draft office memorandum containing the following sentence: See e.g. 18 U.S.C. § 588 (1998); 13 U.S.C. § 12 (1994); Lineman v. Fawcett, 689 U.S. 214 (1991); Hingel v. Brown, 855 U.S. 114 (1987); Smith v. Tenorman, 255 F.2d 2087 (2d Cir. 1997), aff'd, 225 U.S. 3 (1999); Dohr v. Abrams, 255 F. Supp. 2d 651 (D.D.C. 1989); Masters v. Perlman, 23 F.3d 785 (7th Cir. 1986). How would you revise this citation sentence?

   A. The ordering of citations is correct; no changes are necessary.
   B. The citations should be in the following order: See e.g. 18 U.S.C. § 588 (1998); 13 U.S.C. § 12 (1994); Lineman; Smith; Hingel; Masters; Dohr.
   C. The citations should be in the following order: See e.g.13 U.S.C. § 12 (1994); 18 U.S.C. § 588 (1998); Lineman; Hingel; Smith; Masters; Dohr.
   D. The citations should be in the following order: See e.g. 18 U.S.C. § 588 (1998); 13 U.S.C. § 12 (1994); Lineman; Hingel; Dohr; Masters; Smith.
   E. The citations should be in the following order: See e.g. 18 U.S.C. § 588 (1998); 13 U.S.C. § 12 (1994); Lineman; Hingel; Masters; Smith; Dohr.

Answer Key on page 529

8? 5. ALWD Rules for Citing Subdivisions and Pinpoint Cites: Quiz

Assume the following citations appear in court documents.

1. Choose the correct citation for information on page 347 of <u>Beckwith v. United States</u>.

    A. <u>Beckwith v. United States</u>, 425 U.S. 341, 347 (1976).
    B. <u>Beckwith v. United States</u>, 425 U.S. 341, at 347 (1976).
    C. <u>Beckwith v. United States</u>, 425 U.S. 341, p. 347 (1976).
    D. <u>Beckwith v. United States</u>, 425 U.S. 341-47 (1976).

2. Choose the citation without an error.

    A. Christina M. Fernandez, <u>A Case-by-Case Approach to Pleading Scienter Under the Private Securities Litigation Reform Act of 1995</u>, 97 Mich. L. Rev. 2265, p. 2271 (1978).
    B. <u>Sciolino v. City of Newport News</u>, 480 F.3d 642 (4th Cir. 2007) (Wilkinson, J., dissenting, 654).
    C. <u>State v. Bradshaw</u>, 457 S.E.2d 456, 457, 459 (W. Va. 1995).
    D. <u>Codd v. Velger</u>, 429 U.S. 624 to 626 (1977).

3. Choose the citation without an error.

    A. 459 <u>State v. Bradshaw</u>, 457 S.E.2d 456 (W. Va. 1995).
    B. <u>Miranda v. Arizona</u>, 384 U.S. 436, 440 (1966).
    C. <u>Bishop v. Wood</u>, 426 U.S. 341 (1976) ("Fourteenth Amendment is not a guarantee against incorrect or ill-advised personnel decisions") 349.
    D. <u>State v. Mullens</u>, 172, 650 S.E.2d 169 (W. Va. 2007).

4. Choose the correct citation for information on page 2082 of the Michigan Law Review.

    A. Kim Scheppele, <u>Foreword: Telling Stories</u>, 87 Mich. L. Rev. 2073 (1989), 2082.
    B. Kim Scheppele, <u>Foreword: Telling Stories</u>, 2082, 87 Mich. L. Rev. 2073 (1989).
    C. Kim Scheppele, <u>Foreword: Telling Stories</u>, 87 Mich. L. Rev. 2073, 2082 (1989).
    D. Kim Scheppele, <u>Foreword: Telling Stories</u>, 87 Mich. L. Rev. 2073 at 2082 (1989).

5. Choose the correct citation for information on pages 479, 481, 485 in <u>Edwards v. Arizona</u>.

    A. <u>Edwards v. Arizona</u>, 451 U.S. 477, 479, 481, and 485 (1981).
    B. <u>Edwards v. Arizona</u>, 451 U.S. 477-85 (1981).
    C. <u>Edwards v. Arizona</u>, 451 U.S. 477 (1981) 479, 481, 485.
    D. <u>Edwards v. Arizona</u>, 451 U.S. 477, 479, 481, 485 (1981).

Answer Key on page 529

8? 6.   ALWD Rules for Short Form Citations: Quiz

Assume the following citations appear in court documents.

1. Choose the correct short citation for <u>Orozco v. Texas</u>, 394 U.S. 324, 327 (1969), if it is the only source in immediately preceding citation and cited page 327.

    A. <u>Id.</u>
    B. <u>Orozco v. Texas</u>, at 327.
    C. <u>Id.</u> at 327.
    D. <u>Orozco</u>, at 327.

2. Choose the correct short citation for <u>Orozco v. Texas</u>, 394 U.S. 324, 327 (1969), if the same cite was used three citations earlier.

    A. <u>Orozco v. Texas</u>, 394 U.S. at 327
    B. <u>Orozco</u>, 394 U.S. 324, 327.
    C. <u>Id.</u> at 327.
    D. <u>Orozco</u>, 394 U.S. at 327.

3. Choose the correct short citation for <u>Sciolino v. City of Newport News</u>, 480 F.3d 642, 654 (4th Cir. 2007), Judge Wilkinson's dissenting opinion, if the previous citation is from the same case but cites the majority.

    A. <u>Id.</u> at 654 (Wilkinson, J., dissenting).
    B. <u>Sciolino v. City of Newport News</u>, 480 F.3d 642, 654 (4th Cir. 2007) (Wilkinson, J., dissenting).
    C. Sciolino, 480 F.3d 642 at 654 (Wilkinson, J., dissenting).
    D. <u>Id.</u> (Wilkinson, J., dissenting) at 654.

4. Choose the correct short citation for 30 U.S.C. § 1330(a)(1) (2000) if the previous citation is 30 U.S.C. § 1331 (2000).

    A. 30 U.S.C. § 1330(a)(1) (2000).
    B. <u>Id.</u> (a)(1).
    C. <u>Id.</u> § 1330(a)(1).
    D. <u>Id.</u> at § 1330(a)(1).

5. Choose the correct short citation for Katherine Crytzer, You're Fired! Bishop v. Wood: When Does a Letter in Former Public Employee's Personnel File Deny a Due Process Liberty Right?, 16 Geo. Mason L. Rev. 447, 450 (2009), if it was used three citations earlier.

    A. Crytzer, <u>You're Fired!</u>, at 450.
    B. Crytzer, <u>supra</u>, at 450.
    C. Crytzer, 16 Geo. Mason L. Rev at 450.
    D. <u>Id.</u> at 450.

6. Choose the correct short citation for Deborah L. Rhode, <u>Justice and Gender</u> 56, 70-71 (Harv. U. Press 1989), if the immediately preceding cite is for the same source on page 60.

    A. <u>Id.</u> at 70-71.
    B. Rhode, <u>id.</u> at 70-71.
    C. Rhode, <u>Justice and Gender</u>, at 70-71.
    D. Rhode, <u>supra</u>, at 70-71.

7. Choose the correct short citation for <u>Orozco v. Texas</u>, 394 U.S. 324, 327 (1969), if it is one of three sources in the immediately preceding citation and cited on page 329.

    A. <u>Id.</u> at 327.
    B. <u>Orozco v. Texas</u>, at 327.
    C. <u>Id.</u> 394 U.S. 324, 327.
    D. <u>Orozco</u>, 394 U.S. at 327.

Answer Key on page 529

?? 7. ALWD Abbreviations: Quiz

Assume the following citations appear in court documents.

1. The following case appears in a textual sentence. Choose the answer that abbreviates the case name correctly.

    A. <u>NLRB v. General Hospital, Inc.</u>, 61 U.S. 3 (1951).
    B. <u>NLRB v. General Hosp., Inc.</u>, 61 U.S. 3 (1951).
    C. <u>N.L.R.B. v. General Hospital, Inc.</u>, 61 U.S. 3 (1951).
    D. <u>NLRB v. General Hospital, Incorporated</u>, 61 U.S. 3 (1951).

2. The following Ninth Circuit Court case appears in a citation sentence. Choose the answer that abbreviates the case name correctly.

    A. <u>Sunnyside Memorial School v. County Housing Department</u>, 537 F.2d 361, 366 (9th Cir. 1976).
    B. <u>Sunnyside Mem'l. Sch. v. County Hous. Dep't.</u>, 537 F.2d 361, 366 (9th Cir. 1976).
    C. <u>Sunnyside Meml Sch. v. County Hous. Dept</u>, 537 F.2d 361, 366 (9th Cir. 1976).
    D. <u>Sunnyside v. Mem'l Sch. v. County Hous. Dep't</u>, 537 F.2d 361, 366 (9th Circuit 1976).
    E. Both b and c are correct.

3. Choose the correct citation for the Federal Register.

    A. Importation of Dairy Products, 60 Federal Register 50379 (Sept. 29, 1995).
    B. Importation of Dairy Products, 60 F.R. 50379 (September 29, 1995).
    C. Importation of Dairy Products, 60 Fed. Reg. 50379 (Sept. 29, 1995).

D. Importation of Dairy Products, 60 Fed.Reg 50,379 (September 29, 1995).

4. Choose the correct citation for Rule 12(b)(2) of the Federal Rules of Civil Procedure.

    A. Fed. Rule Civ. P. 12(b)(2).
    B. Fed. R. Civ. P. 12(b)(2).
    C. Fed R Civ P 12(b)(2).
    D. Federal Rule of Civil Procedure 12(b)(2).

5. Choose the correct citation for an article in the George Mason Law Review.
    A. Kathy Crytzer, <u>Meeting of the Minds</u>, 16 Geo. Mason L. Rev. 447, 450 (2000).
    B. Kathy Crytzer, <u>Meeting of the Minds</u>, 15 G.M. L. Rev. 447, 450 (2000).
    C. Kathy Crytzer, <u>Meeting of the Minds</u>, 15 Geo. Mason L.R. 447, 450 (2000).
    D. Kathy Crytzer, <u>Meeting of the Minds</u>, 16 Geo Mason L Rev 447, 450 (2000).

Answer Key on page 530

---

8. ALWD Rules for Citing Cases: Quiz

Assume the following citations appear in court documents.

1. Choose the correct citation for <u>United States v. MacDonald</u>, decided in the Fourth Circuit Court of Appeals in 1976.

    A. 531 F.2d 196, 199, <u>United States v. MacDonald</u>, (4th Cir. 1976).
    B. <u>United States v. MacDonald</u>, 531 F.2d 196, 199 (4th Cir. 1976).
    C. <u>United States v. MacDonald</u>. 531 F.2d 196. 199 (4th Cir. 1976)
    D. <u>U.S. v. MacDonald</u>, 531 F.2d 196, 199 (4th Cir. 1976).

2. Choose the correct citation for Commonwealth of Pennsylvania v. Ferrone, decided in the Pennsylvania Superior Court in 1982. (Assume this citation appears in a court document submitted to a Pennsylvania court.)

    A. <u>Commonwealth v. Ferrone</u>, 448 A.2d 637 (Pa. Super. 1982).
    B. <u>Commonwealth of Pennsylvania v. Ferrone</u>, 448 A.2d 637 (Pa. Super. Ct. 1982).
    C. <u>Commonwealth of Penn. v. Ferrone</u>, 448 A.2d 637 (Pa. Super. 1982).
    D. <u>Penn. v. Ferrone</u>, 448 A.2d 637 (Pa. Super. Ct. 1982).

3. Choose the correct citation for <u>Miranda v. Arizona</u> in the United States Reports.

    A. <u>Miranda v. Arizona</u>, 384 S. Ct. 436 (1966).
    B. <u>Miranda v. Arizona</u>, 384 U.S. 436 (S. Ct. 1966).
    C. <u>Miranda v. Arizona</u>, 384 U.S. 436 (1966).
    D. <u>Miranda v. Arizona</u>, 384 U.S. 436 (U.S. 1966).

4. Choose the correct citation for <u>Johnson v. Seiler</u> decided by the Fourth Circuit Court of Appeals and reported in the Second Edition Federal Reporter.

    A. <u>Johnson v. Seiler</u>, 225 F.2d 308 (4th Cir. 1998).

    B. <u>Johnson v. Seiler</u>, 225 F.2d 308 (4th Cir. 1998).

    C. <u>Johnson v. Seiler</u>, 225 F.2d 308 (4th Circuit 1998).

    D. <u>Johnson v. Seiler</u>, 225 S.E.2d 308 (4th Cir. 1998).

5. Choose the correct citation for Justice Scalia's dissenting opinion in Jamison v. Blueline Railroad.

    A. <u>Jamison v. Blueline R.R.</u>, 338 U.S. 25, 47 (2004) (Scalia, J., dissenting) (rejecting Court's conception of the exclusionary rule).

    B. <u>Jamison v. Blueline R.R.</u>, 338 U.S. 25, 47 (2004). (Scalia, J., dissenting) (rejecting Court's conception of the exclusionary rule).

    C. <u>Jamison v. Blueline R.R.</u>, 338 U.S. 25, 47 (2004) (rejecting Court's conception of the exclusionary rule) (Scalia, J., dissenting).

    D. Jamison v. Blueline R.R., 338 U.S. 25, 47 (2004 Scalia J., dissenting) (rejecting Court's conception of the exclusionary rule).

6. Choose the correct citation for the unreported case of <u>Chavez v. Norton</u>, available on Lexis.

    A. <u>Chavez v. Norton</u>, No. 02-3924, 2004 U.S. App. LEXIS 2598713, 220 (3d Cir. Oct. 14, 2004).

    B. <u>Chavez v. Norton</u>, No. 02-3924, No. 02-3924, 2004 U.S. App. LEXIS 2598713 at *220 (3d Cir. Oct. 14, 2004).

    C. <u>Chavez v. Norton</u>, No. 02-3924, 2004 U.S. App. LEXIS 2598713, *220 (3d Cir. Oct. 14, 2004).

    D. <u>Chavez v. Norton</u>, No. 02-3924, 2004 U.S. App. LEXIS 2598713, at *220 (3d Cir. Oct. 14, 2004).

Answer Key on page 530

☺? 9. ALWD Rules for Citing Constitutions: Quiz

Assume that the following citations appear in court documents.

1. Choose the correct citation format for the Fifth Amendment to the U.S. Constitution.

    A. U.S. Const. Amend. V.

    B. United States Constitution, amendment V.

    C. U.S. Const. amend. V.

    D. U.S. Const. amend V.

2. Which one of these citations to Article I, Section 1, of the Kansas Constitution is correct?

    A. Kan. Const. art. I, § 1.

    B. Kan. Const. art. I, sec. 1.

C.   Ka. Const. art. I, § 1,

D.   Kansas Constitution, art. 1, § 1.

3.   What is the correct short citation format for Article II of the U.S. Constitution if it was cited in the immediately preceding section?

A.   Art. II.

B.   U.S. Const. II.

C.   II.

D.   Id.

4.   Choose the correct format for citing the Eighteenth Amendment to the U.S. Constitution (repealed in 1933).

A.   U.S. Const. Amend. XVIII (repealed 1933).

B.   U.S. Const. amend. XVIII (repealed 1933).

C.   U.S. Const. amend. XVIII.

D.   U.S. Const. amend. XVIII, repealed 1933.

5.   What is the correct citation format for Article II, Section 3, of the Pennsylvania Constitution?

A.   Pa. Const. art. II, § 3.

B.   Pen. Const. art. II, § 3.

C.   Pa. Const. Art. II, § 3.

D.   Pen. Const. art 2, § 3.

Answer Key on page 531

8? 10.   ALWD Rules for Citing Statutes: Quiz

Assume that the following citations appear in court documents.

1.   In the citation 28 U.S.C. § 585 (2000), what does the "28" signify?

A.   The section number of the statute

B.   The title number of the statute in the United States Code

C.   The session of Congress that enacted the statute

D.   The number of provisions in the cited statute

2.   Choose the correct full citation for Title 42, Section 1975, of the United States Code.

A.   42 USC § 1975 (2000).

B.   42 U.S.C. § 1975.

C.   42 U.S.C. § 1975 (2000).

D.   42 U.S.C. §1975 (2000).

3. If using a short citation to refer to the statute from question 2, which one of the following options is an acceptable format?

    A. § 1975.

    B. 42 U.S.C.

    C. U.S.C. § 1975.

    D. 42.

4. Which of the following citations to the Internal Revenue Code is NOT correctly formatted?

    A. 26 U.S.C. § 153 (2000).

    B. I.R.C. § 153 (2000).

    C. 26 U.S.C. § 291 (2000).

    D. Int. Rev. Code § 291 (2000).

5. Choose the preferred citation format for the Indiana Code.

    A. Ind. Code § 3-5-1-1 (2008).

    B. Ind. Code Ann. § 3-5-1-1 (West 2006).

    C. Ind. Code Ann. § 3-5-1-1 (LexisNexis 2006).

    D. In. Code § 3-5-1-1 (2008).

6. Choose the correct citation for Federal Rule of Civil Procedure 11(a)(5).

    A. F.R.C.P. 11(a)(5).

    B. Fed R Civ P 11(a)(5).

    C. Fed. R. Civ. P. 11(a)(5).

    D. F.R.C.P. § 11(a)(5).

Answer Key on page 531

8? 11. ALWD Citations for Administrative and Executive Materials: Quiz

Assume that the following citations appear in court documents.

1. Which of the following citations to title 40, section 49.9861, of the Code of Federal Regulations is correct?

    A. 40 Code Fed. Reg. § 49.9861 (1999).

    B. 40 Code Fed. Reg. §49.9861 (1999).

    C. 40 C.F.R. § 49.9861 (1999).

    D. 40 C. F. R. § 49.9861 (1999).

2. Choose the correct short form citation to title 40, section 49.9861, of the Code of Federal Regulations.

    A. 40 C.F.R. § 49.9861 (1999)

    B. 40 C.F.R. at § 49.9861

    C. 40 C.F.R.

    D. 49.9861.

3. A rule is published on page 25684 of volume 74 of the Federal Register, but it has not yet been entered into the Code of Federal Regulations. Choose the correct citation for that rule.

    A. Airworthiness Directives, 74 Fed. Reg. 25684 (May 30, 2009) (to be codified at 14 C.F.R. pt. 39).
    B. Airworthiness Directives, 74 F.R. 25,684 (May 30, 2009) (to be codified at 14 C.F.R. pt. 39).
    C. Airworthiness Directives, 74 Fed. Reg. 25,684 (to be codified at 14 C.F.R. pt. 39).
    D. Airworthiness Directives, 74 Fed.Reg. 25684 (May 30, 2009) (to be codified at 14 C.F.R. pt. 39).

4. Which of the following citations to volume 24, page 2,834, of the Virginia Register of Regulations (dated June 9, 2008) is correct?

    A. 24 Va. Register 2,834 (June 9, 2008).
    B. 24 V.R.R. 2834 (June 9, 2008).
    C. 24 Va. Reg. Regs. 2834.
    D. 24 Va. Reg. Regs. 2,834 (June 9, 2008).

5. Choose the correct citation for a 1982 advisory opinion from the United States Attorney General, volume 43, page 369.

    A. 43 Op. Attorney General 369 (1982).
    B. 43 Op. Att'y Gen. 369 (1982).
    C. 43 Op. Att'y. Gen. 369 (1982).
    D. 43 Op. Atty. Gen. 369 (1982).

6. Presidential Executive Order 12001 is not in the Code of Federal Regulations, but it is found in volume 4, page 33709 of the Federal Register. Which of the following citations is correct?

    A. Exec. Order No. 12,001, 42 Fed. Reg. 33,709 (June 29, 1977).
    B. E.O. No. 12,001, 42 Fed. Reg. 33,709 (June 29, 1977).
    C. E.O. No. 12,001, 42 F.R. 33,709 (June 29, 1977).
    D. Exec. Or. No. 12001, 42 Fed. Reg. 33709 (June 29, 1977).

Answer Key on page 531

12. ALWD Citations for Books, Reports, and Other Nonperiodic Materials: Quiz

Assume that the following citations appear in court documents.

1. Choose the correct citation to page 171 of The Nine: Inside the Secret World of the Supreme Court, by Jeffrey Toobin.

    A. The Nine: Inside the Secret World of the Supreme Court 171 (Anchor Books, 2007) (2007) J Toobin.

    B. Toobin, J., <u>The Nine: Inside the Secret World of the Supreme Court</u> 171 (2007).

    C. Jeffrey Toobin, <u>The Nine: Inside the Secret World of the Supreme Court</u>, 171 (2007).

    D. Jeffrey Toobin, <u>The Nine: Inside the Secret World of the Supreme Court</u> 171 (Anchor Books 2007).

2. Which of the following citations to the tenth edition of <u>A History of the Modern World</u> to 1815, by R.R. Palmer, Joel Colton, and Lloyd Kramer (listed in this order on the title page), is correct?

    A. R.R. Palmer et al., <u>A History of the Modern World to 1815</u> (10th ed. McGraw-Hill, 2006).

    B. R.R. Palmer et al <u>A History of the Modern World to 1815</u> (10th ed. 2006).

    C. R.R. Palmer, Joel Colton and Lloyd Kramer, <u>A History of the Modern World to 1815</u> (10th ed.).

    D. Joel Colton, Lloyd Kramer & R.R. Palmer, <u>A History of the Modern World to 1815</u> (10th ed.).

3. Choose the correct citation to volume 2 of Michael Burlingame's <u>Abraham Lincoln: A Life</u>, published in 2008.

    A. Michael Burlingame, <u>Abraham Lincoln: A Life</u> vol. 2 (Johns Hopkins U. Press 2008).

    B. Michael Burlingame, <u>Abraham Lincoln: A Life</u> 2 (2008).

    C. 2 Michael Burlingame, <u>Abraham Lincoln: A Life</u> (Johns Hopkins U. Press 2008).

    D. Vol. 2 Michael Burlingame, <u>Abraham Lincoln: A Life</u> (2008).

4. Choose the correct citation for an originally unpublished letter from Alexander Hamilton to John Jay dated November 26, 1775, published on page 43 of <u>Alexander Hamilton: Writings</u>.

    A. Ltr. from Alexander Hamilton to John Jay (Nov. 26, 1775), in <u>Alexander Hamilton: Writings</u> 43 (2001).

    B. Letter to John Jay (Nov. 26, 1775), in <u>Alexander Hamilton: Writings</u> 43 (2001).

    C. Letter from Alexander Hamilton to John Jay (November 26, 1775), in <u>Alexander Hamilton: Writings</u> 43 (2001).

    D. Ltr. from Alexander Hamilton to John Jay (Nov. 26, 1775), in <u>Alexander Hamilton: Writings</u> 43 (Library of America 2001).

5. Which citation to the ninth edition of <u>Black's Law Dictionary</u>, published in 2009, is correct?

    A. <u>Black's Law Dictionary</u> (9th ed., West 2009).

    B. <u>Black's Law Dictionary</u> (9th ed. 2009).

    C. <u>Black's Law Dictionary</u> (9th edition 2009).

    D. <u>Black's Law Dictionary</u> (9th ed., West 2009).

Answer Key on page 532

? 13. ALWD Rules for Citing Periodical Materials: Quiz

Assume that the following citations appear in court documents.

1. Which of the following citations to a June 1, 2009, article on page E2 of the *San Francisco Chronicle* is correct?

    A. Peter Hartlaub, SFJazz Show Gets to the Roots, S.F. Chron., June 1, 2009, at E2.
    B. Peter Hartlaub, <u>SFJazz Show Gets to the Roots</u>, S.F. Chron. E2 (June 1, 2009).
    C. Hartlaub, Peter, <u>SFJazz Show Gets to the Roots</u>, S.F. Chron., June 1, 2009, at E2.
    D. Peter Hartlaub, <u>SFJazz Show Gets to the Roots</u>, <u>S.F. Chron</u>., June 1, 2009, at E2.

2. Choose the correct citation to an April 2009 article by Eugene Volokh that appeared in volume 97 of the Georgetown Law Journal.

    A. Eugene Volokh, <u>Symbolic Expression and the Original Meaning of the First Amendment</u>, 97 Georgetown Law Journal 1057 (2009).
    B. Eugene Volokh, <u>Symbolic Expression and the Original Meaning of the First Amendment</u>, 97 Law J. 1057 (2009).
    C. Eugene Volokh, <u>Symbolic Expression and the Original Meaning of the First Amendment</u>, 97 Geo. L.J. 1057 (2009).
    D. Eugene Volokh, <u>Symbolic Expression and the Original Meaning of the First Amendment</u>, 97 J. 1057 (2009).

3. Which citation to a March 2007 student-written note, signed by Adrian Barnes and published in volume 1 the Columbia Law Review, is correct?

    A. Note, <u>Do They Have to Buy from Burma? A Preemption Analysis of Local Antisweatshop Procurement Laws</u>, 107 Colum. L. Rev. 426 (2007).
    B. Adrian Barnes, Note, <u>Do They Have to Buy from Burma? A Preemption Analysis of Local Antisweatshop Procurement Laws</u>, 107 Col. L.R. 426 (2007).
    C. Adrian Barnes, note, <u>Do They Have to Buy from Burma? A Preemption Analysis of Local Antisweatshop Procurement Laws</u>, 107 Colum. L. Rev. 426 (2007).
    D. Adrian Barnes, Student Author, <u>Do They Have to Buy from Burma? A Preemption Analysis of Local Antisweatshop Procurement Laws</u>, 107 Colum. L. Rev. (2007).

4. Choose the correct citation to a nonstudent-written book review by Derrick A. Bell, Jr., reviewing <u>Just Schools: The Idea of Racial Equality in American Education</u> by David L. Kirp. The review appeared in the Texas Law Review in August 1983.

    A. Derrick A. Bell, Jr., <u>School Desegregation Postmortem</u>, 62 Tex. L. Rev. 175 (1983) (reviewing <u>Just Schools: The Idea of Racial Equality in American Education</u>).

B. Derrick A. Bell, <u>School Desegregation Postmortem</u>, 62 Tex. L. Rev. 175 (1983) (reviewing David L. Kirp, <u>Just Schools: The Idea of Racial Equality in American Education</u> (1982)).

C. Derrick A. Bell, Jr., <u>School Desegregation Postmortem</u>, 62 Tex. L. Rev. 175 (1983) (reviewing David L. Kirp, <u>Just Schools: The Idea of Racial Equality in American Education</u> (1982)).

D. Derrick A. Bell, Jr., <u>School Desegregation Postmortem</u>, 62 Texas L.R. 175 (1983) (reviewing David L. Kirp, <u>Just Schools: The Idea of Racial Equality in American Education</u> (1982)).

Answer Key on page 532

⚇? 14. ALWD Rules for Citing Electronic Media: Quiz

Assume that the following citations appear in court documents.

1. Choose the correct citation format for a case that is unreported but is available on Westlaw and has been assigned a unique database identifier. There are no page numbers assigned to this case, but cite to screen two of the case.

    A. <u>Fenstermacher v. Telelect, Inc.</u>, No. 90-2159-O, 1992 WL 175114, at *2 (D. Kan. July 17, 1992).

    B. <u>Fenstermacher v. Telelect, Inc.</u>, 1992 WL 175114 at *2 (D. Kan. July 17, 1992).

    C. <u>Fenstermacher v. Telelect, Inc.</u>, No. 90-2159-O, 1992 WL 175114 at *2 (D. Kan. July 17, 1992).

    D. <u>Fenstermacher v. Telelect, Inc.</u>, No. 90-2159-O, 1992 WL 175114, at *2 (D. Kan. 1992).

    E. Both B and C are correct.

2. Which of the following citations to Baldwin's Kentucky Revised Statutes Annotated, as found on Westlaw is correct? Note that the Kentucky Statutes are current on Westlaw through the end of the 2008 legislation.

    A. Ky. Rev. Stat. Ann. § 38.100 (West, 2008).

    B. Ken. Stat. Ann. § 38.100 (West, Westlaw through 2008 legislation).

    C. Ky. Rev. Stat. Ann. § 38.100 (WL current through 2008 legislation).

    D. Ky. Rev. Stat. Ann. 38.100 (West, Westlaw through 2008 legislation).

3. The following New York Times article is available only on the Internet and is not available in traditional print format. Choose the correct citation format.

    A. Matthew Saltmarsh, Interest Rates Held Steady in Europe, N.Y. Times, June 4, 2009, http://www.nytimes.com/2009/06/05/business/%20global/05euro.html?hpw.

    B. Matthew Saltmarsh, <u>Interest Rates Held Steady in Europe</u>, N.Y. Times (June 4, 2009), http://www.nytimes.com/2009/06/05/business/global/05euro.html?hpw (accessed Oct. 12, 2010).

    C. Matthew Saltmarsh, <u>Interest Rates Held Steady in Europe</u>, N.Y. Times, June 4, 2009, available http://www.nytimes.com/2009/06/05/business/ global/05euro.html?hpw.

    D. Matthew Saltmarsh, <u>Interest Rates Held Steady in Europe</u>, New York Times, June 4, 2009, http://www.nytimes.com/2009/06/05/business/ global/05euro.html?hpw.

4. The following article is available both in the print version of the New York Times and online. Choose the correct parallel citation.

    A. David Jolly, <u>Despite Devaluation Fear, Latvia Stands by Currency</u>, N.Y. Times, June 4, 2009, at B4, http://www.nytimes.com/2009/ 06/05/ business/global/05latvia.html?hpw.

    B. David Jolly, <u>Despite Devaluation Fear, Latvia Stands by Currency</u>, N.Y. Times, at B4, available http://www.nytimes.com/2009/ 06/05/business/global/05latvia.html?hpw (June 4, 2009).

    C. David Jolly, <u>Despite Devaluation Fear, Latvia Stands by Currency</u>, N.Y. Times, June 4, 2009, at http://www.nytimes.com/2009/ 06/05/business/global/05latvia.html?hpw.

    D. David Jolly, <u>Despite Devaluation Fear, Latvia Stands by Currency</u>, N.Y. Times B4 (June 4, 2009), http://www.nytimes.com/2009/06/05/business/global/05latvia.html?hpw (accessed Oct. 12, 2010).

5. Choose the correct citation to a fictional e-mail from George Ferman, Assistant Dean at Georgetown Law, to Alex Aleinikoff, Dean of Georgetown Law.

    A. E-mail from George Ferman, Asst. Dean, Georgetown L., to Alex Aleinikoff, Dean, Georgetown L. (Oct. 1, 2009, 08:15:01 EST) (on file with author).

    B. E-mail from George Ferman, Georgetown Law, Assistant Dean, to Alex Aleinikoff, Georgetown Law, Dean (Oct. 1, 2009, 08:15:01 EST) (on file with author).

    C. George Ferman, Asst. Dean, Georgetown L., to Alex Aleinikoff, Dean, Georgetown L. (Oct. 1, 2009, 08:15:01 EST) (on file with author).

    D. E-mail from George Ferman to Alex Aleinikoff (Oct. 1, 2009, 08:15:01 EST) (on file with author).

6. Which of the following citations to a commercial audio recording is correct?

    A. U2, <u>The Joshua Tree</u> (1987).

    B. U2, <u>The Joshua Tree</u> (Island Records).

    c. U2, CD, <u>The Joshua Tree</u> (Is. Recs., Inc. 1987).

    D. U2, <u>The Joshua Tree</u> (1987) (Island Records).

Answer Key on page 533

C.   *ALWD Citation Self-Assessment*

INSTRUCTIONS: This self-assessment is designed to test your knowledge of the basic citation rules of ALWD covered in chapter 5. Read through the document, taking note of the numbered and highlighted passages. Each number and highlighted passage represents a question about which you should decide whether the citation is correct as is or whether a change is needed. If a change is needed, please make the correct change in citation format. When you are finished, check your work against the answer key on pages 533-537. The answer key also indicates for each item the applicable citation rule or form. This review will help you to assess your understanding of the ALWD citation forms and to more quickly and accurately provide citations for your own documents.

Civil Action No. 02-2332

UNITED STATES COURT OF APPEALS
FOR THE ELEVENTH CIRCUIT

DR. CHARLES OSSINING, Appellant,

v.

HARRISON BRUBAKER, ET AL., APPELLEES

ON APPEAL FROM UNITED STATES DISTRICT COURT
FOR THE SOUTHERN DISTRICT OF ALABAMA

BRIEF OF RESPONDENT

STATEMENT OF ISSUES PRESENTED FOR REVIEW

    I.   Whether an inmate, exhibiting no medical condition warranting special treatment, and having received adequate care for all documented symptoms, has an Eighth Amendment claim when, following self-diagnosis of a rare condition, the prison declined his request for a special diet and further unnecessary testing.

    II. Whether the trial court correctly found an inmate's First Amendment rights were not violated when the Warden reviewed and denied individual publications according to prison regulations in response to the unreasonable burden placed upon the prison's resources.

STATEMENT OF THE CASE

<u>Nature of the Case</u>

    This is an appeal of summary judgment in a prisoner's rights case. Respondents request that summary judgment be affirmed as there are no genuine issues of fact in dispute, and that appellant's 42 U.S.C. § 1983 complaint be dismissed as treatment did not violate prisoner's constitutional rights. Appellant brings his claims under the First and Eighth Amendments #1 U.S. Const. Amend. I; #2 U.S. Const. amend. VIII.

#1   Keep as is/Change

#2   Keep as is/Change

Procedural History

Ossining alleges violations of his First and Eighth Amendment rights by the prison. The United States District Court for the Southern District of Alabama granted the defendant's motion for summary judgment. The District Court concluded that plaintiff's receiving of publications caused unreasonable burdens on the resources of the prison and that the prison was not deliberately indifferent to any serious medical needs of the plaintiff. #3 Ossining v. Brubaker, No. CIV.A.02-2332, 2003 U.S. Dist. LEXIS 5130 at *1 (S.D. Ala. Jan. 6, 2003).

#3   Keep as is/Change

STATEMENT OF FACTS

The prisoner, Dr. Charles Ossining, was convicted of Medicare fraud, mail fraud, and making false claims to the government. At the time of Ossining's incarceration in January 2002, a routine medical examination revealed he was in good health, without any notations of medical problems. (Brubaker Aff. 7.) After his arrival, Ossining received a considerable number of medical journals and newsletters pertaining to allergies. (Brubaker Aff. 8.) Ossining specifically ordered informational brochures concerning various types of allergies and treatments for the purpose of disseminating this information to other prisoners. (Ossining Aff. 4.) By the end of March, the infirmary reported a significant increase in prisoner visits: 15% higher than the same quarter a year before, and requests for allergy testing increased 100%. More than half of these requests were declined as these prisoners showed no symptoms warranting testing. Many inmates requesting allergy testing indicated Ossining had suggested they be tested for various allergies. (Brubaker Aff. 9.) Proper allergy diagnosis has been shown to require extensive testing #4 J. Expert, Allergy on the Net, 5 New Eng. J. Med. 9, 10 (2002), at http://www.nejm.org/expert/v5/allergy.html.

#4   Keep as is/Change

The medical staff could not accommodate all incoming requests for allergy testing, leading to agitation of prisoners and strain on medical resources. (Brubaker Aff. 9, 10.) Additionally, the prison cafeteria received an influx of complaints, as well as special requests and disorderly conduct, requiring additional guards for security. (Brubaker Aff. 11.) Based on these events, Brubaker, the longtime warden of the prison, rejected certain publications addressed to Ossining as detrimental to the security and resources of the prison, an action authorized by federal regulation 28 C.F.R. § 540.71(b) (2009). #5 I.M. Tough, Warden Power, 15 N.Y.Law Sch. L. Rev. 12, 15-17 (1983).

#5   Keep as is/Change

In March, a blood test revealed Ossining was borderline anemic; he was prescribed iron supplements to combat this condition. (Ossining Aff. 12.) In April, Ossining diagnosed himself as suffering from celiac disease, an extremely rare infection, and claimed he needed an endoscopy to confirm his diagnosis. (Flowers Aff. 6.) Celiac disease can be fatal if not treated properly. #6 Adam Gourna, Celiac Disease: A Killer, New York Times, December 12, 1994, at F3, available at 1994 WL 2321843. Reviewing his blood test results, Dr. Gerta Flowers, a specialist in internal medicine and resident physician at the prison, determined that Ossining did

#6   Keep as is/Change

Citation—Study Aid Material

not exhibit such severe symptoms warranting further investigation and rejected his request for an endoscopy. (Flowers Aff. 7.) In July, Ossining requested a gluten-free diet, claiming only this diet could treat celiac disease. (Ossining Aff. 21.) Dr. Flowers informed the prison that sufficient alternatives in the prison cafeteria were available to Ossining should he prefer to eat a gluten-free diet. (Flowers Aff. 8.) The prison has promised that should Ossining present severe symptoms in the future, it would treat him appropriately. (Brubaker Aff. 15.)

<u>STANDARD OF REVIEW</u>

The issue before this Court is whether the trial court properly applied the law to the facts in granting summary judgment. The court's review of the district court's ruling on a motion for summary judgment is de novo. #7 <u>Pope v. Hightower</u>, 101 F.3d 1382, 1383 (11th Cir. 1996).

#7 Keep as is/Change

<u>SUMMARY OF ARGUMENT</u>

Ossining's First and Eighth Amendment claims fail based on the established facts in the record. With regard to the Eighth Amendment, Ossining shows no evidence of a serious medical need, his treatment by the prison did not violate contemporary standards of decency, and the medical staff was not deliberately indifferent to his condition. #8 U.S. CONST. amend. VIII. As for the First Amendment, because assertion of his rights posed a threat to the security of the prison and created an unreasonable burden on prison resources, Warden Brubaker's rejection of particular publications was justified. #9 Amend. I.

#8 Keep as is/Change

#9 Keep as is/Change

<u>ARGUMENT</u>

The prisoner, Dr. Charles Ossining, is currently serving a five-year sentence for defrauding the federal government. Ossining alleges the prison violated his First Amendment rights by denying him access to professional journals and his Eighth Amendment rights by denying him a gluten-free diet and further testing for a rare disease for which he made a self-diagnosis. While detainees are accorded protections of the Constitution, prisoner's rights are inherently restricted, and some constitutional violations may be acceptable if they serve "legitimate penological interests," such as order, security, and safety. #10 <u>See Thornburgh v. Abbott</u>, 490 U.S. 407-408 (1989). Moreover, as operation of a prison falls under the province of the legislative and executive branches of government, deference should be paid by the courts to appropriate prison authorities regulating this delicate balance between prison security and legitimate rights of prisoners. #11 <u>Turner v. Safley</u>, 482 U.S. 78, 84-85 (1987)

#10 Keep as is/Change

#11 Keep as is/Change

I. PLAINTIFF'S EIGHTH AMENDMENT CLAIM OF CRUEL AND UNUSUAL PUNISHMENT IS WITHOUT MERIT BECAUSE THE PRISONER EXHIBITED NO MEDICAL CONDITION WARRANTING SPECIAL TREATMENT

Ossining fails to present sufficient evidence of a serious medical problem related to being denied a gluten-free diet or evidence that the prison was "deliberately indifferent" to his symptoms, as required for claims under the Eighth Amendment. <u>See</u> #12 <u>Helling</u>, 509 U.S. 25, 29 (1993). In #13 <u>Helling</u>, the Supreme Court established

#12 Keep as is/Change

#13 Keep as is/Change

a two-prong test for proving Eighth Amendment violations. Under the subjective prong (A), the prisoner must show deliberate indifference by the prison toward a serious risk posed to the prisoner. Under the objective prong (B), the prisoner must show that the unreasonable risk of harm he faces is contrary to contemporary standards of decency. #14 Id. at 35-36. Because Ossining received adequate treatment for his ailments and exhibited no medical condition warranting special treatment, he fails both prongs of the Eighth Amendment test.

#14   Keep as is/Change

A. The prison was not deliberately indifferent to prisoner's medical condition when the prison physician reviewed prisoner's blood test results to find no severe symptoms of celiac disease warranting further treatment and the prison menu offered adequate gluten-free alternatives

Under the subjective prong, the prisoner must show (1) the prison had knowledge of a serious risk of harm to him and (2) deliberate indifference by the prison toward this risk. #15 Id. at 35.

#15   Keep as is/Change

1. The prison had no subjective knowledge of any serious risk of harm to the prisoner in denying him a gluten-free diet or in rejecting his request for an endoscopy to further test for celiac disease

Ossining fails to show prison officials knew of and disregarded "an excessive risk to his health or safety." #16 See Farmer v. Brennan, 511 U.S. 825, 837 (1994); 42 U.S.C. § 1983 (2003). As serious complications from celiac disease are rare and Dr. Flowers determined that the prisoner did not present such severe symptoms to warrant further investigation, Ossining fails to show the prison's subjective knowledge of a serious risk of harm when denying him a gluten-free diet and further testing. In #17 Campbell et al. v. Sikes, the plaintiff inmate alleged cruel and unusual punishment when the defendant prison psychiatrist misdiagnosed her with poly-substance abuse disorder when in fact she had a bipolar disorder, a diagnosis unreported in jail records or prior hospitalization records. The court affirmed the grant of summary judgment for the prison because there was no evidence that the psychiatrist knew the prisoner had bipolar disorder, that he knew he misdiagnosed her, or that he knew of a substantial risk of serious harm to the inmate as a result of his treatment. #18 Campbell v. Sikes, 169 F.3d 1353, 1366-68 (1999). Similarly, Ossining fails to present evidence from which a reasonable jury could infer that Dr. Flowers or other prison officials knew he had celiac disease, or knew they were misdiagnosing him, or knew their treatment was grossly inadequate but proceeded with the treatment anyway. As in #19 Campbell, Ossining's medical records did not indicate a prior history of celiac disease and a professional review of his blood did not give Dr. Flowers reason for concern. Therefore, Ossining fails the first part of the subjective prong of the Helling test because the prison exhibits no subjective knowledge of his mistreatment.

#16   Keep as is/Change

#17   Keep as is/Change

#18   Keep as is/Change

#19   Keep as is/Change

2. The prison was not deliberately indifferent toward the medical concerns of the prisoner

Ossining fails to demonstrate his medical treatment by the prison constituted the "unnecessary and wanton infliction of pain," as required to show deliberate indiffer-

#20 Keep as is/Change	
#21 Keep as is/Change	
#22 Keep as is/Change	
#23 Keep as is/Change	
#24 Keep as is/Change	
#25 Keep as is/Change	
#26 Keep as is/Change	
#27 Keep as is/Change	
#28 Keep as is/Change	

ence. #20 Mustave Hurt, Unimaginable Pain, 742 Geo. L.J. 801, 831-32 (2003) (discussing the requirements to show deliberate indifference). In Estelle, the prisoner injured his back while engaged in prison work, claiming deliberate indifference by the prison for failure to perform an X-ray to treat him. The court held that questions concerning forms of treatment are matters of medical judgment, and that failure by prison medical staff to use additional diagnostic techniques beyond ordinary treatment does not constitute deliberate indifference or cruel and usual punishment. #21 Estelle v. Gamble, 429 S. Ct. 97, 107 (1976). Similarly, Dr. Flowers's refusal to order an endoscopy to confirm Ossining's self-diagnosis of celiac disease following her professional review of his blood test results does not constitute deliberate indifference to his medical needs. Ossining offers no evidence that prison medical staff failed to meet appropriate professional standards in determining that his symptoms did not warrant further testing. Moreover, Ossining's difference in opinion from prison officials concerning diagnosis and recommended treatment does not constitute cruel and unusual punishment. #22 See id. at 100; but see Harris v. Thigpen, 941 F.2d 1495, 1505 (11th Cir. 1991)(holding that difference of opinion does constitute cruel and unusual punishment). While an endoscopy may have led to an appropriate diagnosis and treatment for his condition, Ossining fails to show deliberate indifference as medical decisions concerning forms of treatment beyond ordinary care do not constitute cruel and unusual punishment. #23 See Estelle, 429 U.S. 97 at 107.

Denial of Ossining's request for a special gluten-free diet does not constitute deliberate indifference because the prisoner lacks convincing symptoms requiring special treatment. See 25 Op. Off. Leg. Counsel 370, 381-82 (1995). #24 In McElligot v. Goley, 182 F.3d 1248, 1256-1258 (11th Cir. 1999), an inmate with a history of stomach problems was treated by prison doctors with Tylenol, Pepto-Bismol, and an anti-gas medication when experiencing severe intestinal pains, even after it was evident these treatments were not responding to his deteriorating condition. The court held that while prison doctors could not be held liable for failing to diagnose the inmate's colon cancer, the failure to further diagnose and treat severe pain experienced by a prisoner was evidence of deliberate indifference. #25 See McElligot v. Foley, 182 F.3d 1248, 1256-58 (11th Cir. 1999); Noah Lee, Deliberate Indifference: What's It All About? 31 (3d ed. 2001). Unlike the inmate in McElligot, Ossining exhibits no severe symptoms of celiac disease. The prison staff examined Ossining, conducted a blood test, prescribed him iron supplements to overcome his weight loss and psychological depression, and professionally reviewed his blood work to conclude there was nothing seriously wrong with him. Therefore, as the prison exercised professional standards of care in evaluating his health, and as the inmate exhibits no severe symptoms warranting special treatment, Ossining fails to show deliberate indifference to his medical needs. #26 See United States Sent. G.L. Man. §5D2.1(f) (2001).

B. The prison's denial of prisoner's requests for a special gluten-free diet and additional testing for a rare disease do not violate contemporary standards of decency

Under the objective prong, Ossining fails to show his exposure to an unreasonable risk of harm contrary to "contemporary standards of decency." #27 Helling, 509 United States at 36. The objective standard requires showing treatment rising to the level of "serious" deprivation. #28 Campbell, 169 F.3d at 1363. In Rhodes, the

Court held confining two inmates to a single cell did not constitute the "unnecessary and wanton infliction of pain" that violates the Eighth Amendment because inmates suffered only minor deprivations of privileges, not necessities such as essential food, medical care, or sanitation. Only when these "minimal civilized measure of life's necessities" are denied is there basis for an Eighth Amendment violation. #29 Rhodes v. Chapman, 452 U.S 337, 346, 349 (1981). Similarly, Wellville's denial of additional testing and special diet to Ossining when trained medical professionals fail to recognize symptoms requiring such treatment does not constitute deprivation of life's minimal necessities. #30 RESTATEMENT (SECOND) OF TORTS § 931 (1994). Ossining was not denied adequate medical care when he was examined by prison medical staff, had his blood tested and reviewed by Dr. Flowers, and was prescribed iron supplements to combat weight loss and fatigue. Moreover, Ossining was never denied essential food as adequate alternatives remained available in the cafeteria should Ossining prefer a gluten-free diet. Therefore, life's minimal necessities were not denied, and Ossining fails the objective standard as his treatment did not violate contemporary standards of decency.

#29 Keep as is/Change

#30 Keep as is/Change

II. PRISONER'S FIRST AMENDMENT CLAIM IS WITHOUT MERIT BECAUSE WARDEN BRUBAKER REVIEWED AND DENIED PRISONER'S PUBLICATIONS IN RESPONSE TO THE UNREASONABLE BURDEN PLACED UPON THE PRISON'S RESOURCES AS AUTHORIZED UNDER 28 C.F.R. §540.71

As authorized under 28 C.F.R. § 540.71(b), Warden Brubaker legitimately restricted Ossining's right to receive publications deemed "detrimental to the security, good order, or discipline of the institution..." 28 C.F.R. § 540.71. Exercise of constitutional rights within the prison must pay due regard to the order and security of the prison environment. #31 See Turner Railroad v. Safley, 482 U.S. 78, 84-85 (1987). Ossining fails to show Wellville's restrictions on his First Amendment rights were not "reasonably related to legitimate penological interests" as required under the four-part Turner-Thornburgh test. #32 See Id. at 89; See Thornburgh, 490 U.S. at 401. Under Turner-Thornburgh, the Court must consider the following factors: (A) the impact that accommodation of the asserted constitutional right will have on others in the prison; (B) whether the governmental objective underlying the regulations at issue is legitimate and neutral, and whether the regulations are rationally related to that objective; (C) whether the regulation represents an exaggerated response to prison concerns; and (D) whether there are alternative means of exercising the right that remain open to prison inmates at de minimis cost to penological interests. #33 Owen v. Wille, 117 F.3d at 1235 (11th Cir. 1997). As Ossining's exercise of his First Amendment right created an unreasonable burden on resources of the prison and put prison security in jeopardy, restricting his access to medical publications was constitutional because it was reasonably related to a legitimate penological interest.

#31 Keep as is/Change

#32 Keep as is/Change

#33 Keep as is/Change

A. Accommodation of prisoner's asserted First Amendment right would be detrimental to the order and security of the prison, placing an unreasonable burden on the resources of the prison medical facility and cafeteria

The Court should be particularly deferential to the informed discretion of Warden Brubaker given interests in security when Ossining's assertion of his

#34 Keep as is/Change

#35 Keep as is/Change

#36 Keep as is/Change

#37 Keep as is/Change

#38 Keep as is/Change

#39 Keep as is/Change

constitutional right created a "ripple effect" among fellow inmates and prison staff. #34 See <u>U.S. v. White</u>, 490 U.S. 84, 87 (1990). In <u>Turner</u>, a class of inmates challenged prison regulations restricting correspondence between inmates as violations of their First Amendment rights. The court deferred to judgment of correction officials and upheld the regulation as reasonably related to legitimate security interests given the potential for coordinating criminal activity by inmate-to-inmate correspondence, and given the probability of material circulating within the prison in a "ripple effect." #35 See <u>Turner</u>, 482 U.S. at 84-85.

Like <u>Turner</u>, Warden Brubaker determined that Ossining created a "ripple effect," threatening the order and security of the prison while placing an unreasonable burden on prison resources, by circulating publications among prisoners to encourage them to believe they were sick. According to Brubaker, the temporal relationship between Ossining's receipt of medical publications and increased inmate complaints indicates a correlation between the assertion of his constitutional rights and the riling up of prisoners, overtaxing of prison personnel, and additional expenditure of prison resources. #36 <u>Ossining v. Brubaker</u>, No. CIV.A.02-2332, 2003 WL 66432 at *6 (Jan. 6, 2003). Dramatic increases in infirmary visits and requests for allergy testing among inmates, many of whom showed no symptoms warranting testing, support Brubaker's hypothesis. Given the threat to order and cost of additional resources required to accommodate Ossining's assertion of his rights, deference should be given to Brubaker's informed discretion in rejecting these publications.

B. <u>Governmental objective in maintaining prison security is legitimate and neutral, and prison regulations governing the availability of publications to inmates rationally relate to this objective by reducing frivolous medical complaints and special requests</u>

Under the second factor of the <u>Turner-Thornburgh</u> test, the Court must determine whether (1) the governmental objective underlying the regulation at issue is legitimate and neutral, and whether (2) the regulation is rationally related to that objective. #37 <u>State of Alabama v. Carter</u>, 507 U.S. 411, 418 (1992).

1. <u>Protecting prison security is a legitimate and neutral governmental objective</u>

In rejecting Ossining's publications, Warden Brubaker acted pursuant to 28 C.F.R. § 540.71, whose "underlying objective of protecting prison security is undoubtedly legitimate and is neutral with regard to the content of the expression regulated." #38 <u>North West Electric Company v. University of Colorado</u>, 211 U.S. 415, 417 (1991). In <u>Thornburgh</u>, inmates filed a class action against the prison challenging regulations excluding incoming sexually explicit publications. The Court upheld the regulations as maintenance of prison order and security is a legitimate governmental purpose, and because the prison's ban on sexually explicit material was neutrally based on security interests. #39 See cf. <u>Thornburgh</u>, 490 U.S. at 414-15. Like <u>Thornburgh</u>, Ossining's publications were rejected because they created obstacles to the legitimate governmental objective of maintaining prison security. Warden Brubaker's rejection of only those publications deemed a threat to prison security remained "neutral" to the legitimate governmental interest in maintaining security and order. Therefore, Brubaker's exercise of authority under 28 C.F.R. § 540.71 was consistent with the legitimate and neutral objectives underlying the regulation.

2. <u>Application of prison regulation governing the availability of publications to inmates is rationally related to the governmental objective</u>

There is a "valid, rational connection" between the rejection of various publications addressed to Ossining and the legitimate government interests in security and preservation of resources. #40 <u>See</u> <u>Turner</u>, 482 U.S. at 89; see also 28 C.F.R. § 540.71 (2002) (establishing security as legitimate government interest). In <u>Onishea</u>, inmates with HIV brought a class action challenging the prison's segregation of recreational, religious, and educational programs based on prisoners' HIV status. The prison justified its actions claiming the cost of hiring additional guards to monitor the threat of "high-risk" behavior in integrated programs would create an undue financial burden on resources. The Court upheld the segregated programs as rationally related to governmental objectives because "penological concerns such as security and cost are legitimate, and…these are in fact the concerns behind the program requirements that participating prisoners neither create a threat of disorder or unreasonable costs." #41 <u>Onishea v. Hopper</u>, 171 F.3d 1289, 1300 (11th Cir. 1999). Similarly, Brubaker's rejection of certain items addressed to Ossining was rationally related to legitimate governmental interests because of the Warden's concern that these publications created threat of disorder and unreasonable costs for the prison. By rejecting these publications, Warden Brubaker intended to remove obstacles to maintaining security by reducing the agitation of prisoners, easing the burden placed on the prison medical staff, and removing the need for additional guards to maintain order in the cafeteria. Therefore, as security was the underlying concern behind Brubaker's actions, his rejection of Ossining's publications was rationally related to legitimate governmental objectives. #42 <u>See</u> H.R. 81, 108th Cong. (2003) (establishing security as legitimate governmental objective), available at http://thomas.-%20loc.gov/bss/d108/d108laws.html.

C. <u>The prison regulation is not an exaggerated response to prison concerns because alternatives accommodating prisoner's rights at de minimus cost to penological interests are not immediately obvious or feasible</u>

Rejection of prisoner's publications is not an exaggerated response to the threat these items posed to prison resources and security because there are no "obvious, easy alternatives." #43 <u>See</u> Jeremy Stevens, <u>Taking Control</u> 41-42 (Amanda Bradley ed., Scholastic Press 3d ed. 2001). In <u>Spellman</u>, inmates challenged the prison's blanket ban on publications sent to prisoners in administrative segregation on the grounds that the regulation was an exaggerated response to security and safety concerns. The Court held the prison's actions unconstitutional, recognizing alternatives to the blanket ban, such as placing reasonable limits on the quantity of publications permitted in confinement, which still addressed the concerns of security, fire, and sanitation. #44 <u>See</u> <u>Spellman v. Hopper</u>, 95 F.supp.2d 1267, 1286 (M.D. Ala. 1999).

Unlike <u>Spellman</u>, Brubaker rejected only Ossining's medical publications, items deemed a threat to prison security; Brubaker did not blanket ban all publications sent to Ossining. Moreover, unlike <u>Spellman</u>, less restrictive alternatives can be rejected because of reasonably grounded fears they will lead to greater harm or administrative inconvenience. #45 <u>See</u> Alabama Constitution article V, § 9. The resources required to read through every allergy magazine received to eliminate publications

#40 Keep as is/Change

#41 Keep as is/Change

#42 Keep as is/Change

#43 Keep as is/Change

#44 Keep as is/Change

#45 Keep as is/Change

deemed a threat would be too expansive as prisoners have complained of a wide variety of allergies. Also, allowing Ossining to read magazines while in confinement would not come at a de minimus cost to the prison as additional resources would be required to fund such an arrangement. #46 See James King, Costs of Confinement, 28 N. Ill. U. L. Rev. 609, 621-22 (2001). Thus, as less restrictive alternatives are not readily available or feasible, the Warden's actions do not represent an exaggerated response to legitimate penological concerns.

#46 Keep as is/Change

D. The prison restrictions on prisoner's receipt of publications are reasonable as prisoner has alternative means of exercising his First Amendment rights to keep up with developments in his field of work.

Ossining fails the fourth factor of the Turner-Thornburgh test because other means of expression remain available to the prisoner despite imposition of prison regulations restricting his access to certain publications. See Stevens, Taking Control at 45. In Turner, the prison restricted inmate-to-inmate correspondence between prisons to prevent future criminal behavior, a legitimate security concern. The Court held the fourth factor satisfied if any other means of expression remained open to the prisoners, not necessarily other means of communicating with inmates in other prisons. Turner, 482 U.S. at 90, 92. Similarly, Brubaker's application of the regulation merely prohibits publications of particular kind, and does not deprive the prisoner of all means of expression. The prison is not prohibiting Ossining from gaining access to allergy information as he can still receive phone calls and visits from colleagues who can keep him up to date. Moreover, the prisoner is still free to receive a variety of other publications. Alternative means of exercising his First Amendment rights are still available to the prisoner, and therefore, Ossining fails to satisfy the fourth factor.

CONCLUSION

For the above stated reasons, the judgment of the District Court should be affirmed.

Respectfully submitted,

_____

Attorney for Respondents

CERTIFICATE OF SERVICE

I swear on this day, the 28th of February, 2003, that I have served Respondent's brief on Appellant's counsel.

_____

Attorney for Respondents

Answer Key on page 533

IV.   STRATEGIES FOR USING THE BLUEBOOK

The Bluebook is not as intimidating as it appears at first glance. The trick for using it is to learn these three things:

1. the purpose of citation;
2. the design, layout, and basic citation rules of the Bluebook; and
3. some of the often-used rules.

A.   *The Purpose of Bluebook Citation*

Lawyers use citation to provide authority in legal documents and to find the law referenced in legal documents. The Bluebook, officially titled, *The Bluebook: A Uniform System of Citation,* is designed to provide a uniform system of citation rules so that lawyers can easily find and reference legal sources. Eventually, when electronic filings are required with links to each cited source, citation might become obsolete. But until that time, lawyers are required to use citation that permits other lawyers easy access to their references. The Bluebook and ALWD (discussed above) are the most commonly used citation systems. Using correct citation adds credibility to your writing; if a judge can trust your citations, she can also trust your analysis.

B.   *Design, Layout, and Basic Citation Rules of the Bluebook*

1.   Bluebook Design

The introduction in the Bluebook explains the purpose and function of the book. The Bluebook, in general, provides citation formats for scholarly documents, such as law review articles. The "quick reference" on the front inside cover is a cheat sheet for most-often used citations for law reviews. In addition to the rules laid out in the main section of the Bluebook, there are a number of important tables toward the end of the book. There are also an index and a table of contents to help in locating rules.

Most practicing lawyers cite to the law in legal documents, not scholarly articles. The Bluebook section, called the **Bluepages,** provides additional citation rules for court documents and legal memoranda. The Bluepages are organized by legal source (cases, statutes, constitutions, and so on) and provide easy-to-understand formatting and examples. In addition, the Bluepages contain two tables: BT1 for abbreviations in court documents and BT2 for local and jurisdiction-specific citation rules. The "quick reference" on the inside back cover of the Bluebook provides a cheat sheet for most-often used citations for legal documents. (The rules and examples in this book follow the citation rules for court documents unless otherwise noted.)

2. Bluebook Layout

The main highlights of the Bluebook contain the following:

1. The Bluepages, for practicing lawyers, are organized by category:
    - Cases (Rule B4)
    - Statutes, Rules, and Regulations (Rule B5)
    - Constitutions (Rule B6)
    - Court and Litigation Documents (Rule B7)
    - Books and Other Nonperiodic Materials (Rule B8)
    - Journals, Magazine, and Newspaper Articles (Rule B9)
2. **Citation rules,** which are organized by category:
    - Cases (Rule 10)
    - Constitutions (Rule 11)
    - Statutes (Rule 12)
    - Administrative and Executive Materials, including Rules and Regulations (Rule 14)
    - Books, Reports, and Other Nonperiodic Materials (Rule 15)
    - Periodical Materials (Rule 16)
3. **Tables** (on white pages with a blue edge), which lay out specific requirements of:
    - United States Jurisdictions (T1)
      - Federal Judicial and Legislative Materials (T1.1)
      - Federal Administrative and Executive Materials (T1.2)
      - States and the District of Columbia (T1.3)
      - Other United States Jurisdictions (T1.4)
    - Foreign Jurisdictions (T2)
    - Intergovernmental Organizations and Treaty Sources (T3 - T4)
    - Abbreviations for Arbitral Reporter Sources (T5)
    - Abbreviations for Case Names and Court Names (T6 - T7)
    - Abbreviations for Explanatory Phrases and Legislative Documents (T8 - T9)
    - Abbreviations for Geographical Terms (T10)
    - Abbreviations for Judges and Officials and Months (T11 - T12)
    - Abbreviations for Periodicals (T13)
    - Abbreviations for Publishing Terms and Services (T14 - T15)
    - Abbreviations for Document Subdivisions (T16)

In addition, the Bluebook contains a table of contents, which is helpful for finding rules on broad topics, such as law reviews, and an index, which is helpful for finding rules on specific subjects such as pinpoint cites.

3.   Bluebook Basic Citation Rules

a.   Cases (Rule 10)

Citation of a U.S. Supreme Court Case:

Lakeside v. Oregon, 435 U.S. 333, 345 (1978).

Lakeside = plaintiff
Oregon = defendant
435 = reporter volume #
U.S. = reporter abbreviation
333 = first page
345 = specific page
(1978) = date case decided

NOTE: Be sure to include both the first page of the cited case and a specific page if one is referenced.

Citation of a case decided by the U.S. Court of Appeals for the Eleventh Circuit:

Campbell v. Sikes,169 F.3d 1353, 1366-68 (11th Cir. 1999).

Campbell = plaintiff
Sikes = defendant
169 = reporter volume #
F.3d = reporter abbreviation
1353 = first page
1366-68 = specific pages
11th Cir. = court—this is necessary if it's not clear from reporter abbreviation
1999 = date case decided

Short form for cases:

Campbell, 169 F.3d at 1369.

Campbell = plaintiff; use defendant's name in short cite if plaintiff's name is a
   common litigant (i.e., United States)
169 = reporter volume #
F.3d = reporter abbreviation
1369 = specific page

---

b. *Constitutions (Rule 11)*

Citation of Section 2 of the Eighteenth Amendment to the U.S. Constitution:

U.S. Const. amend. XVIII, §2.

U.S. Const. = abbreviation of Constitution
amend. = abbreviation of amendment
XVIII = # of amendment
§ 2 = # of section if applicable

---

c. *Statutes (Rule 12)*

Citation of an entire statute, the Federal Trademark Dilution Act of 1995, as codified in the United States Code:

Federal Trademark Dilution Act, 15 U.S.C. § 1125 (2000).

Federal Trademark Dilution Act = official name
15 = title #
U.S.C. = abbreviation of code
§ 1125 = section #
2000 = date of code edition

Citation of an individual provision of the United States Code:

15 U.S.C. § 1125 (2000).

---
15 = title #
U.S.C. = abbreviation of code
§ 1125 = section #
2000 = date of code edition

Short citation of provision of the United States Code:

15 U.S.C. § 1125 or § 1125.

---
15 = title #
U.S.C. = abbreviation of code
§ 1125 = section #
or § 1125 = section #

---

d.   Rules and Regulations (Rule 14)

Citation of a particular provision of a regulation in the Code of Federal Regulations:

49 C.F.R. § 172.101 (2005).

```
49 = title #
C.F.R. = abbreviation of regulations
§ 172.101 = section #
2005 = date of C.F.R. edition
```

NOTE: Whenever possible, cite all federal rules and regulations to the Code of Federal Regulations (C.F.R.) by title, section, and year.

Short citation of particular provision of a regulation in the C.F.R.:

49 C.F.R. § 172.101 or § 172.101.

```
49 = title #
C.F.R. = abbreviation of regulations
§ 172.101 = section #
or § 172.101 = section #
```

e.   Books (Rule 15)

Citation of treatise:

William L. Prosser & W. Page Keeton, <u>Prosser and Keeton on the Law of Torts</u> § 3.65 (5th ed. 1984).

```
William L. Prosser & W. Page Keeton = full name of 1st and 2nd authors
Prosser and Keeton on the Law of Torts = title of treatise
§ 3.65 = section #
5th ed. 1984—edition—if there is more than one—and date of edition
```

Citation of a particular page in a novel:

J. K. Rowling, <u>Harry Potter and the Sorcerer's Stone</u> 125 (1997).

```
J.K. Rowling—use full name of author unless author uses initials only
Harry Potter and the Sorcerer's Stone = title of book
125 = section or page #
1997 = year published
```

f.   *Periodical Materials (Rule 16)*

Citation of particular pages within a law review article:

Mustave Hurt, <u>Unimaginable Pain</u>, 742 Geo. L.J. 801, 831-32 (2003) (discussing the requirements to show deliverage indifference).

> Mustave Hurt = full name of author
> <u>Unimaginable Pain</u> = title of article
> 742 = journal volume #
> Geo. L.J. = abbreviation of journal
> 801 = first page of article
> 831-32 = specific pages
> 2003 = year published
> (discussing the requirements to show deliberate indifference)—parenthetical
>   describes article or point from article

Citation of an entire magazine article:

J. Madeleine Nash, <u>Fertile Minds</u>, Time, Feb. 3, 1997, at 18.

> J. Madeline Nash = author's full name
> Fertile Minds = title of article
> Time = name of magazine
> Feb. 3, 1997 = cover date
> at 18 = first page

Citation of a newspaper article:

Adam Gourna, <u>Celiac Disease: A Killer</u>, N.Y. Times, Dec. 12, 1994, at F3.

> Adam Gourna = author's full name
> <u>Celiac Disease: A Killer</u> = headline
> N.Y. Times = abbreviation of newspaper
> Dec. 12, 1994 = date
> at F3 = page #

C.   *Often-Used Bluebook Rules*

The following are some of the most-often used rules in the Bluebook citation format. They are provided for practitioners' use in court documents and legal memoranda.

Bluebook Typefaces (Bluepages 1, 2, 7, 8, 9, 13 and Rule 2)

BLUEBOOK RULE	KEY POINTS

B2: Citation Sentences and Clauses: Bluepages Tip
 	
Underscoring or italics may be appropriate in court documents or legal memoranda. However, check your local rules for the court's preference (Table BT2).
 	
    Example: Pope v. Hightower
 	
Rule 2: Typefaces for Law Reviews
	• Practitioners underscore or italicize all case names, including the "v."
	• Where the Bluepages indicates to use underscoring, italics may be substituted. Be consistent with underscoring or italics throughout the document.
	• In law reviews, three typefaces are commonly used:
	  1. Ordinary Roman (plain text)
	  2. Italics
	  3. Large and small capitals
	
	See Rule 2 for specifics.

B8: Books and Other Nonperiodic Materials B9: Journal and Newspaper Articles Example: Killer Tornado, Newsweek, Mar. 3, 1991, at 39.	Underscore or italicize the title of a book or the title of an article appearing in a periodical.

B1: Typeface Conventions
 	
This rule tries to clarify the distinction between the Bluepages typeface and law review typeface. It provides an exclusive list of underscored (or italicized) sources for practitioners.
 	
Words and Phrases Introducing Related Authority
 	
    Example: Red Sox Say Manager's Contract Won't Be Renewed, N.Y. Times, Oct. 27, 2003, available at http://www.nytimes.com/aponline/ sports/AP-BBA-Red-Sox-Little.html.
 	
If not specified as underscored or italicized, practitioners print everything else in ordinary Roman type.
 	
    Example: U.S. Const. amend. XVIII, § 2
	• Underscore or italicize subsequent case history.
	• Underscore or italicize "available at" and other similar words and phrases referring to related authority.
	• Underscore or italicize id. and supra.
	
	Print reporters, services, constitutions, statutes, Restatements, model codes, rules, executive orders, administrative materials, unpublished sources, and treaties in ordinary Roman type.

B7.3: Capitalization in Textual Sentences	• Capitalize "Court" in the following circumstances:
Examples: The Court of Appeals for the First Circuit held … The Supreme Court held … This Court should hold …	1. When naming any court in full; 2. When referring to the U.S. Supreme Court; 3. When referring to the court that will be receiving that document. • Capitalize party designations: Plaintiff, Defendant, Appellant, etc., when referring to those actual parties in your case only.

Bluebook Basic Structure and Signals (Bluepages 2, 3, 11 and Rule 1)

BLUEBOOK RULE	KEY POINTS
B2: Citation Sentences and Clauses Examples: See Jones v. Smith, 345 U.S. 322 (1985). Jones v. Smith, 345 U.S. 322 (1985); see also Cambridge v. Boston, 235 U.S. 412 (1977). Rule 1.1: Citation Sentences and Clauses in Law Reviews Example: [Footnote]2. Other authors have made similar assertions. Cf. Mustave Hurt, Unimaginable Pain, 742 Geo. L.J. 801, 831-32 (2003).	• Citations in court documents and legal memoranda traditionally appear within the text rather than in footnotes or endnotes. A citation within the text can appear in a stand-alone sentence or in a citation clause. • A citation sentence begins with a capital and ends with a period. If it contains multiple citations, it will include semicolons to separate each citation. • A citation clause is set off from the text with commas. • In law reviews, citations appear in footnotes. At times, an author might make an assertion within a footnote; here, a citation should appear in the footnote after the assertion.
B3: Introductory Signals Rule 1.2: Introductory Signals Example: See generally Killer Tornado, Newsweek, Mar. 3, 1991, at 39.	A signal is a sign to the reader indicating the type of authority about to be cited. • Signals that indicate support are no signal, e.g., accord, see, see also, cf. • A signal that suggests a useful comparison is compare … with …. • Signals that indicate contradiction are contra, but see, but cf. • A signal that indicates background material is see generally.
B3.5: Order of Signals Rule 1.3: Order of Signals Example: See Mustave Hurt, Unimaginable Pain, 742 Geo. L.J. 801, 831-32 (2003); see also Killer Tornado, Newsweek, Mar. 3, 1991, at 39. But see Adam Gourna, Celiac Disease: A Killer, N.Y. Times, Dec. 12, 1994, at F3.	• Signals of different types must be grouped in different citation sentences. • When more than one signal is used in a citation, the signals should appear in the order listed in Rule 1.2. • Signals of the same type must be strung together with a single citation sentence and separated by semicolons.

B3.5: Order of Signals Rule 1.4: Order of Authorities Within Each Signal Example: <u>See</u> <u>Turner</u>, 482 U.S. at 89; <u>see also</u> 28 C.F.R. § 540.71 (2002) (establishing security as legitimate government interest).	• Authorities within each signal are separated by semicolons. • General order: constitutions; statutes; treaties; cases; legislative materials; administrative and executive materials; resolutions, decisions, and regulations of intergovernmental organizations; records, briefs, and petitions; secondary materials; cross references. • In addition, the Bluebook has rules regarding the order within each one of these categories. • However, if one authority is more helpful, it should precede the others.
B11: Explanatory Parentheticals Rule 1.5: Parenthetical Information Example: 28 C.F.R. § 540.71 (2002) (establishing legitimate government interest).	• Additional information about a citation is added in a parenthetical at the end of the citation sentence or clause. • The text in a parenthetical need not be a full sentence; omit extraneous words such as "the." • Often, parentheticals begin with a present participle; however, a quotation or short phrase is also appropriate. • Parenthetical information is recommended when the relevance of the cited authority might not otherwise be clear to the reader. • Explanatory parenthetical phrases that do not directly quote the authority often begin with a present participle and usually do not begin with a capital letter. • If the parenthetical information includes one or more full sentences, it should start with a capital letter and end with the correct punctuation. • Explanatory parenthetical phrases come before any citations concerning subsequent history or other related authority. Rule 1.5(b) explains the order in which to present multiple parentheticals within a citation.

Bluebook Subdivisions and Pinpoint Cites (Bluepages 4.1.2 and Rule 3)

BLUEBOOK RULE	KEY POINTS
B4.1.2: Reporter and Pinpoint Citation Rule 3.2(a): Pages, Footnotes, Endnotes, and Graphical Materials Example: <u>Campbell v. Sikes</u>, 169 F.3d 53, 66 (1999). Example: <u>McElligot v. Foley</u>, 182 F.3d 1248, 1256-58 (11th Cir. 1999). Example: <u>Rhodes v. Chapman</u>, 452 U.S. 337, 346, 349 (1981).	• When referring to specific material within a source, include both the page on which the source begins and the page on which the specific materials appear, separated by a comma. • When citing material that spans more than one page, give the inclusive page numbers, separated by a hyphen or dash. Always retain the last two digits, but drop other repetitious digits. • Cite nonconsecutive pages by giving the individual page numbers separated by commas. • Give page number or numbers before the date parenthetical, without any introductory abbreviation. • Use "at" if page number may be confused with another part of the citation. • Use a comma to set off the "at." • If you are referring specifically to material on the first page of a source, repeat the page number. • When citing material within a concurring or dissenting opinion, give only the initial page of the case and the page on which the specific material appears. See B4.1.2.

Bluebook Short Citations (Rule 4)

BLUEBOOK RULE	KEY POINTS
In Bluepages, see specific sections for each appropriate short form (e.g., cases, statutes, and so on). Rule 4.1: "<u>Id.</u>" Example: 1. <u>Helling</u>, 509 U.S. 25, 29 (1993). 2. <u>Id.</u> at 35-36. 3. <u>See id.</u>	• Only use short citation format after an authority has been cited once in full citation format and when the reader will not be confused as to which source is being referenced. • Use <u>id.</u> when citing the immediately preceding authority. Capitalize <u>id.</u> when it appears in the beginning of a citation sentence; do not capitalize <u>id.</u> when it is not the beginning of a sentence. • <u>Id.</u> may not be used to refer to one authority in a preceding footnote if the preceding footnote cites more than one source.

Rule 4.2: "Supra" and "Hereinafter" Example: <u>Hurt</u>, <u>supra</u> note 3, at 8.	• Used to refer to legislative hearings, books, pamphlets, unpublished materials, nonprint resources, periodicals, services, treaties, international agreements, regulations, directives, and decisions of intergovernmental organizations. • Do not use to refer to cases, statutes, constitutions, legislative materials, Restatements, model codes, or regulations. • <u>Supra</u> form consists of the last name of the author, followed by a comma and the word "<u>supra</u>," then the footnote in which the full citation can be found, and the specific volume, paragraph, section, or page numbers cited.

Bluebook Abbreviations (Rule 6, Rule 10, BT1, Tables 1-6)

BLUEBOOK RULE	KEY POINTS
Rule 6.1: Abbreviations	• Abbreviations not found within the Bluebook should be avoided unless they are unambiguous and save substantial space. • Generally, close up adjacent capitals (N.W.), but do not close up single capitals with longer abbreviations (D. Mass.). See Rule 6.1.
Rule 6.2(a) Rule 6.2(c): Section (§) and Paragraph (¶) Symbols	• Spell out numbers zero to ninety-nine, but use numerals for larger numbers. Exceptions to this rule are laid out in Rule 6.2(a). • Spell out the words "section" and "paragraph" in the text. • In citations, the symbols should be used with a space between § or ¶ and the numeral.
Rule 10: Abbreviating Case Names	• Rule 10.2.1(c) addresses abbreviations of all case names whether they appear in text or in citations. • Rule 10.2.2 addresses further abbreviations for case names that appear in citations. • Rule 10.3.2: Reporters

BT1: Abbreviations in Court Documents	• The tables in the back of the Bluebook contain abbreviations for specific jurisdictions as well as for specific terms.
T1: Abbreviations for Specific Jurisdictions	
T6: Case Names and Institutional Authors in Citations	• Rules within the Bluebook will also have specific requirements for that rule.
T7: Court Names	• Example: Rule 10.2 for abbreviating case names.
T8: Explanatory Phrases	
T9: Legislative Documents: T9	
T10: Geographical Terms	
T11: Judges and Officials	
T12: Months	
T13, Periodicals	
T14: Publishing Terms	
T15: Services	
T16: Subdivisions	

Bluebook Cases (Bluepages 4 and Rule 10)

BLUEBOOK RULE	KEY POINTS

B4.1: Full Citation
 	
Rule 10.1: Basic Citation Forms
	• U.S. Supreme Court case:
	  • Example: Thornburgh v. Abbott, 490 U.S. 401, 407-08 (1989).
	• U.S. Court of Appeals case:
	  • Example: Pope v. Hightower, 101 F.3d 1382, 1383 (11th Cir. 1996).
	• Do not use superscripts when abbreviating words like "11th."

B4.1.1: Case Name Rule 10.2: Case Names	• Include only the necessary information in a case name and underline the entire case name up until the comma (do not underline the comma). • Use only the surname. • Omit words indicating multiple parties. Look up the abbreviations required in B4.1.1 and 10.2. Note that 10.2.2 provides extra rules for case names in citation sentences and clauses (as opposed to references to case names in text). 1. When a case name is used in a textual sentence (in text or footnotes), you should follow 10.2.1 (see below). 2. When a case name is used in a citation sentence or clause, you should refer to rules 10.2.1 and 10.2.2 (see below).

Rule 10.2.1: General Rules for Case Names	• Omit words indicating multiple parties, such as "et al.," and all parties other than the first listed on each side.
Example: <u>Harris v. Thigpen</u> *Not:* <u>Harris et al. v. Thigpen, Kramer & Levin</u>. Example: <u>Alabama v. Carter</u>, 507 U.S. 411, 418 (1992). Example: <u>Commonwealth v. Robertson</u> *Not:* <u>Commonwealth of Virginia v. Robertson</u> Example: <u>Montana Moving Co. v. Rhode Island Storage, Inc.</u> *Not:* <u>Montana Moving Co., Inc. v. Rhode Island Storage, Inc.</u>	• Abbreviate only widely known acronyms and the following eight words unless the word begins a party's name: 1. & 2. Ass'n 3. Bros. 4. Co. 5. Corp. 6. Inc. 7. Ltd. 8. No. • Usually omit "The" as the first word of a party's name. • Geographical terms: Omit "State of," "Commonwealth of," and "People of," except when citing decisions of the courts of that state. When citing decisions of the courts of that state, use "State," "Commonwealth," or "People." • Business firms: Omit "Inc.," "Ltd.," "L.L.C.," "N.A.," "F.S.B.," and similar terms if the name also contains a word such as "Ass'n," "Bros.," "Co.," and "R.R."
Rule 10.2.2: Additional Rules for Case Names That Appear in Citations Example: <u>Turner R.R. v. Safley</u> *Not:* <u>Turner Railroad v. Safley</u>. <u>Not:</u> <u>U.S. v. White</u>	• Always abbreviate any word listed in Table 6 (T6) and any geographic term in Table 10 (T10), unless the geographical unit is a named party. • Abbreviate other words of eight letters or more if the result is unambiguous and substantial space is saved. • Do not abbreviate "United States" in the case name when the United States is the actual party. (However, abbreviate United States when it is part of the party's name—e.g., U.S. Steel.)
Rule 10.3.3: Public Domain Format	• United States Court of Appeals for numbered circuits: 2d Cir., 4th Cir. • State Courts: Indicate state and court of decision, but do not include the name of the court if the court of decision is the highest court in the state. Omit jurisdiction if it is unambiguously conveyed by the reporter. • See Table T7 for court abbreviations.
B4.1.2: Reporter and Pinpoint Citation Example: <u>Jones v. Smith</u>, 230 U.S. 432, 434 (1986).	• When providing reporter information, you should provide the volume and abbreviation for the reporter as well as the page on which the opinion begins. • A pinpoint cite or jump cite is a reference to the specific page(s) for your proposition.

B4.1.3: Court and Year of Decision Rule 10.4: Court and Jurisdiction Example: <u>United States v. White</u>, 490 U.S. 84, 87 (1990).	• Give the name of the court and its geographical jurisdiction, abbreviating using Table 1 (T1) or Table 2 (T2), in the parenthetical immediately following the citation. You may omit the name of the jurisdiction and court abbreviation of state courts if it is unambiguously conveyed by the title of the reporter. Do not include the name of the deciding court in the parenthetical when citing the U.S. Supreme Court or the highest court of a state. • Include the year of the decision in the parenthetical. • Cite to the Supreme Court using U.S., not S. Ct., when the U.S. citation is available.
B4 1.5: Weight of Authority and Explanatory Parentheticals Rule 10.6: Parenthetical Information Regarding Cases	• Parentheticals may be used to convey information regarding weight of authority, related authority, or a proposition that is not the holding of majority. • Rule 10.6.3 indicates the correct order of parentheticals: (i) weight of authority, (ii) "quoting" or "citing" parentheticals, and (iii) explanatory parentheticals.

B4.2: Short Form Citation
 	
Rule 10.9: Short Forms for Cases
 	
    Acceptable Examples:
 	
    <u>Jones</u>, 250 S.E.2d at 240. 250 S.E.2d at 240.
 	
    <u>Id.</u> at 35-36.
 	
    See <u>id.</u> at 35-36.
	• A short form is a shortened reference to a citation. You may use a short form if it clearly provides the correct reference, the full citation is provided in the same general discussion, and the full citation can be easily found if the reader wishes to do so.
	• There are a number of acceptable short forms; most of them include "at" with a pinpoint cite.
	• When using a name for a short form, use the first party's name unless it is a geographical term or government name.
	• "<u>Id.</u>" may be used in court documents and legal memoranda to refer to a case cited in the previous citation. When used at the beginning of a citation sentence, capitalize the "i." However, when used in the middle of a citation sentence, do not capitalize the "i." Do not use "<u>supra</u>" to refer to previously cited cases in a court document or legal memorandum.

Bluebook Constitutions (Bluepages 6 and Rule 11)

BLUEBOOK RULE	KEY POINTS

B6: Constitutions
 	
Rule 11: Constitutions
 	
  Example: U.S. Const. amend. XVIII, § 2.
	• Abbreviate United States (U.S.).
	• Abbreviate United States (U.S.) if referring to the federal Constitution, or refer to Table T10 for the appropriate abbreviation if citing a state constitution.
	• Use Const., not CONST.
	• If the constitutional provision has been repealed, amended, or superseded, refer to Rule 11 for appropriate citation format.
	• Short form: Do not use short citation form (other than <u>id.</u>) for constitutions.
	• Cite state constitutions by the abbreviated name of the state and the word "Const."
	• Abbreviate subdivisions of constitutions according to Table 16 (T16).
	    • Example: Ala. Const. art. V, § 9.

Bluebook Statutes (Bluepages 5 and Rule 12)

BLUEBOOK RULE	KEY POINTS

B5: Statutes, Rules, and Regulations
 	
Rule 12.1: Basic Citation Forms for Statutes.
 	
  Example: 42 U.S.C. § 1983 (1994).
 	
  Example: 42 U.S.C. §§ 8401-8405 (2000).
	• Cite current statutes to the official code. (Cite U.S.C., not U.S.C.A. or U.S.C.S.)
	• Place periods in between "U.S.C."
	• Do not underline statute citations.
	• Leave a space between "§" and the cited section numbers.
	• When citing multiple sections, use "§§."
	• Include the year the code was published in a parenthetical.
	• Include the official name of the act when available.

Example for Law Review: IND. CODE § 35-42-5-1 (1998). Example for Practitioner: Mo. Ann. Stat. §565.225(3) (West 2010). Example: 18 U.S.C.A. § 1028 (West 2000 & Supp. 2010)	• Cite to the official federal and state codes whenever possible. The official federal code is the United States Code, "U.S.C." To determine the official code for a particular state, see Table T1. • If citing to a code that is published, edited, or compiled by someone other than state officials, give the name of the publisher, editor, or compiler in the parenthetical phrase (Rule 12.3.1(d)). For example: West (2006). • According to Rule 12.3.1(a), if the statute is commonly cited using a different name or is known by a popular name, give that name and the original section number preceding the normal citation format. • If the statute appears in a supplement or pocket part, cite the statute according to Rule 3.1(c). See Rule 12.3.1(e) for examples of the proper citation format. • If a statute has been invalidated, repealed, or amended, cite it in accordance with Rule 12.7. When citing a current version of a statute that has prior history, you may give the prior history in an explanatory parenthetical phrase according to Rule 12.8. • Some statutes require special citation forms. Rule 12.9 indicates that these include the Internal Revenue Code (12.9.1), ordinances (12.9.2), model codes, restatements, standards, and sentencing guidelines (12.9.5).
B5.1.3: Rules of Evidence and Procedure; Restatements; Uniform Acts	Do not include dates.

Rule 12.9.3: Rules of Evidence and Procedure
 	
Rule 12.9.5: Model Codes, Restatements, Standards, and Sentencing Guidelines
 	
    Examples: Fed. R. Evid. 213 Fed. R. Crim. P. 11.
 	
    Restatement (Second) of Torts § 84 (1989).
 	
    Example: U.S. Sentencing Guidelines Manual § 5D2.1(f) (2001).	

B5.2: Short Forms (for Statutes) Rule 12.10: Short Forms for Statutes Example: 42 U.S.C. § 1221 or § 1221.	• Id. may be used in court documents and legal memoranda to refer to the previously cited statute or to a statute within the same title previously cited. • Use chart from 12.10(b) to determine proper format for named statutes, U.S. Code provisions, state code provisions, and session laws.

Bluebook Administrative and Executive Materials
(Bluepages 5.1.4 and Rule 14)

BLUEBOOK RULE	KEY POINTS
B5.1.4: Administrative Rules and Regulations Rule 14.2: Rules, Regulations, and Other Publications Example: 28 C.F.R. § 540.71 (2003).	Whenever possible, cite all federal rules and regulations to the Code of Federal Regulations (C.F.R.) by title, section or part, and year. • Be sure to cite the most recent edition of C.F.R., according to Rule 14.2(a). • Do not leave spaces between the letters of "C.F.R." • If a federal rule or regulation is known by a common name or is typically cited using a name, indicate that name before the title number, using the format specified in Rule 14.2(a).
Example: Numismatic Products Pricing, 76 FR 417 (Dec 29, 2010).	• According to Rule 14.2(a), if a rule or regulation has not yet been published in C.F.R., cite to the Federal Register. Administrative notices should be cited to the Federal Register.
Example: Flexsteel Industries, Inc., 311 N.L.R.B. 257 (1993).	• Cite to arbitrations and administrative adjudications using the same format for cases in Rule 10. However, according to Rule 14.3.1, case names or administrative adjudications are identified by the first-listed private party, or by the official subject-matter title. Case names of arbitrations are cited according to Rule 10 or, if adversary parties are not named, like administrative adjudications according to Rule 14.3.1(a).
Example: Attorney-General—Secretary of War, 20 Op. Att'y Gen. 740 (1894).	• Advisory opinions from the United States Attorney General or any other government entity are cited according to the "Department of Justice" section in Table T1.2. • Federal tax statutes are cited according to Rule 12.8.1, but other federal taxation materials, including Treasury regulations, determinations, and cases, are cited according to Table T1.2.
Example: Exec. Order No. 12,356, 3 C.F.R. 166 (1983). Example: Proclamation No. 13526, 75 Fed. Reg. 707 (Dec. 29, 2009).	• Presidential executive orders are found in title 3 of C.F.R. and should be cited to C.F.R. according to Rule 14.2, with a parallel citation to the United States Code if therein. However, if an executive order is not found in C.F.R., cite according to the Federal Register. Examples of each citation format can be found under the heading "Executive Office of the President" in Table T1.2. • Patents should be cited according to the patent number and the data the patent was filed, using the format specified in "Department of Commerce, Patent and Trademark Office (USPTO)" in Table T1.2.

B5.2: Short Form Citation	• Use chart in Rule 14.4(c) to determine proper format for regulations.
Rule 14.4: Short Forms for Regulations	• <u>Id.</u> may be used in court documents and legal memoranda to refer to the previously cited regulation or to a regulation within the same title previously cited.
Example: 28 C.F.R. § 540.71 or § 540.71.	

Bluebook Books, Reports, and Other Nonperiodic Materials (Bluepages 8 and Rule 15)

BLUEBOOK RULE	KEY POINTS
B8: Books and Other Nonperiodic Materials Rule 15: Books, Reports, and Other Nonperiodic Materials Example: <u>Noah Lee, Deliberate Indifference: What's It All About?</u> 31 (3d ed. 2001).	• Cite books, reports, and other nonperiodic materials by author, title (underlined), pinpoint page, section or paragraph, edition (if more than one), and date (in parenthetical). • When citing a publication for the first time, give the author's full name as it appears on the publication. However, do not include designations indicating academic degrees such as "Dr." See Rule 15.1. • For works with two authors, give their names in the order in which they are listed on the title page, separated by "&" (Rule 15.1(a)).
Example: Emily Noel et al., <u>The Costs and Benefits of Negligence</u> 56-72 (2d ed, 1988).	• For works with more than two authors, you may use the name of the first author listed followed by "et al." or, where it is important to include all the authors' names and space is not an issue, you may list all of their names, separating the final name with "&"(Rule 15.1(b)).
Example: Jeremy Stevens, <u>Taking Control</u> 41-42 (Amanda Bradley ed., Scholastic Press 3d. ed. 2001).	• Rule 15.2 specifies the format for works with editors or translators. Give the full name of the editor in a parenthetical as it appears in the publication. In the same parenthetical, after the full name of the editor, indicate the editor's title with "ed.," the name of the publisher (if other than the original publisher), and the year of publication. • According to Rule 15.3, give the name of the work according to how it appears on the title page. Refer to Rule 8 to determine which words in a title to capitalize. Do not omit articles from the title.

Example: John T. Smith, Jr., <u>Morality and Law</u> 67 (1965). Example: <u>Blacks Law Dictionary</u> (9th ed. 2009).	• For works that have been published in only one edition, give the year of publication in parentheses (Rule 15.4(a)(i)). For works that have been published in multiple editions, cite the latest edition according to Rule 15.4(a) unless an earlier edition is more relevant • Some works are cited so frequently that they have special citation forms in Rule 15.8. These works include Black's Law Dictionary, American Jurisprudence, and Corpus Juris Secundum.
B8.2: Short Form Citation Rule 15.9: Short Citation Forms Example: Stevens, <u>supra</u>, at 45.	• If the work was cited as the immediately preceding authority, use <u>id.</u> • If the work has been cited in full, but not as the immediately preceding authority, use <u>supra</u>.

Bluebook Periodicals (Bluepages 9 and Rule 16)

BLUEBOOK RULE	KEY POINTS
B9.1.1: Consecutively Paginated Journals Rule 16.4: Consecutively Paginated Journals Example: Mustave Hurt, <u>Unimaginable Pain</u>, 742 Geo. L.J. 801, 831-32 (2003).	• Include author, title of work, volume number, periodical name, first page of work, pages on which cited material appears, and year. • Use Table 13 (T.13) to abbreviate the names of periodicals. • Cite the author's full name as it appears in the publication according to Rule 15.1. • Cite the full title of the article as it appears on the title page of the publication, but refer to Rule 8 for capitalization. • Cite the volume number, followed by the abbreviation of the journal name according to Table T13, and the page number on which the cited material begins. • Indicate the date of publication in a parenthetical.
B9.1.2: Nonconsecutively Paginated Journals and Magazines Rule 16.5: Nonconsecutively Paginated Journals and Magazines Example: <u>Killer Tornado</u>, Newsweek, Mar. 3, 1991, at 39, 40.	• Cite works appearing within periodicals that are separately paginated within each issue by author, title, periodical name, date of issue, and first page of work and/or pages on which material appears. • Use Table 13 (T13) to abbreviate names of periodicals.

B9.1.4: Newspaper Articles Rule 16.6: Newspapers Example: <u>Celiac Disease: A Killer</u>, N.Y. Times, Dec. 12, 1994, at F3.	• Use Table 13 (T13) to abbreviate names of newspapers. • Cite the same as for nonconsecutively paginated periodicals (Rule 16.4), but only the first page of the work need be cited.
Rule 16.7: Student Written Law Review Materials	• If the piece you are citing is student-written, follow Rule 16.7.1(a) if it is signed or 16.7.1(b) if it is unsigned. Be sure to indicate the type of piece you are citing, either a "Note" or "Comment" or some other type of work. • For book reviews by nonstudents, reference Rule 16.7.2. • For book reviews written by students, reference Rule 16.7.1(c). • If the work under review is unclear from the surrounding text, include a second parenthetical following the date of publication identifying the work.

Bluebook Electronic Media (Rule 18)

BLUEBOOK RULE	**KEY POINTS**
Rule 18.2.1: General Internet Principles (a) Sources that can be cited as if to original print source (b) Sources to which the URL should be appended (c) Sources using "available at" to indicate when access is available online	• When an authenticated, official, or exact copy of a source can be found online, citation can be made as if to the original print source (without URL information). Some states have started to discontinue printed official legal sources and instead rely on online versions as the official resource, but the federal government continues to publish official print versions. • Note the Bluebook's definitions of and distinctions among "Authenticated Documents," "Official Versions," and "Exact Copies." • When a cited source is available in print but is so obscure as to be practically unavailable, citation should be as if to the printed source, but append the URL directly to the end of citation to indicate online location of the copy. • If a printed source is available, a parallel citation to an electronic source may be appropriate where it would substantially improve access to the information. Citation should be made to the printed source first and then separately to the electronic source, introduced with the explanation phrase *"available at."*

Rule 18.2.2: Direct Citation to Internet Sources Include: Author, Title, Date (and Time When Relevant), URL	• Cite to an Internet source when the material does not exist in a traditional printed format or when the printed source exists but cannot be found or is practically unavailable because it is so obscure. • Cite to the most stable electronic location. • Include information to facilitate the clearest path of access, including title page, pagination, and publication date as they appear on the website. The URL should be separated by a comma and appended to the end of the citation.
Rule 18.2.3: Parallel Citations to Internet Sources Example: Diana Donahoe, *Strip Searches of Students: Addressing the Undressing of Children in Schools and Redressing the Fourth Amendment Violations,* 75 Mo. L. Rev. (forthcoming 2010), available at http://ssrn.com/abstract=444455.	• When a source is available in a traditional printed medium, you may provide a parallel cite to an Internet source with identical content if it will substantially improve access to the source. • The parallel Internet cite should be introduced with the explanatory phrase *"available at."* Rule 18.2.3(a). • The author, title, pagination, and publication date of the original printed source should be used even when the Internet provides slightly different information. But if the information on the Internet differs materially from the information in the traditional printed source, a parallel citation should not be used. Rule 18.2.3(b). • A parallel citation does not affect the order of authorities. Rule 18.2.3(c).

Rule 18.3.1: Commercial Electronic Databases: Cases	• When case is unreported, but available on widely used electronic database, it may be cited to the database.
Example: <u>Ossining v. Brubaker</u>, No. CIV.A.02-2332, 2003 U.S. Dist. LEXIS 5130, at *1 (S.D. Ala. Jan. 6, 2003).	• Provide the case name, docket number, database identifier, court name, and full date of most recent major disposition.
	• Example: Westlaw: WL Lexis: LEXIS
	• Screen or page numbers, if assigned, should be preceded by an asterisk. Paragraph numbers, if assigned, should be preceded by a paragraph symbol.
	• If the electronic database provides a unique identifying number for the case, remember to provide it following the case name, preceded by "No."
	• If citing to a specific page or screen of an opinion, indicate the page number preceded by an asterisk. If citing to a particular paragraph, indicate the paragraph number preceded by "¶."
	• For addresses, books, periodicals, and other secondary material, refer to Rule 18.3.4.
Rule 18.3.2: Constitutions and Statutes	• Cite statutes according to Rules 12.3 and 12.4.
Example: Mich. Comp. Laws § 22.33 (West, Westlaw through 2003 Sess.).	• In addition, when citing statutes from an electronic database (such as Lexis or Westlaw), give within a parenthetical the name of the database and information about the currency of the database, as provided by the database itself, instead of the year of the code according to Rule 12.3.2.
Example: Mich. Comp. Laws Ann. § 22.33 (Michie, LEXIS through 2003 Legislation).	• Also give the name of the publisher, editor, or compiler unless the code is published, edited, compiled, by or under the supervision of federal or state officials (see Rule 12.3.1(d)).

V. STUDY AIDS—BLUEBOOK CITATION

A. *Bluebook Quick Reference and Checklists*

📝 1. The Bluebook in General: Quick Reference

To use the Bluebook effectively, you should understand the following:

- The purpose of citation
- The design, layout, and basic rules of the Bluebook
- Some often-used rules of the Bluebook

Purpose of Citation

The purpose of citation is to allow lawyers to easily find and reference legal sources.

Design, Layout, and Basic Bluebook Citation Rules

Bluebook Design

- In general, provides citation formats for scholarly documents.
- "Quick Reference" on front inside cover provides most-often used citations for law reviews.
- Bluepages provide citation rules for court documents and legal memoranda.
- "Quick Reference" on back inside cover provides most-often used citations for court documents and legal memoranda.

Bluebook Layout

Citations

- Cases: Rule 10
- Constitutions: Rule 11
- Statutes: Rule 12
- Administrative and Executive Materials, including Rules and Regulations: Rule 14
- Books, Reports, and Other Nonperiodic Materials: Rule 15
- Periodical Materials: Rule 16

Tables

- United States Jurisdictions: T1
  - Federal Judicial and Legislative Materials: T1.1
  - Federal Administrative and Executive Materials: T1.2
  - States and the District of Columbia: T1.3
  - Other Untied States Jurisdictions: T1.4
- Foreign Jurisdictions: T2
- Intergovernmental Organizations and Treaty Sources: T3 and T4
- Abbreviations for Arbitral Reporter Sources: T5

- Abbreviations for Case Names and Court Names: T6 and T7
- Abbreviations for Explanatory Phrases and Legislative Documents: T8 and T9
- Abbreviations for Publishing Terms and Services: T14 and T15
- Abbreviations for Document Subdivisions: T16
- Table of Contents
- Index

Basic Bluebook Citation Rules

- Cases: Rule 10
- Constitutions: Rule 11
- Statutes: Rule 12
- Rules and Regulations: Rule 14
- Books: Rule 15
- Periodical Materials: Rule 16

Often-Used Bluebook Citation Rules

- Typefaces: Bluepages 1, 2, 7, 8, 9, and Rule 2
- Basic Structure and Signals: Bluepages 2, 3, 11 and Rule 1
- Subdivisions and Pinpoint Cites: Bluepages 4.1.2 and Rule 3
- Short Citations: Rule 4
- Abbreviations: Rule 6
- Cases: Bluepages 4 and Rule 10
- Constitutions: Bluepages 6 and Rule 11
- Statutes: Bluepages 5 and Rule 12
- Administrative and Executive Materials: Bluepages 5.1.4 and Rule 14
- Books, Reports, and Other Nonperiodic Materials: Bluepages 8 and Rule 15
- Periodicals: Bluepages 9 and Rule 16
- Electronic Media: Rule 18

---

2. Bluebook Typeface Conventions: Checklist

✓ Bluepages B1 addresses typeface conventions for court documents. In court documents, underline (or italicize) the following:
- Case names
- Titles of books and articles
- Titles of legislative materials
- Introductory signals
- Explanatory phrases introducing subsequent case history
- Words and phrases introducing related authority (such as "quoted in" or "citing")
- Cross-references (such as "<u>id.</u>" and "<u>supra</u>")

✓ Remember to underline the "v." in case names.
✓ Note that citations in law review articles have different typeface conventions than court documents. Bluepages B1 and Rule 2 address these differences.

 3. Basic Structure and Signals for Bluebook Citations: Checklist

✓ Types of Signals: See Rule 1.2.
  - Signals that show support: <u>E.g.</u>, <u>Accord</u>, <u>See</u>, <u>See also</u>, <u>Cf.</u>
  - Signals that suggest a useful comparison: <u>Compare</u> ... <u>with</u> ...
  - Signals that indicate contradiction: <u>Contra</u>, <u>But see</u>, <u>But cf.</u>
  - Signals that indicate background material: <u>See generally</u>
✓ Order of Signals: See Rule 1.3. Signals of the same basic type are strung together within one citation sentence and are separated from each other by semicolons. If there are signals of different types then they must be grouped in separate citation sentences. Follow order in Rule 1.2 (Support, Comparison, Contradiction, and Background).
✓ Order of Authorities Within Each Signal: See Rule 1.4 for more details within each category. Constitutions; Statutes; Treaties and other International Agreements; Cases; Legislative Materials; Administrative and Executive Materials; Resolutions, Decisions, and Regulations of Intergovernmental Organizations; Records, Briefs, and Petitions; Secondary Materials. Cases decided by the same court are arranged in reverse chronological order.
✓ Parenthetical Information explains the relevance of a particular authority to proposition given in the text. See Rule 1.5.
  - Explanatory parenthetical phrases that do not directly quote the authority usually begin with a present participle and usually do not begin with a capital letter.
  - If the parenthetical information includes one or more full sentences, it should start with a capital letter and end with the correct punctuation.
  - Explanatory parenthetical phrases come before any citations concerning subsequent history or other related authority. Rule 1.5(b) explains the order in which to present multiple parentheticals within a citation.

☑ 4. Bluebook Citation Signals: Checklist

Signals in Text	Proposition	Cited Authority and Meaning
SUPPORT		
[No signal]		Directly <u>states</u> proposition.
<u>See</u>; <u>see also</u>		Clearly <u>supports</u>; obviously follows from proposition.
<u>Cf.</u>		Analogous proposition.
<u>E.g.</u>; <u>see, e.g.</u>,		Multiple authorities clearly <u>state</u> the proposition.
CONTRADICTION		
<u>Contra</u>		Directly <u>states</u> contrary proposition.
BACKGROUND		
<u>See generally</u>		Helpful, related background material.
COMPARISON		
<u>Compare</u> … <u>with</u> …		Comparison of cited authorities supports proposition.

5.   Bluebook Rules for Citing Subdivisions and
Pinpoint Cites: Checklist

Rule 3.2(a) address the proper format for citations to specific page numbers:

- Give page number or numbers before the date parenthetical, without any introductory abbreviation.
- Use "at" if page number may be confused with another part of the citation.
- Use a comma to set off the "at."
- If you are referring specifically to material on the first page of a source, repeat the page number.
- When citing material within a concurring or dissenting opinion, give only the initial page of the case and the page on which the specific material appears. See B4.1.2.
- When citing material that spans more than one page, give the inclusive page numbers separated by the en dash (–). Always retain the last two digits but drop other repetitious digits.
- Cite nonconsecutive pages by giving the individual page numbers separated by commas.

————————————

 6.   Bluebook Rules for Short Form Citations:
Checklist

✓ According to Bluepages B4.2 and Rule 4, once you have provided one full citation to an authority, you are free to use a "short form" in later citations to the same authority, so long as (i) it will be clear to the reader from the short form what is being referenced, (ii) the earlier full citation falls in the same general discussion, and (iii) the reader will have little more trouble quickly locating the full citation. General rule: Avoid confusion.
✓ For short form citations to cases, refer to Rule 10.9. Use one party's name, the volume number, reporter designation, and page number.
  • Example: <u>Youngstown</u>, 343 U.S. at 585.
  • Party Name: When using only one party name in a short form citation, use the name of the first party, unless that party is a geographical or governmental unit or other common litigant.
✓ B5.2 and Rule 12.10 gives the short form citation rules for statutes, rules, and regulations.
✓ <u>Id.</u>: Use to refer to the immediately preceding authority (B4.2 and Rules 4.1, 10.9).
  • The "i" in "<u>id.</u>" is capitalized only when it begins a citation sentence.
  • To refer to a different page within the immediately preceding authority, add "at" and the new pinpoint cite.

- _Id._ may be used only when the preceding citation cites to only one source.
✓ _Supra_: See Rule 4.2. Once a work in a periodical, book, legislative hearing, report, unpublished work, or nonprint resource has been fully cited, use _id._ to refer to material cited in the immediately preceding citation. Otherwise, use _Supra_ for legislative hearings, reports, unpublished materials, nonprint resources, periodicals, regulations, etc. that have previously been cited fully. _Supra_ form generally consists of the last name of the author of the work, followed by a comma and the word "_Supra_." Indicate any manner the citation differs from the former (B9.2, Rule 16.9). Example: Reich, _Supra_ note 18, at 6.

☑ 7.   Bluebook Abbreviations: Checklist

✓ Rule 6.1 is the general rule on abbreviations. Tables at the end of the Bluebook contain lists of specific abbreviations:
  - Arbitral Reporters: T5
  - Case Names: T6, Rule 10.2
    - Rule 10.2.1(c) addresses abbreviations of all case names whether they appear in text or in citations.
    - Rule 10.2.2 addresses further abbreviations for case names that appear in citations.
  - Court Names: T7
  - Reporters: T1, Rule 10.3.2
  - Explanatory Phrases: T8
  - Legislative Documents: T9
  - Current Official and Unofficial Codes: T1, Rule 12.3
  - Ordinances: 12.9.2
  - Rules of Evidence and Procedure: 12.9.3
  - Geographical Terms: T10
  - Judges and Officials: T11
  - Months: T12
  - Periodicals: T13, Rules 16.3-16.6
  - Publishing Terms: T14
  - Services: T15
  - Subdivisions: T16
✓ Spacing: Generally, close up adjacent single capitals (e.g., N.W.), but do not close up single capitals with longer abbreviations (e.g., D. Mass.). See Rule 6.1.

☑ 8.   Bluebook Rules for Citing Cases: Checklist

✓ According to Rule 10.1 and Bluepages B4.1, the general citation form for cases includes: Case Name, reporter volume number + reporter abbreviations + first page of case, page # (deciding court + date of decision).
✓ Case Names: Rule 10.2

a. For case names that appear in textual sentences and citation sentences, refer to Rule 10.2.1:
    - Omit all parties other than the first one on each side. Omit words indicating multiple parties, such as "et al." See Rule 10.2.1(a) and B4.1.1.
    - Abbreviate only widely known acronyms that appear in Rule 6.1(b) and these eight words: &, Ass'n, Bros., Co., Corp., Inc., Ltd., and No. See Rule 10.2.1(c).
    - Omit "The" as the first word of a party's name. See Rule 10.2.1(d).
    - Omit "State of," "Commonwealth of," and "People of" unless citing decisions of the courts of that state, in which case only "State," "Commonwealth," or "People" should be retained. See Rule 10.2.1(f).
    - Generally, omit given names or initials of individuals, but not in names or businesses of firms. See Rule 10.2.1(g).
    - Omit business firm designations such as "Inc." if the name of the firm also contains a word that clearly indicates its status as a business firm, such as "Ass'n." See Rule 10.2.1(h).
b. For case names that appear in citations, also refer to Rule 10.2.2. Note that case names in citations generally follow the rules detailed in Rule 10.2.1, with the following modifications:
    - Abbreviate any word that appears in Table T6.
    - Abbreviate states, countries, and other geographical units as they appear in Table T10. However, do not abbreviate geographical units if they are the entire name of a party (including "United States").
    - Abbreviate words of eight letters or more if doing so saves substantial space and the abbreviations are unambiguous.

✓ Reporters: see Rule 10.3.2, B4.1.2, and Table T1. A citation to a reporter should include the volume number of the reporter, the abbreviated name of the reporter as found in Table T1, and the page on which the case begins.

✓ Public Domain Format: see Rule 10.3.3. See Table T7 for court abbreviations.
  - United States Court of Appeals for numbered circuits: 2d Cir., 4th Cir.
  - State Courts: Indicate state and court of decision, but do not include the name of the court if the court of decision is the highest court in the state. Omit jurisdiction if it is unambiguously conveyed by reporter title.

✓ Use dates of decisions according to Rule 10.5 and B4.1.3.

✓ According to Rule 10.6 and B4.1.5, parentheticals may be used to convey information regarding weight of authority, related authority, or a proposition that is not the holding of majority. Rule 10.6.3 indicates the correct order of parentheticals: (i) weight of authority, (ii) "quoting" or "citing" parentheticals, and (iii) explanatory parentheticals.

✓ If a case is unreported but available on electronic media, cite it according to Rules 10.8.1 and 18.

✓ Appropriate short form citations for cases are listed in Rule 10.9 and B4.2.

 9. Bluebook Rules for Citing Constitutions: Checklist

✓ Abbreviate United States (U.S.) if referring to the federal Constitution, or refer to Table T10 for the appropriate abbreviation if citing a state constitution (Rule 11).

✓ Abbreviate "Constitution" as "Const." (Rule 11).

✓ Refer to Table T16 for the appropriate abbreviations of article (art.), amendment (amend.), section (§), and clause (cl.).

✓ If the constitutional provision has been repealed, amended, or superseded, refer to Rule 11 for the appropriate citation format.

✓ <u>Id.</u> is the only acceptable format for short citations to constitutions (Rule 11).

 10. Bluebook Rules for Citing Statutes: Checklist

✓ Cite to the official federal and state codes whenever possible. The official federal code is the United States Code, "U.S.C." To determine the official code for a particular state, see Table T1.

✓ Make sure that the abbreviations of code names are properly formatted. There should be periods and no spaces between the letters "U.S.C." See Table T1 to determine the proper abbreviation formats for state codes.

✓ Use "§" to denote the section number of the code that you are citing. Leave a space between "§" and the section number, and use "§§" if you are citing multiple sections.

✓ Include the date of the code edition cited in a parenthetical following the section number (Rules 12.3.2 and 12.4(e)). If citing to a code that is published, edited, or compiled by someone other than state officials, give the name of the publisher, editor, or compiler in the parenthetical phrase (Rule 12.3.1(d)). For example: (West 2006).

✓ According to Rule 12.3.1(a), if the statute is commonly cited using a different name or is known by a popular name, give that name and the original section number preceding the normal citation format.

✓ If a statute appears in a supplement or pocket part, cite the statute according to Rule 3.1(c). See Rule 12.3.1(e) for examples of the proper citation format.

✓ If a statute has been invalidated, repealed, or amended, cite it in accordance with Rule 12.7. When citing a current version of a statute that has prior history, you may give the prior history in an explanatory parenthetical phrase according to Rule 12.8.

✓ Some statutes require special citation forms. Rule 12.9 indicates that these include the Internal Revenue Code (12.9.1), ordinances (12.9.2), rules of evidence and procedure (12.9.3), uniform acts (12.9.4), and model codes, restatements, standards, and sentencing guidelines (12.9.5).

✓ If a statute is previously cited, you may use a short form of the statute according to Rule 12.10(c). <u>Id.</u> may be used in court documents and legal memoranda if the same statute is previously cited or the statute is within the same title as a previously cited statute.

 ## 11. Bluebook Citations for Administrative and Executive Materials: Checklist

✓ Cite federal rules and regulations (except Treasury materials) to the Code of Federal Regulations (C.F.R.). Rules and regulations found in C.F.R. should be identified by title, section number or part, and year of the code edition cited, using the format specified in Rule 14.2.

    a. Be sure to cite the most recent edition of C.F.R., according to Rule 14.2(a).

    b. Do not leave spaces between the letters of "C.F.R."

✓ If a federal rule or regulation is known by a common name or is typically cited using a name, indicate that name before the title number, using the format specified in Rule 14.2(a).

✓ According to Rule 14.2(a), if a rule or regulation has not yet been published in C.F.R., cite to the Federal Register. Administrative notices should also be cited to the Federal Register.

✓ To use a short citation to identify a rule or regulation, use one of the formats listed in Rule 14.4(c).

✓ Cite to arbitrations and administrative adjudications using the same format for cases in Rule 10. However, according to Rule 14.3.1, case names of administrative adjudications are identified by the first-listed private party, or by the official subject-matter title. Case names of arbitrations are cited according to Rule 10 or, if adversary parties are not named, like administrative adjudications according to Rule 14.3.1(a).

✓ Advisory opinions from the United States Attorney General or any other government entity are cited according to the "Department of Justice" section in Table T1.2.

✓ Federal tax statutes are cited according to Rule 12.9.1, but other federal taxation materials, including Treasury regulations, determinations, and cases, are cited according to Table T1.2.

✓ Presidential executive orders are found in title 3 of C.F.R. and should be cited to C.F.R. according to Rule 14.2, with a parallel citation to the United States Code if therein. However, if an executive order is not found in C.F.R., cite according to the Federal Register. Examples of each citation format can be found under the heading "Executive Office of the President" in Table T1.2.

✓ Patents should be cited according to the patent number and the date the patent was filed, using the format specified in "Department of Commerce, Patent and Trademark Office (USPTO)" in Table T1.2.

 ## 12. Bluebook Citations for Books, Reports, and Other Nonperiodic Materials: Checklist

✓ According to Rule 15.1, when citing a publication for the first time, give the author's full name as it appears on the publication. However, do not include designations indicating academic degrees such as "Dr."
  a. For works with two authors, give their names in the order in which they are listed on the title page, separated by "&" (Rule 15.1(a)).
  b. For works with more than two authors, you may use the name of the first author listed followed by "et al." or, where it is important to include all the authors' names and space is not an issue, you may list all of their names, separating the final name with "&" (Rule 15.1(b)).

✓ Rule 15.2 specifies the format for works with editors or translators. Give the full name of the editor in a parenthetical as it appears in the publication. In the same parenthetical, after the full name of the editor, indicate the editor's title with "ed.," the name of the publisher (if other than the original publisher), and the year of publication.

✓ According to Rule 15.3, give the name of the work according to how it appears on the title page. Refer to Rule 8 to determine which words in a title to capitalize. Do not omit articles from the title.

✓ For works that have been published in only one edition, give the year of publication in parentheses (Rule 15.4(a)(i)). For works that have been published in multiple editions, cite the latest edition according to Rule 15.4(a) unless an earlier edition is more relevant.

✓ Some works are cited so frequently that they have special citation forms in Rule 15.8. These works include Black's Law Dictionary, American Jurisprudence, and Corpus Juris Secundum.

 ## 13. Bluebook Rules for Citing Periodical Materials: Checklist

✓ For consecutively paginated journals (Rule 16.4):
  a. Cite the author's full name as it appears in the publication according to Rule 15.1.
  b. Cite the full title of the article as it appears on the title page of the publication, but refer to Rule 8 for capitalization.
  c. Cite the volume number, followed by the abbreviation of the journal name according to Table T13, and the page number on which the cited material begins.
  d. Indicate the date of publication in a parenthetical.

e. If the piece you are citing is student-written, follow Rule 16.7.1(a) if it is signed or 16.7.1(b) if it is unsigned. Be sure to indicate the type of piece you are citing, either a "Note" or "Comment" or some other type of work.

f. For book reviews written by nonstudents, reference Rule 16.7.2. For book reviews written by students, reference Rule 16.7.1(c). If the work under review is unclear from the surrounding text, include a second parenthetical following the date of publication identifying the work.

✓ For newspaper articles (Rule 16.6):

a. Cite the author's full name as it appears in the publication according to Rule 15.1.

b. Cite the full title of the article as it appears on the title page of the publication, but refer to Rule 8 for capitalization.

c. Abbreviate the title of the newspaper according to Table T13.

d. Indicate the date of the article, abbreviating the month according to Table T12.

e. Indicate the page on which the article appears. Note that only the first page need be identified.

 ## 14. Bluebook Rules for Citing Electronic Media: Checklist

✓ Rule 18 addresses citation to the internet in general.

a. Rule 18.1 provides basic citation forms.

b. Rule 18.2 discusses citation to the internet and general principles. Cite to an internet source when it does not exist in a traditional printed format or when the printed source exists but cannot be found or is practically unavailable because it is so obscure. For a citation to an internet source, include: Authors' names, title of the specific web page (underlined), title of main website page, date (and perhaps time if updated multiple times per day), and the URL. Parallel citations to internet sources (Rule 18.2.3) should be given if doing so will substantially improve access to the document. Give the citation to the primary source, followed by the words "available at" and the URL.

✓ Rule 18.3 addresses case citation formats for documents found on widely used electronic databases.

a. Unreported cases that are available on a widely used electronic database such as LexisNexis or Westlaw can be cited to that database according to Rule 18.3.1.

b. If the electronic database provides a unique identifying number for the case, remember to provide it following the case name, preceded by "No."

c. If citing to a specific page or screen of an opinion, indicate the page number preceded by an asterisk. If citing to a particular paragraph, indicate the paragraph number preceded by "¶."

✓ Rule 18.3.2 addresses constitutions and statutes found on commercial electronic databases.

    a. Cite codes according to Rules 12.3 and 12.4.

    b. When citing a code contained in an electronic database, remember to include a parenthetical that gives information regarding the currency of the statute or constitution as indicated in the database.

✓ Rule 18.3.4 addresses books, periodicals, and other secondary materials.

B. Bluebook Quizzes

⚇? 1. Bluebook Typeface Conventions: Quiz

Assume the following citations appear in court documents.

1. Choose the correct citation for <u>Missouri v. Holland</u>.

    A. <u>Missouri</u> v. <u>Holland</u>, 252 U.S. 416 (1922).

    B. <u>Missouri v. Holland</u>, 252 U.S. 416 (1922).

    C. <u>Missouri v. Holland,</u> 252 U.S. 416 (1922).

    D. Missouri v. Holland, 252 U.S. 416 (1922).

2. Which citation does NOT have an error?

    A. See <u>Brown v. Board of Education</u>, 347 U.S. 438 (1954).

    B. <u>Brown</u>, 347 U.S. at 440.

    C. <u>Clark v. Davis</u>, 533 U.S. 678, 719 (2001) (citing <u>Evanson v. United States</u>, 345 U.S. 206 (1953)).

    D. Matt Corney, Red House (Oxford ed., Penguin Books 1979) (1899).

3. Which citation does NOT have an error?

    A. <u>See id.</u> at 348.

    B. <u>Id. at 348.</u>

    C. <u>See id.</u> at 348.

    D. See <u>id.</u> at 348.

4. Which citation does NOT have an error?

    A. Gretel C. Kovach, Use of False Hiring Data Found in Dallas Schools, N.Y. Times, Nov. 15, 2 A10.

    B. Greg Gelpi, Attorney Still Loves Fighting for Little Guys, <u>Augusta Chron.</u>, Dec. 8, 2008, at B.

    C. David Rudovsky, Police Abuse: Can the Violence Be Contained?, 27 Harv. C.R.-C.L. L. Rev 500 (1992).

    D. Andrew Rosenthal, <u>Medicine and the Law</u>, N.Y. Times, June 15, 1990, at A1.

5. Which citation does NOT have an error?

    A. <u>Sciolino v. City of Newport News</u>, 480 F.3d 642, 647 (4th Cir. 2007) <u>(Wilkinson, J., dissenting.</u>

    B. Id. at 735.

    C. <u>Codd v. Velger</u>, 429 U.S. 624, 627 (1977).

    D. <u>U.S. Const</u>. amend XIV, § 1.

Answer Key on page 537

?   2.   Basic Structure and Signals for Bluebook Citations: Quiz

Assume the following citations appear in court documents.

1. Choose the string citation without an error.

    A. <u>See</u> <u>Edwards v. Arizona</u>, 451 U.S. 477 (1981). <u>But see</u> <u>Berkemer v. Mac-Carty</u>, 468 U.S. 420 <u>Compare</u> <u>Orozco v. Texas</u>, 394 U.S. 324 (1969).

    B. <u>See</u> <u>Edwards v. Arizona</u>, 451 U.S. 477 (1981); <u>but see</u> <u>Berkemer v. McCarty</u>, 468 U.S. 420 (1984).

    C. <u>Edwards v. Arizona</u>, 451 U.S. 466 (1981). <u>See</u> <u>Berkemer v. McCarty</u>, 468 U.S. 420 (1984).

    D. <u>See</u> <u>Edwards v. Arizona</u>, 451 U.S. 477 (1981). <u>But see</u> <u>Berkemer v. Mac-Carty</u>, 468 U.S. 420 (1984).

2. Choose the string citation without an error.

    A. <u>See</u> <u>Edwards v. Arizona</u>, 451 U.S. 477 (1981); <u>State v. Bradshaw</u>, 457 S.E.2d 456 (W. Va. 2 <u>Orozco v. Texas</u>, 394 U.S. 324 (1969).

    B. <u>See</u> <u>Edwards v. Arizona</u>, 451 U.S. 477 (1981); <u>Orozco v. Texas</u>, 394 U.S. 324 (1969).

    C. <u>See</u> <u>State v. Bradshaw</u>, 457 S.E.2d 456 (W. Va. 1995); <u>State v. Singleton</u>, 624 S.E.2d 527 (2005).

    D. <u>See</u> <u>Edwards v. Arizona</u>, 451 U.S. 477 (1981); U.S. Const. amend V.

3. Choose the string citation without an error.

    A. <u>See</u> Greg Gelpi, <u>Attorney Still Loves Fighting for Little Guys</u>, Augusta Chron., Dec. 8, 2008, a <u>Swilley v. Alexander</u>, 629 F.2d 1018, 1020 (5th Cir. 1980).

    B. <u>See</u> 42 U.S.C.A. § 1983 (2009); <u>Swilley v. Alexander</u>, 629 F.2d 1018, 1020 (5th Cir. 1980).

    C. <u>See</u> 42 U.S.C.A. § 1983 (2009); U.S. Const. amend XIV, § 1.

    D. <u>See</u> <u>Cox v. Roskelley</u>, 359 F.3d 1105, 1110 (9th Cir. 2002); <u>Codd v. Velger</u>, 429 U.S. 624, 62 (1977).

4. Choose the citation without an error.

    A. <u>Cox v. Roskelley</u>, 359 F.3d 1105, 1110 (9th Cir. 2002) (holding once stigmatizing information placed into Cox's personnel file, it became public record under Washington law).

    B. ("Nor shall any State deprive person of life, liberty, or property, without due process of the law Const. amend XIV, §1.

    C. Gretel C. Kovach, <u>Use of False Hiring Data Found in Dallas Schools</u> (newspaper ran article after obtaining report, marked highly confidential, through a records request), N.Y. Times, Nov. 15, A10.

    D. U.S. Const. ("Nor shall any State deprive person of life, liberty, or property, without due process law") amend XIV, § 1.

5. Choose the string citation without an error.

    A. <u>See also</u> <u>Miranda v. Arizona</u>, 384 U.S. 436 (1966); <u>see</u> <u>Edwards v. Arizona</u>, 451 U.S. 477 (1984).

    B. <u>See</u> S.C. Const. art. I, § 12; U.S. Const. art. IV, § 1.

    C. <u>See</u> <u>Miranda v. Arizona</u>, 384 U.S. 436 (1966); <u>see</u> <u>Edwards v. Arizona</u>, 451 U.S. 477 (1981).

    D. <u>See</u> <u>State v. Jameson</u>, 461 S.E.2d 67 (W. Va. 1995). <u>But see</u> <u>State v. Green</u>, 310 S.E.2d 48 Va. 1983).

Answer Key on page 538

8? 3. Bluebook Citation Signals: Quiz

You are researching a state water quality issue for a partner at your firm, and you have uncovered a number of authorities that support, contradict, or supplement the following excerpt from a Maryland statute: Factories may not dispose of hazardous materials in the Chesapeake Bay. What signal would you use to best cite each authority described below?

1. A case decided by the Maryland Court of Appeals (the highest court in Maryland) that holds that factories cannot dispose of hazardous materials in Maryland rivers.

    A. No signal

    B. <u>But see</u>

    C. <u>See, e.g.,</u>

    D. <u>Cf.</u>

    E. <u>Contra</u>

2. A law review article that discusses hazardous waste disposal laws in several states on the eastern seaboard, including Maryland.

    A. No signal

    B. <u>See generally</u>

    C. <u>See</u>

    D. <u>Cf.</u>

    E. <u>Contra</u>

3. A Delaware statute that prohibits dumping of hazardous materials in the Chesapeake Bay.

    A. No signal
    B. See generally
    C. Accord
    D. Cf.
    E. See

4. One of several Maryland cases holding that factories may not dispose of hazardous waste in Maryland waters.

    A. No signal
    B. See, e.g.,
    C. See
    D. See generally
    E. Compare … with …

5. A Maryland Court of Appeals case holding that factories may not dispose of hazardous materials in the Chesapeake Bay.

    A. No signal
    B. See
    C. But see
    D. Contra
    E. Cf.

6. A Maryland Court of Appeals case holding that no individual or organization may dispose of polluting materials in the bays or other marshland areas of the state of Maryland.

    A. No signal
    B. Cf.
    C. See
    D. But see
    E. See, e.g.,

Answer Key on page 539

⊗? 4. Bluebook Order and Punctuation of Signals and Citations: Quiz

1. Select the correct citation sentence:

    A. See Matthews v. Potter, 19 P.2d 368 (Cal. 1999). See also Morrison v. Perkins, 56 P.2d 247 (Cal. 2000). But see Smith v. Jennings, 85 P.2d 465 (Cal. 2001).
    B. See Matthews v. Potter, 19 P.2d 368 (Cal. 1999); see also Morrison v. Perkins, 56 P.2d 247 (Cal. 2000); but see Smith v. Jennings, 85 P.2d 465 (Cal. 2001).

C. See also <u>Morrison v. Perkins</u>, 56 P.2d 247 (Cal. 2000); <u>see</u> <u>Matthews v. Potter</u>, 19 P.2d 368 (Cal. 1999). <u>But see</u> <u>Smith v. Jennings</u>, 85 P.2d 465 (Cal. 2001).

D. See <u>Matthews v. Potter</u>, 19 P.2d 368 (Cal. 1999); <u>see also</u> <u>Morrison v. Perkins</u>, 56 P.2d 247 (Cal. 2000). <u>But see</u> <u>Smith v. Jennings</u>, 85 P.2d 465 (Cal. 2001).

2. Which of the following is the correct order and punctuation of signals when more than one signal is used?

   A. <u>See</u>; <u>cf.</u>; but see; <u>see generally</u>.
   B. <u>See</u>; <u>cf.</u> But see. See generally.
   C. <u>See</u>. But see. Cf. See generally.
   D. <u>See</u>; <u>cf.</u> But see; see generally.
   E. <u>See</u>. Cf. But see. See generally.

3. A partner at your firm has asked you to revise a draft office memorandum containing the following sentence: <u>See, e.g.</u>, 18 U.S.C. § 588 (1998); 13 U.S.C. § 12 (1994); <u>Lineman v. Fawcett</u>, 689 U.S. 214 (1991); <u>Hingel v. Brown</u>, 855 U.S. 114 (1987); <u>Smith v. Tenorman</u>, 255 F.2d 2087 (2d Cir. 1997), <u>aff'd</u>, 225 U.S. 3 (1999); <u>Dohr v. Abrams</u>, 255 F. Supp. 2d 651 (D.D.C. 1989); <u>Masters v. Perlman</u>, 23 F.3d 785 (7th Cir. 1986). How would you revise this citation sentence?

   A. The ordering of citations is correct; no changes are necessary.
   B. The citations should be in the following order: <u>See, e.g.</u>, 18 U.S.C. § 588 (1998); 13 U.S.C. § 12 (1994); <u>Lineman</u>; <u>Smith</u>; <u>Hingel</u>; <u>Masters</u>; <u>Dohr</u>.
   C. The citations should be in the following order: <u>See, e.g.</u>,13 U.S.C. § 12 (1994); 18 U.S.C. § 588 (1998); <u>Lineman</u>; <u>Hingel</u>; <u>Smith</u>; <u>Masters</u>; <u>Dohr</u>.
   D. The citations should be in the following order: <u>See, e.g.</u>, 18 U.S.C. § 588 (1998); 13 U.S.C. § 12 (1994); <u>Lineman</u>; <u>Hingel</u>; <u>Dohr</u>; <u>Masters</u>; <u>Smith</u>.
   E. The citations should be in the following order: <u>See, e.g.</u>, 18 U.S.C. § 588 (1998); 13 U.S.C. § 12 (1994); <u>Lineman</u>; <u>Hingel</u>; <u>Masters</u>; <u>Smith</u>; <u>Dohr</u>.

Answer Key on page 540

⚇? 5.   Bluebook Rules for Citing Subdivisions and Pinpoint Cites: Quiz

Assume the following citations appear in court documents.

1. Choose the correct citation for information on page 347 of <u>Beckwith v. United States</u>.

   A. <u>Beckwith v. United States</u>, 425 U.S. 341, 347 (1976).
   B. <u>Beckwith v. United States</u>, 425 U.S. 341, at 347 (1976).
   C. <u>Beckwith v. United States</u>, 425 U.S. 341, p. 347 (1976).
   D. <u>Beckwith v. United States</u>, 425 U.S. 341-47 (1976).

2. Choose the citation without an error.

   A. Christina M. Fernandez, <u>A Case-by-Case Approach to Pleading Sci-enter Under the Private Securities Litigation Reform Act of 1995</u>, 97 Mich. L. Rev 2265, p. 2271 (1978).

   B. <u>Sciolino v. City of Newport News</u>, 480 F.3d 642 (4th Cir. 2007) (Wilkin-son, J., dissenting, 654).

   C. <u>State v. Bradshaw</u>, 457 S.E.2d 456, 457, 459 (W. Va. 1995).

   D. <u>Codd v. Velger</u>, 429 U.S. 624 to 626 (1977).

3. Choose the citation without an error.

   A. 459 <u>State v. Bradshaw</u>, 457 S.E.2d 456 (W. Va. 1995).

   B. <u>Miranda v. Arizona</u>, 384 U.S. 436, 440 (1966).

   C. <u>Bishop v. Wood</u>, 426 U.S. 341 (1976) ("Fourteenth Amendment is not a guarantee against in or ill-advised personnel decisions") 349.

   D. <u>State v. Mullens</u>, 172, 650 S.E.2d 169 (W. Va. 2007).

4. Choose the correct citation for information on page 2082 of the Michigan Law Review.

   A. Kim Scheppele, <u>Foreword: Telling Stories</u>, 87 Mich. L. Rev. 2073 (1989), 2082.

   B. Kim Scheppele, <u>Foreword: Telling Stories</u>, 2082, 87 Mich. L. Rev. 2073 (1989).

   C. Kim Scheppele, <u>Foreword: Telling Stories</u>, 87 Mich. L. Rev. 2073, 2082 (1989).

   D. Kim Scheppele, <u>Foreword: Telling Stories</u>, 87 Mich. L. Rev. 2073 at 2082 (1989).

5. Choose the correct citation for information on pages 479, 481, 485 in Edwards v. Arizona.

   A. <u>Edwards v. Arizona</u>, 451 U.S. 477, 479, 481, and 485 (1981).

   B. <u>Edwards v. Arizona</u>, 451 U.S. 477-85 (1981).

   C. <u>Edwards v. Arizona</u>, 451 U.S. 477 (1981) 479, 481, 485.

   D. <u>Edwards v. Arizona</u>, 451 U.S. 477, 479, 481, 485 (1981).

Answer Key on page 541

⚇? 6.   Bluebook Rules for Short Form Citations: Quiz

Assume the following citations appear in court documents.

1. Choose the correct short citation for <u>Orozco v. Texas</u>, 394 U.S. 324, 327 (1969), if it is the only source in immediately preceding citation and cited page 327.

   A. <u>Id.</u> at 327.

   B. <u>Orozco v. Texas</u>, at 327.

   C. <u>Id.</u> 394 U.S. 324, 327.

   D. <u>Orozco</u>, at 327.

2. Choose the correct short citation for <u>Orozco v. Texas</u>, 394 U.S. 324, 327 (1969), if the same cite was used three citations earlier.

    A. <u>Orozco v. Texas</u>, 394 U.S. at 327

    B. <u>Orozco</u>, 394 U.S. 324, 327.

    C. <u>Id.</u> at 327.

    D. <u>Orozco</u>, 394 U.S. at 327.

3. Choose the correct short citation for <u>Sciolino v. City of Newport News</u>, 480 F.3d 642, 654 (4th Cir. 2007), Judge Wilkinson's dissenting opinion if the previous citation is from the same case but cites the majority.

    A. <u>Id.</u> at 654 (Wilkinson, J., dissenting).

    B. <u>Sciolino v. City of Newport News</u>, 480 F.3d 642, 654 (4th Cir. 2007) (Wilkinson, J., dissenting).

    C. Sciolino, 480 F.3d 642 at 654 (Wilkinson, J., dissenting).

    D. <u>Id.</u> (Wilkinson, J., dissenting) at 654.

4. Choose the correct short citation for 30 U.S.C. § 1330(a)(1) if the previous citation is 30 U.S.C. § 1331 (2000).

    A. 30 U.S.C. § 1330(a)(1) (2000).

    B. <u>Id.</u> (a)(1).

    C. <u>Id.</u> § 1330(a)(1).

    D. <u>Id.</u> at § 1330(a)(1).

5. Choose the correct short cite for Katherine Crystzer, <u>You're Fired!</u> Bishop v. Wood: <u>When Does a Letter in Former Public Employee's Personnel File Deny a Due Process Liberty Right?</u>, 16 Geo. Mason L. Rev 44 (2009), if it was used three citations earlier.

    A. Crystzer, <u>You're Fired!</u>, at 450.

    B. Crystzer, <u>supra</u>, at 450.

    C. Crystzer, <u>You're Fired!</u> Bishop v. Wood: <u>When Does a Letter in a Former Public Employee's Personnel File Deny a Due Process Liberty Right?</u>, 16 Geo. Mason L. Rev 447, 450 (2009)

    D. <u>Id.</u> at 450.

6. Choose the correct short cite for Deborah L. Rhode, <u>Justice and Gender</u> 56, 70-71 (1989), if the immediately preceding cite is for the same source on page 60.

    A. <u>Id.</u> at 70-71.

    B. Rhode, <u>id.</u> at 70-71.

    C. Rhode, <u>Justice and Gender</u>, at 70-71.

    D. Rhode, <u>supra</u>, at 70-71.

7. Choose the correct short citation for <u>Orozco v. Texas</u>, 394 U.S. 324, 327 (1969), if it is one of three sources in the immediately preceding citation and cited on page 329.

    A. <u>Id.</u> at 327.
    B. <u>Orozco v. Texas</u>, at 327.
    C. <u>Id.</u> 394 U.S. 324, 327.
    D. <u>Orozco</u>, 394 U.S. at 327.

Answer Key on page 542

⚇? 7. Bluebook Abbreviations: Quiz

Assume the following citations appear in court documents.

1. The following case appears in a textual sentence. Choose the answer that abbreviates the case name correctly.

    A. <u>NLRB v. General Hospital, Inc.</u>, 61 U.S. 3 (1951).
    B. <u>NLRB v. General Hosp.</u>, Inc., 61 U.S. 3 (1951).
    C. <u>N.L.R.B. v. General Hospital, Inc.</u>, 61 U.S. 3 (1951).
    D. <u>NLRB v. General Hospital, Incorporated</u>, 61 U.S. 3 (1951).

2. The following Ninth Circuit Court case appears in a citation sentence. Choose the answer that abbreviates the case name correctly.

    A. <u>Sunnyside Memorial School v. County Housing Department</u>, 537 F.2d 361, 366 (9th Cir. 1976).
    B. <u>Sunnyside Mem'l. Sch. v. County Hous. Dep't.</u>, 537 F.2d 361, 366 (9th Cir. 1976).
    C. <u>Sunnyside Mem'l Sch. v. County Hous. Dep't</u>, 537 F.2d 361, 366 (9th Cir. 1976).
    D. <u>Sunnyside v. Mem'l Sch. v. County Hous. Dep't</u>, 537 F.2d 361, 366 (9th Circuit 1976).

3. Choose the correct citation for the Federal Register.

    A. Importation of Dairy Products, 60 Federal Register 50,379 (Sept. 29, 1995).
    B. Importation of Dairy Products, 60 F.R. 50,379 (September 29, 1995).
    C. Importation of Dairy Products, 60 Fed. Reg. 50,379 (Sept. 29, 1995).
    D. Importation of Dairy Products, 60 Fed.Reg 50,379 (September 29, 1995).

4. Choose the correct citation for Rule 12(b)(2) of the Federal Rules of Civil Procedure.

    A. Fed. Rule Civ. P. 12(b)(2).
    B. Fed. R. Civ. P. 12(b)(2).
    C. Fed R Civ P 12(b)(2).
    D. Federal Rule of Civil Procedure 12(b)(2).

5.　Choose the correct citation for an article in the George Mason Law Review.

A.　Kathy Crytzer, <u>Meeting of the Minds</u>, 16 Geo. Mason L. Rev. 447, 450 (2000).

B.　Kathy Crytzer, <u>Meeting of the Minds</u>, 15 G.M. L. Rev. 447, 450 (2000).

C.　Kathy Crytzer, <u>Meeting of the Minds</u>, 15 Geo. Mason L.R. 447, 450 (2000).

D.　Kathy Crytzer, <u>Meeting of the Minds</u>, 16 Geo Mason L Rev 447, 450 (2000).

Answer Key on page 543

⚇? 8.　Bluebook Rules for Citing Cases: Quiz

Assume the following citations appear in court documents.

1.　Choose the correct citation for <u>United States v. MacDonald</u>, decided in the Fourth Circuit Court of Appeals in 1976.

A.　531 F.2d 196, 199, <u>United States v. MacDonald</u>, (4th Cir. 1976).

B.　<u>United States v. MacDonald</u>, 531 F.2d 196, 199 (4th Cir. 1976).

C.　United States v. MacDonald. 531 F.2d 196. 199 (4th Cir. 1976)

D.　<u>U.S. v. MacDonald</u>, 531 F.2d 196, 199 (4th Cir. 1976).

2.　Choose the correct citation for <u>Commonwealth of Pennsylvania v. Ferrone</u>, decided in the Pennsylvania Superior Court in 1982. (Assume this citation appears in a court document submitted to a Pennsylvania court.)

A.　<u>Commonwealth v. Ferrone</u>, 448 A.2d 637 (Pa. Super. Ct. 1982).

B.　<u>Commonwealth of Pennsylvania v. Ferrone</u>, 448 A.2d 637 (Pa. Super. Ct. 1982).

C.　<u>Commonwealth of Penn. v. Ferrone</u>, 448 A.2d 637 (Pa. Super. Ct. 1982).

D.　<u>Penn. v. Ferrone</u>, 448 A.2d 637 (Pa. Super. Ct. 1982).

3.　Choose the correct citation for <u>Miranda v. Arizona</u> in the United States Reports.

A.　<u>Miranda v. Arizona</u>, 384 S. Ct. 436 (1966).

B.　<u>Miranda v. Arizona</u>, 384 U.S. 436 (S. Ct. 1966).

C.　<u>Miranda v. Arizona</u>, 384 U.S. 436 (1966).

D.　<u>Miranda v. Arizona</u>, 384 U.S. 436 (U.S. 1966).

4.　Choose the correct citation for <u>Johnson v. Seiler</u> decided by the Fourth Circuit Court of Appeals and reported in the Second Edition Federal Reporter.

A.　<u>Johnson v. Seiler</u>, 225 F.2d 308 (4th Cir. 1998).

B.　<u>Johnson v. Seiler</u>, 225 F.2d 308 (4th Cir. 1998).

C.　<u>Johnson v. Seiler</u>, 225 F.2d 308 (4th Circuit 1998).

D.　<u>Johnson v. Seiler</u>, 225 S.E.2d 308 (4th Cir. 1998).

5. Choose the correct citation for Justice Scalia's dissenting opinion in <u>Jamison v. Blueline Railroad</u>.

    A. <u>Jamison v. Blueline R.R.</u>, 338 U.S. 25, 47 (2004) (Scalia, J., dissenting) (rejecting Court's conception of the exclusionary rule).

    B. <u>Jamison v. Blueline R.R.</u>, 338 U.S. 25, 47 (2004). (Scalia, J., dissenting) (rejecting Court's conception of the exclusionary rule).

    C. <u>Jamison v. Blueline R.R.</u>, 338 U.S. 25, 47 (2004) (rejecting Court's conception of the exclusionary rule) (Scalia, J., dissenting).

    D. Jamison v. Blueline R.R., 338 U.S. 25, 47 (2004 Scalia J., dissenting) (rejecting Court's conception of the exclusionary rule).

6. Choose the correct citation for the unreported case of <u>Chavez v. Norton</u>, available on Lexis.

    A. <u>Chavez v. Norton</u>, No. 02-3924, 2004 U.S. App. LEXIS 2598713, 220 (3d Cir. Oct. 14, 2004).

    B. <u>Chavez v. Norton</u>, No. 02-3924, No. 02-3924, 2004 U.S. App. LEXIS 2598713, at *220 (3d 2004).

    C. <u>Chavez v. Norton</u>, No. 02-3924, 2004 U.S. App. LEXIS 2598713, *220 (3d Cir. Oct. 14, 2004).

    D. <u>Chavez v. Norton</u>, No. 02-3924, 2004 U.S. App. LEXIS 2598713, at *220 (3d Cir. Oct. 14, 2004).

Answer Key on page 544

---

 9.   **Bluebook Rules for Citing Constitutions: Quiz**

Assume that the following citations appear in court documents.

1. Choose the correct citation format for the Fifth Amendment to the U.S. Constitution.

    A. U.S. Const. Amend. V.

    B. United States Constitution, amendment V.

    C. U.S. Const. amend. V.

    D. U.S. Const. amend V.

2. Which one of these citations to Article I, Section 1, of the Kansas Constitution is correct?

    A. Kan. Const. art. I, § 1.

    B. Kan. Const. art. I, sec. 1.

    C. Ka. Const. art. I, § 1,

    D. Kansas Constitution, art. 1, § 1.

3. What is the correct short citation format for Article II of the U.S. Constitution if it was cited in the immediately preceding section?

    A. Art. II.
    B. U.S. Const. II.
    C. II.
    D. Id.

4. Choose the correct format for citing the Eighteenth Amendment to the U.S. Constitution (repealed in 1993).

    A. U.S. Const. Amend. XVIII (repealed 1933).
    B. U.S. Const. amend. XVIII (repealed 1933).
    C. U.S. Const. amend. XVIII (*repealed* 1933).
    D. U.S. Const. amend. XVIII, repealed 1933.

5. What is the correct citation format for Article II, Section 3 of the Pennsylvania Constitution?

    A. Pa. Const. art. II, § 3.
    B. Pen. Const. art. II, § 3.
    C. Pa. Const. Art. II, § 3.
    D. Pen. Const. art 2, § 3.

Answer Key on page 545

⚇? 10.   Bluebook Rules for Citing Statutes: Quiz

Assume that the following citations appear in court documents.

1. In the citation 28 U.S.C. § 585 (2000), what does the "28" signify?

    A. The section number of the statute
    B. The title number of the statute in the United States Code
    C. The session of Congress that enacted the statute
    D. The number of provisions in the cited statute

2. Choose the correct *full* citation for Title 42, Section 1975 of the United States Code.

    A. 42 USC § 1975 (2000).
    B. 42 U.S.C. § 1975.
    C. 42 U.S.C. § 1975 (2000).
    D. 42 U.S.C. §1975 (2000).

3. If using a short citation to refer to the statute from question 2, which one of the following options is an acceptable format?

    A. § 1975.
    B. 42 U.S.C.
    C. U.S.C. § 1975.
    D. 42.

4. Which of the following citations to the Internal Revenue Code is NOT correctly formatted?

    A. 26 U.S.C. § 153 (2000).
    B. I.R.C. § 153 (2000).
    C. 26 U.S.C. § 291 (2000).
    D. Int. Rev. Code § 291 (2000).

5. Choose the preferred citation format for the Indiana Code.

    A. Ind. Code § 3-5-1-1 (2008).
    B. Ind. Code Ann. § 3-5-1-1 (West 2006).
    C. Ind. Code Ann. § 3-5-1-1 (LexisNexis 2006).
    D. In. Code § 3-5-1-1 (2008).

6. Choose the correct citation for Federal Rule of Civil Procedure 11(a)(5).

    A. F.R.C.P. 11(a)(5).
    B. Fed R Civ P 11(a)(5).
    C. Fed. R. Civ. P. 11(a)(5).
    D. F.R.C.P. § 11(a)(5).

Answer Key on page 546

☯? 11. Bluebook Citations for Administrative and Executive Materials: Quiz

Assume that the following citations appear in court documents.

1. Which of the following citations to title 40, section 49.9861 of the Code of Federal Regulations is correct?

    A. 40 Code Fed. Reg. § 49.9861 (1999).
    B. 40 Code Fed. Reg. §49.9861 (1999).
    C. 40 C.F.R. § 49.9861 (1999).
    D. 40 C. F. R. § 49.9861 (1999).

2. Choose the correct short form citation to title 40, section 49.9861 of the Code of Federal Regulations.

    A. 40 C.F.R. § 49.9861 (1999)
    B. 40 C.F.R. § 49.9861
    C. 40 C.F.R.
    D. 49.9861.

3. A rule is published on page 25,684 of volume 74 of the Federal Register, but it has not yet been entered into the Code of Federal Regulations. Choose the correct citation for that rule.

   A. Airworthiness Directives, 74 Fed. Reg. 25,684 (May 30, 2009) (to be codified at 14 C.F.R. pt. 39).
   B. Airworthiness Directives, 74 F.R. 25,684 (May 30, 2009) (to be codified at 14 C.F.R. pt. 39).
   C. Airworthiness Directives, 74 Fed. Reg. 25,684 (to be codified at 14 C.F.R. pt. 39).
   D. Airworthiness Directives, 74 Fed.Reg. 25684 (May 30, 2009) (to be codified at 14 C.F.R. pt. 39).

4. Which of the following citations to volume 24, page 2,834 of the Virginia Register of Regulations (dated June 9, 2008) is correct?

   A. 24 Va. Reg. Regs. 2,834 (June 9, 2008).
   B. 24 V.R.R. 2834 (June 9, 2008).
   C. 24 Va. Reg. Regs. 2834.
   D. 24 Va. Reg. Regs. 2834 (June 9, 2008).

5. Choose the correct citation for a 1982 advisory opinion from the United States Attorney General, volume page 369.

   A. 43 Op. Attorney General 369 (1982).
   B. 43 Op. Att'y Gen. 369 (1982).
   C. 43 Op. Att'y. Gen. 369 (1982).
   D. 43 Op. Atty. Gen. 369 (1982).

6. Presidential Executive Order 12001 is not in the Code of Federal Regulations, but it is found in volume 4 page 33,709 of the Federal Register. Which of the following citations is correct?

   A. Exec. Order No. 12,001, 42 Fed. Reg. 33,709 (June 29, 1977).
   B. E.O. No. 12,001, 42 Fed. Reg. 33,709 (June 29, 1977).
   C. E.O. No. 12,001, 42 F.R. 33,709 (June 29, 1977).
   D. Exec. Order No. 12001, 42 Fed. Reg. 33709 (June 29, 1977).

Answer Key on page 547

☝? 12. Bluebook Citations for Books, Reports, and Other Nonperiodic Materials: Quiz

Assume that the following citations appear in court documents.

1. Choose the correct citation to page 171 of <u>The Nine: Inside the Secret World of the Supreme Court</u>, by Jeffrey Toobin.

   A. <u>The Nine: Inside the Secret World of the Supreme Court</u> 171 (Anchor Books, 2007) (2007) J Toobin.

B.   Toobin, J., <u>The Nine: Inside the Secret World of the Supreme Court</u> 171 (2007).

C.   Jeffrey Toobin, <u>The Nine: Inside the Secret World of the Supreme Court</u>, 171 (2007).

D.   Jeffrey Toobin, <u>The Nine: Inside the Secret World of the Supreme Court</u> 171 (2007).

2.   Which of the following citations to the tenth edition of <u>A History of the Modern World to 1815</u>, by R.R. Palmer, Joel Colton, and Lloyd Kramer (listed in this order on the title page), is correct?

A.   R.R. Palmer et al., <u>A History of the Modern World</u> to 1815 (10th ed. 2006).

B.   R.R. Palmer et al <u>A History of the Modern World to 1815</u> (10th ed. 2006).

C.   R.R. Palmer, Joel Colton and Lloyd Kramer, <u>A History of the Modern World to 1815</u> (10th ed.).

D.   Joel Colton, Lloyd Kramer & R.R. Palmer, <u>A History of the Modern World to 1815</u> (10th ed.).

3.   Choose the correct citation to volume 2 of <u>Michael Burlingame's Abraham Lincoln: A Life</u>, published in 2008.

A.   Michael Burlingame, <u>Abraham Lincoln: A Life</u> vol. 2 (2008).

B.   Michael Burlingame, <u>Abraham Lincoln: A Life</u> 2 (2008).

C.   2 Michael Burlingame, <u>Abraham Lincoln: A Life</u> (2008).

D.   Vol. 2 Michael Burlingame, <u>Abraham Lincoln: A Life</u> (2008).

4.   Choose the correct citation for an originally unpublished letter from Alexander Hamilton to John Jay dated November 26, 1775, published on page 43 of <u>Alexander Hamilton: Writings</u>.

A.   Letter from Alexander Hamilton to John Jay (Nov. 26, 1775), in <u>Alexander Hamilton: Writing</u> 43 (2001).

B.   Letter to John Jay (Nov. 26, 1775), *in* <u>Alexander Hamilton: Writings</u> 43 (2001).

C.   Letter from Alexander Hamilton to John Jay (November 26, 1775), *in* <u>Alexander Hamilton: Writings</u> 43 (2001).

D.   Letter from Alexander Hamilton to John Jay (Nov. 26, 1775) <u>Alexander Hamilton: Writings</u> 43 (2001).

5.   Which citation to the ninth edition of <u>Black's Law Dictionary</u>, published in 2009, is correct?

A.   <u>Black's Law Dictionary</u> (9th ed. 2009).

B.   <u>Black's Law Dictionary</u> (9th ed. 2009).

C.   <u>Black's Law Dictionary</u> (9th edition 2009).

D.   <u>Black's Law Dictionary</u> (9th ed., 2009).

Answer Key on page 548

🕵? 13. Bluebook Rules for Citing Periodicals: Quiz

Assume that the following citations appear in court documents.

1. Which of the following citations to a June 1, 2009, article on page E2 of the *San Francisco Chronicle* is correct?

   A. Peter Hartlaub, SFJazz Show Gets to the Roots, S.F. Chron., June 1, 2009, at E2.

   B. Peter Hartlaub, <u>SFJazz Show Gets to the Roots</u>, S.F. Chron., June 1, 2009, at E2.

   C. Hartlaub, Peter, <u>SFJazz Show Gets to the Roots</u>, S.F. Chron., June 1, 2009, at E2.

   D. Peter Hartlaub, <u>SFJazz Show Gets to the Roots</u>, <u>S.F. Chron.</u>, June 1, 2009, at E2.

2. Choose the correct citation to a June 1, 2009, Op-Ed article by Paul Krugman on page A21 of the New York Times.

   A. Paul Krugman, Op-Ed., <u>Reagan Did It</u>, N.Y. Times, June 1, 2009, at A21.

   B. Paul Krugman, Op-Ed., Reagan Did It, N.Y. Times, June 1, 2009, at A21.

   C. Paul Krugman, <u>Reagan Did It</u>, N.Y. Times, June 1, 2009, at A21.

   D. Paul Krugman, Op-Ed., <u>Reagan Did It</u>, New York Times, June 1, 2009, at A21.

3. Choose the correct citation to an April 2009 article by Eugene Volokh that appeared in volume 97 of the *Georgetown Law Journal.*

   A. Eugene Volokh, <u>Symbolic Expression and the Original Meaning of the First Amendment</u>, 97 Georgetown Law Journal 1057 (2009).

   B. Eugene Volokh, <u>Symbolic Expression and the Original Meaning of the First Amendment</u>, 97 Law J. 1057 (2009).

   C. Eugene Volokh, <u>Symbolic Expression and the Original Meaning of the First Amendment</u>, 97 L.J. 1057 (2009).

   D. Eugene Volokh, <u>Symbolic Expression and the Original Meaning of the First Amendment</u>, 97 J. 1057 (2009).

4. Which citation to a March 2007 student-written note, signed by Adrian Barnes and published in volume 1 the *Columbia Law Review*, is correct?

   A. Note, <u>Do They Have to Buy from Burma? A Preemption Analysis of Local Antisweatshop Procurement Laws</u>, 107 Colum. L. Rev. 426 (2007).

   B. Adrian Barnes, Note, <u>Do They Have to Buy from Burma? A Preemption Analysis of Local Antisweatshop Procurement Laws</u>, 107 Col. L.R. 426 (2007).

C. Adrian Barnes, note, <u>Do They Have to Buy from Burma? A Preemption Analysis of Local Antisweatshop Procurement Laws</u>, 107 Colum. L. Rev. 426 (2007).

D. Adrian Barnes, Note, <u>Do They Have to Buy from Burma? A Preemption Analysis of Local Antisweatshop Procurement Laws</u>, 107 Colum. L. Rev. 426 (2007).

5. Choose the correct citation to a nonstudent-written book review by Derrick A. Bell, Jr., reviewing <u>Just Schools: The Idea of Racial Equality in American Education</u> by David L. Kirp. The review appeared in the Texas L Review in August 1983.

A. Derrick A. Bell, Jr., <u>School Desegregation Postmortem</u>, 62 Tex. L. Rev. 175 (1983) (reviewing David L. Kirp, <u>Just Schools: The Idea of Racial Equality in American Education</u> (1982)).

B. Derrick A. Bell, <u>School Desegregation Postmortem</u>, 62 Tex. L. Rev. 175 (1983) (reviewing David L. Kirp, <u>Just Schools: The Idea of Racial Equality in American Education</u> (1982)).

C. Derrick A. Bell, Jr., <u>School Desegregation Postmortem</u>, 62 Tex. L. Rev. 175 (1983) (reviewing David L. Kirp, Just Schools: The Idea of Racial Equality in American Education (1982)).

D. Derrick A. Bell, Jr., <u>School Desegregation Postmortem</u>, 62 Texas L.R. 175 (1983) (reviewing David L. Kirp, <u>Just Schools: The Idea of Racial Equality in American Education</u> (1982)).

Answer Key on page 549

🔎? 14. Bluebook Rules for Citing Electronic Media: Quiz

Assume that the following citations appear in court documents.

1. Choose the correct citation format for a case that is unreported but is available on Westlaw and has been assigned a unique database identifier. There are no page numbers assigned to this case, but cite to screen two of the case.

A. <u>Fenstermacher v. Telelect, Inc.</u>, No. 90-2159-O, 1992 WL 175114, at *2 (D. Kan. July 17, 1992).

B. <u>Fenstermacher v. Telelect, Inc.</u>, 1992 WL 175114, at *2 (D. Kan. July 17, 1992).

C. <u>Fenstermacher v. Telelect, Inc.</u>, No. 90-2159-O, 1992 WL 175114, at 2 (D. Kan. July 17, 1992).

D. <u>Fenstermacher v. Telelect, Inc.</u>, No. 90-2159-O, 1992 WL 175114, at *2 (D. Kan. 1992).

2. Which of the following citations to Baldwin's Kentucky Revised Statutes Annotated, as found on Westlaw correct? Note that the Kentucky Statutes are current on Westlaw through the end of the 2008 legislation.

   A. Ky. Rev. Stat. Ann. § 38.100 (West, 2008).
   B. Ken. Stat. Ann. § 38.100 (West, Westlaw through 2008 legislation).
   C. Ky. Rev. Stat. Ann. § 38.100 (West, Westlaw through 2008 legislation).
   D. Ky. Rev. Stat. Ann. 38.100 (West, Westlaw through 2008 legislation).

3. The following *New York Times* article is available only on the Internet and is not available in traditional print format. Choose the correct citation format.

   A. Matthew Saltmarsh, Interest Rates Held Steady in Europe, N.Y. Times, June 4, 2009, http://www.nytimes.com/2009/06/05/business/global/05euro.html?hpw.
   B. Matthew Saltmarsh, Interest Rates Held Steady in Europe, N.Y. Times, June 4, 2009, http://www.nytimes.com/2009/06/05/business/global/05euro.html?hpw.
   C. Matthew Saltmarsh, Interest Rates Held Steady in Europe, N.Y. Times, June 4, 2009, *available* http://www.nytimes.com/2009/06/05/business/global/05euro.html?hpw.
   D. Matthew Saltmarsh, Interest Rates Held Steady in Europe, New York Times, June 4, 2009, http://www.nytimes.com/2009/06/05/business/global/05euro.html?hpw.

4. The following article is available both in the print version of the New York Times and online. Choose the correct parallel citation.

   A. David Jolly, Despite Devaluation Fear, Latvia Stands by Currency, N.Y. Times, June 4, 2009, at B4, http://www.nytimes.com/2009/06/05/business/global/05latvia.html?hpw.
   B. David Jolly, Despite Devaluation Fear, Latvia Stands by Currency, N.Y. Times, at B4, *available* http://www.nytimes.com/2009/06/05/business/global/05latvia.html?hpw (June 4, 2009).
   C. David Jolly, Despite Devaluation Fear, Latvia Stands by Currency, N.Y. Times, June 4, 2009, at http://www.nytimes.com/2009/06/05/business/global/05latvia.html?hpw.
   D. David Jolly, Despite Devaluation Fear, Latvia Stands by Currency, N.Y. Times, June 4, 2009, available at http://www.nytimes.com/2009/06/05/business/global/05latvia.html?hpw.

5. Choose the correct citation to a fictional e-mail from George Ferman, Assistant Dean at Georgetown Law to Alex Aleinikoff, Dean of Georgetown Law.

   A. E-mail from George Ferman, Assistant Dean, Georgetown Law, to Alex Aleinikoff, Dean, Georgetown Law (Oct. 1, 2009, 08:15:01 EST) (on file with author).
   B. E-mail from George Ferman, Georgetown Law, Assistant Dean, to Alex Aleinikoff, Georgetown Law, Dean (Oct. 1, 2009, 08:15:01 EST) (on file with author).

    C. George Ferman, Assistant Dean, Georgetown Law, to Alex Aleinikoff, Dean, Georgetown Law (Oct. 1, 2009, 08:15:01 EST) (on file with author).

    D. E-mail from George Ferman to Alex Aleinikoff (Oct. 1, 2009, 08:15:01 EST) (on file with author).

6. Which of the following citations to a commercial audio recording is correct?

    A. U2, <u>The Joshua Tree</u> (1987).

    B. U2, <u>The Joshua Tree</u> (Island Records).

    C. U2, <u>The Joshua Tree</u> (Island Records 1987).

    D. U2, <u>The Joshua Tree</u> (1987) (Island Records).

Answer Key on page 550

C. Bluebook Citation Self-Assessment

INSTRUCTIONS: This self-assessment is designed to test your knowledge of the basic Bluebook citation rules covered in chapter 5. Read through the document, taking note of the numbered and highlighted passages. Each number and highlighted passage represents a question about which you should decide whether the citation is correct as is or whether a change is needed. If a change is needed, please make the correct change in citation format. When you are finished, check your work against the answer key on pages 551-555. The answer key also indicates for each item the applicable citation rule or form. This review will help you to assess your understanding of the Bluebook citation forms and to more quickly and accurately provide citations for your own documents.

Civil Action No. 02-2332

UNITED STATES COURT OF APPEALS FOR THE ELEVENTH CIRCUIT

DR. CHARLES OSSINING, Appellant, v.

HARRISON BRUBAKER, ET AL., APPELLEES

ON APPEAL FROM UNITED STATES DISTRICT COURT FOR THE SOUTHERN DISTRICT OF ALABAMA

BRIEF OF RESPONDENT

STATEMENT OF ISSUES PRESENTED FOR REVIEW

    I.   Whether an inmate, exhibiting no medical condition warranting special treatment, and having received adequate care for all documented symptoms, has an Eighth Amendment claim when, following self-diagnosis of a rare condition, the prison declined his request for a special diet and further unnecessary testing.

   II.   Whether the trial court correctly found an inmate's First Amendment rights were not violated when the Warden reviewed and denied individual publications according to prison regulations in response to the unreasonable burden placed upon the prison's resources.

STATEMENT OF THE CASE

Nature of the Case

    This is an appeal of summary judgment in a prisoner's rights case. Respondents request that summary judgment be affirmed as there are no genuine issues of fact in dispute, and that appellant's 42 U.S.C. § 1983 complaint be dismissed as treatment did not violate prisoner's constitutional rights. Appellant brings his claims under the First and Eighth Amendments #1 U.S. Const. Amend. I; #2 U.S. Const. amend. VIII.

#1 Keep as is/Change

#2 Keep as is/Change

Procedural History

Ossining alleges violations of his First and Eighth Amendment rights by the prison. The United States District Court for the Southern District of Alabama granted the defendant's motion for summary judgment. The District Court concluded that plaintiff's receiving of publications caused unreasonable burdens on the resources of the prison and that the prison was not deliberately indifferent to any serious medical needs of the plaintiff. #3 Ossining v. Brubaker, No. CIV.A.02-2332, 2003 U.S. Dist. LEXIS 5130, at *1 (S.D. Ala. Jan. 6, 2003).

#3 Keep as is/Change

STATEMENT OF FACTS

The prisoner, Dr. Charles Ossining, was convicted of Medicare fraud, mail fraud, and making false claims to the government. At the time of Ossining's incarceration in January 2002, a routine medical examination revealed he was in good health, without any notations of medical problems. (Brubaker Aff. 7.) After his arrival, Ossining received a considerable number of medical journals and newsletters pertaining to allergies. (Brubaker Aff. 8.) Ossining specifically ordered informational brochures concerning various types of allergies and treatments for the purpose of disseminating this information to other prisoners. (Ossining Aff. 4.) By the end of March, the infirmary reported a significant increase in prisoner visits: 15% higher than the same quarter a year before, and requests for allergy testing increased 100%. More than half of these requests were declined as these prisoners showed no symptoms warranting testing. Many inmates requesting allergy testing indicated Ossining had suggested they be tested for various allergies. (Brubaker Aff. 9.) Proper allergy diagnosis has been shown to require extensive testing. #4 J. Expert, Allergy on the Net, 5 New Eng. J. Med. 9, 10 (2002), at http://www.nejm.org/expert/v5/allergy.html.

#4 Keep as is/Change

The medical staff could not accommodate all incoming requests for allergy testing, leading to agitation of prisoners and strain on medical resources. (Brubaker Aff. 9, 10.) Additionally, the prison cafeteria received an influx of complaints, as well as special requests and disorderly conduct, requiring additional guards for security. (Brubaker Aff. 11.) Based on these events, Brubaker, the long-time warden of the prison, rejected certain publications addressed to Ossining as detrimental to the security and resources of the prison, an action authorized by federal regulation 28 C.F.R. §540.71(b). #5 I.M. Tough, Warden Power, 15 N.Y.Law Sch. L. Rev. 12, 15-17 (1983).

#5 Keep as is/Change

In March, a blood test revealed Ossining was borderline anemic; he was prescribed iron supplements to combat this condition. (Ossining Aff. 12.) In April, Ossining self-diagnosed himself as suffering from celiac disease, an extremely rare infection, and claimed he needed an endoscopy to confirm his diagnosis. (Flowers Aff. 6.) Celiac disease can be fatal if not treated properly. #6 Adam Gourna, Celiac Disease: A Killer, New York Times, December 12, 1994, at F3, available at 1994 WL 2321843. Reviewing his blood test results, Dr. Gerta Flowers, a specialist in internal medicine and resident physician at the prison, determined that Ossining did not exhibit such severe symptoms warranting further investigation and rejected his request for an endoscopy. (Flowers Aff. 7.) In July, Ossining requested a gluten-free diet, claiming only this diet could treat celiac disease. (Ossining Aff. 21.) Dr. Flowers

#6 Keep as is/Change

informed the prison that sufficient alternatives in the prison cafeteria were available to Ossining should he prefer to eat a gluten-free diet. (Flowers Aff. 8.) The prison has promised that should Ossining present severe symptoms in the future, it would treat him appropriately. (Brubaker Aff. 15.)

STANDARD OF REVIEW

The issue before this Court is whether the trial court properly applied the law to the facts in granting summary judgment. The court's review of the district court's ruling on a motion for summary judgment is de novo. #7 Pope v. Hightower, 101 F.3d 1382, 1383 (11th Cir. 1996).

#7 Keep as is/Change

SUMMARY OF ARGUMENT

Ossining's First and Eighth Amendment claims fail based on the established facts in the record. With regard to the Eighth Amendment, Ossining shows no evidence of a serious medical need, his treatment by the prison did not violate contemporary standards of decency, and the medical staff was not deliberately indifferent to his condition. #8 U.S. CONST. amend. VIII. As for the First Amendment, because assertion of his rights posed a threat to the security of the prison and created an unreasonable burden on prison resources, Warden Brubaker's rejection of particular publications was justified. #9 Amend. I.

#8 Keep as is/Change

#9 Keep as is/Change

ARGUMENT

The prisoner, Dr. Charles Ossining, is currently serving a five-year sentence for defrauding the federal government. Ossining alleges the prison violated his First Amendment rights by denying him access to professional journals and his Eighth Amendment rights by denying him a gluten-free diet and further testing for a rare disease for which he made a self-diagnosis. While detainees are accorded protections of the Constitution, prisoner's rights are inherently restricted, and some constitutional violations may be acceptable if they serve "legitimate penological interests," such as order, security, and safety. #10 See Thornburgh v. Abbott, 490 U.S. 407-408 (1989). Moreover, as operation of a prison falls under the province of the legislative and executive branches of government, deference should be paid by the courts to appropriate prison authorities regulating this delicate balance between prison security and legitimate rights of prisoners. #11 Turner v. Safley, 482 U.S. 78, 84-85 (1987)

#10 Keep as is/Change

#11 Keep as is/Change

I. PLAINTIFF'S EIGHTH AMENDMENT CLAIM OF CRUEL AND UNUSUAL PUNISHMENT IS WITHOUT MERIT BECAUSE THE PRISONER EXHIBITED NO MEDICAL CONDITION WARRANTING SPECIAL TREATMENT

Ossining fails to present sufficient evidence of a serious medical problem related to being denied a gluten-free diet or evidence that the prison was "deliberately indifferent" to his symptoms, as required for claims under the Eighth Amendment. See #12 Helling, 509 U.S. 25, 29 (1993). In #13 Helling, the Supreme Court established a two prong test for proving Eighth Amendment violations. Under the subjective prong (A), the prisoner must show deliberate indifference by the prison toward a

#12 Keep as is/Change

#13 Keep as is/Change

serious risk posed to the prisoner. Under the objective prong (B), the prisoner must show that the unreasonable risk of harm he faces is contrary to contemporary standards of decency. #14 Id. at 35-36. Because Ossining received adequate treatment for his ailments and exhibited no medical condition warranting special treatment, he fails both prongs of the Eighth Amendment test.

#14   Keep as is/Change

A. The prison was not deliberately indifferent to prisoner's medical condition when the prison physician reviewed prisoner's blood test results to find no severe symptoms of celiac disease warranting further treatment and the prison menu offered adequate gluten-free alternatives

Under the subjective prong, the prisoner must show 1) the prison had knowledge of a serious risk of harm to him and 2) deliberate indifference by the prison toward this risk. #15 Id. at 35.

#15   Keep as is/Change

1. The prison had no subjective knowledge of any serious risk of harm to the prisoner in denying him a gluten-free diet or in rejecting his request for an endoscopy to further test for celiac disease

Ossining fails to show prison officials knew of and disregarded "an excessive risk to his health or safety." #16 See Farmer v. Brennan, 511 U.S. 825, 837 (1994); 42 U.S.C. § 1983 (2003). As serious complications from celiac disease are rare and Dr. Flowers determined that the prisoner did not present such severe symptoms to warrant further investigation, Ossining fails to show the prison's subjective knowledge of a serious risk of harm when denying him a gluten-free diet and further testing. In #17 Campbell et al. v. Sikes, the plaintiff inmate alleged cruel and unusual punishment when the defendant prison psychiatrist misdiagnosed her with poly-substance abuse disorder when in fact she had a bipolar disorder, a diagnosis unreported in jail records or prior hospitalization records. The court affirmed the grant of summary judgment for the prison because there was no evidence that the psychiatrist knew the prisoner had bipolar disorder, that he knew he misdiagnosed her, or that he knew of a substantial risk of serious harm to the inmate as a result of his treatment. #18 Campbell v. Sikes, 169 F.3d 1353, 1366-1368 (1999). Similarly, Ossining fails to present evidence from which a reasonable jury could infer that Dr. Flowers or other prison officials knew he had celiac disease, or knew they were misdiagnosing him, or knew their treatment was grossly inadequate but proceeded with the treatment anyway. Like #19 Campbell, Ossining's medical records did not indicate a prior history of celiac disease and a professional review of his blood did not give Dr. Flowers reason for concern. Therefore, Ossining fails the first part of the subjective prong of the Helling test because the prison exhibits no subjective knowledge of his mistreatment.

#16   Keep as is/Change

#17   Keep as is/Change

#18   Keep as is/Change

#19   Keep as is/Change

2. The prison was not deliberately indifferent toward the medical concerns of the prisoner

Ossining fails to demonstrate his medical treatment by the prison constituted the "unnecessary and wanton infliction of pain," as required to show deliberate indifference. #20 Mustave Hurt, Unimaginable Pain, 742 Geo. L.J. 801, 831-32 (2003) (discussing the requirements to show deliberate indifference). In Estelle, the prisoner

#20   Keep as is/Change

#21 Keep as is/Change

#22 Keep as is/Change

#23 Keep as is/Change

#24 Keep as is/Change

#25 Keep as is/Change

#26 Keep as is/Change

#27 Keep as is/Change

#28 Keep as is/Change

injured his back while engaged in prison work, claiming deliberate indifference by the prison for failure to perform an X-ray to treat him. The court held that questions concerning forms of treatment are matters of medical judgment, and that failure by prison medical staff to use additional diagnostic techniques beyond ordinary treatment does not constitute deliberate indifference or cruel and usual punishment. #21 Estelle v. Gamble, 429 S. Ct. 97, 107 (1976). Similarly, Dr. Flowers' refusal to order an endoscopy to confirm Ossining's self diagnosis of celiac disease following her professional review of his blood test results does not constitute deliberate indifference to his medical needs. Ossining offers no evidence that prison medical staff failed to meet appropriate professional standards in determining that his symptoms did not warrant further testing. Moreover, Ossining's difference in opinion from prison officials concerning diagnosis and recommended treatment does not constitute cruel and unusual punishment. #22 See id. at 100; but see Harris v. Thigpen, 941 F.2d 1495, 1505 (11th Cir. 1991)(holding that difference of opinion does constitute cruel and unusual punishment). While an endoscopy may have led to an appropriate diagnosis and treatment for his condition, Ossining fails to show deliberate indifference as medical decisions concerning forms of treatment beyond ordinary care do not constitute cruel and unusual punishment. #23 See Estelle, 429 U.S. 97 at 107.

Denial of Ossining's request for a special gluten-free diet does not constitute deliberate indifference because the prisoner lacks convincing symptoms requiring special treatment. See 25 Op. Off. Legal Counsel 370, 381-82 (1995). #24 In McElligot v. Goley, 182 F.3d 1248, 1256-1258 (11th Cir. 1999), an inmate with a history of stomach problems was treated by prison doctors with Tylenol, Pepto-Bismol, and an anti-gas medication when experiencing severe intestinal pains, even after it was evident these treatments were not responding to his deteriorating condition. The court held that while prison doctors could not be held liable for failing to diagnose the inmate's colon cancer, the failure to further diagnose and treat severe pain experienced by a prisoner was evidence of deliberate indifference. #25 See McElligot v. Foley, 182 F.3d 1248, 1256-58 (11th Cir. 1999); Noah Lee, Deliberate Indifference: What's It All About? 31 (3d ed. 2001). Unlike McElligot, Ossining exhibits no severe symptoms of celiac disease. The prison staff examined Ossining, conducted a blood test, prescribed him iron supplements to overcome his weight loss and psychological depression, and professionally reviewed his blood work to conclude there was nothing seriously wrong with him. Therefore, as the prison exercised professional standards of care in evaluating his health, and as the inmate exhibits no severe symptoms warranting special treatment, Ossining fails to show deliberate indifference to his medical needs. #26 See United States Sent. G.L. Man. §5D2.1(f) (2001).

B. The prison's denial of prisoner's requests for a special gluten-free diet and additional testing for a rare disease do not violate contemporary standards of decency

Under the objective prong, Ossining fails to show his exposure to an unreasonable risk of harm contrary to "contemporary standards of decency." #27 Helling, 509 United States at 36. The objective standard requires showing treatment rising to the level of "serious" deprivation. #28 Campbell, 169 F.3d at 1363. In Rhodes, the Court held confining two inmates to a single cell did not constitute the "unnecessary and wanton infliction of pain" that violates the Eighth Amendment because inmates suffered only minor deprivations of privileges, not necessities such as essential food, medical care, or sanitation. Only when these "minimal civilized measure of life's necessities" are denied is there basis for an Eighth Amendment violation. #29 Rhodes v. Chapman, 452 U.S 337, 346, 349 (1981). Similarly, Wellville's denial of additional testing and special diet to Ossining when trained medical professionals fail to recognize symptoms requiring such treatment does not constitute deprivation of life's minimal necessities. #30 RESTATEMENT (SECOND) OF TORTS § 931 (1994). Ossining was not denied adequate medical care when he was examined by prison medical staff, had his blood tested and reviewed by Dr. Flowers, and was prescribed iron supplements to combat weight loss and fatigue. Moreover, Ossining was never denied essential food as adequate alternatives remained available in the cafeteria should Ossining prefer a gluten-free diet. Therefore, life's minimal necessities were not denied, and Ossining fails the objective standard as his treatment did not violate contemporary standards of decency.

II. PRISONER'S FIRST AMENDMENT CLAIM IS WITHOUT MERIT BECAUSE WARDEN BRUBAKER REVIEWED AND DENIED PRISONER'S PUBLICATIONS IN RESPONSE TO THE UNREASONABLE BURDEN PLACED UPON THE PRISON'S RESOURCES AS AUTHORIZED UNDER 28 C.F.R. §540.71

As authorized under 28 C.F.R. § 540.71 (b), Warden Brubaker legitimately restricted Ossining's right to receive publications deemed "detrimental to the security, good order, or discipline of the institution..." 28 C.F.R. § 540.71. Exercise of constitutional rights within the prison must pay due regard to the order and security of the prison environment. #31 See Turner Railroad v. Safley, 482 U.S. 78, 84-85 (1987). Ossining fails to show Wellville's restrictions on his First Amendment rights were not "reasonably related to legitimate penological interests" as required under the four-part Turner-Thornburgh test. #32 See Id. at 89; See Thornburgh, 490 U.S. at 401. Under Turner-Thornburgh, the court must consider the following factors: A) the impact that accommodation of the asserted constitutional right will have on others in the prison; B) whether the governmental objective underlying the regulations at issue is legitimate and neutral, and whether the regulations are rationally related to that objective; C) whether the regulation represents an exaggerated response to prison concerns; and D) whether there are alternative means of exercising the right that remain open to prison inmates at de minimis cost to penological interests. #33 Owen v. Wille, 117 F.3d at 1235 (11th Cir. 1997). As Ossining's exercise of his First Amendment right created an unreasonable burden on resources of the prison and put prison security in jeopardy, restricting his access to medical publications was constitutional because it was reasonably related to a legitimate penological interest.

A. Accommodation of prisoner's asserted First Amendment right would be detrimental to the order and security of the prison, placing an unreasonable burden on the resources of the prison medical facility and cafeteria

The Court should be particularly deferential to the informed discretion of Warden Brubaker given interests in security when Ossining's assertion of his constitutional right created a "ripple effect" among fellow inmates and prison staff.

#29 Keep as is/Change

#30 Keep as is/Change

#31 Keep as is/Change

#32 Keep as is/Change

#33 Keep as is/Change

#34 Keep as is/Change

#35 Keep as is/Change

#36 Keep as is/Change

#37 Keep as is/Change

#38 Keep as is/Change

#39 Keep as is/Change

#34 See U.S. v. White, 490 U.S. 84, 87 (1990). In Turner, a class of inmates challenged prison regulations restricting correspondence between inmates as violations of their First Amendment rights. The court deferred to judgment of correction officials and upheld the regulation as reasonably related to legitimate security interests given the potential for coordinating criminal activity by inmate-to-inmate correspondence, and given the probability of material circulating within the prison in a "ripple effect." #35 See Turner, 482 U.S. at 84-85.

Like Turner, Warden Brubaker determined that Ossining created a "ripple effect," threatening the order and security of the prison while placing an unreasonable burden on prison resources, by circulating publications among prisoners to encourage them to believe they were sick. According to Brubaker, the temporal relationship between Ossining's receipt of medical publications and increased inmate complaints indicates a correlation between the assertion of his constitutional rights and the riling up of prisoners, over taxing of prison personnel, and additional expenditure of prison resources. #36 Ossining v. Brubaker, No. CIV.A.02-2332, 2003 WL 66432, at *6 (Jan. 6, 2003). Dramatic increases in infirmary visits and requests for allergy testing among inmates, many of whom showed no symptoms warranting testing, support Brubaker's hypothesis. Given the threat to order and cost of additional resources required to accommodate Ossining's assertion of his rights, deference should be given to Brubaker's informed discretion in rejecting these publications.

B. Governmental objective in maintaining prison security is legitimate and neutral, and prison regulations governing the availability of publications to inmates rationally relate to this objective by reducing frivolous medical complaints and special requests

Under the second factor of the Turner-Thornburgh test, the Court must determine whether 1) the governmental objective underlying the regulation at issue is legitimate and neutral, and whether 2) the regulation is rationally related to that objective. #37 State of Alabama v. Carter, 507 U.S. 411, 418 (1992).

1. Protecting prison security is a legitimate and neutral governmental objective

In rejecting Ossining's publications, Warden Brubaker acted pursuant to 28 C.F.R. § 540.71, whose "underlying objective of protecting prison security is undoubtedly legitimate and is neutral with regard to the content of the expression regulated." #38 North West Electric Company v. University of Colorado, 211 U.S. 415, 417 (1991). In Thornburgh, inmates filed a class action against the prison challenging regulations excluding incoming sexually explicit publications. The Court upheld the regulations as maintenance of prison order and security is a legitimate governmental purpose, and because the prison's ban on sexually explicit material was neutrally based on security interests. #39 See cf. Thornburgh, 490 U.S. at 414-15. Like Thornburgh, Ossining's publications were rejected because they created obstacles to the legitimate governmental objective of maintaining prison security. Warden Brubaker's rejection of only those publications deemed a threat to prison security remained "neutral" to the legitimate governmental interest in maintaining security and order. Therefore, Brubaker's exercise of authority under 28 C.F.R § 540.71 was consistent with the legitimate and neutral objectives underlying the regulation.

2. <u>Application of prison regulation governing the availability of publications to inmates is rationally related to the governmental objective</u>

There is a "valid, rational connection" between the rejection of various publications addressed to Ossining and the legitimate government interests in security and preservation of resources. #40 <u>See</u> <u>Turner</u>, 482 U.S. at 89; see also 28 C.F.R. § 540.71 (2002) (establishing security as legitimate government interest). In <u>Onishea</u>, inmates with HIV brought a class action challenging the prison's segregation of recreational, religious, and educational programs based on prisoners' HIV status. The prison justified its actions claiming the cost of hiring additional guards to monitor the threat of "high-risk" behavior in integrated programs would create an undue financial burden on resources. The Court upheld the segregated programs as rationally related to governmental objectives because "penological concerns such as security and cost are legitimate, and...these are in fact the concerns behind the program requirements that participating prisoners neither create a threat of disorder or unreasonable costs." #41 <u>Onishea v. Hopper</u>, 171 F.3d 1289, 1300 (11th Cir. 1999). Similarly, Brubaker's rejection of certain items addressed to Ossining was rationally related to legitimate governmental interests because of the Warden's concern that these publications created threat of disorder and unreasonable costs for the prison. By rejecting these publications, Warden Brubaker intended to remove obstacles to maintaining security by reducing the agitation of prisoners, easing the burden placed on the prison medical staff, and removing the need for additional guards to maintain order in the cafeteria. Therefore, as security was the underlying concern behind Brubaker's actions, his rejection of Ossining's publications was rationally related to legitimate governmental objectives. #42 <u>See</u> H.R. 81, 108th Cong. (2003) (establishing security as legitimate governmental objective), available at http://thomas.-20loc.gov/bss/d108/d108laws. html.

C. <u>The prison regulation is not an exaggerated response to prison concerns because alternatives accommodating prisoner's rights at de minimus cost to penological interests are not immediately obvious or feasible</u>

Rejection of prisoner's publications is not an exaggerated response to the threat these items posed to prison resources and security because there are no "obvious, easy alternatives." #43 <u>See</u> Jeremy Stevens, <u>Taking Control</u> 41-42 (Amanda Bradley ed., 3d ed. Scholastic Press 2001). In <u>Spellman</u>, inmates challenged the prison's blanket ban on publications sent to prisoners in administrative segregation on the grounds that the regulation was an exaggerated response to security and safety concerns. The Court held the prison's actions unconstitutional, recognizing alternatives to the blanket ban, such as placing reasonable limits on the quantity of publications permitted in confinement, which still addressed the concerns of security, fire, and sanitation. #44 <u>See</u> <u>Spellman v. Hopper</u>, 95 F.supp.2d 1267, 1286 (M.D. Ala. 1999).

Unlike <u>Spellman</u>, Brubaker rejected only Ossining's medical publications, items deemed a threat to prison security; Brubaker did not blanket ban all publications sent to Ossining. Moreover, <u>unlike</u> Spellman, less restrictive alternatives can be rejected because of reasonably grounded fears they will lead to greater harm or administrative inconvenience. #45 <u>See</u> Alabama Constitution article V, § 9. The resources

#40 Keep as is/Change

#41 Keep as is/Change

#42 Keep as is/Change

#43 Keep as is/Change

#44 Keep as is/Change

#45 Keep as is/Change

required to read through every allergy magazine received to eliminate publications deemed a threat would be too expansive as prisoners have complained of a wide variety of allergies. Also, allowing Ossining to read magazines while in confinement would not come at a de minimus cost to the prison as additional resources would be required to fund such an arrangement. #46 See James King, Costs of Confinement, 28 N. Ill. U. L. Rev. 609, 621-22 (2001). Thus, as less restrictive alternatives are not readily available or feasible, the Warden's actions do not represent an exaggerated response to legitimate penological concerns.

#46 Keep as is/Change

D. The prison restrictions on prisoner's receipt of publications are reasonable as prisoner has alternative means of exercising his First Amendment rights to keep up with developments in his field of work

Ossining fails the fourth factor of the Turner-Thornburgh test because other means of expression remain available to the prisoner despite imposition of prison regulations restricting his access to certain publications. See Stevens, Taking Control at 45. In Turner, the prison restricted inmate-to-inmate correspondence between prisons to prevent future criminal behavior, a legitimate security concern. The Court held the fourth factor satisfied if any other means of expression remained open to the prisoners, not necessarily other means of communicating with inmates in other prisons. Turner, 482 S.Ct. at 90, 92. Similarly, Brubaker's application of the regulation merely prohibits publications of particular kind, and does not deprive the prisoner of all means of expression. The prison is not prohibiting Ossining from gaining access to allergy information as he can still receive phone calls and visits from colleagues who can keep him up to date. Moreover, the prisoner is still free to receive a variety of other publications. Alternative means of exercising his First Amendment rights are still available to the prisoner, and therefore, Ossining fails to satisfy the fourth factor.

CONCLUSION

For the above stated reasons, the judgment of the District Court should be affirmed.

Respectfully submitted,

_____

Attorney for Respondents

CERTIFICATE OF SERVICE

I swear on this day, the 28th of February, 2003, that I have served Respondent's brief on Appellant's counsel.

_____

Attorney for Respondents

Appendix A: Answer Keys

I. LEGAL ANALYSIS ANSWER KEYS

A. Quizzes

1. Legal Analysis in General (page 57)

1. T
2. F - Facts often change, and you may need to retrace your steps while collecting facts for a case.
3. T
4. F - If there is consistent common law that predates the statute, it may be applicable to your case.
5. T
6. T
7. T
8. F - Policy arguments are appropriate when existing rules are ambiguous, you have a case of first impression, or you want to bolster your other legal arguments.
9. F - When applying an elements test, you must meet all the elements. When applying a totality test, some elements may be more important than others and not all elements need be met.
10. T
11. F - You should analyze each term within a rule.
12. T
13. F - A proponent of realism makes policy arguments to influence the judge. A proponent of positivism enumerates the applicable legal rules and applies them with legal precedent.
14. T
15. F - Inductive reasoning is used to show why a case is more likely to be decided one way instead of another. Deductive reasoning is used to reach an absolute conclusion.
16. T
17. F - The overarching goal of statutory interpretation is to determine the legislature's intent.
18. T
19. T

20. F - Some judges decline to consider legislative history when interpreting a statute. However, many judges believe that legislative history provides insight to legislative intent.
21. T
22. T
23. F - Circuit courts are the federal courts of appeal. District courts are the federal trial courts.
24. T
25. F - Case holdings, majority opinions, and primary law are binding on lower courts in the same jurisdiction.
26. F - If the holding of a prior case is different from your predicted or preferred outcome, find legally significant differences that distinguish the prior case from your current case.
27. T
28. F - You can include too much Euro. Effective case comparisons include only the legally significant facts.
29. T
30. T
31. F - Use the legal writing formulas as guides in your organizational and thinking processes. Then craft your legal analysis to suit your specific purpose and audience.

2. Binding vs. Persuasive (page 59)

1. D
2. B
3. C
4. A
5. E

II.   THE WRITING PROCESS ANSWER KEY

A. *Quiz*

1. Writing and Rewriting in General (page 122)

1.	F	11.	T
2.	T	12.	F
3.	T	13.	T
4.	T	14.	T
5.	F	15.	T
6.	T	16.	T
7.	F	17.	T
8.	T	18.	F
9.	F	19.	F
10.	F	20.	T

21. F		24. T	
22. F		25. F	
23. T		26. T	

III.   LEGAL DOCUMENTS ANSWER KEYS

A.   *Quizzes*

1.   Memos (page 320)

1. F		34. T	
2. T		35. F	
3. F		36. F	
4. T		37. T	
5. T		38. F	
6. F		39. T	
7. T		40. T	
8. F		41. T	
9. F		42. F	
10. F		43. F	
11. F		44. F	
12. F		45. T	
13. F		46. T	
14. F		47. F	
15. F		48. T	
16. F		49. F	
17. T		50. T	
18. T		51. F	
19. T		52. T	
20. F		53. T	
21. T		54. F	
22. T		55. T	
23. F		56. F	
24. T		57. T	
25. T		58. F	
26. F		59. T	
27. T		60. T	
28. F		61. T	
29. T		62. T	
30. F		63. F	
31. F		64. F	
32. T		65. T	
33. T		66. T	

2. Briefs (page 323)

1.	T		30.	F
2.	F		31.	F
3.	F		32.	T
4.	F		33.	T
5.	T		34.	F
6.	T		35.	T
7.	T		36.	T
8.	T		37.	T
9.	F		38.	F
10.	F		39.	T
11.	T		40.	T
12.	T		41.	T
13.	F		42.	T
14.	T		43.	F
15.	F		44.	T
16.	T		45.	T
17.	T		46.	F
18.	F		47.	T
19.	T		48.	F
20.	F		49.	T
21.	F		50.	T
22.	F		51.	F
23.	F		52.	T
24.	T		53.	T
25.	T		54.	T
26.	F		55.	T
27.	T		56.	F
28.	T		57.	F
29.	T			

3. Persuasive Techniques (page 327)

1.	T		5.	T
2.	T		6.	F
3.	F		7.	F
4.	F		8.	F

4. Oral Argument (page 327)

1.	F		6.	T
2.	T		7.	T
3.	T		8.	T
4.	F		9.	F
5.	F			

5. Client Letters (page 328)

1.	F	8.	T
2.	T	9.	F
3.	F	10.	T
4.	T	11.	F
5.	T	12.	F
6.	T	13.	T
7.	F		

6. Pleadings and Motions (page 329)

1.	T	6.	F
2.	F	7.	T
3.	F	8.	F
4.	T	9.	T
5.	T	10.	T

7. Write-On Competition (page 330)

1.	T	3.	T
2.	F	4.	F

B. Self-Assessments

1. Rewriting a Legal Memo—Self-Assessment (page 331)

1. Effective. The question presented is effective because it provides the jurisdiction ("under"), the legal issue (stalk), and some of the legally significant facts. *See:* Question Presented
2. Ineffective. Although this brief answer provides a short answer ("probably not") and uses the legal terms of art from the stalking statute, the sentence structure is too confusing for the reader. *See:* Brief Answers
3. Ineffective. Here, the language is not objective. Instead, the writer should provide examples to show the reader how Castle acted instead of characterizing his actions. *See:* Statement of Facts
4. Ineffective. The use of the term "this" is vague. The writer could have been more clear, for instance, by writing "this entry."
5. Effective. This roadmap clearly lays out the elements of the stalking law and cites to the statute. *See:* Roadmaps
6. Effective. This topic sentence follows the roadmap and uses the same legal term of art ("follow"). *See:* Topic Sentences

7. Ineffective. Although this case comparison ties the facts of the prior case to the current facts, it would be more effective if the writer explicitly provided the holding of the prior case. *See:* Case Analysis

8. Effective. This mini-conclusion clearly concludes on the element of "follow" and provides reasoning for the reader. *See:* Large-Scale Organization

9. Effective. Here, the writer provides definitions from the statute to interpret its meaning. *See:* Legal Analysis

10. Effective. This case comparison is effective because the writer provides the facts, reasoning, and holding of the prior case and compares them to the facts of her case. *See:* Case Comparisons

11. Effective. This paragraph demonstrates rule-based reasoning using statutory definitions to interpret the meaning of the statute. The writer uses short sentences and clear, simple logic. *See:* Statutory Interpretation

12. Ineffective. This mini-conclusion is not effective because the writer has not finished discussing this element. The paragraph below continues to discuss the issue of consent. *See:* Mini-Conclusions

13. Ineffective. Here the mini-conclusion is inconclusive. If the writer cannot come out one way or the other on a particular issue, she should provide reasons why.

14. Effective. This mini-roadmap clearly lays out the large-scale organization for this section. *See:* Large-Scale Organization

15. Ineffective. This paragraph relies solely on facts. Instead, it should use authority such as case comparisons to create legal arguments. *See:* Legal Analysis

16. Ineffective. It is not clear how this case applies or that the rule it seemingly stands for makes sense.

17. Effective. This topic sentence follows the mini-roadmap and clearly informs the reader of the legal element to be discussed in this paragraph. *See* Topic Sentences

18. Ineffective. Although it is a good idea to present a general rule for the reader, it would have been better if this rule came before the case comparison to provide context for the comparison. In addition, the writer needs to include a citation for this rule. *See:* Legal Analysis

19. Ineffective. This topic sentence does not make it clear to the reader that the paragraph will focus on reasonable fear. *See:* Legal Analysis

20. Effective. This topic sentence clearly focuses the reader on the legal element discussed in the paragraph, and it follows the structure laid out in the mini-roadmap. *See* Topic Sentences

21. Ineffective. Here, the reader is left wondering what happened in these cases. How many incidents did these cases involve, and what were the holdings? Even if the writer decides to leave this string cite (instead of discussing more of these cases in the text), she should at least provide parentheticals for the reader. *See:* Case Analysis

22. Ineffective. Here, the writer seems unable to come to a conclusion. While a conclusion on each issue is not always possible, the writer forces the reader to analyze the issue. *See:* Purpose

23. Ineffective. Here, the writer needs to use this case to illustrate her point. Instead, she makes a number of unsupported assertions and then simply cites a case without applying it. In addition, she uses circular reasoning by stating that the entries are not legitimate if they are harassing and intimidating as she is trying to analyze the element of harassing and intimidating. *See:* Legal Analysis

24. Effective. This part of the conclusion is effective because it is consistent with the brief answer, clearly lays out each element, and gives reasons for the outcome. *See:* Conclusion

25. Ineffective. Here, the writer is unable to provide an answer for the reader. Instead she goes back and forth in her reasoning.

2. Rewriting a Legal Brief—Self-Assessment (page 336)

1. Effective. This pointheading is effective because it accurately conveys the organization of your analysis in a persuasive manner. *See:* Pointheadings

2. Ineffective. Although this subheading does show the organization of the brief by clearly delineating this factor (age and experience), it does not do so persuasively. This subheading could be made more effective by incorporating specific facts from the case. *See:* Pointheadings

3. Ineffective. This issue statement is ineffective because it does not pass the breath test. *See:* Issue Statements

4. Effective. This issue statement is effective because it focuses the reader on the issue of custody, contains persuasive facts, and uses creative word choice (such as detained and summoned) to illustrate those facts. *See:* Issue Statements

5. Effective. This is an effective way to begin your statement of the facts; your theory of the case (that Lance Harbor is a model high school student) is beginning to show already. *See:* Statement of the Case, Theory of the Case

6. Effective. This word choice, while not legally significant, is effective in persuading the court and subtly conveys your theory of the case. *See:* Theory of the Case

7. Ineffective. While it is a good idea to start with the context of the Fifth Amendment, there are a few problems here. First, this opening topic sentence can be more persuasive. Second, the quote might not be the most persuasive technique here—it is not adding much to the argument. Third, a cite to the Fifth Amendment is necessary. *See:* Persuasive Techniques

8. Ineffective. Although this sentence serves as a roadmap to the rest of the brief, it is not written persuasively. *See:* Persuasive Techniques

9. Ineffective. While this paragraph introduces the reader to the element of interrogation, it lacks a roadmap laying out the factors addressed below. Also, if a sentence (such as the second sentence) references

"courts," it should cite to more than one court or use the <u>e.g.</u> signal. *See:* Large-Scale Organization, Signals

10. Effective. This topic sentence effectively conveys the legal factor to the reader in a persuasive manner. *See:* Persuasive Techniques, Large-Scale Organization

11. Ineffective. This case comparison is ineffective for a number of reasons. First, the paragraph focuses on functional equivalent; therefore, the case comparison should be limited to the functional equivalent discussion. Second, the second sentence assumes the reader is familiar with the <u>Innis</u> case; as a result, the reader is left wondering what the case has to do with handicapped children. Third, the tie between the facts of Lance Harbor's case and <u>Innis</u> are not clear to the reader. *See:* Case Comparisons

12. Ineffective. This case comparison can be improved in a number of ways. First, a topic sentence focusing the reader on the legal point of the comparison would be helpful. Second, the rule of law (knowledge of unusual susceptibility) is hidden mid-paragraph; instead, it would be helpful for that information to appear closer to the beginning of the paragraph to set up the legal context for the reader. Third, the comparison is wordy; by tightening up the language, the reader would have a concise comparison. Fourth, there are two case comparisons on the same issue (this one and <u>Innis</u> above); it might have made more sense to address them together. *See:* Case Comparisons

13. Ineffective. These two sentences sound more like a roadmap in a scholarly article than a roadmap in a brief. In addition, they are not necessary here if the two issues have been clearly delineated in the issue statements and the context at the beginning of the argument section. *See:* Briefs

14. Ineffective. Although this case comparison uses the facts, reasoning, and holding of the prior case to compare to Harbor's facts, it could be more concise. The reader identifies two considerations in <u>Gilmore</u>: (1) whether D volunteered the information and (2) whether the officer asked questions or initiated conversation—the comparison could be made clearer and more concise by identifying which of the Harbor facts match up with each consideration, rather than saying that both considerations are met, and then providing a slew of facts? *See:* Case Comparisons

15. Ineffective. This context for the custody section is ineffective for a number of reasons. The second, third, and fourth sentences could be combined to make a concise, coherent sentence defining the standard. Also, the roadmap provided is not persuasive and it identifies five factors while only three are addressed below. *See:* Conciseness, Persuasive Techniques

16. Effective. This topic sentence is effective because it persuasively addresses an argument from the other side without sounding too defensive and without drawing attention to the other side's argument. *See:* Persuasive Techniques

17. Effective. This case comparison is effective because it concisely compares the prior case to Harbor's case and subtly attacks the other side's argument that the familiar location of the principal's office makes it unlikely that the defendant was in custody. *See:* Case Comparisons

18. Ineffective. The topic sentence needs to be rewritten so that it is not so wordy by deleting "this is ..." In addition, the next sentence is wordy and awkward—delete "the court stated that what is of." Next, the case comparison needs facts from <u>Turner</u> to compare to the Harbor facts. *See:* Conciseness, Case Comparisons

19. Ineffective. This topic sentence is too generic; it could be placed on any brief on this topic. *See:* Persuasive Techniques

20. Ineffective. This list of factors is not written persuasively. In addition, it does not address the factors discussed below. If a roadmap is provided, it should be followed. *See:* Persuasive Techniques, Large-Scale Organization

21. Ineffective. This case comparison would be more effective if it included more detail. The reader has no idea what the court's reasoning or holding was in <u>E.A.H.</u> so it is difficult to follow the comparison. *See:* Case Comparisons

22. Ineffective. While this topic sentence focuses the reader on the elements, it is not persuasive. *See:* Persuasive Techniques

23. Ineffective. While this topic sentence is persuasive, the word, "kid" is inappropriate in a formal brief. *See:* Briefs

24. Effective. This conclusion effectively requests relief from the appellate court. *See:* Conclusions

IV.   EDITING ANSWER KEYS

A.   *Quizzes*

1.   Active vs. Passive Voice (page 370)

1. B	4. B
2. A	5. B
3. A	6. A

2.   Affect vs. Effect (page 370)

1. Affect	4. Effect
2. Effect	5. Effect
3. Effect	6. Affect

3. Although vs. While (page 371)

1. Although	4. Although
2. While	5. While
3. Although	6. While

4. Apostrophes (page 371)

1. B	5. B
2. A	6. B
3. A	7. A
4. B	8. A

5. Because vs. Since (page 372)

1. Since	3. Because
2. Because	4. Since

6. Capitalization (page 373)

1. C	4. B
2. B	5. B
3. A	6. C

7. Commas (page 374)

1. C	4. D
2. B	5. C
3. B	6. C

8. Due to (page 375)

1. Improper	3. Improper
2. Proper	

9. Farther vs. Further (page 375)

1. Further	4. Farther
2. Farther	5. Further
3. Farther	

10. Sentence Fragments (page 375)

1. Fragment
2. Complete
3. Complete
4. Fragment

5. Fragment
6. Complete
7. Complete

11. Grammar (page 376)

1. T
2. F
3. F
4. T
5. F
6. F
7. T
8. T
9. F
10. T
11. T
12. F

13. F
14. F
15. F
16. F
17. F
18. F
19. F
20. T
21. F
22. T
23. F
24. T

12. Hyphens (page 377)

1. A

2. C

13. Indefinite Pronouns (page 378)

1. B
2. A
3. C

4. A
5. C
6. B

14. Legalese (page 378)

1. B

2. A

15. Modifiers (page 379)

1. B
2. A
3. B

4. B
5. B
6. B

16. Nominalizations (page 379)

1.	A	4.	B
2.	A	5.	B
3.	B	6.	B

17. Numbers and Quantities (page 380)

1.	Fewer	5.	Many
2.	Less	6.	Fifteen
3.	Fewer	7.	Fifteen
4.	Much	8.	15

18. Parallel Structure (page 381)

1.	Parallel	4.	Not parallel
2.	Not parallel	5.	Parallel
3.	Parallel	6.	Not parallel

19. Quotation Marks (page 381)

1.	A	3.	B
2.	A	4.	A

20. Semicolons and Colons (page 382)

1.	A	3b.	A
2.	B	3c.	A
3a.	B	4.	B

21. That vs. Which (page 382)

1.	Which	4.	That
2.	That	5.	Which
3.	That	6.	That

22. Verb Tense (page 383)

1.	Was	3.	Is
2.	Was		

23. Who, Whom, and Whose (page 383)

1.	Whom	6.	Who
2.	Whom	7.	Whom
3.	Who	8.	Whose
4.	Whom	9.	Who's
5.	Who		

B. Self-Assessment

1. Editing (Grammar) Self-Assessment (page 385)

1. Change. First Amendment. *See:* Capitalization

2. Change. Capitalize titles only when a personal name follows (e.g., Warden Brubaker). *See:* Capitalization

3. Change. prisoner's constitutional rights. *See:* Apostrophes

4. Change. First and Eighth Amendment. *See:* Capitalization

5. Change. district court. *See:* Capitalization

6. Change. concluded. *See:* Conciseness

7. Change. the prison was. *See:* Pronouns

8. Change. Medicare fraud, mail fraud, and making false claims to the government. *See:* Commas

9. Change. number. *See:* Numbers and Quantities

10. Change. to disseminate allergy information to other prisoners. *See:* Conciseness

11. Keep as is. : *See:* Semicolons and Colons

12. Keep as is. 15%. *See:* Numbers and Quantities

13. Change. long-time. *See:* Dashes

14. Change. Note that a blood test is not concerned—Ossining is. Concerned with his condition, Ossining sought a blood test in March, which revealed he was borderline anemic. *See:* Misplaced and Dangling Modifiers.

15. Change. diagnosed himself. *See:* Redundancy

16. Keep as is. In reviewing Ossining's blood test results, Dr. Gerta Flowers. *See:* Misplaced and Dangling Modifiers

17. Change. Dr. Flowers promised she would treat Ossining appropriately if he presented severe symptoms in the future. *See:* Conciseness

18. Keep as is. *de novo. See:* Italics

19. Change. Ossining's First and Eighth Amendment claims fail. *See:* Conciseness

20. Change. Ossining showed no evidence that (1) he had a serious medical need; (2) the prison violated contemporary standards of decency; or (3) the medical staff was deliberately indifferent to his condition. *See: Parallel Structure*

21. Change. <u>Advanced question</u>. Usually, you should avoid nominalizations. Warden Brubaker justifiably rejected the particular publications. How-

ever, keep as is in text if the writer wishes to downplay the rejection. *See:* Nominalizations

22. Keep as is. five-year. *See:* Hyphens

23. Change. Dr. Charles Ossining, a prisoner, is currently serving a five-year sentence for fraud of the federal government. *See:* Sentence Fragments.

24. Change. Although. *See:* Although vs. While

25. Change. ," *See:* Quotation Marks

26. Change. courts. *See:* Capitalization

27. Change. Ossining presents no evidence. *See:* Strong Subject-Verb Combinations

28. Change. the denial of. *See:* Nominalizations

29. Keep as is. Supreme Court. *See:* Capitalization

30. Change. two-prong. *See:* Hyphens

31. Keep as is. : *See:* Semicolons and Colons

32. Change. [omit]. *See:* Clearly vs. Obviously

33. Keep as is. ." *See:* Quotation Marks

34. Change. In <u>Campbell v. Sikes</u>, the inmate alleged cruel and unusual punishment when the prison psychiatrist misdiagnosed her with the wrong disorder. *See:* Conciseness

35. Change. The court granted summary judgment. *See:* Active vs. Passive Voice.

36. Change. Like the medical records in <u>Campbell</u>, Ossining's medical records. *See:* Comparisons

37. Change. because. *See:* Because vs. Since.

38. Change. does not. *See:* Contractions

39. Change. simply to confirm. *See:* Split Infinitives

40. Keep as is. gluten-free. *See:* Hyphens

41. Change. deliberate. *See:* Terms of Art

42. Change. Tylenol, Pepto-Bismol. *See:* Capitalization

43. Keep as is. further. *See:* Farther vs. Further

44. Change. Under the objective prong, Ossining fails to show his exposure to an unreasonable risk of harm contrary to "contemporary standards" of decency." *See:* Active vs. Passive voice.

45. Keep as is. did not. *See:* Verb Tense

46. Keep as is. does. *See:* Verb Tense

47. Change. [omit]. *See:* Legalese

48. Keep as is. ..." *See:* Quotation Marks

49. Change. It is not the "Exercise of constitutional rights" that must pay due regard; it is the prison. The prison must pay due regard to the order and security of the prison environment in order to allow the exercise of constitutional rights. *See:* Subject-Verb Agreement

50. Change. consider. *See:* Nominalizations

51. Keep as is. ; *See:* Semicolons and Colons

52. Change. A class of inmates challenged prison regulations restricting correspondence between inmates as violations of its First Amendment rights. *See:* Subject-Verb Agreement

53. Change. by. *See:* Conciseness

54. Change. effect. *See:* Affect vs. Effect

55. "ripple effect"; he threatened. *See:* Quotation Marks

56. Change. incitement. *See:* Nominalizations

57. Change. whom. *See:* Who, Whom, and Whose

58. Change. "of which the." *See:* Who, Whom, and Whose

59. Change. The Court upheld the regulations because maintenance of prison order and security is a legitimate governmental purpose and because the prison's ban on sexually explicit material was neutrally based on security interests. *See:* Commas

60. Change. because they created. *See:* Nominalizations

61. Change. its. *See:* It's vs. Its

62. Change. no quotation marks for block quotes with over 50 words. *See:* Quotation Marks

63. Change. Keep as is. was. *See:* Subject-Verb Agreement

64. Keep as is. By rejecting these publications, Warden Brubaker intended to remove obstacles. *See:* Misplaced and Dangling Modifiers

65. Change. Therefore, Brubaker's rejection of Ossining's publications was rationally related to a legitimate governmental objective—prison security. *See:* Conciseness

66. Change. claiming. *See:* Conciseness

67. Keep as is. , *See:* Commas

68. Change. that. *See:* That vs. Which

69. Keep as is. : *See:* Semicolons and Colons

70. Change. because. *See:* Conciseness

71. Change. rewrite sentence. *See:* Sentence Fragments

72. Keep as is. among. *See:* Numbers and Quantities

73. Change. if. *See:* Conciseness

74. Change (no comma). *See:* Commas

75. Keep as is. who. *See:* Who, Whom, and Whose

76. Keep as is. First Amendment. *See:* Capitalization

V. CITATION ANSWER KEYS

A. *ALWD Quizzes*

1. ALWD Typeface Conventions (page 427)

1. B - The comma that follows the case name should not be italicized or underlined (Rule 12.0).

2. B - This is the correct citation according to Rules 12.0 and 12.20(b). The comma that follows the case name should not be italicized or underlined.

3. A - The introductory signal and "id." are properly underlined according to Rule 44.6(b).

4. D - This is the correct typeface format according to Rule 23.1(d).

5. C - This is the correct typeface format according to Rule 12.2(a).

2. Basic Structure and Signals for ALWD Citations (page 428)

1. B - This citation uses the proper format for signals according to Rules 44.8(a) and 44.3. Authorities should be separated with a semi-colon and one space (Rule 45.2).

2. B - This citation uses the correct order of authorities according to Rule 44.8(a). For cases from the same court, cases should be cited in reverse chronological order (Rule 45.3(h)).

3. B - This citation uses the correct order of authorities according to Rule 45.4(a). Statutes should be cited before cases (Rule 45.4(a)).

4. A - The explanatory parenthetical is correctly placed and formatted according to Rules 46.2(a) and 46.3.

5. D - This citation uses signals correctly according to Rules 44.8(a), (c), 44.3, and 45.2. For cases from the same court, cases should be cited in reverse chronological order (Rule 45.3(h)).

3. ALWD Citation Signals (page 429)

1. D - This is the correct signal according to Rule 44.3.

2. B - This is the correct signal according to Rule 44.3.

3. C - This is the correct signal according to Rule 44.3. The Maryland statute is in accord with the Delaware statute (Rule 44.3).

4. B - This is the correct signal according to Rule 44.3.

5. A - This is the correct signal according to Rule 44.3. Signals should not be used when the cited authority directly supports the stated proposition.

6. C - This is the correct signal according to Rule 44.3.

4. ALWD Order and Punctuation of Signals and Citations (page 431)

1. B - This is the correct citation sentence according to Rule 44.8(a).

2. A - This is the correct citation sentence according to Rules 44.8(a) and 44.3.

3. C - This is the correct citation sentence according to Rules 45.4(a) and 44.3. Federal statutes should be cited sequentially by title number and section number.

5. ALWD Rules for Citing Subdivisions and Pinpoint Cites (page 432)

1. A - According to Rules 12.1 and 12.5(b), this is the correct format for a citation to specific material within a case.

2. C - According to Rules 5.4, 12.1, and 12.5(b), this is the correct citation.

3. B - According to Rules 5.4, 12.1, and 12.5(b), this is the correct citation.

4. C - According to Rule 5.2(b)(2), this is the correct format to a citation to specific material from a law review article.

5. D - According to Rule 5.4, this is the proper format for a citation to nonconsecutive pages.

6. ALWD Rules for Short Form Citations (page 433)

1. A - According to Rules 12.20(a) and 11.3(b)(1) and (e), this is the correct short form citation to a case that is the only source in the immediately preceding citation and that cites the same page number.

2. D - According to Rule 12.20(b), this is the correct short form citation to a case that was not in the immediately preceding citation.

3. A - According to Rules 12.11(a) and 11.3(e), this is the correct short form citation.

4. D - According to Rule 14.6, this is the correct short form citation.

5. C - According to Rule 23.2(b), this is the correct short form citation.

6. A - According to Rules 23.2(a) and 11.3(b)(1), this is the correct short citation.

7. D - <u>Id.</u> should not be used if there is more than one source in the immediately preceding citation. See Rules 11.3(b)(1) and (4)(a).

7.   ALWD Abbreviations (page 434)

1. A - The abbreviations in this citation are correct according to Rule 12.2(e)(7).

2. E - The abbreviations in this citation are correct according to Appendix 3, Part E, General Abbreviations.

3. C - "Fed. Reg." is the proper abbreviation for the Federal Register according to Rule 19.3.

4. B - This is the correct abbreviation for the Federal Rules of Civil Procedure according to Rule 17.1.

5. A - "Geo. Mason L. Rev." is the proper abbreviation for the George Mason Law Review according to Appendix 5, Abbreviations for Legal Periodicals.

8.   ALWD Rules for Citing Cases (page 435)

1. B - The reporter is correctly cited according to Rule 12.4(a)(1) and the Fourth Circuit is correctly abbreviated according to Appendix 4(B), Federal Courts.

2. A - This is the correct citation according to Rule 12.4(b), Appendix 1 (under Pennsylvania), and Appendix 1B, State Appellate Court Decisions.

3. C - "U.S." is the correct abbreviation for the United States Reports and is the official reporter for United States Supreme Court decisions according to Rule 12.4(c) and Appendix 1, Federal Materials.

4. B - The reporter is correctly cited according to Rule 12.4(a)(1) and Appendix 1, Federal Materials. The Fourth Circuit is correctly abbreviated according to Appendix 4(B), Federal Courts.

5. A - The parenthetical information in this citation is properly formatted according to Rules 12.11(a), 46.2(a), and 46.3.

6. A - The parenthetical information in this citation is properly formatted according to Rules 12.12(a), (b), and (d).

9. ALWD Rules for Citing Constitutions (page 436)

1. C - This is the correct citation format according to Rule 13.2. "Const." and "amend." are correctly abbreviated according to Appendix 3, General Abbreviations, C and E.

2. A - This is the correct citation format according to Rule 13.2(a), and "Kan." is correctly abbreviated according to Appendix 3, General Abbreviations, B.

3. D - This is the correct citation format according to Rules 11.3(b) and 13.4.

4. B - This is the correct citation format according to Rules 13.2, 13.3, and Appendix, 3 General Abbreviations, C and E.

5. A - This is the correct citation format according to Rule 13.2(a), and "Pa." is correctly abbreviated according to Appendix 3, General Abbreviations, B.

10. ALWD Rules for Citing Statutes (page 437)

1. B - According to Rule 14.2, the number preceding the abbreviation of the relevant code signifies the title number of the statute.

2. C - This is the correct citation format according to Rule 14.2.

3. A - This is an acceptable short form citation according to Rule 14.6.

4. D - This citation format is not correct.

5. A - This is the correct citation format according to Appendix 1, Primary Sources by Jurisdiction.

6. C - This is the correct citation format according to Rule 17.1.

11. ALWD Citations for Administrative and Executive Materials (page 438)

1. C - This is the correct citation format for C.F.R. provisions according to Rule 19.1.

2. B - According to Rule 19.2, this is the correct alternate short form citation.

3. A - According to Rule 19.3(e), this is the correct citation format for a regulation that has not yet been entered into the Code of Federal Regulations.

4. A - According to Rule 20.3 and Appendix 1, Primary Sources by Jurisdiction, this is the correct format for a citation in the Virginia Register of Regulations.

5. D - This is the proper citation format for an advisory opinion according to Rule 19.7.

6. D - This is the proper citation format for an Executive Order according to Rule 19.9.

12. ALWD Citations for Books, Reports, and Other Nonperiodic Materials (page 439)

1. D - The author's name is correctly formatted (Rule 22.1), the title is correctly formatted (Rule 22.1), the page number is correctly formatted (22.1(c). The publisher information should also be included (Rule 22.1(i)).

2. A - In citing books with more than two authors, use the author's name followed by "et al." according to 22.1(a), and include a comma and one space after the edition and before the publisher's name (Rules 22.1(f), (i)).

3. A - This is the correct citation format according to Rule 22.1. The volume number appears after the book title (Rule 22.1 (c)).

4. D - In citing an originally unpublished letter, begin the citation with the phrase "Ltr. from," (Rule 32.1(a)). Cite the rest of the letter according to Rule 32.3, 22.1(l), or 22.1(m). The publisher information should also be included (Rule 22.1(i)).

5. D - This is the correct citation according to Rule 25.1.

13. ALWD Rules for Citing Periodical Materials (page 441)

1. B - This is the correct citation for a newspaper according to Rule 23.1(d).

2. C - This is the correct citation for a journal article according to Rule 23.1 and Appendix 5, Abbreviations for Legal Periodicals.

3. D - This is the correct citation for a journal article according to Rule 23.1(a) and Appendix 5, Abbreviations for Legal Periodicals.

4. A - This is the correct citation for a nonstudent-written book review according to Rule 23.1(b)(2).

14. ALWD Rules for Citing Electronic Media (page 442)

1. E - This is the correct citation format for unreported cases available on Westlaw according to Rule 12.12(b). According to Rule 12.12(d), the docket number is not a required element for cases published on Lexis-Nexis or Westlaw.

2. C - This is the correct citation format according to Appendix 1, Primary Sources by Jurisdiction, and Rule 14.5.

3. B - This is the correct citation format for an article found on the Internet according to Rules 23.1(d), 38.2, and 40.1.

4. D - This is the correct citation format for a parallel citation according to Rules 23.1(d), 38.2, and 40.1.

5. A - This is the correct citation format for a personal e-mail message according to Rule 41.1(d).

6. C - This is the correct citation format for a commercial recording according to Rule 34.1.

B. ALWD Self-Assessment

1. ALWD Citation Self-Assessment (page 444)

1. Change. Answer: U.S. Const. amend. I;. Explanation: Rule 13.2, abbreviate and use lowercase letters for designations such as "article" or "amendment."

2. Keep as is. Answer: U.S. Const. amend. VIII. Explanation: Rule 13.2, abbreviate and use lowercase letters for designations such as "article" or "amendment."

3. Keep as is. Answer: Ossining v. Brubaker, No. CIV.A.02-2332, 2003 U.S. Dist. LEXIS 5130 at *1 (S.D. Ala. Jan. 6, 2003). Explanation: Rules 12.12(a), (b), and (d). The docket number is optional in citing cases from Lexis or Westlaw. Careful: Many jurisdictions do not allow citations to unpublished cases.

4. Change. Answer: Judith Expert, Allergy on the Net, 6 New Eng. J. Med. 9, 10 (2002) (available at http://www.nejm.org/expert/v5/allergy.html). Explanation: Rule 23.1(a), use the author's full name. Rule 38.1(b), include electronic source information in a parenthetical after the print source.

5. Change. Answer: Irving M. Tough, Warden Power, 16 N.Y. L. Sch. L. Rev. 12, 15-17 (1983). Explanation: Rule 23.1(a), use the author's full name. Abbreviate the name of the periodical using Appendix 5.

6. Change. Answer: Adam Gourna, Celiac Disease: A Killer, N.Y. Times F3 (Dec. 12, 1994) (available at 1994 WL 2321843). Explanation: Rule 23.1(d), abbreviate newspaper names using Appendix 3 or 5. Rule

23.1(e), after the abbreviated newspaper name, give the page on which the article starts. Rule 23.1(f), place the abbreviated date in a parenthetical. Rule 38.1(b), include electronic source information in a parenthetical after the print source.

7. Change. Answer: <u>Pope v. Hightower</u>, 101 F.3d 1382, 1383 (11th Cir. 1996). Explanation: Rule 12.6(a), no superscript in court name.

8. Change. Answer: U.S. Const. amend. VIII. Explanation: Rule 13.2, do not use all capitals in citing amendments.

9. Change. Answer: <u>Id.</u> Explanation: Rule 13.4, use <u>id.</u> as a short form citation for constitution provisions when appropriate.

10. Change. Answer: <u>See</u> <u>Thornburgh v. Abbott</u>, 490 U.S. 401, 407-08 (1989). Explanation: Rule 12.5(a), after the reporter abbreviation, give the page on which the case begins. Any pinpoint references follow, separated by a comma.

11. Change. Answer: <u>Turner v. Safley</u>, 482 U.S. 78, 84-85 (1987). Explanation: Rule 43.1(a), a citation sentence begins with a capital letter and ends with a period.

12. Change. Answer: <u>Helling v. McKinney</u>, 509 U.S. 25, 29 (1993). Explanation: Rule 12.20, use a short citation form only if you have previously cited the case in full.

13. Keep as is. Answer: <u>Helling</u>. Explanation: Rule 12.20, case that has been cited in full in the same general discussion may be referred to by one of the parties' names without further citation.

14. Change. Answer: <u>Id.</u> at 35-36. Explanation: Rule 11.3, italicize or underline <u>id.</u> Rule 12.20, generally, the case name may be omitted if the reader will have no doubt about the case to which the citation refers.

15. Keep as is. Answer: <u>Id.</u> at 35. Explanation: Rule 12.20, generally, the case name may be omitted if the reader will have no doubt about the case to which the citation refers.

16. Change. Answer: <u>See</u> 42 U.S.C. § 1983 (2003); <u>Farmer v. Brennan</u>, 511 U.S. 825, 837 (1994). Explanation: Rule 45.4(a), cite statutes before cases within the same signal. Rule 12.2(a), italicize or underline case names.

17. Change. Answer: <u>Campbell v. Sikes</u>. Explanation: Rule 12.2(c), omit words indicating multiple parties, such as "et al."

18. Change. Answer: <u>Campbell v. Sikes</u>, 169 F.3d 1353, 1366-68 (11th Cir. 1999). Explanation: Rule 12.6, include the name of the court within the parenthetical, unless the name of the reporter clearly indicates which court decided the case.

19. Change. Answer: <u>Campbell</u>,. Explanation: Rules 12.2(a) and 12.20, italicize short case names.

20. Keep as is. Answer: Mustave Hurt, <u>Unimaginable Pain</u>, 742 Geo. L.J. 801, 831-32 (2003) (discussing the requirements to show deliberate indifference). Explanation: Rule 23.1.

21. Change. Answer: <u>Estelle v. Gamble</u>, 439 U.S. 97, 107 (1976). Explanation: Rule 12.4(c), cite to U.S., if therein; otherwise cite to S. Ct., L. Ed., or U.S.L.W., in that order of preference.

22. Keep as is. Answer: <u>See</u> <u>id.</u> at 100, <u>but see</u> <u>Harris v. Thigpen</u>, 941 F.2d 1495, 1505 (11th Cir. 1991) (holding that difference of opinion does constitute cruel and unusual punishment). Explanation: Rule 44.8(c), separate different signals and their citations with a semicolon.

23. Change. Answer: <u>See</u> <u>Estelle</u>, 429 U.S. at 107. Explanation: Rule 12.20, use only the pinpoint page number in short form case citations.

24. Keep as is. Answer: <u>McElligot v. Goley</u>, 182 F.3d 1248, 1256-1258 (11th Cir. 1999), OR <u>McElligot v. Goley</u>, 182 F.3d 1248, 1256-58 (11th Cir. 1999). Explanation: According to Rule 5.3, you may drop the last two digits of page numbers or keep them.

25. Change. Answer: <u>See</u> <u>id.</u>; Noah Lee, <u>Deliberate Indifference: What's It All About?</u> 31 (3d ed., Biking 2001). Explanation: Rule 22.1(i), in citing books, include the publisher's name within the parenthetical. Rule 45.4(a), cite primary sources such as cases before secondary sources such as books. A short cite would be appropriate for the case assuming it was correctly referenced in the immediate previous citation (the full citation would also be correct).

26. Change. Answer: <u>See</u> <u>U.S. Sentencing Guidelines Manual</u> § 5D2.1(f) (2001). Explanation: Rule 27.5, cite U.S. sentencing guidelines as shown in the examples in Rule 27.5. Rule 6.2, use a space after a section symbol.

27. Change. Answer: <u>Helling</u>, 509 U.S. at 36. Explanation: Rule 12.4, abbreviate case reporters as shown in Appendix 1.

28. Keep as is. Answer: <u>Campbell</u>, 169 F.3d at 1363. Explanation: Rule 12.20, a short form is used after the first time a case is cited in full in the document.

29. Keep as is. <u>Rhodes v. Chapman</u>, 452 U.S. 337, 346, 349 (1981). Explanation: Rule 12.5(b), cite nonconsecutive pages by giving the individual page numbers separated by commas.

30. Change. Answer: <u>Restatement (Second) of Torts</u> § 931 (1994). Explanation: Rule 27.1(a), use upper- and lowercase letters and italic type when citing the title of a Restatement.

31. Change. <u>See</u> <u>Turner R.R. v. Safley</u>, 482 U.S. 78, 84-85 (1987). Explanation: Rule 12.2, abbreviate words in case names according to Appendix 3, unless doing so would cause confusion for the reader.

32. Change. Answer: <u>See</u> <u>id.</u> at 89; <u>Thornburgh</u>, 490 U.S. at 401. Explanation: Rule 45.1, signals of the same basic type must be strung together within a single citation sentence and separated by semicolons. Rule 11.3(d), when <u>id.</u> does not start a new sentence, use a lowercase "i." Rule 12.20, italicize or underscore short case names.

33. Change. Answer: <u>Owen v. Wille</u>, 117 F.3d 1235, 1235 (11th Cir. 1997). Explanation: Rule 12.5(b), when referring specifically to the first page of a source, repeat that page number.

34. Keep as is. Answer: <u>See</u> <u>U.S. v. White</u>, 490 U.S. 84, 87 (1990). Explanation: Rule 12.2(g) now permits the use of "U.S." or "United States" when referring to the name of a party in a case citation.

35. Keep as is. Answer: <u>See</u> <u>Turner</u>, 482 U.S. at 84-85. Explanation: Rule 12.20, a short form is used after the first time a case is cited in full in the document.

36. Change. Answer: <u>Ossining v. Brubaker</u>, No. CIV.A.02-2332, 2003 WL 66432 at *6 (S.D. Ala. Jan 6, 2003). Explanation: Rule 12.12(a)(2), if the database identifier does not clearly indicate which court decided the case, add the court's abbreviation before the date within the parenthetical. Careful: Many jurisdictions do not allow citation to unpublished cases.

37. Change. Answer: <u>Ala. v. Carter</u>, 507 U.S. 411, 418 (1992). Explanation: Rule 12.2(h)(2), omit "State of" in case names except when citing decisions of the courts of that state. Abbreviate state names according to Appendix 3.

38. Change. Answer: <u>N.W. Elec. Co. v. Univ. of Colo.</u>, 211 U.S. 415, 417 (1991). Explanation: Rule 12.2, abbreviate words in case names according to Appendix 3, unless doing so would cause confusion for the reader.

39. Change. Answer: <u>Thornburgh</u>, 490 U.S. at 414-15. Explanation: Rule 44.3, introductory signals. <u>See cf.</u> is not a signal in any circumstance.

40. Change <u>See</u> <u>Turner</u>, 482 U.S. at 89; <u>see also</u> 28 C.F.R. § 540.71 (2002) (establishing security as legitimate government interest). Explanation: Rule 44.6(b), italicize or underline signals.

41. Keep as is. Answer: <u>Onishea v. Hopper</u>, 171 F.3d 1289, 1300 (11th Cir. 1999). Explanation: Rule 12.1.

42. Change. Answer: <u>See</u> H.R. 81, 108th Cong. (Jan. 4, 2003) (available at http://thomas.-%201oc.gov/bss/d108/d108laws.html) (establishing security as legitimate governmental objective). Explanation: Rule 38.1.

43. Change. Answer: <u>See</u> Jeremy Stevens, <u>Taking Control</u> 41-42 (Amanda Bradley ed., 3d ed., Scholastic Press 2001). Explanation: Rule 22.1(d) and (f), place the editor's name first, the edition second, the publisher's name third, and the year of publication last.

44. Change. Answer: <u>See</u> <u>Spellman v. Hopper</u>, 95 F. Supp. 2d 1267, 1286 (M.D. Ala. 1999). Explanation: Rule 12.4, abbreviate reporter names according to Appendix 1.

45. Change. Answer: <u>See</u> Ala. Const. art. V, § 9. Explanation: Rule 13.2, abbreviate the name of the constitution and designations such as "article" or "amendment."

46. Keep as is. Answer: <u>See</u> James King, <u>Costs of Confinement</u>, 28 N. Ill. U. L. Rev. 609, 621-22 (2001). Explanation: Rule 23.1(d), abbreviate periodical names according to Appendix 5.

C. *Bluebook Quizzes*

1. Bluebook Typefaces Conventions (page 486)

1. B - Correct.
   A is incorrect. The entire case name, including the "v." is underlined. See Rules B2 and B1.
   C is incorrect. The comma after the case name should not be underlined. See Rules B2 and B1.
   D is incorrect. The case name should be underlined. See Rules B2 and B1.

2. B - Correct.
   A is incorrect. Introductory signals are underlined. See Rules B1 and B3.3.
   C is incorrect. The word "citing" should be underlined. Words and phrases introducing related authority are underlined. See Rule B1.
   D is incorrect. The title of the book, "Red House" should be underlined. See Rule B1.

3. A - Correct.
   B is incorrect. Only the "id." is underlined, not the page reference. See Rules 10.9 and B1.
   C is incorrect. The space between "See" and "Id." should not be underlined. See Rules 10.9, B2, and B7.
   D is incorrect. Introductory signals are underlined according to Rule B1.

4. D - Correct.
   A is incorrect. The title of the article should be underlined. See Rules 16.6, B9.1.4, and B1.
   B is incorrect. The newspaper's name should not be underlined, but the title of the article should be. See Rules 16.6, B9.1.4, and B1.
   C is incorrect. The name of the author should not be underlined, but the title of the article should be. See Rules 16.6, B9.1.1, and B1.

5. C - Correct.

A is incorrect. The parenthetical information should not be underlined. See Rules B4.1.5 and B11.

B is incorrect. "Id." should be underlined. See Rules 10.9 and B1.

D is incorrect. "U.S. Const." should not be underlined. See Rules 11, B6, and B1.

2. Basic Structure and Signals for Bluebook Citations (page 487)

1. D - Correct.
   A is incorrect. The citation with "Compare" should come before "But see." See Rule 1.3 and B3. Compare should also be used with "with."
   B is incorrect. There should be a period between the two citations and the "b" in "but see" should be capitalized. See Rule 1.3 and B3.
   C is incorrect. The two citations should not be separate sentences but part of the same citation sentence separated by a semicolon. See Rule 1.3 and B3.

2. B - Correct.
   A is incorrect. Orozco should come before Bradshaw because Supreme Court cases come before state cases. See Rules 1.4 and B3.
   C is incorrect. Singleton should come before Bradshaw because the citations should be in reverse chronological order. See Rules 1.4 and B3.
   D is incorrect. Constitutions come before cases in citation sentences. See Rules 1.4 and B3.

3. B - Correct.
   A is incorrect. Cases come before secondary sources. See Rules 1.4 and B3.
   C is incorrect. Constitutions come before cases. See Rules 1.4 and B3.
   D is incorrect. Supreme Court cases should come before court of appeals cases. See Rules 1.4 and B3.

4. A - Correct.
   B is incorrect. Parenthetical information does not come before the citation. See Rules 1.5, B3, and B11.
   C is incorrect. Parenthetical information comes at the end of the citation. See Rules 1.5, B3, and B11.
   D is incorrect. Parenthetical information comes at the end of the citation. See Rules 1.5, B3, and B11.

5. D - Correct.
   A is incorrect. The "See" citation should come before "See also." See Rules 1.2, 1.3, and B3.
   B is incorrect. The U.S. Constitution comes before state constitutions. See Rules 1.4 and B3.
   C is incorrect. This citation string needs only the first "see." See Rules 1.2 and B3.

3. Bluebook Citation Signals (page 488)

1. D - Correct. (<u>See</u> would also be correct.)
   A is incorrect. Use no signal when directly quoting an authority (see Rule 1.2(a)).
   B is incorrect. "<u>But see</u>" is used when contradicting an authority (see Rule 1.2(a)).
   C is incorrect. Use "<u>See, e.g.,</u>" when the cited authority states the proposition (see Rule 1.2(a)).
   E is incorrect. Cited authority is not contrary to the proposition (see Rule 1.2(c)).

2. B - Correct.
   A is incorrect. Use no signal when directly quoting an authority (see Rules 1.2(a) and B3.1).
   C is incorrect. Cited authority does not clearly support the proposition (see Rules 1.2(a)).
   D is incorrect. Use this signal when the cited authority is different from the proposition but analogous to it (see Rules 1.2(a)).
   E is incorrect. Cited authority is not contrary to the proposition (see Rule 1.2(c)).

3. C - Correct.
   A is incorrect. Use no signal when directly quoting an authority (see Rule 1.2(a)).
   B is incorrect. Use "<u>See, e.g.,</u>" when the cited authority states the proposition (see Rule 1.2(a)).
   D is incorrect. Use this signal when the cited authority is different from the proposition but analogous to it (see Rule 1.2(a)).
   E is incorrect. Cited authority does not clearly support the proposition (see Rule 1.2(a)).

4. B - Correct.
   A is incorrect. Use no signal when directly quoting an authority (see Rule 1.2(a)).
   C is incorrect. Use e.g. when you want to tell the reader there are several cases even if you do not cite all of them.
   D is incorrect. Use "<u>See, e.g.,</u>" when the cited authority states the proposition (see Rule 1.2(a)).
   E is incorrect. <u>Compare</u>...<u>with</u>... is used when comparison of the authorities will offer support for a proposition (see Rule 1.2(a)).

5. A - Correct.
   B is incorrect. Cited authority directly states the proposition. It does not offer support for the proposition (see Rule 1.2(a)).
   C is incorrect. Use "<u>But see</u>.," when cited authority supports a proposition contrary to the main proposition(see Rule 1.2(c)).
   D is incorrect. Cited authority is not contrary to the proposition (see Rule 1.2(c)).

E is incorrect. Cited authority is not analogous to the proposition. It directly states it (see Rule 1.2(a)).

6. C - Correct.
A is incorrect. Use no signal when directly quoting an authority (see Rule 1.2(a)).
B is incorrect. Cited authority is not analogous to the proposition. It directly states it (see Rule 1.2(a)).
D is incorrect. Use "<u>But see</u>.," when cited authority supports a proposition contrary to the main proposition (see Rule 1.2(c)).
E is incorrect. Use "<u>See, e.g.,</u>" when the cited authority states the proposition (see Rule 1.2(a)).

4. Bluebook Order and Punctuation of Signals and Citations (page 489)

1. D - Correct.
A is incorrect. Signals of the same basic type—supportive—must be strung together within a single citation sentence and separated by semi-colons according to Rule 1.3.
B is incorrect. Signals of different must be grouped in different citation sentences according to Rule 1.3.
C is incorrect. When "<u>See</u>" is used, it should appear before "<u>See also</u>" in a citation sentence according to Rules 1.3 and Rule 1.2.

2. B - Correct.
A is incorrect. According to Rule 1.3, signals of different types must be grouped in different citation sentences. Only signals of the same basic type are strung together within a single citation sentence and separated by semi-colons.
C is incorrect. According to Rule 1.3, signals of the same basic type—supportive and comparative—are strung together within a single citation sentence and separated by semi-colons.
D is incorrect. According to Rule 1.2, "<u>Cf</u>" should be before "<u>But see</u>".
E is incorrect. According to Rule 1.3, signals of the same basic type—supportive and comparative—are strung together within a single citation sentence and separated by semi-colons. In addition signals should be in lower case when used to begin a citation clause.

3. C - Correct.
A is incorrect. The ordering of citations should be changed.
B is incorrect. 13 U.S.C. § 12 (1994) should be cited before 18 U.S.C. § 588 (1998) according to Rule 1.4 (b). Statues in U.S.C. should be in progressive order of U.S.C. title.
D is incorrect. 13 U.S.C. § 12 (1994) should be cited before 18 U.S.C. § 588 (1998). Statues in U.S.C. should be in progressive order of U.S.C. title (Rule 1.4 (b)).

E is incorrect. 13 U.S.C. § 12 (1994) should be cited before 18 U.S.C. § 588 (1998). Statues in U.S.C. should be in progressive order of U.S.C. title (Rule 1.4 (b)).

5. Bluebook Rules for Citing Subdivisions and Pinpoint Cites (page 490)

1. A - Correct.
   B is incorrect. Do not use "at" unless the page number may be confused with another part of the citation. See Rules 3.2 and B4.1.2.
   C is incorrect. Use "p." or "pp." only in internal cross-references. See Rules 3.2 and B4.1.2.
   D is incorrect. Use a comma between the first page of the case and the pinpoint cite: 341, 347. See Rules 3.2 and B4.1.2.

2. C - Correct.
   A is incorrect. Do not use "p." See Rules 3.2 and B9.1.1.
   B is incorrect. The page number does not go in the parenthetical information but after "642." See Rules 3.2 and B4.1.2.
   D is incorrect. See Rules 3.2 and B4.1.2.

3. B - Correct.
   A is incorrect. The page number does not go at the beginning of the citation. See Rules 3.2 and B4.1.2.
   C is incorrect. The page number does not go at the end of the citation but is separated by a comma after "341." See Rules 3.2 and B4.1.2.
   D is incorrect. The page number does not come before the reporter abbreviation. See Rules B4.1.2 and 3.2.

4. C - Correct.
   A is incorrect. The page number does not go at the end of the citation but follows a comma after "2073." See Rules 3.2 and B9.1.1.
   B is incorrect. The page number follows a comma after "2073." See Rules 3.2 and B9.1.1.
   D is incorrect. There is no need to use "at," and the page number should be separated by a comma. See Rules 3.2 and B9.1.1.

5. D - Correct.
   A is incorrect. Do not use "and." See Rules 3.2 and B4.1.2.
   B is incorrect. Cite nonconsecutive page numbers by giving individual page numbers separated by commas. See Rules 3.2 and B4.1.2.
   C is incorrect. the page numbers should be separated by commas and appear after "477." See Rules 3.2 and B4.1.2.

6.   Bluebook Rules for Short Form Citations (page 491)

1. A - Correct.
    B is incorrect. Do not repeat the case name if the same case is cited in the preceding citation. Use Id. instead. See Rules 4.1, Rules 10.9, and B4.2.
    C is incorrect. See Rules 4.1, Rules 10.9, and B4.2.
    D is incorrect. See Rules 4.1, Rules 10.9, and B4.2.

2. D - Correct.
    A is incorrect. Do not repeat the full case name if the case is cited in one of the preceding five footnotes. See Rules 10.9 and B4.2.
    B is incorrect. There is no need to put "324" after "U.S."; instead use "U.S. at 327." See Rules 10.9 and B4.2.
    C is incorrect. Do not use Id. unless the case is the only source in the preceding citation. See Rules 10.9 and B4.2.

3. A - Correct.
    B is incorrect. Do not use the full citation if the same case is the only source in the previous citation. See Rules 10.9(b) and B4.2.
    C is incorrect. See Rules 10.9(b) and B4.2.
    D is incorrect. The page number comes before the parenthetical information. See Rules 10.9(b) and B4.2.

4. C - Correct.
    A is incorrect. Do not use the full citation for different provisions within the same title. See Rules 12.10 and B5.2.
    B is incorrect. The citation needs to include the different provision. See Rules 12.10 and B5.2.
    D is incorrect. Do not use "at." See Rules 12.10 and B5.2.

5. B - Correct.
    A is incorrect. Use "supra" instead of the title. See Rules 16.9 and B9.2.
    C is incorrect. Do not use the entire citation but instead use supra. See Rules 16.9 and B9.2.
    D is incorrect. Do not use Id. unless the work is in the immediately preceding authority. See Rules 16.9 and B9.2.

6. A - Correct.
    B is incorrect. Do not repeat the author's name if the same source appears in the immediately preceding citation. See Rules 15.10 and B8.2.
    C is incorrect. There is no need to give the book title. See Rules 15.10 and B8.2.
    D is incorrect. Do not use supra if the source is in the immediately preceding citation. See Rules 15.10 and B8.2.

7. D - Correct.
    A is incorrect. Do not use Id. if there is more than one source in the immediately preceding citation.

B is incorrect. Do not cite both party names in a short citation unless the reference to only one party's name would be ambiguous. See Rules 10.9 and B4.2.

C is incorrect. See Rules 10.9 and B4.2

7. Bluebook Abbreviations (page 493)

1. A - Correct.

   B is incorrect. In a textual sentence, "Hospital" should not be abbreviated according to Rule 10.2.1(c).

   C is incorrect. According to Rule 6.1(b), omit the periods between letters of entities with widely recognized initials, such as NLRB, in text, in case names, and as institutional authors.

   D is incorrect. Incorporated should be abbreviated "Inc" according to Rule 10.2.1 (c).

2. C - Correct.

   A is incorrect. In a citation sentence, "Memorial" should be abbreviated "Mem'l," "School" should be abbreviated "Sch.," "Housing" should be abbreviated "Hous.," and "Department" should be abbreviated "Dep't." See Rules 6.1 and 10.2.2, and Table T.6.

   B is incorrect. There should not be periods after "Mem'l" and "Dep't." See Rules 6.1 and 10.2.2, and Table T.6.

   D is incorrect. "Circuit" should be abbreviated "Cir." See Rule 6.1 and Table T.7.

3. C - Correct.

   A is incorrect. Do not fully spell out "Federal Register. See Rules 14.1 and 14.2, and Table T.9.

   B is incorrect. "F.R." is not the correct abbreviation for "Federal Register," and "September." should be abbreviated. See Rules 14.1 and 14.2, and Tables T.9 and T.12.

   D is incorrect. There is a space between "Fed." and "Reg.," and September is abbreviated "Sept." See Rules 6 and 14.1, and Tables T.9 and T.12.

4. B - Correct.

   A is incorrect. "Rule" should be abbreviated. See Rule 12.9.3 and Table T.9.

   C is incorrect. Each abbreviated word should have a period after it. See Rule 12.9.3 and Table T.9.

   D is incorrect. "Federal," "Rule," "Civil," and "Procedure" all need to be abbreviated. See Rule 12.9.3 and Table T.9.

5. A - Correct.

   B is incorrect. "George Mason" is improperly abbreviated. See Table T.13 and Rule 16.4.

   C is incorrect. "Law Review" is improperly abbreviated. See Table T.13 and Rule 16.4.

D is incorrect. The periods after "Geo," "L," and "Rev" are missing.
See Table T.13 and Rule 16.4.

8.   Bluebook Rules for Citing Cases (page 494)

1. B - Correct.
    A is incorrect. The reporter information comes after the case name.
    See Rule 10.3.
    C is incorrect. Do not use periods except for at the end of the citation.
    See Rule 10.
    D is incorrect. Do not abbreviate "United States" when it stands alone
    as a named party. See Rules 10.2.2 and B4.1.1.

2. A - Correct.
    B is incorrect. Omit "of Pennsylvania." See Rule 10.2.1(f).
    C is incorrect. Omit "of Penn." See Rule 10.2.1(f).
    D is incorrect. Use "Commonwealth" instead of "Penn." See Rule
    10.2.1(f).

3. C - Correct.
    A is incorrect. "S. Ct." is not the correct reporter abbreviation for the
    United States Reports nor is the Supreme Court Reporter the official
    reporter. See Rule 10.4 and Table T1.
    B is incorrect. Remove "S. Ct." See Rule 10.4 and Table T1.
    D is incorrect. Remove "U.S." before the date. See Rule 10.4 and Table
    T1.

4. B - Correct.
    A is incorrect. The letters "th" should not be in superscript. See Rule
    10.4 and Table T1.
    C is incorrect. Abbreviate "Circuit." See Rule 10.4 and Tables T1 and
    T7.
    D is incorrect. "S.E.2d" stands for "South Eastern Reporter, Second Edi-
    tion," not "Federal Reporter, Second Edition." See Rule 10.4 and Table
    T1.

5. A - Correct.
    B is incorrect. The parenthetical information is part of the citation
    sentence and thus should not be separated by a period. See Rule 10.6.
    C is incorrect. The parenthetical information is the incorrect order. See
    Rule 10.6.2.
    D is incorrect. Weight of authority goes in a separate parenthetical
    than the date. See Rule 10.6.1.

6. D - Correct.
    A is incorrect. Screen or page numbers, if assigned, should be preceded
    by an asterisk. See Rules 10.8.1 and 18.3.1.
    B is incorrect. Give the full date of the decision. See Rules 10.8.1 and
    18.3.1.

C is incorrect. Citation is missing "at" before the page number. See Rules 10.8.1 and 18.3.1.

9. Bluebook Rules for Citing Constitutions (page 495)

1. C - Correct.

   A is incorrect. The first letter of "Amend." should not be capitalized according to Rules B6 and 11.

   B is incorrect. United States" and "Constitution" should be abbreviated according to Rules B6 and 11, and "amendment" should be abbreviated according to Table T16.

   D is incorrect. This choice is incorrect because there should be a period following the abbreviation of "amendment," according to Table T16.

2. A - Correct.

   B is incorrect. According to Table T16, in this context, the correct abbreviation for section is the symbol "§."

   C is incorrect. According to Table T10, "Kan." is the correct abbreviation for "Kansas."

   D is incorrect. "Kansas" should be abbreviated "Kan." according to Table T10, and "Constitution" should be abbreviated "Const." according to Rules B6 and 11.

3. D - Correct.

   A is incorrect. Id. is the correct short citation format for constitutions according to Rule 11.

   B is incorrect. Id. is the correct short citation format for constitutions according to Rule 11.

   C is incorrect. Id. is the correct short citation format for constitutions according to Rule 11.

4. B - Correct.

   A is incorrect. According to Rules B6 and 11, "Amend." should not be capitalized.

   C is incorrect. According to Rule 11, "repealed" should not be italicized in this citation format.

   D is incorrect. According to Rule 11, there must be parentheses around "repealed 1933."

5. A - Correct.

   B is incorrect. "Pa." is the correct abbreviation of "Pennsylvania" according to Table T10.

   C is incorrect. "Art." should not be capitalized according to Rules B6 and 11.

   D is incorrect. "Pa." is the correct abbreviation of "Pennsylvania" according to Table T10, and the Roman numeral II should be used rather than the Arabic number 2 according to Rules B6 and 11.

10. Bluebook Rules for Citing Statutes (page 496)

1. B - Correct.
   A is incorrect. The "28" refers to the title number of the statute. The number following the abbreviation of the statute is the section number.
   C is incorrect. The "28" refers to the title number of the statute.
   D is incorrect. The "28" refers to the title number of the statute.

2. C - Correct.
   A is incorrect. There should be periods in between the letters "U.S.C."
   B is incorrect. A short form citation for a statute may omit the date of the code edition cited according to Rule 12.10, but a full citation must include the date of the code edition.
   D is incorrect. There should be a space between "§" and the cited section number.

3. A - Correct.
   B is incorrect. This option omits the section number of the statute, which must always be included in a short citation.
   C is incorrect. Two acceptable short form citations are 42 U.S.C. § 1975 or § 1975.
   D is incorrect. This is an incomplete short form citation. Instead, according to Rule 12.10, the short form citation could read 42 U.S.C. § 1975.

4. D - Correct.
   A is incorrect. This citation is properly formatted. The Internal Revenue Code can be cited as Title 26 of the United States Code.
   B is incorrect. This citation is properly formatted. According to Rule 12.9.1, in citations to the Internal Revenue Code, "26 U.S.C." may be replaced with "I.R.C."
   C is incorrect. This citation is properly formatted.

5. A - Correct.
   B is incorrect. This is the correct citation form for West's Annotated Indiana Code, but it is not the preferred statutory compilation for the Indiana Code.
   C is incorrect. This is the correct citation form for Burns Indiana Statutes Annotated on LexisNexis, but it is not the preferred statutory compilation for the Indiana Code.
   D is incorrect. The correct abbreviation for "Indiana Code" is "Ind. Code."

6. C - Correct.
   A is incorrect. According to Rule 12.9.3, the correct abbreviation for a Federal Rule of Civil Procedure is "Fed. R. Civ. P."
   B is incorrect. There should be periods following each of the terms in the abbreviation of the Federal Rules of Civil Procedure.

D is incorrect. According to Rule 12.9.3, the correct abbreviation for a Federal Rule of Civil Procedure is "Fed. R. Civ. P." In addition, there should be no "§" before the rule number

11. Bluebook Citations for Administrative and Executive Materials (page 497)

1. C - Correct.
   A is incorrect. According to Rules B5.1.4 and 14.2, the correct abbreviation for the Code of Federal Regulations is "C.F.R."
   B is incorrect. According to Rules B5.1.4 and 14.2, the correct abbreviation for the Code of Federal Regulations is "C.F.R.," and there should be a space between "§" and the section number.
   D is incorrect. There should be no spaces between the letters in "C.F.R."

2. B - Correct.
   A is incorrect. This citation is properly formatted. However, it is not an acceptable short form citation according to Rule 14.4.
   C is incorrect. The section number must be included in any short form citation (Rule 14.4).
   D is incorrect. There must be a "§" before the section number (Rule 14.4).

3. A - Correct.
   B is incorrect. As indicated in Rule 14.2(a), the correct abbreviation for the Federal Register is "Fed. Reg."
   C is incorrect. You must include the date of the Federal Register that you are referencing, according to Rule 14.2(a).
   D is incorrect. There must be a space between "Fed." and "Reg." and a comma in the page number "25,684" (Rule 14.2(a)).

4. D - Correct.
   A is incorrect. According to Rule 6.2, there should not be a comma in numbers with fewer than five digits.
   B is incorrect. According to Table T.1, the correct abbreviation for the Virginia Register of Regulations is "Va. Reg. Regs."
   C is incorrect. When citing to an administrative register, you must include the month, day, and year of its publication.

5. B - Correct.
   A is incorrect. According to Table T1.2, "Attorney General" should be abbreviated to read "Att'y Gen."
   C is incorrect. According to Table T1.2, there should not be a period following the abbreviation "Att'y."
   D is incorrect. There should be an apostrophe in the abbreviation "Att'y" as indicated in Table T1.2.

6. A - Correct.

B is incorrect. The correct abbreviation for a presidential executive order is "Exec. Order," according to Table T1.2.

C is incorrect. The correct abbreviation for a presidential executive order is "Exec. Order," according to Table T1.2, and the correct abbreviation for the Federal Register is "Fed. Reg."

D is incorrect. According to Rule 6.2, numbers with five or more digits require commas.

12. Bluebook Citations for Books, Reports, and Other Nonperiodic Materials (page 498)

1. D - Correct.

A is incorrect. The name of the author is misplaced. According to Rules B8.1 and 15.1, the author's name should precede the title of the book.

B is incorrect. Include the author's full name as it appears on the publication, according to Rules B8.1 and 15.1.

C is incorrect. There should not be a comma separating the title of the publication and the page cited).

2. A - Correct.

B is incorrect. There should be a period following "al." and a comma separating "et al." and the title of the book.

C is incorrect. While it is acceptable to list all three authors' names according to Rules B8.1 and 15.1(b), use an ampersand (&) instead of "and" between the second and third authors' names.

D is incorrect. The authors should be listed in the order in which their names appear on the title page of the publication, according to Rules B8.1 and 15.1(b).

3. C - Correct.

A is incorrect. The volume number is incorrectly placed. It should precede the author's name, according to Rules B8.1 and 15.3.

B is incorrect. The volume number is incorrectly placed. It should precede the author's name, according to Rules B8.1 and 15.3.

D is incorrect. According to Rules B8.1 and 15.3, the volume number should be indicated by "2." Omit the abbreviation "vol." before the "2."

4. A - Correct.

B is incorrect. According to Rule 15.5.2(b), a letter should be identified both by the sending party and the receiving party.

C is incorrect. November should be abbreviated "Nov."

D is incorrect. According to Rule 15.5.2(b), identify the letter as included in a collection of works by using the term "in."

5. B - Correct.

A is incorrect. Do not use superscript in referencing a numbered edition of a publication.

C is incorrect. Edition should be abbreviated to read "ed." according to Rules B8.1 and 15.8.

D is incorrect. There should not be a comma between "ed." and "2009" according to Rules B8.1 and 15.8.

13. Bluebook Rules for Citing Periodicals (page 500)

1. B - Correct.
   A is incorrect. The title of the article should be underlined according to Rules B9.1.4 and 16.3.
   C is incorrect. The author's name should be cited as it appears in the newspaper, according to Rule 15.1.
   D is incorrect. According to Rule B1, the title of a publication should be underlined in the text of a document, but not in a citation.

2. A - Correct.
   B is incorrect. The title of the article should be underlined according to Rules B9.1.4 and 16.3.
   C is incorrect. According to Rule 16.6(a), designate Op-Ed articles with "Op-Ed." between the name of the author and the title of the article.
   D is incorrect. Abbreviate the name of periodicals according to Table T.13 for periodicals and Table T.10 for geographic locations.

3. C - Correct.
   A is incorrect. Abbreviate the title of the periodical according to Table T.13.
   B is incorrect. Abbreviate the title of the periodical according to Table T.13.
   D is incorrect. According to Table T.13, there should not be a space between the letters "L." and "J."

4. D - Correct.
   A is incorrect. If a student-written note or comment is signed, Rules B9.1.3 and 16.7.1(a) indicate that you must list the author's full name before the designation of the work as a "note" or "comment."
   B is incorrect. According to Table T.13, the correct abbreviation for the Columbia Law Review is "Colum. L. Rev."
   C is incorrect. The designation of the piece, "Note," should be capitalized according to Rules B9.1.3 and 16.7.1.

5. A - Correct.
   B is incorrect. According to Rule 15.1, include designations such as "Jr." when citing an author's full name.
   C is incorrect. Titles of books should be either underscored or italicized in citations according to Rule B1.
   D is incorrect. According to Table T.13, the correct abbreviation for the Texas Law Review is "Tex. L. Rev."

14. Bluebook Rules for Citing Electronic Media (page 501)

1. A - Correct.

    B is incorrect. If a case in LexisNexis or Westlaw has been assigned a unique database identifier, include that number following the case name (Rule 18.3.1).

    C is incorrect. Screen or page numbers in unreported opinions should be preceded by an asterisk according to Rule 18.3.1.

    D is incorrect. When citing unreported opinions, give the full date of the opinion as it appears in Westlaw or LexisNexis, including month, day, and year (Rule 18.3.1).

2. C - Correct.

    A is incorrect. According to Rule 18.3.2, when citing a code contained in an electronic database, give a short description regarding the currency of the database as provided by the database itself, rather than just the year of publication.

    B is incorrect. According to Table T.1, the correct abbreviation to Baldwin's Kentucky Revised Statutes Annotated is "Ky. Rev. Stat. Ann."

    D is incorrect. See Rules 3.2 and B4.1.2.

3. B - Correct.

    A is incorrect. The title of the article should be underlined.

    C is incorrect. According to Rule 18.2.2, the Internet URL should be appended directly to the end of the citation, not preceded by "available at."

    D is incorrect. The name of the publication should be abbreviated to "N.Y. Times."

4. D - Correct.

    A is incorrect. Include the phrase "available at" before the parallel internet citation according to Rule 18.3.2.

    B is incorrect. The date of the article should go after the name of the publication but before the page number on which the article is found.

    C is incorrect. The phrase "available at" should be italicized.

5. A - Correct.

    B is incorrect. According to Rule 17.2.4, the respective titles of the sender and recipient should precede the organization or institution that each one works for.

    C is incorrect. According to Rule 17.2.4, e-mails should be identified by the words "E-mail from" preceding the name of the sender.

    D is incorrect. Identify the sender and recipient of an e-mail using the title and employer of each (Rule 17.2.4).

6. C - Correct

    A is incorrect. Include the name of the recording company in a parenthetical following the name of the album, according to Rule 18.7.1.

B is incorrect. According to Rule 18.7.1, include the date of release in a parenthetical, along with the name of the recording company. D is incorrect. According to Rule 18.7.1, the name of the recording company should precede the date of release, and both should be included in one parenthetical.

D. *Bluebook Self-Assessment*

1. Bluebook Citation Self-Assessment (page 504)

1. Change: Answer: U.S. Const. amend. I;. Explanation: Rule 11.

2. Keep as is. Answer: U.S. Const. amend. VIII. Explanation: Rule 11.

3. Keep as is. Answer: <u>Ossining v. Brubaker,</u> No. CIV.A.02-2332, 2003 U.S. Dist. LEXIS 5130, at *1 (S.D. Ala. Jan. 6, 2003). Explanation: Rule 18.3.1, Commercial Electronic Databases, cases; when a case is reported but unavailable on a widely used electronic database, then it may be cited to that database.

4. Change. Answer: Judith Expert, <u>Allergy on the Net</u>, 5 New Eng. J. Med. 9, 10 (2002), <u>available at</u> http://www.nejm.org/expert/v5/allergy.html. Explanation: Rule 18.2, Author; use the author's full name. Bluepages B2; you may substitute underscoring for italics.

5. Change. Answer: Irving M. Tough, <u>Warden Power</u>, 15 N.Y.L. Sch. L. Rev. 12, 15-17 (1983). Explanation: Rule 16.1, Author; use the author's full name. Bluepages B2; you may substitute underscoring for italics. Rule 16, Periodical Materials; abbreviate journal names using Table T13: Periodicals.

6. Change. Answer: Adam Gourna, <u>Celiac Disease: A Killer</u>, N.Y. Times, Dec. 12, 1994, at F3, <u>available at</u> 1994 WL 2321843. Explanation: Rule 16.6, Newspapers. Rule 16.6(e), Commercial electronic databases. T13 Months.

7. Change. Answer: <u>Pope v. Hightower</u>, 101 F.3d 1382, 1383 (11th Cir. 1996). Explanation: Rule 10, Cases No Superscript.

8. Change. Answer: U.S. Const. amend. VIII. Explanation: Rule 11, Constitutions.

9. Change. Answer: U.S. Const. amend. VIII. Explanation: Rule 11, constitutions do not use a short citation form (other than <u>id.</u>) for constitutions.

10. Change. Answer: <u>See</u> <u>Thornburgh v. Abbott</u>, 490 U.S. 401, 407-08 (1989). Explanation: Rule 10, Cases. Rule 3.2(a), when referring to specific material within a source, include both the page on which the source begins and the page on which the specific materials appear, separated by a comma.

11. Change. Answer: <u>Turner v. Safley</u>, 482 U.S. 78, 84-85 (1987). Explanation: Rule 1.1(b)(i); citation sentences start with a capital letter and end with a period.

12. Change. Answer: <u>Helling v. McKinney</u>, 509 U.S. 25, 29 (1993). Explanation: Rule 10.9, Short Forms for Cases; only use a short form if you have previously cited the case.

13. Keep as is. Answer: <u>Helling</u>. Explanation: Rule 10.9(c), Short Forms for Cases in Text; a case that has been cited in full in the same general discussion may be referred to by one of the parties' names without further citation.

14. Change. Answer: <u>Id.</u> at 35-36. Explanation: Rule 4.1, "<u>Id.</u>" Use <u>id.</u> when referring to immediate prior reference. Always underscore <u>id.</u> (including the period).

15. Keep as is. Answer: <u>Id.</u> at 35. Explanation: Rule 10.9, Short forms for cases. Rule 4.1, use <u>id.</u> when referring to immediate preceding authority. Bluepages, always underscore <u>id.</u> (including the period).

16. Change. Answer: <u>See</u> 42 U.S.C. § 1983 (2003); <u>Farmer v. Brennan,</u> 511 U.S. 825, 837 (1994). Explanation: Rule 1.4, Order of Authorities Within Each Signal.

17. Change. Answer: <u>Campbell v. Sikes</u>. Explanation: Rule 10.2.1(a), Case Names in textual Sentences; omit words indicating multiple parties, such as "et al."

18. Change. Answer: <u>Campbell v. Sikes</u>, 169 F. 3e 1353, 1366-68 (11th Cir. 1999). Explanation: Rule 10.4, Court and Jurisdiction. Rule 3.2(a), Page numbers.

19. Change. Answer: <u>Campbell</u>. Explanation: Bluepages, Case names; underscore or italicize all case names.

20. Keep as is. Answer: Mustave Hurt, <u>Unimaginable Pain</u>, 742 Geo. L.J. 801, 831-32 (2003) (discussing the requirements to show deliberate indifference). Explanation: Introductory Rule I.4 (g), Typical Legal Citations Analyzed; Periodical materials. Rule 16, Periodical Materials. Table T13, Periodicals; journal abbreviations.

21. Change. Answer: <u>Estelle v. Gamble</u>, 429 U.S. 97, 107 (1976). Explanation: Rule 10, Cases. Table T1, cite to U.S., if therein; otherwise cite to S. Ct., L. Ed., or U.S.L.W. in that order of preference.

22. Change. Answer: <u>See id.</u> at 100. <u>But see</u> <u>Harris v. Thigpen</u>, 941 F.2d 1495, 1505 (11th cir. 1991) (holding that difference of opinion does constitute cruel and unusual punishment). Explanation: Rule 1.3, Order of Signals; signals of different types must be grouped in different citation sentences.

23. Change. <u>See</u> <u>Estelle</u>, 429 U.S. at 107. Explanation: Rule 10.9, Short Forms for Cases. Bluepages, Short Forms in Court Documents and Legal Memoranda.

24. Change. Answer: <u>McElligot v. Foley</u>, 182 F.3d 1248, 1256-58 (11th Cir. 1999), Explanation: Rule 3.2. When citing material that spans more than one page, retain the last two numbers, but drop any other repeating digits.

25. Keep as is. Answer: <u>See id.</u>; Noah Lee, <u>Deliberate Indifference: What's It All About?</u> 31 (3d ed. 2001). Explanation: Rule 15, Books, Reports, and Other Nonperiodic Materials. Rule 15.4, Edition, Publisher, Date. Rule 1.4, Order of Authorities Within Each Signal; authorities within each signal are separated by semicolons; cases before books. Bluepages, B8, Sources and Authorities: Books and Other Nonperiodic Materials. A short cite for McElligot would be appropriate if the full citation was correctly given in previous sentence (the full citation would also be correct).

26. Change. Answer: <u>See</u> U.S. Sentencing Guidelines Manual § 5D2.1(f) (2001). Explanation: Rule 12.9.5, Model Codes, Restatements, Standards, and Sentencing Guidelines. Rule 6.2(c), Sections & Paragraph Symbols; when the symbols are used, there should be a space between § and the numeral.

27. Change. Answer: <u>Helling</u>, 509 U.S. at 36. Explanation: Rule 10.9, Short Forms for Cases. Table T1: United States Jurisdictions; for Supreme Court, cite to U.S.

28. Keep as is. Answer: <u>Campbell</u>, 169 F.3d at 1363. Explanation: Rule 10.9, Short Forms for Cases. Rule B4.2, Short Forms.

29. Keep as is. Answer: <u>Rhodes v. Chapman</u>, 452 U.S. 337, 346, 349 (1981). Explanation: Rule 3.3(d), Multiple Pages, Footnotes, and Endnotes; cite non-consecutive pages by giving the individual page numbers separated by commas.

30. Change. Answer: Restatement (Second) of Torts § 931 (1994). Explanation: Rule 12.9.5, Model Codes, Restatements, Standards, and Sentencing Guidelines. Bluepages, see B1 for typefaces in legal documents vs. journals.

31. Change. Answer: <u>See</u> <u>Turner R.R. v. Safley</u>, 482 U.S. 78, 84-85 (1987). Explanation: Rule 20.2.2, Case Names in Citations; always abbreviate any word listed in Table T.6.

32. Change. Answer: <u>See id.</u> at 89; <u>Thornburgh</u>, 490 U.S. at 401. Explanation: Bluepages B2, Citation Sentences and Clauses in Court Documents. Rule 1.3, Order of Signals; signals of the same basic type must be strung together within a single citation sentence and separated by semicolons.

33. Change. Answer: <u>Owen v. Wille</u>, 117 F.3d 1235, 1235 (11th Cir. 1997). Explanation: Rule 3.3(a), Pages, Footnotes, Endnotes, and Graphical Materials; when referring specifically to the first page of a source, repeat the page number.

34. Change. Answer: <u>See</u> <u>United States v. White</u>, 490 U.S. 84, 87 (1990). Explanation: Rule 10.2.2, Case Names in Citations; do not abbreviate "United States."

35. Keep as is. Answer: <u>See</u> <u>Turner</u>, 482 U.S. at 84-85. Explanation: Rule 10.9, Short Forms for Cases. Rule 3.3(d), Multiple pages, Footnotes, Endnotes; when citing material that spans more than one page, give the inclusive page numbers, separated by a hyphen or dash. Always retain the last two digits, but drop other repetitious digits.

36. Change. Answer: <u>Ossining v. Brubaker</u>, No. CIV.A.02-2332, 2003 WL 66432, at *6 (S.D. Ala. Jan. 6, 2003). Explanation: Rule 18.3.1, Commercial Electronic Databases, cases; provide the case name, docket number, database identifier, court name, and full date of the most recent major disposition of the case.

37. Change. Answer: <u>Alabama v. Carter</u>, 507 U.S. 411, 418 (1992). Explanation: Rule 10.2.1(f), Geographical Terms; omit "state of" except when citing decisions of the courts of that state, in which case only "State" should be retained.

38. Change. Answer: <u>N.W. Elec. Co. v. Univ. of Colo.</u>, 211 U.S. 415, 417 (1991). Explanation: Rule 10.2.2, Case Names in Citations; always abbreviate any word listed in Table T6; abbreviate states, countries, and other geographical units as indicated in Table T10, unless the geographical unit is a named party.

39. Change. Answer: <u>Thornburgh</u>, 490U.S. at 414-15. Explanation: Rule 1.2, Introductory Signals. <u>See</u> <u>cf.</u> is not a signal in any circumstance.

40. Change. <u>See</u> <u>Turner</u>, 482 U.S. at 89; <u>see also</u> 28 C.F.R. § 540.71 (2002) (establishing security as legitimate government interest). Explanation: Rule 1.2, Introductory Signals. Rule 1.3, Order of Signals. Rule 1.4, Order of Authorities Within Each Signal. Rule 1.5, Parenthetical Information.

41. Keep as is. Answer: <u>Onishea v. Hopper</u>, 171 F.3d 1289, 1300 (11th Cir. 1999). Explanation: Rule 10, Cases. Bluepages B2, Citation Sentences and Clauses; citation sentences begin with capital letters and end with periods. Rule 1.1, Citation Sentences and Clauses in Law Review Footnotes.

42. Change. Answer: <u>See</u> H.R. 81, 108th Cong. (2003) (establishing security as legitimate governmental objective), <u>available at</u> http://thomas.-%20loc.gov/bss/d108/d108laws.html. Explanation: Rule 18.2, The Internet. Rule 18.2.3(c), Parenthetical Information; explanatory and other parentheticals should be placed after the date information for that aspect of the citation to which the parenthetical pertains. Rule 13.2(a), Unenacted federal bills and resolutions.

43. Change. Answer: <u>See</u> Jeremy Stevens, <u>Taking Control</u> 41-42 (Amanda Bradley ed., Scholastic Press, 3d ed. 2001). Explanation: Rule 15, Books, Reports, and Other Non-periodic Materials; cite books by author,

editor and/or translator. Rule 15.2, Editor or Translator; give the full name of the editor/ translator, publisher, edition, and date of publication in that order. Separate the editor/ translator from other publication information with a comma.

44. Change. Answer: <u>See</u> <u>Spellman v. Hopper</u>, 95 F. Supp. 2d 1267, 1286 (M.D. Ala. 1999). Explanation: T.1F., Supp 2d has spaces.

45. Change. Answer: <u>See</u> Ala. Const. art. V, § 9. Explanation: Rule 11, Constitutions; cite state constitutions by the abbreviated name of the state and the word "Const." Abbreviate subdivisions of constitutions according to Table T.17.

46. Keep as is. Answer: James King. <u>Costs of Confinement</u>, 28 N. Ill. U. S. Rev. 609, 621-622 (2001). Explanation: Rule 16, Periodical Materials. Rule 16.4, Consecutively Paginated Journals; cite works found within periodicals that are consecutively paginated throughout an entire volume by author, title of work, volume number, periodical name, first page of the work and page or pages on which specific material appears, and year enclosed in parenthesis at the end of the citation. Table T13: Periodicals.

Appendix B

TABLE OF CONTENTS WITH SCREEN NUMBERS

Note: The first column indicates the print book page number, and the second column indicates the ebook screen number.